Advances in
Bond Analysis &
Portfolio Strategies

Advances in Bond Analysis & Portfolio Strategies

Edited by

Frank J. Fabozzi

Visiting Professor
Alfred P. Sloan School of Management
Massachusetts Institute of Technology
and
Managing Editor
The Journal of Portfolio Management

and

T. Dessa Garlicki

Consultant

Probus Publishing Company
Chicago, Illinois

Library of Congress Cataloging in Publication Data Available

ISBN 0-917253-62-0

Printed in the United States of America

1   2   3   4   5   6   7   8   9   0

CONTENTS

CONTRIBUTORS

Marcelle Arak, Ph.D., Vice President, Capital Markets Analysis, Citicorp Investment Bank

Lawrence N. Bader, Vice President, Bond Portfolio Analysis, Salomon Brothers Inc

Richard Bookstaber, Ph.D., Vice President, Morgan Stanley and Co., Inc.

Raj Daryanani, Research Analyst, Capital Markets Analysis, Citicorp Investment Bank

Chris P. Dialynas, Principal, Pacific Investment Management Company

Philip Fischer, Ph.D., Vice President, Public Finance, Citicorp Investment Bank

Philip H. Galdi, C.P.A., Vice President, Structured Investments Group, Merrill Lynch Capital Markets

Laurie Goodman, Ph.D., Vice President, Capital Markets Analysis, Goldman Sachs & Co.

Michael R. Granito, Ph.D., Managing Director, J.P. Morgan Investment Management, Inc.

Hal Heaton, Ph.D., Assistant Professor of Finance, Brigham Young University

Susan Mara Hunter, Senior Associate, Mortgage Securities Research, Goldman, Sachs & Co.

David P. Jacob, Research Manager, Fixed Income Analytical Research, Morgan Stanley and Co., Inc.

Cal Johnson, Ph.D., Vice President, Salomon Brothers Inc

Frank J. Jones, Ph.D., Managing Director, Kidder, Peabody & Company, Inc.

Thomas E. Klaffky, Managing Director, Salomon Brothers Inc.

Robert W. Kopprasch, Ph.D., C.F.A., Director, Salomon Brothers Inc

Beth A. Krumholz, Assistant Vice President, Kidder, Peabody & Co., Inc.

Peter C. Lambert, Assistant Vice President, Western Asset Management Company

Terence C. Langetieg, Ph.D., Vice President, Bond Portfolio Analysis, Salomon Brothers Inc

Gary D. Latainer, Fixed Income Analytical Research, Morgan Stanley and Co., Inc.

Martin L. Leibowitz, Ph.D., Managing Director, Bond Portfolio Analysis Group, Salomon Brothers Inc

Graham Lord, Ph.D., Manager, Mathtech, Inc.

William J. Marshall, Ph.D., Vice President, Fixed Income Division, Goldman, Sachs & Co.

Richard W. McEnally, Ph.D., C.F.A., Meade H. Willis Sr. Professor of Investment Banking, University of North Carolina-Chapel Hill

James F. Meisner, Vice President, Merrill Lynch Capital Markets

Sharmin Mossavar-Rahmani, Vice President, Fidelity Management Trust Company, Boston

Scott M. Pinkus, Vice President and Co-Director, Mortgage Securities Research, Goldman, Sachs & Co.

John A. Richards, Vice President, Merrill Lynch Capital Markets

Edgar A. Robie, Jr., Managing Director, Western Asset Management Company

Richard Roll, Ph.D., Vice President and Co-Director, Mortgage Securities Research, Goldman, Sachs & Co.

Michael R. Rosenberg, Ph.D., Vice President and Manager, International Fixed Income Research Department, Merrill Lynch

Robert A. Smith, Vice President, The First Boston Corporation

Peter B. Taggart, Assistant Vice President, The First Boston Corporation

Armand H. Tatevossian, Senior Analyst, Salomon Brothers Inc

James A. Tilley, Ph.D., F.S.A., Principal, Fixed Income Analytical Research, Morgan Stanley and Co., Inc.

Alfred Weinberger, Vice President, Bond Portfolio Analysis, Salomon Brothers Inc

Richard Williams, Research Analyst, Credit Suisse First Boston Limited

PREFACE

The objective of this book is to present recent developments in bond analysis and portfolio strategies. The book is *not* an introduction to fixed income securities or to bond portfolio management. It is a rigorous review of the latest analytical tools designed to capture opportunities in the capital markets. This book also examines new approaches to asset/liability management and bond portfolio management.

OVERVIEW OF THE BOOK

Asset management is undertaken in three main steps. First, the objectives and policy guidelines are established by the fund sponsor. For institutions such as pension funds and life insurance companies, these objectives may be a cash flow specification to satisfy a single period (bullet) liability or multiple period liabilities. For institutions such as banks and thrifts, the objective may be to lock in a minimum interest rate spread over the cost of funds. While for others, such as investment companies, the investment objective may be to maximize return. Setting policy begins with asset allocation among major asset classes (such as, equities, fixed income securities, real estate vehicles, venture capital, and foreign securities) so as to achieve the specified objectives. Client and regulatory constraints must be considered in establishing investment policy. It is against these investment objectives and policy that the investment manager will be evaluated.

In the second step, a portfolio strategy is selected so as to best achieve a specified investment objective. In the case of bond portfolio management, portfolio strategies can be broadly classified as either active portfolio strategies or structured portfolio strategies. Essential to all active portfolio strategies is expectations about the direction of interest rates and yield spreads between market sectors. In contrast, structured portfolio strategies reduce, if not eliminate, interest rate anticipation and focus on sector and security selection.

Once a portfolio strategy has been selected, the manager proceeds, in the third step, to choose the optimal combination of individual securities to implement the strategy. Typically, the manager can choose from an infinite number of portfolios. For a given portfolio strategy, the manager will seek an efficient portfolio; that is, one designed to provide the greatest return for a given level of risk. Constructing an efficient portfolio requires analysis and valuation of the individual securities.

The three sections of this book reflect these three main steps in asset management. The six articles in Section I cover portfolio objectives, asset allocation and performance evaluation. Richard McEnally describes portfolio objectives and management policies for bond investors. Chris Dialynas explores the active bond management process, contrasting it with passive management. He argues that regardless of whether active or passive management is selected, success is dependent upon "good long-term economic forecasting and a thorough understanding of the mathematical dynamics of fixed income obligations." The selection of a performance bogey also depends on similar considerations plus an understanding of the liability structure. Edgar Robie and Peter Lambert explain how *normal portfolios* can be used as a basis for evaluating portfolio performance with respect to stated investment objectives. While the convention in managing money is to think in terms of asset returns, Martin Leibowitz emphasizes the fact that pension fund liabilities also are sensitive to changes in interest rates. While a decline in interest rates may have a favorable impact on asset returns, the adverse impact on interest-sensitive liabilities (which he refers to as "liability returns") could actually result in a reduction in a fund's surplus status. The implication is that fund managers should not think of the process of asset allocation in terms of stock/bond ratios but, instead, in terms of a total duration approach which allows for the measurement and control of interest rate risk. The principal concepts of this article are extended in the article by Terence Langetieg, Lawrence Bader, Martin Leibowitz and Alfred Weinberger, who show how to measure the effective duration of pensions liabilities under FASB 87. In the last article in Section I, William Marshall demonstrates how portfolio insurance can be used to preserve the value of interest-sensitive assets relative to interest-sensitive liabilities under FASB 87.

The eight articles in Section II deal with the analysis and valuation of fixed income securities and debt options. By examining the appropriate pricing, volatility characteristics and historical returns of Treasury zero-coupon bonds, Thomas Klaffy provides an analytical framework for judging the relative merits and shortcomings of these instruments. Scott Pinkus, Susan Mara Hunter and Richard Roll describe the mortgage market, the characteristics of mortgage backed securities and develop an analytical framework for their valuation.

The central problem in security valuation is the pricing of a stream of contingent cash flows or claims. Graham Lord, David Jacob and James Tilley provide an analytical framework for pricing fixed income securities with contingent cash flows and then go on to analyze the price sensitivity of that stream with respect to changes in interest rates. This theme is carried over to the next article where Gary Latainer and David Jacob provide a framework for valuing and analyzing the performance characteristics of callable bonds. Robert Smith and Peter Taggart discuss the structure of floating rate notes, methods of analysis and portfolio strategies using floating rate notes. Richard Williams explains and evaluates the various measures used to value floating rate notes. The last two articles in Section II deal with the valuation of debt options. James Meisner and John Richards present a generalized form of the Black-Scholes option pricing model and examine the duration and convexity measures for options on fixed income securities. In the last article in Section II, Michael Granito proposes a simplified framework for deriving European bond option values employing only information about the equilibrium shape of the yield curve.

Section III focuses on various portfolio strategies. Sharmin Mossavar-Rahmani discusses the motivations for indexation, its advantages and disadvantages, and current methodologies for indexation, including enhanced indexation strategies and tracking error. A further discussion of indexing is provided by Philip Galdi who provides an overview of the theories and techniques involved in establishing and managing an indexed fixed income portfolio. Michael Granito proposes a strategy which he refers to as "duration averaging," in which he demonstrates that under some simplifying assumptions about the behavior of the yield curve, a money manager can "derive an exact formula for the performance of this strategy that is simple, highly intuitive and likely to represent an attractive tradeoff for many investors, especially those who would invest in a bond index fund." Robert Kopprasch, Cal Johnson and Armand Tatevossian describe hedging techniques and the use of synthetic assets to enhance portfolio returns. General guidelines for setting up and constructing an international bond portfolio, and a framework for designing an active global bond portfolio strategy are discussed by Michael Rosenberg. How the Treasury bond and note futures contracts can be used for both duration management and asset allocation is explained by Frank Jones and Beth Krumholz. The pricing efficiency of the Municipal Bond Index futures contract and its relative hedging efficiency are evaluated by Richard Bookstaber and Hal Heaton. The motivation for trading the municipal/Treasury bond futures spread, known as the "MOB," is explained by Marcelle Arak, Philip Fischer, Laurie Goodman and Raj Daryanani in the last article in this section.

ACKNOWLEDGMENTS

We would like to express our appreciation to the contributors. In addition, we wish to thank Fred Price (Bear Stearns) and Michael Smirlock (Wharton School) who gave generously of their time to review portions of this book. We are particularly grateful to Sharmin Mossavar-Rahmani (Fidelity Management Trust Company, Boston) for her insightful comments on several of the articles and her guidance in the organization of this book. Jean Marie De-Jordy provided assistance at various stages of this project. Last, but certainly not least, we are grateful to Probus Publishing Company for its encouragement and support.

Frank J. Fabozzi

T. Dessa Garlicki

PORTFOLIO OBJECTIVES, ASSET ALLOCATION, AND PERFORMANCE EVALUATION

ARTICLE 1

RICHARD W. MCENALLY is Meade Willis Professor
of Investment Banking at the University of North Carolina.
He holds a B.S. degree from Washington and Lee
University, while his M.B.A. and Ph.D. are from
the University of North Carolina. He was formerly on the
faculty of the University of Texas at Austin. He is a
Chartered Financial Analyst, and is president of a firm,
The Financial Analysts Review, that prepares candidates
to take the CFA examinations. He is also on the board of
directors of the JP group of mutual funds. His research
and teaching interests include investment banking and
investment management, with emphasis in the latter on
fixed income securities, quantitative stock selection, and
portfolio construction.

PORTFOLIO OBJECTIVES AND MANAGEMENT POLICIES FOR FIXED INCOME INVESTORS

Richard W. McEnally, Ph.D., C.F.A.
Meade H. Willis Sr. Professor of Investment Banking
University of North Carolina–Chapel Hill

On the face of it, fixed income securities are not very attractive investment media. They require that the investor surrender money up front in return for a *promise* of uneven quality to receive a stream of future cash benefits, usually spread out over the far distant future, with the certain knowledge that if the security is held for its entire life the benefits will never exceed those initially promised and may be less.[1,2] Given this limitation, it is worthwhile

---

[1] In speaking with student groups about bonds I often call their attention to the fact that thirty- and forty-year bonds are routinely issued, and ask them to contemplate how old they will be and what year it will be when the initial investment is paid back at maturity. This approach is not entirely fair, because (as the concept of duration has taught us) the payoff at maturity is a comparatively unimportant component of the bond's value. But it is sobering nonetheless.

[2] In practice many fixed income securities contain prepayment options, such as the right of the issuer to refund early, but these nearly always work to the benefit of the issuer rather than the investor.

5

to inquire about the conditions under which an investor might reasonably invest in fixed income securities.

Fixed income investment appears to make sense under three different sets of portfolio objectives: seeking current income, attempting to accumulate value over time, and going for holding period returns.

I. INVESTING FOR CURRENT INCOME

The traditional, conventional basis for investing in bonds has always been to provide a reasonably steady, high, and highly reliable stream of spendable income, where *income* is equated with coupon receipts. This goal is typified by the portfolio of an eleemosynary institution from which only the cash income can be spent, or by the portfolio of an income-beneficiary-remainderman trust where priority attaches to the income objective. Fixed income securities are a classic investment medium for such portfolios. Provided the portfolio is well diversified, both respect to issues and maturities, the income stream can virtually be counted on in the senses that the cash *will* come in and it will come in at a level that changes only slowly as interest rates vary through time. Moreover, the income will be larger than other investment media can provide, at least initially. The notion of bonds as a "widows and orphans" investment is as reasonable as it is commonplace.

When the objective shifts to some combination of income and growth of income and/or growth of principal, the case for bonds is not compelling. The dividend stream of a diversified portfolio of common stocks is also highly reliable and relatively insensitive to interest rate fluctuations,[3] and it will almost surely grow over time along with the value of the underlying principal.[4]

[3] For example, a review of data for the Standard & Poor's 500 reveals that over the period 1926 through 1981 there were only nine years when these common stocks showed an absolute year-to-year decrease in dividends, with the maximum decrease of 38.1 percent occurring in 1933; since World War II there have been only four years of dividend decrease, with the largest of these, a decrease of 4.1 percent, occurring in 1952.

[4] Over the years 1926–1981 the dividends paid on the Standard & Poor's 500 grew at an average annual rate of 2.4 percent. Over a surprisingly long span in

With respect to portfolio management practices, investment for current income is undemanding—indeed, the real dangers are that the portfolio will be totally ignored on the one hand, or managed more aggressively than it should be on the other! Clearly, the monitoring and control of credit risk is paramount. Maturity management designed to minimize fluctuations in income and avoid the risk of rolling over large quantities of maturing bonds in low interest rate environments is important, and for this reason the traditional "laddered" maturity structure—in which approximately equal quantities of bonds mature at fairly regular intervals—certainly makes sense (unless the manager can forecast interest rate highs years in advance, which seems unlikely). For similar reasons bond refunding can be a problem, especially because the temptation in managing for current income is to go for high coupon issues, and thus call risk should be watched carefully. The primary opportunity for active management probably lies in the area of swapping, both among broad sectors of the bond market or among substantially identical securities, to take advantage of what are viewed as transient yield aberrations.

II. INVESTING FOR ACCUMULATION OF VALUE

A second portfolio objective that rationally leads to fixed income securities investment is to accumulate value over time, especially when the time horizon is not extremely long or the tolerance for uncertainty is low. References to this as a "funding" portfolio objective capture its nature very well. In this context all intermediate

---

this period—from 1926 through 1958—the S & P 500 dividend yield actually exceeded the yield on Moody's Aaa corporate bonds. Since 1958 this relationship has been reversed, but even so, through 1976, dividend growth was such that money initially invested in the stocks would have been earning more cash income than money invested in bonds after eight years, on average. (In fairness, it should be noted that for funds invested in stocks at the beginning of three years prior to 1976—1969, 1972, and 1973—as of the end of 1985 the dividend return had still not caught up with the bond yield that would have resulted from investing in bonds at the beginning of these years, and because of the high yields on bonds compared to stocks since 1976 money invested in stocks at the beginning of any of these years would still be earning less.)

cash throw-offs of the portfolio are reinvested. No substantive distinction is made between value that accumulates from coupon flows, from the reinvestment of intermediate flows, or from appreciation of the "built-in" variety resulting from discounted securities converging on their redemption prices. The goal is simply to have a portfolio value at the end of the investment horizon that equals or exceeds some target expectation. While in practice there may be a *schedule* of horizons and target expectations, these are easily accommodated within the accumulation scheme provided withdrawals are unrelated to coupon receipts or changes in value over short intervals.

A prototypical example of such an accumulating portfolio results from the occasional practice in pension management of identifying a group of retired beneficiaries and setting aside a package of assets to fund their projected benefits. Another representative example arises when a municipality, say, floats a bond issue to fund a specific project and invests the proceeds in a portfolio designed to generate just enough cash to meet progress payments as they become due. Both these examples represent liquidating portfolios of a short-run nature. IRA accounts and employee benefit plans at the stage where contributions exceed benefit payments are also accumulating portfolios, but ones where the horizon is longer and greater uncertainty regarding future values are usually tolerated in return for an expectation of higher future value.

Because of the highly reliable nature of their flows (or perfectly reliable nature, in the case of U.S. Treasury issues), fixed income securities are an ideal investment medium for accumulating portfolios when the horizon is short or risk aversion is high. By proper choice of specific securities it is often possible to assemble a portfolio whose actual flows just match the pattern of funds needs, and thus there is no reinvestment and no reinvestment rate risk, nor is there any price risk. This approach has come to be known as *portfolio dedication.*

The bad music begins when it is infeasible or excessively expensive in terms of foregone returns to match the built-in flows from portfolio securities with funds needs. Under these circumstances, the "other" flows—those flows that result from reinvesting intermediate cash flows, from selling bonds, from called bonds, and the like—become important, and these flows are anything but highly predictable. By holding bonds of sufficiently short maturity it is usually possible to finesse price uncertainty, but reinvestment of intermediate flows is another matter. Such reinvestment and the rate at which reinvestment occurs, or *reinvestment rate risk,* are critical in portfolios that are accumulating value over the long run.

An alternative approach to managing reinvestment rate risk is to match the duration of the portfolio assets and the investment horizon in the operation known as *portfolio immunization.*[5] In this approach the portfolio is structured so that reinvestment rate risk and price risk should just offset each other, causing the realized return to just equal the yield at which the portfolio was originally immunized regardless of subsequent interest rate movements. Aside from implementational issues, the big problems with immunization are the highly defensive nature of the operation and the lack of fixed income securities with durations as long as investment horizons that are routinely encountered. The implication of the former problem is that immunization may not be the most desirable portfolio management practice in terms of returns foregone for risk avoided, while the latter suggests that securities other than fixed income securities may be appropriate investments.

Despite the recent popularity of dedication and immunization, it is probably fair to say that most accumulating portfolios—and certainly most *long run* accumulating portfolios—are not managed in a manner that formally deals with reinvestment rate risk. Instead, either by ignorance or design it is implicitly assumed that reinvestment considerations will average out over time. At the one extreme the portfolio may be managed in an essentially passive manner, with heavy emphasis on long-term securities and fairly consistent portfolio composition in terms of quality, sector allocation, and the like. At the other extreme it may be run in an aggressive manner, with "bets" on interest rate movements via maturity structure shifts or on other dimensions of the portfolio. In this way the portfolio may shade over into one managed for holding period returns, as discussed below. But what typifies all such portfolios is

[5]A useful review of immunization is provided by G.O. Bierwag, George C. Kaufman, and Alden Toevs, "Duration: Its Development and Use in Bond Portfolio Management," *Financial Analysts Journal,* July/August, 1983, pp. 15–35.

greater tolerance for risk, including reinvestment rate risk, than under the highly defensive strategies.

If the time horizon is reasonably long *and* risk tolerances are not extremely low, then investment media other than bonds may be more suitable for accumulating portfolios. It is well known that common stocks have had higher geometric mean periodic rates of return than bonds over long runs of history, and most observers feel that this will be the experience in the future. Moreover, common stocks with growing dividend streams tend to have longer durations than coupon bonds. It follows, therefore, that common stock investment will result in greater accumulation of value than fixed income securities over the long run, and they may better lay off reinvestment rate risk as well.[6,7]

With respect to portfolio management, appropriate techniques depend upon the level of aggressiveness that is tolerable. For defensive dedicated or immunized portfolios, about the only opportunity to add value through management is to engage in swaps to exploit temporary security or sector mispricing in a manner that does not change the basic dimensions of the portfolio. Cash flow

[6] For further discussion of the geometric mean and value accumulation, see my treatment in "Latane's Bequest: The Best of Portfolio Models," *The Journal of Portfolio Management,* Winter, 1986, pp. 21–30. With respect to the obvious question of what constitutes the "long run," using the Ibbotson-Sinquefeld data to examine the period 1926–1981, one finds only 13 out of 52 possible five-year periods in which high corporate bonds (Moody's Aaa corporates) had greater total returns than common stocks (Standard & Poor's 500); for U.S. Treasury bonds, there are also only 13 such periods. If the horizon is lengthened to ten years, common stocks dominated corporate bonds in 36 out of 47 possible periods, and dominated Treasury issues in 40 of the possible periods. Over this span of years the longest period over which someone who bought stocks would be behind someone who invested in corporate bonds was 21 years, with the holding period beginning in 1930. The longest equivalent period with Treasuries was 16 years, beginning in the same year. See Roger G. Ibbotson and Rex A. Sinquefeld, *Stocks, Bonds, Bills, and Inflation: The Past and the Future* (Charlottesville, Virginia: The Financial Analysts Research Foundation, 1982.)

[7] The relevance of the long durations of common stocks to investing for the long run are discussed by Peter L. Bernstein in a superb but unpublished speech delivered to the Institutional Investor Annual Pension Fund Conference in New York City on February 19, 1984, entitled "What Does Long-Term Investing Really Mean?"

shocks such as might result from an unexpected call are especially troublesome, and exposure to this type of disruption should be monitored closely. For less defensive portfolios, the range of options is wide. Many will be managed in an essentially passive manner, using indexing or what amounts to indexing. Such a strategy, with its implied laddering of maturities, has the effect of minimizing reinvestment rate shocks by exposing funds for reinvestment to a wide variety of interest rate environments. Substitution and sector swapping is consistent with such a strategy. With increasing aggressiveness, the sky is the limit. In particular, large bets on interest rates, quality sectors, and the like may be justified provided the manager is believed to have the "touch" and the portfolio can bear the risk. But even at this level of aggressiveness reinvestment considerations and the factors that enter into it—such as exposure to refunding call—are critical.

A particular technique for dealing with accumulating portfolios, "contingent immunization," is of interest not so much for the technique itself as for the message it conveys about reinvestment rate risk.[8] In contingent immunization the portfolio is managed actively so long as the combination of its value and prevailing interest rates are such that if immunized its terminal value would exceed some predetermined accumulation goal; if a point is reached at which its immunized terminal value would only just attain the goal then active management is supposed to cease and the portfolio is to be immunized. Obviously this is nothing more than active management accompanied by a resolution to cease active management if it does not pay off. What is interesting about the technique is that it calls attention in a forceful way to reinvestment considerations. With contingent immunization the portfolio value can have increased substantially, but if the rollover rate of interest (akin to the reinvestment rate) has gone down sufficiently the portfolio will not be adequate to reach the accumulation objective; the portfolio can have depreciated, but if the rollover rate has risen sufficiently, the accumulation outlook will have improved. The message is that

[8] Contingent immunization is a product of Salomon Brothers, Inc. For a detailed exposition see Martin L. Leibowitz and Alfred Weinberger, "The Uses of Contingent Immunization," *Journal of Portfolio Management,* Fall, 1981, pp. 51–55.

with accumulation portfolios, enhancement of value is not enough.
The manager should always worry about reinvestment rates, and
always concentrate on the value to which the portfolio will accumulate.

III. INVESTING FOR HOLDING
PERIOD RETURNS

The holding period return, or total return, is simply the ending
value of the portfolio plus cash received from investments during
the holding period, all divided by the beginning-of-period value of
the portfolio. In investing for holding period returns, the objective
is to maximize the return that is achieved in each period commen-
surate with the risk that is assumed.

Fixed income portfolios are often managed for holding period
returns, and sometimes this emphasis is justified. But in some circumstances the holding period return objective is not really appropriate even though it is the objective for which the portfolio is
managed, and in many circumstances it is not really *the* objective
for which the portfolio is managed even though it is the *nominal*
objective.

Investing for holding period returns would appear to make the
most sense under two obvious conditions: first, no legal or institutional differentiation exists between return from cash receipts and
return from price appreciation; and second, no particular intention exists to reinvest cash thrown off by the portfolio in fixed
income securities or even to remain invested in fixed income securities.[9] Therefore, for example, an aggressive investor might place
funds in bonds in the anticipation that interest rates are going to
decline, with the expectation that these funds would be moved
to another investment medium such as common stocks after the
decline occurs. Under these circumstances the holding period

---

[9] Differential taxation of capital gains and ordinary income, such as existed
prior to the tax reform legislation of 1986, does not constitute an institutional
difference in the first sense; such differentiation would simply underscore the
need to look at *after-tax* holding period returns. The point in the text is intended to refer to situations where the differentiation alters spending or consumption decisions.

return objective and fixed income investment appear to be entirely compatible. Some fixed income investment may also be appropriate to diversify portfolios of other types of assets that are properly managed for holding period returns, such as *balanced* closed-end or mutual funds.[10]

In other circumstances the compatibility may not be so great. Publicly marketed bond funds and the fixed income component of employee benefit funds are two prime examples of portfolios that are nominally managed for holding period returns. The total rate of return is certainly the criterion by which the portfolio performance is usually evaluated, and it seems to be the objective with which most managers of such portfolios are preoccupied. However, undue emphasis on the holding period return objective, especially in the short run, can lead to decisions that the owners, beneficiaries, or sponsors of such portfolios might not view with approval in the proverbial situation in which they "know all the facts."

Consider the position of many managers of bond fund portfolios over the past five years, a period of dramatic interest rate decline. If the manager had anticipated at least a portion of this decline then the purely total return-oriented portfolio would have consisted of long bonds of low coupon. However, many managers of such portfolios over this interval were hesitant to shift into low coupon issues because of the income that would have been foregone in the interim. At the present time (mid-1986), when more is probably to be feared than hoped for in terms of future interest rate movements, many managers of these portfolios would like to shorten their maturities. However, doing so will result in realizing heretofore unrealized capital gains and rolling the money over into lower yielding securities, thereby adversely affecting the income stream once again. For this reason many managers have resisted wholesale restructuring. They realize that even though

[10] A number of authors have dealt with the portfolio diversification implications of different types of fixed income securities. See, e.g., my piece in the *Journal of Financial and Quantitative Analysis* for September, 1973, "Portfolio-Relevant Characteristics of Long Term Marketable Securities," pp. 565–585; Gordon J. Alexander, "Mixed Security Testing of Alternative Portfolio Selection Models," *Journal of Financial and Quantitative Analysis,* December, 1977, pp. 817–832; or William F. Sharpe, *Investments,* Third Edition (Englewood Cliffs, New Jersey: Prentice-Hall, 1985), p. 346.

holding period returns may be the nominal objective of such funds, many of the investors are actually in them for income they generate. Therefore they are willing to compromise on the holding period return objective in return for the spendable income objective.

A similar situation is arising in pension portfolios, which are probably best viewed as accumulating portfolios even though often they too are nominally managed for holding period returns. Because of lower borrowing costs and the fact that the Internal Revenue Service effectively subsidizes the retirement of debt via cash tender offers, many corporations are now making tender offers for their high coupon debt that is not currently refundable.[11] Since such offers are made at prices above the current market price of the bonds, they have the effect of enhancing the holding period return of the portfolio that holds them if the tender offer is accepted. However, some pension fund managers are examining their reinvestment alternatives and concluding that the fund will be better off over the long run if the tenders are *not* accepted.

The point, therefore, is that there are relatively few fixed income portfolios for which total returns should be the overriding objective, including two types that are often offered as examples of portfolios with this objective. The more common case is one in which holding period returns can be thought of as a secondary objective, one that should be pursued as long as it is not incompatible with the primary objective of the portfolio. The incompatibility appears to be least for accumulating portfolios. Over any given horizon, value in such portfolios must necessarily accumulate at a *rate* equal to the geometric mean of the holding period returns that are realized within that interval. As long as future holding period returns are not sacrificed for future returns there is no problem. (Accumulation of dollar value is another matter; if cash additions to the portfolio are being made over time, it is better for the holding period returns to be loaded toward the end of the horizon.) Given the general movement of interest rates, which of

[11] For a discussion of the economics of such tendering operations and the implications for investors, see Andy J. Kalotay, "Refunding Considerations for High-Coupon Debt," in *CFA Readings in Fixed Income Securities* (Charlottesville, Virginia: The Institute of Chartered Financial Analysts, 1985), pp. 136–144.

course is beyond the control of the portfolio manager, the objective of seeking holding period returns is a reasonable one.[12]

Investing for holding period returns is straightforward in principle even though it may be difficult in practice. The goal is simply to construct the portfolio that will show the largest appreciation over the holding period considering both the market's expectations regarding future bond prices or rates *and* the existing structure of bond prices or rates. In other words, the emphasis should be on identifying mispricing in the marketplace. Interest rate plays, which have come to dominate total return investing, illustrate the relevance of these considerations. The manager may have a certain expectation regarding future interest rates, and this expectation may suggest an appropriate portfolio composition in terms of maturity, coupon, and the like to exploit the move towards the expected rates. But first it is necessary to check the pricing of these characteristics in the marketplace. It may be that the manager's expectations are so commonly held that the anticipated future pricing is already built in to the existing structure of yields and prices—and in fixed income investing, as in equity investing, the largest rewards will go to the manager who can identify and exploit errors in the consensus expectation of the future.

Mispricing may also be identifiable in other "large ways"—along dimensions of bond quality, type of security, call protection, or any other measurable characteristic of fixed income securities—or in "small ways," such as differing yields on substantially identical securities. Scenario or "what if" analysis should clearly play a large role in investing for holding period returns, as should constant attention to patterns of pricing in the marketplace. If the manager's strength of conviction is sufficiently great, then the result should be portfolios that are structured with *bullet* maturities and equivalent concentration along other dimensions.

---

[12] In a recent article, "Rethinking Our Thinking About Interest Rates," *Financial Analysts Journal*, March/April, 1985, pp. 62–67, I argue that declines in interest rates are generally counterproductive from the viewpoint of the accumulating investor because of the implications for reinvestment. However, I also observe that managers should seek to increase value or avoid loss as much as possible given the interest rate environment that exists, and conclude that holding period returns can be valid means of evaluating the portfolio manager.

ARTICLE 2

CHRIS P. DIALYNAS is a Principal of Pacific Investment
Management Company of Newport Beach, California,
which specializes in institutional bond management. He
earned a degree in economics from Pomona College and an
MBA in Finance from the University of Chicago.

THE ACTIVE DECISIONS IN THE SELECTION OF PASSIVE MANAGEMENT AND PERFORMANCE BOGEYS

Chris P. Dialynas
Principal
Pacific Investment Management Company

The asset allocation decision is perhaps a plan sponsor's most important decision. Within the scope of that decision, the selection of investment managers and performance bogeys are critical. Traditional asset allocation methods are based on studies of relative returns and risk over long periods of time. Performance periods, however, both for the plan itself and the investment manager entrusted with the funds, are based upon relatively short time spans. As such, there is an inherent inconsistency in the process.

In this article the active bond management process will be explored and contrasted with the "passive management" option. We will also examine the differences in index composition. Performance inferences will be made based exclusively on the index composition and the future economic environment. We will see that successful bond management, be it active or passive, depends upon good long-term economic forecasting and a thorough understanding

19

of the mathematical dynamics of fixed income obligations. Likewise, selection of a performance bogey depends upon similar considerations as well as the liability structure of the plan itself.

I. ACTIVE BOND MANAGEMENT

Active management of bond portfolios capitalizes on changing relations among bonds to enhance performance. Volatility in interest rates and changes in the amount of volatility induce divergences in the relative price between bonds. Since volatility, by definition, allows for opportunity, the fact that during the first half of 1986, active bond managers as a class have under-performed the passive indexes in one of the most volatile bond markets in the past 50 years seems counter-intuitive. What has gone wrong?

Active bond managers each employ their own methods for relative value analysis. Common elements among most managers are historical relations, liquidity considerations, and market segmentation. Market segmentation allegedly creates opportunities and historical analysis provides the timing cue. Unfortunately, since the world is in perpetual motion and constant evolution, neither market segmentation nor historical analysis is able to withstand the greater forces of change. Both methods, either separately or jointly, are impotent. The dramatic increase in volatility experienced in recent years implies the world is turning and evolving more quickly. Paradoxically, many active managers are using methods voided by volatility to try to capitalize on volatility.

The mistakes of active bond managers have been costly. As a result, a significant move from active to passive (or indexed) management is in progress. Does this move make sense? To understand why the indexes have outperformed active managers, we need to dissect the active and passive portfolios and reconstruct the circumstances. We will see that the composition of the indexes and the circumstances produced a dynamic combination that was most difficult to beat.

While a variety of bond market indexes are popular today, only two were notable throughout the present business cycle. The Shearson Lehman Government Corporate (SLGC) bond index was the most popular and the Salomon High Grade Long Term Bond

Index was the traditional measure. Our focus will be primarily on the SLGC Index. We will conclude with a comparison of the different indexes and their respective performance expectations given various interest rate movements.

The SLGC Index

The SLGC is primarily composed of government and agency securities. The composition of the index is detailed below:

	6/1980	6/1984	6/1986
U.S. Government	43.38	61.54	63.27
Agency	18.93	14.46	11.35
Corporates	30.72	18.54	18.74
Finance	6.93	5.47	6.55

The SLGC is constructed such that its composition is representative of the relative distribution of securities in the market. Since the government issues the vast majority of debt, it is not surprising that the index holds such a high and increasing proportion of government securities. The index must, by definition, "buy" the debt. With the exception of some of the 30-year government bonds issued during this period, virtually all of the government and agency debt held in the index is noncallable. Because of this, between 1980 and 1986 the index became increasingly call-protected. We will see that the callable/noncallable distribution is the most important distinguishing feature between the index and the managers.

Performance Characteristics of Callable and Noncallable Bonds

Exhibit 1 characterizes the expected performance characteristics of callable and noncallable bonds under different market environments. The market environments are described by two parameters, the direction of interest rates and the volatility of rates.

EXHIBIT 1
Expected Performance Characteristics for Callable and Noncallable Bonds under Different Market Environments

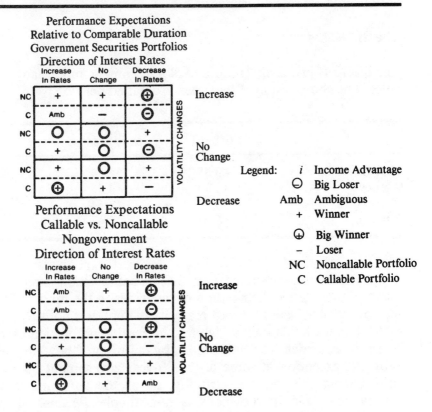

Performance Expectations
Relative to Comparable Duration
Government Securities Portfolios

Performance Expectations
Callable vs. Noncallable
Nongovernment

Legend:
i	Income Advantage
⊖	Big Loser
Amb	Ambiguous
+	Winner
⊕	Big Winner
–	Loser
NC	Noncallable Portfolio
C	Callable Portfolio

Callable bonds do well in rising rate environments and decreasing volatility environments. Decreases in volatility have the profound direct effect of reducing the value of the call option imbedded within the callable bond. Since the bond holder has effectively sold the option, as its value is reduced by the lower volatility, the total value of the bond increases independent of any interest rate movement.

Callable bonds do better than noncallable bonds in increasing rate environments because the higher rates cause the option to go out of the money. As the option goes out of the money its value diminishes and the bond's value increases. The option value

EXHIBIT 2
Call Features of the Bond Universe

Issue Type	Refunding Protection	Call Protection	Refunding Price
Treasury	Maturity*	Maturity	NA
Traditional agency	Maturity	Maturity	NA
Traditional agency	Ten Years	None	Premium
Traditional utility	Five Years	None	Premium
Traditional finance	Ten Years**	None	Premium
GNMA Pass-thru	None	None	100
FNMA Pass-thru	None	None	100
FHLMC PC	None	None	100
CMO	None	None	100
Title XI	None***	None***	100***

*Some 30 year Government Bonds were issued with 25 years of call-protection.
**A decline in receivables may permit an immediate par call.
***Default negates any refunding or call-protection.

decline cushions the bond price decline induced by higher rates, thereby reducing the *effective duration* of the bond. The effective duration of the bond decreases as rates increase, and the callable bond outperforms the noncallable bond whose duration is relatively inelastic.

Noncallable bonds perform better than callable bonds in decreasing rate and increasing volatility environments. Their effective duration increases in decreasing rate environments since, exclusive of credit risk considerations, the noncallable bonds are more *convex*[1]; i.e., their *rate* of price increase outpaces that of the comparable duration callable bonds. As the volatility of interest rates increases, noncallable bonds will command a premium, and since the noncallable bonds are more convex, they appreciate exclusively because of their relative convexity advantage. Exhibit 2 lists the call features of bonds by various issuers.

[1] Convexity is the measure of that portion of a bond's price change (as yields change) that is not explained by the bond's duration.

A Look at Market Volatility

It is helpful to examine the volatility of the bond market to make inferences about performance attributes. Exhibit 3 displays the volatility of the bond market as described by the 6 month moving average of the 12 month standard deviation of total return on 30 year U.S. Treasury bonds.

Unprecedented, high volatility has been experienced in the bond market during the past decade. Not only has volatility been high but the degree of variation in volatility has been high. It is *volatility change* that influences the value of options which, in turn, cause relative performance differences between callable and noncallable portfolios.

EXHIBIT 3
Volatility of Rate of Return on 30-Year Bond
6-Month Moving Average of 12-Month Standard Deviation

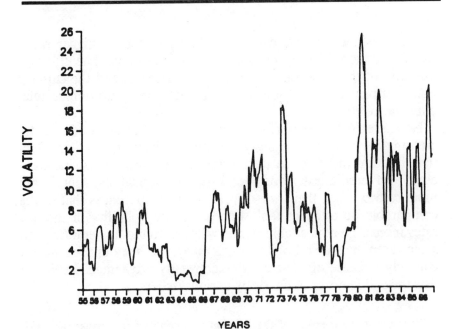

A Look at Interest Rates

The final piece of the puzzle is the direction of interest rates. Exhibit 4 depicts the movement of rates over the last eleven years. We observe dramatic changes in the absolute level of rates. As such changes occur, the relative values of callable and noncallable bonds change. Lower rates work to the advantage of noncallable bonds and higher rates to the advantage of callable bonds.

II. A LOOK AT RECENT HISTORY

Exhibit 5 shows the historical performance of callable and non-callable bonds from 1976 to 1986. The volatility of the bond market increased from about 4 percent in 1976 to about 20 percent

---

EXHIBIT 4
Yield to Maturity on Current Long Bond
January 1976 to June 1986

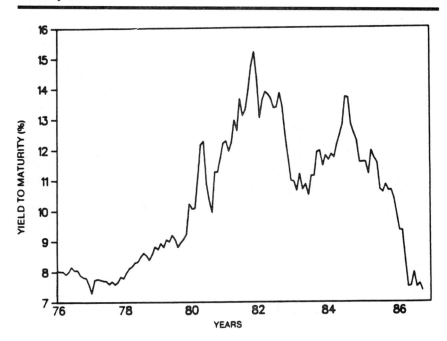

EXHIBIT 5
Performance Differences between Callable and Noncallable Bonds during Prior Periods

Portfolio Composition	1976–1982 Interest Rates Increased Volatility Increased	1982–1986 Interest Rates Declined Volatility Unchanged	1976–1986 Interest Rates Declined Slightly Volatility Increased
Callable	–	(–)	–
Noncallable	+	(++)	+

The interest rate increase from 8% to 14¹/₂% moved the call features out of the money which swamped the change from 4% to 20% in volatility. However while that effect caused relative spread ratios to decline, nominal spreads actually increased. Thus, non-callable portfolios outperformed callable bond portfolios by a small margin during this period. See Appendix I.

The steep decline in interest rates and the virtually unchanged level of high volatility favored noncallable over callable portfolios by a wide margin. The options became in the money and shortened the duration of the callable portfolio, revealing the dramatic effects of negative convexity!

While interest rates declined only modestly, the tremendous increase in volatility served to make the option more valuable. A countervailing effect of callable issues' income advantage does not offset their decrease in principal value created by the option over short investment horizons.

in 1982. In the period from 1976 to 1982, volatility ranged between 2 percent and 20 percent. In the period from 1982 to 1986, volatility was never less than 7 percent. Over the complete period from 1976–1986, average volatility tripled. This information alone would favor bond portfolios containing the *fewest* callable securities. However, all else equal, we would prefer noncallable portfolios during the period from 1976–1982 and callable ones during the 1982–1986 period. (See Appendix I.)

Yields on long-term government bonds increased from 8 percent in 1976 to 14½ percent in 1982. In the 1982 to 1986 period, rates dropped from 14½ percent to 7.25 percent. The range in rates from 1976 to 1982 was 8 to 14½ percent. The range for the latter period was 7¼ percent to 14½ percent. We would expect portfolios containing callable securities to do best during the first period and portfolios containing call-free bonds to do best during the latter period.

III.   THE IMPLICIT FORECASTS OF VOLATILITY AND INTEREST RATES

Most active bond managers are sector managers or sector rotaters. They hold portfolios composed of a high proportion of non-government securities. These portfolios are short the call options or, viewed alternatively, long portfolios of callable bonds. Combining this observation with the preceding historical analysis, it is obvious that, adjusting for durational differences, most active managers under-performed the indexes during the first 6 months of 1986. Few people seem to have anticipated the magnitude of the change in interest rates and the profound increase in realized volatility. Both of these forecast errors were important detractors from performance. Even those managers who correctly forecasted the change in interest rates terribly underestimated the combined impact of increased volatility and declining rates on the value of the option. Thus, their selection of bonds was inconsistent with their forecast.

Bond management necessarily requires an interest rate forecast, a volatility forecast and a set of analytical models which calculate the future value of individual securities and portfolios of securities based upon those forecasts. It is the confluence of volatility movement and interest rate movement that affects bond values.

Similarly, the decision to move from active to passive management or from passive to active is necessarily predicated upon an implicit forecast of both interest rates and volatility. Moreover, the choice of index as a bogey for active managers or as a source of investment value contains within it an implicit forecast of both rates and volatility.

The choice of indexes today (long government rates at 7 1/2 percent) is a choice of buying or selling convexity and duration. Convex portfolios, such as the SLGC, hold a high percentage of non-callable bonds. Portfolios with little convexity, such as the Shearson Lehman Aggregate Index[2] (SL AG) hold many callable bonds. Thus the durations of convex portfolios move inversely with market rates, whereas the durations of non-convex portfolios may, perversely, change in the same direction as rates.

Simply stated, in today's world, the SLGC is a convex portfolio and the SL AG is not as convex.[3] As such, the SLGC yields less than the SL AG and is much more sensitive to changes in interest rates and changes in volatility. However, if rates decline from here, the SL AG index will under-perform the SLGC by a significant margin—just as many active managers have done recently—because its duration will not increase and may actually decrease. We compare expected performance characteristics in Exhibit 6.

The expected differences in portfolio performance are largely the result of the one-dimensional nature of duration as a descriptive risk variable. Portfolios with a high proportion of bonds containing imbedded call options which are at or near the money perversely influence duration when interest rates change. Rate increases initially cause an *increase* in portfolio durations and rate decreases cause a *decrease* in portfolio durations. The aggregate indexes, today, represent portfolios with this unconventional durational attribute because they contain a high proportion of callable bonds at or near the money. Portfolios described in terms of both

[2] The Shearson Lehman Aggregate Index includes mortgage pass-throughs in its composition.

[3] See Appendix II for an explanation.

EXHIBIT 6
Expected Performance Characteristics Compared

Interest Rates	Unch.	Rise	Fall	Unch.	Unch.	Rise	Rise	Fall	Fall
Volatility	Unch.	Unch.	Unch.	Rises	Falls	Rises	Falls	Rises	Falls
Index which Performs Best	SL AG	SL AG	SLGC	SLGC	SL AG	Ambiguous (SL AG) **	SL AG	SLGC	Ambiguous (SLGC) **

**Interest rate movements are usually the prevailing force. The index in parenthesis would therefore dominate unless the interest rate movement was very small and the volatility movement great.

duration and convexity have greater explanatory power since their risk parameters have been more fully defined.

Implicit within a move to passive management is both a volatility and an interest rate forecast. The move to passive management reinforces Say's Law, which holds that supply creates its own demand. Passive investment portfolios have done well in spite of their investment criterion which holds as its main tenet—buy that which is produced independent of price or value considerations. Passive, narrow indexes, such as the SLGC, have even done well recently because of the circumstances—radically lower rates and increased volatility, both of which benefitted call-protected portfolios. The past is prologue . . . today's investment choice will be judged by tomorrow's circumstances.

The compositional and structural differences between the narrow and aggregate indexes are, today, very pronounced. Previously, while compositionally distinct, their structural similarities caused highly correlated performance results. The performance characteristics of the two indexes will now differ to a greater degree than has been previously experienced. In fact, the aggregate index will experience a gradual, unpredictable lengthening in duration as the high percentage of low duration premium mortgages are prepaid and refinanced with current coupon longer duration mortgages. This lengthening will occur quite independently of any changes in interest rates.

Those who are required to select a performance bogey for their fund have a difficult choice. The bogey performs the role of directing the risk of the assets. The choice involves a trade-off between a bogey that: (1) replicates the proportional distribution of bonds in the market, (2) has risk characteristics complementary to the liability structure of the assets, and (3) has a relatively neutral market bias associated with it. Unfortunately, no bogey satisfies all of these requirements, and the trade-offs can be costly.

The choices are difficult. Ultimately, correct macroeconomic forecasts will dominate the active/passive choice. Will volatility increase or diminish and when? Will rates go up or down and when? What is it that influences volatility? How do interest rate changes and volatility changes trade off? When does the volatility/ interest rate forecast favor one index over the other? These are the tough questions that should be addressed.

APPENDIX I

The Subtle Disparities between Nominal and Relative Yields

The rules presented in this article may be partially violated when large movements in interest rates occur. Interest rate movements induce many influences on bond prices. The two primary effects of rates and volatility were discussed in this article. Other effects, while normally modest, take on greater importance as the change in interest rates is magnified. A simple example is presented below:

Yield Ratio	Reference Yield	Inter-market Yield	Nominal Yield Spread	Break even Ratio
1.3	5%	6.5	1.50	1.30
1.3	10%	13.00	3.00	1.15
1.3	15%	19.50	4.50	1.10

Investors normally demand premiums in percentage terms whereas both performance and actual money made or lost is defined in nominal terms. As such, since interest rates serve as our reference parameter, large changes in this parameter cause contradictory results between nominal and relative spreads. As we observe in the table above, at constant relative spreads, nominal spreads change dramatically. By inference, portfolios which correctly forecast relative spreads can lose in both the performance arena and the bottom line tally.

APPENDIX II

The SL AG and the SLGC have exhibited a high historical correlation. The high correlation was violated during the first half of 1986. It is important to understand why the high correlation existed and why it diverged in 1986 to better understand tomorrow's expected correlation.

It was previously noted that the major distinction between the SLGC and the SL AG is the inclusion of mortgages in the SL AG.

As such, we must determine whether these securities' options were at the money, in the money or out of the money to determine their effect on portfolio convexity. The simplest framework we can utilize to evaluate the effect on convexity is a pricing framework. Mortgages selling at a discount exhibit positive convexity and higher durations, whereas other mortgages exhibit low or negative convexity and lower durations.

From Exhibit 7 we observe that in 1982 all mortgages were at par or a discount. In 1984 most mortgages were at a discount. The situation differed in June 1986 in that very few mortgages are priced at a discount. This means that the SL AG exhibited a non-callable character through 1984 and most of 1985, but reversed late in 1985. At that point it took on negative convexity and a callable character. Today it has that callable character and therefore, a shorter effective duration. In fact, in contrast to non-callable indexes, its duration will decrease as rates *decline* and increase as rates increase.

EXHIBIT 7
Percent of Outstanding GNMA's Priced At or Below Par

June/ 1978	79	June/ 1980	81	June/ 1982	83	June/ 1984	85	June/ 1986 (Line)
96.8	100	97.4	100	97.1	71.6	95.7	48.0	34.9

ARTICLE 3

EDGAR A. ROBIE, JR. is a Managing Director with Western Asset Management Company in Los Angeles, California. His responsibilities include coordination of the firm's investment strategy, quantitative development and product innovation. Mr. Robie earned his B.S.B.A. in Finance at Nichols College and his M.B.A. in Finance and Economics from Babson College.

PETER C. LAMBERT is an Assistant Vice President with Western Asset Management Company in Los Angeles, California. His responsibilities include the development and management of passive portfolio products and the application of quantitative methodologies to active fixed income portfolio strategy. Mr. Lambert earned his B.A. in Philosophy from the University of California at Santa Cruz and his M.B.A. in Finance and Economics from the University of California at Los Angeles.

FIXED INCOME NORMAL PORTFOLIOS AND THEIR APPLICATION TO FUND MANAGEMENT

Edgar A. Robie, Jr.
Managing Director
Western Asset Management Company

and

Peter C. Lambert
Assistant Vice President
Western Asset Management Company

With the increased volatility of the bond markets and the plethora of management styles, plan sponsors who have a portion of their assets invested in the fixed income markets have found themselves carefully scrutinizing both the manager's investment process and his performance. Such evaluation usually takes the form of total return measurement and its comparison to market indices or other portfolios from the manager's "peer group." Total return measurement tells a sponsor little about a manager's investment process and its contribution to the total return. Moreover, this focus on short-term total return leads to a situation in which manager performance is measured against a bogey that is inappropriate for the task. The result is not only that performance is incorrectly evaluated but that the original rationale for including fixed income investments in the fund is forgotten. What is needed is a benchmark that accurately reflects the objectives of a manager's portfolio and its contribution to the total fund.

The purpose of this article is to propose the use of normal portfolios as a practical tool for the objectification and quantification of a fixed income manager's investment process and to demonstrate the applicability of its use in fund management. The identification of a manager's normal portfolio provides a basis for evaluating portfolio performance with respect to its stated objectives.

Until quite recently, the use of the normal portfolio concept has been confined to equity managers and fund sponsors. The notion of specifically identifying the goals of fixed income portfolio management and relating the portfolio's short-term performance to its long-term goals was suggested by Leibowitz in an article which establishes the usefulness of "baseline" or normal portfolios.[1]

In that same article it was suggested that the investment process may be characterized by four major steps.[2] The process could also be illustrated as shown in Exhibit 1.

The first step involves the plan sponsor's allocation of funds to broad asset classes (e.g., fixed income). The second step involves the selection of managers according to their investment processes identified by their long-run exposure to specific market characteristics. The third step is the manager's active management process in which portfolio holdings are adjusted vis-a-vis their long-run exposure in response to current market conditions. The fourth step reviews and evaluates the contribution of the strategic decisions to the manager's stated objectives in order to ensure that the portfolio performance and associated risk are in line with the sponsor's original expectations.

[1] Martin L. Leibowitz, "Goal Oriented Bond Portfolio Management," *Journal of Portfolio Management*, Summer 1979, pp. 13–18.
[2] *Ibid.*

EXHIBIT 1
Overview of the Investment Management Process

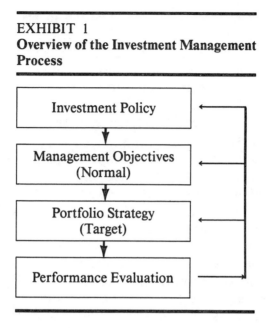

I. THE EVOLUTION OF THE NORMAL PORTFOLIO

The construction of the normal portfolio includes the definition and quantification of both the passive and active components of the manager's investment process. It begins with the identification of the broad universe of investable fixed income securities and, proceeding through several stages, establishes the average exposures to specific market characteristics (e.g., duration, sector, coupon and quality) over a long-run investment horizon. Because it is often difficult for managers to articulate their investment process and identify these average, long-run characteristics, it may be useful to consider the investment process in three stages. These stages correspond to portfolios whose attributes can be defined with increasing specificity and reflect the strategic decision-making process inherent in active management. These three stages may be defined as follows:

1. *Definition of the benchmark portfolio.* This is the appropriate universe of investable fixed income securities from which the

manager selects securities for inclusion in his portfolios. For practical application it is usually sufficient to use one (or a combination) of the several publicly available bond indices (e.g. The Salomon Brothers Broad Investment-Grade Bond Index, the Shearson/Lehman Composite Index or the Merrill Lynch High Yield Index). Plan sponsors have traditionally used these "portfolios" as benchmarks for evaluating managers' total rate-of-return performance.

2. *Identification of the manager's normal portfolio.*   This portfolio represents the set of "passive" or "neutral" investment positions which best depicts the manager's long-run strategy and average exposures to market characteristics. Through its exposure to market characteristics such as duration, sector, coupon and quality, the normal portfolio serves as the best predictor of the expected risk and return of the manager's portfolios. The normal portfolio captures the essence of a manager's long-run investment style and so serves as a point of reference for evaluating the success of his active investment decisions.

3. *Identification of the target portfolio.*   The target portfolio is an objective depiction of the manager's investment strategy at a given point-in-time. The target portfolio's deviations from the normal portfolio represent the manager's responses to current market conditions. The target portfolio is the manager's optimal portfolio at a given point-in-time based upon his expectations and constrained by his overall investment policy or style.

These three stages of portfolio construction mirror the underlying investment process and provide a framework for use in constructing the normal portfolio.

II. CONSTRUCTION OF THE NORMAL PORTFOLIO

The construction of a manager's normal portfolio is no simple task. It requires the manager to identify his long-run objectives and to distinguish between the passive and active components of his investment style. The first step is to characterize the manager's investment philosophy from which his investment process or "style" is derived. Such a characterization might include the following statements of objectives:

1. As a broad-scale or "core" fixed income manager, the fixed income component of an investment fund is a "stabilizing force" which should be relatively free from the volatility and economic risks associated with the equity components of the fund. To this end, the investment philosophy calls for holdings in most of the major sectors of the fixed income markets but excludes lower quality securities. Emphasis should be on those sectors which consistently offer opportunities to capture excess returns by exploiting inefficiencies.

2. The fixed income component of a client's fund should be a provider of stable cash flow that may be depended upon under virtually any economic condition. Consequently, investment concentration is in those securities which provide stable total returns irrespective of the current interest rate environment.

3. Recognizing the impossibility of consistently predicting the movement of interest rates, the investment strategy limits unnecessary exposure to interest rate risk. Hence, our portfolios will, on average, maintain a duration equal to that of the benchmark portfolio; at no time will a portfolio's duration deviate from the duration of the benchmark portfolio by more than 20 percent.

Using such general objectives as guidelines, the next step is to specifically identify the manager's exposure to sectors of the fixed income market. A manager's sector exposures may be thought of as his "preferred habitat" for making active investment decisions. A further requirement of the normal portfolio definition is that its holdings reflect the average holdings in a manager's portfolios over a relatively long period of time.

The following is an example of how a manager's investment exposure to the broad market sectors may be characterized. Note that sector weightings are specified with respect to the benchmark portfolio and that the stated rationale for each sector exposure supports this manager's overall investment policy and objectives.

Normal Portfolio Characteristics

A. *Governments & Agencies* (Underweighting: 25%; SBBI[3] = 57%): A deliberate under-allocation is made to governments and agencies in the normal portfolio as they traditionally do not provide the yields available from other sectors. However, due to the liquidity of this sector, they provide a convenient means of effecting changes in portfolio duration. They also provide additional diversification to the portfolio and mitigate a portion of the credit risk assumed in other market sectors.

B. *Corporates* (Overweighting: 30%; SBBI = 22%): A substantial emphasis on corporates in the normal portfolio is due to the attractive opportunities provided by inefficiencies which exist within this sector (i.e., credit perception, structural qualities and technical factors) as well as the generous yield-to-maturity characteristics of the sector.

C. *Mortgage Pass-Throughs* (Overweighting: 40%; SBBI = 21%): A high concentration is allocated to mortgage pass-throughs in the normal portfolio due to both the securities' cash-flow characteristics which provide generous yields compared to other broad market sectors and the numerous inefficiencies created by the continual introduction of new types of mortgage securities.

D. *Cash Equivalents* (Strategic Allocation: 5%; SBBI = 0%): While cash equivalents constitute a small fraction of the normal portfolio, as a sector it provides funds for investment opportunities and added flexibility in making the duration decision.

E. *Duration* (Equal to benchmark; may vary ± 20%): The Duration of the normal portfolio is equal to the benchmark (SBBI) portfolio. In times in which no strong convictions can be made about the direction of interest rates, a neutral position (normal portfolio duration = benchmark portfolio duration) represents the point at which economic and volatility risk equal that of the market.

The normal portfolio characteristics stated above provide an example of how any fixed income manager may go about constructing his

---

[3] Salomon Brothers Broad Investment-Grade Bond Index.

own normal portfolio. Depending upon a particular manager's investment objectives and strategies, more specific characterizations may be required. Some managers may maintain explicit concentrations in some subsector of the broad sectors mentioned. For instance, a manager's exposure to corporate bonds may be primarily concentrated in the utility sector; the manager's normal portfolio should reflect this fact. Similarly, a manager who desires a high-level of call protection may exclude high-coupon bonds priced at a premium to par.

A note of caution is appropriate here; when constructing a normal portfolio to be compared with one of the existing benchmark indices, it is crucial that all characteristics be specified according to the same methods of calculation. For instance, when determining the duration of the mortgage pass-through component, one's prepayment assumptions must match those used in the calculation of the benchmark portfolio's durations.

III. FUNCTIONS OF THE
NORMAL PORTFOLIO

The use of normal portfolios by fixed income investment managers provides a tremendous amount of information about the investment process that has previously been extremely difficult for the fund sponsor to define. We highlight three ways that the normal portfolio can contribute to the dialogue between the fund sponsor and his managers:

The normal portfolio:

1. Provides a mutual vantage point from which the success of a manager's active investment decisions can be evaluated with respect to the stated objectives of the fund.
2. Serves as the appropriate benchmark against which a manager's actual returns should be compared.
3. Provides an analytic description of a manager's investment process which a sponsor may employ to assess the appropriateness of a particular manager's style to his fund's overall investment objectives.

IV. EVALUATION OF ACTIVE MANAGEMENT

Given that the normal portfolio depicts a manager's long-term "neutral" or "passive" investment strategy, departures from the normal portfolio represent his strategic (active) investment decisions. Such departures are made in response to changes in current market conditions with the expectation of capturing excess returns or of protecting the value of the portfolio in adverse market conditions. The increasing tendency to focus on short-term total returns may cause managers to accept greater risks in pursuit of short-term returns than is appropriate in view of the fund's overall investment objectives. The use of a normal portfolio allows a manager's active investment strategies to be evaluated in terms of their contribution to the fund's overall risk and return profile.

The sum effect of a manager's active strategies on the portfolio's composition is embodied in the target portfolio discussed above. This portfolio may be illustrated by a matrix showing the percentage of the portfolio that is invested in each sector and the distribution of the durations of each of the sector holdings as in Exhibit 2.

The target portfolio serves as the model around which a manager's fully discretionary portfolios are constructed and maintained. As market conditions change, the composition of the target portfolio will adjust to take advantage of those changes.

Recent technological developments have resulted in quantitative tools that allow for the decomposition of a fixed income portfolio's return into its several sources.[4] Similar capabilities have been available for use in equity portfolios since the early 1970s.[5] One such "return attribution" system provides a method for attributing returns to the "external" interest rate environment and to the components of the active management process; maturity/duration management, sector/quality management and individual security selection.

Performing a return attribution analysis on both the normal and the target portfolios allows one to determine the marginal value

[4] Gifford H. Fong, Charles Pearson, and Oldrich Vasicek, "Bond Performance: Analyzing Sources of Return," *Journal of Portfolio Management,* Spring 1983, pp. 46–50.

[5] Eugene F. Fama, "Components of Investment Performance," *Journal of Finance,* June 1972, pp. 551–67.

EXHIBIT 2
Portfolio Characteristics Matrix
January 1986

Sector	Benchmark	Normal	Duration Distribution					Target	Average Duration
			0–1	1–3	3–5	5–7	7+		
Governments & Agencies	60	25		10	5			15	
Mortgage Instruments	20	40				30	10	40	
Corporates	20	30				25	5	30	
Cash & Cash Equivalents	0	5	15					15	
Target Portfolio			15	10	5	55	15	100	5.1 Yrs.
Normal Portfolio			10	20	20	30	20	100	4.6 Yrs.
Benchmark Portfolio			1	33	32	12	22	100	4.6 Yrs.

Percent of Portfolio

added by deviations from the normal portfolio. To the extent that such deviations add to the portfolio's risk exposure, the contribution of the added risk to portfolio returns can be assessed. Using the normal portfolio as a guide allows the portfolio manager to focus more clearly on his day-to-day activities on the fund sponsor's behalf.

V. THE NORMAL PORTFOLIO AS THE MANAGER'S APPROPRIATE BOGEY

While choosing the correct benchmark index is an important first step towards meaningful performance evaluation, the normal portfolio improves upon indices in that it is a customized benchmark for a particular manager. If we accept the normal portfolio as representative of the passive component of a manager's strategy that could be adopted as is, and view the active management decisions as deviations from his "normal" strategy, then the normal portfolio is the correct benchmark against which a manager's performance should be measured. To the extent that the returns on a manager's target or actual portfolios exceed those earned by his normal portfolio, then his active management strategies may be considered successful. However, if a manager's returns are less than those of his normal portfolio, he would have been better-off investing in a portfolio designed to replicate the characteristics of the normal portfolio.

We have tracked the normal portfolio described above for the six year period beginning January 1, 1980 and ending December 31, 1985. The returns on this normal portfolio were compared to the benchmark portfolio, in this case the Salomon Brothers Broad Investment-Grade Bond Index, and to a composite portfolio of 10 fully discretionary portfolios which serves as a proxy for the target portfolio. Over this period, the normal portfolio returned 49 basis points above the benchmark index on an annualized basis; the proxy target portfolio returned another 127 basis points more than the normal portfolio on the same annualized basis. While the total rate-of-return volatility of the normal portfolio was slightly higher than that of the benchmark index (13.29 percent vs. 12.18 percent in annual standard deviation), the volatility of the target portfolio was less than that of both the normal and benchmark portfolios

EXHIBIT 3A
Risk/Return Analysis
January 1, 1980–December 31, 1985

Sector/Portfolio	Annual Geometric Mean Return	Annual Standard Deviation
Treasury/Agency*	13.75	9.94
Corporates*	14.20	15.03
Mortgage Pass-throughs*	15.04	15.89
3-Month T-Bill	10.31	1.17
SBBI*	13.99	12.18
Normal Portfolio	14.48	13.29
Target Portfolio	15.75	11.59

* Source: Salomon Brothers Inc

EXHIBIT 3B
Risk/Return Analysis
January 1, 1980–December 31, 1985

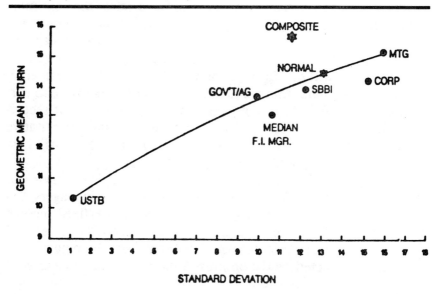

(11.59 percent). These results are summarized in Exhibits 3A and 3B along with the comparable statistics for the four broad sectors.

In this example, the active strategies followed by the managers, as exemplified by the proxy target portfolio, have decidedly been successful. Not only has total rate-of-return volatility been reduced (in accordance with the manager's stated objectives presented in Exhibit 3), but returns have been significantly enhanced.

VI. USING THE NORMAL PORTFOLIO
TO SELECT MANAGERS

As fund sponsors increase the number of managers in a multiple-manager environment, the aggregate holdings of the fund's active managers tend to resemble the market portfolio of investable assets. While this provides the fund with the benefits of maximum risk diversification, it mitigates the original intention of hiring "specialty" managers. In short, as the fund assumes the risk profile of the market, it will assume the market's return profile.

The normal portfolio describes the manager's average or "normal" exposure to market characteristics. As such, it is the best prediction of the expected risk and return of a manager's portfolio. To the extent that a plan sponsor attempts to select the "optimal" mix of managers for a multiple-manager fund, the normal portfolio is the best available input to such a process. Sponsors can use managers' normal portfolios to select the allocations to various managers that will provide the fund with the desired diversification benefits while maintaining a greater than market exposure to certain characteristics (e.g., high-yield securities or discount securities). A combination of qualitative judgement and quantitative techniques may be used to select that mix of managers which best fits the overall goals and objectives of the fund.

Using mean-variance optimization techniques, the sponsor can determine the most efficient allocation to his active managers. Exhibit 4 shows the normal risk/return profiles of six fixed income managers and the correlation among them based on five years of quarterly returns. In order to ensure that some minimum number of managers is selected by the optimizer, the maximum allocation to any one manager may be constrained by an appropriate percentage. Exhibit 5 and 6 have constrained the maximum allocation to 25

EXHIBIT 4
Manager Risk/Return Profiles

	Return	Standard Deviation	Correlation					
			(1)	(2)	(3)	(4)	(5)	(6)
Manager 1	18.92%	5.05%	1.000					
Manager 2	14.49	4.39	.766	1.000				
Manager 3	15.06	5.28	.750	.965	1.000			
Manager 4	17.11	6.50	.748	.945	.920	1.000		
Manager 5	14.81	5.46	.706	.926	.935	.954	1.000	
Manager 6	15.92	5.22	.785	.966	.978	.949	.942	1.000

percent and 33 percent, which provides for a minimum of four or three different managers, respectively.

These exhibits show how managers are eliminated as the allocation constraint is increased from 25 percent to 33 percent. In Exhibit 5 a manager can hold no more than 25 percent of the corpus and in Exhibit 6 no more than one third of the corpus. As the risk and expected return increase, the weaker performing managers are eliminated. This analysis suggests that greater returns can be achieved (50 basis points) for about the same level of risk with

EXHIBIT 5
Optimization Results and Efficient Frontier
(25% Allocation Constraint)

	Allocations									
	Min. Risk	(2)	(3)	(4)	(5)	(6)	(7)	(8)	(9)	Max. Return
Manager 1	25.0	25.0	25.0	25.0	25.0	25.0	25.0	25.0	25.0	25.0
Manager 2	25.0	25.0	25.0	25.0	25.0	25.0	25.0	25.0	15.1	0.0
Manager 3	17.2	22.0	21.2	16.9	13.4	8.7	4.0	0.0	9.9	25.0
Manager 4	0.0	0.0	3.8	8.1	11.6	16.3	21.0	25.0	25.0	25.0
Manager 5	12.4	3.0	0.0	0.0	0.0	0.0	0.0	0.0	0.0	0.0
Manager 6	20.4	25.0	25.0	25.0	25.0	25.0	25.0	25.0	25.0	25.0
Expected Return	16.0	16.1	16.2	16.3	16.3	16.4	16.5	16.6	16.7	16.8
Std. Deviation	4.7	4.7	4.8	4.8	4.9	4.9	5.0	5.0	5.1	5.2

EXHIBIT 6
Optimization Results and Efficient Frontier
(33% Allocation Constraint)

	Min. Risk	(2)	(3)	(4)	(5)	(6)	(7)	(8)	(9)	Max. Return
					Allocations					
Manager 1	33.0	33.0	33.0	33.0	33.0	33.0	33.0	33.0	33.0	33.3
Manager 2	33.0	33.0	33.0	30.2	25.1	19.7	15.6	11.0	5.8	0.0
Manager 3	16.0	8.5	0.3	0.0	0.0	0.0	0.0	0.0	0.0	0.0
Manager 4	0.0	0.0	0.0	3.8	8.9	14.3	18.4	23.0	28.2	33.3
Manager 5	13.4	10.4	0.7	0.0	0.0	0.0	0.0	0.0	0.0	0.0
Manager 6	4.6	15.1	33.0	33.0	33.0	33.0	33.0	33.0	33.0	33.3
Expected Return	16.2	16.2	16.4	16.5	16.7	16.8	16.9	17.0	17.2	17.3
Std. Deviation	4.6	4.6	4.6	4.7	4.8	4.9	5.0	5.1	5.2	5.3

fewer as opposed to a greater number of managers. The reduction in managers is further enhanced by lower fees and transaction costs. The sponsor may choose which efficient mix of managers is right for his fund.

The point of this example is to show how the information provided by managers' normal portfolios can be used with quantitative techniques to select the optimal mix of managers. The allocation of funds to each manager should, in the aggregate, provide the risk and return characteristics desired for the fixed income component of the fund.

VII. SUMMARY

Normal portfolios can be extremely useful to both the plan sponsor and the manager. Advantages of using this approach include defining the investment process of the manager and eliminating fuzzy generalities, providing a mutual vantage point for interpreting the *actual* returns and increasing the level of discussion between the sponsor and the manager. The normal portfolio is an objective point of reference which ensures continuity of understanding over any investment horizon between the sponsor and his managers.

ARTICLE 4

MARTIN L. LEIBOWITZ is a Managing Director of Salomon Brothers Inc where he is in charge of the Bond Portfolio Analysis Group.

Dr. Leibowitz received his bachelor's and master's degrees from the University of Chicago and his doctorate in mathematics from New York University.

Dr. Leibowitz co-authored a book on bonds entitled *Inside the Yield Book,* which was jointly published by Prentice-Hall and the New York Institute of Finance.

In recent years, Dr. Leibowitz and his group have been active in the development of a variety of structured portfolio techniques. In particular, Dr. Leibowitz played a key role in the design and the development of the Salomon Brothers Broad Investment-Grade Bond Index. His latest work includes a series of papers on asset allocation.

LIABILITY RETURNS: A NEW PERSPECTIVE ON ASSET ALLOCATION*

Martin L. Leibowitz, Ph.D**

Managing Director,
Bond Portfolio Analysis Group
Salomon Brothers Inc

By any performance standard, the bond and stock markets have provided extraordinary returns recently. Among the ranks of professional investment managers, there may be some mixed feelings as managers compare themselves with the broad market return indexes. Few managers of real-life portfolios with real-life clients have found themselves totally free from the return-dampening influences of portfolio cash, call/refunding effects, prepayments, or the cautionary impulses that naturally arise after a rally that

* Although the information in this article has been obtained from sources which Salomon Brothers Inc believes to be reliable, we do not guarantee its accuracy, and such information may be incomplete or condensed. All opinions and estimates included in this article constitute our judgment as of this date and are subject to change without notice. This article is for information purposes only and is not intended as an offer or solicitation with respect to the purchase or sale of any security.

** The author would like to express his appreciation to his colleagues, Dr. Steven Mandel and Andrew Feigenberg, for their help in constructing the performance analyses, and to Professor Lawrence Fisher for his valuable suggestions.

51

thunders forward for one record-setting week after another. While money managers may have mixed feelings, there is a much more consistent view among their sponsor clients: elation! In particular, pension fund sponsors—virtually regardless of their pattern of asset allocation—have seen their assets surge to giddy levels. With such superb absolute performance, it may seem almost petty to quibble when their managers' relative performance falls somewhat short of the broad market indexes.

The general euphoria among sponsors may be somewhat short-sighted. Assets are not the only component of the pension fund structure that have grown apace during the same time period. Quietly and without the fanfare of broadly cited performance numbers, the cost of pension liabilities has also exploded. This extraordinary growth in liability costs—this high level of "liability returns"—has been fueled by the same dramatic decline in interest rates that has driven the historic rally in bonds and stocks.

The net impact varies greatly from one fund to another. However, in many cases, the liability return has far outdistanced the fund's asset growth. The "liability portfolio," after all, is relatively free from the return-dampening factors that restrain the asset portfolio—liabilities are unfettered by those calls/refundings, prepayments, cautionary and/or frictional cash components, etc.

In this article, we will discuss these "liability returns" and how they compare with market performance recently and longer historical periods. This analysis is consistent with the "liability framework" discussed in a study on total portfolio duration.[1] These concepts have major implications for the structure of the asset allocation process for pension funds. In particular, one clear finding is that for many pension funds, interest rate volatility is a key—if not an overriding—risk factor affecting surplus status. Since a fund's total portfolio duration provides a measure of control for this risk, asset allocations should be chosen with at least some consideration of the resulting total duration value. More pointedly, the process of asset allocation should be expressed not in stock/bond ratios, as is the current general practice, but in terms of equity weightings and "total portfolio duration."

[1] Martin L. Leibowitz, *Total Portfolio Duration: A New Perspective on Asset Allocation.* New York: Salomon Brothers Inc, February 1986.

I. RISK AND RETURN IN A LIABILITY FRAMEWORK

The traditional approach to asset allocation within a pension fund focuses on the return/risk characteristics of various market asset classes. There is rarely an explicit orientation to the liability framework that defines the fund's ultimate purpose. Historically, the long-term nature and statistical character of the pension liabilities has often blurred the true importance of the asset/liability approach in this area.

New FASB initiatives and the greater potential for fund terminations have recently provided compelling reasons for a greater sensitivity to the behavior of the liability side of the pension balance sheet. Still, it appears that considerable progress needs to be made in developing asset allocation frameworks that integrate asset return/risk profiles with the "performance" characteristics of liabilities.

In another study, we developed a procedure for computing a comprehensive value for the interest rate sensitivity of a portfolio that included stocks as well as bonds.[2] We showed how this "total portfolio duration" value could then be related to the interest rate sensitivity of the liabilities. The emphasis was on gauging the net interest rate risk for a given asset allocation. To estimate the duration for the stock market, we explored the volatility and correlation characteristics of the S&P 500 relative to the Salomon Brothers Broad Investment-Grade Bond Index. One of the surprising results from these empirical studies was that the S&P duration value turns out to be far lower than the generally accepted values that have been derived from dividend discount models.

In this article, we turn from the risk dimension to the return dimension. The "returns" from representative pension liabilities (that is, the changes in the present value of future benefits) are compared with returns from the S&P 500 and the Salomon Brothers Broad Investment-Grade Index. Again we encounter some surprising results.

While the asset returns of both classes have done rather well over the 6¼-year period beginning January 1, 1980 (and spectacu-

---

[2] *Ibid.*

larly well recently), the "return on the liabilities" has also been extremely high.

In fact, the liability returns from the long-duration "active lives" liability schedule far exceed the stellar performance of both the stock and bond markets. In more concrete terms, this means that for significant classes of pension fund situations, there has been an actual shrinkage in the true economic surplus just as asset performance has been forging ahead at a historic pace.

II. MARKET RETURNS AND ASSET DURATIONS

As a first step, it might be worthwhile to update the historical results from the previous study. Basically, those numbers were based upon monthly returns achieved from January 1, 1980 through November 1, 1985. Exhibit 1 depicts the returns by fixed-income components over this period together with the subsequent five months to March 31, 1986. In Exhibit 2, the total return figures for the Broad Index are compared with the returns from the S&P 500.

Exhibit 3 updates the rolling volatilities over trailing one-year periods for these two markets. The average volatilities over the entire span now comes in at 9.40 percent for the Broad Market Index and 14.34 percent for the S&P 500.

The rolling one-year correlations show a different story. As shown in Exhibit 4, the correlation for the last 12 months investigated has surged to a high value of 0.78. This is virtually as high a correlation as there has been for any 12-month period over the past 6¼ years. This high level is consistent with the intuition of many market participants that lower interest rates have been a particularly direct driving force behind the current stock market rally.

This high correlation level has several implications. For example, Exhibit 5 shows the scatter pattern for S&P returns versus changes in the ten-year Treasury rates. A regression line for the entire period is shown. Because of the high weight assigned to the earlier period, this regression reflects an empirical duration of 2.47, which is close to the 2.41 value found earlier using the January 1980 to November 1, 1985 data. The overall correlation of 0.38 is only marginally different from the earlier value of 0.34.

EXHIBIT 1
Salomon Brothers Broad Index Returns, January 1980–March 1986

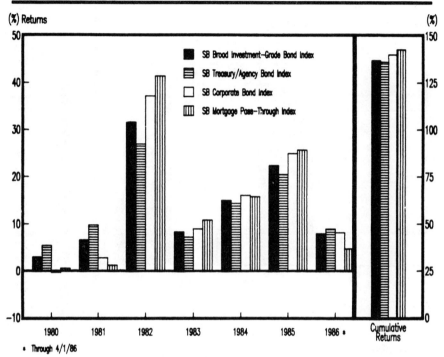

(%) Returns   (%)

Legend:
■ SB Broad Investment-Grade Bond Index
≣ SB Treasury/Agency Bond Index
□ SB Corporate Bond Index
Ⅲ SB Mortgage Pass-Through Index

1980   1981   1982   1983   1984   1985   1986 •   Cumulative
                                                      Returns
• Through 4/1/86

In Exhibit 6, the scattergram is shown for the trailing 12 months ending April 1, 1986. Although statistical reliability is compromised by using such a small number of data points, the results are nonetheless startling. The correlation, of course, is 0.78, corresponding to the last point plotted on Exhibit 4, and the duration is 6.18, more than twice as great as the duration estimated over the entire 6¼-year period. Moreover, the last five months of data reflect an even stronger enhancement of this trend.

There is no reason to believe that the stock market duration should be stable over time; in fact, our intuitions suggest that the duration could be significantly greater during some market periods than others. The current period appears to be one of them.

EXHIBIT 2
Equity and Fixed-Income Returns, January 1980–March 1986

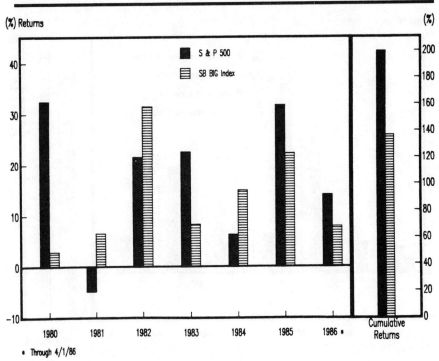

(%) Returns

S & P 500
SB BIG Index

1980   1981   1982   1983   1984   1985   1986 •   Cumulative Returns

• Through 4/1/86

III. LIABILITY STRUCTURES FOR PENSION PLANS

Basically, a pension plan can be viewed as having two types of liabilities: active lives and retired lives. These two classes have quite different characteristics.

The retired lives represent employees who are retired and currently receiving benefits as well as terminated pensioners who will receive deferred benefits. A snapshot of the benefit payments that would be actuarially scheduled to be paid out to a fixed pool of such retirees would have the general pattern that is exhibited in Exhibit 7. With such a frozen pool of existing retirees, the benefits typically decline over time in accordance with mortality tables.

EXHIBIT 3
**Rolling One-Year Volatility, Fixed-Income and Equity Markets,
1981–1986**

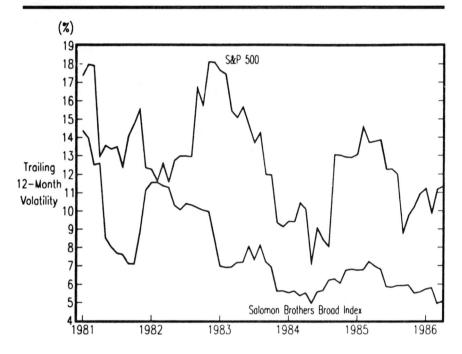

This pattern, therefore, reflects a front-end loading that typically declines on an "exponential basis" with the passing years.

In contrast, the "active lives" component of the pension liability reflects current employees who have vested (or accrued but unvested) interests in future benefits. For members of this class, the receipt of payments is deferred until some actuarially specified retirement time. Consequently, the projected schedule of benefit payments for active lives will begin to build up with those who are about to retire and then grow to a peak that represents the bulk load of future retirement benefits. This flow is backloaded and includes some very long-term flows. A representative schedule of benefits for an active lives liability is shown in Exhibit 8.

The actuarial procedure for determining these patterns is detailed, complex and highly customized to the individual fund's

EXHIBIT 4
**Rolling One-Year Correlations, Fixed-Income and
Equity Markets, 1981–1986**

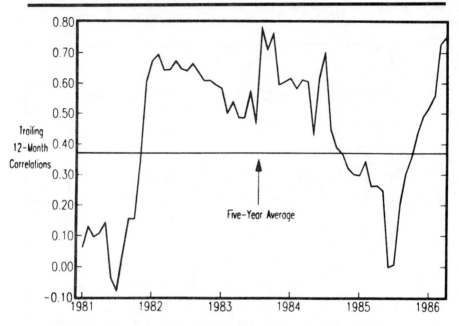

circumstance. Many sources of complication arise in practice. In particular, the active lives projections clearly depend upon a whole host of assumptions regarding future benefit/payroll statistics. Different active lives schedules may be used for the same payroll for different actuarial and reporting purposes. Moreover, there are sure to be interactions with the inflation rate, which will then feed back into any more refined duration calculations.

The flow of future contributions can also have a profound effect on interest rate sensitivity. The fixed flow of nominal dollar payout, depicted in Exhibit 8, admittedly captures none of these important effects: It is for illustrative purposes only. Our sole intention is to indicate the typical shape of this pattern without trying to venture too far into areas that we will leave to the true professionals in this field—the actuaries.

EXHIBIT 5
**The S&P Return Versus Change in Ten-Year Treasury Yield,
January 1980–March 1986**

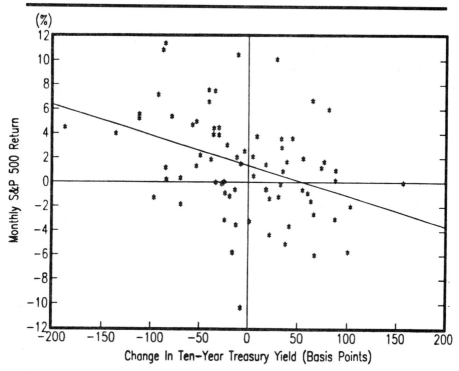

Change In Ten-Year Treasury Yield (Basis Points)

IV. LIABILITY RETURNS

It has often been remarked that semantics can alter patterns of thought. In this case, it is common to speak of the return from assets and to contrast it with the cost of liabilities. While the expression "return" has a dynamic connotation (certainly for any market participant), the term "cost" tends to imply a well-defined and relatively unchanging value. This semantic distinction has tended to obscure the structural similarity between assets and liabilities in the asset allocation equation. In particular, we are already accustomed to how changes in the market environment can lead to better or worse returns for different asset classes. This over-

EXHIBIT 6
**The S&P Versus Change in Ten-Year Treasury Yield,
April 1985–March 1986**

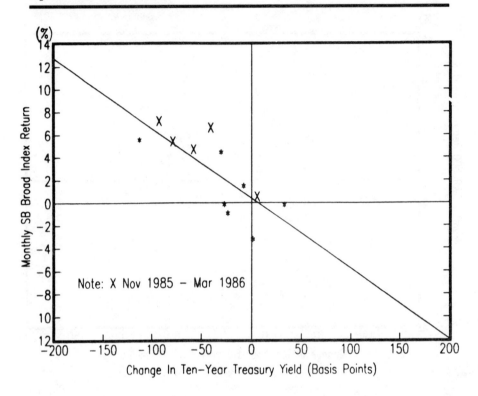

emphasis on the asset return side of the equation tends to obscure a broader view that would also include concomitant changes in a more comprehensive measure of the fund's status—the surplus function, that is, the difference between the market value of the assets and the present value of the liabilities. To address this imbalance, the impact of market changes on the cost of the liabilities should be investigated. In practice, this can be an intricate process to carry out for a specific fund. However, at least one facet of this effect can be readily explored—the impact of changing interest rates on the present value of a prescribed liability stream.

In fact, to turn this discussion around and to introduce a more comfortable terminology, we suggest that changes in the liabilities' cost be viewed as a kind of negative return. By defining this

EXHIBIT 7
Retired Lives Liability Schedule (Dollars in Millions)

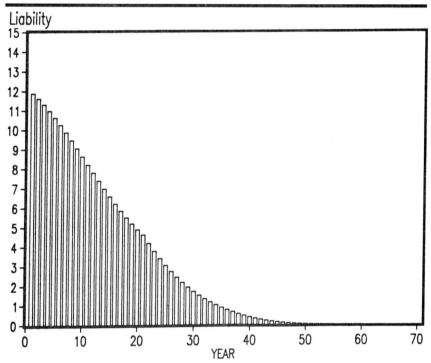

Liability

YEAR

"liability return" properly, a measure that is directly comparable with asset returns can be obtained. Thus, for a given fund, to the extent that the asset return matches the liability return over a given period, the funding status would remain in balance (at least for the initial set of liabilities). To proceed in this direction, we simply define the liability return as follows:

$$\frac{\left(\begin{array}{c}\text{Discounted Present}\\\text{Value of Liability}\\\text{End of Period}\end{array}\right) - \left(\begin{array}{c}\text{Discounted Present}\\\text{Value of Liability}\\\text{Beginning of Period}\end{array}\right) + \left(\begin{array}{c}\text{Liabilities Discharged}\\\text{During the}\\\text{Period}\end{array}\right)}{\left(\begin{array}{c}\text{Discounted Present}\\\text{Value of Liability}\\\text{Beginning of Period}\end{array}\right)}$$

EXHIBIT 8
Active Lives Liability Schedule (Dollars in Millions)

Liability

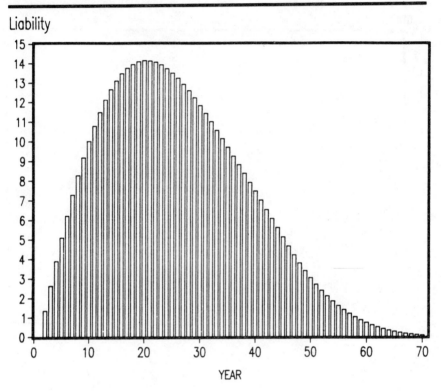

YEAR

In this formulation, we refer to the liabilities that existed at the beginning of the period—that is, this return calculation does not incorporate additional liabilities that may accrue during the course of each period.

As an example of this calculation, suppose the retired lives liabilities depicted in Exhibit 7 were subject to a market discount rate of 8 percent at the beginning of the year, resulting in a present value of $100 million. The first-year benefits of $11.87 million are paid out over the course of the year. At the end of the period, the remaining schedule is then discounted at a new market rate of 7 percent, resulting in a year-end present value of $102.86 million.

The liability return in this case would therefore be equal to the following:[3]

$$\frac{\$102.86 \text{ Million} - \$100 \text{ Million} + \$11.87 \text{ Million}}{100} = 14.73\%$$

In the past, actuarial smoothing and the highly lagged process for revision of actuarial valuation rates contributed to the perception that the present value of the liabilities had little immediate bearing on fund management. In such an environment, the liability return calculation would have limited appeal. In the new environment, however, rate-driven changes in the value of liabilities can be of great and immediate significance to the pension plan and the sponsor organization. The new FASB regulations argue clearly in the direction of using a market-sensitive discount rate to value the liabilities. In addition, with the increasingly routine consideration of potential annuity purchases, the fluctuating cost of these liabilities takes on the hard bite of a real dollars-and-cents impact. With these trends, the concept of liability return has become far more relevant today than it has ever been in the past.

V. LIABILITY PERFORMANCE

This model for liability returns can be applied retrospectively to develop performance results for the changing costs of liabilities over various historical periods. To carry out this analysis, the structure of the flows for each evaluation point, together with a discounting mechanism, must be specified. Consider, for example, the retired lives schedule in Exhibit 7. Suppose that the discounting mechanism corresponded to a uniform interest rate approximated by the ten-year new A Industrial rate.[4]

On January 1, 1980, this interest rate stood at 11.13 percent. Applied to the retired lives flow of Exhibit 7, it yields a present value of $81.82 million and a modified duration of 5.87 years.

---

[3] This result ignores intraperiod compounding.

[4] Lawrence Bader, Managing Director of William M. Mercer-Meidinger, Inc., suggested this rate as a convenient but crude proxy for annuity rates.

During January 1980, approximately $1 million would have been paid out to beneficiaries, and the remaining flow (aged one month) could then be discounted at the ten-year A new Industrial rate on February 1, 1980—12.00 percent. This results in a February 1, 1980 value of $77.60 million. Using our simplified liability return format, we find that the "return" for this retired lives liability amounts to −3.94 percent.

It is interesting to compare this number with the Broad Index return for January 1980, which is −3.03 percent. A large part of this difference is explained by the difference in the duration between the two flows—with its shorter duration, the Broad Index was less vulnerable to the increase in interest rates. Thus, for that month, an asset portfolio corresponding to the Broad Index would have gained some ground relative to this retired lives liability.

Next, a liability stream that begins February 1, 1980 is required. This could be achieved in several ways, including simply aging the original stream from the prior month's calculation. However, for simplicity's sake and to retain a consistent archetype over time, we assume that the retired lives on February 1, 1980 has the exact same (unaged) shape as depicted in Exhibit 7. Given this assumption, the liability return for each succeeding month can be computed, and a comparison with the Salomon Brothers Broad Market Index Returns can be developed. This comparison is shown in Exhibit 9.

In 1980 and 1981, the retired lives component turned in slightly lower returns than the Broad Index. In 1982, the Broad Index returns were an excellent 31 percent, but were surpassed by the 41 percent liability return. The returns in 1983 were roughly comparable. In 1984, 1985 and the first three months of 1986, however, the liability returns pulled ahead of the Broad Index. Exhibit 9 also shows the S&P equity returns throughout the same period. Over the full 75-month period, the cumulative liability return exceeded the growth in the Broad Index but fell short of the S&P's growth. A $100-million fund that was in perfect balance in January 1980 would have a surplus of $36 million today if it had been invested totally in stocks, but would have incurred a $26-million deficit if it had been invested totally in the Broad Index. It should be noted, however, that this result is highly period specific.

EXHIBIT 9
Retired Lives Liability Returns, January 1980–March 1986

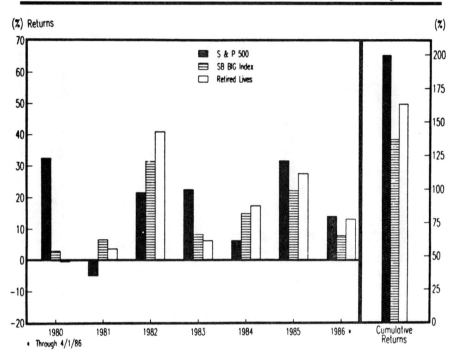

(%) Returns

* Through 4/1/86

Moreover, the impact of asset and liability returns upon the surplus clearly depends upon the initial surplus condition. Thus, if a fund is in balance—that is, the market value of assets equals the present value of liabilities—market returns over a period can be directly offset against liability returns to determine the net surplus change. However, for a fund with a large starting surplus, the market returns will affect an asset base that is larger than the initial liability value, and appropriate adjustments must be made to find the surplus change.

The same approach can be applied to the active lives, with performance results shown in Exhibit 10. The active lives liability on January 1, 1980 had a theoretical duration of 12.59 years—considerably longer than the retired lives liability or the Broad Market

---

EXHIBIT 10
Active Lives Liability Returns, January 1980–March 1986

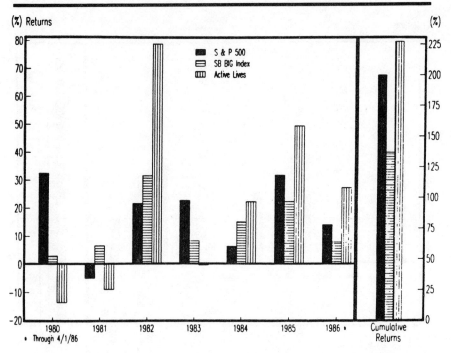

(%) Returns   (%)

* Through 4/1/86

Index. This longer duration could be expected to lead to more volatile liability returns; as Exhibit 10 indicates, this proves to be true. For example, in 1980, the active lives liability return was −13.48 percent. Thus, an investor in the Broad Market Index with only a +2.90 percent return over this period would have enjoyed a whopping increase in surplus value to 16.38 percent, due primarily to the huge decline in the present value of the liabilities.

In contrast, during 1982 the decline in interest rates caused the present value of the active lives schedule to soar by almost 80 percent. This was a multiple of the returns available in either the S&P 500 or the Broad Market Index. Therefore, it would have been virtually impossible for any fund with a large active lives component to avoid serious erosion in its surplus function in 1982. Some surplus erosion was also likely in 1984, 1985 and for the first three months of 1986. Thus, even despite the great performance of both stocks and bonds in the first three months of 1986, the surplus of virtually every active lives fund would have eroded because of the soaring costs of these liabilities.

VI.   INTEGRATED LIABILITY RETURNS

For purposes of clarity, this analysis focused first on pure retired lives liabilities and then on pure active lives liabilities. In practice, a pension fund will have a liability structure that consists of a dynamic combination of both types of liabilities. In fact, the actual schedule can be complex and can change in ways that are unique to an individual fund. To gain insight into a more realistic pattern

EXHIBIT 11
Integrated Liability Schedule, 60% Retired/40% Active
(Dollars in Millions)

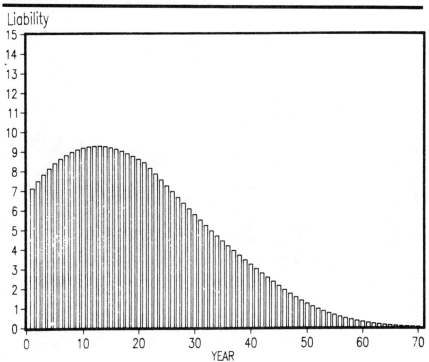

of liability returns, it can be useful to explore the "performance" of an integrated benefits structure consisting of a well-defined combination of both retired and active lives (see Exhibit 11). The present value of this combined flow comprises 60 percent retireds and 40 percent actives, based upon their respective present values under a discount rate of 8 percent. (Again, any actual fund will have a complex and changing combination of liability structures that usually can be identified only through an intensive actuarial study. Our purpose here is to take a simple archetype liability and compare its liability returns with those of stocks and bonds.) Proceeding with the integrated flow illustrated in Exhibit 11 and again applying the ten-year new A Industrial rates as a discounting proxy, one achieves the performance results shown in Exhibit 12.

To the extent that this archetype is at all representative, the

---

EXHIBIT 12
Integrated Liability Returns, January 1980–March 1986

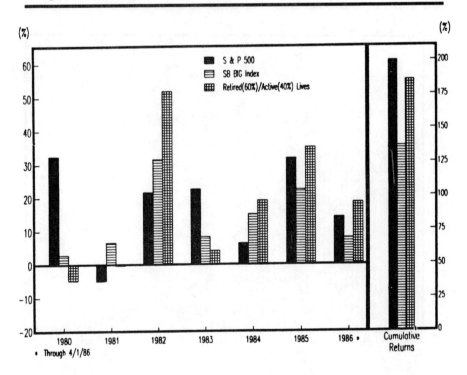

results are most intriguing. First, over the entire 75-month period, the performance of the bond market would have fallen significantly below the increased costs in this liability structure. S&P returns fared somewhat better than the combined liabilities. In three of the past four calendar years (as well as in the first quarter of 1986), the integrated liability returns actually outdistanced the pure equity returns themselves.

VII. COMPARISON WITH STOCK/BOND PORTFOLIOS

Few portfolios consist totally of all stocks or all bonds. To obtain more representative results, the integrated liability should be compared with a fund allocation that includes both stocks and bonds. For these purposes, we arbitrarily formulated a fund with 60 percent invested in the S&P 500 and the remaining 40 percent deployed in the Broad Index. The performance results are depicted in Exhibit 13.

It is discomforting, to say the least, that over the entire period, the fund returns did not pull ahead of the liability performance. This shortfall led to an enlarged deficit of about 11 percent over the 75-month period. But a closer look at the period-by-period returns suggests even greater cause for concern. In 1982, the liability return far exceeded the fund's asset performance. In 1984 and 1985, the liability performance again ran ahead of the asset performance. Perhaps more seriously, for the first three months of 1986, there was a sizable 6.6 percent shortfall between the asset performance and that of the combined liability schedule.

VIII. THE DURATION OF LIABILITIES

Many of the above results can be traced to the fundamental interest rate sensitivity of the liability streams. The pro forma modified duration is quite long for the liabilities: 5.87 years for the retireds, 12.59 years for the actives, and 8.20 years for the integrated flows (all as of January 1, 1980). However, a more meaningful measure of interest rate volatility would be the effective duration relative to

EXHIBIT 13
Portfolio and Integrated Liability Returns, January 1980–March 1986

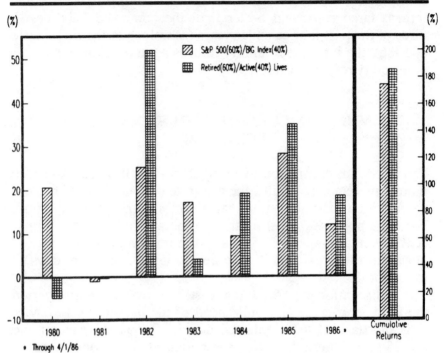

* Through 4/1/86

a consistent interest rate benchmark. Since we have used the ten-year Treasury rate as a benchmark in computing the effective duration of the Broad Index and the S&P 500, it is natural to adopt it again for the liability side. In Exhibits 14, 15 and 16, the liability returns for each of the 75 months are plotted against corresponding changes in the ten-year Treasury. The regression line provides a measure of the effective duration values—5.71 for retireds, 12.35 for actives, and 7.84 for the integrated schedule.

The effective durations are close to the pro forma duration values. This is hardly surprising. While there is a certain quality spread variation between the discounting rate (ten-year new A Industrials) and the benchmark rate (ten-year Treasuries), liability streams are free from some of the "adverse convexity problems" that encumber corporate bonds, mortgage securities, agencies, and even certain Treasury issues, especially in times of low interest

EXHIBIT 14
Effective Duration of Retired Lives Liability

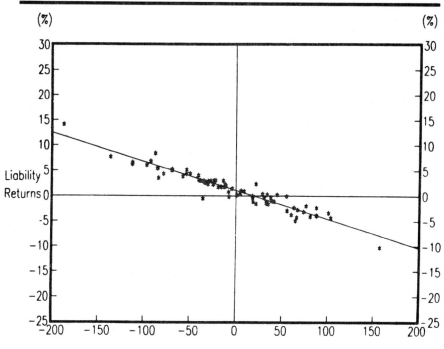

Change in Ten-Year Treasury Yield (Basis Points)

rates. In this sense, duration value tends to be a better gauge for a liability's volatility than for an actual bond portfolio's volatility.

The point is that the volatility of the integrated flows far exceeds the duration values for the Broad Index. The equity durations are even lower yet. It is possible that with the increased correlation between bonds and stocks in recent periods, the S&P 500 duration may be greater than its historical average value, but a fund with typical allocations in stocks and/or bonds would still have a lower duration than these archetype liabilities. This duration gap would naturally make the fund surplus vulnerable to lower interest rates.

Indeed, past performance results indicate that this is exactly what occurred. When interest rates rose, as they did in 1980 and 1981, the liability returns were low, often leading to increases in the surplus. In contrast, when interest rates fell, the value of the

EXHIBIT 15
Effective Duration of Active Lives Liability

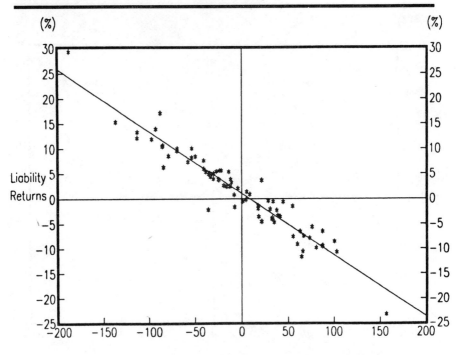

Change in Ten-Year Treasury Yield (Basis Points)

liabilities rose and typically exceeded stock and bond market returns. The pattern shown in Exhibits 9, 10 and 12 is no coincidence, but may reflect a rather fundamental and dangerous "liability trap."

Thus, in terms of surplus growth, the net performance of a pension fund may be most vulnerable precisely when fund sponsors and/or managers encounter the most favorable market returns and are enjoying ample growth in the market value of their portfolios.

IX. ALLOCATIONS USING "TOTAL PORTFOLIO DURATIONS"

These performance results provide striking evidence of the vulnerability of the pension fund surplus in today's markets. The high

EXHIBIT 16
Integrated Liability Schedule

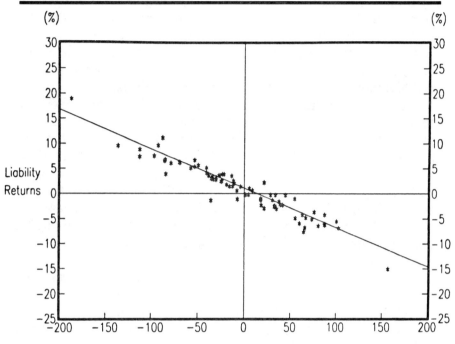

Change in Ten-Year Treasury Yield (Basis Points)

level of interest rate volatility and the long duration of representative liability schedules create the potential for wide variations in liability returns. While surplus is not the only yardstick that determines pension fund allocations, it is certainly becoming increasingly important in light of recent developments in the accounting/ actuarial environment.

Traditional asset allocation procedures generally do not address this question of surplus vulnerability. Stocks are usually ascribed both a higher expected return and a higher volatility than bonds. Over longer horizon periods, this places equities on the "asset of choice" pedestal. However, too high an equity component engenders unacceptably high levels of volatility in portfolio value. The bond component is therefore added as a sort of bland "filler" to cut portfolio variability down to tolerable levels. In many of these approaches, the "fixed-income component" is defined as some benchmark bond or bond market index that is taken to have an essentially constant duration. With this static choice for "fixed income," the bond component is prized primarily as a predictably dull "volatility dilution agent." Thus, in traditional allocation procedures, the sole decision variable is the magnitude of the equity component. The bond component basically becomes a derived residual that follows from the primary equity decision.

This traditional approach fails to address three major facets of today's pension and market environment. First, it focuses solely on asset return, without any explicit treatment of liability return, liability risk or the resultant surplus vulnerability. Second, it fails to recognize the high level of interest rate volatility that now appears endemic. (Even within the traditional framework itself, this rate volatility erodes the role of "bonds" as risk-dampening agents.) Third, it does not recognize a major development in the capital markets over the past decade—the spectrum of new instruments that allows the practical construction of fixed-income portfolios that span an extremely wide range of durations. (While this is true for conventional bonds and zero-coupon instruments, the range obviously expands even further when futures and options can be applied.) In a certain sense, for large funds, the range of (duration) risk levels readily available for the fixed-income component may be much wider than the practical (beta) risk range available for the equity component.

From the viewpoint of the liability/surplus framework, these problems can be addressed only through a revised asset allocation process that explicitly models the interest rate risk characteristics of all fund components—bonds, equity, liabilities, etc. This makes the total portfolio duration an important risk measure for the asset side. This framework would have implications for return enhancement as well as for risk control. Thus, for certain interest rate scenarios within a tactical allocation, the liability return could potentially become a significant positive contributor to surplus.

In any case, the total duration approach would begin to allow for measurement and control of interest rate risk. Together with the wide range of duration vehicles available in the market, this presents the fund with the opportunity to adjust the duration of the bond component to achieve a desired level of overall fund exposure to rate movements. Thus for a given equity weighting, the duration of the bond component can be selected to achieve vastly different target durations for the total portfolio. For example, with 60 percent in equities, the 40 percent "fixed-income" portion can be invested in cash equivalents for a total portfolio duration under one year, or in longer instruments to achieve total duration beyond six years. For the same fixed proportion invested in bonds, different bond portfolios can clearly lead to vastly different "total portfolio durations" for the overall fund. (Once the equity weighting is determined, the second decision can be stated in terms of either the bond component duration or the duration target for the total portfolio.)

Thus without transforming the allocation process into a highly modeled form based upon the surplus function, it becomes clear that there are compelling reasons to make some simple changes in the traditional way of even thinking about asset allocation. The range of choices in the bond component is so wide and so important that a simplistic "stock/bond ratio" is no longer appropriate. Rather, the fund sponsor should recognize that there are two semi-independent choices—the equity weighting and the portfolio duration for the total fund. (This is very different from the traditional framework, where the equity weighting basically dictates all facets of the fund allocation.) These two choices are clearly related. The portfolio duration can provide some risk compensation for the equity weighting. In the final analysis, the overall vulnerability of both the portfolio value and the surplus will depend upon the equity weight and the duration of the fixed-income component.

A comprehensive liability framework would ultimately form the most desirable basis for a more sophisticated asset allocation model. At the very least, the semantics of the allocation process should be modernized so that decisions are framed in terms of equity weightings and "total portfolio durations."

ARTICLE 5

TERENCE C. LANGETIEG is a Vice President of Salomon Brothers Inc, where he works in the Bond Portfolio Analysis Group. Prior to his present position, Mr. Langetieg was an Associate Professor in the Department of Finance and Business Economics at University of Southern California, where he was responsible for teaching coursework in Corporate Finance, Investments, Financial Institutions and Quantitative Analysis. Mr. Langetieg has a B.A. in Philosophy, and M.S. and Ph.D. degrees in Finance, from the University of Wisconsin.

Mr. Langetieg's scope of research and outside consulting has encompassed the subjects of bond pricing and investment, pension regulation and management, mortgage pricing, bank financial management, option pricing, and mergers.

LAWRENCE N. BADER is a Vice President of Salomon Brothers Inc, where he works in the Bond Portfolio Analysis Group. He previously was a Managing Director at William M. Mercer-Meidinger Inc., an employee benefits and compensation consulting form. Mr. Bader received his B.A. in Mathematics from Yale University, where he was elected to Phi Beta Kappa, and did graduate work in economics at Gonville and Cains College, Cambridge University. He is a Fellow of the Society of Actuaries, has served as Vice Chairman of the American Academy of Actuaries Committee on Pension Actuarial Principles and Practices, and is a member of numerous other actuarial organizations. He is also the only actuarial member of the AICPA Committee on Accounting for Pension Plans and Pension Costs.

MARTIN L. LEIBOWITZ *(See biography in the previous article.)*

ALFRED WEINBERGER is a Vice President in The Bond Portfolio Analysis Group of Salomon Brothers Inc, where he is involved in the development of new approaches to problems in asset/liability management for a variety of financial institutions. He has extensive experience in the areas of immunization and dedicated portfolios and wasan originator with Martin L. Leibowitz of the fixed-income portfolio management technique known as Contingent Immunization.

Prior to joining Salomon Brothers, Mr. Weinberger was an Assistant Treasurer in the Investment Department of the Sun Life Assurance Company of Canada. He holds Master's degrees in electrical engineering and business and has had papers published in the *Journal of Portfolio Management* and the *Financial Analysts Journal*.

MEASURING THE EFFECTIVE DURATION OF PENSION LIABILITIES*

Terence C. Langetieg Ph.D.
Vice President
Bond Portfolio Analysis
Salomon Brothers Inc

Lawrence N. Bader
Vice President
Bond Portfolio Analysis
Salomon Brothers Inc

Martin L. Leibowitz Ph.D.
Managing Director
Bond Portfolio Analysis
Salomon Brothers Inc

Alfred Weinberger
Vice President
Bond Portfolio Analysis
Salomon Brothers Inc

*Although the information in this article has been obtained from sources which Salomon Brothers Inc believes to be reliable, we do not guarantee its accuracy, and such information may be incomplete or condensed. All opinions and estimates included in this article constitute our judgment as of this date and are subject to change without notice. This article is for information purposes only and is not intended as an offer or solicitation with respect to the purchase or sale of any security.

In this article, we develop a framework for measuring the interest rate sensitivity of pension liabilities under the new reporting requirements of Financial Accounting Standards Board (FASB) Statement 87, which applies to corporate sponsors of defined-benefit pension plans. Before FASB 87, interest sensitivity could be "managed" to a considerable extent because of the latitude permitted in selecting the actuarial discount rate. FASB 87, however, requires plan sponsors to use market interest rates in the actuarial valuation of pension liabilities. In particular, FASB's requirement of "mark-to-market" liability valuation introduces a new volatility, with the possibility of substantial adverse fluctuations on both the income statement and the balance sheet.[1]

Efforts to stabilize reported pension obligations were formerly focused on stabilizing assets. Liabilities, while subject to fluctuations from changes in plan demographics, were not subject to interest rate shocks. In fact, the generally conservative approach to selecting the actuarial interest assumption and the secular upward trend in interest rates often made it possible to offset increases in reported pension liabilities due to plan changes or other factors simply by raising the interest assumption. With liabilities under control, the plan sponsor could turn to the asset side and manage the asset volatility with a combination of actuarial smoothing techniques and investment strategies that were often independent of the liability structure and liability risk.

FASB 87 requires a valuation of pension liabilities based on market interest rates and significantly reduces the ability to smooth changes in assets and liabilities. Furthermore, under the new reporting requirements, volatility in market interest rates will be transmitted, via changes in pension assets and pension liabilities, to the income statement and, for deficit plans, to the balance sheet. In the future, asset management will occur in a setting that recognizes not only the sponsor's long-term risk and return objectives but also the short-term implications for the income statement and the balance sheet.

---

[1] Note that the relevant rules for funding pension plans, set forth in the Internal Revenue Code and ERISA regulations, have not changed, and funding patterns therefore need not be subject to the same interest sensitivity as accounting results.

The key to meeting long- and short-term objectives successfully is to develop a new perspective in which assets and liabilities are jointly managed to control surplus volatility.[2] The integrating link between assets and liabilities is interest rate risk. The most important aspect of surplus management is the control of the effective duration of the pension surplus, which in turn reflects the combined interest rate sensitivities of pension assets and pension liabilities.

I. MEASUREMENT OF PENSION LIABILITIES UNDER FASB 87

Accurate measurement of the effective duration of pension liabilities is now essential. Without such measurement, it is virtually impossible to gain control of surplus volatility and its consequences for the balance sheet, or expense volatility and its consequences for corporate earnings. The effectiveness of protective asset-allocation strategies, such as immunization or dynamic hedging, depends critically on accurate measurement of the interest rate sensitivities of both pension liabilities and pension assets.

In this article, we examine three types of pension liability, each with different interest sensitivity: the accumulated benefit obligation (ABO); the projected benefit obligation (PBO); and the service cost.

The Accumulated Benefit Obligation

The ABO is the actuarial value of all benefits earned to date. It is used in several ways:

- Many plan sponsors and participants consider it the minimum level of benefit security: Plan assets should at least cover all benefits earned to date.

[2] For a discussion of the volatility and interest rate sensitivity of the pension surplus in recent years, see Martin L. Leibowitz, *Surplus Management: A New Perspective on Asset Allocation,* New York: Salomon Brothers Inc, October 1986.

- It is the focus of disclosure under FASB 36, the standard that governed pension reporting before FASB 87, and continues to be disclosed under the new standard.

- It offers a measure of the cost of terminating the plan, although various adjustments may be applicable on an actual termination. Subject to these adjustments, it is useful in estimating the cash available to the firm through a termination/reversion or the deficiency that would have to be made up if an underfunded plan was terminated.

- It becomes the basis of a balance sheet liability under FASB 87. Beginning in 1989, any shortfall of pension assets against the ABO must be recorded on the balance sheet. (There is no corresponding balance sheet asset for overfunding.)

The Projected Benefit Obligation

Like the ABO, the PBO reflects benefits earned to date, but it also reflects the effect of future salary increases on those benefits. This is demonstrated in the following example:

The plan used for illustration provides a benefit of 2 percent of final salary for each year of service. Consider an employee with ten years of service, currently earning $20,000 but with a projected final salary of $50,000 at age 65. The ABO reflects an annual pension benefit equal to 20 percent of his $20,000 salary, or $4,000. The calculation of the PBO, however, recognizes that when the employee retires, the 20 percent benefit already earned will apply to a $50,000, rather than a $20,000 salary, so the employee's annual pension benefit is taken as $10,000, rather than $4,000.

The PBO is also used in several ways:

- FASB 87 continues to require the disclosure of the ABO, but it shifts the focus to the PBO. FASB 87 requires the new disclosure of the PBO as well as the critical assumptions used in its calculation.

- It measures the current value of the firm's pension liability for an *ongoing plan*. (In contrast, the ABO is closer to the termination liability.) Therefore, the PBO can be used by securities analysts to assess the full extent of the firm's pension liability.

The impact of this new disclosure requirement on securities prices remains to be seen.

- It is a key figure in determining the annual pension expense under FASB 87. At the date of compliance with FASB 87, the PBO surplus (or deficit) is reflected in future pension expenses on an amortized basis. A PBO surplus will decrease future pension expenses, whereas a PBO deficit will increase future expenses. Subsequent changes in the PBO surplus resulting from plan amendments or actuarial gains or losses are amortized in the calculation of annual expense.

- An acquisition accounted for under the purchase method requires the recording of an asset (or liability) corresponding to the amount of overfunding (or underfunding) of the PBO in the acquired company's plans.

The Service Cost

The service cost is the value of benefits earned during the current year and represents the increment to the PBO resulting from the employee's current service. It is an important component of the annual pension expense.

Each of these three measures of the pension liability has a different interest rate sensitivity. Interest sensitivities, or effective durations,[3] can range from 0 to 20 or more, depending on several factors:

- The benefit formula (flat benefit, final salary and career average salary).

- Benefit indexing for cost-of-living adjustments (COLAs) related to either automatic COLA provisions or recurring ad hoc adjustments.

- The demographics of the work force, including the age distribution, years of service, salary levels, and other factors.

---

[3] An effective duration of 20 means that a 1 percent (100-basis-point) change in the interest rate results in a change of approximately 20 percent in the value of the liability.

- Actuarial assumptions regarding retirement, turnover and mortality.

- The level of interest rates.

- The relationships among the salary growth rate, the general inflation rate and interest rates.

II. THE INTEREST RATE SENSITIVITY OF PENSION LIABILITIES

A change in interest rates can affect pension liabilities in two ways: First, there is "discount rate sensitivity"—like the value of stocks, bonds and other cash flow streams, the value of pension liabilities is sensitive to changes in the discount rate. Under FASB 87, the actuarial discount rate is the rate inherent in the price that an insurance company would charge to settle the liability through an annuity purchase. That rate reflects current market yields on high-grade bonds. As market interest rates change, annuity purchase rates and the actuarial discount rate also change. Thus, the actuarial present value of the pension obligation is sensitive to changes in market interest rates, just as any fixed-income security would be.

Second, there is "pension benefit sensitivity"—the interest sensitivity of the pension benefit itself. Interest rate changes are often associated with changes in inflation expectations. Estimates of future benefit payments are linked to inflation when benefit payments are pay-related or adjusted for changes in the cost of living. To the extent that future inflation, interest rates and pension benefits are positively correlated, there will be a compensatory effect on interest rate sensitivity. Inflation-driven salary increases lead to higher benefit payments, but inflation also reduces present values because of higher discount rates. This counterbalancing effect reduces the overall interest rate sensitivity of pension liabilities.

These interest sensitivities have always existed in an economic sense; FASB 87 has only heightened the awareness and concern about them, by requiring a market-based valuation and by giving balance sheet status to pension liabilities.

To illustrate these two types of interest sensitivity, we will examine the measures of the firm's actuarial pension liability that are reported under FASB 87: the ABO, PBO, and the service cost. Without a COLA provision, the interest rate sensitivity of the ABO is entirely the result of its discount rate sensitivity. Since the ABO measures only accrued benefits and does not reflect future salaries, the benefit stream associated with the ABO is based entirely on the current salary or salary history; therefore, the ABO has no "pension benefit sensitivity" to changes in interest rates.

The PBO and the service cost exhibit both discount rate sensitivity and pension benefit sensitivity. Since their interest rate sensitivities are based on a projection of future salaries, the benefit streams are uncertain. Changes in the inflation rate are likely to affect both future salaries and the associated pension benefits.

Our analysis will include a consideration of variations in plan provisions, including the COLA provision. With a COLA provision, the ABO develops pension benefit sensitivity to interest rate changes, and the pension benefit sensitivities of the PBO and service cost are magnified. But as pension benefit sensitivity increases, the overall interest sensitivity of the liability measures decreases. Lastly, we will also consider alternative employee demographics.

III. AN ILLUSTRATIVE PENSION PLAN: PLAN PROVISIONS, ACTUARIAL ASSUMPTIONS AND EMPLOYEE DEMOGRAPHICS

A pension plan's interest sensitivity depends on the age/service/pay characteristics of the work force; plan provisions; and assumptions about turnover, mortality, salary increases, retirement, and other events. Simplified provisions and assumptions will be used to illustrate the measurement of interest rate sensitivity; the conclusions, however, are applicable to virtually all defined-benefit plans.

Like many existing defined-benefit plans, the pension plan we will use provides benefits based on final salary. Specifically, the retirement pension is equal to 2 percent of final salary for each year of service. This benefit is payable annually, beginning at age 65 and continuing for the remainder of the retiree's life, with no survivor benefits. The basic plan does not include adjustments for inflation in retirement years; however, a COLA provision will be examined later.

Pension plans provide varying benefits to employees who terminate service before they reach retirement age, depending on length of service and the reason for terminating. For simplicity, the basic plan is assumed to provide all employees who terminate before age 65 a deferred benefit at age 65 that is equal to 90 percent of the benefit accrued at the termination date.

Because of the simplified plan provisions, it is not necessary to make detailed assumptions about rates of death, disability, termination, and voluntary change of jobs before age 65. The probability of survival to age 65 is shown in Exhibit 1, and actuarial mortality probabilities for the retirement years are shown in Exhibit 2.[4]

Participants' salaries are assumed to increase in real terms with age. A participant hired at age 20 is assumed to earn a real or inflation-adjusted salary of $10,000 annually, growing to $32,253 at age 65. The nominal growth in salary is equal to the real growth plus an adjustment for inflation. The analysis ignores any salary lags and differences between expected and actual inflation. The effect is that the salary is assumed to increase according to the real scale shown in Exhibit 3, plus an adjustment for expected inflation.

The active employee population used in our illustration is a "normal group, (which) represents a reasonably mature and stable group that is projected to continue to grow. It is typical of many large companies."[5] The age distribution for this normal group is shown in Exhibit 4. A typical retiree group was developed with the age distribution shown in Exhibit 5; at a 10 percent interest rate,

[4] See Dan M. McGill, *Fundamentals of Private Pensions* (Homewood, IL: Richard D. Irwin, 1984) and Harold R. Greenlee, Jr. and Alfonso D. Keh, "The 1971 Group Annuity Mortality Table," *Transactions of the Society of Actuaries*, 23, 1971, pp. 569–604.

[5] The active employee population is Employee Group A from *Pension Cost Method Analysis,* American Academy of Actuaries, 1985.

EXHIBIT 1
Probability of Remaining in Active Service to Age 65

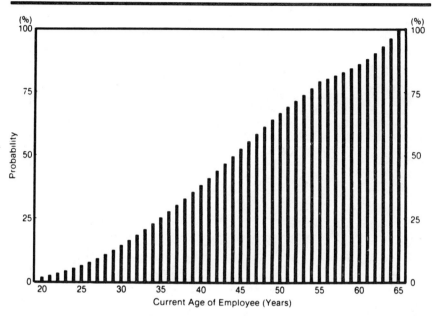

Current Age of Employee (Years)

the ABO of the retiree group is assumed to be half that of the active employees, or one third of the total ABO.

IV. EFFECTIVE DURATION OF THE ABO

Under FASB 87, the ABO achieves balance sheet status: If the market value of pension assets falls below the ABO, the deficit is reported on the balance sheet. Deficits are measured plan by plan; overfunding in one plan cannot be used to offset underfunding in another. Thus, FASB 87 motivates the firm to keep all plans in a surplus condition. To avoid balance sheet fluctuations caused by volatility in the ABO, the firm must devise new asset-allocation strategies to offset adverse fluctuations in the ABO. A necessary first step in developing an effective asset allocation is to measure the interest sensitivity of the ABO.

EXHIBIT 2
Probability of Surviving from Age 65 to Indicated Age

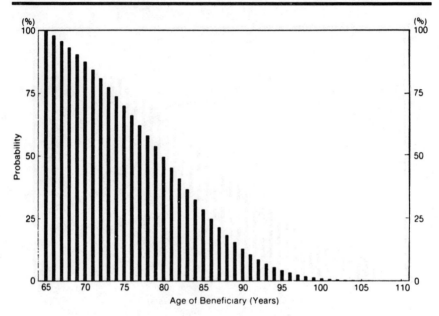

Under FASB 87, the ABO represents the actuarial present value of accrued benefits, calculated according to the plan formula. In our example, the benefits for the ABO calculation are based on the current salary and the accumulated years of service:

$$\text{Benefit} = \text{Current Salary} \times \text{Years of Service} \times 2\% \qquad (1)$$

The actuarial value of the benefit stream is based on four factors:

- The annual benefit at age 65;
- The value at age 65 of an annuity paid until death, based on a mortality table (see Exhibit 2) and a market-based discount rate;
- An actuarial adjustment for the probability that the employee will not survive to age 65 to receive the benefit (see Exhibit 1); and

---

EXHIBIT 3
Current Salary Scale

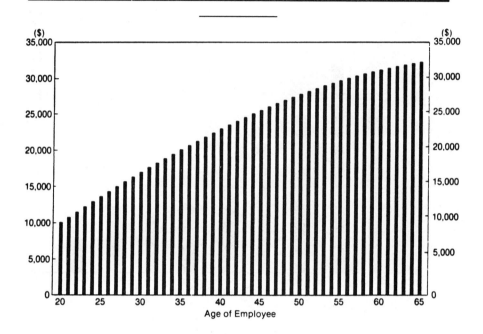

• A discount for interest from the employee's current age to age 65.

The actuarial value of the ABO is summarized as follows:

$$\begin{array}{c} \text{ABO with Respect} \\ \text{to Benefits Payable} \\ \text{at Age 65} \end{array} = \text{Benefit} \times \begin{array}{c} \text{Probability} \\ \text{of Survival} \\ \text{to Age 65} \end{array}$$

$$\times \begin{array}{c} \text{Present Value of} \\ \text{Annuity Starting} \\ \text{at Age 65} \end{array} \times \begin{array}{c} \text{Interest Discount} \\ \text{from Current Age} \\ \text{to Age 65} \end{array}$$

Consider a worker at age 55 with ten years of service and a current salary of $29,703. Using Equation (1) the worker's benefit at age 65 is $5,941 (29,703 × 10 × .02). Suppose the appropriate market interest rate is 10 percent. Using the mortality probabilities shown in

EXHIBIT 4
Age Distribution of Active Participants

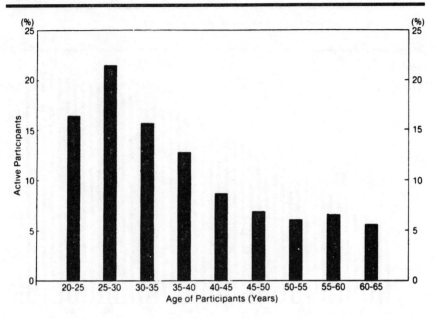

Exhibit 2, the present value at age 65 of a $1 life annuity is $7.7065. The probability that a 55-year-old worker will reach retirement age in active service is 79.1 percent (see Exhibit 1). Therefore, the ABO for this worker, excluding benefits payable in the event of termination before age 65, is equal to the following:

$$\text{ABO (Active to Age 65)} = \$5,941 \times .791 \times 7.7065 \times \frac{1}{1.10^{10}}$$

$$= \$13,963 \tag{3}$$

Under the plan, participants terminating before age 65, for any reason, are assumed to receive an average of 90 percent of the accrued normal retirement benefit based on the appropriate salary. If 79.1 percent of 55-year-old workers remain in service to age 65, 20.9 percent will exit early. Therefore, with respect to benefits payable on termination before age 65, the ABO is equal to the following:

EXHIBIT 5
Age Distribution of Retired Participants

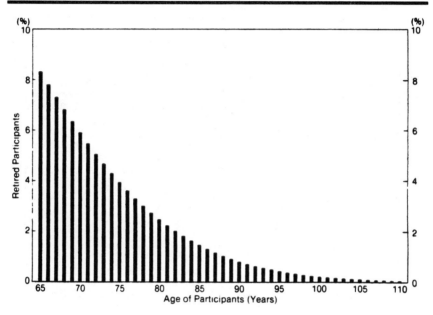

$$\text{ABO (Exits before Age 65)} = .90 \times \$5,941 \times .209 \times 7.7065 \times \frac{1}{1.10^{10}}$$

$$= \$3,320 \qquad (4)$$

The total of the amounts in equations 3 and 4 is equal to the ABO for an employee at age 55 with ten years of service:

$$\text{ABO (Age 55 with 10 Years of Service)} = \$13,963 + \$3,320 = \$17,283 \quad (5)$$

The calculation for workers at other ages is similar, yielding an ABO of \$110,176,283 for a work force of 10,000 active participants and retirees. Without a COLA, the projected cash flow stream for the ABO is independent of interest rates, so its calculation at any interest rate is straightforward (see Exhibit 6). The ABO at interest rates from 5 percent to 15 percent, for retired and active participants separately and combined, is shown in Exhibit 7. At a 5 percent interest rate, retirees account for only 22 percent of

EXHIBIT 6
Forecast ABO Cash Flows—Active Participants, Retirees, and All Participants (Dollars in Millions)

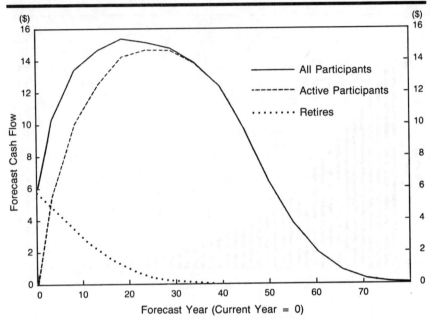

the total liability; at a 10 percent rate, they account for 33 percent, and at a 15 percent rate, they account for 42 percent of the totals.

To determine the ABO's interest sensitivity, suppose the interest rate increases from 10 percent to 10.01 percent. At 10.01 percent, the ABO drops by .1050 percent to $110,060,580. This represents an interest rate sensitivity comparable to that of a bond with a duration of 10.50. In other words, the current value of this liability stream changes by approximately 10.50 percent for a 1 percent change in the level of interest rates. If interest rates increase (or decrease) by 2 percent, we can expect the current value of the ABO to fall (or rise) by approximately 21 percent (2 × 10.50 percent), and so forth. Compared with almost all fixed-income investments, the ABO's interest sensitivity is extremely high.

The ABO's duration for the active and retired components is shown separately at different interest rate levels in Exhibit 8. At a 10 percent interest rate, the duration for the retired component is

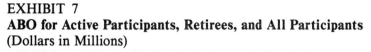

EXHIBIT 7
ABO for Active Participants, Retirees, and All Participants
(Dollars in Millions)

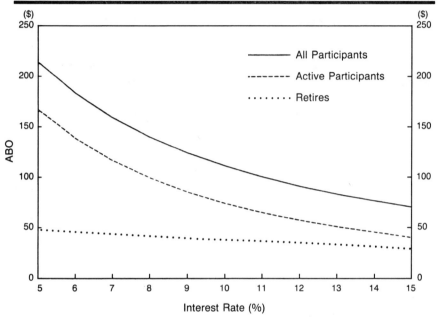

4.42, while the duration for the active component is 13.54. This large difference reflects the fact that the active participants' cash flow is more distant than that of the retirees (see Exhibit 6). The retired component comprises participants currently receiving benefits; its cash flows are weighted heavily over the next ten years. On the other hand, the active component has an average age of 36; therefore, the average active participant has 29 years to retirement, and the duration of the resulting benefit stream is much higher.

FASB 87 requires the use of a market-based interest rate in actuarial calculations. For plans that have an ABO deficit, an ABO sensitivity of the magnitude indicated here raises the potential for large fluctuations on the corporate balance sheet. Many firms may choose to develop an asset-allocation strategy to hedge the current ABO surplus or deficit against adverse changes in interest rates. A fund consisting of a dedicated portfolio for retirees—who have a relatively short duration—and a typical unmatched portfolio for

EXHIBIT 8
Effective Duration of the ABO for Active Participants, Retirees, and All Participants

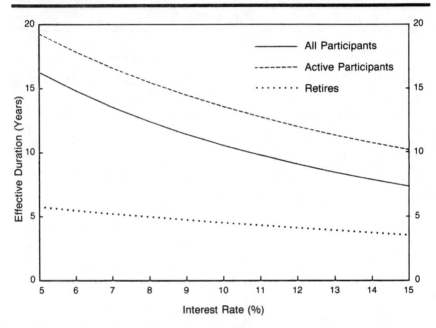

active participants—who have a duration of 13.54 in this example—will be highly vulnerable to surplus impairment during a period of declining interest rates.

V.   EFFECTIVE DURATION OF THE PBO

The ABO represents the firm's current pension liability on a termination basis and has balance sheet significance under FASB 87. For a firm that intends to terminate in the near term, the PBO is of little significance. However, if the firm intends to maintain a defined-benefit retirement plan indefinitely, the PBO is a much better gauge of the current value of the firm's future obligations. If the firm is to make good on its defined-benefit promises, it must fund toward the PBO, rather than the ABO. For the ongoing plan with a long horizon, the "economic surplus" is equal to the market value of pension assets minus the PBO. Therefore, strategies for hedging the economic surplus must focus on the PBO's interest sensitivity.

The actuarial value of the PBO can be obtained in a fashion similar to that used for the ABO. In the PBO calculation, however, a projected benefit[6] is used, and it must reflect projected salary increases based on merit, longevity and inflation.[7] The benefit for the PBO calculation is the following:

$$\text{Benefit} = \frac{\text{Projected Salary at Age}}{\text{65 or at Exit Age}} \times \frac{\text{Current Years}}{\text{of Service}} \times 2\% \qquad (6)$$

Consider a 55-year-old worker who is currently earning $29,703 and who is expected to earn $32,285 at age 65 in current dollars (see Exhibit 3). Suppose the current interest rate is 10 percent, reflecting an expected inflation rate of 5.75 percent. The final salary of this worker is projected to be $56,468 ($32,285 \times 1.0575^{(65-55)}$). Using the projected salary and the benefit formula in Equation (6), the 55-year-old worker with ten years of service has a PBO benefit at age 65 equal to $11,294, compared with the ABO benefit of only $5,941.

The projected exit salary must also be determined for workers who terminate before age 65. The probabilities of continuing in service (see Exhibit 1) can be used to determine the probability of exit at each age. These probabilities are then applied to the corresponding salaries to determine the benefit amounts and actuarial liabilities. The formula in Equation (6) must be applied to each exit age; thus, the PBO calculation is more complicated than the ABO calculation.

The PBO and ABO for active participants at different ages are compared in Exhibit 9. For retirees, the PBO and ABO are the same. Since the current salary is close to the projected retirement salary for older workers, the ABO is very close to the PBO. For younger workers, however, the difference between the ABO and

[6] This benefit is projected in terms of salary, but not in terms of additional 2 percent benefit units, which may be credited for years of future service.

[7] The PBO must also reflect benefit increases based on a COLA clause, if one exists, and must reflect future benefit liberalizations if the firm has a substantive commitment to such increases.

EXHIBIT 9
ABO and PBO for Active Participants (Dollars in Thousands)

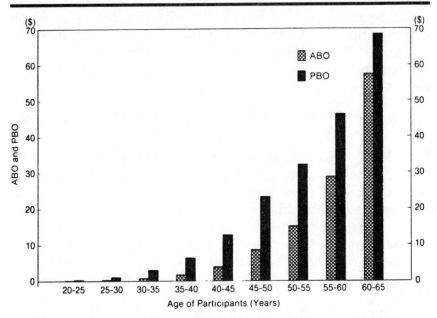

the PBO is quite dramatic, since the difference between current salary and the projected retirement salary is very large.

The projected cash flows of the PBO and ABO for the current work force of 10,000 plus retirees are shown in Exhibit 10. The PBO's cash flows are larger, since they are based on future salaries. The average maturity of the PBO's cash flow is also more distant than the ABO's. This is because the difference between projected and current salary is greatest for younger workers, and the more distant cash flows are associated with the retirement of the younger workers. In sum, the anticipation of future salary levels both increases the amount of the PBO relative to the ABO and extends its average maturity.

The PBO's Discount Rate Sensitivity

To determine the interest sensitivity of the PBO, we must specify how the projected cash flows will change as interest rates change.

EXHIBIT 10
Forecast Cash Flows—ABO Versus PBO (Dollars in Millions)

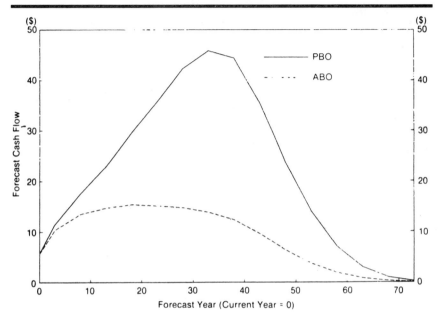

First, suppose that the PBO's cash flows are invariant with respect to changes in interest rates. In this case, the PBO's interest sensitivity is due entirely to discount rate sensitivity. For the cash flow stream shown in Exhibit 10, the PBO is $167,323,234 when discounted at 10 percent. Discounting the same cash flow stream at 10.01 percent, the PBO is $167,090,800. Thus, a one-basis-point change in the interest rate produces a .1389 percent change in the PBO. Assuming that future salaries are independent of interest rate changes, it follows that the duration of pension liabilities is 13.89. This is substantially higher than the 10.50 duration calculated for the ABO, because of the greater weight the PBO assigns to younger employees through the projection of salaries. When benefits are salary related but invariant to interest rate changes, the PBO's duration is always higher than the ABO's (see Exhibit 11).

EXHIBIT 11
**Effective Duration of the ABO and the PBO—Constant
Pension Benefits**

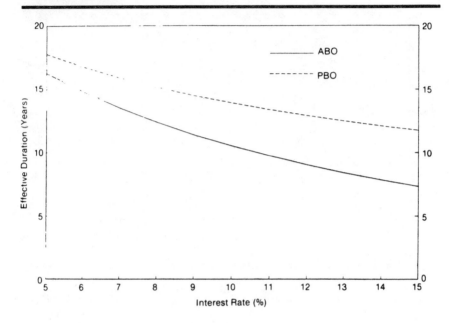

The PBO's Pension Benefit Sensitivity

For most salary-based plans, the assumption that future pension payments are independent of interest rates is questionable. Interest rate changes—and, over the long run, salary increases—generally reflect changes in anticipated inflation. While actual changes in inflation rates, interest rates and salary growth rates are not perfectly correlated, a 1 percent increase in the *anticipated* inflation rate is likely to increase expectations for both salary growth rates and interest rates by 1 percent, at least over the long run.

The next PBO duration calculation is based on the assumption that the change in interest rates is matched by an equal change in the rate of salary inflation. The real salary scale in Exhibit 3 remains unchanged. In the short run, it is unlikely that a change in interest rates will be matched by an equal change in salary growth rates. For the long forecasting horizon required in the PBO calculation, however, it is more plausible to assume this than to assume that cash flows are constant.

Again suppose the interest rate increases from 10 percent to 10.01 percent. At 10 percent, the PBO is equal to $167,323,234. If the interest rate rises to 10.01 percent, the PBO drops to $167,090,800 (a .1389 percent decrease) *before* pension benefit sensitivity is considered. If there is a corresponding .01 percent increase in the salary inflation rate, the PBO moves back up to $167,216,880, for a net decline in value of .0636 percent. The increase in the salary growth rate offsets about half the effect of the increase in the discount rate.[8] Thus, when salary growth rates and interest rates move together, the PBO has the same interest sensitivity as a bond with a fixed cash flow stream and a duration of 6.36. This 6.36 duration is significantly less than the duration of 13.89 obtained when the PBO cash flows are fixed and insensitive to interest rate changes.

It is interesting that the PBO's inflation-adjusted duration of 6.36 is also substantially less than the ABO's interest sensitivity of 10.50. The cash flow profiles in Exhibit 10 might imply a higher interest sensitivity for the PBO, since it clearly has a longer average maturity. The PBO does have a higher discount rate sensitivity. When the pension benefit sensitivity is considered, however, with expected salary growth rates perfectly correlated with interest rates, the PBO turns out to be less interest sensitive than the ABO. This relationship is shown in Exhibit 12 over a range of interest rates.

VI. THE EFFECTIVE DURATION OF THE SERVICE COST

The service cost—a key element of pension expense—can be thought of as a PBO for benefits newly earned during the year. This new or incremental PBO is clearly of longer duration than the

---

[8] Changes in the salary growth rate are assumed to be exactly equal to changes in the interest rate, but the PBO is still sensitive to interest rate changes. The residual sensitivity exists because benefits are not adjusted for inflation during the retirement years nor are benefits adjusted during preretirement years for those workers who leave the work force before retirement.

EXHIBIT 12
Effective Duration of the ABO and PBO—Interest-Sensitive Benefits

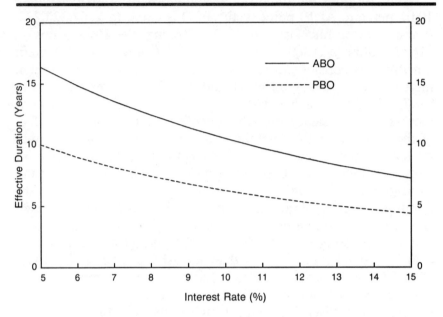

existing PBO. The existing PBO includes retirees, with their short duration, while the service cost does not, since retirees are no longer earning benefits. The existing PBO is also more heavily weighted toward older workers, because of their higher accumulation of service units. In the service cost calculation, each worker is weighted by only one service unit. For example, a 60-year-old worker might have a weighting of 40 years of service in the PBO calculation but only one year of service in the service cost calculation—the same as a new, 20-year-old employee.

The duration of the service cost for the final-pay plan, assuming benefit sensitivity, is shown in Exhibit 13. As noted, the duration of the service cost is somewhat above the PBO's, but not as high as the ABO's. Exhibit 14 shows the effective duration of the service cost at different interest rates for the pay-related plan and a flat benefit plan (that is, a plan without benefit payment sensitivity). When benefits are held constant, the effective duration ranges from about 26 at low interest rates to 12 at high interest rates.

EXHIBIT 13
Effective Duration of the Service Cost, ABO, and PBO—Interest Sensitive Benefits

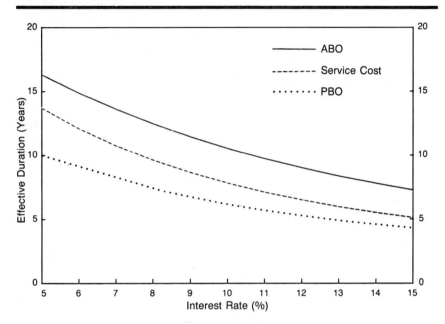

When benefit payment sensitivity is introduced, the effective duration is about halved, ranging from 13 to 5. Since salary growth is not likely to be correlated perfectly with interest rates, many plans will probably have a service cost duration of 10 to 15. With such a high interest sensitivity, a 2 percent change in rates could produce a 20–30 percent change in the service cost. This level of volatility is significantly larger than that of the more manageable pre-FASB 87 pension expense.

VII. THE EFFECTS OF ALTERNATIVE PLAN PROVISIONS

There is a limitless number of benefit formulas, and we believe it useful to consider how variations affect liability duration. We will now examine flat benefit plans, career-average pay plans and COLAs.

Plans with Flat Benefits

Plans for union or other hourly paid employees are typically independent of pay, providing a fixed amount of pension, such as $20 monthly for each year of service. The $20 figure could be adjusted periodically as a result of negotiations or, in a nonunion plan, unilateral changes. Unless the employer has a "substantive commitment" to such changes, however, they are not anticipated in the FASB 87 accounting.

The durations of the ABO are generally slightly longer than those of pay-related plans. In a pay-related plan, younger workers earn benefits at the same rate as older workers, but their longer durations get somewhat less weight because they tend to be lower paid. A duration of 10.79 for the flat benefit plan at a 10 percent interest rate is shown in Exhibit 14. This is marginally higher than the 10.50 duration of the pay-related plan.

Since flat benefit plans do not involve salary projections, the PBO is the same as the ABO. The PBO has no pension benefit sensitivity unless the plan has a COLA provision; therefore, it has a significantly higher duration than the PBO of a pay-related plan. (A firm might, however, find it desirable to manage an adjusted PBO that reflects expected benefit increases, although FASB 87 does not require current recognition.) At a 10 percent interest rate, the duration of the flat benefit plan is 10.79—70 percent higher than the 6.36 duration of the pay-related plan (see Exhibit 14).

The duration of a flat benefit plan's service cost is also significantly higher than that of a pay-related plan because of the absence of benefit payment sensitivity. At a 10 percent interest rate, the duration is 122 percent higher for the flat benefit plan (17.23 versus 7.77) (see Exhibit 15).

Plans Based on Career-Average Salary

The benefit formula introduced in Equation (6) is a final-pay formula, relating benefits to the participant's pay at the time of retirement. Most final-pay plans relate benefits to pay averaged over a period of three or five years. This lessens the pension benefit sensitivity slightly, since the effect of salary inflation is reduced during the averaging period. With a lower benefit sensitivity, there is a

EXHIBIT 14
**Effective Duration of the ABO and PBO—Flat Benefit Versus
Pay-Related Benefit**

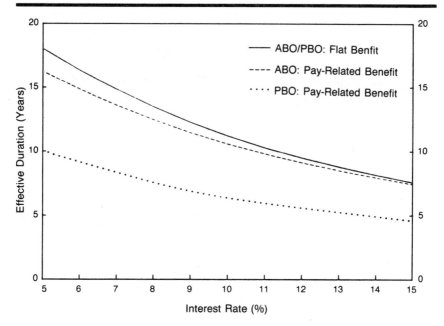

slight increase in the overall interest sensitivity of the PBO and service cost. There is no effect on the ABO's interest sensitivity, since the ABO's cash flows are constant (in the absence of a COLA provision).

The reduction in pension benefit sensitivity is far more significant for career-average pay formulas, which relate benefits to pay averaged over the participant's entire career. These plans have benefit sensitivities that are about half the sensitivities of final-pay plans, so the overall interest sensitivities of the PBO and service cost tend to be about halfway between those of the flat-benefit and final-pay formulas.

Plans with COLA Provisions

The preceding examples assumed that pensions are fixed at retirement, with no automatic COLA provision. FASB 87 requires

EXHIBIT 15
**Effective Duration of the Service Cost—Flat Benefit Versus
Pay-Related Benefit**

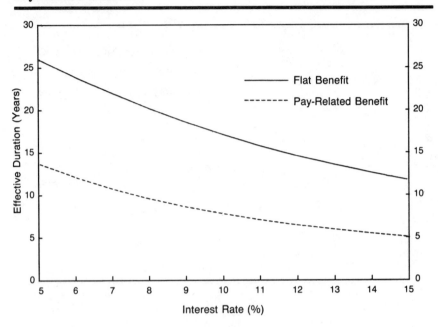

advance recognition of both automatic indexing and ad hoc increases for which the plan sponsor has a "substantive commitment." When changes in the interest rate are caused by inflation
in the cost of living, a COLA provision reduces the effective durations of the ABO, PBO and service cost significantly. The COLA
provision introduces pension benefit sensitivity, which partially
offsets the actuarial discount sensitivity.

While many firms make it a practice to grant periodic increases
to retirees, few grant the full amount implied by the inflation rate,
either by automatic indexing or ad hoc increases. Therefore, the
following example assumes that each 1 percent change in interest
rate is associated with a .5 percent increase in anticipated cost-of-
living increases, and that salary growth assumptions move in
tandem with interest rates. The values of the ABO, PBO and service cost for the final-pay plan with and without a COLA provision are shown in Exhibits 16 and 17. At a 10 percent interest

EXHIBIT 16
ABO and PBO for Plans With and Without a COLA Provision
(Dollars in Millions)

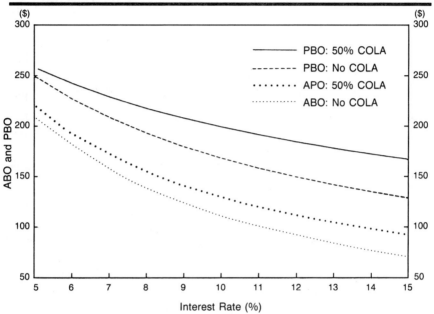

rate—implying a 5.75 percent inflation rate in the example—these values are approximately 20 percent higher with a 50 percent COLA provision.

Effective durations with and without a COLA provision are shown in Exhibits 18 and 19. At a 10 percent interest rate, a COLA provision reduces the ABO's duration from 10.50 to 8.39, the PBO's duration from 6.36 to 4.16, and the service cost's duration from 7.77 to 5.50. By tying pension benefits to inflation in the postretirement years, the COLA increases pension benefit sensitivity and reduces overall interest rate sensitivity by 20–35 percent.[9]

---

[9] As a theoretical point, note that if salary inflation, the COLA provision and the discount rate all reflect inflation equally, and if the COLA begins at the date of service termination rather than retirement, then pension benefit sensitivity would exactly offset the discount rate sensitivity, and the effective durations of the PBO and the service cost would be zero.

EXHIBIT 17
Service Cost for Plans With and Without a COLA Provision
(Dollars in Millions)

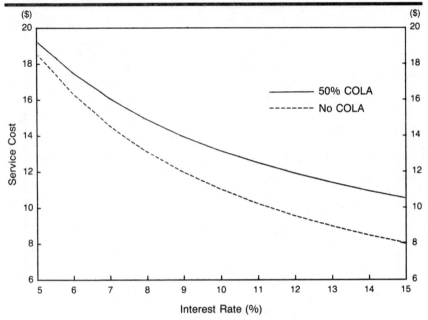

VIII. THE EFFECTS OF ALTERNATIVE
EMPLOYEE DEMOGRAPHICS

Naturally, duration depends on the age distribution of the employees. In Exhibit 19, we compare the group we have used thus far with two other groups.[10] Each group is assigned a retiree population with the same age distribution as in Exhibit 5, but scaled to an appropriate size. The characteristics of the three groups are compared in Exhibit 20.

The ABO's duration of the three groups for the pay-related plan without a COLA provision is shown in Exhibit 21. As might be expected, the "Older Group" has a lower duration, while the

---

[10] The other two groups are Group D—"Older Group with Long Service"—and Group H—"New Group (typical of emerging high-technology companies)"— also from *Pension Cost Method Analysis.*

EXHIBIT 18

Effective Duration of the ABO and PBO for Plans With and Without a COLA Provision

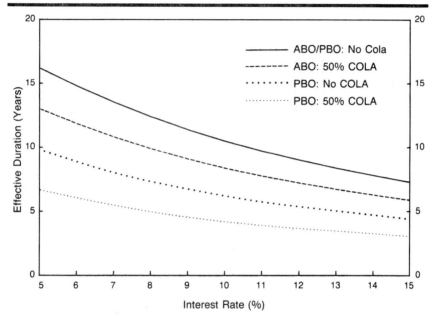

"New Group" has a higher duration. The ABO's duration for the Normal Group and the Older Group are nearly equal; however, the duration for the New Group is 40 percent higher (14.6 versus 10.5, at a 10 percent interest rate).

The effective durations of the PBO and the service cost for the three groups are shown in Exhibits 22 and 23. While the PBO's duration is slightly higher for the New Group, the difference in duration between groups is only one year at a 10 percent interest rate. The service cost's durations are also very close for all three groups, with a maximum difference of one year at very low interest rates. Overall, the durations of both the PBO and the service cost are relatively insensitive to group demographics, at least for these three groups.[11]

---

[11] The demographics of a particular plan may differ significantly from those of the Normal Group, Older Group and New Group. In particular, many mature plans have retiree populations, which represent a much larger proportion of

EXHIBIT 19
Effective Duration of the Service Cost for Plans With and Without a COLA Provision

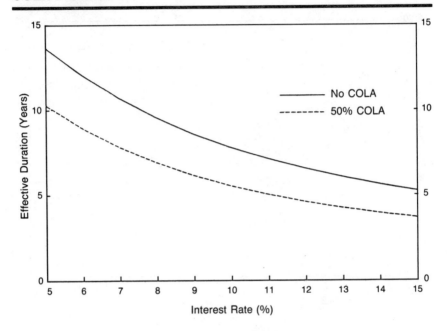

IX. DEVELOPING AN INTEGRATED APPROACH FOR SURPLUS MANAGEMENT

FASB 87 has added several new concerns to the pension plan sponsor's already difficult task. Traditionally, the plan sponsor selected an asset-allocation policy to balance the advantages of a lower average funding cost provided by a high-return strategy against the disadvantages of uncertain investment performance. Typically, the sponsor would take a long-term perspective, since short-term performance had little effect on earnings or on the balance sheet, given the use of actuarial smoothing techniques. Under FASB 87, an asset-allocation policy will have new short-term implications

the PBO than in the groups illustrated here. Thus, it is possible that a particular plan's interest sensitivity can exhibit unique characteristics not reflected in these examples.

EXHIBIT 20
Characteristics of Different Plan Participant Groups

	Average Age (Years)	Average Service (Years)	Retire ABO as Percentage of Active ABO (10% Discount Rate)
Normal Group	36.3	7.7	50%
Older Group	40.2	13.4	100%
New Group	38.9	4.3	10%

for both the balance sheet and the income statement. In particular, FASB 87's requirement of mark-to-market liability valuation may produce substantial adverse fluctuations in both the pension surplus and pension expense.

To develop an effective asset-allocation policy under FASB 87, the sponsor must adopt an integrated approach in which the assets

EXHIBIT 21
Effective Duration of the ABO for Different Age Groups

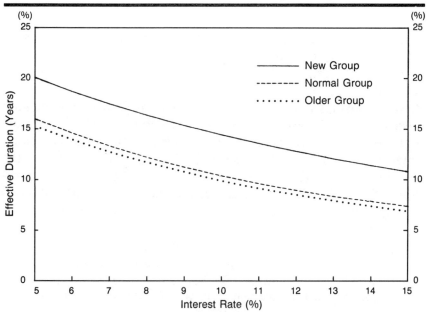

EXHIBIT 22
Effective Duration of the PBO for Different Age Groups

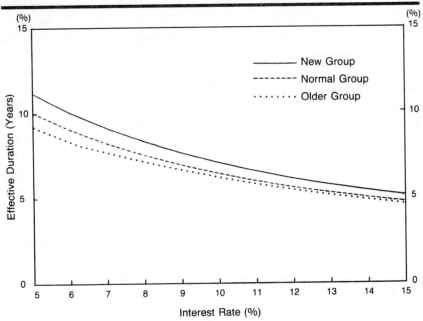

and liabilities are managed together, rather than separately, with the objective of controlling the interest rate sensitivity of the surplus and the resulting balance sheet and expense volatilities. Toward this end, we recently introduced a conceptual framework, termed "surplus management," that integrates the asset-allocation decision with a market-valued pension liability.[12] The integrating link between assets and liabilities is interest rate risk. The plan's interest rate risk is best measured by the effective duration of the pension surplus. The pension surplus can be thought of as a portfolio with a "long" position in pension assets and a "short" position in pension liabilities, from which the interest sensitivity of the

[12] See Martin L. Leibowitz, *Total Portfolio Duration: A New Perspective on Asset Allocation,* New York: Salomon Brothers Inc, February 1986 and "Liability Returns: A New Perspective on Asset Allocation," the previous article in this book, for an extended discussion of the effective duration of the pension assets, pension liabilities and the pension surplus.

EXHIBIT 23
Effective Duration of the Service Cost for Different Age Groups

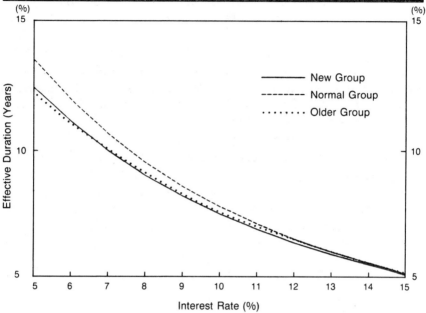

surplus is readily determined. Of course, successful control of interest rate risk requires accurate measurement of the effective duration of pension assets and pension liabilities. With an integrated approach to surplus management, an asset-allocation strategy can be designed to manage the new balance sheet and expense volatilities introduced by FASB 87, as well as the traditional long-term risk and return objectives.

To apply these concepts in practice, plan sponsors must think through their objectives clearly. For example, the difference between the interest sensitivities of the ABO and PBO makes it impossible to hedge both simultaneously. Therefore, a sponsor concerned about managing its surplus must decide whether it is more important to control near-term balance sheet volatility by managing the interest sensitivity of the ABO, or to control longer-term volatility by managing the interest sensitivity of the PBO. When benefits are nominal and constant, the PBO's effective duration is longer than the ABO's; however, it may be difficult to construct an asset portfolio that has a sufficiently high duration to match the durations of either the ABO or PBO. Of course, a shortfall in duration on the asset side exposes the surplus to a loss (or gain) if interest rates fall (or rise). When benefits are salary related and interest sensitive, the effective duration of the PBO may be shorter than that of the ABO. In this case, the appropriate hedging strategy is to hold very long-term assets if the sponsor's priorities are short term, and hold relatively shorter-term assets if the sponsor's priorities are long term.

The objective of managing expense volatility introduces additional complexity. The pension expense under FASB 87 comprises several components, all with different interest sensitivities: service cost, changes in the PBO surplus ("actuarial gains and losses"), and interest on the surplus. Certain smoothing techniques are also permitted. The management of pension expense volatility is an important issue that is worthy of future research.

ARTICLE 6

WILLIAM MARSHALL is vice president of the Fixed Income Division at Goldman Sachs & Co. Prior to joining Goldman Sachs in 1985, Dr. Marshall was Professor of Finance at Washington University, where he obtained a Ph.D. in 1977. Dr. Marshall has also taught at the University of Michigan and Stanford University. He has published extensively on topics related to fixed income portfolio management.

PORTFOLIO INSURANCE: LIMITING THE EXPOSURE OF ACTIVELY MANAGED PENSION FUNDS UNDER STATEMENT OF FINANCIAL ACCOUNTING STANDARDS NO. 87

William J. Marshall, Ph.D.
Vice President
Fixed Income Division
Goldman, Sachs & Co.

Portfolio insurance is an asset allocation method that limits the downside risk of a portfolio—the risk that performance will fall short of a minimally acceptable target—without sacrificing the potential to participate in superior market performance. For many institutional investors, risk equates with the likelihood of failure to achieve some critical level of performance, often performance relative to a benchmark portfolio of assets or liabilities. This article demonstrates the use of portfolio insurance to preserve the value of assets relative to liabilities, where the values of both vary over time with market conditions.

The notion of risk that underlies portfolio insurance differs significantly from that implicit in other portfolio theoretic asset allocation methods. Mean-variance models, for example, equate risk with potential variation of actual from expected rate of return. The mean-variance investor's risk might be expressed as the probability that actual and expected return differ by more than, say, 100 basis points. An investor who chooses portfolio insurance will have identified a specific level of performance as critical. For that investor, risk can be expressed as the likelihood that the actual performance will fall short of the critical standard.

Although the methods we describe are appropriate to a variety of problems, we will focus in this article on asset allocation for a defined benefit pension plan. While the desire to protect funded status has already attracted many pension fund managers to portfolio insurance, recent changes in accounting for defined benefit pension plans have created a sense of urgency for its consideration. The newly issued Statement of Financial Accounting Standards No. 87 (hereafter, FAS 87) dramatically alters pension accounting by requiring that pension liabilities be "marked to market." Under FAS 87, the impact of volatile pension performance on a sponsor's financial statements could overwhelm operating results. Portfolio insurance can be used to limit these effects without sacrificing the opportunity to prosper from active investment management.

The key to the use of portfolio insurance with a volatile benchmark, such as a market sensitive liability portfolio, is the appropriate identification of an asset or portfolio to serve as the riskless, reserve asset. Where portfolio insurance is used to put a floor on asset value, cash is easily identified as the riskless asset. In contrast, cash is risky if held to fund liabilities that vary in value with market conditions, as in the case of defined benefit pension liabilities. Thus the riskless assets in the portfolio insurance programs we describe move with liabilities as markets change. Duration matched bond portfolios are prominent in this application since many institutional investors have nominal liabilities that are fixed in time.

Many approaches to portfolio insurance mimic the dynamic hedging of an option and, unfortunately, require elaborate technology for implementation. Recently, however, Fischer Black and

Robert Jones[1] and others have introduced an intuitive, rule-based method of portfolio insurance that removes the technological barriers that have kept many managers from using portfolio insurance. Their method can be readily adapted to address the problem at hand.

The remainder of this article is organized as follows: Section I introduces the concept of portfolio insurance. After reviewing the general approach, we consider the application of portfolio insurance where the performance benchmark reflects market sensitive liabilities. We then describe the implementation of a simplified approach to portfolio insurance. Section II analyzes FAS 87 and demonstrates the special appeal of portfolio insurance to the plan sponsor subject to the new rules. We consider the modeling of pension liabilities under FAS 87 and the identification of a reserve asset for the portfolio insurance program. Section III provides a numerical example of the application of portfolio insurance under FAS 87. We offer some concluding remarks in Section IV.

I. PORTFOLIO INSURANCE

Portfolio insurance is a method of asset allocation that maximizes the likelihood that predetermined minimum acceptable performance objectives will be achieved no matter what course markets take. Portfolio insurance is attractive because it limits downside risk. If failure to meet a performance objective is "ruinous," some form of insurance is a necessity. In less severe circumstances, the confidence that comes from having a portfolio insurance program in place may permit more aggressive management and correspondingly higher expected returns.

In principle, a variety of methods can be used for limiting downside risk. By definition, investment in a riskless asset portfolio provides that protection. That approach precludes active management and limits the opportunities to enjoy the higher expected returns generally associated with risky portfolios. Nevertheless, structured bond portfolios, for example, are often constructed to limit risk.

---

[1] Fischer Black and Robert Jones, *A Simplified Approach to Portfolio Insurance,* New York: Goldman, Sachs & Co., 1986.

Some financial assets are designed to furnish the same sort of protection that attracts investors to portfolio insurance. For example, convertible bonds provide the upside associated with equity positions while limiting downside to the performance of a bond. Put options held in conjunctions with equities also limit downside risk. Alternatively, and equivalently, one can invest in riskless assets and hold call options on risky assets. Unfortunately, strategies employing these assets for large, active and diversified portfolios would be cumbersome and costly. The instruments may not even exist in sufficient supply.

The ideal strategy would be to obtain a blanket put option on a risky portfolio in its entirety, an option that would remain in force as the composition of the portfolio changed. Portfolio insurance can be thought of as synthesizing that blanket put option.

Many writers of options have learned to hedge their exposure by synthesizing an offsetting position in the cash or futures markets. This approach is termed "delta hedging," since it involves matching the "deltas," or the volatilities of option prices relative to price changes of the underlying instruments. Portfolio insurance is essentially delta hedging without the offsetting option position. The idea is to hold the portfolio that synthetically duplicates the performance characteristics of a desired blanket put option. Unfortunately, delta hedging requires complex analytical and empirical analysis, as do conventional approaches to portfolio insurance.

Essential Features

However, portfolio insurance can be provided by asset allocation methods that are straightforward and require no elaborate technology. Consider the essential features that characterize portfolio insurance:

1. A portfolio insurance program is a rule-based method of allocating resources between risky and riskless assets. The rule depends only on the value of the portfolio. Views on markets and predictions of performance may influence the *choice* of risky assets, but not the *allocation* between risky and riskless assets.

2.   The allocation rule causes the portion of the portfolio allocated to the riskless asset to increase as the value of the portfolio falls, and to decline as the value of the portfolio rises.

3.   The rule causes the portfolio to be entirely invested in the riskless asset before the critical downside threshold is reached.

Any asset allocation method with these features provides portfolio insurance.

A Simplified Approach

In their paper, Black and Jones describe a simple, efficient, intuitive and quite powerful approach with the features described above. Below, we define the key components of their approach using the example in Exhibits 1 and 2 for clarification.

1.   *The Floor:* The floor is the minimum acceptable level of performance. It can be absolute, e.g., a portfolio value of $10 million, or relative, e.g., 90 percent of the value of a specific market index. In this example, the floor is $900.

2.   *The Cushion:* The cushion is the difference between the portfolio value and the floor. In this example, the cushion is $100.

3.   *The Reserve Asset:* The reserve asset is riskless. If the floor is absolute, the reserve asset is cash or near-cash assets with no credit risk. If the floor is relative, the reserve asset is an asset or portfolio that will perfectly track the benchmark on which the floor is based.

4.   *The Active Asset:* The active asset refers to any holdings other than the reserve asset. The active asset might be an equity portfolio, a high yield bond portfolio, mortgages, commodities—anything that an active manager might hold. Moreover, the composition of the active asset can change depending, for example, on market views.

5.   *The Exposure:* The exposure of a portfolio is the dollar value of holdings of the active asset. In this example, the exposure is $600.

6.   *The Multiple:* The multiple is the ratio of the exposure to the cushion. In this example, the multiple is 6.

EXHIBIT 1
A Simple Portfolio Insurance Program

Initial Portfolio Value:	$1,000	
Floor:	900	
Cushion:	$ 100	
Multiple:	6	
Exposure:	$ 600	
Tolerance:	10.00%	

Portfolio Allocation at Various Prices

Price of Active Asset	$ 71.45	$ 83.12	$ 98.33	$ 100.00	$ 101.67	$ 110.43	$ 112.27
Old Portfolio							
Active	$ 79.70	$ 205.72	$ 590.00	$ 600.00	$ 610.00	$ 982.41	$1,080.85
Reserve	832.46	725.66	400.00	400.00	400.00	94.74	14.22
Total	$ 912.16	$ 931.38	$ 990.00	$1,000.00	$1,010.00	$1,077.15	$1,095.07
Floor	(900.00)	(900.00)	(900.00)	(900.00)	(900.00)	(900.00)	(900.00)
Cushion	$ 12.16	$ 31.38	$ 90.00	$ 100.00	$ 110.00	$ 177.15	$ 195.07
New Portfolio							
Active	$ 72.95	$ 188.29	$ 540.00		$ 660.00	$1,062.94	$1,094.87
Reserve	839.21	743.09	450.00		350.00	14.22	0.00
% Active	8%	20%	55%		65%	99%	100%
% Reserve	92%	80%	45%		35%	1%	0%

EXHIBIT 2

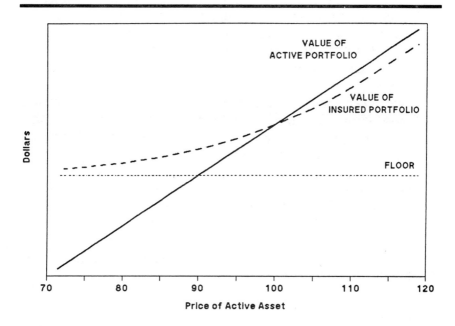

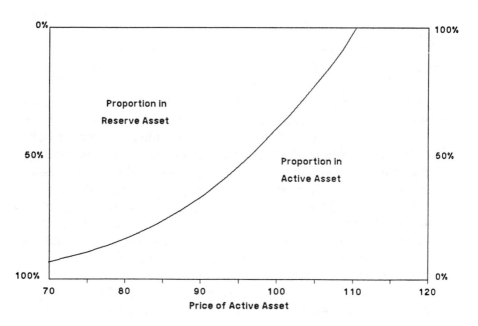

Portfolio insurance is accomplished in a strikingly simple manner: simply choose a multiple to be maintained. For example, the following rule constitutes a portfolio insurance program: if market changes cause the multiple to differ by 10 percent from 6, undertake a trade that restores the multiple of 6. The deviation tolerated between trades is called:

7. *The Tolerance:* The multiple is permitted to vary from the target within the range of the tolerance. One can link the tolerance to the price of the active asset, the cushion, or the multiple. The latter two will accommodate a flexible floor.

This approach has the required features of a portfolio insurance program. It is rule-based. The allocation to the riskless asset varies inversely with the value of the portfolio, since it varies inversely with the cushion. Finally, as the cushion approaches zero, so does the exposure; the portfolio will be entirely invested in the riskless asset before the floor is reached.

An Example

The example presented in Exhibits 1 and 2 will clarify these concepts. When the program is initiated, the portfolio has a value of $1,000 and a cushion of $100. $600 is invested in the active asset, which has a price of $100. (The portfolio is composed of 60 percent active asset and 40 percent reserve asset.)

Trades are to be undertaken to restore the multiple if the cushion changes by 10 percent. As the price of the active asset falls, the first trade would occur at $98.33. The multiple is restored, resulting in an allocation of $540 to the active asset. The percentage breakdown is 55 percent active asset and 45 percent reserve asset. Further loss of value would result in corresponding reductions in holdings of the active asset. At a price of $83.12, the portfolio is allocated 20 percent active asset and 80 percent reserve asset. At a price of $71.45, the allocation is 8 percent active asset and 92 percent reserve asset. The allocation to the active asset will approach zero as the price of the active asset approaches zero.

As the price of the active asset rises, so does the allocation to the active asset. Assuming trading at all the intervening points where the tolerance is reached, the allocation at a price of $101.67 is 65 percent active asset and 35 percent reserve asset. At a price of $110.43, the allocation is 99 percent active asset and 1 percent reserve asset. At any price above $112.27, the portfolio is entirely in the active asset.

The relation between the value of the active asset and the value of the insured portfolio is most easily seen in the graph in Exhibit 2. As the price of the active asset increases from $100, the value of the insured portfolio increases at a slightly lesser rate because the portfolio is not entirely in the active asset. For price movements beyond $112, the portfolio is entirely in the active asset and the active asset and the insured portfolio appreciate at the same rate.

The insurance effect is evident for prices under $100. At each trade as price falls, less of the portfolio is invested in the active asset. Each subsequent decline has less effect than its immediate predecessor. The value of the insured portfolio approaches, but does not penetrate, the floor of $900.

The graph of portfolio value against price in Exhibit 2 shows clearly the option-like character of portfolio insurance. Similar payoff curves would be obtained for two option positions: (1) long the reserve asset plus a call on the active asset, or (2) long the active asset plus a put on the active asset.

The Cost of Portfolio Insurance

Of course, the protection obtained from portfolio insurance has a cost, as does a put option—a cost that is not apparent in the example. As with an option, the cost depends on volatility. However, while the cost of an actual option depends on *expected volatility* for the term of the option, the cost of portfolio insurance depends on *actual volatility* during the term.

Consider Exhibit 3, which extends our earlier example. In Case One, the price of the active asset falls from $100 to $98.33 causing a rebalancing trade from 6 units to 5.49 units of the active asset. Then the price returns to $100. Even with no transaction costs, the insured portfolio has lost value, going from $1000 to $999.15. Why? Because more of the active asset was held during the decline than during the recovery. Essentially, the insured portfolio "buys high and sells low."

EXHIBIT 3
The Cost of Portfolio Insurance

	Case One			Case Two		
	Date 1	Date 2	Date 3	Date 1	Date 2	Date 3
Price of Active Asset	$ 100.00	$ 98.33	$100.00	$ 100.00	$ 101.67	$100.00
Old Portfolio						
Active	$ 600.00	$590.00	$549.15	$ 600.00	$ 610.00	$649.18
Reserve	400.00	400.00	450.00	400.00	400.00	350.00
Total	$1,000.00	$990.00	$999.15	$1,000.00	$1,010.00	$999.18
Floor	(900.00)	(900.00)	(900.00)	(900.00)	(900.00)	(900.00)
Cushion	$ 100.00	$ 90.00	$ 99.15	$ 100.00	$ 110.00	$ 98.18
Units of Active	6.00	6.00	5.49	6.00	6.00	6.49
New Portfolio						
Active		$540.00			$ 660.00	
Reserve		450.00			350.00	
Units of Active		5.49			6.49	

The same effect is evident in Case Two, where the price of the active asset rises then declines. More of the active asset is bought at the higher price, so more is lost as price regresses. The insured portfolio declines in value to $999.18.

The greater the volatility of the active asset, the greater will be the cost of portfolio insurance. Essentially, something is lost with each price reversal that causes a trade. Of course, wider tolerances would reduce these costs. However, wider tolerances also reduce the effectiveness of the program, increasing the chance that the floor is penetrated before an adjustment is made, and increasing the lag in participation in price appreciation.

In summary, a simple approach to portfolio insurance can be used to protect against "ruinous" losses at a cost that varies with the volatility of the active asset. The next section explores the "ruinous" implications of FAS 87. A simulation of portfolio insurance within the context of FAS 87 is reported later in this article.

II. STATEMENT OF FINANCIAL ACCOUNTING STANDARDS NO. 87

Recently, the Financial Accounting Standards Board promulgated Statement of Financial Accounting Standards No. 87 and required adoption no later than fiscal 1987. FAS 87 radically alters the accepted methods of representing pension expense and pension liabilities in a plan sponsor's financial statements. Under FAS 87, pension assets and the benefits promised to workers are to be marked to the market annually. Changes in these values will directly affect reported pension expense. Moreover, any deficit of pension assets relative to promised benefits will be reported as a liability.

The concern over FAS 87 stems from the potential volatility that pension plan performance will add to the financial statements of many plan sponsors. Not only are asset values volatile, but promised benefits have roughly the valuation characteristics and potential price volatility of a 30-year bond. For firms with large plans relative to operations, the financial statement impact of FAS 87 could be great.

The remainder of this section explains the major features of FAS 87. We will ignore details that are not central to the issues at hand. Our purpose is not to provide a thorough critique of FAS 87 or to argue its importance, but to provide sufficient background so that the use of portfolio insurance to limit its impact can be understood.[2]

FAS 87 applies to defined benefit pension plans. Under such a plan, a firm incurs an obligation to pay its workers certain benefits after they retire. Benefits may be linked to average or final pay (e.g., 30 percent of average pay over the five years preceding retirement) or based on a flat rate (e.g., $200 per year for each year of service). It is important to note that in neither case does the firm's obligation depend on the performance of any assets set aside to fund the plan.

Plan Assets and Liabilities

For reporting purposes, two measures of a firm's pension liability are calculated: the *accumulated benefit obligation* and the *projected benefit obligation*. Each is calculated by predicting the payments that will be made year by year to retiring workers. Actuarial assumptions about mortality and similar considerations influence both.

The accumulated benefit obligation represents the benefits owed if the firm was to terminate the plan or discontinue operations. It is based on service to the date of calculation and pay level at that date. The projected benefit obligation is a growing concern measure of pension liability. It is based on service to the date of calculation and an assumed level of pay at time of retirement. The two measures are the same for flat rate plans, but differ for pay-related plans.

Inflation will affect accumulated and projected benefit obligations differently. The accumulated benefit obligations depends only on the prevailing pay level. The projected benefit obligation depends on prevailing pay levels and the assumed rate of future inflation. All else equal, both will change from year to year with

[2] Amy Stevens, *Statement of Financial Accounting Standards No. 87: Tempest in a Teapot?*, New York: Goldman, Sachs & Co., 1986.

actual inflation. In addition, the projected benefit obligation will change as the inflation assumption changes.

Both the accumulated and the projected benefit obligations are discounted present values, based on cash outflows calculated as described above. While some discretion is allowed, the alternative discount rates permitted by FAS 87 are all market related; indeed, a principal objective of FAS 87 is to assure use of realistic rates for valuing pension liabilities. The prevailing rate of interest on long-term bonds is one alternative, and a determinant of the other permissible discount rates.

FAS 87 also requires that the chosen discount rate and the assumed rate of inflation used to determine the projected benefit obligation be consistent. Although we will not dwell on the implications of the requirement here, it is important for determining the market sensitivity of projected benefit obligations.

Under FAS 87, pension expense and funded status depend on what is referred to as the "market related value" of plan assets. The market related value of plan assets differs from actual market value because certain smoothing techniques are permitted. Eventually, however, any change in market value will be fully reflected in market related value.

Pension Expense

Under FAS 87, pension expense (also referred to as net periodic pension cost) is sensitive to the market valuation of pension assets and promised benefits. Pension expense is calculated from the following components:

1. *Interest cost:* the change in the projected benefit obligation resulting from the passage of time.
2. *Service cost:* the change in projected benefit obligation resulting from service during the period.
3. *The expected return on plan assets:* the change in the value of plan assets expected during the period.
4. *Gain or loss:* unamortized changes in projected benefit obligation or in the value of plan assets resulting from changes in assumptions and deviations of actual from assumed experience.
5. *Various transition costs and other occasional adjustments.*

Components 4 and 5 can be ignored for our purposes, since the volatility of expense comes almost entirely from the first three components. Component 4 is subject to smoothing that will mitigate its effect. Component 5 is not market sensitive.

For our purposes, pension expense can be calculated as:

$$
\begin{array}{l}
\text{Interest cost} \\
+\ \text{Service cost} \\
\underline{-\ \text{Expected return on assets}} \\
=\ \text{Net periodic pension cost}
\end{array}
$$

Of principal concern are interest cost and the expected return on plan assets. Service cost represents an expense of doing business during the period. It will vary from year to year with inflation, but so will all the costs of doing business. In contrast, interest cost and expected return on assets represent the market performance of what are essentially financial claims: pension benefits incurred because of prior years' service and the assets held to fund those benefits.

Capping Pension Expense

The primary source of variation in pension expense will be changes in interest cost that are not offset by changes in expected return on assets. We can represent these two components as:

Return on assets = Asset rate   × Plan assets

Interest cost   = Benefit rate × Projected benefit obligation

In general, the methods of determining the benefit rate and the asset rate under FAS 87 are such that these rates will be highly correlated. Most variation in expense will be due to changes in the value of plan assets and in the projected benefit obligation.

Portfolio insurance can be used to limit the potential increase in pension expense from year to year by reducing the likelihood that the projected benefit obligation will rise by more than the increase in plan assets. The reserve asset in the portfolio insurance program would be a hedge portfolio chosen to match the market sensitivity of the projected benefit obligation. As the spread between asset value and projected benefit obligation narrows (becomes less positive), assets would be shifted into the hedge portfolio.

The choice of a hedge portfolio is complex and depends on the assumptions used to calculate the projected benefit obligation. The simplest case is where the inflation assumption reflected in the projected benefit obligation is insensitive to market rates of interest. Exhibit 4 depicts a typical pension benefit stream. The duration of that stream, calculated using the rate on 30-year Treasury bonds, would be about ten years. The appropriate hedge portfolio would be a duration matched portfolio. Indeed, assumptions allowed under FAS 87 would permit a perfect hedge. If the market rate used to calculate the projected benefit obligation is the rate on an asset that can be held, then that asset constitutes a perfect hedge instrument, one with no basis risk.

EXHIBIT 4
Typical Pension Liability Stream

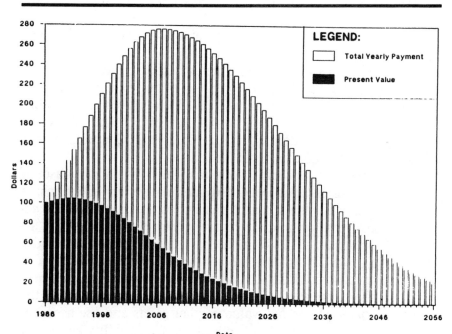

If the inflation assumption used to calculate the projected benefit obligation will vary with the market rate of interest, the cash flows in Exhibit 4 are not constant, and the duration of the stream is not meaningful. To see this, suppose that the inflation assumption were to be adjusted annually to equal the then-prevailing discount rate minus 3 percent. That rule is consistent with the view that the real rate of interest is constant. It can be shown that under these conditions the duration of the projected benefit obligation would be zero. Changes in the discount rate would be exactly offset by changes in the predicted cash flows.

For cases that lie between the two extremes considered above, we can calculate an effective duration of the projected benefit obligation and choose a hedge portfolio to serve as the reserve asset. If the inflation assumption or the discount rate does not relate directly to a tradable financial instrument, the hedge portfolio will minimize but not eliminate all basis risk. Consequently, the portfolio insurance program will be imperfect.

Protecting Funded Status

Pension cost represents the present value of expected future payments of promised benefits. Typically, sponsors contribute assets to a pension plan from time to time as costs are incurred. Those assets are intended to fund all or part of future benefit payments. The contributions, no matter how great, do not discharge the liability of a sponsor; his liability is for the actual payment. Thus, the sponsor retains an economic and legal interest in the performance of plan assets and liabilities over time.

Prior to FAS 87, a liability was recognized by the sponsor if cumulative pension cost exceeded cumulative contributions; a pension asset was recognized if the opposite was true. This accounting treatment ignored the market performance of pension assets and liabilities. FAS 87 addresses that perceived oversight. Specifically, FAS 87 includes the additional requirement that a liability be recognized if the funded status of the plan becomes negative. For the purpose of this requirement, the funded status is the difference between the fair value of plan assets and the accumulated benefit obligation. Thus, under FAS 87, a liability can result from either insufficient contributions or inadequate performance of assets relative to liabilities.

Presuming that initial funding is adequate, a portfolio insurance program can be structured that will protect the funded status under FAS 87. The floor in the program will be the accumulated benefit obligation, which will vary in value with market conditions. The key element determining the effectiveness of the program will be the choice of a reserve asset. The market value of that asset should closely track the accumulated benefit obligation.

Recall that the accumulated benefit obligation is the present value of benefits that will be paid, based on services previously rendered and current salary levels. In contrast to the projected benefit obligation, the accumulated benefit obligation does not depend on an inflation assumption. Thus, the principal source of variation in the accumulated benefit obligation will be changes in the discount rate.

The hedge portfolio that constitutes the reserve asset in the portfolio insurance program will have a duration equal to the duration of the accumulated benefit obligation. Moreover, the hedge portfolio should be chosen such that its yield varies closely with the discount rate applied to calculate the accumulated benefit obligation. Again the choice of discount rate is crucial in determining the effectiveness of the hedge. If the discount rate is a market rate, that asset can be held as the reserve asset. Otherwise, some basis risk will be present.

With the reserve asset chosen, the portfolio insurance program can be implemented as described earlier. A simulation on historical data of a portfolio insurance program intended to protect funded status is reported in Section III.

Funded Status and Pension Cost

Can a portfolio insurance program be designed that will simultaneously protect funded status and limit pension cost? Yes, but probably not as successfully as if only one or the other is of concern.

The programs described above focus on the market performance of pension assets and pension liabilities for promised benefits. The difficulty in designing a program directed at both cost and funded status arises because the two calculations use different measures of asset and liability values. Market related value of plan assets is used to calculate pension cost, while fair value is used to determine funded status. The former method may incorporate various smoothing methods, while fair value is a contemporary market valuation. Without smoothing, the two will be closely correlated.

The real barrier to hedging both pension cost and funded status is the treatment of promised benefits. Pension cost is based on the projected benefit obligation, while funded status depends on the accumulated benefit obligation. The difference between the two is the application of an inflation assumption to salary levels to calculate the projected benefit obligation. The difference between the estimated cash payments used in the accumulated benefit obligation and those used in the projected benefit obligation will be greater the more distant the date of payment, that is, because of the compounding effect of the inflation assumption. Thus, the duration of the projected benefit obligation will tend to be longer.

However, a link between the inflation assumption and the discount rate will shorten the duration of the projected benefit obligation. Indeed, we saw earlier that the projected benefit obligation can have a duration of zero under certain assumptions permitted by FAS 87.

Clearly, the projected benefit obligation and the accumulated benefit obligation need not perform identically as the market rate of interest varies. So in general, a portfolio insurance program that addresses both pension cost and funded status with equal effectiveness will not exist. If both are important, it will be necessary to weigh the tradeoffs when designing a program.

III. PROTECTING FUNDED STATUS

In their study, Black and Jones simulate a portfolio insurance program designed to protect funded status. The results of their simulation are a valuable source of insight into the determinants of the cost and performance of portfolio insurance.

The following assumptions are made for the simulation:

1. *Initial portfolio value:* $100 million.
2. *Floor:* the accumulated benefit obligation, which is initially $90 million. For simplicity, we assume that the accumulated benefit obligation varies in value exactly as does the long-term Treasury bond.
3. *Active asset:* the S&P 500 Index.
4. *Reserve asset:* at any time, the then-current long-term Treasury bond. The reserve asset provides a perfect hedge for the accumulated benefit obligation.
5. *Multiple:* 6.
6. *Tolerance:* 10% variation from target exposure.
7. *Trading costs:* 0.5% of the value of a trade.

To provide a benchmark, we also show the performance of a constant mix portfolio indicative of traditional pension fund allocations: 60 percent in the S&P 500 and 40 percent in the current 10-year Treasury bond. The constant mix portfolio was rebalanced whenever the S&P 500 moved 2 percent, a criterion roughly equivalent to the tolerance of the portfolio insurance program. Trading costs were assumed to be the same as for the insured portfolio, 0.5 percent.

The findings from the simulations are reported in Exhibit 5. Eight trials were undertaken, corresponding to successive, overlapping five-year periods between 1975 and 1985. For each of these periods, *Part One* reports the values of the portfolio and floor for the alternative allocations, along with various trading statistics. *Part Two* reports year to year performance of the portfolio insurance program.

The final values for the floor range from $198 to $83. Clearly, the accumulated benefit obligation is a volatile financial instrument. Yet, *Part Two* shows that the portfolio insurance program successfully protected the surplus in each year.

We cannot easily assess the costs of portfolio insurance from performance, but we can get a sense of the relations determining cost. Recall that there are two components of cost: the actual charge for executing the transaction and the opportunity cost of buying high and selling low as prices reverse. Both increase in proportion to the dollar volume of trades.

EXHIBIT 5
Simulation Results for Five-Year Portfolio Insurance Strategies

Active Asset: S&P 500
Reserve Asset: 30-Year Treasury Bonds

Initial Portfolio Value:	$100
Floor:	90
	$ 10
Cushion:	
Multiple:	6
Exposure:	$ 60
Tolerance:	10.00%
Trading Cost:	0.50%

Part One:

								Constant Mix		
	Insured Portfolio's	Final	Final	Final			Total Trading	Strategies Using 10-Year Bonds		
Years	Final Value	Floor	Cushion	Exposure	Buys	Sells	Cost	100% S&P	60% S&P	10% S&P
1974-78	$115.25	$114.10	$1.15	$ 7.37	7	85	$1.46	$123.30	$126.90	$129.35
1975-79	192.46	111.69	80.77	192.46	3	0	0.38	198.73	166.24	131.57
1976-80	151.63	98.00	53.63	151.63	47	44	4.21	191.64	159.79	125.41
1977-81	121.53	83.03	38.50	121.53	37	33	2.59	146.86	128.76	107.25
1978-82	175.32	122.36	52.96	175.32	19	16	1.70	192.87	173.76	148.47
1979-83	211.08	123.22	87.86	211.08	8	5	0.77	222.08	192.89	157.48
1980-84	151.17	143.82	7.35	41.40	61	66	5.63	199.38	189.00	171.90
1981-85	198.16	197.59	0.57	3.18	86	109	2.24	198.71	207.83	215.19

Part Two:

To the End of	From the Beginning of . . .												
	1974	1975	1976	1977	1978	1979	1980	1981	1982	1983	1984	1985	Sept. 1986
1974	$0.53												
1975	1.40	$ 34.42											
1976	1.70	48.38	$11.79										
1977	0.98	37.40	6.80	$ 5.69									
1978	1.15	48.71	7.98	6.67	$ 11.75								
1979	2.61	80.77	18.14	15.17	27.53	$ 24.37							
1980	5.03	147.30	53.63	45.00	67.99	64.22	$31.88						
1981	1.24	134.40	45.93	38.50	60.29	56.65	25.86	$2.50					
1982	0.24	137.33	20.94	17.15	52.96	48.26	6.06	0.49	$1.95				
1983	0.58	204.59	55.89	44.97	93.24	87.86	14.60	1.17	4.70	$27.75			
1984	0.29	204.77	47.73	37.91	89.14	83.29	7.35	0.59	2.36	22.13	$5.11		
1985	0.28	269.57	62.47	49.59	117.16	109.44	7.09	0.57	2.27	28.30	4.92	$9.69	
Sept 86	0.13	280.74	46.98	30.49	114.29	105.38	3.27	0.26	1.05	14.08	2.27	4.48	$4.48

Source: *Simplifying Portfolio Insurance for Corporate Pension Plans*, Fischer Black and Robert Jones, New York: Goldman, Sachs and Company, 1986.

The simulation provides two excellent, albeit seemingly quite different, examples of "cheap" portfolio insurance. Consider the period 1975–1979. During 1975, the cushion increased to $34, with only three buys. The year ended with the portfolio allocated entirely to the S&P 500. The portfolio participated fully in the increase in the S&P 500 over the subsequent four years. The portfolio insurance was virtually costless: the insured portfolio underperformed the S&P 500 by approximately $6.27.

Now, consider the period 1974–1978. During 1974, the cushion declined to $0.53. That is about as close to the floor as an insured portfolio can get. At that point, the portfolio was concentrated in the reserve asset. The large number of subsequent trades involved no dollar volume, and thus cost little. It is as if the portfolio immediately moved to the floor. Over the entire period, the insured portfolio underperformed the S&P 500 by approximately $8.05.

Portfolio insurance is "expensive" when the cushion is volatile, with reversals in market direction. For example, the cushion of the insured portfolio begun in 1976 had shrunk to $6.80 by the end of 1977. The allocation to the S&P 500 had declined accordingly. Consequently, the insured portfolio underperformed the S&P during the rally over the next three years. The final value of the S&P 500 exceeded that of the insured portfolio by $40.01.

As we discussed earlier, the cost of an actual option depends on expected volatility and can be determined in advance of purchase. In contrast, the cost of portfolio insurance depends on actual volatility and cannot be known until the period is over. The results of the simulations suggest the range of cost that might be experienced, but they are not sufficiently comprehensive to be taken as evidence of average cost.

Of course, the decision to undertake portfolio insurance must be made on the basis of expected volatility and expected cost. The risk that actual and expected volatility differ is borne by the portfolio insurer.

IV. CONCLUDING REMARKS

Portfolio insurance is an asset allocation method that provides an important alternative for the asset-liability manager. We have seen that a portfolio insurance program can be designed that protects the equity position in a portfolio with market sensitive assets and market sensitive liabilities. Moreover, the technology required to implement such a program is well within the reach of any asset-liability manager.

More specifically, we have seen that portfolio insurance can be used to reduce the impact of FAS 87 on the financial statements of pension plan sponsors. The problem is a difficult one, compared to a strictly economic problem, since we must analyze the impact of alternative choices of actuarial and accounting assumptions. The benefits of the analysis may be great: we suspect that many plan sponsors will conclude that their exposure under FAS 87 is intolerable without some protection in place.

ANALYSIS AND VALUATION OF THE INSTRUMENTS

ARTICLE 7

ARTICLE 7

THOMAS E. KLAFFKY is a Managing Director of the Bond Portfolio Analysis Group at Salomon Brothers Inc in New York, where he is involved with various forms of fixed income portfolio strategy. He has paid particular attention to the optimization of portfolio structures ranging from cash matching and immunization to index-fund replication on both single currency and a multi-currency basis.

After joining the firm in 1976, he was named a Vice President in 1979 and a Managing Director in 1986.

Mr. Klaffky received a B.A. degree in economics from C.W. Post College in 1975 and an M.B.A. degree in finance from New York University in 1976.

Mr. Klaffky has written research publications on coupon stripping, covering such topics as pricing, volatility and historical rates of return on CATS, STRIPS, and other zero-coupon bonds.

ANALYSIS OF TREASURY ZERO-COUPON BONDS*

Thomas E. Klaffky
Managing Director
Salomon Brothers Inc

During the past several years, an amazing number of new types of securities have been developed in the bond market. "Standard" terms and covenants have given way to newer and more innovative terms, such as variable interest rates, warrants and original-issue discounts. Most of these securities have arisen from investors' propensity to invest in securities that fulfill specific functions in their investment strategies. For example, an investor who buys a bond with warrants attached does so to maximize total return in a falling interest rate environment, while an investor who buys floating-rate securities wants to maintain a market-sensitive cash flow. The specific needs of investors, coupled with their tolerance

*The author wishes to thank Robert W. Kopprasch, Frances L. Sirianni and John D. Plum for their many valuable contributions to this article. Thanks also go to Linda Aloia and Laura Davey for their work on the article.

143

for risk, have promoted a new market environment in which it is now possible to tailor a portfolio to the specific cash flow needs and risk exposure of virtually any investor. Within this new context of financial innovation, zero-coupon bonds provide unique flexibility for investors to structure their investments to meet individual portfolio requirements.

While issuers have raised many billions of dollars through the direct issuance of zero-coupon bonds, this amount is far exceeded by "coupon stripping"—the process of separating the interest payments of a bond from the principal amount that is due at maturity. Once separated, each coupon, as well as the principal amount (the "corpus"), represents a different single-payment claim due from the issuer of the security. Each single-payment claim, then, becomes tantamount to a zero-coupon bond.

By "stripping" a bond, a yield curve of zero-coupon bonds can be created, each maturity of which may be used independently. For example, if $1 million par amount of a 12 percent bond due in ten years was stripped, the result would be a series of 20 semiannual zero-coupon bonds, each with a par value of $60,000, and one ten-year zero-coupon bond with a par value of $1 million.

Coupon stripping has historically revolved around the U.S. Treasury bond market, in which the supply of securities is abundant and the problems associated with callability and sinking funds may be conveniently avoided.

This article will focus on the market for Treasury zero-coupon bonds, which are zero-coupon bonds originated through stripping Treasury bonds. Because of the size and homogeneity of this market, it is possible to apply theoretical techniques to the analysis of Treasury zero-coupon bonds and implement those techniques in an actual market environment. In this article, we will study the appropriate pricing of zero-coupon bonds, their volatility characteristics and their historical returns. Through this process, we hope to give investors the tools with which to judge the relative merits and shortcomings of zero-coupon bonds.

I.   A BRIEF HISTORY OF TREASURY ZEROS

Coupon stripping would seem to require the use of "physical" securities—securities in bearer form with coupons attached. In this way, each investor could receive a physical coupon or corpus attesting to ownership of that payment. The original process of coupon stripping, in fact, did require the availability of physical bonds. The process of delivering and insuring physical coupons, however, soon became too cumbersome to be practical and fostered the need for a more reasonable method of stripping bonds—a process more consistent with the trading and delivery mechanisms of other markets.

In August 1982, Treasury zeros were introduced in "receipt" form by Merrill Lynch (TIGRs) and by Salomon Brothers Inc (CATS).[1] To originate receipts, a Treasury bond is deposited in a bank custody account, and receipts are issued attesting to an ownership in a portion of the underlying bond (each portion represented a coupon or principal payment). These receipts, in registered rather than physical form, are then sold to a variety of investors. Upon the maturity of a receipt, the custodian pays the investor from the cash flow of the underlying bond.

The custodial arrangement solved the problems of insurance and physical delivery of coupons, and within months, several receipts were introduced, each sponsored by a different dealer and each carrying a different name. In addition to TIGRs and CATS, TRs, COUGARs, LIONs, GATORs, TBRs, ETRs, and several other products were soon vying for investors' attention.[2] Although there were subtle differences among these receipts, they all basically represented ownership of the pieces of a bond held by a custodian.

The receipt products were a huge success. Over the August 1982–December 1984 period, more than $125 billion par amount

---

[1] Treasury Investment Growth Receipts (TIGRs), are the proprietary product of Merrill Lynch, Pierce, Fenner & Smith. Certificates of Accrual on Treasury Securities (CATS), are the proprietary product of Salomon Brothers Inc.

[2] Treasury Receipts (TRs) can be originated by any of several depositors acceptable to the custodian bank. COUGARs are the proprietary product of A. G. Becker Paribas Inc.

Lehman Investment Opportunity Notes (LIONs) are the proprietary product of Lehman Government Securities.

Government and Agency Term Obligations (GATORs) are the proprietary product of Moseley, Hallgarten, Estabrook & Weeden Inc.

Treasury Bond Receipts (TBRs) are the proprietary product of E.F. Hutton & Company Inc.

Easy Growth Treasury Receipts (ETRs) are the proprietary product of Dean Witter Reynolds Inc.

of receipts was originated. Of this amount, CATS and TRs led the way with approximately $45 billion each, TIGRs followed with more than $27 billion, and the other receipts totaled nearly $10 billion. The demand for zero-coupon receipts placed an overwhelming strain on the raw materials of this market—Treasury bonds. Traditional yield spread relationships changed as "strippers" sought high-coupon Treasury bonds to transform into receipts, and auctions for new Treasury bonds were frequently dominated by dealers attempting to get enough whole bonds to satisfy the demand for the pieces. The U.S. Treasury, while not directly participating, benefited from coupon stripping as their interest costs fell in proportion to the strong demand for newly auctioned Treasury bonds.

In early 1985, the U.S. Treasury announced that it intended to have a more direct role in coupon stripping by introducing the Separate Trading of Registered Interest and Principal of Securities (STRIPS). Under the STRIPS program, selected Treasury bonds became eligible to be separated and to have their coupons and corpora maintained in the book-entry system operated by the Federal Reserve banks. Since none of the receipts is eligible to be maintained in this book-entry system, the transfer of STRIPS between investors can be facilitated much more easily than that of receipts. Furthermore, to increase the ability to strip bonds, the U.S. Treasury simultaneously announced that 30-year Treasury bonds (traditionally callable after 25 years) would no longer carry a call option.

With the STRIPS program, the U.S. Department of the Treasury decided not to directly issue zero-coupon bonds; all Treasury auctions continue to take place in the traditional manner. Rather, the STRIPS program was designed to facilitate the secondary market stripping of specified Treasury notes and bonds into their individual interest and principal components. With official sponsorship by the U.S. Treasury, STRIPS seemed destined to become the basis of value for all zero-coupon bonds.

The introduction of STRIPS virtually ended the origination of additional receipts, and although CATS, TRs and TIGRs still trade in the secondary market, all receipts are now priced relative to STRIPS. Exhibit 1 shows the market for Treasury zeros as of August 29, 1986, and from this chart, it is evident that STRIPS

EXHIBIT 1
Par Value of Treasury Zeros Outstanding, August 29, 1986
(Dollars in Billions)

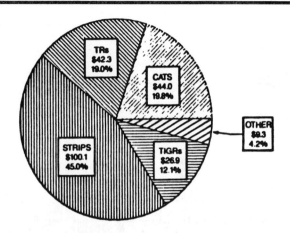

already dominate the market for Treasury zeros. Moreover, since STRIPS are traded by many bond dealers, this instrument has become more marketable than any of the receipts.

Exhibit 2 shows the par amount of Treasury zeros outstanding by maturity as of August 29, 1986. The availability of Treasury zeros is not limited to one section of the maturity spectrum; Treasury zeros are available throughout the 30-year maturity spectrum of the U.S. Treasury bond market. This availability makes Treasury zeros useful for a wide range of portfolio strategies, such as cash matching and immunization. This spectrum of maturities, coupled with their marketability, makes Treasury zeros an important and flexible addition to the universe of securities available to investors.

II. THE PRICING OF TREASURY ZEROS

In August 1982, when the first TIGRs and CATS were introduced, widespread uncertainty developed about the "appropriate" value of Treasury zeros. Should each zero have the same yield as that of its underlying Treasury bond? Should each have the same yield as

EXHIBIT 2
**Par Amount of Treasury Zeros Outstanding by Maturity,
August 29, 1986** (Dollars in Billions)

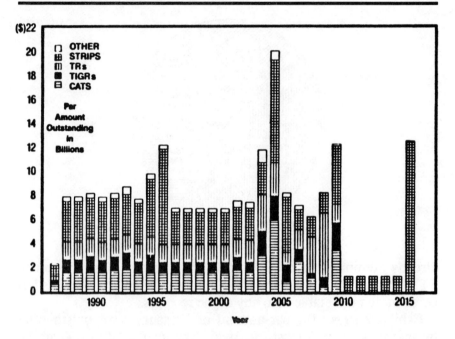

the Treasury bond of the same maturity or, possibly, of the same duration? It became clear that traditional standards of value were inappropriate when discussing Treasury zeros and that additional concepts were needed to help market participants determine whether or not these zeros were fairly priced.

The concept of yield to maturity was developed many years ago in the fixed-income market in an attempt to give relative values to bonds with different coupons and different maturities. The yield to maturity is the rate that equates the present value of a bond to the future payments of interest and principal. Yield to maturity serves as a basis of comparison, a benchmark for historical reference and a measure of value between quality or coupon sectors of the market. A shortcoming of this concept, however, is that it is a single rate that is applied to all of the cash flows from a bond, regardless of when they occur. This shortcoming becomes relevant when discussing coupon stripping because yield to maturity, being a single rate, cannot accurately evaluate all of the component cash flows from a bond—each of which falls due at a different time.

Let us assume that a two-year Treasury bond has a yield to maturity of 7.5 percent and that a ten-year Treasury bond has a yield to maturity of 8.5 percent. What is the appropriate yield to maturity for a Treasury zero that matures in six months? If the Treasury zero was stripped from the two-year bond, one could argue that the appropriate yield should be 7.5 percent; one could also argue that the appropriate yield should be 8.5 percent, if the Treasury zero was stripped from the ten-year bond. Alternatively, one could argue that the appropriate yield should approximate that of a six-month Treasury bill rather than that of either a two-year or a ten-year bond.

A Treasury zero should have a yield to maturity that is based on its time to maturity rather than on its origin. In other words, a six-month Treasury zero should have one price and one yield to maturity regardless of the price or yield of the bond from which it was stripped. The traditional par bond Treasury yield curve, therefore, is inadequate as a basis for determining the appropriate yield levels of zero-coupon bonds.

A yield curve is needed where every point represents the yield to maturity of a zero-coupon bond to its maturity date. In academic literature, this zero-coupon yield curve is known as the "theoretical spot rate curve," and using statistical methods, it is possible to calculate this spot rate curve from the par bond yield curve.[3] Most simplistically, an equilibrium spot rate curve should value each component of cash flow in an internally consistent fashion, so that all Treasury par bonds have the same value as the sum of their parts. Exhibit 3 shows the simple calculation of a spot rate. Given that a one-year par bond has a coupon (and yield to maturity) of 10 percent, we can see that by discounting each coupon and the corpus at the yield to maturity of 10 percent, we arrive at a total price of $1,000,000.

However, if we observe that the six-month Treasury bill has a yield of 5 percent (not 10 percent) and we conclude that the value

---

[3] In some academic literature, the theoretical spot rate curve is known as the term structure of interest rates.

EXHIBIT 3
Break-Even Spot Rates (10%, 12-Month Bond @ 100)

Years	Payment	Present Value @10%	Spot Rate	Present Value @Spot Rates	Difference in Present Values
0.5	$ 50,000	$ 47,619	5.000%	$ 48,780	$1,161
1.0	50,000	45,351	10.128[a]	45,296	– 55
1.0	1,000,000	907,030	10.128[a]	905,924	– 1,106
Total	$1,100,000	$1,000,000		$1,000,000	$ 0

[a] 12-Month break-even spot rate (10.128%).

of a six-month bill, a zero-coupon security, is a reasonable proxy for the appropriate value of a six-month coupon, we find that we must discount the 12-month payment at a rate higher than the bond's yield to maturity (10.128 percent in this case, or approximately 13 basis points higher than the bond's yield to maturity) to maintain the equilibrium price of $1,000,000. The six- and 12-month points on the spot rate curve are, therefore, 5 percent and 10.128 percent, respectively.

Continuing the example (see Exhibit 4), we find that the 18-month par bond has a coupon and yield to maturity of 15 percent. Once again, if we discount all payments at the bond's yield to maturity of 15 percent, the total price equals $1,000,000.

By discounting the six- and 12-month payments at the spot rate appropriate for the term of each, we can again solve for the break-even rate on the remaining payment, 15.537 percent, or approximately 54 basis points more than the bond's yield to maturity. Similarly, we can calculate a break-even spot rate for each maturity and arrive at a theoretical spot rate curve.[4]

Although it has long been possible to calculate theoretical spot rates, the market for Treasury zeros makes it possible to compare the theory with the reality. The yield curve that has developed for these zero-coupon bonds from actual trading activity bears a striking resemblance to the theoretical spot rate curve. In fact, in many areas of the maturity spectrum, actual trades frequently take place

[4] In practice, calculating spot rates from actual securities is more complex.

EXHIBIT 4
Break-Even Spot Rates (15%, 18-Month Bond @ 100)

Years	Payment	Present Value @15%	Spot Rate	Present Value @Spot Rates	Difference in Present Values
0.5	$ 75,000	$ 69,767	5.000%	$ 73,171	$3,403
1.0	75,000	64,900	10.128	67,944	3,044
1.5	75,000	60,372	15.537[a]	59,922	− 450
1.5	1,000,000	804,961	15.537[a]	798,963	− 5,998
Total	$1,225,000	$1,000,000		$1,000,000	$ 0

[a] 18-Month break-even spot rate (15.537%).

at interest rates virtually identical to the theoretical spot rate.

If we may assume that the theoretical spot rate curve is a reasonable proxy for the Treasury zero yield curve, we may address the question of how Treasury zeros should be valued in different interest rate environments. This should allow a portfolio manager to assess quickly the approximate yield level for zero-coupon securities merely by observing the par bond Treasury yield curve.

Upward-Sloping Yield Curve

Let us assume that Exhibit 5 represents the par yield curve. In this situation, the yield curve is not only upward sloping, but it also has a constant slope; that is, yield to maturity and coupon increase as a direct function of a lengthening of maturity. As might be expected from our previous examples, this yield curve shape leads to a spot rate curve where each spot rate must be higher than the corresponding yield of a par bond to the same maturity.

Exhibit 6 shows this comparison, where the spot rate curve eventually approaches infinity as maturity increases. As maturity increases along this yield curve, and coupon level and yield to maturity rise accordingly, the initial payments of all par bonds are being discounted at yield levels lower than their yields to maturity. Since these early payments constitute much of the bond's present value, the later payments must be discounted at increasingly higher rates to maintain the equilibrium pricing of $1,000,000 per par bond.

EXHIBIT 5
Upward-Sloping Yield Curve

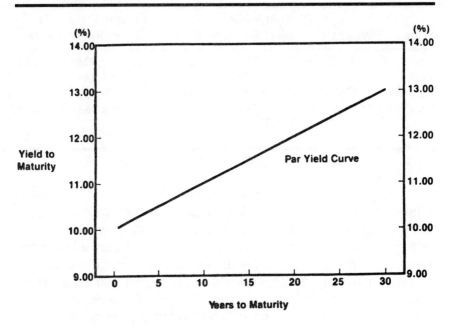

Other Par Yield Curve Shapes

Likewise, a downward-sloping par yield curve would necessitate a spot rate curve where each spot rate would have to be lower than the yield of the par bond to the same maturity. Exhibit 7 shows this relationship.

Yield curves are rarely as simple as being purely upward or downward sloping. Exhibit 8 shows a "positive" yield curve and its corresponding spot rate curve. This positive yield curve is a combination of an upward-sloping yield curve and a flat yield curve.

As we can see in Exhibit 8, out to ten years the spot rate curve and the par yield curve have much the same relationship as the one displayed in Exhibit 6. However, after the ten-year maturity when the par yield curve becomes flat, the spot rate curve begins to converge with the par yield curve. Therefore, as Exhibit 8 shows, the spot rate curve will increase only as long as the par yield curve increases.

EXHIBIT 6
Upward-Sloping Yield Curve and Theoretical Spot Rate Curve

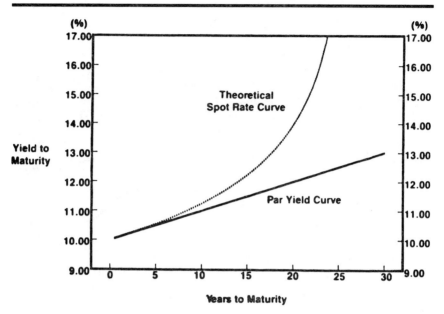

Exhibit 9 shows the opposite effect with an "inverted" yield curve that is basically the mirror image of Exhibit 8. In general, the flatter the par yield curve, the more that spot rates will resemble yields on par bonds, and the more inverted or positive the yield curve, the more that spot rates will differ from yields on par bonds.

III. THE VOLATILITY OF TREASURY ZEROS

As investors have employed investment strategies that involve combinations of Treasury zeros with other securities, a need has arisen to understand the price volatility of Treasury zeros. While many aspects of their volatility can be derived from traditional bonds, there are some features of zero-coupon bonds that deserve special emphasis. This section will address the analytical aspects of pricing Treasury zeros, given a particular yield level or yield change.

EXHIBIT 7
Downward-Sloping Yield Curve and Theoretical Spot Rate Curve

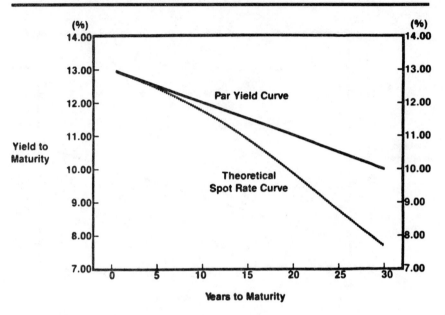

Volatility can be measured and expressed in several ways, and it is important to specify the measure to avoid confusion. Sometimes volatility is expressed in dollar terms, as measured by the "price value of .01" (basis point).[5] This measure is important in hedging, for example, when the dollar price fluctuation of one position must be offset by another.[6] In other situations—such as when trying to maximize or minimize total change in value because of an expected change in interest rates—the percentage price fluctuation is most important.

Suppose that we price a series of hypothetical Treasury zeros, each one six months longer in maturity than the previous one,

[5] Many investors also use the "yield value of 1/32 point" when attempting to offset the absolute change in one position with the absolute change in another position.

[6] For more information see Robert W. Kopprasch, *Introduction to Interest Rate Hedging,* New York: Salomon Brothers Inc, November 1982.

EXHIBIT 8
"Positive" Yield Curve and Theoretical Spot Rate Curve

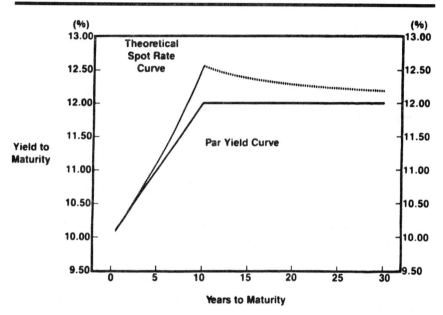

until we reach the Treasury zero that matures in 30 years. See Exhibit 10 for graph of the prices at a yield of 11 percent.

As is evident, a longer maturity results in a lower price.[7] At a different yield, say 10 percent, the basic shape would be similar, but the prices at 11 percent would always lie below those at 10 percent. A comparison of these curves is shown in Exhibit 11.

Note that for short-maturity Treasury zeros, prices are very similar, even with a 100-basis-point difference in yield. This occurs because the proceeds of the Treasury zeros will be received shortly, and even an extremely high yield cannot drive the price too far below par.

---

[7] The graph demonstrates this at a constant yield of 11 percent. Logic dictates that this would hold, because a security that pays earlier is worth more than one that pays the same amount later. Only with negative forward interest rates can longer-maturity zero-coupon bonds have higher prices than shorter zero-coupon bonds. An illogical situation has occasionally arisen as strong demand for corpus STRIPS has driven their price above the price of shorter-maturity coupon STRIPS.

EXHIBIT 9
"Inverted" Yield Curve and Theoretical Spot Rate Curve

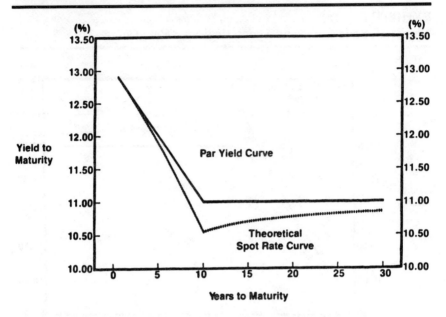

EXHIBIT 10
Treasury Zeros—Price versus Maturity (11% Yield to Maturity)

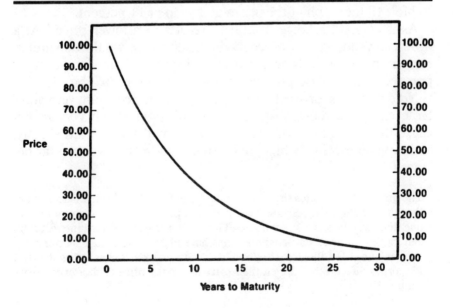

EXHIBIT 11
Treasury Zeros—Price versus Maturity
(10% and 11% Yields to Maturity)

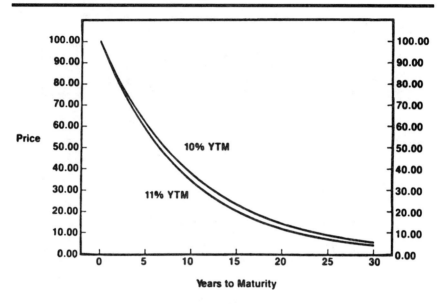

At the other extreme (for long-maturity Treasury zeros), prices are also fairly close in dollar terms. This is understandable if we consider long-term zeros, for example, with maturities of 30 years. At a yield of 10 percent or 11 percent, each price is less than six points; thus, the difference between the price at 10 percent and the price at 11 percent must be small, just as it is at the short end of the maturity scale.

If we measure volatility as the absolute price change given a change in rates, we can use Exhibit 11 as a guide. The difference between the two curves represents the change in price resulting from a 100-basis-point change in yield. Thus, the vertical distance between the lines can be considered as "the price value of 100.01s" (see Exhibit 12). The dollar value of the price change is highest somewhere in the eight- to 12-year maturity range.[8]

---

[8] This range varies somewhat at different interest rate levels.

EXHIBIT 12
Treasury Zeros—Price Value of 100 .01s
(10% Yield to Maturity versus 11% Yield to Maturity)

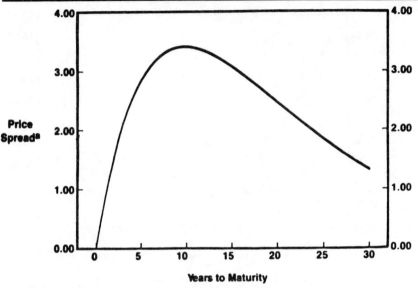

^a Price at 10% yield to maturity minus price at 11% yield to maturity.

ᵃ Price at 10% yield to maturity minus price at 11% yield to maturity.

Those who prefer to measure volatility using the yield value of a
$1/32$ point will find that this figure is at its lowest in the eight- to
12-year maturity range, again indicating maximum absolute price
volatility in that range.

This is shown in Exhibit 13, measured at an 11 percent yield
level. Thus, Treasury zeros in the eight- to 12-year maturity sector
change in price by more dollars (or points) per bond than either
longer- or shorter-maturity Treasury zeros for a constant change in
yield.

Percentage Price Volatility

The greater absolute price volatility of eight- to 12-year Treasury
zeros does not mean that they have a greater percentage volatility
than longer Treasury zeros. Although longer Treasury zeros have

EXHIBIT 13
Treasury Zeros—Yield Value of 1/32 Point at 11% Yield to Maturity

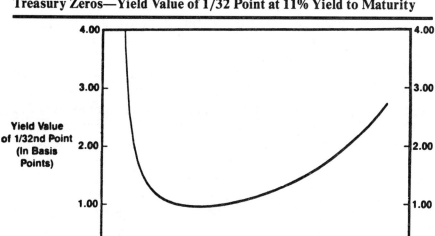

lower absolute price volatility per bond, they also have a much lower price than eight- to 12-year Treasury zeros; thus, the total percentage price fluctuation (per dollar invested) is greater for longer Treasury zeros, assuming equal yield movements.

This should not surprise readers familiar with the notion of duration, which, among other things, can be used as an estimate of percentage price volatility. Most bond market participants know that the Macaulay duration of a zero-coupon bond equals its maturity.[9] Thus, longer-maturity zero-coupon bonds should have higher percentage price volatility than shorter ones. This will be demonstrated for yields of 10 percent and 11 percent, using the values in Exhibits 11 and 12.

[9] There are actually two measures of duration. The first, known as Macaulay duration, is used in immunization. The Macaulay duration of a zero-coupon bond is equal to its maturity. The "modified duration" that relates percentage price change to a change in rates is simply the Macaulay duration divided by $(1 + \text{yield}/\text{frequency})$.

Exhibit 14 lists, for selected maturities, the prices of Treasury zeros at yields of 10 percent and 11 percent, the difference between those prices in absolute and percentage terms, and the modified duration. The absolute price change per bond is maximized in the ten-year maturity sector, as shown in Exhibit 12. In percentage terms, however, the longest maturity delivers the greatest change in market value for a given yield change. To put this into perspective, consider an investment of $100 million. At a yield to maturity of 11 percent, a $100-million investment translates into a par amount of $292-million ten-year Treasury zeros or $2,484-million 30-year Treasury zeros. If rates drop from 11 percent to 10 percent, ten-year Treasury zeros provide a gain of approximately $9.97 million, while 30-year Treasury zeros increase by $32.99 million.

The modified duration provides a reasonable approximation of the percentage price change for a 100-basis-point yield change. The accuracy of modified duration apparently deteriorates in the longer maturities, but it is quite accurate for smaller yield changes. For example, if a 30-year zero-coupon bond changes in yield from 11 percent to 10.90 percent, the actual percentage change is 2.88 percent, compared with the duration-based prediction of 2.84 percent.

Therefore, for equal yield changes, maximum dollar price volatility occurs near the ten-year maturity, but maximum percentage price change occurs in the longest maturities.

Yield Volatility

Thus far, we have discussed the price volatility of Treasury zeros with respect to changes in yield. In effect, we have measured the price sensitivity of various zero-coupon maturities to a single, uniform change in the level of interest rates. If we could be sure that yields would move in a parallel fashion, our discussion of volatility could end here. However, yield spreads change, and yield moves are not always parallel. As we will see, even when the par bond yield curve undergoes a parallel shift, zero-coupon bonds may not respond with a parallel shift. Therefore, to measure total volatility, we must examine both price volatility and yield volatility.

EXHIBIT 14
Treasury Zeros—Effect of Maturity on Volatility

					Years to Maturity			
	1–Yr.	5–Yr.	8–Yr.	10–Yr.	12–Yr.	15–Yr.	20–Yr.	30–Yr.
Price of 11%	89.845	58.543	42.458	34.273	27.666	20.064	11.746	4.026
Price at 10%	90.703	61.391	45.811	37.689	31.007	23.138	14.205	5.354
Absolute Price Change	0.858	2.848	3.353	3.416	3.341	3.074	2.459	1.328
Percentage Price Change	0.995%	4.860%	7.897%	9.967%	12.076%	15.321%	20.935%	32.986%
Modified Duration (Years)	0.948	4.739	7.583	9.479	11.374	14.218	18.957	28.436

Parallel Yield Moves.   Exhibit 15 shows the price sensitivity of five- and 20-year Treasury zeros over a wide range of interest rates. For easy comparison, we have assumed that both issues have a yield to maturity of 11 percent, and that the initial investment in each security is $100 million. Exhibit 16 shows the effects of an immediate change in interest rates from 11 percent to 9 percent. This move in interest rates changes the value of the five-year Treasury zeros to $110.0 million, while altering the value of the 20-year Treasury zeros to $146.4 million. As we learned earlier, for a given change in yields, the 20-year Treasury zeros are more volatile per dollar invested. Furthermore, these results are reasonably predictable using the modified durations in Exhibit 14.

Nonparallel Yield Moves.   If we now impose a change in the yield spread between these two securities, the results can be

EXHIBIT 15
Price Sensitivity of Five- and 20-Year Treasury Zeros

Yield to Maturity

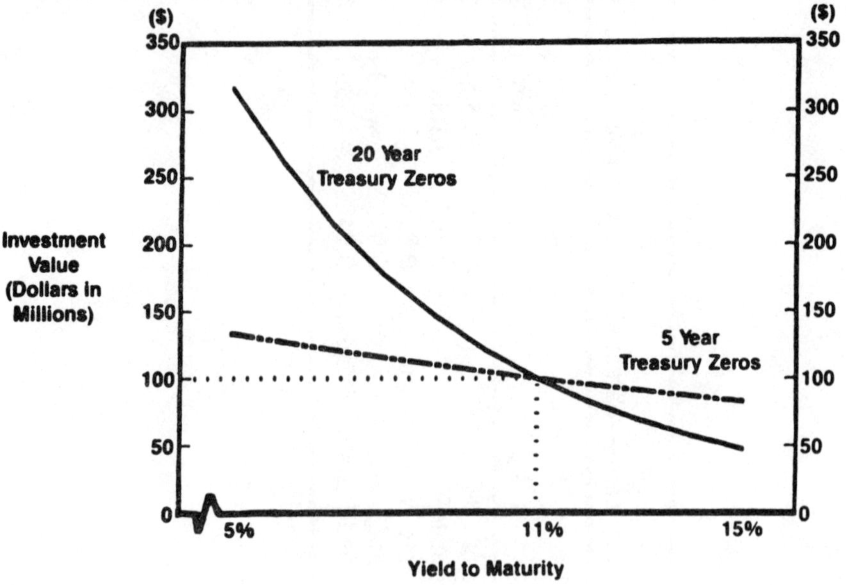

EXHIBIT 16

Impact of a 200-Basis-Point Yield Move on the Investment Value of Five-Year and 20-Year Treasury Zeros

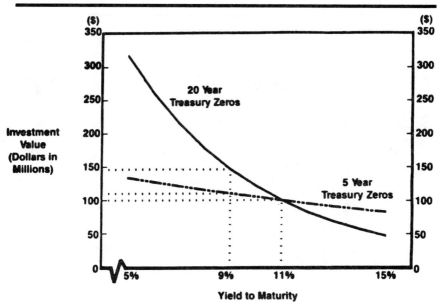

significantly different. Exhibit 17 shows a yield change in the five-year Treasury zeros of −200 basis points, to 9 percent, and change in the 20-year Treasury zeros of −300 basis points, to 8 percent.

Under this assumption, where the yield spread widens to 100 basis points, the value of the five-year Treasury zeros still increases to $110.0 million, but now the value of the 20-year Treasury zeros rises to $177.3 million, a gain from the previous example of more than $30 million.[10]

---

[10] This change in yield spread does not have to occur as a result of an inversion in the entire yield curve. It could possibly result from a humped yield curve, where yields on five-year bonds are greater than yields on either shorter or longer securities.

EXHIBIT 17
Impact of a Nonparallel Yield Move on Five- and 20-Year Treasury Zeros

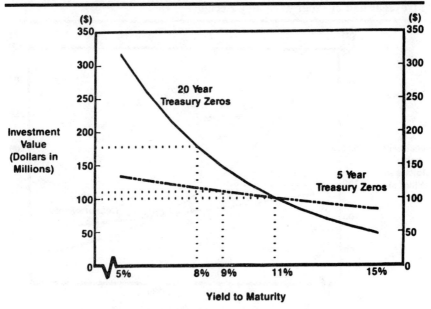

IV. YIELD CURVE CHANGES

We have now discussed price sensitivity of Treasury zeros to given yield changes and have determined that yield spread changes can significantly affect total volatility. Now we will examine how changes in the level and shape of the par yield curve might affect the theoretical spot rate curve. In so doing, it becomes evident that yield spreads are likely to change between zero-coupon bonds and par bonds and between various maturities of zero-coupon bonds. (In each example, the beginning levels are defined as 1 and the ending levels are defined as 2.)

Parallel Par Yield Curve Moves

Let us begin by moving the par yield curve uniformly up by 200 basis points and studying the impact on the theoretical spot rate curve. Exhibits 18 and 19 show that this parallel shift in the

EXHIBIT 18
Impact of a Parallel Shift in a Par Yield Curve on the Theoretical Spot Rate Curve

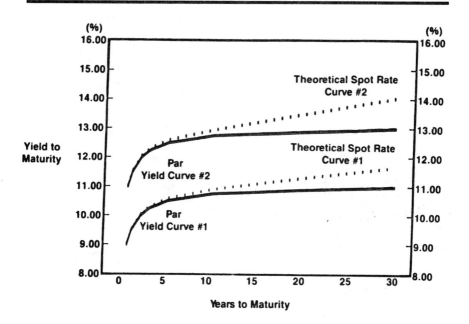

Years to Maturity

yield curve creates somewhat surprising results with respect to spot rates. One might be tempted to assume that a parallel shift in the par yield curve (with no change in shape) would lead to a parallel shift in the theoretical spot rate curve. However, we find that although the shape of the two par yield curves is identical, the spot rates lie further above the par yield curve in the higher interest rate environment. Exhibit 19 illustrates this relationship vividly by focusing on the spread between spot rates and par yields.

The 200-basis-point change in the par yield curve increases the yield spread across all maturities (to a new maximum of more than 100 basis points in year 30).

This relationship between par yields and spot rates is significant, because it shows that the shape of the theoretical spot rate curve is a function not only of the shape of the underlying par yield curve, but also of the absolute level of interest rates.

EXHIBIT 19
Impact of a 200-Basis-Point Shift in a Par Yield Curve on the Yield Spread Between the Par Yield Curve and the Theoretical Spot Rate Curve

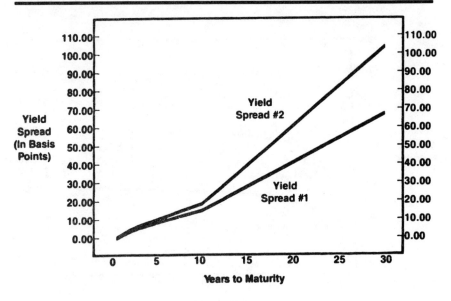

An Increasingly Positive Yield Curve

Second, we will examine a nonparallel change in interest rates and study another potential effect on the relative yield levels of zero-coupon bonds. Exhibit 20 shows a change in the shape of the par yield curve and its effect on the theoretical spot rate curve that, in effect, makes the par yield curve more positively sloped. The increasingly positive slope of the par yield curve necessarily raises the slope of the theoretical spot rate curve. However, the change in the slope of the theoretical spot rate curve appears to be more severe than that in the slope of the par yield curve. As mentioned earlier, the flatter the par yield curve, the more that spot rates will resemble yields on par bonds, and the more inverted or positive the par yield curve, the more that spot rates will differ from yields on par bonds. Because of this relationship, the long-term yields of the theoretical spot rate curve in this example rise significantly, even

EXHIBIT 20
Impact of a Change in the Slope of a Par Yield Curve on the Theoretical Spot Rate Curve

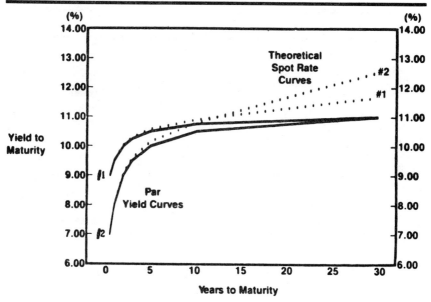

though the long-term yields of the par yield curve remain almost constant.

An Inverted Yield Curve

Third, we will examine the effects of changing from a positively sloped yield curve to an inverted yield curve. Exhibit 21 shows a change in yields of 400 basis points in the shortest par maturities and no change in the longest par maturities.

The effect of this "mirror image" change in the shape of the par yield curve is very nearly a "mirror image" change in the shape of the theoretical spot rate curve. The potential impact of such a yield change is somewhat startling, in that an increase in par yields gives rise to a decrease in theoretical spot rates across much of the maturity spectrum.

The spread relationship between various zero-coupon bonds

EXHIBIT 21
**Impact of an Inversion in a Par Yield Curve on the
Theoretical Spot Rate Curve**

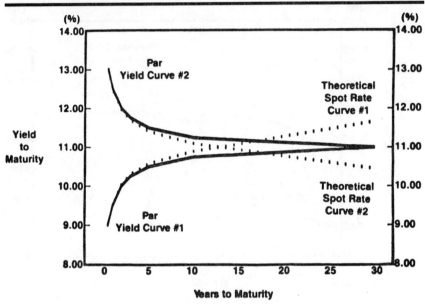

changes dramatically in this example, and an investor who expects this yield curve scenario must be aware of this potential change in spread. In effect, given a desire to maximize total return and given this scenario of interest rate changes, an investor would profit the most by investing in long Treasury zeros—the securities with the greatest percentage price volatility and the greatest favorable yield volatility. To many investors, this result is completely counterintuitive, because the yield scenario is basically bearish.

An Inverted Yield Curve at Higher Yield Levels

Finally, let us examine a very bearish scenario. In this example (see Exhibit 22), we have moved short par yields up by 600 basis

EXHIBIT 22
**Impact of an Inversion of a Par Yield Curve on the Theoretical Spot
Rate Curve at Higher Yield Levels**

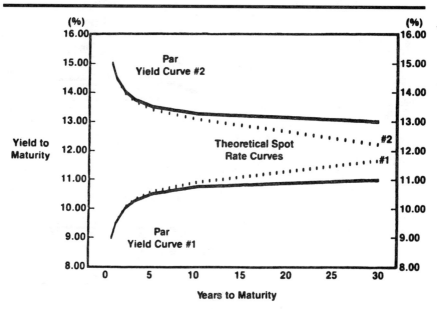

points and long par yields up by 200 basis points. In effect, we
have combined the parallel shift with the yield curve inversion.
The change in the shape and level of the par yield curve gives rise
to a much smaller change in the theoretical spot rate curve. For
example, as the 30-year par yield moves up by 200 basis points, the
30-year Treasury zero yield increases by only 55 basis points. This
dampening effect of the yield curve change can be very significant
when measuring total volatility of zeros, because it implies that in
certain scenarios (both bullish and bearish), zeros can have a yield
volatility that differs not only from that of other zeros, but also
from that of the rest of the market.

Exhibit 23 shows the actual Treasury yield curve, the theoretical
spot rate curve and the STRIPS yield curve for the end of 1985. It
is interesting to note that for maturities earlier than 20 years,

EXHIBIT 23
U.S. Treasury Yield Curve and its Corresponding Theoretical Spot Rate Curve, December 31, 1985

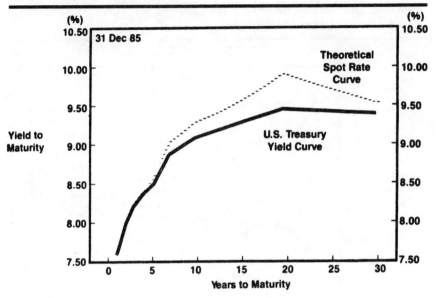

U.S. Treasury Yield Curve and STRIPS Yield Curve

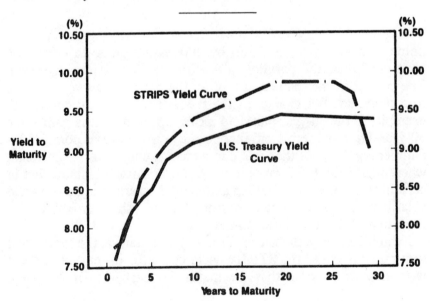

EXHIBIT 23 (*Continued*)

STRIPS Yield Curve and Theoretical Spot Rate Curve

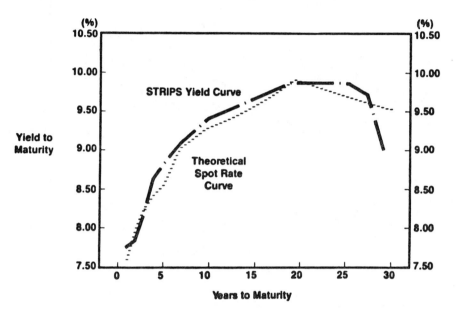

where the Treasury yield curve slopes upward, theoretical spot rates lie increasingly above the yields on Treasury bonds. From the 20- to 30-year maturities, where the Treasury yield curve slopes downward, the theoretical spot rate curve also slopes downward, again exaggerating the change. Throughout the maturity spectrum, however, STRIPS yields lie very close to the levels that spot rate theory would predict. The longest maturity of the STRIPS yield curve, the 30-year corpus, is the lone exception to the close relationship that exists between STRIPS and theoretical spot rates throughout the maturity spectrum. Because of strong demand from certain investors (primarily in Japan), the corpus STRIPS tend to trade richer (lower in yield) than coupon STRIPS of similar maturity.

On August 29, 1986, interest rates were significantly lower than they were on December 31, 1985 (see Exhibit 24). Over the first

EXHIBIT 24
U.S. Treasury Yield Curve and Its Corresponding Theoretical Spot Rate Curve, August 29, 1986

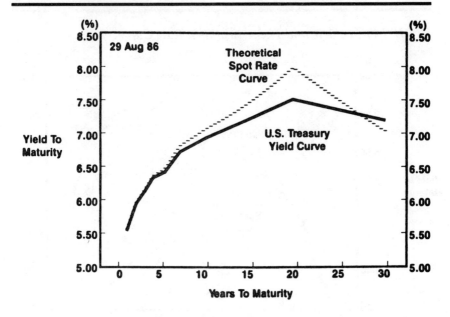

U.S. Treasury Yield Curve and STRIPS Yield Curve

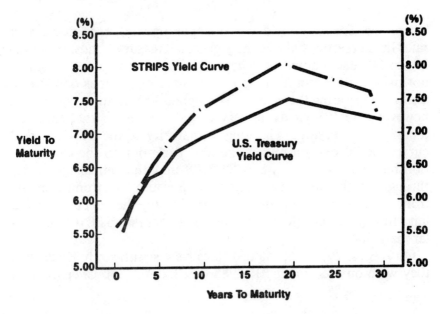

EXHIBIT 24 (*Continued*)

STRIPS and Theoretical Spot Rate Curve

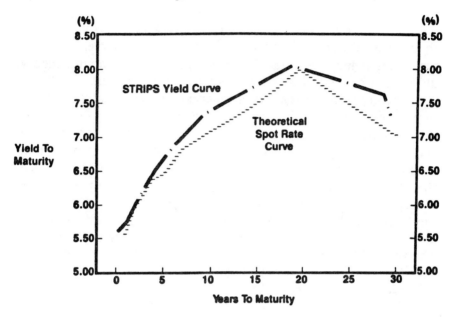

eight months of 1986, yields on long-term Treasuries fell by approximately 200 basis points while yields on short-term Treasuries fell by approximately 175 basis points. In general, although interest rates fell significantly, the shape of the Treasury yield curve remained relatively stable. As we learned earlier, a parallel decline in the Treasury yield curve should cause the yield spread between spot rates and par bonds to narrow. In other words, as the Treasury bond yields decline in unison, theoretical spot rates should be expected to decline even more. For most maturities beyond five years, however, the yield spread between STRIPS and theoretical spot rates was wider at the end of August than it was at the beginning of 1986. As Treasury yields fell, STRIPS yields did not fall more, they fell less.

By understanding the relationships between Treasury bonds and spot rates, investors have a basis for determining relative values among zero-coupon bonds. Investors, however, should not blindly employ any model of relative values. In the market for Treasury zeros, and in virtually every other market, there are occasionally factors that will reduce the ability of any model to fully reflect value.

A question often arises as to why the Treasury zero yield curve should ever differ from the theoretical spot rate curve. In effect, the question may be restated, "Why does (or why should) theory differ from reality?" There are probably several answers.

Before giving those answers, a general comment should be made. In practice, actual trading levels have been remarkably close to the theory, given the many factors affecting both the Treasury bond and Treasury zero markets, and given the dramatic changes that have occurred in the level of interest rates. Indeed, if one had been able to predict accurately the changes that have taken place in the Treasury yield curve since the introduction of Treasury zeros, one would be able to explain many of the changes that have occurred in the Treasury zero market. Nevertheless, there are some reasons why the yields of Treasury zeros differ (and perhaps should differ) from theoretical spot rates, such as:

1. Liquidity Premium. Treasury zeros are generally less liquid than Treasury bonds; as a result, investors demand more yield when buying Treasury zeros. The equilibrium spot rate concept does not consider yield differences that compensate for liquidity. An investor who places a large premium on portfolio flexibility may be willing to pay for liquidity by purchasing Treasury bonds, and longer-term investors can take advantage of this liquidity premium by purchasing Treasury zeros. In a cash-matched portfolio, for example, where cash flow is more important than is portfolio flexibility, it makes sense to sell expensive bonds and buy Treasury zeros to produce the same level of cash flow at a lower cost.[11]

2. Supply and Demand. Since the origination of Treasury zeros, the demand has been consistently strong for longer-maturity zeros. In part, this demand has arisen from long-term investors attempting to capture historically high interest rates and, partly, from short-term investors attempting to maximize total return by

---

[11] For more information see Martin Leibowitz and Alfred Weinberger, *Optimal Cash Flow Matching,* New York: Salomon Brothers Inc, August 1981.

investing in volatile securities. With coupon stripping, it is not possible to create long-maturity Treasury zeros without also creating short- and intermediate-maturity Treasury zeros. The activity in coupon stripping has repeatedly supplied more short- and intermediate-maturity Treasury zeros than investors have demanded, and this excess supply has led to an increase in the spread between these Treasury zeros and the corresponding theoretical spot rates.

3. Investor Expectations. Since zero-coupon bonds are widely regarded as being more volatile than Treasury bonds of equal maturity, short-term investors will generally attempt to purchase Treasury zeros when they expect interest rates to fall. Likewise, investors will generally sell volatile securities when they expect interest rates to rise. Reflecting this investor preference, Treasury zeros will tend to move less (in yield) than will the general market. In other words, when interest rates drop significantly (and investors begin to believe that there is more probability that rates will go up than down), the yield spread between Treasury zeros and theoretical spot rates will tend to increase. The yield spread change of 1986 is most probably the result of adverse investor expectations.

4. Limitations of Spot Rate Theory. The theoretical spot rate curve is somewhat inconsistent with reality. The idea of the theoretical spot rate curve is quite simple: The sum of the pieces should equal the whole. If yields on Treasury zeros differ from theoretical spot rates, the theory states, there is room for arbitrage. According to this arbitrage argument, if whole bonds are cheaper than the price of the component pieces, investors will buy the bonds and sell the pieces. Likewise, if the component pieces are cheaper than the bonds, investors will buy the pieces and sell the bonds.

To date, this arbitrage has worked in only one direction. Dealers have bought bonds and sold the pieces, because some bonds are cheaper than the value of their pieces. Few investors have effected the opposite arbitrage (selling the bond and buying the pieces), even though the opportunity for this arbitrage ("reconstruction") has existed. If the market is rewarding investors to do so, they should sell their expensive bonds and buy the component pieces. Only when there are active participants on both sides of this arbitrage will the Treasury zero yield curve resemble the theoretical spot rate curve more precisely.[12]

V. HISTORICAL RETURNS

As the Treasury yield curve changes in different market environments, the theoretical spot rate curve should help portfolio managers to determine the appropriate yield level for Treasury zeros. Furthermore, by combining an understanding of the volatility characteristics of zero-coupon bonds with an expected change in interest rates, a portfolio manager should be able to assess value among a wide variety of alternative investments. It should be interesting, then, to review the rates of return that have been achieved by holders of Treasury zeros over the past few years in order to determine how these securities have performed when compared with some investment alternatives.

From our earlier discussion about volatility, we know that Treasury zeros are more volatile than are Treasury bonds of the same maturity. As a result, time-to-maturity cannot accurately be used as a basis for comparing investments. Conversely, duration is a useful measure by which investments may be compared, based on their percentage price volatility.

Exhibits 25–28 show the rates of return that have been produced by Treasury zeros from year-end 1982 through August 1986. Time to maturity gives little insight into the difference between rates of return, and duration is a more valuable tool to be used to compare rates of return.

In 1983 (see Exhibit 25), when all interest rates rose by approximately 150 basis points, the highest rates of return were realized from the shortest securities. Long-term securities returned significantly less than short-term securities, and when each is viewed against its maturity, Treasury bonds performed far better than did

---

[12] In practice, there is little incentive to "reconstruct" a Treasury bond from STRIPS, because the U.S. Treasury will not currently exchange a bond for the pieces. If the U.S. Treasury allows reconstruction at some future date, the arbitrage will begin to work effectively in both directions, and the STRIPS yield curve should draw closer to the theoretical spot rate curve.

EXHIBIT 25
Historical Returns, Dec. 31, 1982–Dec. 30, 1983

U.S. Treasury and CATS Yield Curves

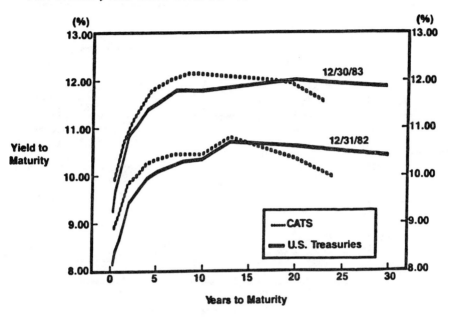

Annual Rates of Return by Maturity

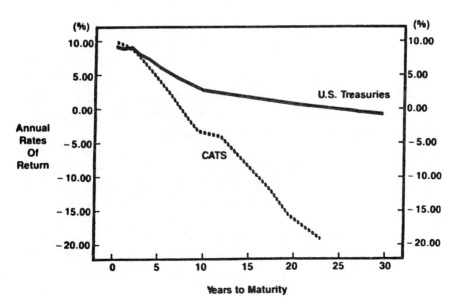

EXHIBIT 25 (*Continued*)

Annual Rates of Return by Duration

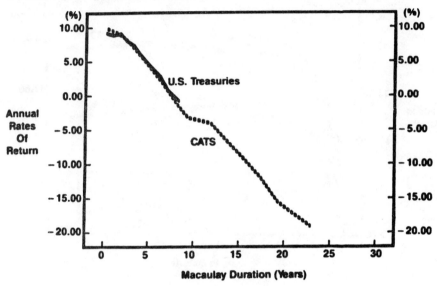

Treasury zeros. When each security is viewed against its duration, however, the rates of return are virtually identical. It should come as no surprise that the longest Treasury zero achieved a rate of return of −20 percent, while the longest Treasury bond achieved a rate of return of −1 percent, because the duration of the Treasury zero is almost 2.5 times as great as the duration of the Treasury bond, even though they have similar maturities.

In 1985 (see Exhibit 27) and through August 1986 (see Exhibit 28), the rate-of-return patterns were similar to those displayed in 1983. As interest rates changed by a similar magnitude across the maturity spectrum, the rates of return achieved during 1985 and again in 1986 were similar when each security was viewed against its duration. In both years, the highest rates of return were achieved from the securities with the longest duration—Treasury zeros. In 1984 (see Exhibit 26), yields did not change by very much and the

EXHIBIT 26
Historical Returns, Dec. 30, 1983–Dec. 31, 1984

U.S. Treasury and CATS Yield Curves

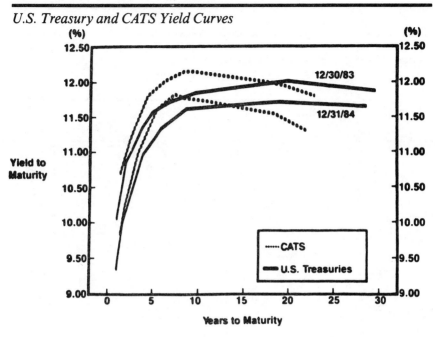

Annual Rates of Return by Maturity

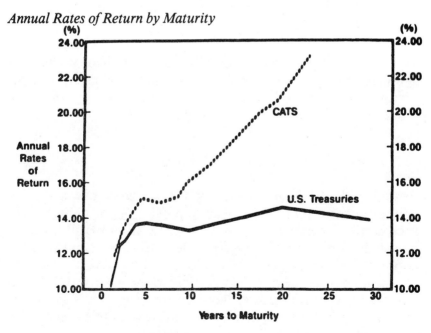

EXHIBIT 26 (*Continued*)

Annual Rates of Return by Duration

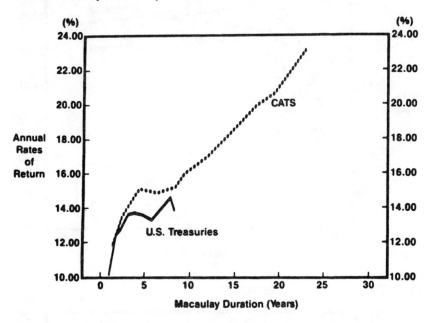

changes that took place were focused more in the shape of the yield curves rather than in the level of interest rates. As a result, the rates of return produced by Treasury zeros exceeded the rates of return produced by Treasury bonds of equal duration.

VI. CONCLUSION

Investors in the 1980s are constantly bombarded by new and innovative investment vehicles designed to provide opportunities to enhance portfolio performance. In many cases, it is difficult to accurately assess the value of these securities within the context of the entire fixed-income market. In one sense, zero-coupon bonds are nothing more than one more new vehicle whose value is difficult to evaluate. In a broader sense, however, Treasury zeros bring the entire market into perspective by providing a unique mechanism for evaluating every cash flow of every bond.

EXHIBIT 27
Historical Returns, Dec. 31, 1984–Dec. 31, 1985

U.S. Treasury and CATS Yield Curves

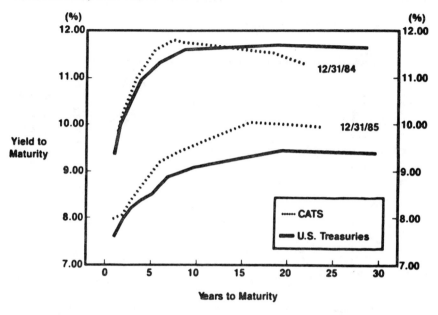

Annual Rates of Return by Maturity

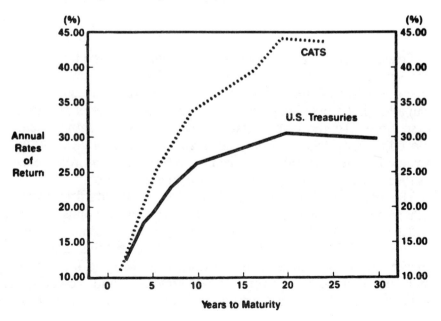

EXHIBIT 27 (*Continued*)

Annual Rates of Return by Duration

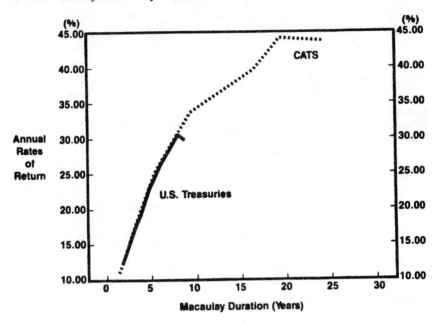

Treasury zeros are the raw materials from which the bond market is made. By providing the price and yield of cash flows that are free of credit risk, reinvestment risk and call risk, Treasury zeros can allow investors to construct the value of any series of promised cash flows. To the extent that Treasury zeros are actually employed to evaluate and reconstruct the components of different investments, the Treasury zero yield curve should gain prominence as the standard of value for all fixed-income securities.

The Treasury yield curve has long been the standard by which other bonds are measured. It is common to hear of bonds trading "50 basis points off the ten year" or "100 basis points over the long bond." The Treasury yield curve has deserved this important market position because it has historically been the most basic standard of risk-free interest rates. A Treasury bond, however, is nothing more than one possible collection of Treasury zeros;

EXHIBIT 28
Historical Returns, Year to Date, Dec. 31, 1985–Aug. 29, 1986

U.S. Treasury And STRIPS Yield Curves

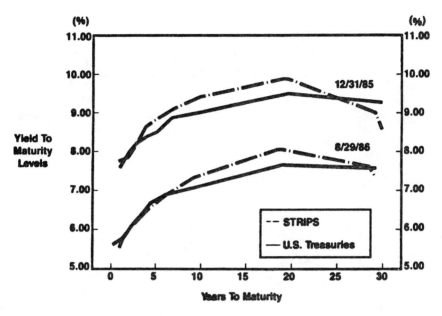

Year-to-Date Rates of Return by Maturity

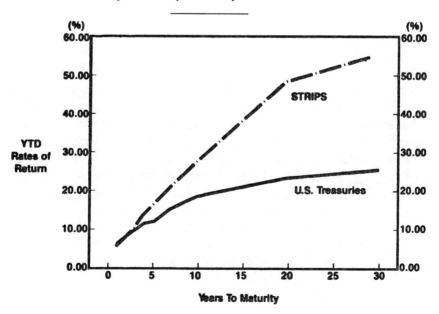

EXHIBIT 28 (*Continued*)

Year-to-Date Rates of Return by Duration

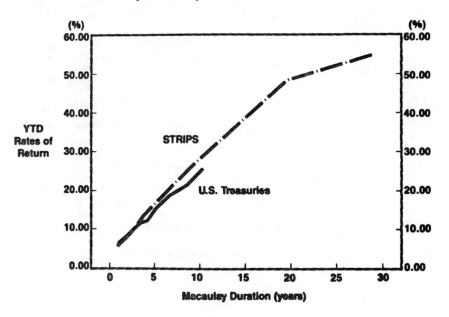

therefore, the Treasury yield curve is no longer the most basic standard of value.

In the long run, when Treasury zeros have more liquidity and when Treasury zeros may be freely exchanged for Treasury bonds, the Treasury zero yield curve should provide the most basic series of risk-free interest rates and, as such, should become *the* yield curve. When this happens, we will no longer need to infer theoretical spot rates from Treasury par bonds: It will be quite to the contrary. Because we will have *observable* spot rates, we will more likely infer the theoretical yield level for Treasury par bonds. Even investors with no interest in zero-coupon bonds should understand Treasury zeros thoroughly, because as this market continues to develop, Treasury zeros may become the driving force behind the evaluation of the entire fixed-income market.

ARTICLE 8

SCOTT PINKUS is a vice president and Co-Head of the Mortgage Securities Research Department at Goldman, Sachs & Company. Prior to joining Goldman Sachs in March of 1986, he was at Morgan Stanley, where he founded and managed the Mortgage Research Group. Mr. Pinkus also helped develop and later managed the Mortgage-Backed Securities Research Department at Merrill Lynch from 1980 to 1984. Mr. Pinkus has also held positions at the Federal Home Loan Bank of San Francisco and the Federal Reserve Bank of Philadelphia. He holds an MBA and a BS in Economics from the Wharton School of the University of Pennsylvania.

SUSAN MARA HUNTER is a senior research associate in the Mortgage Securities Research Department at Goldman, Sachs & Co. where she is primarily responsible for sales and trading support. Prior to working at Goldman, Sachs & Co., she worked at Morgan Stanley, Merrill Lynch, and the Federal Home Loan Mortgage Corporation. She holds a Bachelor of Arts in Economics from Bucknell University and a Masters in Business Administration from George Washington University.

RICHARD ROLL is vice-president for new product development in the mortgage finance department at Goldman, Sachs & Co and co-director of the Mortgage Securities Research Group. Prior to joining Goldman Sachs, Dr. Roll held the Allstate Insurance chair in finance at the Graduate School of Management, U.C.L.A. He has published two books and over fifty papers in technical journals. He is an associate editor of the *Journal of Finance,* the *Journal of Financial Economics,* and the *Journal of Portfolio Management.* He is currently president of the American Finance Association.

AN INTRODUCTION TO THE MORTGAGE MARKET AND MORTGAGE ANALYSIS

Scott M. Pinkus
Vice President and Co-Director
Mortgage Securities Research
Goldman, Sachs & Co.

Susan Mara Hunter
Senior Associate
Mortgage Securities Research
Goldman, Sachs & Co.

Richard Roll, Ph.D.
Vice President and Co-Director
Mortgage Securities Research
Goldman, Sachs & Co.

The mortgage-backed securities market has developed rapidly since the late 1970s. Thrift institutions had been the primary sources of mortgage money, but in the late 1970s and early 1980s, investors who had not traditionally invested in mortgages began to play a greater role in housing finance. Recognizing attractive opportunities, these new investors began to include mortgage securities in their fixed income portfolios. The influx of these new investors has altered the traditional mortgage business and has forced a closer examination of the issues related to pricing and valuing mortgage securities.

This article describes the characteristics of mortgage securities and develops an analytic framework for their valuation. It discusses the various methods currently used to price mortgage securities and gives some insights into future trends in valuation analysis. The article highlights the institutional and market realities of investing in these securities, as these factors are critical for developing an effective understanding of the securities as well as for creating investment or trading strategies.

I.   MORTGAGE CHARACTERISTICS

A mortgage is a loan secured by some form of real property. While there are mortgages secured by such things as airplanes, locomotives, and financial assets, the most common security for a mortgage is real estate. The real property, such as a house, can be claimed by the lender (the mortgagee) if the borrower (the mortgagor) fails to make payments to the lender as required by the loan contract. The overall credit quality of a mortgage, therefore, depends on both the credit of the borrower and the market value of the property securing the loan.

The most active market for mortgages has been for those backed by single-family residences. Residences for one to four families are considered to be "single-family" homes. While the markets for mortgages backed by multifamily developments and commercial properties are expected to grow substantially over the next several years, they are currently only in the early stages of development.

Single-family Mortgages

Until recently, most single-family mortgages had the same basic characteristics: an original term to maturity of 30 years, a fixed contractual interest rate, and a monthly payment amount that remains constant over the entire term of the loan. The monthly payments on such a loan consist of some principal as well as all of the interest due each month. The monthly payments are fixed so that the principal payments made each month will completely repay the loan principal balance by the final maturity. As can be seen in Exhibit 1, the monthly payment in the early years consists mainly of interest, but as the loan ages, gradually more and more of the payment goes toward paying off the principal balance of the loan.

Fixed Rate.   The *30-year, fixed rate, level pay mortgage* structure was established by the Federal Housing Administration (FHA) in the 1930s and was the dominant type of mortgage for almost 50 years. Borrowers had few choices about the maturities, rate structures, or payment structures on the mortgages they used to finance their homes. While widely accepted, this mortgage structure tended to create problems for borrowers and lenders alike. Borrowers found that they could not qualify for mortgages when interest rates were high. For traditional lenders, long-term mortgages created a mismatch between the maturities of their assets and the maturities of their liabilities. The net interest spreads on their portfolios were, therefore, highly cyclical; when interest rates rose the lenders' costs of financing would rise faster than the yields on their assets, and when rates fell the costs of their liabilities would fall faster than the yields on their assets.

The problems with the traditional mortgage became particularly acute in the late 1970s and early 1980s when interest rates skyrocketed. Few borrowers were able to qualify for new mortgages and the spreads between the yields on lenders' assets and liabilities began to evaporate. Alternative mortgage structures were developed to allow more borrowers to be able to afford mortgages, even when interest rates are high, and to provide lenders with a better hedge against changes in their costs of funds. Today, prospective borrowers can select from an almost overwhelming array of mortgages with different maturities, interest rate structures, and payment structures.

The *15-year, fixed-rate, level pay mortgage* appeals to many borrowers who prefer shorter term obligations. The *graduated payment mortgage* (GPM) has a fixed-rate, but the monthly payments increase annually by a fixed percentage for the first several years of the mortgage (usually five years) before leveling off and remaining fixed throughout the remaining term of the loan. For the first few years of a GPM's life, therefore, the borrower makes a lower monthly payment than would be made on a traditional

EXHIBIT 1
Distribution of Mortgage Cash Flows (12% Mortgage)

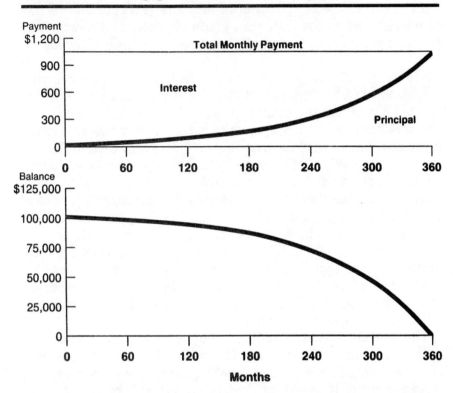

mortgage with the same interest rate. Because of the artificially low monthly payments, the amount of interest that is *paid* on the GPM in the early years is not sufficient to cover the amount of interest that is *accrued* on the mortgage; the difference is added to the principal balance of the mortgage. Rather than amortizing the loan's principal balance steadily over the term of the mortgage, therefore, GPMs have *negative amortization* for the first few years of their lives. The *growing equity mortgage* (GEM) is similar to the GPM in that the scheduled monthly payments increase over time. The monthly payment amount on a GEM, however, is always sufficient to cover the interest accrued each month and the increased payment goes toward faster reduction of the loan's principal balance.

Adjustable Rate. The alternative mortgage instrument that has so far had the greatest impact on the mortgage market is the *adjustable rate mortgage* (ARM). The contractual interest rate on an ARM is tied to some published interest rate index and the mortgage rate will change at designated adjustment intervals as the index changes. ARMs currently available in the market differ in many ways. Some of the key features are described below.

Index: Currently, the most popular indices in the United States are the constant maturity 6-month, 1-year, 3-year, and 5-year Treasury indices published by the Federal Reserve, as well as the Federal Home Loan Bank of San Francisco (eleventh district) Cost of Funds index (COFI). The cost of funds index is the average book cost of funds of thrift institutions who are members of the eleventh district of the Federal Home Loan Bank System (California, Arizona, and Nevada).

The various indices can perform **very** differently as interest rates change over time. In general, the shorter the term of the instrument tracked by the index, the more volatile the index will be. The index based on the constant maturity 5-year Treasury, for example, will generally be less volatile than the index based on the constant maturity 1-year Treasury. Since the Cost of Funds index is based on the book cost of funds, it is not entirely sensitive to current market conditions and it tends to lag current interest rates.

Margin: The margin is the amount by which the interest rate on an ARM exceeds the index rate. If the index in a particular month is 9 percent, for example, and the margin is 225 basis points, the interest rate on the mortgage in that month would be 11.25 percent.

Rate and Payment Adjustment Periods: The length of the period between rate adjustment dates is usually, but not always, the same as the maturity of the ARM index; ARMs indexed to the 1-year Treasury, for example, usually adjust annually. The rate adjustment period usually, but not always, corresponds to the payment adjustment period. There are ARMs, however, with semi-annual rate adjustments tied to changes in the 6-month Treasury, that have payments that adjust annually.

Rate Caps: Most ARMs have limits as to the amount by which the mortgage interest rate can change at each adjustment date and/ or over the life of the loan. These caps alter the extent to which the mortgage rate adjusts to the index. The periodic caps usually limit both increases and decreases in the mortgage rate, while the lifetime cap usually limits only the highest rate the mortgage can reach.

Payment Caps: Some ARMs have limits as to the percent by which a mortgage's monthly payment can increase on any given payment adjustment date from the prior month's payment. Often, but not always, ARMs with payment caps allow for negative amortization to absorb the difference between the amount of interest that is being accrued on the mortgage and the amount of interest that is included in the mortgage payment.

Multifamily Mortgages

Multifamily loans are those secured by properties housing more than four families. These loans are structured in several different ways. Many multifamily mortgages have scheduled maturities of 180 months, but pay principal each month based on a 360-month amortization schedule; the principal remaining at maturity is repaid in full as a balloon payment. Such a loan usually cannot be prepaid during the first few years of the loan's life. The "lock-out" periods on these loans usually last for about 4.5 to 5 years. Not all multifamily mortgages have these features, however. Some fully amortize over their lives and do not have balloon payments at maturity. Others do not have lock-out periods prohibiting prepayments during the early years of the lives of the loans.

Commercial Mortgages

Commercial mortgages are backed by properties such as shopping centers, hotels, office buildings, and industrial complexes. There has been very little standardization in the commercial mortgage market. The market for these mortgages has been relatively undeveloped because of the diversity of mortgage structures, underwriting standards, types and quality of collateral, etc. The recent establishment of rating standards by Standard & Poor's for securities backed by commercial mortgages should help to increase the homogeneity of these mortgages.

II. THE SECONDARY MARKET
FOR MORTGAGES

Long before mortgage-backed securities were created, mortgages were bought and sold by investors as whole loans, or unsecuritized mortgages. In general, most of these transactions took place between lenders in capital deficit areas and lenders in capital surplus areas. Lenders with loan demand exceeding their deposit flow would sell their loans to lenders with deposit flow exceeding their loan demand. Many other large investors, however, were not involved in this market because of the specialized and extensive underwriting and operational capabilities these investments required.

Advantages of Securitized Mortgages

Mortgage-backed securities were created primarily to simplify the trading of mortgage instruments and thereby encourage wider participation in the market by investors who had not traditionally invested in these instruments. Mortgage securities generally provide investors several advantages over unsecuritized mortgages, some of which are described below.

Additional Insurance Protection. The security of an individual mortgage loan involves two factors: the borrower's ability to make payments and the market value of the property that the lender can claim if the borrower defaults on the loan. While the existence of FHA insurance or private mortgage insurance on a loan reduces potential losses, it does not guarantee timely payments each month during delinquency and foreclosure and may not, in certain cases, completely eliminate the risk of loss of principal. The mortgage-backed security structure solves this problem by adding an additional layer of insurance at the security level. The Government National Mortgage Association (GNMA), for instance, guarantees the timely payment of principal and interest each month on its securities, a guarantee that is backed by the full faith and credit of the U.S. Treasury. Regardless of what happens to the individual FHA or VA mortgages underlying a GNMA pool, the investor is assured of timely payments each month and need not be concerned with the credit quality of individual loans or lenders.

Quality Underwriting Standards. The mortgages that can be used to back federal agency mortgage securities must conform to standard underwriting guidelines which provide investors with the assurance that the loans collateralizing their securities are investment quality. Investors need not go through the often tedious process of evaluating the individual loans in a pool, as the loans are all underwritten during the securitization process.

Settlement Process. Settlement procedures on mortgage-backed securities have been standardized through the Public Securities Association (PSA). These procedures specify such things as the types of securities that can be delivered, the range of principal balances that can be delivered, and the standard settlement dates for mortgage-backed securities. Whole loan settlements, on the other hand, are often problematic because of the lack of standard procedures for these transactions.

Payment Process. An investor holding a mortgage-backed security need not collect monthly payments on each individual mortgage loan underlying a pool, but instead receives a single check based on the investor's pro rata share of the entire pool.

Use as Collateral. Mortgage-backed securities can be used as collateral for a number of different types of borrowings. While whole loans can be used as collateral for some types of borrowings, they are not as widely accepted as securitized mortgages nor are the borrowing costs usually as attractive as when securities are used as collateral.

Market Liquidity. The market for mortgage-backed securities is far more liquid than the market for unsecuritized loans. Large blocks of mortgage securities can be traded in a matter of seconds with bid/offer spreads of $1/8$th of a point or less. While the market for whole loans is growing, it can still be very difficult to buy or sell these loans as quickly or with the execution available in the securities market.

Pass-through Securities

Pass-through securities are issued against pools of mortgages and the cash flows generated by the mortgages are passed from the servicers of the underlying loans to the holders of the securities on a monthly basis. The investors receive payments comprised of scheduled principal and interest and any unscheduled payments of principal (resulting from prepayments and defaults) that may have occurred. While there have been many pass-through securities issued by private corporations, the most widely held mortgage pass-throughs are those guaranteed by firms that are often thought of as agencies of the U.S. government: the Government National Mortgage Association (GNMA), the Federal National Mortgage Association (FNMA), and the Federal Home Loan Mortgage Corporation (FHLMC).[1] While the basic structures of the GNMA, FNMA, and FHLMC securities are very similar, they differ in many ways that influence how they are valued in the market. Exhibit 2 highlights some of these differences. The following sections describe the significance of these differences in security valuation.

Guarantee.   GNMA, FNMA, and FHLMC all guarantee the principal balances of their securities. GNMA and FNMA, however, guarantee *timely* payment of principal and interest, while FHLMC provides this additional guarantee on a relatively limited portion of its pools. The strength of the guarantee of payment becomes particularly important when the mortgages underlying the securities are experiencing significant defaults. GNMA and FNMA investors would continue to receive interest and principal amortization payments in such an environment, while most FHLMC investors would receive interest only.

Mortgage Collateral.   The mortgages underlying the different types of securities differ in many ways that can affect security valuation.

- *Mortgage Insurance:* Securities backed by mortgages that are VA guaranteed or FHA insured (all GNMAs and a few FNMAs and FHLMCs) have a different level of credit risk than do securities backed by privately insured (conventional) mortgages. FHA/VA-backed securities also tend to prepay slower

[1] FNMA and FHLMC are not actually agencies of the U.S. government, but are private corporations that were created by Acts of Congress. Only GNMA has a guarantee of payment backed by the full faith and credit of the U.S. government.

EXHIBIT 2
MBS Program Comparison

	GNMA I	GNMA II	FHLMC-Regular	FHLMC-Guarantor	FNMA
Guarantee	Timely payment of principal and interest		Timely payment of interest, ultimate payment of principal	Some pools timely payment of principal and interest; other pools timely payment of interest, ultimate payment of principal	Timely payment of principal and interest
Mortgage Collateral:					
Insurance	FHA/VA		Conventional and FHA/VA	Conventional and FHA/VA	Conventional and FHA/VA
Payment Structure	Fixed rate, GPM, Buydown, ARM		Fixed rate, ARM	Fixed rate, ARM	Fixed rate, ARM, GEM, GPM
Property Type	Single-family, Multifamily, Mobile Home		Single-family, Multifamily	Single-family, Multifamily	Single-family, Multifamily
Maximum Original Maturity	15, 30, 40 years		15, 30 years	15, 30 years	15, 30, 40 years
Pooling Requirements:					
Mortgage Coupons	50 bp above security rate	Between 50 and 150 bp above security coupon rate	No Requirement	All mortgage rates must be higher than the security coupon rate and must be within 200 bp of each other	Mortgage rates usually are at least 25 or 37.5 bp (depending on type of servicing lender performs) above security coupon and they must be with 200 bp of each other
Mortgage Age	All loans must be originated within one year of each other and within one year of the GNMA commitment date		Conventional Loans: No Limits. FHA/VA Loans: Loans must be at least 12 mos. old for pools issued prior to April 1986; no limits for pools issued after April 1986	Conventional Loans: No Limits. FHA/VA Loans: Loans must be at least 12 mos. old for pools issued prior to April 1986; no limits for pools issued after April 1986	Conventional Loans: No Limits. FHA/VA Loans: Loans must be at least 12 mos. old for pools issued prior to April 1986; no limits for pools issued after April 1986
Mortgage Maturities	At least 90% of the pool's original principal balance must be in mortgages with maturities of 20 years or more in the 30-year program		No Requirements	No Requirements	No Requirements
Pool Information:					
Mortgage Coupons	50 bp over security rate	No Information	WAC as of issue date for some pools, no information for other pools	WAC as of issue date for some pools, no information for other pools	WAC as of issue date
Mortgage Age	No Information		No Information	No Information	No Information
Mortgage Maturities	Final Maturity		WAM as of issue date for some pools; final maturity for all pools	WAM as of issue date for some pools; final maturity for all pools	WAM as of issue date and final maturity for all pools
Payment Delay Penalty	14 days	19 days	44 days	44 days	24 days

than securities backed by conventional mortgages because the mortgages can be assumed and, it is believed, because FHA/VA borrowers tend to be less mobile than borrowers with conventional mortgages.

- *Mortgage Payment Structure:*   While the bulk of the mortgage pass-through securities currently outstanding is backed by fixed rate, fixed payment, fully amortizing mortgages, there is a growing population of securities backed by alternative mortgage structures such as GPMs, ARMs, and balloon mortgages.

- *Original Maturity:*   The mortgages backing pass-through securities can have different original maturities. Most have original maturities of either 15 or 30 years. The length of the maturity will affect the size of the amortization payments for mortgages of a given age and possibly the rate at which they will prepay.

Payment Delay.   The payment delay refers to the length of time between the date borrowers make their monthly payments to lenders and the date investors holding the securities backed by these loans receive the monthly payments. This is an interest-free delay because investors stop earning interest on any principal repaid in a month as of the date the payment is made to the lender. (For calculating security interest payments, the pass-through structure assumes that all principal payments occur on the first day of the month). Because of this interest-free period, the longer a security's payment delay, the lower its yield will be relative to other securities with the same coupon and price. Conversely, for two securities with the same coupon and yield, the security with the longer payment delay will have a lower price than the security with the shorter payment delay.

Pooling Requirements.   Each security program has different requirements regarding the characteristics of the mortgages that can be pooled together. In general, the more homogeneous the loans, the easier it is to predict how the pool will perform as it ages and as economic conditions change.

- *Mortgage Rates:*   Mortgages with different mortgage rates will prepay differently in response to changes in interest rates. The higher the mortgage rate, the more sensitive a loan's prepayment rate will be to changes in interest rates. The greater the diversity of the mortgage rates included in a pool, the more difficult it is to predict the amount and timing of the pool's principal payments.

- *Mortgage Ages:* As mortgages age, they tend to prepay faster as a result of such things as homeowners relocating, trading up or down in house sizes, etc. The more diverse the ages of the loans included in a pool, the more difficult it is to predict how the pool's prepayments will vary as the pool ages.

- *Mortgage Maturities:* For two mortgages with the same coupon rate, the mortgage with the shorter remaining term will have greater monthly amortization payments than the mortgage with the longer remaining term. As will be discussed later, if the mortgages in a pool have very different remaining terms, it is difficult to determine how much of a pool's total monthly principal payment is amortization and how much is prepayment. It is, therefore, difficult to analyze the pool's historical payment experience and to predict how it is likely to behave in the future.

Pool Information Provided. Depending on the requirements of a pass-through program, the characteristics of the loans underlying a pass-through security can be widely disparate. In most cases, however, the information published about a pool does not adequately indicate the extent to which the characteristics of the underlying loans are different. While combining heterogeneous loans in a pool makes it very difficult to predict how the pool is likely to repay, it becomes even more complicated when the information that is provided about the pool does not adequately describe the characteristics of the underlying loans. The amount of information provided for the various pools differs by security program.

- *Mortgage Coupons:* The only security program for which there is perfect certainty as to the mortgage rates underlying a pool is the GNMA I program; all of the mortgages backing a GNMA I pool must have mortgage rates of exactly 50 basis points over the security coupon rate. For all other mortgage pass-through pools, the most detailed information that is available is the weighted average coupon rate (WAC) on the underlying mortgages as of issue date. It is probable, however, that a pool's WAC will change as the pool ages and the loans in the pool amortize and prepay. For several types of pools, no mortgage rate information is provided, except the maximum range of mortgage rates allowed to be pooled together given a security program's pooling requirements.

- *Mortgage Ages:*   No pass-through program currently provides detailed information about the ages of the mortgages in a specific pool. The pooling requirements for each program represent the only information that is available.

- *Mortgage Maturities:*   The exact distribution of mortgage maturities included in a pool is generally unavailable. Usually, the most information that is provided is the weighted average maturity (WAM) on the underlying mortgages as of issue date. As with a pool's WAC, it is highly probable that a pool's WAM will change as the pool ages and the loans in the pool amortize and prepay. For many pools, the only maturity information that is available is the final maturity of the pool, which is the maturity date of the loan with the longest maturity in the pool. Clearly, this statistic provides very little information about the distribution of the maturities in a pool and, therefore, how the loans are likely to perform in the future.

Collateralized Mortgage Obligations [2]

While pass-through securities pay investors their pro rata share of the principal and interest payments made on the mortgages backing a security through the maturity of the security, Collateralized Mortgage Obligations (CMOs) allocate the cash flows generated by the underlying mortgages to several different classes of investors.

---

[2] For a detailed discussion of CMOs, see Richard Roll, "Collateralized Mortgage Obligations: Characteristics, History, Analysis," in *Mortgage-Backed Securities: New Strategies, Applications and Research,* Frank J. Fabozzi, ed., Chicago: Probus Publishers, 1987.

Most of the existing issues have four classes of bonds, or "tranches." The principal payments produced from the underlying mortgages are paid to the different tranches in sequence.

In the traditional CMO structure, investors in the first class of a CMO receive all of the principal payments on the underlying mortgages until the first class is completely repaid. Investors in each successive class receive no principal until each of the earlier classes is completely repaid. Investors in each class, except any accrual classes, receive only interest payments while investors in the earlier classes are receiving principal. In the majority of CMO issues, the last tranche is an accrual class ("Z-bond") which receives no cash payments at all until the earlier tranches are fully retired. Instead, the face amount of the Z-bond accretes at its stated coupon rate. When the other tranches have been retired, the Z-bond investors begin to receive both coupon payments (on the then higher principal balance) and principal payments received from the remaining collateral.

As with pass-through securities, the timing of the principal payments on CMOs is sensitive to the prepayments on the mortgages backing the securities. Unlike pass-through securities, CMOs are considered to be debt on the books of the issuers. CMOs generally do not make payments to investors on a monthly basis, but pay quarterly or semi-annually.

Stripped Mortgage-Backed Securities[3]

Stripped mortgage-backed securities (SMBSs) are securities formed by segregating the principal and interest payments on a pool of mortgages. Unlike CMOs, which divide mortgage principal payments among different classes of bonds with varying maturities, SMBSs divide the mortgage principal and interest payments unequally among different classes of securities, each of which has a maturity equal to the maturity of the underlying pool of mortgages. There are two types of SMBSs currently outstanding: those backed by relatively low coupon mortgage pools whose market prices are

[3] For a detailed discussion of stripped mortgage-backed securities, see Richard Roll, "Stripped Mortgage-Backed Securities," New York: Goldman Sachs Mortgage Securities Research, July 1986.

below par and others backed by mortgage pools with relatively high coupons such that the current market values of the underlying mortgages are above par.

In an SMBS backed by discount coupon mortgages, the mortgage pool is used to construct both a very low coupon, deep discount security and a high coupon, premium security. Each class of the resulting SMBS receives one-half of each dollar of principal paid on the underlying mortgages, but the interest is divided unequally. A $100 million pool with a 9 percent coupon (9.5 percent rate on the underlying mortgages), for example, could be stripped into two classes, one $50 million class receiving one-third of the interest and another $50 million class receiving two-thirds of the interest. This would create a $50 million security with a 6 percent coupon rate and a $50 million security with a 12 percent coupon rate. The discount SMBS would benefit from the prepayments on mortgages 350 basis points higher than the SMBS coupon rate. The prepayments on the premium SMBS would be considerably lower and less interest rate sensitive than the prepayments on comparable coupon securities, because the mortgages underlying this security would be 250 basis points lower than the SMBS rate.

SMBSs that have been structured using premium coupon collateral have had two types of classes: one class with claim to most of the mortgage pool's principal balance and to some of the interest generated by the pool, and another class with claim to a very small portion of the pool's principal balance and to some of the pool's interest payments. As an example, a $100 million pool of mortgages with an 11 percent coupon rate (11.5 percent rate on the underlying mortgages) could be stripped to form a $99 million class (99 percent of the total principal) that receives 4.95 percent of the interest generated by the mortgage pool, and a $1 million class (1 percent of the total principal) that receives 6.05 percent of the interest produced by the mortgage pool. The $99 million first class would have a coupon rate of 5 percent (4.95 ÷ .99), while the $1 million second class would have a coupon of 605 percent (6.05 ÷ .01). The first class is a seemingly ordinary mortgage pass-through security with a 5 percent coupon. The second class is effectively an "interest-only" security because the amount of principal returned is trivial compared to the coupon payments.

The first class of an SMBS backed by premium collateral is a deep discount security whose value is enhanced by fast prepayments. Since there is such a big difference between the security coupon rate and the rates on the underlying mortgages, this security will normally trade at a higher price than a comparable coupon security with otherwise equivalent features, because the mortgages underlying the SMBS will prepay faster than the mortgages backing generic discount securities.

Since the bulk of the payments received by the second class of an SMBS backed by premium collateral are comprised of interest on the underlying pool of mortgages, this security is highly sensitive to the timing of the prepayments on the pool; the higher the prepayments the less interest this class receives. With most fixed income securities, the price of a security falls when interest rates rise, because the present value of the future cash flows decreases with the higher discount rate. With the "interest-only" SMBSs, however, the price of the security can be expected to increase as interest rates rise (within a certain range of interest rates), because the rising rates cause prepayments to fall, increasing the security's cash flows enough to offset the effects of the higher discount rate. After a certain point, however, further increases in interest rates have a relatively small effect on prepayment rates, so the price of the SMBS begins to fall with further increases in interest rates.

III. MORTGAGE PRINCIPAL PAYMENTS

One of the biggest risks associated with any type of mortgage-backed security is the uncertainty regarding the timing of principal payments on the mortgages underlying the security. The actual cash flow an investor receives from a mortgage-backed security depends on the amortization schedules and the termination pattern (resulting from prepayments and defaults) of the many individual mortgages included in the pool.

Since mortgage security investors are assured of the ultimate repayment of the principal balance of a pool, the actual pattern of cash flows from the pool will not affect the yield on their investments if the security is purchased at its parity price (i.e., the par value adjusted for the effect of the delay in monthly payments).

If the security is purchased at any other price (at a discount or premium), however, the investor's yield will vary significantly depending on the timing of the repayment of the principal balance through principal amortization payments and principal prepayments.

Exhibit 3 shows the principal amortization payments of an 8 percent mortgage and a 12 percent mortgage, both with remaining terms of 30 years. The principal payments on these mortgages increase each month at a rate equal to the mortgage rate divided by 12. For either mortgage, therefore, the older the mortgage, the greater its amortization payments. The principal amortization payments on the 8 percent mortgage are higher than on the 12 percent rate mortgage until year 22. Since the monthly principal payments on the 12 percent mortgage increase at a faster rate than do the principal payments on the 8 percent mortgage, eventually the

EXHIBIT 3
Amortization Principal Payments
8% and 12% Mortgages ($100,000 Original Balance)

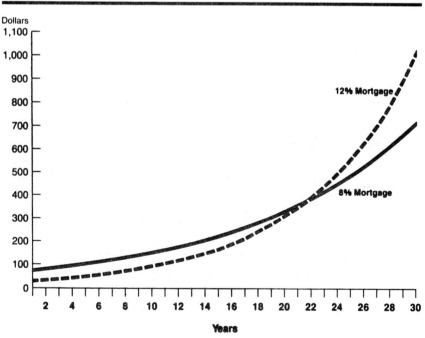

amortization payments on the 12 percent mortgage catch up with and then exceed the payments on the 8 percent mortgage.

While principal amortization payments on a single mortgage loan are predictable, it is difficult, if not impossible, to predict when a mortgage will prepay and the timing of a mortgage's pre-payment can have a significant impact on its yield. As is shown in Exhibit 4, when a new 11 percent mortgage is priced at par (100 percent), its yield will be equal to its coupon rate of 11 percent, regardless of whether it prepays in the fifth, twelfth, or twentieth year, or even runs to maturity. If, on the other hand, the mortgage is priced at a discount (such as 85 percent), the yield increases as the time the mortgage is outstanding is reduced. The yield on the mortgage will be higher if the loan prepays in its fourth year, for example, than if it prepays in its twelfth year. This occurs because

---

EXHIBIT 4
Yield to Termination on a New 11% Mortgage at Various Secondary Market Prices (Discount, Par, Premium)

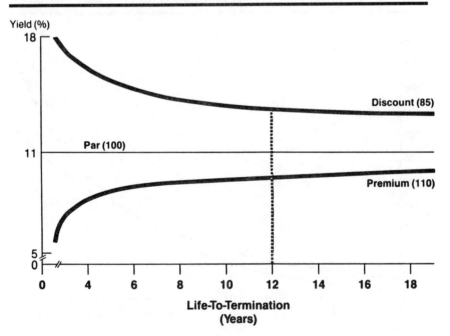

the value of the discount from par (15 percent) is recouped over a shorter period of time. The investor may have paid only 85 percent of the outstanding principal balance of the loan, but the investor will receive 100 percent of the principal balance when the loan is repaid. The earlier the 15 percent discount is received, the higher the yield will be. If the mortgage is priced at a premium, on the other hand, its yield *decreases* as the time until the loan is terminated shortens. In this case, the investor pays a premium over par for a relatively valuable stream of monthly coupon payments which, by ending prematurely at the time of prepayment, reduces the return on the premium paid, and thus, the yield on the total investment.

As is shown in Exhibit 5 the *magnitude* of the discount on a mortgage affects the relationship between the yield and the assumption about when the loan will be repaid. As would be

EXHIBIT 5
Yield to Termination on a New GNMA 11% Priced at 98 and 88

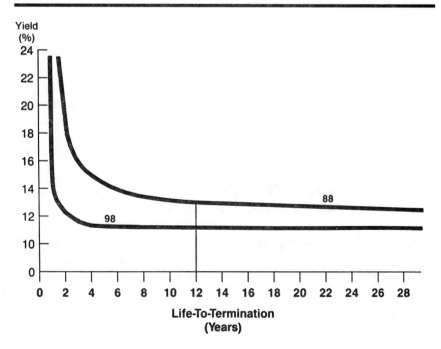

expected, the farther away from par a mortgage is priced, the more sensitive the mortgage's yield will be to the length of time the mortgage is outstanding. The greater the discount, the greater the absolute and percentage increase in yield that will result from an early termination. The yield assuming a 12-year prepayment, for example, on an 11 percent mortgage is 11.25 percent when it is priced at 98, and 12.95 percent when it is priced at 88. When the prepayment is assumed to occur in the fourth year, however, the yield of the mortgage priced at 98 increases by 2.1 percent to 11.49 percent, while the yield of the mortgage priced at 88 increases by almost 15 percent to 14.86 percent.

It is important to note that, while the *yield to maturity* on a mortgage priced near par will be insensitive to the timing of principal payments, the *total return* from such an investment probably will be sensitive to principal payments. Prepayments tend to increase as interest rates fall because there is a greater incentive to refinance mortgages with high rates at lower market rates and there is a reduced disincentive to prepay loans with relatively low rates. The increased cash flow on an MBS that result from faster prepayments must then be reinvested at lower market interest rates. The cumulative influence of reinvesting the cash flows at lower rates can, over time, have a major impact on the total return of the investment, regardless of its purchase price. Conversely, when prepayments slow in a rising rate environment, the cash flows that can be reinvested at higher rates are reduced, thus diminishing the total return on the investment.

IV.   ESTIMATING PRINCIPAL PAYMENTS ON A POOL OF MORTGAGES

Any valuation of mortgage securities must incorporate a projection of future scheduled and unscheduled principal payments on the underlying mortgage loans. Estimating each of these components of a security's principal payments can be particularly problematic. The following sections describe some of the methods used to project mortgage principal payments and discuss some of the advantages and shortcomings of these methods.

Measuring and Estimating Prepayments

Terminations can be caused by either prepayments or defaults. The net effect to the pass-through investor is virtually identical: the investor receives principal payments over and above those resulting from normal amortization. The following sections will refer to both types of unscheduled principal payments as prepayments.

Life Estimates. The simplest approach to estimating prepayments on a pool of mortgages is to assume that nothing but amortization is received on the pool for some specified period of time after which the remaining balance on the pool prepays in full. For years, the standard prepayment assumption used to quote yields on mortgage-backed securities was a 12-year life assumption. This convention assumes that all of the loans backing a mortgage security are brand new 30-year mortgages whose cash flows consist of interest and scheduled amortization of principal for 12 years and full prepayment of the remaining principal balance at the end of the twelfth year.

There are several problems with this approach to estimating prepayments on mortgage securities. Many of the securities outstanding in the market today are significantly seasoned, so the assumption that they are all new can understate the principal amortization that will be received on these securities. Also, this convention was adopted during a period of relatively stable interest rates when the range of mortgage rates outstanding was narrow. In the current environment, with more volatile interest rates and a wide range of security coupons outstanding, the assumption of full prepayment after 12 years cannot be applied to all mortgage securities. While an individual mortgage generates level payments of interest and scheduled principal until it prepays in full (unless it has partial prepayments), this pattern does not hold true for the pools of mortgages backing mortgage securities, where prepayments can be expected to be distributed over time as different loans in the pool prepay.

FHA Experience. In order to avoid the shortcomings inherent in using life estimates to predict prepayments on mortgage securities, many market participants turned to using the average prepayment

experience observed by the Actuarial Division of the Federal
Housing Administration on FHA insured mortgages. "FHA experience" represents the average prepayment and default experience
of all FHA-insured single-family, 30-year mortgages over many
years. Each FHA series consists of 30 termination balances, one
for each year of a 30-year mortgage's life, representing the portion
of a pool's original balance that would be outstanding at the end of
each year if the pool prepaid according to the average FHA experience. From these balances it is possible to derive prepayment rates
showing the average percentage of FHA loans that prepaid in each
year of their life relative to the total number of loans of the same
age outstanding at the beginning of the period. While the FHA
experience series provides a benchmark for viewing the prepayment experience of a group of mortgages as they age, these base
rates are often adjusted to reflect expectations for higher or lower
prepayments in the future. If it is expected that prepayments on a
particular pool will be twice as fast as those implied by the base
FHA experience series, for example, one would adjust the FHA
series accordingly and refer to the prepayment distribution as "200
percent FHA."

While using FHA experience as a benchmark to predict prepayments is far superior to using a point life estimate, there are still
many problems associated with using FHA experience as a model
of prepayments. One problem relates to the way the underlying
data are aggregated. Exhibit 6 illustrates the breakdown of the
FHA experience series released in 1981. The prepayment rate for
the first year of a mortgage's life is derived from the percentage of
mortgages originated in the years 1957 through 1981 that prepaid
after one year. Thus, a mortgage written at the beginning of 1957
would be examined at the end of 1957 to see whether it prepaid in
its first year, one written in 1958 would be examined at the end of
1958, and so on. Since the prepayment rates for each of the succeeding years of a mortgage's life are derived in a similar manner,
the number of distinct observation years included in each sample
declines from 25 for the first year's prepayment rate (from mortgages originated between 1957 and 1981) to one year of observations for the 25th year's prepayment rate (from mortgages originated in 1957 only). The prepayment rates for the early years of a
mortgage's life, therefore, are based on the experience of mortgages

EXHIBIT 6
Breakdown of FHA Experience (Figures Released in Spring 1982)

Age in Years	Origination Years	Observation Years	Number of Years Observed	Prepayment Rates
1	1957-1981	1957-1981	25	1.13
2	1957-1980	1958-1981	24	3.77
3	1957-1979	1959-1981	23	5.17
4	1957-1978	1960-1981	22	5.73
5	1957-1977	1961-1981	21	6.21
6	1957-1976	1962-1981	20	6.80
7	1957-1975	1963-1981	19	7.12
8	1957-1974	1964-1981	18	7.23
9	1957-1973	1965-1981	17	7.00
10	1957-1972	1966-1981	16	6.69
11	1957-1971	1967-1981	15	6.59
12	1957-1970	1968-1981	14	6.43
13	1957-1969	1969-1981	13	6.12
14	1957-1968	1970-1981	12	5.86
15	1957-1967	1971-1981	11	5.59
16	1957-1966	1972-1981	10	5.34
17	1957-1965	1973-1981	9	5.10
18	1957-1964	1974-1981	8	4.89
19	1957-1963	1975-1981	7	4.67
20	1957-1962	1976-1981	6	4.40
21	1957-1961	1977-1981	5	4.11
22	1957-1960	1978-1981	4	4.94
23	1957-1959	1979-1981	3	5.78
24	1957-1958	1980-1981	2	6.68
25	1957	1981	1	7.62
26-30	Forecasted Data Points		0	

originated at the various market rates that existed between 1957 and the early 1980s, while the prepayment rates in the later years represent only the experience of mortgages originated in the late 1950s and early 1960s, when rates were uniformly low, mortgages that were thus less likely to prepay in the high interest rate environment of the late 1970s and early 1980s.

The FHA has historically updated the series every one or two years by incorporating the most recent experience of both old and newly-originated loans into the series. Beginning with the series released in 1984, however, the series includes only the experience of loans originated since 1970. By removing the experience of the very old FHA loans from the data, the newer FHA series better reflects the more recent prepayment experience and reduces, though does not eliminate, the bias built into the earlier series. Since the newer FHA series includes only the experience of mortgages originated between 1970 and 1983, however, the average prepayment rates calculated for years 14 through 30 of the series were not based on actual experience, but were estimated.

In addition to the bias caused by the aggregation of the FHA data and the confusion related to the periodic updating of the FHA experience series, there also exists a more obvious and fundamental problem associated with the way the data are averaged. While the relationship between the actual coupon rate on a mortgage and current market rates has a significant impact on prepayments, the FHA experience ignores this important relationship. Each series is the average prepayment experience of a group of loans with a wide range of coupon rates prepaying in vastly different interest rate environments. The prepayment rates on 8 percent mortgages originated in a rising rate environment will be considerably different than the prepayment rates on 17 percent mortgages originated in a falling rate environment, but the FHA experience does not capture these differences.

Conditional Prepayment Rates (CPRs).   The use of conditional or constant prepayment rates (CPRs) to measure prepayments on mortgage securities has gained popularity over the last several years. A conditional prepayment rate (CPR) is the percentage of principal outstanding at the beginning of a period that prepays during that period. The term "CPR" usually refers to an annualized prepayment rate, while the terms constant monthly prepayment (CMP) and single monthly mortality (SMM) refer to the unannualized monthly prepayment rate.[4] These statistics reflect the actual prepayment experience of mortgage securities and are pure numbers that can be easily interpreted, understood, and monitored on a historical basis.[5]

The greatest disadvantage in using a single CPR for estimating

[4] $CPR = 1 - [1 - (CPM/100)]^{12}$

[5] For a further discussion of the CPR approach and the methodologies for calculating historical CPRs, see Scott M. Pinkus and Evan B. Firestone, "Mortgage Securities: Predicting Prepayments," *Mortgage Banker,* December 1983.

future prepayments on a mortgage security is, not surprisingly, the greatest strength of using the FHA experience: a single prepayment rate applied over the entire remaining term of a security cannot accurately capture the influences of aging on prepayments during the early years of a mortgage's life. At a constant interest rate level, prepayments on a new mortgage pool can be expected to increase during the first several years of its life, before leveling off. While a series of CPRs could be used to reflect better the varying influence of prepayments on mortgages cash flows over the life of a security, estimating the appropriate CPRs is a difficult and often subjective process.

It is reasonably accurate to use a single CPR to estimate prepayments for seasoned pools of mortgages and for pools with coupon rates above the current market level, because mortgage age has much less of a significant influence on prepayments for pools backed by these types of mortgages. The difference between the mortgage rate on the loans in the pools and the current market mortgage rate is the dominant influence on prepayments. This difference will determine the extent of the incentive to refinance a high rate mortgage for a new mortgage with a lower rate. For older mortgages, this difference will determine the degree of a borrower's disincentive to prepay a relatively low rate mortgage. This disincentive can lead a borrower to postpone a desired move; permit a loan to be assumed (if allowed); or take out a second, or wrap-around, mortgage rather than refinancing an existing loan when greater leverage is desired.

By regularly monitoring the historical prepayment experience of the securities issued under the major pass-through programs, it is possible to observe the effects of changing interest rates on prepayments. It is possible to isolate the differing influences of mortgage aging and changing interest rates by segregating homogeneous securities (such as GNMA 30-year, single-family pass-throughs) by coupon and approximate mortgage age.

The PSA Prepayment Model. The PSA standard prepayment model was developed by the Public Securities Association (PSA), which consists of major dealers in the mortgage-backed securities and Treasury markets. The PSA model was created primarily to provide standardization to the prepayment models used to price new CMO issues. To date, this model has been used almost exclusively for analyzing CMOs and is not widely used to analyze pass-through securities.

The PSA model represents a compromise between the FHA experience and constant prepayment methods of predicting mortgage prepayments. Like FHA experience, the prepayments incorporated in the PSA model vary with the assumed age of the mortgages underlying a security. During the first 30 months of a mortgage's life, PSA prepayments increase linearly; 100 percent PSA provides for a .2 percent (per annum) prepayment in the first month which increases by .2 percent in each succeeding month until it reaches 6 percent in month 30. After month 30, the PSA model stays at 6 percent for the remainder of the mortgage's life. After month 30, therefore, using PSA is exactly the same as using a constant CPR.

As with using either FHA experience or a CPR, the PSA model does not explicitly account for the effect of the current level of interest rates relative to the coupon rate on the mortgage. Instead, the recommended procedure is to use a PSA "multiple." A multiple such as 200 percent PSA, for example, might be appropriate for a mortgage selling at a premium, while a multiple such as 50 percent PSA might be appropriate for a mortgage selling at a discount.

Econometric Models.[6] It is possible to derive an econometric model to predict mortgage prepayments from the detailed historical prepayment and default experience of any large portfolio of individual mortgage loans or mortgage securities. The key factors that influence mortgage prepayment rates (such as mortgage coupon rates, future market interest rates, and mortgage age) can be explicitly considered as variables in such a model. This avoids having to make arbitrary or subjective adjustments to a prepayment assumption, as is required with the use of life estimates, FHA experience, or with the PSA model.

By determining the statistical relationships between one or several independent variables and the dependent variable to be

---

[6] For a further discussion of this approach as applied to the Federal Home Loan Mortgage Corporation's mortgage portfolio, see Helen F. Peters, Scott M. Pinkus, and David J. Askin, "Figuring the Odds: A Model of Prepayments," *Secondary Mortgage Markets*, May 1984.

forecasted, an econometric model acts as a formal proxy for the informal evaluation techniques employed by an experienced decision maker. Econometric modeling offers a systematic and statistically sound method of estimating prepayments, but it requires explicit estimates of the future values of a number of variables which are often themselves difficult to forecast. Many investors are unfamiliar with a number of the variables that could be included in such a model (e.g., regional migration patterns, average home costs, housing starts, etc.). Furthermore, the statistical relationships that proved meaningful during the 1960s, 1970s, or early 1980s may not hold true in the current interest rate environment and can even be misleading for predicting behavior today.

Amortization Principal Payments [7]

In order to calculate accurately the scheduled principal payments for a mortgage security, it is necessary to know the mortgage rate and maturity of each of the mortgages in the pool. Because this information is rarely available, it is necessary to make assumptions about the distribution of the maturities and mortgage rates given the information that is available. As was discussed earlier, the most detailed maturity information that is generally available for any mortgage security is the weighted average maturity (WAM) of the mortgages in a pool as of the pool's issue date. This information is provided for all FNMA securities and for FHLMC Guarantor securities issued after June 1983. For all GNMA securities and for all FHLMC securities issued prior to July 1983, however, the only maturity information available is the final maturity date of the mortgage with the longest remaining term as of the pool's issue date.

Exhibit 7 illustrates how estimates of principal amortization payments can vary when the exact distribution of the maturities on the individual mortgages in a pool is not known. In this hypothetical example, a $3 million pool has a final maturity at issue date of 350 months. While the pool's WAM is approximately 283 months, the actual maturities range from 200 to 350 months. If all of the

[7] See Scott M. Pinkus and Susan D. Mara, "Measuring the Maturity of a Mortgage Security: When is a WAM not a WAM?" *Mortgage Banker*, February 1985.

EXHIBIT 7
Impact of Maturity Distribution on Estimated Principal Payments

	Pool Maturity Distribution (12% Mortgages)			
Principal Balance	% of Pool's Total Balance	Maturity (Months)	Scheduled Principal Payment	% of Pool's Total Payment
$1,000,000	33.3%	200	$1,583.28	65.1%
1,000,000	33.3	300	532.24	21.9
1,000,000	33.3	350	317.01	13.0
$3,000,000	100.0%	283	$2,432.53	100.0%

Estimated Scheduled Principal Payments	
Maturity Assumptions	Scheduled Principal Payment
Final Maturity (350 months)	$ 951.03
Weighted Average Maturity (283 months)	1,909.74
Actual Scheduled Principal	2,432.53

mortgages in the pool are assumed to have the same maturity as the pool's final maturity, the pool's next scheduled principal payment would be calculated as $951.03. Using the WAM as a single maturity assumption for the pool, the scheduled principal payment would be calculated as $1,909.74. Both of these payment amounts, however, are substantially different from the $2,432.53 total scheduled principal that would actually be paid on the underlying mortgages. The greater the dispersion of the maturities on the loans in a pool, the less useful the published maturity information will be in calculating the pool's scheduled principal payments.

If a pool's scheduled principal payments are misestimated because the actual distribution of maturities on the underlying loans is not known, the amount of prepaid principal calculated for the pool will also be incorrect. (Principal prepayments are calculated as the principal paid in excess of the amount of principal scheduled to have been paid.) To the extent a pool's historical scheduled principal payments are *understated* by using either the pool's WAM or final maturity, the pool's prepayment experience will be *overstated*.

Exhibit 8 illustrates a hypothetical pool's total principal payment for a given month, together with the breakdown of amortization payments and prepaid principal that would be calculated under two different maturity assumptions: the *final maturity* of the pool and the *original weighted average maturity* adjusted for seasoning. The interaction between the maturity assumption and the calculation of prepayments can be clearly seen. The longer the remaining term to maturity is assumed to be, the smaller the portion of total principal payments that is considered to be scheduled principal, and the greater the portion that is assumed to be prepaid principal. When comparing the historical prepayment experience of different pools, therefore, it is critical to consider the maturity assumption that was made when the prepayment rates were calculated. While the prepayment rate calculated for a pool using its WAM is likely to be lower than one calculated for a similar pool for which a WAM is unavailable and a final maturity was used, the total principal payments on the two pools could, in fact, be identical.

EXHIBIT 8
Impact of Maturity Assumption on Prepayment Estimates and Projected Yields

FNMA 8%

Security Principal Balance: $1,000,000
Final Maturity: 300 Months
Adjusted WAM: 200 Months

	Final Maturity	Adjusted WAM
Total Principal Payment:	$5,000.00	$5,000.00
Assumed Amortization Principal:	968.94	2,282.88
Estimated Prepaid Principal:	$4,031.06	$2,717.12
Conditional Prepayment Rate (CPR):	4.7%	3.2%
Assumed Price:	77.25	77.25
Projected Yield:*	12.29%	12.77%

* The projected cash flow yields are based on the maturity assumptions shown and the historical CPRs calculated using those maturity assumptions.

Exhibit 8 also shows that when a shorter remaining term is assumed (the adjusted WAM) and a lower prepayment rate is calculated for the pool, the yield produced when that prepayment rate is projected over the same remaining term is actually the higher of the yields shown. Conversely, the lower yield results when the longer remaining term (the final maturity) and a higher prepayment rate are assumed for the future. Clearly, the faster amortization schedule that is implicitly projected when the shorter maturity is assumed more than offsets the impact of the lower prepayment rate in the yield calculation.

Principal Payments: Generic Versus Pool Specific Trades

There are two distinct approaches to handling the uncertainty of principal payments when evaluating mortgage securities, differing largely with the way the mortgage-backed securities are bought or sold. Mortgage securities can be traded on a *generic* basis or on a *pool specific* basis. A generic trade is one in which the specific pools that will be delivered are not identified at the time of the trade, and any pool of the same security type with the agreed upon coupon rate can be delivered at the specified price. Securities can also be traded on a specified pool basis. In these instances, the pools that must be delivered are those that were identified at the time of the transaction.

When evaluating a generic transaction, future principal payments on the securities are usually estimated based on either the average characteristics of all securities similar to those being examined or based on a reasonable worst case scenario of the characteristics of the securities that could be delivered against the trade. When evaluating a generic trade involving FNMA 8 percent securities priced at a discount, for example, an investor could assume that the securities that will be delivered will have the same average age and average historical prepayment experience as the averages for the population of FNMA 8 percent securities, or the investor could assume that only newly originated securities will be delivered with longer than average remaining terms and slower than average prepayment rates.

For a specified pool transaction, the parties involved have the advantage of knowing the actual characteristics of the individual pools being traded as well as the historical principal paydown experience of each pool. While this information can be useful when evaluating a potential transaction, its value is often overestimated. The historical prepayment experience of a particular pool is only relevant to the extent it provides insight into how the pool will prepay in the future. Many market participants jump to the conclusion that a "fast-pay" pool, one that has historically prepaid at a faster rate than the average for similar pools, will continue to prepay at a faster than average rate. The historical prepayment data on a pool must be carefully evaluated to determine how *consistently* the pool prepaid faster or slower than the average for similar securities, and over what time period. If a pool has a fast 12-month average prepayment rate, for example, but a monthly prepayment history showing little or no prepayments in most months with only a few months with large prepayments, it cannot be assumed that the pool will have faster than average prepayments in the future. It is possible, on the other hand, that a pool will consistently prepay faster than average as a result of the specific characteristics of the mortgages in the pool (the location of the loans, the maturities of the loans, the mortgage rates, etc.).

Exhibit 9 shows the actual prepayment experience of two specific GNMA 8 percent pools, as well as the average experience of all GNMA 8 percent pools. Pool 10747 had prepayments that were consistently faster than the generic averages, indicating that the pool may be somewhat more valuable than a generic pool. Pool 10749, on the other hand, had only one prepayment over the last nine months and, in fact, had not had another prepayment since 1979. The fact that the 6- and 12-month average prepayment rates on pool 10749 were faster than the average for all GNMA 8 percent pools is really irrelevant when one considers the pool's monthly prepayment experience.

V. VALUING MORTGAGE SECURITIES

Determining when a security has a value relative to other securities is a subjective process that in many ways depends on what a portfolio manager is trying to accomplish. Many investors use estimated yields as a basis for valuing different securities. If the yield

EXHIBIT 9
Generic Versus Pool Specific Prepayment Data

	All GNMA 8% Pools "Generic Data"	GNMA 8%-Pool 10747 "Consistently Fast"	GNMA 8%-Pool 10749 "Sporadic Prepayments"
Mar 1985	2.3% CPR	5.0% CPR	0% CPR
Feb 1985	2.4	11.0	0
Jan 1985	2.3	5.6	0
Dec 1984	2.3	0	0
Nov 1984	2.3	8.2	47.4
Oct 1984	2.0	11.5	0
Sep 1984	2.6	3.8	0
Aug 1984	3.0	0	0
July 1984	3.7	15.0	0
Summary Statistics:			
3-mo avg	2.3% CPR	7.2% CPR	0% CPR
6-mo avg	2.3	7.0	10.2
12-mo ave	2.8	5.2	5.3
Avg to date	3.4	7.5	7.5

on a particular mortgage-backed security, using an estimated prepayment rate, is greater than the estimated yield on another security, the first security is often thought to be more valuable. Other differences between the securities, such as their relative price volatilities, prepayment risk, liquidity, or credit quality, however, can more than offset any yield advantage when viewed within a risk-return framework. The following sections discuss some of the factors that should be considered when evaluating the relative value of mortgage securities.

Forward Prices[8]

Unlike most other types of securities, mortgage-backed securities can be bought and sold for delivery several months later than the

[8] See Susan D. Mara, "Pricing Mortgage-backed Securities in the Forward Market," in *Mortgage-Backed Securities: New Strategies, Applications and Research.*

date of the transaction. The forward delivery market is necessary because of the nature of the mortgage origination process. The pricing of forward transactions should reflect the cost of financing the securities between two settlement dates, given the return from holding the securities during this period. Often, however, the pricing does not appear to reflect this "cost of carry." In such situations, the market demand for a certain type of security for delivery in a particular month may have driven up the price for that security relative to the price for the same security for delivery in a later month. It is important to recognize when these conditions exist in order to take advantage of any arbitrage opportunities that may be created.

In general, the forward delivery market for mortgage-backed securities exists primarily to facilitate the origination of mortgage loans and their packaging as securities for sale in the secondary market. Mortgage lenders often commit to originate and sell loans at specified rates several months before the loans are actually closed. To hedge themselves against interest rates rising between the time they set a rate and the time they sell the loans, mortgage originators will often commit to securitize and sell the loans for delivery on a future date, thus locking in the current sale price of the loans.

Market forces tend to ensure that the difference between the price of a security for delivery in one month and its price for delivery in a later month will provide a return on the security equal to the returns available from investing in other instruments between the two delivery dates. Frequently, however, the demand for a particular security for delivery on a specific date exceeds the supply of that security, driving up the security's price for the first delivery date relative to its price for the later delivery date. When this happens, the difference between the two prices reflects an implied cost of carry that is lower than comparable market rates, creating arbitrage opportunities.

The implied cost of carry associated with a particular price differential can be calculated by considering all of the factors that affect the return from holding the mortgage-backed security between the two delivery dates:

- security coupon income during the period;
- security price level;

- difference between the security prices on the two delivery dates;
- recovery of any price discount or premium through scheduled and unscheduled principal payments;
- number of days between the two delivery dates;
- number of days of accrued interest paid on the security delivered on the first date relative to the number of days of accrued interest paid on the security delivered on the second date;
- reinvestment of security cash flows between the delivery dates;
- and security payment delay penalty.

It is important to be aware of the costs of carry implied by the prices for securities for delivery in different months in order to recognize when securities can be sold for an unusually high price in one month and/or purchased in another month at a cheaper price level.

Relative Price Volatility and Implied Duration[9]

The total return on a mortgage security over a relatively short-term horizon is usually very dependent on changes in the market value of the security over the horizon. Portfolio managers who actively manage their fixed income portfolios attempt to improve their short-term performance by anticipating the direction and, to a lesser extent, the magnitude of future price movements. If they believe rates will rise, these investors will try to reduce the average price volatilities of their portfolios, as measured by the durations on their securities. If they expect that rates will fall, they will try to increase the volatilities of their holdings by lengthening the average durations of their portfolios.

Using the traditional cash flow duration measure for estimating the price volatility of a mortgage security, however, can be seriously misleading. Since the traditional measure is based on a

---

[9] For a detailed discussion of the price volatility and duration characteristics of mortgage securities, see Scott M. Pinkus and Marie A. Chandoha, "The Relative Price Volatility of Mortgage Securities," *Mortgage-Backed Securities: New Strategies, Applications and Research.*

security's future cash flows, it is necessary to estimate future prepayments on a mortgage security in order to calculate its duration. Prepayments on a mortgage security, however, are themselves extremely sensitive to changes in interest rates. Even if it was possible to predict accurately what the future prepayments of a mortgage security would be if interest rates remain stable at their current levels, these estimates would be of limited value since interest rates are unlikely to remain stable over the life of the security. While duration has become a standard measure of interest rate sensitivity for most fixed income portfolio managers, it is necessary to alter the approach and broaden the concept to account properly for the interest-sensitive nature of the cash flows on a mortgage security.

The historical price relationships of mortgage securities offer some clues about how these securities are likely to perform in different interest rate environments. Exhibit 10 shows the price relationship between the GNMA 8 and GNMA 13 over the period of January 1, 1984 through January 1, 1986. The price relationship between these securities was not linear over that period, but can be better represented by a slightly curved line. The degree of curvature in the line representing their price relationship increases significantly after the price of the GNMA 13 reaches par and becomes a premium. This indicates that the price volatility relationship between the GNMA 8 and GNMA 13 coupons changes at different price levels, and these changes become more rapid as the price of the GNMA 13 rises above par. The GNMA 13 becomes less and less volatile relative to the GNMA 8 as it trades at higher price levels, particularly in the premium area.

As was discussed before, the current level of interest rates will determine the extent of a borrower's incentive to prepay an existing high-rate mortgage and refinance the balance with a new, lower-rate loan. For older, low-rate mortgages, the current level of interest rates will determine the extent of a mortgagor's disincentive to pay off a relatively desirable loan. Current coupon securities, those priced just below par, are generally backed by mortgages recently originated at current market rates. Securities with coupons higher than the current coupon rate, therefore, are more likely to be prepaid than the current coupon, while securities with coupons below the current coupon are less likely to be prepaid.

EXHIBIT 10
Historical Price Relationship* GNMA 8 vs. GNMA 13

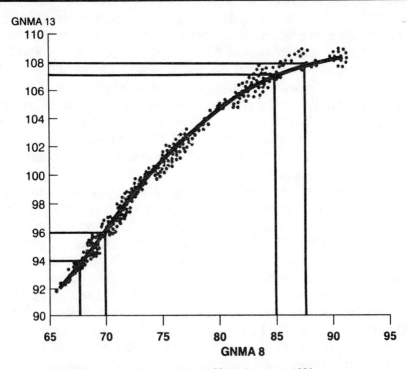

*Using daily prices from January 1, 1984 to January 1, 1986

The prepayment risk associated with current or higher coupon mortgage securities is in many ways analogous to that of a callable bond or any security with an implicit call option that is at or in the money. The risk that a mortgage security will prepay increases rapidly as the difference between the security's coupon and the current coupon increases, as the option to call the bonds at par becomes more in the money. The price volatility of a mortgage security, therefore, will reflect the market's changing assessment of this risk.

Regression analysis can be used to measure the impact of this prepayment risk on the price volatility of securities with coupon rates above or below the current coupon. Exhibit 11 shows

EXHIBIT 11
GNMA Relative Price Volatility Curve
Volatilities Estimated Relative to Current Coupon GNMA
(January 1, 1984–October 1, 1986)

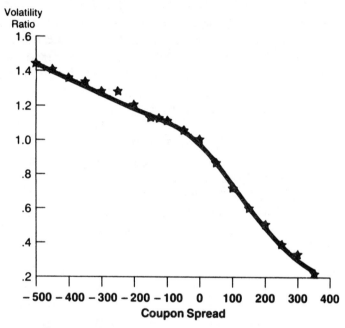

* Regression Estimates ("b")

the results of regressing the percentage price changes of GNMA securities with different coupon spreads versus the current coupon against the percentage price changes of the current coupon GNMA. As is clear from this graph, GNMAs with coupons that are below the current coupon have prices that are more volatile than the prices of the current and higher GNMA coupons (i.e., high relative price volatility ratios). Also, the relative price volatility curve shown in the exhibit is relatively flat for the discount coupons, but falls sharply for coupons at the current coupon level and higher. As interest rates fall and the difference between a security's coupon and the current coupon becomes greater, the prepayment risk associated with the security increases substantially as the implicit call option becomes in the money. The deeper in the money the call option becomes, the less volatile is its price with respect to the current coupon GNMA.

While the graph in Exhibit 11 reflects the price volatilities of different GNMA coupons relative to the price volatility of the current coupon GNMA, it is also useful to be able to compare the price volatilities of mortgage-backed securities relative to other types of fixed income securities. Since duration is the measure of interest rate sensitivity most commonly used for fixed income securities, it is appropriate to develop a measure for mortgage securities that can be directly related to duration. It is possible to calculate an "implied duration" for mortgage securities by estimating the price volatility of a given GNMA (such as the current coupon) relative to another fixed income instrument for which the standard duration measure is meaningful, such as the 10-year Treasury. Given the duration of the 10-year Treasury and the observed historical price volatility of the Treasury relative to the GNMA, it is possible to calculate what the duration of the GNMA would have to be to produce the observed relative price volatility, given the following relationship:

$$\begin{array}{c}\text{Relative Price Volatility}\\\text{of the 10-year Treasury}\\\text{to the Current Coupon GNMA}\end{array} = \frac{\text{Duration of}\ \text{10-year Treasury}}{\begin{array}{c}\text{Implied Duration of}\\\text{Current Coupon GNMA}\end{array}}$$

Once the implied duration of the current coupon GNMA has been calculated, the implied durations of GNMAs with higher or lower coupons can be determined from the relative price volatility curve show in Exhibit 11. The volatility estimates on this curve are indexed to the benchmark GNMA, the current coupon, which was assigned a value of one. By assigning the benchmark GNMA a value equal to its implied duration and rescaling the curve accordingly, it is possible to create an implied duration curve for GNMAs with coupons above or below the current coupon. Exhibit 12 illustrates the GNMA implied duration curve estimated over the time period of April 1986 through October 1986.

Implied durations are based on actual market data and, therefore, the market's implicit valuation of the prepayment option on these securities. Portfolio managers can use implied durations to

EXHIBIT 12
GNMA Implied Duration/Coupon Curve*
(April 1, 1986–October 1, 1986)

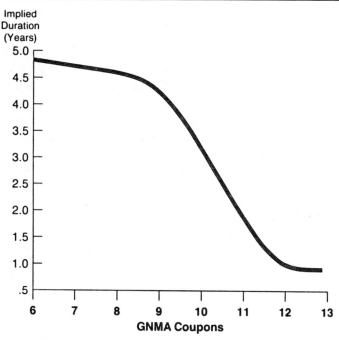

Implied
Duration
(Years)

GNMA Coupons

* Closing Prices as of October 17, 1986.

compare the true interest rate sensitivities of mortgage securities to those of other fixed income securities and to manage more effectively the interest rate exposure of any portfolio that includes mortgage securities.

Options Pricing Theory

A mortgage is really a hybrid security consisting of a long position in an annuity (the mortgage's scheduled principal and interest payments) and a short position in a call option on the annuity (the borrower's option to prepay the mortgage at any time). The risks and returns from holding the mortgage can be partitioned and allocated to the two parts. The option entitles the borrower to retire some or all of the annuity at any point in time. It is a "call" option because prepayment is tantamount to purchasing the annuity from the investor (who is effectively short the call) for a predetermined exercise price of approximately par.

The annuity portion of a mortgage is subject to the same risks as a portfolio of Treasuries, the only uncertainty being due to changes in the level and shape of the yield curve. The option portion of the mortgage presents a more complex pricing problem. An option's market value depends on the market value of the underlying cash asset, a relationship that is non-linear.

Exhibit 13 shows two curves relating option value to portfolio value. The upper curve depicts the option value if mortgage borrowers could be expected to exercise "rationally." This curve is bounded below at zero. It rises with the value of the mortgage's

EXHIBIT 13
Actual and Rational Prepayment Options

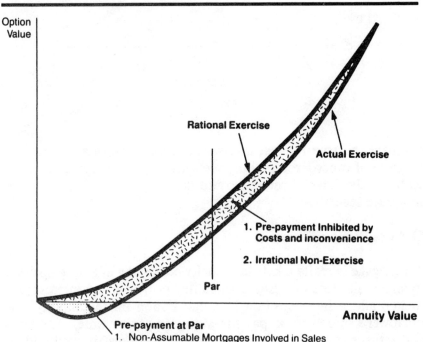

annuity portion. At high values of the annuity, the option value moves one for one with the annuity value. In this range, the option is said to be "in the money" because the market value of the annuity exceeds the exercise price. At low values of the annuity, the option is out of the money. Its exercise at this point would actually bring a net loss since the value of the asset received would be less than the exercise price.

The lower curve depicts what actually happens in the mortgage market. Borrowers do not always prepay "rationally." For various reasons, they may prepay when the option is out of the money, when the current level of mortgage rates is higher than the rates on their mortgages. Similarly, they may not prepay when it is clearly advantageous to do so, when current rates on new mortgages are well below the rate on the old mortgage. Such behavior implies that the market value of the prepayment option is consistently below the value of a "rational" option price. Since the mortgage investor has sold the option to the borrower, the combined value of the mortgage annuity and the option is higher than it would be if prepayments were always made on rational economic grounds.

The total value of the mortgage consists of the annuity portion less the option portion. This is shown in Exhibit 14. The upper curve in this figure depicts the response of the annuity portion to interest rates.

The lower curve gives the total value of the mortgage, annuity less option, at different interest rate levels. The mortgage value departs significantly from the annuity curve as rates decline. This is the region of "negative convexity" which is due to the prepayment option moving more deeply into the money. There is actually an upper bound on the mortgage value as rates decline. It is reached when the option's value begins to move one for one with the value of the annuity.

The difference between the annuity and mortgage curves in Exhibit 14 is related to the variability over time of the yield on current coupon mortgages which is, in turn, related to the general variability of interest rate levels (i.e., interest rate volatility). Higher volatility induces a larger difference between mortgage value and annuity value at low levels of interest rates. This is due to the fact that an option's value is positively related to the volatility

---

EXHIBIT 14
Annuity Value and Mortgage Value

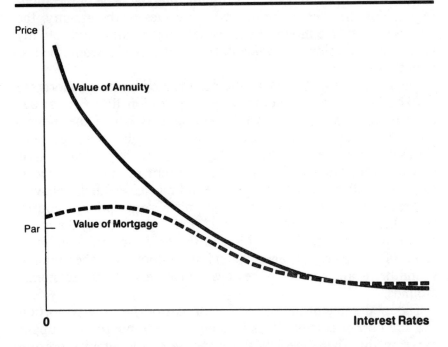

of the underlying asset. Since the value of the prepayment call option is deducted from the annuity's value when calculating the mortgage's value, the mortgage will be worth less when interest rates are volatile relative to, say, otherwise equivalent Treasuries. An increase in the variability of interest rates, therefore, will cause mortgage yields to widen with respect to Treasuries, even in the absence of a change in the level of interest rates or in expected prepayment rates.

Considering the performance characteristics of mortgage securities within an options pricing framework offers valuable insight into some of the more subtle factors that influence their performance, such as interest rate volatility and the slope of the yield curve. While the prepayment option in a mortgage security is in many ways analogous to a pure call option, the irrationality in the exercise of the prepayment makes it far more difficult to value. Fundamental to any valuation of the prepayment option, therefore, is an estimate of the sensitivity of prepayments to changes in interest rates.

Total Return Analysis

A yield to maturity assumes that a security will be held to maturity and all of the security's cash flows will be reinvested at the security's internal rate of return. Because of these assumptions, this measure has limited value for investors who intend to sell the security before maturity and for those who wish to see the effects of changes in interest rates on the value of their holdings. Total return analysis measures all of the factors that can affect the value of an investor's position as of the end of a specified holding period:

- coupon income;

- recovery of any purchase discount or premium;

- reinvestment income earned on any principal and interest payments received during the holding period;

- and any price appreciation or depreciation on the security balance remaining at the end of the horizon.

Yields to maturity often provide misleading information about the relative values of different mortgage securities. Total returns calculated using reasonable assumptions usually produce better insights into the risk/return profiles of the securities. As an example, on July 29, 1986, the GNMA 11 had the highest yield to maturity (using projected CPRs) of any other GNMA (see Exhibit 15), and on this basis the GNMA 11 appeared very attractive. On a total return basis, however, the GNMA 11 did not appear nearly as attractive.[10]

Because the prepayment rate on the GNMA 11 was expected to increase by more if interest rates fell than it would decrease if interest rates rose, the GNMA 11 would underperform other GNMA securities if rates did anything but remain stable. Exhibit 16 shows

[10] See Susan Mara Hunter, "The Risk of Owning GNMA 11s in the Current Market," New York: Goldman Sachs Mortgage Securities Research, August 1986.

EXHIBIT 15
GNMA Projected Yields (As of 7/29/86)

Coupon	Price	Rem. Term	Projected* CPR	Projected Yield (CBE)
7.5	92-28	245	6.0	8.95
8	94-12	245	6.0	9.17
8.5	95-19	259	6.0	9.43
9	97-01	294	5.0	9.63
9.5	99-20	291	5.5	9.69
10	102-26	332	4.0	9.70
10.5	105-22	348	4.0	9.77
11	106-01	330	10.0	9.83
11.5	106-05	325	25.0	9.17
12	106-22	336	30.0	9.01
12.5	106-26	324	37.0	8.74
13	107-12	322	40.0	8.58
13.5	107-29	321	40.0	8.76
14	108-08	310	45.0	8.37

* Projected CPR assuming a stable interest rate scenario over the remaining term of the security.

1-year total returns on GNMA 8, 9, 11, 11.5, and 12 coupons under three interest rate scenarios: stable rates, rates rising by 100 basis points, and rates falling by 100 basis points. The prepayment rates on the securities were assumed to start at the beginning prepayment rate and to change linearly over the holding period to the terminal prepayment rate shown for each scenario. The securities were assumed to be sold at the end of the holding period at their beginning yields to maturity, or that yield plus or minus 100 basis points, depending on the interest rate scenario. The securities' cash flows were assumed to be reinvested at 6.5 percent under all scenarios.

In order to evaluate the risk/reward tradeoffs of owning the securities under different interest rate scenarios, it is helpful to calculate expected averages of the total returns, weighting the return

EXHIBIT 16
Total Returns

Coupon	Price	Rem. Term	Beg. CPR	CPR			1-Year Total Returns(CBE)[*]		
				-100	0	+100	-100	0	+100
8	94-12	245	6.0	6.5	6.0	5.5	13.61	9.00	4.46
9	97-01	294	5.0	5.5	5.0	4.5	14.61	9.44	4.37
11	106-01	330	10.0	30.0	10.0	6.0	8.10	9.56	6.22
11.5	106-05	325	25.0	37.0	25.0	7.0	8.35	8.80	10.60
12	106-22	336	30.0	40.0	30.0	10.0	8.26	8.61	11.49

[*] Using a 6.5 reinvestment rate under all scenarios.

of each security in a given scenario by the probability of that scenario's occurrence. Exhibit 17 shows several of these weighted returns, with probabilities somewhat arbitrarily assigned to each interest rate scenario to reflect different biases or expectations about future market conditions. The stable scenario assumes that there is

EXHIBIT 17
Weighted Total Returns (CBE)

Coupon	Neutral	Stable	Bullish	Bearish
8	9.02	9.02	10.17	7.88
9	9.47	9.47	10.76	8.20
11	7.96	8.36	8.00	7.53
11.5	9.25	9.14	9.03	9.59
12	9.45	9.24	9.16	9.96

Neutral = 33% -100; 33% 0; 33% +100
Stable = 25% -100; 50% 0; 25% +100
Bullish = 50% -100; 25% 0; 25% +100
Bearish = 25% -100; 50% 0; 50% +100

a 50 percent chance of rates remaining stable, a 25 percent chance of rates rising, and a 25 percent chance of rates falling. The bullish scenario assumes that there is a 50 percent chance of rates falling, a 25 percent chance of rates remaining stable, and a 25 percent chance of rates rising. The bearish scenario assumes that there is a 50 percent chance of rates rising, a 25 percent chance of rates remaining stable, and a 25 percent chance of rates falling. The neutral scenario assumes that there is an equally likely chance of rates rising, falling, or remaining stable.

Under each of these weighted scenarios, the GNMA 11 does worse than all of the other securities shown. While the GNMA 11 outperforms the other securities if there is a 100 percent chance of rates remaining stable, as long as there is any significant chance of rates either rising or falling, the 11 underperforms the other securities; the risk of poor performance if rates change overwhelms the slight advantage the 11 has if rates remain stable. The yields to maturity on these securities did not capture the sensitivity of their returns to changes in interest rates. Total return analysis provides a better indication of how the securities are likely to perform in different interest rate environments.

VI.   CONCLUSION

In recent years, the mortgage securities market has become increasingly complex in terms of the types of mortgages created, the structures of the securities issued, and the methods of analysis used to assess the value of these instruments. To be successful in this market environment, it is essential that an investor have a good grasp of the structural characteristics of the securities as well as of their underlying mortgage collateral. It is important to recognize how the various features can affect the valuation of these instruments, particularly since market participants are increasingly basing their evaluations on the specific characteristics of an individual mortgage pool. In addition, one must be familiar with the different forms of analysis available in order to understand how the market is likely to evaluate these securities and to assess how they might perform under different market conditions.

The mortgage market will probably continue to grow more complex over the next several years as market participants develop new products, structures, and analytical techniques to take advantage of the immense profit opportunities in this market. These opportunities will undoubtedly continue to produce an environment conducive to both innovation and change.

ARTICLE 9

GRAHAM LORD is a Manager in the Economics Department at Mathtech (Mathematica) and is also Adjunct Professor at the Graduate School of Business of New York University. Dr. Lord was formerly a member of Morgan Stanley's Fixed Income Analytical Research Department after having worked as an actuary at Metropolitan Life. Prior to that he was Professor of Actuarial Science, Statistics and Operations Research at Université Laval, Québec.

DAVID P. JACOB is a vice president in the Fixed Income Research Department at Morgan Stanley & Co. where his responsibilities include the research and development of fixed income products and risk management techniques. During the past four years at Morgan Stanley he has done research in the areas of futures, options, mortgage-backed securities, callable bonds, high yield bonds and asset liability management for insurance companies. He has a BA in mathematics from Queens College and received his MA in mathematics, MBA in finance, and advanced certificate in accounting from New York University.

JAMES A. TILLEY is a Principal in the Fixed Income Division at Morgan Stanley & Co. He heads a group of coverage officers who manage Morgan Stanley's overall relationship with the investment organizations of large insurance companies and a group of professionals who provide consulting services to insurance companies regarding investment strategy and asset/liability management. He has published numerous papers and articles on asset/liability management, the valuation of interest-sensitive cash flows, and methods to manage investment risk. Mr. Tilley has a Ph.D. in Physics from Harvard University. He is a Fellow of the Society of Actuaries and has served on its Board of Governors.

THE VALUATION OF FIXED INCOME SECURITIES WITH CONTINGENT CASH FLOWS

Graham Lord, Ph.D.
Manager
Mathtech, Inc.

David P. Jacob
Research Manager
Fixed Income Analytical Research
Morgan Stanley and Co., Inc.

and

James A. Tilley, Ph.D., F.S.A.
Principal
Fixed Income Analytical Research
Morgan Stanley and Co., Inc.

This article addresses the central problem of security valuation—the pricing or valuation of a stream of contingent cash flows or claims. Any financial instrument, or indeed any financial institution, can be thought of as a stream of cash flows. For a bond, the coupon and the principal payments comprise the cash flow stream.

For a European option, a payment at the exercise date equal to the option's intrinsic value at that time is the only cash flow. For a financial institution, a key component of net worth is determined by analyzing the stream of net cash flows that results from deducting liability cash flows from asset cash flows. Once the stream of cash flows can be priced, it is straightforward to analyze the price sensitivity of that stream with respect to changes in interest rates and thus to compute its duration, convexity and other indexes of interest rate sensitivity.[1]

In all but the simplest cases the values of the cash flows to be priced are explicity dependent on the value of one or more exogeneous variables. The value of an European option on a particular stock at a specific date is a function of the value of the underlying stock. The future cash flow of a callable bond is determined by the levels of future interest rates amongst other factors. For a complex instrument such as a mortgage-backed security the cash flow is dependent on a whole host of economic and demographic variables.

Though models for pricing contingent claims first appeared in the 1960s, it was the seminal paper of Black and Scholes[2] that provided the greatest stimulus to the work on theoretical pricing models. Black and Scholes developed a continuous-in-time and distribution-dependent model for valuing an European call option on a stock. Their model has been extended by others and applied to a variety of contingent claims including bonds and mortgage-backed securities.

Inherent in almost all these models are the following assumptions. Markets are frictionless in that there are no transaction costs or taxes, and securities are infinitely divisible. There are no institutional restrictions in that short sales are permitted. (The borrowing and the lending rates are identical.) There are no arbitrage opportunities in that all riskless securities have the same return per unit invested.

The preceding are also usually assumed in the alternative approaches which restrict trading to occur only at discrete points

---

[1] For definitions of the indexes see David P. Jacob, Graham Lord and James A. Tilley, *Price, Duration and Convexity of a Stream of Interest-Sensitive Cash Flows,* New York: Morgan Stanley Fixed Income Analytical Research, April 1986.

[2] Fischer Black and Myron Scholes, "The Pricing of Options and Corporate Liabilities," *Journal of Political Economy,* 81, no. 3, May/June 1973, pp 637–54.

in time. Common to a number of the latter models is a binomial structure describing the security price process. The binomial model, originally suggested by Sharpe[3] and first expanded upon by Cox, Ross and Rubinstein[4] has been adapted to pricing debt options and underlies approaches developed for applications particularly in investment banking and in the insurance industry. These various attempts have shortcomings in that they violate put-call parity, or do not guarantee an arbitrage-free environment, or produce negative interest rates, or imply the existence of stochastically dominant securities, or otherwise do not model reasonable yield curve behavior.

In this article a methodology for discounting or valuing interest-sensitive cash flows of fixed income instruments is developed which overcomes the inadequacies of these earlier models. Section I reviews some preliminary definitions and fundamental properties. The theoretical framework for valuing path-independent as well as path-dependent cash flows is presented in Section II. Section III discusses the application of the model not only to specific generic assets but also to certain interest-sensitive insurance products. The application considered in detail is to the pricing of put bonds. A summary is presented in Section IV.

I. FIXED AND CERTAIN CASH FLOWS

The simplest and hence the most fundamental cash flow to value is that of a zero-coupon bond. If the term to maturity of the zero-coupon bond is n periods and its par value is $1, then its price[5] will be the n-period discount factor $B^{(n)}$ which is given by:

$$\text{Price} = B^{(n)} \equiv \left(\frac{1}{1 + r^{(n)}}\right)^n \tag{1}$$

[3] William F. Sharpe, *Investments,* Englewood Cliffs, N.J.: Prentice Hall, 1978.

[4] John C. Cox, Stephen A. Ross, and Mark Rubinstein, "Options Pricing: A Simplified Approach," *Journal of Financial Economics,* September 1979, pp. 229–263.

[5] Price, present value and market value are terms used interchangeably throughout.

From this equation it can be seen that the spot rate of interest, $r^{(n)}$, expressed on a per-period basis, is the yield to maturity of the zero-coupon bond. Should the par value be equal to $CF^{(n)}$ rather than \$1, the price of the zero will be the product of $CF^{(n)}$ times the discount factor: the price will be $CF^{(n)} \times B^{(n)}$. A more complex cash flow stream, where the value is $CF^{(n)}$ at time periods $t = 0, 1, \ldots, n$, can be decomposed into the sum of zero-coupon bonds of par value $CF^{(0)}, CF^{(1)}, CF^{(2)}, \ldots, CF^{(n)}$ corresponding to maturities of $0, 1, 2, \ldots, n$ periods, respectively. The present value of the general stream will then be the sum of the present values of the component zero-coupon bonds:

$$\text{Price} = \sum_{t=0}^{n} CF^{(t)} \cdot B^{(t)} \tag{2}$$

For a par bond (par = \$1) with coupon $c^{(n)}$ and whose maturity is in n periods, Equation (2) becomes the following:

$$1 = B^{(n)} + c^{(n)} \cdot \sum_{t=1}^{n} B^{(t)} \tag{3}$$

Equation (3) provides a relationship between the yield (coupon rate) of a par bond and the yields on zero-coupon bonds, the latter being generally referred to as spot rates. For each possible term from 1 through n periods, the corresponding par bond will define an equation of the form of (3). The resulting system of n equations establishes a relationship between all the par bond yields, known collectively as the yield curve, and all the zero-coupon yields, known collectively as the term structure of interest rates. The system permits the term structure to be derived from the yield curve and vice versa.[6]

Durations and Convexities of Fixed and Certain Cash Flows

The time-weighting and the time-squared-weighting of the present values in Equation (2) leads to the following definitions of duration and convexity that are commonly employed as measures of the price sensitivity of fixed and certain cash flows streams to changes in interest rates.

$$\text{Duration} = [\Sigma t \cdot CF(t) \cdot B(t)] / \text{Price} \tag{4}$$

$$\text{Convexity} = [\Sigma t^2 \cdot CF(t) \cdot B(t)] / \text{Price} \tag{5}$$

[6] In practice, spot rates derived from the yield curve can differ from the yields on traded zero-coupon bonds.

Duration measures a security's price sensitivity to interest rates; and convexity measures the sensitivity of a security's duration to interest rates.

It is important to realize that these definitions are inappropriate when the cash flows are interest-sensitive: they will give distorted measures of price movement. To distinguish them from more general definitions the values from Equations (4) and (5) are often identified as the "Macaulay" duration and convexity. (Note Macaulay's own definition used yield-to-maturity in place of the spot rates.)

II. INTEREST-SENSITIVE CASH FLOWS

In order to value a stream of interest-sensitive cash flows, one has to make assumptions as to how interest rates change as time passes. This includes an assumption about how volatile the level of rates will be and how the term structure will change in shape. It will be assumed that interest movements can be closely approximated by a discrete binomial process represented by the lattice shown in Exhibit 1.

Discrete points of time are marked on the horizontal axis. The periods can be years, half-years, quarters, months, or anything else desired. The cash flows are assumed to occur only at these points in time, not between any of the periods. With each node in the lattice is associated an entire spot rate curve—the yields to maturity for all zero-coupon bonds. The term structure at any one point in time jumps to one of two others at the next point in time—either to the "up" state or to the "down" state. The lattice is connected because the two paths "up, down" and "down, up" emanating from any one node always lead to a single node two periods hence. A graphic representation of the volatilies of interest rates is the vertical spacings of the nodes.

Path-Independent Cash Flows

A stream of interest-sensitive cash flows is *path-independent* if each component in the stream may depend on interest rates prevailing at the time the cash flow occurs but does not depend on the interest rates of any previous period. A typical European option is

---

EXHIBIT 1
Lattice of Interest Rates

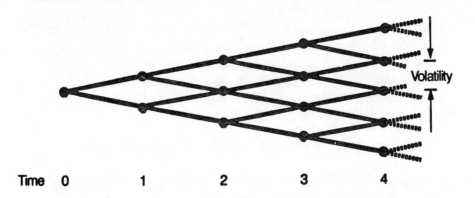

Time   0   1   2   3   4

an example. When the cash flows are a function only of the nodes at which they occur and not of the paths followed to reach those nodes, the present value problem can be solved by working backwards through the lattice. A calculation is required only for every node in the lattice, not every path. This is fortunate because the number of nodes grows as the square of the number of time periods whereas the number of paths through the lattice grows exponentially with the number of periods. However, the solution to the path-independent problem also shows how to solve the more general path-dependent problem.

The key to computing the present value of the entire lattice pattern of cash flows is to realize that one needs only to determine the procedure for a single vertex, and then merely repeat the calculation starting from the latest time period and work backwards one period at a time to the beginning of the earliest time period. Exhibit 2 shows a single vertex.

The node where the upper and lower branches join is labelled O, for "origin," the node at the end of the upper branch U for "up," and the node at the end of the lower branch D for "down." Let MV_U be the discounted value of U of all future cash flows occurring on the portion of the lattice emanating from node U. Similarly, let MV_D be the discounted value at node D of all future cash flows occurring on the portion of the lattice emanating from node D. Next, suppose that the cash flow occurring at node U is CF_U and

---

EXHIBIT 2
Determining the Present Value

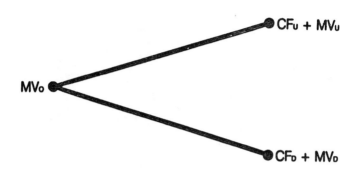

$CF_U + MV_U$

MV_O

$CF_D + MV_D$

that the cash flow occurring at node D is CF_D. Finally, let MV_O represent the present value at node O of all future cash flows occurring on the portion of the lattice emanating from node O. The problem is to express MV_O as a function of the variables MV_U, CF_U, MV_D, CF_D, and the term structure at nodes O, U, and D. The fundamental building blocks or discounting factors needed for the calculation are illustrated in Exhibit 3.

In a binomial model of interest rate movements, there are two factors at each node in the lattice. The "up factor" is a financial instrument that pays $1 one period from now if interest rates move to the up state and nothing if interest rates move to the down state. Conversely, the "down factor" pays $1 one period from now if interest rates move to the down state and nothing if interest rates move to the up state. The up factor is an elementary put option and the down factor is an elementary call option. Q_U will denote the price of the up factor and Q_D the price of the down factor. These prices are the present values of the simple payoff function depicted in Exhibit 3.

Assume for the moment the values of the factors are known throughout the lattice. Then MV_O can be determined by decomposing the cash flow and market value pattern at the U and D nodes into Q_U scaled by $(CF_U + MV_D)$ and Q_D scaled by $(CF_D + MV_D)$. This description is captured in Equation (6), and shown in Exhibit 2.

$$MV_O = (CF_U + MV_U) \cdot Q_U + (CF_D + MV_D) \cdot Q_D \qquad (6)$$

EXHIBIT 3
Fundamental Discounting Factors

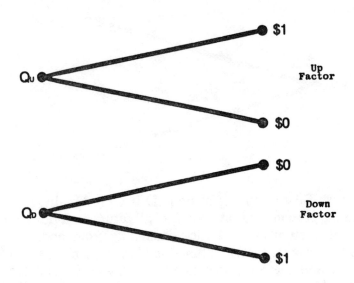

Determination of the Discounting Factors

This involves writing down equations that express the values of zero-coupon bonds in terms of the factors values. Exhibit 4 shows how a one-period zero-coupon bond is represented on the lattice—payoffs of \$1 one period hence, regardless of the final node. Because the price of the one-period zero-coupon bond at node O is $B_O^{(1)}$, Equation (6) implies:

$$B_O^{(1)} = 1 \cdot Q_U + 1 \cdot Q_D \qquad (7)$$

In a similar fashion, a two-period zero-coupon bond can be represented on the lattice as shown in Exhibit 5—payoffs of \$1 two periods hence regardless of the final node. Equation (6) applied twice yields an expression for $B_O^{(2)}$, the price of the two-period zero-coupon bond at the origin. The following equation represents the result of the two steps:

$$B_O^{(2)} = B_U^{(1)} \cdot Q_U + B_D^{(1)} \cdot Q_D \qquad (8)$$

EXHIBIT 4
Determining the Fundamental Discounting Factor Values

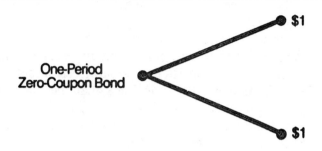

Equations (7) and (8) can be solved for the values of Q_U and Q_D that apply at node O. Continuation of the argument above, results in the following general equation, valid for any positive integer n:

$$B_O^{(n)} = B_U^{(n-1)} \cdot Q_U + B_D^{(n-1)} \cdot Q_D \qquad (9)$$

Equation (9) for $n = 1, 2 \ldots$ expresses relationships among the term structure at the nodes O, U, and D that must hold if a consistent

EXHIBIT 5
Determining the Fundamental Discounting Factor Values

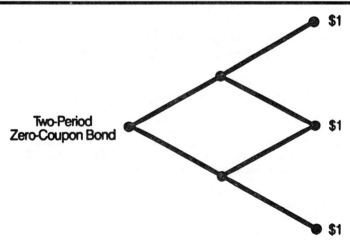

solution is to be found for Q_U and Q_D at node O. Corresponding equations at other nodes cause the term structures at nodes throughout the lattice to be similarly related. This grand system of equations is the mathematical statement of the relationships among security prices that must hold if single-period and multi-period riskless arbitrages are to be eliminated in a binomial lattice. Option pricing models constructed without forcing these relationships will lead to inaccurate and inconsistent option prices, a fact often uncovered for such models when one finds that the put-call parity relationship for European options is not satisfied.[7]

The values of the discounting factors at each node of the binomial lattice are then found by solving the above system by dynamic programming techniques subject to constraints guaranteeing non-negativity of the solutions and constraints ensuring the lack of security dominance. This requires "centering" the portion of the lattice emanating from a given node on the forward rates derived from the term structure at that node.

Path-Dependent Cash Flows

The variables P_U and P_D at node O are defined as follows:

$$P_U = Q_U \cdot (1 + r_O^{(1)})$$
$$P_D = Q_D \cdot (1 + r_O^{(1)})$$

$$(10)$$

where $r^{(1)}$ is the one-period spot rate at node O. It can be seen from Equations (1), (7), and (10) that P_U and P_D satisfy $P_U + P_D = 1$. Also, $P_U > O$ and $P_D > O$. P_U and P_D are called "arbitrage probabilities."[8] Equation (6) can be rewritten in the following very useful and intuitive form:

$$MV_O = P_U \cdot (CF_U + MV_U) \cdot B_O^{(1)} + P_D \cdot (CF_D + MV_D) \cdot B_O^{(1)} \quad (11)$$

---

[7] For a full discussion of the potential problems in pricing debt options, see R. Bookstaber, D. Jacob, and J. Langsam, *Pitfalls in Debt Option Models,* New York: Morgan Stanley Fixed Income Analytical Research, April 1986.

[8] These are independent of any subjective probabilities of rates moving up or down. For further discussion of these "probabilities" see R. Bookstaber, D. Jacob, and J. Langsam, "Arbitrage-Free Pricing of Options on Interest-Sensitive Instruments," *Advances in Futures and Options Research,* Vol. 1 Part A, 1986.

Equation (11) states that the present value at node O can be calculated by "probability-weighting" the present value at the nodes U and D and then discounting the result to node O using the one-period spot rate application at node O.

The preceding equation is the key to finding the present value of a stream of path-dependent cash flows. Ideally one would use Equation (11) to price all paths. However, as mentioned earlier, the number of paths grows exponentially with the number of periods. Thus, from a practical standpoint, the full set of paths through the lattice cannot be used and a sample must be drawn. The cash flows are then projected along each path in the sample and discounted to the origin using the sequence of one-period spot rates applicable to the path. These discounted values are realizations of the random variable whose expected value is the desired price. The expected value or weighted mean of the sample is then an estimator for the market value. The utilization of variance-reduction techniques in the selection of the sample results in price estimates within 0.5 percent of the exact value using samples of only 1000 to 2000 paths.

Exhibit 6 shows the prices derived from the model compared to the market prices for a selection of current coupon and discount bonds with maturities of seven and ten years. The yield curve used is the Treasury curve of April 16, 1986: 5.95 percent, 6.06 percent, 6.14 percent, 6.35 percent, 6.42 percent, 6.52 percent, 6.65 percent, 6.76 percent, 6.95 percent, 7.21 percent and 7.12 percent for terms of 90-days, 6 months, 1-year, 2, 3, 4, 5, 7, 10, 20, and 30

EXHIBIT 6
Comparison of Market and Model Prices

		Model Price	
Instrument	Market Price	Sample Size 512	Sample Size 1024
7-year zero	62.59	62.64	62.62
7-year current coupon, 6.76%	100.00	100.06	100.03
10-year zero	50.05	50.12	50.05
10-year current coupon, 6.95%	100.00	100.12	100.01

years, respectively. The length of a period in the model is taken to be a quarter of a year. For each of these fixed and certain, cash flow examples the error in the model price is well within the .5 percent bound and reduces with an increase in the size of the sample drawn from the 2^{40} lattice paths.

Duration and Convexities

Whereas Equations (4) and (5) are correct for calculating duration and convexity of fixed and certain streams of cash flow, they cannot be used for securities with path-dependent cash flows.

The generalization of these definitions of duration and convexity to the situation of interest-sensitive cash flows can be done by computing how the present value and duration of the cash flow stream change when the term structure of interest rates is changed. The more general equations given below can be shown to be equivalent to the more familiar definitions (4) and (5) when the cash flow is fixed and certain.

$$\text{Duration} = -\Delta \, \text{Price} / (\Delta i) \cdot \text{Price} \tag{12}$$

$$\text{Convexity} = -(\Delta \, \text{Duration} \cdot \text{Price}) / (\Delta i) \cdot \text{Price} \tag{13}$$

In the context of the lattice framework, this means that to calculate duration a new shocked term structure must be used to generate a new lattice and then a new price calculated using either the backward induction method for path-independent cash flows or the sampling method for path-dependent cash flows. Equation (12) can now be employed to find the duration. Similarly, to calculate convexity the initial term structure is shocked twice and the change in duration is calculated and used in Equation (13).

Exhibit 7 illustrates the above procedure applied to the examples of the previous exhibit for the larger sample size. Since the cash flows of each of the bonds considered are fixed and certain, the Macaulay duration and convexity as defined by Equations (4) and (5) serve as a correct basis for comparison.

The Appendix illustrates the method in detail for a simple floating rate note instrument. For that example the cash flows are path independent and so the floating rate note can be easily priced using Equation (6) directly. The Appendix also indicates how to proceed when the sampling procedure is employed.

EXHIBIT 7
Comparison of Durations and Convexities

Instrument	Macaulay		Model	
	Duration (years)	Convexity (years^2)	Duration (years)	Convexity (years^2)
7-year zero	7.00	49.00	6.99	48.98
7-year current coupon, 6.76%	5.68	38.69	5.68	36.67
10-year zero	10.00	100.00	9.99	100.14
10-year current coupon, 6.95%	7.34	65.01	7.33	65.08

III. APPLICATIONS

The pricing framework described in the prior section can be used to value any stream of cash flow that can be expressed as a function of time and interest rates. A fixed pay instrument's cash flow is independent of the level or path of interest rates. Examples of such instruments would be U.S. Treasury bills and notes, structured settlement liabilities of an insurance company, and fixed payments to a closed group of retirees. In terms of the lattice structure the cash flow would be identical at any given point in time regardless of the level of the node or path to the node. Although the methodology can be used to price fixed pay assets and liabilities and would produce the same values obtained by the standard cash flow discounting procedures, it would be inefficient for these situations. The real usefulness of this model is demonstrated when the cash flows vary with interest rates. This section describes the variety of instruments that can be analyzed with this model and then shows a detailed application of the model to put bonds.

The cash flow from floating rate assets and liabilities is by definition a function of interest rates. In its simplest form the cash flow from a floater is determined from one point on the yield curve which corresponds to the beginning of the period. An example would be a ten-year floating rate note that semi-annually pays the 6-month Treasury bill rate. The first payment is based on the initial 6-month rate, the payment at the end of the first year is based on the 6-month rate at mid-year, and so on. At reset points, that is, immediately following a cash flow, the price of this security would be par (credit considerations aside). The cash flow from this type of floater is a simple example of a security with interest sensitive but path independent payments. Complicated alternatives to this kind of floating rate mechanism can be easily constructed. (Another example is provided in the Appendix.) For example, the model described above could be used to price a security which, on an annual basis, pays 120 percent of the greater of the average 10-year Treasury note for the last four months or the average 6-month Treasury bill rate for the last four months. This floater's cash flow is not only interest sensitive and path dependent but also yield curve shape dependent. Unlike for fixed pay securities, conventional pricing methodology cannot be applied here.

Options on fixed income instruments are another example of securities with interest-sensitive cash flow. The European style option, which does not permit early exercise, will generate a cash flow based upon the difference between the option's strike price and the value of the underlying security on the expiration date of the option. The strike price is a fixed number, but the price of the underlying security is a function of interest rates. The cash flow generated from this type of option is interest-sensitive but path-independent. While there are several approaches to pricing options currently in use in the financial community, none of these appear to, under reasonable yield curve dynamics, eliminate the potential arbitrages across securities—a fundamental condition of option pricing. The model described in this article on the other hand assures that there is no arbitrage across securities and thus produces results that satisfy the so called put-call parity relationship.

The American style option, which allows the holder to exercise prior to the expiration date gives rise to cash flows that are both interest-sensitive and path-dependent. The path dependency can be seen as follows. Consider two paths of interest rates along one of which early exercise occurs and along the other of which exercise occurs at expiration. Now assume that at expiration date the paths coincide. The cash flow at that point for the path in which early exercise occurs will necessarily be 0. The cash flow at that point for the other path will be a function of the difference between the price of the underlying security and the strike price. Once the cash flow is described, the model can be used to correctly discount them and thereby value the option.

The insurance industry is replete with products whose cash flow is both interest-sensitive and path-dependent. For instance, consider the typical single premium deferred annuity (SPDA). The marketplace for this product demands that policyholders' accounts be credited at current intermediate term rates. On the other hand policyholders have the option to withdraw funds at book value less surrender charges, which may reflect the upfront expenses of the product, but almost never take into account declines in market value of the supporting assets. To the extent that the credited rate lags behind market rates, policyholder lapses will occur. The path dependency in the cash flow is the result of several factors. First, policyholder lapse rates are usually a function not just of today's interest rate environment but of rates in prior periods as well. Second, the balance in the insurer's accounts will differ if rates first rise and then fall or vice versa. Thus even if the lapse rate is the same at some point, the balance to which it is applied differs leading to differing cash flows. To value the SPDA liability one must build a lapse rate function to describe the cash flow and then apply the generalized discounting procedure.[9]

Put Bonds

A put bond is a bond with an option attached that gives the investor the right to put the bond back to the issuer at par on a specified expiration date. The most typical domestic put bond structure is a bond with a ten-year maturity and a European-style put option with five years to expiration. If interest rates drop, the investor will let the option expire unexercised since the bond will then be priced above par. If interest rates rise, the investor will exercise the put option receiving par for a bond selling at a discount.

From the standpoint of applying the model, the cash flow from the put bond can be viewed in two ways. First, the put bond can be decomposed into its two component securities, a fixed-pay bond

[9] For a further discussion see Chapter 9 by James A. Tilley in *Controlling Interest Rate Risk,* Robert B. Platt, ed. New York: John Wiley and Sons, Inc., 1986.

and a European put option on a fixed-pay bond. The cash flow from the bond is non-interest-sensitive and non-path-dependent and can be priced using the lattice. The European put option is an example of an interest-sensitive path-independent cash flow. The option's only cash flow occurs at the end of the fifth year. It will be equal to the strike price of the option less the value of the bond on that date. Since the bond's future cash flows are independent of prior rates, its value is path-independent. With this first view of the cash flow, the price, duration and convexity are determined for each of the two components and then combined.

Exhibit 8 shows the model values for a generic put bond at different yields.[10] The bond has a 10-year maturity with a European put at par in 5 years. Since the put option increases in value as interest rates rise, the put bond has a lower duration than a similar bond without the put. Moreover, the put option causes duration to drop more readily (as rates rise) than a bond without the put. Thus, its convexity is higher. However, as rates reach higher levels, the convexity of the put option becomes negative causing the put bond to be less convex than the non-putable bond. This happens because at very high rates the put bond begins to act more like a 5-year bond than a 10-year bond.

Rather than considering the cash flow from the put bond as though one had two securities, suppose one looks at the combined cash flow. When thought of as a unit the put bond's cash flow is, in fact, path-dependent.[11] Exhibit 9 shows the two ways in which the put bond's cash flow can be viewed.

For the first 4½ years of the bond's life, the cash flow is non-interest-sensitive. Then at the end of year 5, the cash flow will be either the strike price of the option plus a coupon payment or simply a coupon payment. After the end of year 5 the cash flow will depend upon whether or not the put option is exercised. This

---

[10] There was a large flurry of put bond issues at the end of 1984. Since then rates have dropped significantly making the associated put options essentially worthless and causing the bonds to trade as if there were no put options. Since the intent of this example is not to demonstrate relative value but to show how the cash flow model can be used, a generic issue is used to illustrate the effects of the options.

[11] This is because the fixed pay bond matures after the expiration date of the put option.

EXHIBIT 8
Price, Duration, and Convexity
10-Year Bond with 5-Year European Put
9.0% Coupon, Strike at 100

Yield on Bond Without Put	Price			Duration			Convexity		
	Bond Without Put	Put	Bond With Put	Bond Without Put (years)	Put (years)	Bond With Put (years)	Bond Without Put (years²)	Put (years²)	Bond With Put (years²)
7.0%	$114.21	$1.10	$115.31	7.0	−72.6	6.3	61	2738	86
7.5	110.42	1.48	111.90	7.0	−61.6	6.1	60	1746	82
8.0	106.80	2.01	108.81	6.9	−52.5	5.8	59	1073	78
8.5	103.32	2.49	105.82	6.9	−47.4	5.6	59	695	74
9.0	100.00	3.13	103.13	6.8	−38.8	5.4	58	417	69
9.5	96.82	3.75	100.56	6.7	−34.1	5.2	57	235	64
10.0	93.77	4.33	98.10	6.7	−30.4	5.0	57	106	59
10.5	90.85	5.04	95.88	6.6	−26.6	4.9	56	7	54
11.0	88.05	5.68	93.73	6.6	−23.5	4.7	55	−68	48

EXHIBIT 9
Decomposition of a Put Bond

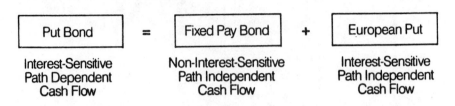

Put Bond	=	Fixed Pay Bond	+	European Put
Interest-Sensitive Path Dependent Cash Flow		Non-Interest-Sensitive Path Independent Cash Flow		Interest-Sensitive Path Independent Cash Flow

can be seen in Exhibit 10, where the cash flow at the middle node at the end of 5½ years will depend upon rates in the prior period. Whether one prices the cash flow via the components or as a unit, the value will be the same.

IV. SUMMARY

Pricing fixed and certain cash flows is straightforward. With the increased volatility of interest rates, and the proliferation of securities whose cash flow is not only uncertain but correlated with the current level, and, in some cases, the prior history of rates, the traditional valuation method of discounting cash flows is incorrect.

To value such securities, a generalized pricing framework has been developed that is consistent with term structure theory and arbitrage pricing, the basis for valuing options. Using this approach, all securities whose cash flow can be described as a function of

EXHIBIT 10
Put Option Cash Flow Diagram

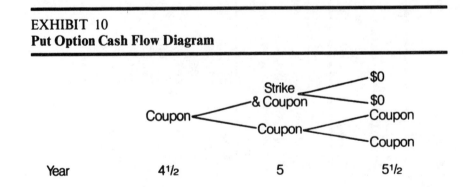

Year	4½	5	5½

interest rates can be priced. Moreover, with a pricing model in hand, one can compute durations and convexities, which are critical for the proper management of today's complicated assets and liabilities.

APPENDIX

A Simple Pricing Example: The Case of a Floating Rate Note.

The techniques described in Section II will now be applied to price a floating rate note whose term is 1½ years. Its rate is reset every 6 months to equal the new 6 month rate effective at that point in time.

Adherence to the binomial process implies there will be two possible interest rate environments or states of the world at the end of six months, three states after one year and four states at the end of one-and-one-half years. The spot rate curves generated for this example are shown in Exhibit 11. The initial yield curve, equal to 7.65 percent, 7.84 percent, and 8.22 percent (bond equivalent) for terms of six months, one year and one-and-one-half years, respectively, will change in structure as determined by the volatility assumptions taken and the arbitrage-free conditions imposed. The first component of each vector is the 6-month spot rate, the second component the 12-month spot rate and the third component the

EXHIBIT 11
Term Structure (Bond Equivalent Spot Rates)

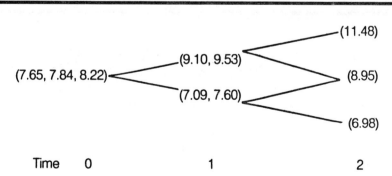

| Time | 0 | 1 | 2 |

18-month spot rate, all on a bond equivalent basis. Only those rates whose terms fall within the one-and-one-half year total period are shown.

The floating rate note's cash flow at each attainable state during the 1½ year period is given in Exhibit 12.

The values of the discounting factors are derived by means of Equations (7) and (8). For example, if Q_U and Q_D are the up and the down values at the origin of the lattice, then the equations that hold are:

$$Q_U + Q_D = \frac{1}{1.03825}$$

$$\frac{Q_U}{1.0455} + \frac{Q_D}{1.03545} = \frac{1}{1.079933}$$

Here 3.825 percent, 4.550 percent and 3.545 percent are equal to one half of the bond equivalent rates of 7.65 percent, 9.10 percent and 7.09 percent. (The number 1.079933 is equal to the reciprocal of the annual effective one-year rate. In terms of the notation of Equation (1) it is $B^{(2)}$.) The solution of the simultaneous equations above is $Q_U = .45445$ and $Q_D = .50871$. The other discounting factors have been similarly derived and are shown in Exhibit 13.

Now, the asset can be priced by discounting back through the lattice period by period employing recursively Equations (10) and (11). At each node, the market value of the remaining possible cash flows is determined. For example, to determine the market value at

EXHIBIT 12
Cash Flows

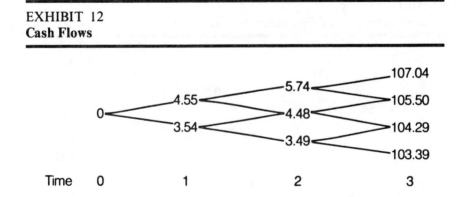

| Time | 0 | 1 | 2 | 3 |

EXHIBIT 13
One Period Discounting Factors

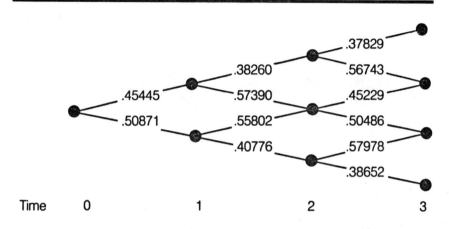

| Time | 0 | 1 | 2 | 3 |

the uppermost node after one year has elapsed (time equal to 2 periods) Equation (11) gives:

$$(107.04 \cdot 0.37829) + (105.50 \cdot 0.56743) = 100.36.$$

Then this present value of $100.36 plus the cash flow of $5.74, i.e., a total of $106.10, is the (rounded) present value after one year of all future and current cash flows which stem from the uppermost node.

The last recursion made in the lattice is from the end to the beginning of the first six-month period. The final market value thus derived of $100.98 is the price of the floating rate note.

Exhibit 14 shows for each node of the lattice the present values of future cash flows plus current payments. An alternate way by which the price of the asset could have been calculated would have been to sample paths through the lattice, and then, for each path, to discount the resulting stream of cash flows by the successive one-period spot rates back to the origin of the lattice. For each segment of a path there is an associated arbitrage probability defined by Equation (10). The product of these probabilities for the path gives, relative to the other paths chosen, the appropriate weight to be used in determining the expected value of the discounted stream.

EXHIBIT 14
Present Values of Current and Future Cash Flows

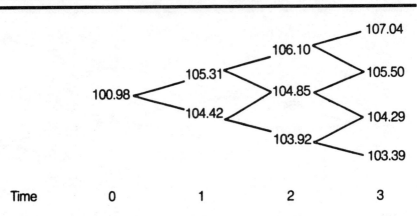

| Time | 0 | 1 | 2 | 3 |

To illustrate the latter method, the price of the note will be recalculated by sampling paths in the lattice. Since there is a total of only eight paths, all will be used. The first path followed rises along the upper boundary of the lattice and results in cash flows of $4.55, $5.74 and $107.04. The path is identified as "up-up-up." The one-period spot rates to be used for discounting along this path are 7.65 percent, 9.10 percent, and 11.48 percent (bond equivalent). The present value of this up-up-up stream is then:

$$((\$107.04 \cdot (1.0574)^{-1} + \$5.74) \cdot (1.0455)^{-1} + \$4.55)$$
$$\cdot (1.03825)^{-1} = \$102.93$$

Exhibit 15 gives the present values for all the paths, together with the associated path arbitrage probabilities and, in the final column, the calculation of the asset's current market price.

Since the sampling is complete (all paths were taken) it is not surprising that the prices obtained by the two methods are identical (apart from rounding).

When the number of periods is large and when the cash flows are path-dependent, it becomes necessary to draw a subset from the universe of all paths through the lattice and to subsequently value, as illustrated above, the interest-sensitive cash flow for the subset.

By employing Equations (12) and (13), the duration and the convexity of the note are found to be 0 years and 0 years-squared,

EXHIBIT 15
Price Determination by Weighted Paths

Path	Path Present Value	Percentage Weight	Weighted Present Value
up-up-up	$102.93	7.55%	$ 7.77
up-up-down	101.59	11.32	11.50
up-down-up	101.53	13.38	13.58
up-down-down	100.47	14.93	15.00
down-up-down	100.43	16.10	16.17
down-up-up	101.51	14.42	14.64
down-down-up	100.40	13.38	13.43
down-down-down	99.59	8.92	8.88
		100.00%	$100.97

respectively. These results could have been alternatively deduced by noting that since the one-period spot rates are used for the discounting, the present value of the asset is consequently insensitive to a one-time shape-preserving shock of the initial term structure: the duration and the convexity are zero. For the more common floating rate note where the coupon for a six-month period is set equal to the six-month rate at the beginning of the period, the duration equals one half a year and the convexity is .25 years-squared.

ARTICLE 10

GARY LATAINER, a Vice-President in the Fixed Income Research Group, is a fixed income portfolio strategist at Morgan Stanley. In addition to his responsibilities for developing portfolio strategies for institutional customers, he is also responsible for the group's portfolio optimization products.

Prior to joining Morgan Stanley in 1982, Gary was a Portfolio Manager at the Equitable Life Assurance Society of the United States. He holds an M.B.A. in finance from New York University and undergraduate degrees in economics and statistics, also from New York University.

DAVID P. JACOB is a vice president in the Fixed Income Research Department at Morgan Stanley & Co. where his responsibilities include the research and development of fixed income products and risk management techniques. During the past four years at Morgan Stanley he has done research in the areas of futures, options, mortgage-backed securities, callable bonds, high yield bonds and asset liability management for insurance companies. He has a BA in mathematics from Queens College and received his MA in mathematics, MBA in finance, and advanced certificate in accounting from New York University.

MODERN TECHNIQUES FOR ANALYZING VALUE AND PERFORMANCE OF CALLABLE BONDS

Gary D. Latainer
Vice President
Fixed Income Analytical Research
Morgan Stanley and Co., Inc.

and

David P. Jacob
Research Manager
Fixed Income Analytical Research
Morgan Stanley and Co., Inc.

Call features can significantly affect the performance of a fixed income portfolio. Investors in callable bonds receive higher nominal yields relative to non-callable bonds, but are faced with uncertain cash flow patterns due to the call option that they have written to the issuer. Since most corporate debt is callable, a thorough understanding of the performance characteristics of these bonds is essential for fixed income managers.

Investors traditionally have evaluated callable bonds by comparing them to non-callable bonds having either the same maturity or a maturity of the first call date. If interest rates decline, a callable bond will underperform a non-callable bond of the same maturity, but will outperform a non-callable bond maturing on the first call date. The reverse is true if rates rise. This information, while useful, is, in our view, insufficient from a portfolio management perspective. It does not, for example, tell a manager whether a particular callable bond represents a good value. Furthermore, it does not tell the manager the interest rate sensitivity of a particular callable bond and therefore does not allow a manager seeking a specific duration target to determine the best bonds for meeting that target.

This article seeks to address these issues by providing a framework for valuing and analyzing the performance characteristics of callable bonds. The framework allows us to properly price, measure the duration of, and, most importantly, determine the return profile for any callable bond. The portfolio manager can then examine the return profile of a bond to determine whether it is consistent with portfolio objectives. Within this framework, investors can compare any two bonds, regardless of how dissimilar their call features may be.

The article is divided into six sections. Section I provides an overview of the valuation of callable bonds. Any callable bond can be decomposed into a non-callable bond plus a call option on this non-callable bond that the investor has written to the issuer. By using option pricing methodology to value the call option, investors can determine a fair value for the callable bond. Section II focuses on the duration properties of callable bonds. The call feature affects the responsiveness of a callable bond to interest rate changes and therefore its duration. Section III translates the valuation and duration analysis of the first two sections into a total return context. We analyze the return profiles of typical callable bonds in the marketplace and also analyze the impact of mispricings on the return profiles. In general, a callable bond will outperform a non-callable bond of equivalent duration when interest rates are relatively stable, but will underperform such a bond when rates either rise or fall by a sufficient amount. In Section IV, we test the real world applicability of our framework by examining whether trading opportunities have been present that could have provided investors with the possibility of earning incremental returns from identifying mispriced callable bonds. While not present at all times, such opportunities are available sufficiently often to make searching for them a worthwhile exercise for the portfolio manager. Section V discusses a number of portfolio management applications for callable bonds, including their use in immunized bond portfolios. Finally, Section VI concludes the article.

We wish to emphasize several points regarding the focus of this article. Firstly, it is not an article on option pricing. Option pricing theory is discussed only to the extent necessary for the reader to understand the factors affecting a callable bond's value. Secondly, many bonds have a number of refunding provisions that interact to influence the bond's value. We address only the issue of call for refunding purposes. The impact of possible cash call, sinking fund provisions, and maintenance and replacement funds are not discussed in this article. Finally, while the article is presented mainly from the viewpoint of the active manager concerned with total return, many other fixed income managers should find this article applicable.

I. THE VALUATION OF CALLABLE BONDS

The tremendous volatility of interest rates in recent years has resulted in the availability of a wide range of coupons in the fixed income marketplace. This has created greater opportunities for bond managers, but has also made their jobs more difficult. How can managers determine, for example, whether current coupon bonds callable after 10 years are attractive relative to discount bonds, or whether premium bonds with five years of call protection are attractive relative to current coupon bonds with three years of call protection? A sound basis for valuing callable bonds is essential to answering such questions.

The Components of a Callable Bond

Callable bonds can be analyzed by dividing them into their component parts. A callable bond can be thought of as a combination of a long position in a non-callable bond and a short position in a call option that the investor has written to the issuer. The non-callable bond (underlying bond) has the same contractual cash flows as the callable bond, while the call option is written on the contractual cash flows occurring from the bond's first refunding date.

Since a callable bond can be broken down into these two components, its value can likewise be broken down into the value of these two components. That is, the market price of a callable bond should equal the price of the underlying non-callable bond less the price of the call option. This relationship is shown in Exhibit 1. Because the investor receives a premium for writing the call, the option price enters negatively into the pricing relationship and callable bonds therefore carry higher yields than the underlying non-callable bonds otherwise would. The greater is the option's value, the lower is the price on the callable bond and the higher is its yield.

Factors Affecting the Call's Value

The value of the call option that the investor has written is dependent upon complex interrelationships among a number of variables. Option pricing models can be used to quantify these relationships and thereby determine a "fair" value for the call. While we do not discuss such models here, it is useful to examine the variables that go into these models and the ways in which these variables affect the option's value. The variables can be grouped into the characteristics of the underlying noncallable bond, the specifics of the call schedule, and external market factors.

Basically, those variables that increase the likelihood of call increase the value of the call option. Most of these relationships are

EXHIBIT 1
Basic Principles of Valuation

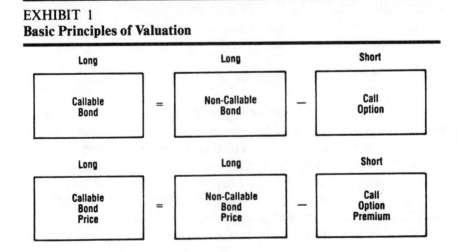

obvious to investors. The higher is the coupon and the lower is the yield on the underlying bond, for example, the more valuable is the call option. Likewise, the lower is the initial call price and the longer is the period over which the issuer can call the bond (generally, the longer is the maturity of the bond), the more valuable is the call option. Call options will also be more valuable the shorter is the period of call protection. This is because the shorter is the period of call protection, the greater is the present value of the cash flows that the issuer can call away from the investor.

In addition to the above factors, two general bond market characteristics affect the value of the call option. These are the volatility of interest rates and the shape of the yield curve. The more volatile are interest rates, the greater is the chance that they will drop to a level low enough to make calling the bond attractive to the issuer and the more valuable will be the call. Perhaps the least obvious factor affecting the call option's value is the shape of the yield curve. The higher are short-term rates relative to long-term rates, the more valuable is the call. This implies that as the yield curve steepens (flattens) callable bonds will be worth more (less), that is carry lower (higher) yields. This relationship makes sense when one considers that market participants often purchase callable bonds on a yield to call basis. If callable bond yields did not fall as short-term rates fell, high coupon callable bonds would be extremely attractive on a yield to call basis relative to non-callable short-term bonds.

Given the number of factors that influence the call option's value, it becomes clear that an option pricing model is needed to properly value the call. Only by using an option pricing model can investors evaluate such tradeoffs as lower call price for extra call protection or extra call protection for higher coupon.

Interestingly, investors seem to exhibit biases towards certain of these factors and place less emphasis on others. Investors are highly aware of coupon. Most investors, for example, require extra yield when trading from a lower to a higher coupon. Unless an issue is very near its call date, however, much less emphasis is placed on call protection. Yet extra call protection can be extremely valuable to an investor.

To see this, consider two typical issues in the marketplace—a 20-year 12 percent industrial issue callable after 10 years and a 40-year 12 percent telephone issue callable after five years. An investor receives almost 70 percent of the industrial's cash flows (in present value terms) prior to call date, but less than 45 percent of the telephone's cash flows prior to call date. The call on the telephone is therefore worth considerably more than that on the industrial and, other things being equal, the investor should demand extra yield on the telephone issue. Some Canadian issues are available carrying very high coupons, but because they generally have at least ten years of remaining call protection, their call features are worth relatively little.[1]

Call-Adjusted Yield

We turn now to determining whether a callable bond is fairly priced. We are concerned here only with identifying whether a bond is a good value, not whether it should be included in a portfolio.[2] A particular bond may be cheap, yet still be unsuitable for an investor's portfolio if it has the wrong performance characteristics.

Assume, for the moment, that we have used an option model and know the price of the call. Recall that a callable bond's price is equal to the price of the underlying non-callable, less the price of the call option. We can express this pricing relationship somewhat differently as:

$$\text{Price of Non-Callable Bond} = \text{Price of Callable Bond} + \text{Price of Call Option}$$

That is, the price of the underlying non-callable bond is simply the sum of the price of the callable bond and the price of the call option. Since we know the price of the call option and the market explicitly prices the callable bond, we can easily calculate the price of the underlying non-callable. The market, by the level at which it prices the callable bond, is actually implying a price for the underlying non-callable bond. Given this price, we can calculate the yield to maturity on the underlying non-callable bond. We refer to this yield as the "call-adjusted" yield. This is the yield at which the market is

---

[1] The value of the call feature on long Treasury issues for which there are 25 years of call protection is almost negligible for this reason.

[2] Value in this context means current relative value compared to other bonds, not value on an historic basis.

EXHIBIT 2
Call-Adjusted Yield—Example

Assumptions

30-year, 12% coupon bond, callable after 5-years at 110.
Bond is priced at par to yield 12%.
Option premium is estimated to be $1.89.

Calculation

Price of Callable Bond	$100.00
+	
Option Premium	1.89
Price of Non-Callable Bond	$101.89 → Call-Adjusted Yield = 11.77%

---

implying the callable bond would trade if it were non-callable. It can be thought of as the yield received for the underlying credit of the security. Exhibit 2 provides an example of a call-adjusted yield calculation. The call-adjusted yield of 11.77 percent shown in the exhibit represents the implied yield on a non-callable 30-year 12 percent coupon bond, given that the callable bond is trading at par. Note that call-adjusted yield is a very different concept from yield to call.

Call-adjusted yield is the key to locating value in callable bonds because it nets out the impact of callability and allows an issue to be evaluated solely on a credit basis.[3] Investors should ask whether the call-adjusted yield on a bond is the level at which a non-callable bond of the same issuer would actually trade. If it is, the callable bond is fairly priced; if the call-adjusted yield is higher, the callable bond is cheap; if the call-adjusted yield is lower, the callable bond is rich. At times, issues can be so mispriced that their call-adjusted yields trade through Treasuries.

Besides its usefulness in locating value in individual bonds, call-adjusted yield is a sound basis for comparison across bonds, particularly across bonds of widely different coupon or call features. Many issuers have several issues outstanding of similar maturity,

---

[3] We recognize that many bonds have additional provisions besides call and credit affecting their values, but ignore these provisions for this discussion.

but with different coupons or call schedules. Because of these differences, the issues will carry different yields. On a call-adjusted basis, however, they should have the same yield, as their underlying credit is obviously the same. We have sometimes observed, however, two issues of the same issuer with call-adjusted yields over 100 basis points apart. Section IV presents the results of a study based on such comparisons.

The use of call-adjusted yield can best be illustrated through a specific example. Consider the two bonds in Exhibit 3.[4] The BC Hydro's have a much higher coupon than the South Central Bell's, but also have over 11 years of call protection remaining while the South Central's have almost no remaining call protection. The two bonds are trading five basis points apart on a yield to maturity basis. When proper account is taken of the respective call features and the two bonds are compared on the basis of their call-adjusted yields, the BC Hydro's appear to offer much better value. As a non-callable investment due in 2011, the BC Hydro's provide a yield 72 basis points above that of the 30-year Treasury. The South Central's, on the other hand, yield only 12 basis points above the 30-year Treasury as a non-callable bond due in 2020. The market is thus providing 60 basis points of additional yield for the underlying credit of the BC Hydro's relative to the South Central's. Most investors would agree that such a difference is not currently warranted. Longer call protection more than offsets a higher coupon in this case.

EXHIBIT 3
Callable Bond Summary Example*

BC Hydro 15 1/2 Due 11-15-11, Callable 11-15-96 @ 106.64

Yield to Maturity	12.30% (+ 100 vs. 30-year)
Call-Adjusted Yield	12.02% (+ 72 vs. 30-year)

South Central Bell 12 7/8 Due 10-1-20, Callable 10-1-85 @ 110.39

Yield to Maturity	12.25% (+ 95 vs. 30-year)
Call-Adjusted Yield	11.42% (+ 12 vs. 30-year)

---

*These bonds are priced as of 5-15-85.

[4] The bonds are priced as of May 15, 1985.

Although a bond represents a good value, it may still be an unsuitable issue for an investor's portfolio. Regardless of how cheap a bond may be, unless its interest rate sensitivity is consistent with a portfolio's objectives, it may be a poor investment. Many portfolios are managed towards specific duration targets. The next section focuses on the duration properties of callable bonds.

II. DURATION CHARACTERISTICS OF CALLABLE BONDS

Duration was first developed as an alternative measure of the life of a series of known cash flows. It was considered an improvement over time to maturity, which ignores the timing and size of all cash flows except for the final principal payment at maturity. Duration has a far more important use though for portfolio managers; namely, it can serve as an index for any security's price sensitivity to interest rate changes.[5] For example, a security with an eight-year duration has about twice the price sensitivity to interest rate changes as a security with a four-year duration.

Duration and Uncertain Cash Flows

For a bond whose cash flows are known with certainty, an investor can use a standard duration calculation to estimate its price sensitivity. The cash flows from a bond that is subject to call, however, are uncertain. Because this uncertainty is interest rate related, the duration of the security will be affected. The short call option reduces a bond's price sensitivity to interest rate movements. Determining the duration of a callable bond involves determining the degree to which the short call affects price sensitivity.[6]

At the extremes, the duration of a callable bond can be easily estimated. When interest rates are very high, the call date is far away, and there is a substantial call premium, the duration of a

---

[5] For a discussion of duration and its uses see Alden L. Toevs, *Uses of Duration Analysis for the Control of Interest Rate Risk,* New York: Morgan Stanley, January 1984.

[6] See Alden L. Toevs, "Interest Rate Risk and Uncertain Lives," *Journal of Portfolio Management,* Spring 1985, pp 45-56.

callable bond is approximately the same as that of an equivalent (same coupon, maturity, and credit quality) non-callable bond. This is because the option is nearly worthless and will have little impact on the bond's price movement. Another way of seeing this is to note that in such an environment the cash flows are nearly certain out to maturity. At the other extreme, when interest rates are low, the call date is nearby, and there is little or no call premium, the bond is nearly certain to be called and duration to call date then provides a good approximation of the bond's price sensitivity.

In most situations, however, it is difficult to know what constitutes a very high or very low interest rate environment for a particular call date, call premium schedule, and interest rate volatility. A bond's price movement, therefore, generally will not mirror that of a security with a duration equal to its duration to call or its duration to maturity. For example, consider a 27-year bond with a 12 percent coupon callable after two years at a price of 109.60. At an 11 percent yield, the duration to maturity is 9.0 years and the duration to call is 1.8 years. Which duration should the money manager use to draw a performance profile for this security? The correct answer is neither; the true price sensitivity lies somewhere in between.

Call-Adjusted Duration

When such uncertainty is present, standard duration calculations are inappropriate. Instead, it is necessary to estimate a bond's price sensitivity by calculating a "call-adjusted" duration. The call-adjusted duration is the price sensitivity of the callable bond taking into account the impact of the short call option. Just as it can be used to determine the value of the call, an option model can be used to determine the amount by which the bond's price sensitivity is reduced by the call.

Call-adjusted duration must be computed numerically, rather than through a closed form formula.[7] Since duration is a measure of price sensitivity with respect to interest rates it can be approximated for any security by the following formula:

---

[7] This is because there is no known closed form formula for an American option on a fixed income security.

$$D = \frac{-\Delta P}{P} \times \frac{(1 + y/2)}{\Delta y}$$

where ΔP is the change in price of the bond corresponding to a small change in interest rates Δy, P is the current price of the bond, and y is the current bond-equivalent interest rate. For callable bonds, the y used in computing the call-adjusted duration is the bond-equivalent yield on the underlying non-callable bond and P is calculated using an option pricing model.

Consider again the prior example of trying to estimate the price sensitivity of a 27-year bond with a 12 percent coupon, callable after 2 years at 109.60. If the underlying security has a yield of 11 percent, the call-adjusted duration would be approximately 6.6 years. In a 9 percent interest rate environment the call-adjusted duration would be approximately 4.4 years.[8] In both cases, the bond's duration is measured between its duration to maturity and duration to call date. These numbers also show that the more valuable is the call option, the larger is the reduction in the bond's duration from its duration to maturity.

To analyze how a bond will perform in a changing interest rate environment one must look beyond a bond's current duration. For nearly all bonds, duration changes as rates change. Ideally one would like the duration of a bond to fall as rates rise (to minimize capital loss) and to increase as rates fall (to maximize capital gain). This is the case for non-callable bonds. Many investors apply the term positive convexity to these favorable duration properties.[9] The call feature of a bond tends to reduce the duration of the bond as rates fall because it increases the likelihood that the cash flows will only occur out to the first call date. Since a callable bond is a combination of a short call option and a non-callable bond, these two components compete to change its duration in opposite directions as rates change. As a result, the duration of a callable bond may or may not increase (decrease) as rates fall (rise). If the call option is more dominant, a callable bond's duration can shorten as rates fall and lengthen as rates rise. Even if its duration does

---

[8] We have assumed an annual yield volatility of 12 percent.

[9] Although the duration of a zero coupon bond is constant, its modified duration is not. It, too, therefore has positive convexity.

increase (decrease) as rates fall (rise), it will do so by a lesser amount than for an equivalent duration non-callable bond. Thus, relative to a non-callable bond, a callable bond will have less favorable duration characteristics. This has important implications for the relative performance of these securities.

We illustrate these duration concepts through two bonds that are representative of many issues available in the marketplace. They are:

1. a 12 percent coupon, 30-year issue, callable after 5 years at 109.60, and
2. a 12 percent coupon, 10-year issue, callable after 7 years at 100.

Exhibit 4 shows the duration (call-adjusted) at various yield levels of the first bond (a typical long-term bond) at issue, after three years and after four years. The top line shows the duration of the bond at issue. The duration is relatively stable, ranging between roughly six and seven years over a wide band of interest rates. This relative stability actually evidences the fact that the duration of the bond is

EXHIBIT 4
Duration at Various Yield Levels
30-Year 12% Coupon Bond Callable After 5 Years at 109.6

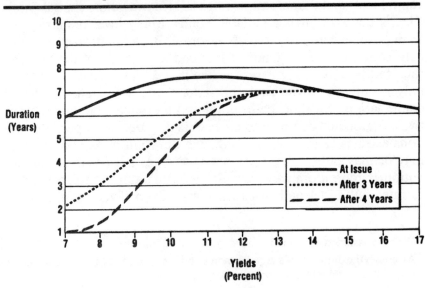

affected by the call. While duration does not drop very much even in an 8 percent interest rate environment, an equivalent non-callable bond's duration would have risen to about 11 years. The difference will become apparent in the performance graphs of the following section. The middle line of Exhibit 4 shows the duration of the 30-year bond three years after issue. Here duration drops off dramatically as interest rates fall. The dropoff is even more obvious when only one year of call protection remains (bottom line). Investors frequently apply the term negative convexity to this type of unfavorable duration behavior. Long-term current coupon bonds that have little remaining call protection often exhibit a high degree of negative convexity because the cash flows associated with these bonds are very uncertain. Even a moderate change in rates can greatly increase or decrease the likelihood of call. In fact, the duration behavior can sometimes be worse for a current than for a high coupon bond when there is little remaining call protection. Since high coupon bonds will almost certainly be called, even if rates move upward somewhat, their durations are more stable (close to duration to call) as interest rates change.

Exhibit 4 highlights not only the importance of changing rate levels, but the importance of the passage of time on a callable bond's duration. The duration characteristics of the 30-year bond worsen significantly as time passes. As the call protection winds down, a much greater proportion of the bond's cash flows become callable. The call feature, therefore, becomes more valuable and impacts duration to a greater extent.

Exhibit 5 shows a duration picture for the second bond (a typical intermediate bond). Duration is shown at issue, after three years and after six years. The duration of this bond behaves similarly to that of a non-callable bond when there are seven years of call protection and the call is not very valuable. However, when one year of call protection remains, duration can drop off dramatically as rates fall.

To make the above duration concepts more concrete reconsider the two bonds described in Exhibit 3. As shown in Exhibit 6, the BC Hydro's have a nominal duration of 8.1 years compared to the South Central's 8.4 years. However, on a call-adjusted basis these durations are 7.6 years and 5.5 years, respectively. Although the BC Hydro's have a substantially higher coupon, their 11 years of call

EXHIBIT 5
Duration at Various Yield Levels
10-Year 12% Coupon Bond Callable After 7 Years at 100

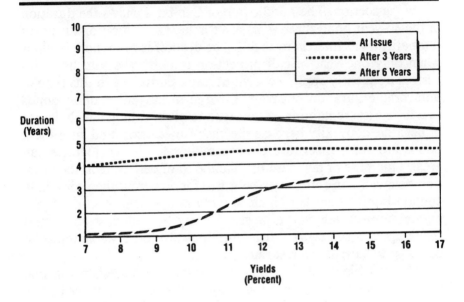

EXHIBIT 6
Callable Bond Summary Example

BC Hydro 15 ¹/₂ Due 11-15-11, Callable 11-15-96 @ 106.64

Duration to Maturity	8.1 years
Call-Adjusted Duration	
Current Rate Levels	7.6 years
Rates 100 Basis Points Higher	7.3 years
Rates 100 Basis Points Lower	8.0 years

South Central Bell 12 ⁷/₈ Due 10-1-20, Callable 10-1-85 @ 110.39

Duration to Maturity	8.4 years
Call-Adjusted Duration	
Current Rate Levels	5.5 years
Rates 100 Basis Points Higher	6.4 years
Rates 100 Basis Points Lower	3.8 years

protection results in the call-adjusted duration being only half a year less than the nominal duration, compared to a difference of nearly three years for the South Central issue. The manner in which the durations change as interest rates change is even more important than the initial call-adjusted durations. The South Central issue has very unfavorable duration properties. Duration declines (increases) substantially as rates fall (rise) from current levels. The BC Hydro's duration, on the other hand, changes in a favorable way as rates change. In Section III we will show how to evaluate these duration properties in terms of performance and integrate them with the value concepts of Section I.

III. PERFORMANCE PROPERTIES OF CALLABLE BONDS

Although many callable bonds do not have favorable duration properties, they should not automatically be excluded from portfolios. Investors are compensated for the risk of the callable bond by the option premium that they receive for writing the call. This translates into a higher yield on a callable security relative to a non-callable security of the same issuer.

Active managers are interested in the total returns that can be anticipated on any bond. To evaluate the total return prospects of a callable bond, a manager must take into account the tradeoff between its extra yield and its possibly unfavorable duration properties. This can be accomplished by analyzing the bond's performance profile relative to other bonds. Investors frequently compare callable bonds to non-callable bonds of the same maturity. As the previous section showed, these bonds may have very different interest rate sensitivities. A more appropriate comparison is between the callable bond and a non-callable bond of the same duration. This comparison is consistent with the thinking of most active managers, for whom duration is a primary consideration in portfolio decisions.

Representative Return Profiles

We analyze the same two bonds in this section as in the previous section. They are:

1. a 12 percent coupon, 30-year issue, callable after 5 years at 109.60, and
2. a 12 percent coupon, 10-year issue, callable after 7 years at 100.

Our analysis assumes a six-month holding period. We further assume that the yield on the underlying non-callable bonds is 12 percent and that the yield curve is upward sloping.

Consider first the 30-year, 12 percent bond with five years of call protection. Its call-adjusted duration when the underlying non-callable yields 12 percent is 7.4 years. Exhibit 7 shows how this bond would perform relative to a non-callable bond of the same initial duration by graphing the differential total return on the bonds. If interest rates are relatively stable, remaining within a band of about 100 basis points on either side of current rate levels, the callable bond provides a better total return than the same duration non-callable bond. In this range of rates, the extra yield on the callable bond adequately compensates for the undesirable duration properties of the bond. Beyond this range of rate moves, the non-

EXHIBIT 7
6-Month Performance Relative to Equivalent Duration Non-Callable 30-Year 12% Coupon Bond Callable After 5 Years at 109.6

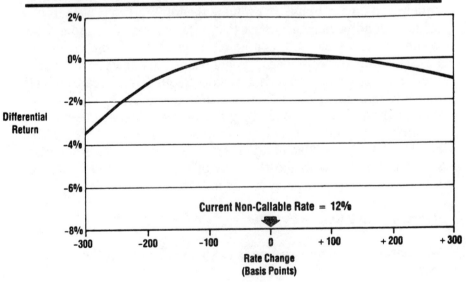

callable bond outperforms the callable bond and does so by an increasingly larger amount the larger the rate change. This is because with larger rate moves, the adverse duration properties and associated price sensitivities of the callable bond then dominate its higher stated yield. A key point is that the callable bond underperforms the non-callable for both a rise and a fall in interest rates of more than 100 basis points. The underperformance for a rise in rates is often surprising to investors. It occurs because the non-callable bond's duration shortens to a much greater extent than does the callable bond's duration as rates rise. Another point that may surprise investors is that this return profile is for a current, rather than a high coupon bond. Although a bond may be trading below its call price today, the call feature should not be ignored in evaluating its potential returns.[10]

Exhibit 8 shows the performance of the same bond after four years have passed. The bond now has only one year of call protection remaining. The general picture is the same—the callable outperforms the equivalent duration non-callable when rates are relatively stable, but underperforms it when rates move significantly in either direction. In this case, the extra return has increased somewhat from the case of the bond with five years of call protection, reflecting the fact that the stated yield increases as the bond loses its call protection. However, the underperformance becomes even more dramatic, particularly as interest rates decline. This occurs because the bond's duration drops rapidly as interest rates fall and its price appreciation falls short of the price appreciation from the non-callable bond.

At first glance, these differential return profiles may appear unattractive. One should not necessarily draw this conclusion, however. Under certain circumstances, these bonds may represent very appropriate portfolio holdings. An investor anticipating relatively stable interest rates, for example, should buy callable bonds, as this will increase total return should his rate forecast prove

---

[10] An investor can reshape this return profile by rebalancing his portfolio to always maintain its desired duration characteristics. In so doing, the investor would increase convexity but would also sacrifice yield. In fact, by continuous rebalancing, an investor "buys back" the call he has written to the issuer and realizes the same returns on the callable bond as on the same duration non-callable bond.

EXHIBIT 8
6-Month Performance Relative to Equivalent Duration Non-Callable
26-Year 12% Coupon Bond Callable After 1 Year at 109.6

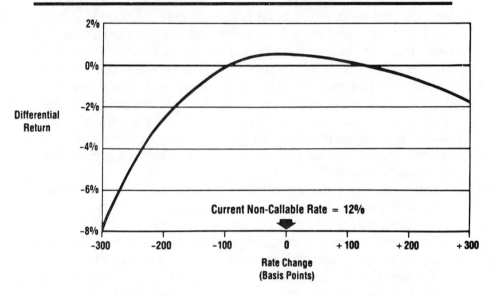

correct. Also, many active managers are measured against performance bogeys that contain callable bonds having these same return
profiles. Eliminating this type of bond from a portfolio therefore
involves taking interest rate volatility risk relative to the performance bogey.[11]

The Impact of Mispricings

Exhibits 7 and 8 assumed that the callable bonds were fairly priced,
i.e., that the investor has received the correct amount of extra yield
for writing the call option to the issuer. The attractiveness of the
performance profiles can change greatly if the bond is initially mispriced. This is illustrated by Exhibits 9 and 10.

[11] A manager who constructs a portfolio of non-callable bonds of the same duration as the stated duration of one of the bond indices will actually have a
portfolio with more price sensitivity than the index.

EXHIBIT 9
6-Month Performance Relative to Equivalent Duration Non-Callable
30-Year 12% Coupon Bond Callable After 5 Years at 109.6
Priced 50 Basis Points Rich

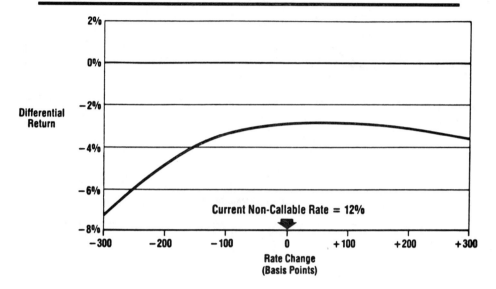

Exhibit 9 shows the performance profile of the callable bond with five years of call protection remaining, but assumes that the bond is priced 50 basis points too richly. That is, the call-adjusted yield on this bond is 50 basis points less than the actual yield on a non-callable bond of the same issuer.[12] We assume further that this mispricing corrects so that by the end of the six months, the bond's call-adjusted yield is equal to the actual yield on the non-callable bond. In this case, even if interest rates do not move, the callable bond's spread will widen and it will underperform the equivalent duration non-callable. The cheapening of the bond more than offsets the yield premium that is received for writing the call. When rates do move significantly, the callable bond underperforms by an even greater amount than previously because the adverse duration properties are now compounded by the cheapening of the bond. While there is no assurance that the mispricing of the bond will

[12] The bond may or may not be rich on an historic basis.

EXHIBIT 10
6-Month Performance Relative to Equivalent Duration Non-Callable
30-Year 12% Coupon Bond Callable After 5 Years at 109.6
Priced 50 Basis Points Cheap

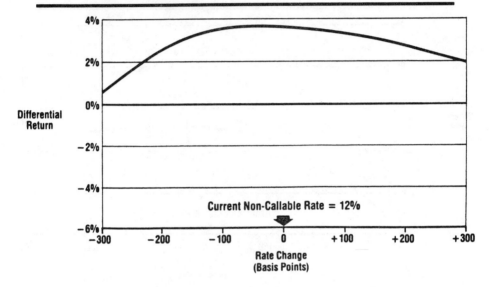

correct over six months, the performance profile of the bond if it does correct is so unattractive that such bonds should almost always be excluded from a portfolio.[13]

On the other hand, a callable bond that is cheap can be attractive despite its adverse duration properties. Exhibit 10 shows the performance profile for a bond that is priced 50 basis points cheaply, assuming again that the mispricing corrects over the six months. Recall that the fairly priced callable bond provided incremental return relative to a non-callable for a range of rate moves of 100 basis points on either side of current rate levels. When the bond is cheap, however, the range over which the callable bond provides incremental return widens to more than 300 basis points upward or downward from current rate levels. The richening of the bond here

---

[13] An exception might be if the investor anticipates a tender for the bond and expects it to richen even further.

more than offsets its adverse duration properties. Any issue for which such a price correction is anticipated is almost always a good selection to include in a portfolio.[14]

While the differential performance profiles shown so far have illustrated only a current coupon long bond, they are representative of almost any callable bond. The basic differences among bonds can be described in terms of the range of interest rate moves over which incremental returns are provided, the amount of incremental return when rates remain in this range, and the degree of underperformance when rates move outside this range. Compared to the differential performance profile of a current coupon issue, a higher coupon bond generally provides more incremental return over a shorter

---

EXHIBIT 11
6-Month Performance Relative to Equivalent Duration Non-Callable
10-Year 12% Coupon Bond Callable After 7 Years at 100

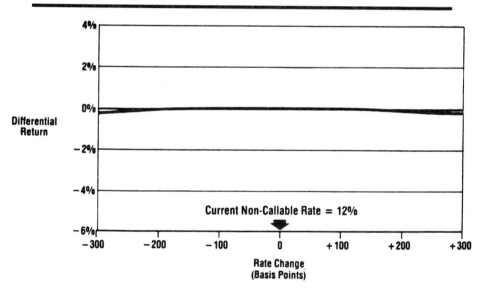

---

[14] Even in the absence of favorable price correction, the extra yield on a cheap bond increases total return. However, price correction is the more important element over short time periods. In Exhibit 10, for example, the extra yield added about 25 basis points to total return over six months, while the price correction added about 300 basis points to total return.

rate range, but underperforms the same duration non-callable by a greater amount outside that rate range.

To complete this section, we show the performance profiles for a current coupon intermediate issue. At issue, the impact of callability on performance is almost nil for this bond (Exhibit 11). The long period of call deferment and the lack of price volatility of the security that can be called (a three-year bond) lead to the call option being worth very little and thus having only a minor impact on duration. The bond's performance is almost identical to that of a non-callable. As time passes and the call protection winds down, the performance profile begins to resemble those seen earlier. With only one year of call protection remaining (Exhibit 12), the extra return earned when rates are stable becomes more apparent, as does the underperformance for interest rate shifts.

EXHIBIT 12
6-Month Performance Relative to Equivalent Duration Non-Callable
4-Year 12% Coupon Bond Callable After 1 Year at 100

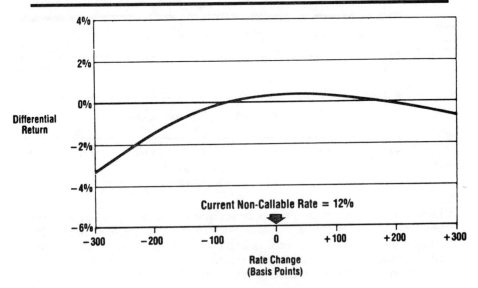

IV. HISTORICAL ANALYSIS—LOCATING
VALUE IN THE MARKETPLACE

The performance profiles shown in Section III offer a guide to structuring portfolios that provide value and are consistent with investment objectives. In particular, the attractiveness and un-attractiveness of the cheap and rich pictures, respectively, suggest that investors manage towards duration targets or execute duration based swaps by identifying rich or cheap bonds on a call-adjusted yield basis. But this approach can only be useful if the marketplace eventually reaches the same conclusions as to value as does the analytical framework. If this is so, we would expect bonds that are rich or cheap to correct in price and provide the differential re-turns shown in the performance profiles. If, on the other hand, a bond is identified as rich or cheap but the market never recog-nizes the fact, its price will not correct and it will not perform as expected.

To test the usefulness of this framework, we have compared the returns on issues that were identified as overvalued on a call-adjusted yield basis with the returns on issues that were identified as undervalued on a call-adjusted yield basis. If undervalued bonds can outperform overvalued bonds, we can have confidence in the analytical framework. To isolate the impact of callability, we compared pairs of bonds of similar maturity of the same issuer. Net of their call features, two bonds of the same issuer and matu-rity should have the same value, that is the same call-adjusted yield. We considered two bonds mispriced when their call-ad-justed yields differed by at least 25 basis points. This guideline was used because it provides a level of comfort that the issues are actually mispriced, given the uncertainty of the inputs to any op-tion pricing model. An unbiased test must also account for the interest rate movements that took place over the historical period by comparing returns between two bonds of the same duration. Since the durations of the two bonds in each comparison pair were typically different, we combined the longer duration bond with a cash position to equate durations. All of the issues in our study were long telephone issues, because such bonds have "clean" re-funding provisions (no sinking fund provisions or separate cash call provisions).[15] We compared total returns over six-month holding periods, as this is a commonly used time frame for active managers.

Exhibit 13 summarizes the results of this test. The exhibit compares, for each six-month time period, the average return on bonds that were identified as undervalued and the average return on bonds that were identified as overvalued. It also shows the frequency with which the call-adjusted yield measure identified the better performing bond. On average, bonds that were identified as cheap on the basis of call-adjusted yield provided incremental returns over six-month periods of 1.27 percent relative to bonds that were identified as rich on this basis. To the manager measured in terms of relative performance, adding such an amount to a portfolio's return is highly significant. Furthermore, the cheap bond provided a higher total return (adjusted by duration) 70 percent of the time.

While these results confirm the usefulness of call-adjusted yield numbers for analyzing securities, they also suggest that managers should not expect to earn incremental return over every six-month time period. A bond that is cheap may provide an inferior return to a rich bond if it cheapens further. This was the case in the second half of 1982, when high coupon bonds were cheap at the start of the period, but even cheaper at the end of the period. But the results do suggest that mispricings eventually correct; no one class of coupons remains consistently overvalued or undervalued. By the middle of 1983, most of the high coupon bonds that had been cheap were rich on the basis of call-adjusted yield.

A complete listing of the pairs of bonds used in the study is contained in the appendix. While there were too many pairs to discuss each in detail, it is interesting to focus on one example. Consider two Southwestern Bell issues, the 11 3/8s due 1/15/2020 and the 16 1/8s due 9/18/2021. Exhibit 14 summarizes yield, dura-

---

[15] Although there are no other refunding provisions, tax and coupon effects are still present. Generally, the combination of these effects results in discount bonds trading more richly than premium bonds. Total return investors, however, should not subsidize after-tax investors. If they can, in the absence of call risk, consistently take advantage of the higher yields available on premium bonds, they should do so.

EXHIBIT 13
Identifying Value from Call-Adjusted Yields

Time Period	General Interest Rate Trend	Cheaper Coupon Class[1]	Total Return Undervalued Bonds[2]	Total Return Overvalued Bonds[2]	Differential Return	Frequency of Better Performance[3]
January 1982–June 1982	Rising	High	7.71%	5.97%	1.74%	8/8
July 1982–December 1982	Falling	High	27.29	30.21	-2.98	0/9
January 1983–June 1983	Stable	High	9.64	5.46	4.18	11/11
July 1983–December 1983	Rising	Low	2.33	2.65	-.32	3/7
January 1984–June 1984	Rising	Low	-.36	-2.99	2.63	9/9
July 1984–December 1984	Falling	Low	17.83	16.42	1.41	3/4
Average 6-month results			10.37%	9.10%	1.27%	34/48

[1] Indicates, in general, whether the higher or the lower coupon bond in each mispriced pair was cheaper on a call-adjusted basis.

[2] Average total return (duration-weighted) assuming equal par weighting in all bonds.

[3] Indicates the number of times the bond identified as cheap provided the greater total return, relative to the total number of mispricings identified.

EXHIBIT 14
Analysis of Southwestern Bell Issues

Time Period	Issue		Starting Yield to Maturity (%)	Ending Yield to Maturity (%)	Starting Call-Adjusted Yield (%)	Ending Call-Adjusted Yield (%)	Actual Duration (Years)	Call-Adjusted Duration (Years)	Total Return (%)	Duration Adjusted Total Return (%)
1/1/82–6/30/82	11 3/8	1-15-20	15.05	15.45	14.81	15.27	6.78	6.33	5.02	5.07
	16 1/8	9-18-21	16.27	16.28	15.70	15.63	6.35	5.46	8.01	8.01
7/1/82–12/31/82	11 3/8	1-15-20	15.45	12.20	15.27	11.84	6.53	6.20	32.45	28.55
	16 1/8	9-18-21	16.28	13.81	15.63	12.98	6.35	5.33	24.99	24.99
1/1/83–6/30/83	11 3/8	1-15-20	12.20	12.30	11.84	11.91	8.16	6.92	5.22	5.06
	16 1/8	9-18-21	13.81	13.39	12.98	11.68	7.40	5.53	9.80	9.80
1/1/84–6/30/84	11 3/8	1-15-20	13.07	14.59	12.85	14.33	7.66	6.95	-3.39	.08
	16 1/8	9-18-21	13.74	14.89	12.13	13.76	7.41	4.27	-.58	-.58
7/1/84–12/31/84	11 3/8	1-15-20	14.59	12.60	14.33	12.36	6.91	6.38	21.60	17.41
	16 1/8	9-18-21	14.89	13.87	13.76	12.24	6.90	4.74	15.58	15.58

tion, and total return information for these two bonds over time. In some periods, the 11 3/8s were cheap and the 16 1/8s rich, while the reverse was true in other periods.

At the start of 1982, the call-adjusted yield on the 16 1/8s was 89 basis points cheaper than that of the 11 3/8s. The high coupon bond represented better value at this time. The spread narrowed to 36 basis points by the middle of the year and the 16 1/8s provided a higher return over these six months. The 16 1/8s were still cheap, but over the second half of the year they became cheaper as the spread between the call-adjusted yields widened to 114 basis points during the market rally. The 16 1/8s provided a lower return, despite initially being cheap relative to the 11 3/8s. During the first half of 1983, the mispricing between the two issues corrected, with the 16 1/8s yielding 23 basis points less than the 11 3/8s on a call-adjusted basis by the middle of the year. The 16 1/8s provided a much greater total return over this period, reflecting the price correction. At the beginning of 1984 the bonds were again mispriced, but this time the 11 3/8s were cheap relative to the 16 1/8s. Over the next six months, the spread of call-adjusted yields narrowed from 72 basis points to 57 basis points and the 11 3/8s provided a greater total return. By the end of 1984, the bonds were again fairly priced, having call-adjusted yields just 12 basis points apart. With the price correction, the return on the 11 3/8s exceeded that on the 16 1/8s over this period.

V. APPLICATIONS TO PORTFOLIO MANAGEMENT

Sections I to III of this article developed an analytical framework for callable bonds while the historical tests of Section IV confirmed the usefulness of this framework. Our discussion has so far focused on individual bonds in an isolated context. In this section, we incorporate our analysis into a portfolio context, discussing how fixed income managers can apply the analysis to enhance portfolio performance. We first discuss the active manager measured on a relative performance basis, then the immunized manager with a fixed return target.

Active Managers

Most active bond managers are regularly evaluated in terms of how their total returns compare to those of some market index. While they utilize a variety of styles in trying to outperform the indices, almost all managers search for "value" as part of their approaches. The search for value encompasses a number of dimensions, the most widespread being analysis of the shape of the yield curve, fundamental credit analysis, and sector/quality spread analysis. Quantitative analysis of call features is a less widely used tool in the search for value and for that very reason should be incorporated into the portfolio management process.

The simplest stage of applying the analysis is to use it for bond selection, where call-adjusted yield information can enhance the familiar rich/cheap analysis. Since a call-adjusted yield represents the yield that is received for the underlying non-callable, it is a measure of the yield received for undertaking the particular degree of credit risk appropriate to the security. Call-adjusted yields, therefore, provide valid comparisons between different issues of a single issuer, between bonds of different issuers, and between corporate issues and government issues.

Most clear-cut is the comparison between several issues of the same issuer, where the call-adjusted yields should be approximately the same. Bonds that are rich on this basis should almost always be sold and bonds that are cheap on this basis should almost always be purchased. Unfortunately, there will frequently be times when no mispricings of this type are present.

A wider comparison can be made among issuers, combining callability analysis with fundamental credit analysis. Bonds with valuable call features (high coupon, short period of call protection, etc.) will always look cheap relative to those with less valuable call features on a naive comparison of yields to maturity. Yet this comparison may be misleading and may not reflect actual value. The difference in call-adjusted yields between two issuers, on the other hand, should reflect the perceived credit differences between them. Call-adjusted yields often reveal mispricings that a comparison of stated yields does not. For example, the BC Hydro and the South Central Bell issues analyzed earlier were priced 5 basis points apart on stated yields, but 60 basis points apart on call-adjusted yields.

Comparing call-adjusted yields to yields on Treasury securities may likewise reveal important information. Again, the South Central Bell issue appeared to offer an attractive spread based on its stated yield (95 basis points over the 30-year Treasury), but a rather unattractive spread in terms of what the investor actually received for the underlying credit (call-adjusted yield of 12 basis points over the 30-year Treasury). Occasionally, a bond's call-adjusted yield will be lower than the yield on a comparable Treasury. This is a clear signal that the bond is overpriced and should be sold.[16]

Besides their usefulness in comparing the current values of bonds, call-adjusted yields provide a sound number to use in historical spread analysis. Traditional spread analysis is distorted by the impact of callability, because when issues have markedly different call features, their spreads may widen or narrow as interest rates change even though the market perceives no difference in the fundamental values of the issuers. A spread history of call-adjusted yields isolates changes due to changes in underlying fundamentals, thereby identifying bonds that offer good value on an historical basis.

Using call-adjusted yields in this way, a manager may develop a list of buy and sell candidates. But before rushing out to buy all the cheap bonds and sell all the rich bonds, it is important that the manager consider the broader picture of setting a duration and convexity target for the portfolio. That is, a manager should not mechanically alter a portfolio through value trades without recognizing the duration and convexity impact of the trades. Suppose, for example, cheap bonds have call-adjusted durations of eight years and rich bonds have call-adjusted durations of six years. A proceeds trade out of the rich bonds into the cheap bonds involves lengthening the portfolio's duration by two years. Unless this is the manager's intention, adjustments must be made. Many managers adjust for this by duration-weighting their trades, combining the longer bond with a cash position in order to retain the same interest rate sensitivity. When doing duration-matched trades with callable bonds, the bonds should be weighted by their call-adjusted durations, rather than their stated durations.

---

[16] An investor seeking the return pattern of the callable corporate issue can achieve it more cheaply by buying a Treasury and writing an option against it in this case.

More effective use can be made of these analytical techniques by examining portfolios in total rather than looking at individual bonds. A manager wishes to construct the best portfolio to meet a set of objectives and duration-weighting individual trades through the appropriate cash positions may not be the most efficient way of doing this. A more sophisticated approach is to take actions in one part of the portfolio that offset actions in another part of the portfolio. This is best shown through a hypothetical example.

Suppose there is a shortage of non-callable intermediate paper and such paper is therefore trading richly. Suppose callable intermediate paper, on the other hand, is trading cheaply and finally, suppose the long sector of the bond market is fairly valued. Consider a manager who is somewhat bullish and therefore has structured a

EXHIBIT 15
6-Year Duration Portfolio with Expected Poor Performance

Bond	Call-Adjusted Yield	Call-Adjusted Duration		
		Current Rate Levels	100 b.p. Rate Rise	100 b.p. Rate Decline
7-year, 10.5%, non-callable	10.50%	5.1	5.1	5.2
26-year, 11.5%, callable in one year at 108	11.25%	7.0	7.4	5.7
Portfolio average*	10.91%	6.0	6.2	5.4

6-Year Duration Portfolio with Expected Good Performance

Bond	Call-Adjusted Yield	Call-Adjusted Duration		
		Current Rate Levels	100 b.p. Rate Rise	100 b.p. Rate Decline
7-year 13%, callable in four years at 100	11.00%	4.8	4.7	4.6
24-year, 8.5%, callable immediately at 106	11.25%	8.8	8.4	9.2
Portfolio average*	11.11%	6.0	5.8	6.0

* Weighted to achieve 6-year duration.

6-year duration portfolio consisting of the two bonds in the upper half of Exhibit 15. This portfolio is unlikely to produce very good performance. Firstly, the intermediate issue is trading richly and therefore presents the risk of cheapening. Secondly, the portfolio shortens in duration as interest rates fall, thus failing to provide the upside the manager sought in targeting the 6-year duration.

Now consider the alternative portfolio shown in the bottom half of Exhibit 15. This portfolio offers better value, because the call-adjusted yield of the callable intermediate issue is greater than the yield of the non-callable intermediate issue. Furthermore, since the duration of this portfolio does not shorten as interest rates fall, it can be expected to provide better upside performance than the first portfolio. Using computer-based techniques it is possible to analyze a range of portfolios in this way, so as to determine the portfolio most consistent with the manager's objectives.

Even when two portfolios offer similar value, a manager can still employ callability analysis to refine a portfolio. Many managers structure portfolios along the lines of one of the major bond indices and do not alter durations based on interest rate forecasts. However, such managers may alter the ways in which they obtain their durations. While uncomfortable with making forecasts on the direction of rates, these managers may be comfortable with making forecasts of the likely range of rates. For example, a manager may believe that interest rates will neither rise nor fall by more than 100 basis points over the next six months. In that case, the performance profiles of Section III suggest that the manager obtain the target duration by tilting the portfolio towards higher coupon callable bonds, as these bonds will provide incremental return over this rate range. A number of other "bets" of this type can be made without changing a portfolio's duration.

Immunized Managers

Immunized managers have traditionally shunned current or high coupon callable bonds because they are uncertain of how to measure the duration of these bonds. Since duration matching is the key element of immunization, the avoidance of such issues should not be surprising. Most immunized portfolios are therefore constructed using non-callable bonds or callable bonds whose coupons are below some "conservative" maximum. In the latter case, the impact of callability is assumed to be negligible and the call is ignored. Many times these restrictions result in a rather limited universe of potential bonds for the portfolio, or a universe of bonds that is richly priced. An expanded universe of bonds would allow an immunized manager greater flexibility both in terms of initial portfolio construction and ongoing management.

The techniques for analyzing callable bonds presented in this article imply that there is a place for callable bonds in immunized portfolios. Section II showed that it is possible to compute the duration of callable bonds, thereby overcoming the major objection to their use. But there are a number of other considerations present when using callable bonds for immunization that are not present when only non-callables are used.

Firstly, immunized portfolios must not only be matched in duration to liabilities, but must also have at least as much positive convexity as the liabilities. Although the duration of a callable bond can be measured, it may not move favorably with changes in interest rates. Given a time period between portfolio rebalancings, there will be a range of rate movements over which an immunized portfolio of callable bonds increases in value to a greater extent than do the liabilities. Beyond this range, the portfolio will experience a shortfall in value relative to the liabilities. Secondly, the yield target that is obtained when immunizing with callable bonds is less obvious than with non-callables. A key point is that the stated yield to maturity on the bonds is not the yield that can be captured through immunization. In fact, if the bonds are fairly priced, the appropriate target return is the rate applicable to non-callable bonds of the target duration and same credit quality. Thirdly, immunization with callable bonds involves greater exposure to the risk of non-parallel shifts in the yield curve. For example, callable bonds may fall in value and liability values may not change if short rates increase but long rates are stable.[17]

Despite these caveats, callable bonds can frequently be included in immunized portfolios. Most importantly, if these bonds can be

---

[17] By matching both duration and convexity, investors can reduce the risk of non-parallel yield curve shifts. Combining callable corporate bonds with long zero coupon Treasuries is one way of doing this.

obtained more cheaply on a call-adjusted yield basis than non-callable or discount bonds, the manager can add incremental return to an existing portfolio or offer a higher initial target return through their use. Furthermore, many callable issues have positive convexity and will exhibit favorable price responsiveness. Even if the bonds are not cheap relative to non-callables, the expanded universe creates more swap opportunities and a greater ability to add value through ongoing management.

VI. CONCLUSION

Recent years have seen an increasing performance pressure placed on fixed income managers. This has led managers to search for new and creative ways to add to portfolio returns. We believe the framework for analyzing callable bonds presented in this article is a particularly useful technique for this purpose.

This article has focused on the analysis of call for refunding. Many bonds have a number of provisions through which they can be retired. Of course, call features represent only one factor affecting a portfolio's performance. The portfolio management process must consider the broad spectrum of factors affecting total return, such as the shape of the term structure, fundamental credit valuation, relative quality spreads, and so on. We will continue to seek new insights into these topics in a way that can help managers add that degree of incremental return necessary to achieve consistently good performance.

APPENDIX
CALLABLE BOND RETURN ANALYSES

January 1982–June 1982

Issue			Yield to Maturity 1/1/82 (%)	Yield to Maturity 6/30/82 (%)	Call Adjusted Yield 1/1/82 (%)	Call Adjusted Yield 6/30/82 (%)	Actual Duration (Years)	Call Adjusted Duration (Years)	Total Return (%)	Duration Adjusted Total Return (%)
Bell Tel of Pa	11 7/8	4-15-20	15.15	15.40	14.89	15.18	6.90	6.35	5.97	6.05
	15 1/8	4-15-21	15.90	16.02	15.39	15.52	6.57	5.68	7.18	7.18
Michigan Bell Tel	8 1/8	6-1-15	14.95	15.25	14.91	15.22	7.23	7.13	5.48	5.74
	15 3/4	5-1-21	16.16	16.25	15.63	15.71	6.51	5.69	7.50	7.50
Mountain States Tel	11 1/4	11-1-19	15.15	15.50	14.95	15.34	6.95	6.55	5.34	5.57
	15 3/4	8-5-21	16.13	16.27	15.57	15.71	6.28	5.50	7.18	7.18
New England Tel	12.20	5-15-17	15.55	15.80	15.34	15.62	6.81	6.35	6.20	6.24
	15 1/4	6-15-18	16.15	16.22	15.71	15.77	6.63	5.85	7.64	7.64
New York Tel	8 7/8	6-15-18	14.83	15.05	14.75	14.97	7.27	7.08	5.94	6.12
	15 5/8	7-15-21	16.04	16.15	15.52	15.63	6.26	5.50	7.27	7.27
Pacific Tel & Tel	12.70	11-15-19	16.05	16.25	15.86	16.09	6.61	6.18	6.79	6.78
	15	11-1-20	16.65	16.55	16.35	16.21	6.34	5.84	8.87	8.87
Southern Bell Tel	10.90	12-1-19	15.05	15.30	14.75	15.15	6.66	6.18	5.89	5.96
	16	11-1-21	16.17	16.17	15.58	15.51	6.59	5.67	8.05	8.05
Southwestern Bell	11 3/8	1-15-20	15.05	15.45	14.81	15.27	6.78	6.33	5.02	5.27
	16 1/8	9-18-21	16.27	16.28	15.70	15.63	6.35	5.46	8.01	8.01

July 1982–December 1982

Issue			Yield to Maturity 7/1/82 (%)	Yield to Maturity 12/31/82 (%)	Call Adjusted Yield 7/1/82 (%)	Call Adjusted Yield 12/31/82 (%)	Actual Duration (Years)	Call Adjusted Duration (Years)	Total Return (%)	Duration Adjusted Total Return (%)
Bell Tel of Pa	11 7/8	4-15-20	15.40	12.20	15.18	11.74	6.79	6.36	32.93	29.73
	15 1/8	4-15-21	16.02	13.28	15.52	12.46	6.52	5.64	27.75	27.75
Michigan Bell Tel	8 1/8	6-1-15	15.25	11.70	15.22	11.63	7.10	7.02	38.05	31.22
	15 3/4	5-1-21	16.25	13.65	15.71	12.86	6.48	5.59	26.49	26.49
Mountain States Tel	11 1/4	11-1-19	15.50	12.20	15.34	11.87	6.80	6.49	34.02	28.95
	15 3/4	8-5-21	16.27	13.59	15.71	12.74	6.23	5.37	26.39	26.39
New Jersey Bell	8 1/4	2-15-16	15.05	11.60	15.01	11.52	6.88	6.79	35.96	30.69
	14 5/8	3-1-21	15.87	13.16	15.38	12.41	6.46	5.65	27.23	27.23
New York Tel	8 7/8	6-15-18	15.05	11.70	14.97	11.57	7.17	7.00	36.18	28.66
	15 5/8	7-15-21	16.15	13.50	15.63	12.72	6.22	5.33	26.12	26.12
Ohio Bell Tel	9	11-1-18	15.05	11.75	14.96	11.61	7.04	6.86	35.07	31.04
	12 5/8	2-1-20	15.55	12.50	15.26	11.94	6.52	5.95	30.46	30.46
Southern Bell Tel	10.90	12-1-19	15.30	11.85	15.15	11.47	6.98	6.63	36.33	30.62
	16	11-1-21	16.17	13.69	15.51	12.85	6.51	5.44	25.56	25.56
South Central Bell	9 5/8	3-1-19	15.07	11.70	14.96	11.50	6.85	6.61	34.93	32.41
	12 7/8	10-1-20	15.56	12.55	15.25	11.98	6.68	6.06	30.65	30.65
Southwestern Bell	11 3/8	1-15-20	15.45	12.20	15.27	11.84	6.53	6.20	32.45	28.55
	16 1/8	9-18-21	16.28	13.81	15.63	12.98	6.35	5.33	24.99	24.99

January 1983–June 1983

Issue			Yield to Maturity 1/1/83 (%)	Yield to Maturity 6/30/83 (%)	Call Adjusted Yield 1/1/83 (%)	Call Adjusted Yield 6/30/83 (%)	Actual Duration (Years)	Call Adjusted Duration (Years)	Total Return (%)	Duration Adjusted Total Return (%)
Bell Tel of Pa	11 7/8	4-15-20	12.20	12.13	11.74	11.57	8.40	6.80	6.61	6.25
	15 1/8	4-15-21	13.28	12.85	12.46	11.19	7.74	5.75	9.79	9.79
Michigan Bell Tel	8 1/8	6-1-15	11.70	12.10	11.63	12.05	9.00	8.71	2.54	3.22
	15 3/4	5-1-21	13.65	13.35	12.86	11.97	7.59	5.81	8.94	8.94
Mountain States Tel	11 1/4	11-1-19	12.20	12.30	11.87	11.95	8.46	7.25	5.27	5.09
	15 3/4	8-5-21	13.59	13.41	12.74	12.02	7.39	5.71	7.92	7.92
New England Tel	12.20	5-15-17	12.45	12.22	12.02	11.60	8.29	6.75	8.02	7.65
	15 1/4	6-15-18	13.69	12.84	13.11	11.10	7.67	6.10	13.31	13.31
New Jersey Bell	8 1/4	2-15-16	11.60	11.80	11.52	11.72	8.77	8.44	4.10	4.23
	14 5/8	3-1-21	13.16	12.75	12.41	11.27	7.69	5.60	9.52	9.52
New York Tel	8 7/8	6-15-18	11.70	11.85	11.57	11.73	9.00	8.50	4.58	4.54
	15 5/8	7-15-21	13.50	12.97	12.72	11.22	7.38	5.79	10.39	10.39
Ohio Bell Tel	9	11-1-18	11.75	11.90	11.61	11.78	8.84	8.30	4.61	4.57
	12 5/8	2-1-20	12.50	12.35	11.94	11.59	8.00	6.45	7.29	7.29
Pacific Tel & Tel	12.70	11-15-19	12.89	12.30	12.47	11.51	8.06	6.62	11.08	10.12
	16 1/8	4-1-21	14.19	13.53	13.60	12.07	7.25	5.74	11.68	11.68
Southern Bell Tel	10.90	12-1-19	11.85	11.89	11.47	11.49	8.77	7.44	5.58	5.29
	16	11-1-21	13.69	13.28	12.85	11.57	7.57	5.66	9.78	9.78
South Central Bell	9 5/8	3-1-19	11.70	11.92	11.50	11.74	8.67	7.97	4.02	4.09
	12 7/8	10-1-20	12.55	12.37	11.98	11.55	8.13	6.63	7.62	7.62
Southwestern Bell	11 3/8	1-15-20	12.20	12.30	11.84	11.91	8.16	6.92	5.22	5.06
	16 1/8	9-18-21	13.81	13.39	12.98	11.68	7.40	5.53	9.80	9.80

July 1983–December 1983

Issue			Yield to Maturity 7/1/83 (%)	Yield to Maturity 12/31/83 (%)	Call Adjusted Yield 7/1/83 (%)	Call Adjusted Yield 12/31/83 (%)	Actual Duration (Years)	Call Adjusted Duration (Years)	Total Return (%)	Duration Adjusted Total Return (%)
Bell Tel of Pa	11 7/8	4-15-20	12.13	12.90	11.57	12.56	8.43	6.79	.26	2.04
	15 1/8	4-15-21	12.85	13.15	11.19	11.60	7.96	4.32	4.18	4.18
New England Tel	12.20	5-15-17	12.22	13.07	11.60	12.75	8.41	6.37	-.23	1.39
	15 1/4	6-15-18	12.84	13.37	11.10	12.08	8.09	4.48	2.54	2.54
New Jersey Bell	8 1/4	2-15-16	11.80	12.57	11.72	12.52	8.63	8.29	-.05	2.15
	14 5/8	3-1-21	12.75	13.21	11.27	12.05	7.90	4.75	3.01	3.01
New York Tel	8 7/8	6-15-18	11.85	12.67	11.73	12.60	8.90	8.42	-.54	2.10
	15 5/8	7-15-21	12.97	13.32	11.22	11.70	7.65	4.50	3.94	3.94
Pacific Tel & Tel	15	11-1-20	12.82	13.27	10.96	11.85	8.02	3.91	3.09	3.09
	16 1/8	4-1-21	13.53	13.72	12.07	12.12	7.56	4.43	5.37	5.29
South Central Bell	9 7/8	9-15-18	12.00	12.72	11.82	12.57	8.50	7.63	.50	1.60
	12 7/8	10-1-20	12.37	13.12	11.55	12.64	8.23	5.81	.65	.65
Southwestern Bell	11 3/8	1-15-20	12.30	13.07	11.91	12.85	8.10	6.78	.53	1.76
	14 1/4	12-10-20	12.72	13.43	11.54	12.69	8.20	4.97	1.16	1.16

January 1984–June 1984

Issue		Yield to Maturity 1/1/84 (%)	Yield to Maturity 6/30/84 (%)	Call Adjusted Yield 1/1/84 (%)	Call Adjusted Yield 6/30/84 (%)	Actual Duration (Years)	Call Adjusted Duration (Years)	Total Return (%)	Duration Adjusted Total Return (%)
Bell Tel of Pa	11 7/8 4-15-20	12.90	14.46	12.56	14.29	7.98	6.92	-4.06	-.90
	15 1/8 4-15-21	13.15	14.71	11.60	14.03	7.80	4.67	-3.71	-3.71
Michigan Bell Tel	8 1/8 6-1-15	12.87	14.33	12.84	14.32	8.29	8.18	-3.83	.26
	15 3/4 5-1-21	13.57	14.92	12.14	14.11	7.62	4.60	-2.04	-2.04
Mountain States Tel	11 1/4 11-1-19	13.12	14.59	12.93	14.49	7.92	7.34	-3.33	.41
	15 3/4 8-5-21	13.51	14.99	11.82	14.15	7.41	4.25	-2.65	-2.65
New England Tel	12.20 5-15-17	13.07	14.59	12.75	14.41	7.94	6.72	-3.68	-1.14
	15 1/4 6-15-18	13.37	15.00	12.08	14.41	7.81	4.89	-4.01	-4.01
New Jersey Bell	8 1/4 2-15-16	12.57	14.03	12.52	14.01	8.16	8.02	-3.86	-.07
	14 5/8 3-1-21	13.21	14.72	12.05	14.15	7.65	4.78	-3.23	-3.23
New York Tel	8 7/8 6-15-18	12.67	14.45	12.60	14.43	8.39	8.13	-6.03	-.32
	15 5/8 7-15-21	13.32	15.05	11.70	14.40	7.46	4.16	-4.21	-4.21
Pacific Tel & Tel	12.70 11-15-19	13.24	14.79	12.86	14.60	7.86	6.57	-3.67	-.57
	15 11-1-20	13.27	15.04	11.85	14.54	7.77	4.39	-4.83	-4.83
Southern Bell Tel	12 7/8 10-5-20	13.06	14.59	12.57	14.33	7.85	6.18	-3.64	-.95
	16 11-1-21	13.64	14.94	12.03	13.94	7.59	4.40	-1.67	-1.67
Southwestern Bell	11 3/8 1-15-20	13.07	14.59	12.85	14.33	7.66	6.95	-3.39	.08
	16 1/8 9-18-21	13.74	14.89	12.13	13.76	7.41	4.27	-.58	-.58

July 1984–December 1984

Issue			Yield to Maturity 7/1/84 (%)	Yield to Maturity 12/31/84 (%)	Call Adjusted Yield 7/1/84 (%)	Call Adjusted Yield 12/31/84 (%)	Actual Duration (Years)	Call Adjusted Duration (Years)	Total Return (%)	Duration Adjusted Total Return (%)
Bell Tel of Pa	11 7/8	4-15-20	14.46	12.45	14.29	12.11	7.21	6.75	22.67	19.09
	15 1/8	4-15-21	14.71	13.07	14.03	11.12	7.06	5.41	19.27	19.27
Mountain States Tel	11 1/4	11-1-19	14.59	12.56	14.49	12.35	7.21	6.90	22.88	17.08
	15 3/4	8-5-21	14.99	13.65	14.15	11.97	6.74	4.70	16.50	16.50
Southern Bell Tel	12 7/8	10-5-20	14.59	12.68	14.33	12.12	7.11	6.49	21.83	17.72
	16	11-1-21	14.94	13.77	13.94	12.18	7.00	5.00	14.32	14.32
Southwestern Bell	11 3/8	1-15-20	14.59	12.60	14.33	12.36	6.91	6.38	21.60	17.41
	16 1/8	9-18-21	14.89	13.87	13.76	12.24	6.90	4.74	15.58	15.58

ARTICLE 11

ROBERT SMITH is a market analyst in the taxable Fixed Income Research Group of The First Boston Corporation. As a specialist in money market securities, he is responsible for assessing relative value among the wide variety of short term investment opportunities, floating rate notes, and T-bill and Eurodollar Futures. He is also the author of First Boston's *Money Market Review.*

Prior to joining The First Boston Corporation, Bob worked at General Mills Inc., where he was manager of corporate finance. He received his M.B.A. in finance from the University of Illinois, and B.A. from Indiana University.

PETER B. TAGGART is an Assistant Vice President and Portfolio Manager with First Boston Asset Management Corporation. He joined First Boston in 1984 as a member of the Fixed Income Research Group where he developed quantitative models for fixed income sales and trading. Mr. Taggart has developed models for floating rate securities, corporate bonds, zero coupon instruments, and high yield securities. He moved to the Asset Management Group in 1985.

Prior to joining First Boston, Mr. Taggart was an analyst at Commodities Corporation.

Mr. Taggart graduated from Colgate University in 1980, receiving a B.A. with Honors in Computer Science.

U.S. FLOATING RATE NOTES: STRUCTURE, ANALYSIS, AND PORTFOLIO STRATEGIES

Robert A. Smith
Vice President
The First Boston Corporation

Peter B. Taggart
Assistant Vice President
The First Boston Corporation

U.S. floating rate notes (floaters or FRNs) gained popularity in the late seventies and early eighties as defensive securities. In rising interest rate environments, they protected investors from the dramatic price volatility of fixed rate debt instruments. Since then, the market has matured considerably: floating rate formulas have been refined, and investors have learned to use these instruments to enhance as well as protect returns. For example:

- FRNs can be used as defensive securities. They exhibit less price volatility than fixed rate investments of comparable maturity and credit.

- FRNs are accepted by multisector investors as a higher yielding, fully manageable alternative to traditional money market instruments.

- Floating rate securities can be combined with interest rate swaps and futures to create synthetic fixed rate securities.

- FRNs are an increasingly important part of asset and liability management, especially for financial managers who match fund floating rate assets with shorter maturity money market liabilities.

- Various analytical methods have been developed to value floaters. These methods allow investors to compare FRN investment opportunities with others available in both the fixed and floating rate markets.

This article reviews and updates information available on the U.S. floating rate product.[1] A brief history of floaters is presented in Section I. The structural variables and how they affect price volatility and value is discussed in Section II. Section III presents analytical methods. A few important portfolio strategies using floaters are outlined in Section IV.

I. HISTORY OF FLOATING RATE NOTES

A floating rate note is a debt instrument that pays a variable (or floating) coupon based on an interest rate index such as Treasury bills, the London Interbank Offered Rate (LIBOR), or commercial paper. The FRN market has grown considerably since 1974, with issuance volume rising from $1.3 billion in 1974 to $9.1 billion in 1985. Increasingly, issuers and investors have sought to replace traditional long-term, fixed rate debt with securities having variable interest rates and shorter maturities. FRNs enable issuers to fund interest rate sensitive assets, to refinance variable rate bank debt at a net savings, or to take advantage of either declining interest rates or a positively sloped yield curve.

Exhibit 1 shows the three periods of increased activity for floating rate notes: 1974, 1978–79, and 1982–85. Each of the three periods came on the heels of increased interest rate volatility. Each surge of issuance produced improvements in the product.

[1] For information on Euro FRNs, see Susan Ziobro *Euro Floating Rate Notes 1985 Market Review,* London: Credit Suisse First Boston, March 1986.

The first group of U.S. floating rate notes had maturities of 15 to 20 years, semiannual coupon adjustments and payments, and coupons that refixed at a spread over 3-month Treasury bills. Issues that remain outstanding from this group are currently putable and callable on payment dates.

After a three-year lull in issuance, a second group of floaters reached the U.S. market in 1978 and 1979. These issues had maturities ranging from 8 to 30 years, and were structured to reset and pay interest semiannually. They did not include a put option, but some were convertible into fixed rate bonds. Investors found these securities more attractive than earlier issues because they reset off the longer maturity, and usually higher yielding, 6-month Treasury issue.

The third wave of floating rate securities, those issued since the early 1980s, have had maturities of 3 to 15 years and greater

EXHIBIT 1
U.S. Floating Rate Security Issuance 1974–1985

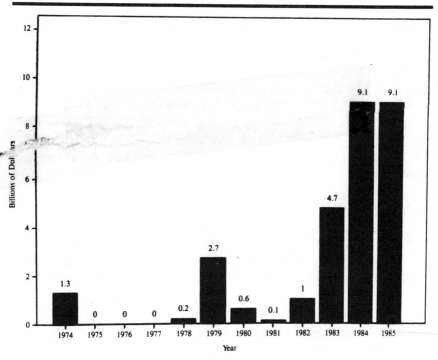

variation in structure than their predecessors. These issues have featured refinements aimed at reducing price volatility: monthly and quarterly coupon payments, weekly coupon resets, and a LIBOR index.

II. STRUCTURE OF FLOATING RATE NOTES

Floating rate notes experience lower price volatility than do fixed rate securities, given the same issuer and maturity. They accomplish this by periodically adjusting coupon levels. FRN coupons are reset to equal an index rate plus or minus a predetermined margin. The price of a floater will fluctuate, however, when the coupon level alone does not compensate investors for credit risk. The more accurately a floater's coupon adjusts to compensate investors for credit risk, the lower the issue's price volatility.

Structural variables that affect FRN price volatility are:

- index and margin
- maturity
- coupon refix frequency

In addition to these parameters, some issues contain caps, collars, floors, or conversion features, which further modify price volatility. Other structural variables, such as coupon payment frequency and delay, do not affect price volatility but do affect a floater's yield and value. These two features are discussed at the end of this section.

Index and Margin[2]

The combination of index and margin is the most critical structural variable to examine when investing in a floating rate note. Together, they determine current and anticipated coupon income

[2] For a more thorough discussion of index and margin, see Neal Soss, "Floating Rate Securities: The Choice of Interest Index," in *Floating Rate Instruments*, Frank Fabozzi ed., Chicago: Probus Publishing Company, 1986, pp. 221–232.

of the issue and establish the basis for price evaluation. An index that reflects the issuer's industry fundamentals, cost of funds, and credit quality will reduce price volatility, because it will help maintain the floater's coupon at a level that is comparable to the general industry's cost of funds.

Index: Issuers of U.S. floating rate notes have relied primarily upon two indices: U.S. Treasury bills and LIBOR. Half of U.S. floaters outstanding have a Treasury bill index, 36 percent are based on LIBOR, and 7 percent have the option to use either. Other indices, including commercial paper, certificates of deposit (CDs), and prime rate account for the remainder.

Treasury Bill Index: The Treasury bill bond equivalent yield is the most frequently used index for U.S. floaters. Typically, issuers have used the bond equivalent yield of the 3- or 6-month Treasury bill as determined in the weekly auctions and announced by the Treasury. Issues based on Treasury bills add a margin to the index rate to calculate coupon levels. This margin is a premium that investors receive for accepting the credit risk of the issuer. Interest is paid on an actual/actual or 30/360 basis.

LIBOR Index: The London Interbank Offered Rate (LIBOR) is the second most predominant refix index in U.S. floaters. LIBOR rates are quoted by the major London banks when offering Eurodollar deposits to one another. While LIBOR reflects the costs of Eurodollar deposits for terms ranging from overnight through five years, the most popular LIBOR rates used for coupon resets are the 3- and 6-month rates. In practice, most LIBOR based coupons are determined by referring to the rate set by a specific reference bank or group of banks at 11:00 A.M. London time. Interest is paid on an actual/360 basis.

Index Relationships: Historically, floating rate notes indexed to Treasury bills have experienced greater price volatility than issues based on LIBOR. This difference in volatility results from the difference in credit sensitivity of the indices: LIBOR is more sensitive to global credit risk than are Treasury bills.

Treasury bills are considered a riskless security. LIBOR, on the other hand, reflects the global banking community's cost of attracting deposits, a cost that includes a yield premium added to the Treasury bill rate for credit risk. When investor confidence in the banking system is strong, this credit premium is reduced and the spread between Treasuries and LIBOR (the TED spread) narrows. When confidence wanes, such as during the Argentinian debt crisis in 1982 or the Continental Illinois crisis in 1984, the TED spread widens.

Many FRN issuers are financial institutions. Accordingly, when the TED spread is widening or narrowing, investors are demanding greater or lesser yields for accepting the credit risk of these FRN issuers. A floater based on LIBOR will automatically adjust its coupon income to market-determined levels for the credit risk of financial institutions. On the other hand, the coupon of a floater based on Treasury bills will not respond to these changes in credit. Its price must adjust to provide the comparable yield to maturity (YTM).

Exhibit 2 illustrates the inherent price volatility of a Treasury bill indexed floater. The top half of this exhibit shows the prices since 1984 of two floating rate notes. These floaters have similar credit quality and maturity. The major difference between these issues is that one resets based on 3-month LIBOR and the other on 3-month Treasury bills. The bottom half of the exhibit contains the TED spread since 1982.

The Citicorp Treasury bill based floater experienced greater price deterioration than the Irving LIBOR based FRN during the summer of 1984. The price deterioration was caused by a widening of the TED spread through August 1984. Consequently, banks had to pay more to attract deposits. The LIBOR indexed FRN was providing the market-determined YTM through coupon income. The Treasury bill indexed issue had to decline in price in order to maintain a competitive YTM.

Margin: Most FRNs reset their coupons at a fixed spread over an index rate. This spread is called the quoted margin, and serves to provide different coupon levels for investments based on the same index. The quoted margin equalizes issuer credit variations by providing greater coupon income for weaker credits.

Quoted margins are usually expressed in basis points (e.g.,

EXHIBIT 2
Price Volatility due to Index Rate

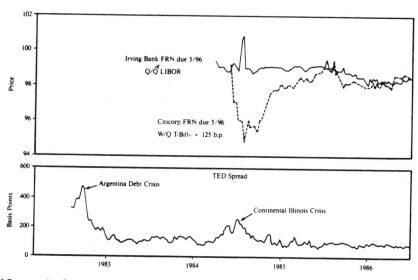

*Quarterly/Quarterly

Treasury bills plus 50 b.p.), but some FRNs refix at a percentage of their index (e.g., 110 percent of LIBOR). Several issues have refix margins that change over time. The margin might be 100 b.p. over Treasury bills for the first few years, then drop to 75 b.p., and ultimately drop to 50 b.p.

For some FRNs issued after 1982, the coupon refix formula incorporates several index rates and margins. A $1.5 billion Kingdom of Sweden issue resets its coupon at the 3-month CD rate plus 55 b.p. or prime rate minus 40 b.p., whichever is lower at the time of refix.

"Reverse" floaters were introduced in 1986. These issues refix their coupons by subtracting an index rate from a fixed interest rate. For example, one Citicorp FRN issued in 1986 resets its coupon at 17 3/8 percent minus the current 6-month LIBOR rate.

Issuer Credit Quality: The combination of index and margin must reflect the credit quality of the individual issuer in order to maintain an issue's price near par. Since these structural parameters are set at issuance, subsequent changes in the credit of the issuer will likely result in price movement of the security. Exhibit 3 shows the price volatility of a U.S. floating rate note due to credit deterioration of the issuer.

The Phillips Petroleum floating rate note resets its coupon quarterly based on the 3-month LIBOR rate. The price of the Phillips floater, however, declined as a result of the steep drop in oil prices. Investors feared that Phillips would have difficulty servicing its interest expense as its revenues declined. In response, its senior debt rating was lowered from Baa3/BBB to Ba1/BBB in March 1986; consequently, investors demanded a greater yield premium from this issue. The only way for the issue to provide this increased yield premium was through a lower price.

EXHIBIT 3
Price Volatility due to Issuer Credit

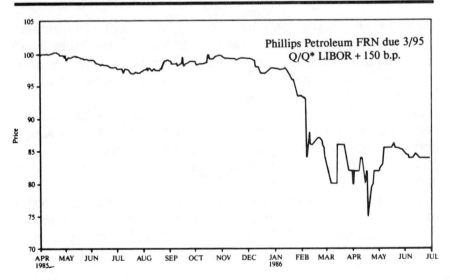

Phillips Petroleum FRN due 3/95
Q/Q* LIBOR + 150 b.p.

*Quarterly/Quarterly

Maturity

The maturity (or put or call date, if applicable) of a floating rate note is a secondary structural variable for determining price volatility. A floater with a longer time to maturity will experience a greater magnitude of price movement than a similar issue with a shorter time to maturity. This relationship between maturity and price volatility is explained by modified duration.

Modified duration is the present value weighted average cash flow of an investment, divided by a factor.[3] The percentage price change of a security is equal to the negative of the security's modified duration multiplied by the required change in yield. For example, a 5-year fixed rate bond with a modified duration of 4.1 years will decline by 4.1 percent if interest rates rise by 100 b.p. $(-4.1 \times .01 = -.041)$. A security with a longer time to maturity will typically have a longer modified duration, and thus experience greater price volatility, than a shorter maturity issue.

In contrast to a fixed rate bond, the coupon reset mechanism of FRNs prevents price deterioration due to rising interest rate levels. An increase in the general level of interest rates will raise a floater's yield by way of a higher coupon rate. A floater will decline in price, however, when investors need an increased yield premium due to a perceived weakening in issuer credit relative to its floater index. This yield increase can not be provided through the FRN coupon mechanism.

The modified duration of a floating rate note is technically impossible to calculate, since the future cash flows are not known with certainty. Using the same cash flows assumed for the floater's yield to maturity (YTM), however, a modified duration can be derived. This modified duration will explain the magnitude of FRN price movement due to changes in credit premiums. If investors demand an additional 10 b.p. in credit premium, then a floater with a modified duration of 4.1 years will decline in price about .41 percent.

Exhibit 4 illustrates the impact of modified duration on price volatility by comparing the prices of two Citicorp issues, due in

---

[3] The factor is the quantity (1 + yield/annual coupon payment frequency).

EXHIBIT 4
Price Volatility due to Modified Duration

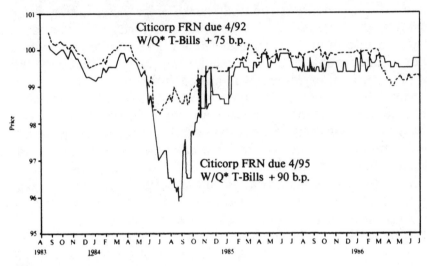

*With Quarterly

1992 and 1995, respectively. These issues have the same credit quality, reset index and frequency, payment frequency, and put price, and have similar refix spreads. The major difference is their retirement (put) dates. The Citicorp '92 was putable on 4/10/86 while the Citicorp '95 is putable on 4/10/89.

The exhibit shows that the prices of both Citicorp issues declined below par as the spread between LIBOR and Treasury bills widened in 1984. Since both issues are indexed to Treasury bills, their prices dropped in order to maintain the yield to retirement (put) date of these issues at a level consistent with the LIBOR market. The Citicorp '95 issue declined more than the '92 issue, however, because of its longer time to put and longer modified duration.

Coupon Refix Frequency

The periodic reset of a floater's coupon to current market levels reduces price volatility by shortening the periods during which coupon income can vary from market levels. All else equal, a shorter refix period reduces the likelihood that a coupon will vary from market levels.

U.S. FRN coupon rates refix on weekly, monthly, quarterly, semiannual, and annual bases. Quarterly reset issues are most commonly based on LIBOR, while issues that reset weekly or semiannually are most frequently based on Treasury bills. Monthly and annual refix issues can be found using each index.

Historically, floating rate notes with more frequent coupon resets have shown greater price stability than those that reset their coupon levels less frequently. Exhibit 5 compares the price volatility of two Citicorp Aa1/AA rated floaters with different reset frequencies. The weekly reset issue has maintained far greater price stability than the semiannual reset issue.

EXHIBIT 5
Price Volatility due to Refix Frequency

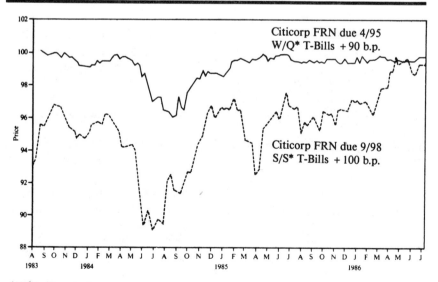

*With Quarterly

**Semiannual

Coupon Payment Frequency

Floaters offer monthly, quarterly, semiannual, and annual payments. The timing of a floater's cash flow has an impact upon the effective yield: for the same nominal coupon rate, more frequent coupon payments will result in a higher effective yield. This increase in effective yield is due to the reinvestment of cash flows.

Exhibit 6 displays the impact of payment frequency for coupon rates from 6 percent to 10 percent. For example, a monthly paying security with a coupon rate of 8 percent would provide an effective yield of 8.14 percent due to reinvestment of the monthly coupon income. The same security making semiannual payments would provide an effective CBE yield of only 8.00 percent.

Coupon Payment Delay

The end of the coupon period does not necessarily correspond to the coupon payment date. For example, most weekly refix/quarterly pay FRNs have a delay period of 6 to 16 days. A payment delay reduces effective yield because a coupon does not accrue interest between the end of the coupon period and the payment date. Exhibit 7 shows the effect of 6- and 16-day delays on quarterly paying floaters with 6 percent, 8 percent, and 10 percent coupon rates. The 10 percent coupon issue would yield 10.13 percent with no payment delay, while a 16-day delay on the same issue would reduce the yield to 10.09 percent.

EXHIBIT 6
Impact of Coupon Payment Frequency (Corporate Bond Equivalent)

	Frequency of Coupon Payments				
Coupon Rate	Daily*	Monthly	Quarterly	Semiannually	Annually
6%	6.09%	6.08%	6.05%	6.00%	5.91%
8	8.16	8.14	8.08	8.00	7.85
10	10.25	10.21	10.13	10.00	9.76

*FRNs do not pay daily. Daily payments are included here only for comparison to overnight repo rates or federal funds rates.

EXHIBIT 7
Impact of Coupon Payment Delay (Corporate Bond Equivalent)

Coupon Rate	No Delay	6-Day Delay	16-Day Delay
6%	6.05%	6.04%	6.03%
8	8.08	8.07	8.06
10	10.13	10.11	10.09

III. ANALYTICAL METHODS

The goal of floating rate security analysis is to provide a standard measurement of value. The measurement should enable investors to compare floating rate securities with other floating rate securities as well as with fixed rate securities. It must take into account the current market price, expected future interest rates, and all structural variables of the issue. Two commonly used floater valuation techniques are yield to maturity (YTM) and YTM spread analysis. Both are typically expressed as corporate bond equivalents.

Yield to Maturity (YTM)

The standard bond market method of quantifying cash flows is the yield to maturity formula.[4] Yield to maturity is the rate which, when used to discount the future coupon and principal payments back to the settlement date, produces the settlement cost, including any accrued interest. This method of analysis can be applied to floating rate as well as fixed rate securities.

YTM can be computed for fixed rate instruments because future coupon income is known. In order to compute yield to maturity for floating rate instruments, future coupon income must be estimated.

Exhibit 8 compares the cash flows of two securities, one fixed rate and one floating rate. Each security has two and one-third

---

[4]For a more technical discussion of valuation methods, see David Muntner, "Analysis of Floating Rate Securities," in *Floating Rate Instruments*, Frank Fabozzi, ed., Chicago: Probus Publishing Company, 1986, pp. 203–220.

EXHIBIT 8
Cash Flows for a Fixed Rate and a Floating Rate Security

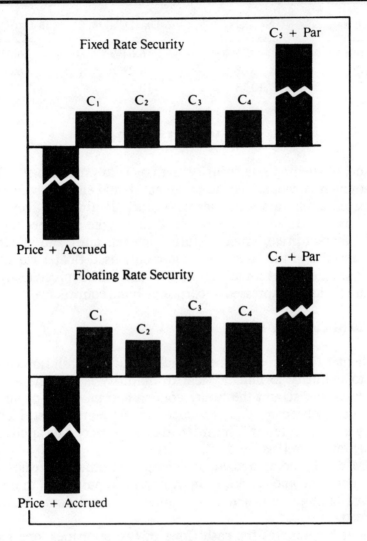

years to maturity and makes semiannual coupon payments. The payments above the horizontal line represent cash inflows; the one below the line (the first payment) represents a cash outflow equal to the cost of the security, including accrued interest. At maturity, the additional income is due to the return of principal.

For the fixed coupon security, the five equal coupon payments are known. In contrast, only the first coupon payment of a floating rate security may be known. An estimate of the security's index rate must be made for future coupon dates. A single rate is normally selected as the average expected rate for the index. The floater may therefore have uneven cash flows, since the accrued interest and first coupon payment for the floating rate security will be determined by one coupon rate (the current coupon) and all of the subsequent coupon payments will be computed using a second coupon rate (determined by the coupon refix formula).

The U.S. corporate bond market assumes semiannual compounding of interest and uses 30/360 accounting. The benefit of presenting YTM on a bond equivalent basis is that it facilitates comparisons to most fixed rate securities. If the alternative investment makes interest payments on a monthly, quarterly, or annual basis, the YTM formula can be adjusted to provide a yield on the same basis.

Many floating rate securities include redemption features that are important to issuers and investors. Call dates and call prices or put dates and put prices can be included in the yield to maturity formulation. The analysis is modified to end at the call date or put date and the corresponding price is substituted when it is not par. Investors usually assume that premium securities will be called by the issuer while discount securities will be put back to the company on the put date.

YTM Spread Analysis

The earliest calculations used to analyze floating rate securities sought to compare the return of the floater to the return of the index. This method makes the most sense when all of the securities being considered use the same index for establishing new coupon rates (e.g., 3-month LIBOR or 6-month Treasury bills). As the floater market has grown, frequent issuers have been using both the U.S. and European markets, a variety of indices, and a variety of coupon refix formulas. Consequently, yield spread calculations in floating rate security analysis have become less valuable. To address the difficulties in the early formulations of yield spreads, two formulas have been developed—YTM Spread, used in the United States, and Discounted Margin, used in Europe.[5]

YTM spread is the difference between the YTM of the floating rate security and that of the index rate. The return of the index rate is the expected return obtained by rolling over investments in the index, and can be computed like the YTM of the FRN. It uses the short-term index rate as the first coupon and the assumed short-term future index rate in place of future coupon rates. This yield must be expressed on the same compounding basis as that of the floating rate security.

Using the yield to maturity calculation, investors can now accurately calculate the yield spread (or the expected incremental return) of the floating rate security over the expected return of the index rate.

IV. PORTFOLIO STRATEGIES

Investors have found a variety of uses for floating rate securities. Floaters offer higher yields than traditional money market securities. They may be used to create securities with certain attributes (e.g., credit quality, issuer, maturity) that otherwise are unavailable in the cash market. Arbitragers may match fund FRNs to lock in profits. What follows is a discussion of three major portfolio strategies for floating rate notes: enhancing money market returns, creating synthetic fixed rate investments, and arbitraging among cash and money market securities.

Enhancing Money Market Returns

Floating rate notes have higher yields than traditional money market securities, but have similar interest rate risk. Consequently, money market investors find floaters attractive. A floater will outperform money market alternatives over a given holding period, assuming price amortization consistent with the YTM calculation.

Exhibit 9 compares the yield of a Chase '95 LIBOR based FRN

---

[5] For a discussion of Discounted Margin, see Richard Williams, "Floating Rate Notes: Methods of Analysis," which is the next article in this book.

EXHIBIT 9
Comparison of Yields

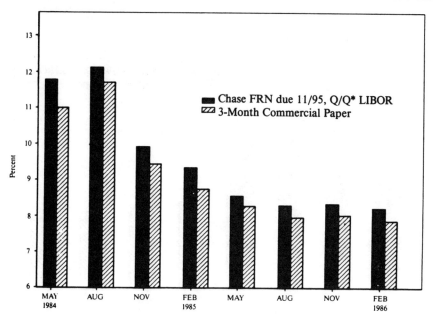

*Quarterly/Quarterly

with that of 3-month commercial paper for the past two years. The Chase issue provided a higher yield than commercial paper in all quarters, and an average 45 basis point annual yield advantage over the entire period.

Exhibit 10 shows that while the Chase floater had a higher yield than commercial paper, its quarterly total returns fluctuated relative to those of commercial paper. In the quarters beginning May and August 1984, this Chase floater experienced slight price deterioration. Its total return was less than that of commercial paper as a result. This price deterioration was reversed in the next two quarters, allowing the floater to outperform commercial paper by a significant margin in this period.

Exhibits 9 and 10 illustrate two important FRN strategies for money market investors. First, floaters can be used as a core holding group when investors need an effective duration similar to

EXHIBIT 10
Comparison of Annualized Returns

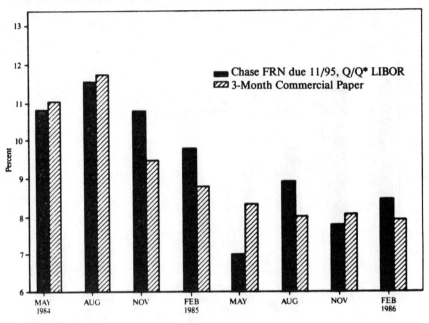

*Quarterly/Quarterly

short-term investments. While quarter-to-quarter returns may fluctuate, investors who can hold floaters for longer periods historically have obtained higher returns than those generated with money market alternatives. In the example above, the Chase FRN provided .16 percent greater annual return than commercial paper over two years.

Second, aggressive investors can achieve superior returns by owning floaters as they appreciate in price. The price of an FRN will rise when issuer credit quality is improving relative to Treasuries when Treasury bills are the index and relative to the banking industry when LIBOR is the index. The total return earned from an appreciating issue will be much greater than that provided by money market securities. Conversely, the total return from a depreciating issue may be less than that provided by money market securities. While the total return of the Chase issue was only slightly better than that of commercial paper, the Chase returns were significantly better in four of the eight quarters. For example, in the 3-month period starting in August 1985, the Chase floater outperformed the commercial paper by 1.30 percent on an annualized basis.

Creating Synthetic Fixed Rate Securities

While money market investors may find floaters attractive as a high yielding alternative to traditional short-term investments, the use of FRNs should not be limited to the short end of the portfolio. Investors who maintain a longer duration portfolio may also find these issues rewarding as part of a synthetic alternative to the fixed rate bond market. Synthetic fixed rate securities may enable the investor either to obtain a yield for a given credit that is higher than that available on comparable fixed rate issues or to create a specific asset/duration combination that is unavailable in the cash market.

Synthetic fixed rate securities can be created by combining floating rate notes with either asset-based interest rate swaps or financial futures. Since FRNs have short durations, they will decline little in price due to movement of the general level of interest rates. At the same time, floaters have credit risk that is similar to that of fixed rate securities of the same issuer with the same maturity. By adding duration to the FRN, the synthetic security will perform similarly to fixed rate issues in all interest rate environments.

Asset-Based Interest Rate Swaps. An interest rate swap allows investors to change the duration of their portfolios with only minimal increases in credit risk. Investors agree to make payments based on the differential between two interest indices, with no principal amount involved. When investors agree to make payments based on a short-term floating rate index and receive fixed payments, they lengthen the duration of their investment portfolio. Conversely, by agreeing to pay the longer-term fixed rate and receive the floating, the duration of the portfolio is shortened.

To create a synthetic fixed rate issue using an interest rate swap, investors agree to swap floating for fixed rate payments. This floating for fixed swap adds to the duration of the FRN.

Exhibit 11 shows a transaction combining a Citicorp Person-to-Person floating rate note and an interest rate swap. The floater is a weekly reset, quarterly paying instrument that carries a coupon of 3-month Treasury bills + 125 b.p. and matures on 5/10/96. It is priced at 98.625. The next payment is due on 7/01/86.

The notional amount of the swap is equal to the face value of the FRN. The investor has agreed to make quarterly payments based on the weekly average interest rate of 3-month Treasury bills and receive an amount equal to the interest rate of the 10-year Treasury note. In addition, the swap outflows are timed to occur on the same dates as the floater coupon payments.

The result of this combination is a synthetic 10-year corporate security. The credit risk and duration of this synthetic are similar to those of a fixed rate 10-year Citicorp issue. The synthetic security, however, provides a YTM of 9.16 percent, compared to the 8.85 percent YTM for the fixed rate Citicorp Person-to-Person 8 3/4 issue of 3/01/98.

EXHIBIT 11
Interest Rate Swap with a Floating Rate Note

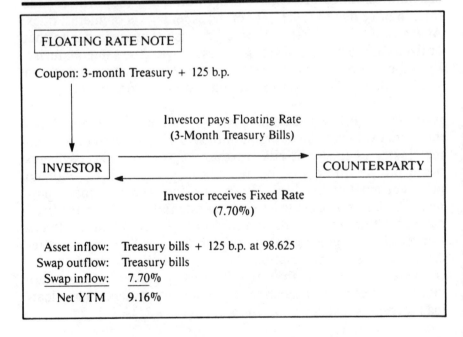

FLOATING RATE NOTE

Coupon: 3-month Treasury + 125 b.p.

Investor pays Floating Rate
(3-Month Treasury Bills)

INVESTOR   COUNTERPARTY

Investor receives Fixed Rate
(7.70%)

Asset inflow: Treasury bills + 125 b.p. at 98.625
Swap outflow: Treasury bills
Swap inflow: 7.70%
Net YTM   9.16%

Basis risk between the FRN coupons and the interest rate swap has been eliminated in this example. Both floating rate payments, the coupon inflow from the floater and payment outflow from the swap, are based on the same index and are timed to occur on the same day. Investors may choose to accept basis risk when they feel that they are justly compensated for it.

Investors need to evaluate the trade-offs between similar swaps before deciding to accept the basis risk of coupon flows that are not based on the same index. Exhibit 12 presents two swaps. The LIBOR based swap provides a 9 basis point advantage to the investor. Should the spread between LIBOR and Treasury bills (the TED spread) widen, the LIBOR based swap would become less advantageous, perhaps even providing a lower return than its alternative. Should the TED spread narrow, the LIBOR based swap would become more advantageous. The choice of swap in this case depends on the investor's outlook for credit spreads, since the yield advantage is so small.

Financial Futures.[6] The second method of constructing a synthetic fixed rate security is to combine a floating rate note with a long position in interest rate futures. Like interest rate swaps,

---

EXHIBIT 12
Comparison of Interest Rate Swaps

	Treasury Based Swap	LIBOR Based Swap
Floating Index (Pay)	3-month T-Bills (−6.25%)	3-month LIBOR (−7.06%)
Fixed Rate Index (Receive)	10-year T-Notes (+7.70%)	10-year T-Notes + 90 b.p. (+8.60%)
Net Result	+1.45%	+1.54%

---

[6] For a more thorough discussion of investment strategies with financial futures to create synthetic securities, see *Money Market Futures Synthetics,* New York: First Boston Corporation, August 1986.

interest rate futures increase or decrease duration without significantly affecting credit risk. By adding a long position in note or bond futures to a long position in floaters, the duration of the combination can be increased to equal that of comparable maturity, fixed rate corporate issues.

The advantage of synthetic securities using futures is provided by capturing the convergence of the basis between cash and futures. In a positively sloped yield curve environment, debt futures will trade at a discount to the underlying cash securities, reflecting the value of carry available to holders of cash securities but not available to holders of futures. This difference is called the basis. As the delivery date of the futures contract nears, the value of carrying cash securities to that date will diminish and cash and futures prices will converge. This convergence provides the additional return to an investor who holds an FRN and a long futures position.

Exhibit 13 shows the construction of a synthetic corporate bond. This synthetic uses the Citicorp Person-to-Person FRN of 5/10/96 and September Treasury note futures as an alternative to the fixed rate Citicorp Person-to-Person 8 3/4s of 3/01/98. The synthetic issue has a duration and credit risk similar to that of the fixed rate security.[7]

In creating a synthetic security, the number of futures contracts is chosen such that the effective duration of the synthetic is the same as the cash alternative. The cheapest deliverable Treasury note will determine the effective duration of the futures contract.[8]

Exhibit 14 shows the historical convergence in the basis between Treasury notes and Treasury note futures over successive 2-month periods. The starting basis used in this exhibit is the difference between the prices of Treasury note futures and the cheapest to deliver Treasury note three months before the futures contract expires. The ending basis is the same measurement one month before contract expiration. After two months of the possible 3-month

---

[7] For the purpose of this example, the call features of the fixed rate note have been ignored. In practice, call features may have a significant effect on total return.

[8] This assumes that the cheapest deliverable note is also the most likely to be delivered.

EXHIBIT 13
Structure of Fixed Rate vs Synthetic Securities

	Citicorp 8¾ '98	Citicorp FRN '96
Settlement	9/02/86	9/02/86
Price	98.934	99.500
Yield	8.90%	6.63%
Interest Payments	Semiannual	Quarterly*
Refix Index	N.A.	3-month Treasury
Refix Spread	N.A.	125 b.p.
Modified Duration	7.13 years	N.A.
Maturity	3/01/98	5/10/96
Futures		
Settlement	N.A.	9/02/86
Delivery Month		December 1986
Purchase Price		103.313
Number of Contracts per $1,000,000 of Investment		14

*Coupons are paid on an actual/365 day basis, with the base Treasury rate assumed to be 5.26%.

holding period, the average convergence has been 64 percent. Because the futures and the cheapest to deliver Treasury note have always converged, investors can sell or swap the futures before delivery to benefit from a portion of the convergence. This historical pattern suggests that convergence is approximately linear.

Exhibit 15 compares the total return of the synthetic issue with that of the corporate security over a 3-month holding period. The example assumes that yield levels and intermarket spreads remain constant, and that the futures basis converges linearly. The synthetic issue outperforms the fixed term security as a result of the cash flow generated by the futures as they converge with the deliverable Treasury note.

Exhibit 16 compares the same Citicorp fixed rate and synthetic investments issue under changing interest rate environments.

EXHIBIT 14
Convergence of Treasury Note Futures and Deliverable Notes

Start Date	Starting Basis	End Date	Ending Basis	% Convergence
10/01/82	1.58%	11/30/82	.55%	65%
1/04/83	2.30	2/28/83	1.32	42
3/31/83	1.27	5/31/83	.86	32
7/01/83	.91	8/31/83	.48	47
10/01/83	.94	11/30/83	.32	66
1/04/84	.96	2/28/84	.15	84
4/02/84	1.35	5/31/84	.40	70
7/02/84	.89	8/31/84	.02	98
10/01/84	1.09	12/03/84	.78	28
1/04/85	1.30	2/28/85	.62	52
4/01/85	1.48	5/31/85	.36	76
7/01/85	1.77	8/30/85	.11	94
10/01/85	1.38	11/29/85	.34	75
Average				64%

Again, we assume yield spreads are constant and that the futures will converge linearly. In addition, we assume that there is no change in the deliverable Treasury note issue, and that the indicated yield changes occur on 9/03/86.

Arbitrage

A third major use of FRNs is arbitrage. Investors can lock in profits and insulate themselves from interest rate movements by matching their liabilities with appropriate floating rate notes. For example, a financial institution that finances itself at LIBID can lock in a current yield advantage by investing in a floater that pays LIBOR + 15 basis points. Refix index, refix date, payment dates, maturity, and payment calculations should all be considered when doing this.

To illustrate the importance of matching payment considerations, Exhibit 17 compares arbitrage income using different refix

EXHIBIT 15
Comparison of Total Returns: Citicorp Fixed Rate and Synthetic Issues, 9/02/86–12/01/86 Cash Flow for Fixed Rate Citicorp Issue

Date	Event	Cash Flow
9/02/86	Buy Citi 8¾ '98	− 98.93 (principal) − .02 (1 day accrued interest)
12/01/86	Sell Citi 8¾ '98	98.92 (principal) 2.19 (90 days of accrued interest)
	IRR	8.91 %(CBE)

Cash Flow for Synthetic Citicorp Issue

Date	Event	Cash Flow
9/02/86	Buy Citi FRN '96	− 99.500 (principal) − 1.124 (63 days of accrued interest)
	Buy 1.4 T-note futures @ 103.313	−
10/01/86	Receive coupon payment	1.641
12/01/86	Sell Citi FRN '96	99.500 (principal) 1.088 (61 days of accrued interest)
	Sell 1.4 T-note futures @ 104.469*	1.619
	IRR	13.32 %(CBE)

*The price of the futures is determined by the 11³/₄ '93 (the cheapest to deliver issue), which has a delivery factor of 1.1924. With yields unchanged, it is priced at 125.188 on December 1, 1986. Linear convergence would leave the basis at 20/32nds of a point, which is 25% of the initial 80/32nds basis on September 2, 1986.
The futures price is therefore (125.188 − 0.625)/1.1924 = 104 − 15, or 104.469.

EXHIBIT 16
Comparison of Total Returns:
Citicorp Fixed Rate and Synthetic Issues, 9/02/86–12/01/86
Changing Interest Rates

Interest Rate Change	Citicorp Fixed	Citicorp Synthetic	Synthetic Advantage
+ 100 b.p.	− 17.93%	− 15.48%	2.45%
+ 50	− 5.06	− 2.20	2.86
0	8.91	13.32	4.41
− 50	24.10	28.60	4.50
− 100	40.61	45.11	4.50

EXHIBIT 17
Comparison of Arbitrage Returns

	Refix on Last Day of Month	Refix on Fifth Day of Month
Index	1-month LIBOR	1-month LIBOR
Quoted Margin	15 b.p.	15 b.p.
Price	100	100
Payment Frequency	Monthly	Monthly
Accrual Basis	Act/360	Act/360
Accrual Beginning	1/02/86	1/02/86
Accrual Ending	3/31/86	3/31/86
First Payment Date	1/31/86	1/05/86
Annualized Return (Corporate Bond Equivalent)	8.39%	8.33%
Assumed Cost	8.12%	8.12%
Arbitrage Profit	.27%	.21%

dates. In the first case, income is based on LIBOR as recorded for the last day of each month. The alternative case provides LIBOR as recorded on the fifth day of each month. In both instances, the assets pay monthly on the refix dates (in arrears). All other factors are the same.

In each instance, an arbitrager would receive one-month LIBOR + 15 basis points from January through March 1986. The returns for the two issues, however, are not the same. The movement of interest rates during this period resulted in a lower return for the asset that reset on the fifth of the month.

If the arbitrager had been seeking to offset a LIBID liability that reset on the last day of each month, the choice between the two assets above would become significant. The 0.06 percent difference in return would have been one-quarter of the total arbitrage profit. The highly leveraged nature of arbitrage requires that all payment details be similarly considered.

ARTICLE 12

RICHARD WILLIAMS graduated from the University of Manchester Institute of Science and Technology (UMIST) in 1981. He has a B.Sc. (Hon) in Mathematics and a M.Sc. in Systems and Control. While studying for his first degree, he gained the first prize for his course in each year and was UMIST top graduate in 1981.

Prior to joining CSFB, Richard worked for a software house, Scicon Ltd, where he was involved in defense systems development. He joined CSFB Research in September 1985 to extend the software capabilities of the department. He has since moved into a market analyst role specializing in Floating Rate Notes.

FLOATING RATE NOTES: METHODS OF ANALYSIS

Richard Williams
Research Analyst
Credit Suisse First Boston Limited

Early attempts to value *floating rate notes* (FRNs) resulted in a proliferation of methods. Many of these methods provided different and frequently misleading measures of FRN value. Two methods in particular—the *simple margin* (SM) and the *discounted margin* (DM)—are now widely accepted as standard in the Euro-FRN markets.[1] Another method[2]—the *yield to maturity spread* (YTM spread)—based on bond yield calculation methods and targeted at U.S. floating rate products, gives very similar results.

The purpose of this article is to explain the development of these methods and to show that they do indeed provide the most realistic and consistent measures of value. Using simple examples, the methods are compared to other possible measures of value to show their superiority.

The formulae suggested in this article have been endorsed and recommended for use in evaluating floating rate notes by the European Bond Commission of the European Federation of Financial Analyst Societies ('EFFAS'). Attention is particularly drawn

[1] For information see Steven Mobbs, *Eurodollar Floating Rate Notes Evaluation Techniques*, London: Credit Suisse First Boston Research, November 1984.

[2] For information see David Muntner, *Analysis of Floating Rate Securities*, New York: The First Boston Corporation, Fixed Income Research, August 1985.

to the methods of the discounted margin (money market basis) and the YTM spread (bond market basis).

The article is presented in two sections. Section I describes the development of each method. Many possible alternatives are considered and methods failing to pass tests of consistency are rejected. It has been written with simplicity in mind. Section II examines the development of the recommended formulae in greater detail. Specific applications of some of the more complex methods are also described, e.g., perpetuals. This section is written to enable the mathematically minded to appreciate the construction of the formulae recommended and the problems with those discarded. All recommended formulae are listed in Appendix A.

FRN analytical techniques fall into two groups—simple and complex. Examination of the simple techniques reveals that only one provides a consistent measure of FRN value—the simple margin. More realistic measures of value are achieved using more complex analysis techniques. Two methods provide the most consistent results—the discounted margin and the floating rate security yield to maturity.

I.   MEASURES OF FRN VALUE

FRN coupon payments are linked to one or more of many market index rates (e.g., LIBOR, Treasury bills). An obvious measure of value, therefore, is the return given by the FRN above or below its market index rate. Existing FRN analysis provides a range of methods for calculating this difference in return on 'margin' value. These methods are reviewed in this section to identify those which provide a consistent measure.

The margin techniques used to value floating rate securities were developed initially in Europe where investors have traditionally viewed FRNs as close substitutes for other money market instruments. Therefore, the margin values represent the difference in return between an FRN and an equivalent money market investment.

The U.S. market has adopted a different approach and FRNs have been treated as an alternative to conventional bond market investments. As a result, a comparable measure of investment return is required. A version of the conventional bond market yield to maturity is appropriate for this purpose.

For a value to be useful, it is essential that it is consistent through time. In other words, if there is no change in the value of an FRN from one day to the next, then the measure of its value should not exhibit any sudden, major change. It can be shown that for many proposed margin techniques this stability condition is not satisfied.

Existing methods can be described as falling into two groups— simple and complex. The simple methods sacrifice precision for ease of computation while the more complex methods provide a more realistic, yet more difficult to calculate, assessment. First, a recommended version of a simple margin measure is developed by considering the range of possible measures and eliminating those that do not satisfy stability and consistency conditions. An examination of the more complex methods is presented next. These methods avoid some of the restrictive assumptions made during the simple margin analysis.

Simple Measures of FRN Value

The primary aim of a simple measure of FRN value is to estimate the return from the note. Furthermore, since this return often is compared with that of its index rate, the value should be given in terms of an amount (margin) over or under the return from the index rate. The simple approach avoids any forecasting of future interest rates and coupon values.

A simple margin value is defined as the average cash return per annum on the FRN throughout its life compared with its index rate. How one can determine this value follows.

The FRN investor receives a return over or under the FRN's base rate, which can be expressed as a quoted margin per year. Furthermore, the value of any difference between the price and the redemption value can be considered to be received in equal amounts per annum over the life of the FRN (i.e., it is amortized in a straight line over the life of the note). The simple margin is the sum of these two components:

$$\text{Simple Margin (SM)} = \frac{\text{Redemption Value (RV)} - \text{Price (P)}}{\text{Life}}$$

$$+ \text{Quoted Margin (QM)}$$

Example: An FRN with a redemption value of 100, a quoted margin of 25 basis points (0.25 percent) over six-month LIBOR and a remaining life of 10 years, which is trading at a price of 99, has a simple margin of:

$$\text{Simple Margin} = \frac{100 - 99}{10} + 0.25$$

$$= 0.35 \text{ (or 35 basis points)}$$

FRN Life. The life of an FRN is measured in years from the date of purchase (settlement) to the final maturity date of the note (or the put or call date, when appropriate). However, it may not be sufficient simply to use the number of calendar years, as interest may be accrued according to various accounting conventions.

For consistency, time should be measured in the same manner as used by the accounting convention for the note's index rate. Index rate accounting follows the general form:

$$\text{Return} = \text{Index rate} \times \frac{\text{Number of days elapsed}}{\text{Number of days in the year}}$$

U.S. corporate bond accounting uses a measurement of bond days elapsed,[3] which results in a year consisting of twelve 30-day months. Thus, the number of days in the year is assumed to be 360. U.S. government bond accounting uses the actual number of days elapsed and a 365-day year convention. Money market accounting uses the actual number of days elapsed with a 360-day year convention.

Since the Euro-FRN market calculates its margin relative to money market indices, it is normal practice to use:

$$\frac{\text{Actual number of days elapsed}}{360}$$

when defining formulae. Any formulae presented can easily be converted to other accounting conventions.

Simple Margin Formula Variations. The basic simple margin formula for FRNs:

---

[3] See Appendix A for the method of calculating "bond days elapsed."

$$SM = \frac{RV - P}{Life} + QM$$

is acceptable at the issue date or on coupon dates. Between coupon dates, however, any difference between the coupon and current market rates will influence the FRN's attractiveness and this should be reflected by any measure of value. The effect of the difference between price and redemption value on simple margin is dependent upon the following two factors:

(a) A capital gain/loss,
(b) The additional/reduced cost of financing the FRN due to the change in the index rate from its value when the coupon was last fixed.

The simple margin equation above reflects only the capital gain/loss component of return. The formula therefore should be adjusted to account for the difference between the current coupon and prevailing market rates.

Existing methods adjust the simple margin formula by adjusting the cost of the FRN at settlement forward to the next coupon date when the coupon is brought in line with market rates. Thus, the revised simple margin formula is:

$$SM = \frac{RV - Adjusted\ Price}{Life} + QM$$

The precise formulation of the simple margin has been the subject of widespread disagreement, as it raises the following questions:

i.   Should the adjusted price be calculated by carrying the gross price forward to the next coupon date at the index rate of the note or at the index rate plus some margin?
ii. Should the adjusted price be carried forward accruing value based on par or based on the price actually paid?
iii. Should life be measured as the time from the next coupon date to maturity or the time from settlement to maturity?

When calculating the adjusted price, three rates of carry forward have been suggested. These are the index rate, the index rate plus the quoted margin and the index rate plus the simple margin itself.

The three possible rates of carry combine with questions i, ii and iii to give twelve possible ways of calculating a simple margin:

Carry Forward at		Index Rate		Index Rate plus Quoted Margin		Index Rate plus Simple Margin	
Adjust on a Base of		Actual Price	Par	Actual Price	Par	Actual Price	Par
Amortize over	Life from settlement	(a)	(b)	(c)	(d)	(e)	(f)
	Life from next coupon	(g)	(h)	(i)	(j)	(k)	(l)

Section II examines the formulae for the simple margin that result from each of the above possibilities. Two of the formulations are shown to be equivalent (see Section II), which leaves eleven possible variants for a simple margin formula.

Carrying the price forward using a base of par means that any interest earned between settlement and the next coupon date is calculated as a percentage of par value. As a result, the value is carried forward in a straight line to the next coupon date. Using a base of the price paid means that further interest may compound on any accrued interest earned prior to settlement, i.e., value is not carried forward in a straight-line. Exhibit 1 displays the divergence of the two approaches to compounding value.

The basic simple margin formula assumes straight-line amortization over the life of the bond. Intuitively, therefore, compounding value in a straight-line is more consistent with the simple margin concept.

Consistency and Stability.   For the simple margin to be useful, it must provide consistent values over time. In other words, if there is no change in the value of an FRN from one day to the next, then the simple margin should not exhibit any major change. For example, consider an FRN with a constant price of 100, a redemption value of 100 and a quoted margin of 25 basis points, paying interest at constant intervals. In addition, assume that the index rate is a constant LIBOR of 8 percent. One can plot the value of simple margin as time passes for each formula. This is done in Exhibit 2.

EXHIBIT 1
Interest Compounding—Straight Line vs. Non-Straight Line

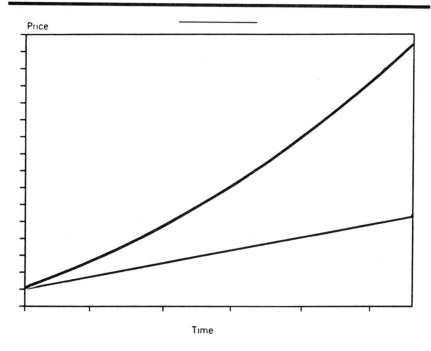

One can see that for the FRN in the example above (constant price of par, index rate at 8 percent) there will be no capital gain or loss. Hence, the simple margin should be approximately the same as the quoted margin. Note, however, that formulations (a), (b), (g) and (h) exhibit significant changes of value at or around the coupon date of the FRN and therefore can be rejected. This phenomenon is explained in Section II.

For the remaining formulations, where the price is not equal to par an element of capital gain/loss must be included in the simple margin. As the life of the FRN gets shorter, the capital gain per unit of time becomes a more significant part of simple margin value. For example, if the price is constant at 99, there is a capital gain element to the simple margin. As the life gets shorter, this element of capital gain is received over a shorter period of time and hence becomes more valuable. The simple margin should in-

EXHIBIT 2
Simple Margin Formulations Example with price at par

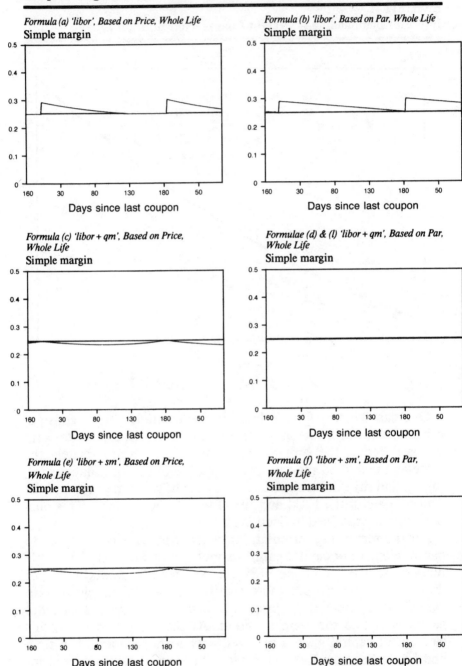

Formula (a) 'libor', Based on Price, Whole Life
Simple margin

Days since last coupon

Formula (b) 'libor', Based on Par, Whole Life
Simple margin

Days since last coupon

Formula (c) 'libor + qm', Based on Price, Whole Life
Simple margin

Days since last coupon

Formulae (d) & (l) 'libor + qm', Based on Par, Whole Life
Simple margin

Days since last coupon

Formula (e) 'libor + sm', Based on Price, Whole Life
Simple margin

Days since last coupon

Formula (f) 'libor + sm', Based on Par, Whole Life
Simple margin

Days since last coupon

EXHIBIT 2 (*Continued*)

Formula (g) 'libor', Based on Price,
Remaining Life
Simple margin

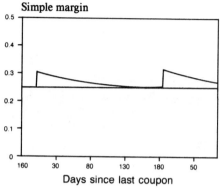

Days since last coupon

Formula (h) 'libor', Based on Par,
Remaining Life
Simple margin

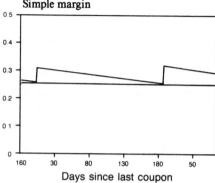

Days since last coupon

Formula (i) 'libor + qm', Based on Price,
Remaining Life
Simple margin

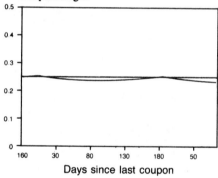

Days since last coupon

Formula (j) 'libor + qm', Based on Par,
Remaining Life
Simple margin

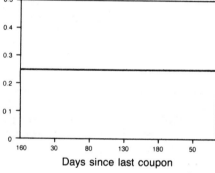

Days since last coupon

Formula (k)'libor + sm', Based on Price,
Remaining Life
Simple margin

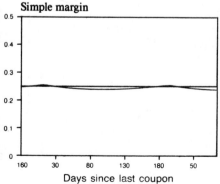

Days since last coupon

crease to reflect this. However, the simple margin growth should occur in a smooth manner. The simple margin histories for the remaining formulae are plotted in Exhibit 3 using a constant price of 99.

All of the remaining formulae except formula (d) and (l) exhibit sudden jumps in value around the FRN's coupon date. Therefore, all formulae except (d) and (l) can be rejected. Section II of this article shows that formulation (d) and (l) provides the following prescription for simple margin:

$$\text{Simple Margin} = \frac{RV - ((P+A) + (I+QM) \times (d/360) - \text{Coupon})}{\text{Life}} + QM$$

where RV = Redemption value
  P = Net price
  A = Accrued interest
  I = Index rate to next coupon date
  QM = Quoted margin
  d = Days to next coupon date
  Life = Number of years to FRN maturity (measured as actual/360)
  Coupon = Next coupon payment

EXHIBIT 3
Simple Margin Formulations Example with Price at 99

Formula (c) 'libor + qm', Based on Price,
Whole Life
Simple margin

Formula (e) 'libor + sm', Based on Price,
Whole Life
Simple margin

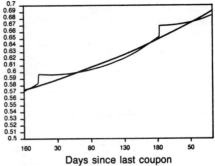

Days since last coupon   Days since last coupon

EXHIBIT 3 (*Continued*)

Formulae (d) & (l) 'libor + qm', Based on Par, Whole Life

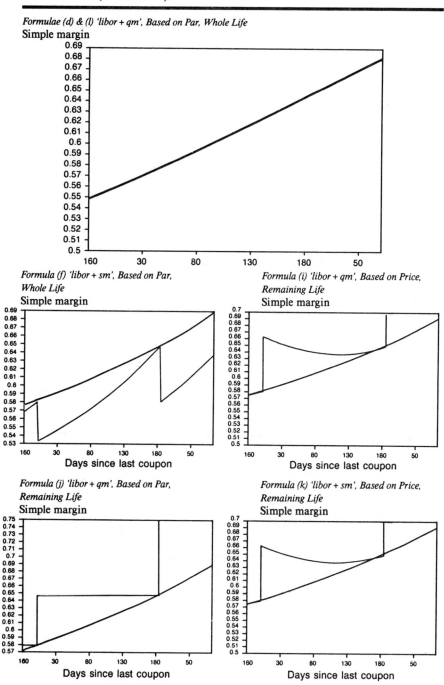

Simple margin

Formula (f) 'libor + sm', Based on Par, Whole Life
Simple margin

Days since last coupon

Formula (i) 'libor + qm', Based on Price, Remaining Life
Simple margin

Days since last coupon

Formula (j) 'libor + qm', Based on Par, Remaining Life
Simple margin

Days since last coupon

Formula (k) 'libor + sm', Based on Price, Remaining Life
Simple margin

Days since last coupon

The stability of formula (d) or (l) can be further demonstrated by examining its behavior through time for scenarios where the yield curve structures shown in Exhibit 4 are used.

The following cases are considered in Exhibits 5, 6, and 7:

- Constant price = 101, (i) Index rate constant
  - (ii) Index rate decreasing
  - (iii) Index rate increasing
- Constant price = 100, (i) Index rate constant
  - (ii) Index rate decreasing
  - (iii) Index rate increasing
- Constant price = 99, (i) Index rate constant
  - (ii) Index rate decreasing
  - (iii) Index rate increasing

EXHIBIT 4
LIBOR Curves

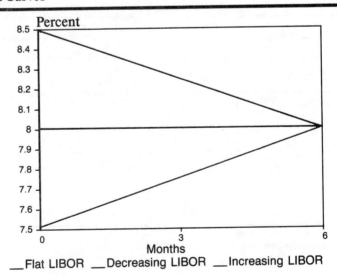

___Flat LIBOR ___Decreasing LIBOR ___Increasing LIBOR

EXHIBIT 5
For Constant Price = 101

Simple margin (settlement price = 101)

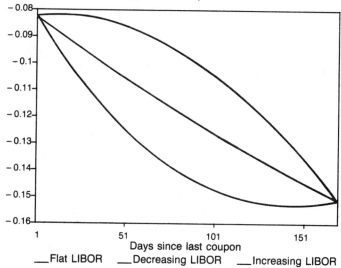

_____Flat LIBOR   _____Decreasing LIBOR   _____Increasing LIBOR

EXHIBIT 6
For Constant Price = 100

Simple margin (settlement price = 100)

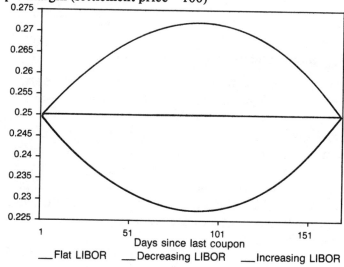

_____Flat LIBOR   _____Decreasing LIBOR   _____Increasing LIBOR

EXHIBIT 7
For Constant Price = 99

Simple margin (settlement price = 99)

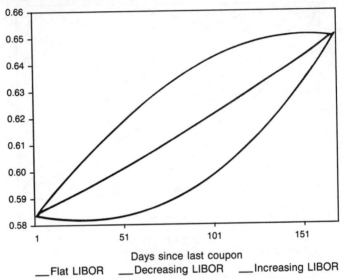

Days since last coupon
___Flat LIBOR   ___Decreasing LIBOR   ___Increasing LIBOR

The graphs of the simple margin through time demonstrate that it meets the earlier intuitive requirements, namely the following:

- There are no sudden jumps (or discontinuities) in value.

- When the price is par and interest rates are constant, there is no capital gain or loss element to the simple margin.

- Any constant capital gain element of the simple margin becomes more significant as the life of the FRN gets shorter.

Note that the simple margin tracks changes in the index rate in a stable manner. The value of the simple margin is expected to change as the index rate moves away from the coupon rate between coupon dates. Furthermore, when the price is constant at par, the simple margin should return to the quoted margin again as the FRN approaches a coupon date where the coupon will again be consistent with the index.

As the index rate increases, so the cost of financing the FRN increases. This will reduce the element of capital gain and hence the simple margin. In other words, as the index rate to the next coupon date increases one expects the simple margin to fall between coupon dates, and as the index rate decreases we expect the simple margin to increase. Exhibits 5, 6, and 7 show that this is achieved by the selected formula.

This formula prompts the following definition for simple margin. *The simple margin is the average cash return on the FRN through its life compared with its index rate, with both returns calculated on a base of par.*

It follows that if the *discount/premium of the note to par is amortized in a straight line throughout the life of the FRN, the cash return will be the index rate plus the simple margin between any two coupon dates and also between settlement and the first coupon date.*

Simple Margin Drawbacks. It has been shown that the recommended simple margin formula is the most accurate and consistent of possible simple margin formulae. However, it suffers from two drawbacks.

1. *The simple margin formula does not take into consideration the current yield effect on the price of the FRN since coupon payments received on the FRN are given the same weight if the price is above or below par.* This does not fully reflect the value to the investor of buying an FRN below par nor the cost to the investor of buying an FRN above par. This effect understates the coupon value for notes trading below par and overstates it for notes trading above par.

2. *The discount/premium of the bond is amortized to par in a straight line over the life of the FRN, rather than discounted at a constantly compounded rate.* For a note trading below par, the associated capital gain is thus distributed evenly over its life. This distorts the simple margin value, since the gain is received only at maturity. Therefore, the resulting cash payment has a lower present value than that calculated to be the sum of gains assumed using the simple margin formula. This effect overstates the rate of amortization for FRNs trading below par and understates it for FRNs trading above par.

Complex Measures of FRN Value

To overcome the drawbacks of simple margin, more complex valuation techniques must be employed. Attempts have been made to remove the first drawback of simple margin highlighted above but with little success. An example is the *adjusted total margin* (ATM) technique. ATM suffers from discontinuity problems similar to those observed in some of the earlier simple margin analysis. An examination of the ATM method appears in Appendix B.

Greater success has been achieved by analysis that solves both of the simple margin drawbacks at the same time. Two methods are now recognized as providing stable, consistent measures of FRN value. The methods are both very similar to the yield to maturity method used in conventional bond analysis.

The first method is the *discounted margin* method[4]. The discounted margin was developed in the European markets where FRN investments are compared to money market investments. It builds upon the idea of the simple margin by providing a measure of return over/under the index rate of the note. The second method is the *floating rate security yield to maturity* (YTM)[5]. The YTM was developed in the United States where FRN investments are considered alongside bond market investments. The YTM is an FRN equivalent of the conventional bond market yield to maturity.

These more complex methods combine the known elements of FRN value to the next coupon date with anticipated future interest rate values. The current yield effect is overcome by basing all calculations on the price actually paid for the note. The problems of using straight line amortization are avoided by discounting all future cash flows back to a present value at the appropriate rate.

Discounted Margin. In order to overcome the drawbacks of the simple margin calculation the following additional features of the FRN are considered:

---

[4] For additional information see Steven Mobbs, *Eurodollar Floating Rate Notes Evaluation Techniques.*

[5] For additional information see David Muntner, *Analysis of Floating Rate Securities.*

- The cash flows of the FRN beyond the first coupon payment,
- Future interest rate values.

The margin value is calculated in a manner similar to the conventional bond market yield to maturity. Yield to maturity is the rate of discount which, when applied to all future cash flows of a bond, equates the sum of the discounted cash flows to the cost of the bond. Thus, a working definition of the discounted margin is the difference between this rate of discount and the index rate of the note. The discounted margin can therefore be calculated using:

Discounted Margin = Rate of Discount (R) – Index Rate

where R is the rate of discount such that:

FRN Cost = Sum of discounted cash flows.

Since the index rate (and hence the cash flows) for all coupon periods following the first coupon received are unknown at the settlement date, an appropriate index rate must be assumed.

Consider analyzing an FRN investment using the conventional yield to maturity method. The discount rate for all coupon periods would then be equal to the assumed index rate plus the discounted margin. This implies however, that it is possible to invest at a rate appropriate to a full coupon period for the period to the first coupon, e.g., invest at a six-month rate for a period of two months. How, therefore, should discounting of the part coupon period to the first coupon payment be handled? The selection of an appropriate discount rate is not immediately clear. An alternative, equivalent approach[6] is to carry the price of the FRN forward to the next coupon date. The next step is to perform the discounting process on the remaining whole periods using the assumed index rate plus the discounted margin, as discussed above.

Carrying the price forward to the next coupon date raises questions similar to those posed when developing the simple margin.

(a) What index rate should be used, the actual rate for the part period or the average assumed rate that will be used in the discounting process?

---

[6] To see the equivalence of the two approaches see Section II of this article.

(b) Should the index rate be used alone or should the price be carried forward using the index rate plus quoted margin or discounted margin?

(c) Should interest to the next coupon date be simple or compound?

There is no question of carrying the price forward on a base of par, since this has been identified as a drawback of the simple margin evaluation. The combinations suggested by questions a, b and c above result in twelve possible formulations for a discounted margin evaluation method, shown in Exhibit 8.

Recall that the impetus for developing a margin measure of value is for comparison of the returns from the FRN with its index rate. The money market convention is to use a simple interest calculation for part period price adjustment. All quoted money market interest rates are consistent with simple interest calculations. Therefore, to maintain a consistent approach to the development of a discounted margin formula, the price should be carried forward using a simple interest calculation. Formulations (vii)–(xii) will not therefore be considered.

Consistency and Stability. Once again the measure of value must be stable through time. The remaining formulations, (i)–(vi), can be checked using the following simple example.

Example: Consider an FRN with a payment schedule of 100 days to the first coupon, 182 days to the second and 183 to the final coupon. Let the price be constant at 99.90, the quoted

EXHIBIT 8
Possible Formulations for a Discounted Margin Evaluation Method

Carry Forward Using	Index Rate		Index Rate plus Quoted Margin		Index Rate plus Simple Margin	
Index Rate Used	Actual	Assumed	Actual	Assumed	Actual	Assumed
Interest Gain — Simple	(i)	(ii)	(iii)	(iv)	(v)	(vi)
Compound	(vii)	(viii)	(ix)	(x)	(xi)	(xii)

margin be 25 basis points, and the index rate to the next coupon be constant.

The results are shown in the six graphs in Exhibit 9. It can be seen from these that sudden jumps in value occur at the first coupon date for all formulae except formula (v). Since the example is for an FRN that does not increase in value at this date, the formulations are clearly invalid. One can therefore reject all formulae except (v).

Note that formula (v) provides a stable measure of value. Suppose, however, that another assumed index rate is selected. One can examine the values given by formula (v) for a range of different assumed rates. These are shown in Exhibit 10.

Formula (v) retains a consistent, stable value for a range of assumed index rates. In other words, for notes trading close to par the discounted margin (formula (v)) is relatively independent of small changes in the assumed rate. For notes trading away from par, formula (v) shows some dependence upon the assumed rate. This dependence is consistent with the reinvestment rate assumptions about future interest rates made by the investor when selecting an assumed rate.

Derivation of Discounted Margin Formula

Consider the return from an FRN investment in two ways. The value of the investment at the maturity of the note should be the same whichever view is taken. To obtain a defining formula for discounted margin the following two views are equated:

View 1: To obtain the same return on a money market investment as from the FRN, the cost of the FRN to the investor needs to be invested at the index rate plus the discounted margin. Such an investment could be rolled forward through each coupon period to the maturity of the FRN. This provides one view of the expected return from the FRN.

View 2: This view considers each cash flow from the FRN, reinvested at the index rate plus the discounted margin from the date it is paid to the maturity of the note. A second measure of the final value from the FRN investment is thus the sum of these reinvested cash flow values plus the redemption value of the note.

EXHIBIT 9
Variations in Discounted Margin—Formulae (i)–(vi)

Formula Version (i)
Discounted Margin

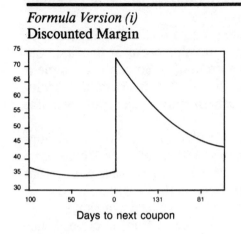

Days to next coupon

Formula Version (ii)
Discounted Margin

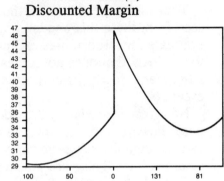

Days to next coupon

Formula Version (iii)
Discounted Margin

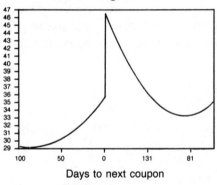

Days to next coupon

Formula Version (iv)
Discounted Margin

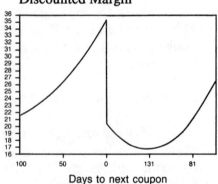

Days to next coupon

Formula Version (v)
Discounted Margin

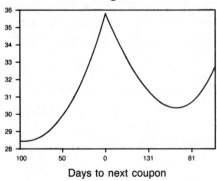

Days to next coupon

Formula Version (vi)
Discounted Margin

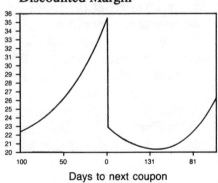

Days to next coupon

Assumed Index Rate = 9%
Discounted Margin

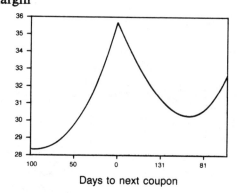

Days to next coupon

Assumed Index Rate = 10.00%
Discounted Margin

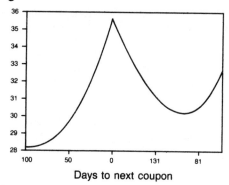

Days to next coupon

Assumed Index Rate = 11.00%
Discounted Margin

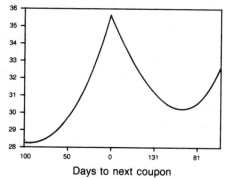

Days to next coupon

Equating the values from View 1 and View 2 provides a formula for evaluating the discounted margin. This formula is variant (v) discussed earlier. The derivation of the formula is discussed in more detail in Section II. Possible variations of the formula are also presented.

The discounted margin compares the return of the FRN with that of the index rate. It is therefore meaningful to compare two FRNs using the discounted margin only if they are both based upon the same index rate, paying out with the same frequency. Comparison of notes based on different indices, using the discounted margin, takes no account of the spread between the two indices. Furthermore, comparison of two FRNs based upon the same index rate and paying out with the same frequency will clearly require the same index rate assumption for each FRN.

As will be shown in Section II, the discounted margin formula is:

$$(P+A) \times \left(1 + \frac{(I+DM)}{100} \times \frac{d_1}{360}\right) - C_1 = \frac{(I_a+QM) \times (d_2/360)}{\left(1 + \frac{(I_a+DM)}{100} \times \frac{d_2}{360}\right)}$$

$$+ \frac{(I_a+QM) \times (d_3/360)}{\left(1 + \frac{(I_a+DM)}{100} \times \frac{d_3}{360}\right) \times \left(1 + \frac{(I_a+DM)}{100} \times \frac{d_2}{360}\right)} + \cdots$$

$$\cdots + \frac{((I_a+QM) \times (d_n/360)) + RV}{\left(1 + \frac{(I_a+DM)}{100} \times \frac{d_n}{360}\right) \times \cdots \cdots \times \left(1 + \frac{(I_a+DM)}{100} \times \frac{d_2}{360}\right)}$$

where P + A = Price plus accrued, the cost of the note at settlement

I = Index rate for the period from settlement to next coupon

I_a = Assumed index rate for the life of the note

QM = Quoted margin

DM = Discounted margin

d_1 = Number of days from settlement to next coupon

$d_2, \ldots, d_n$ = Number of days in 2nd, ...,nth coupon period

RV = Redemption value

This is clearly a complex formula. The value of the discounted margin is usually found by using an iterative technique, such as

Newton—Raphson Iteration.[7] The need to know the exact number of days in each coupon period is a particularly onerous feature of the formula above. This requirement can be removed without loss of accuracy by assuming that coupon payments are made at equal intervals throughout a 365.25 year. This constant coupon period approach is described in Section II. A similar technique has been developed, which enables direct calculation of the discounted margin. This equivalent technique is also presented in Section II.

The stability of the formula when subjected to different values of assumed rate has already been demonstrated. Exhibit 11 demonstrates the effect of changes in price, next coupon value, redemption value, maturity, index rate to the next coupon and quoted margin.

The discounted margin is defined such that, if the discounted margin remains constant throughout the life of the note, then the investor's return between any two coupon dates and also between settlement and the first coupon date will be the index rate plus the discounted margin.

Yield to Maturity. The yield to maturity (YTM) value was developed to provide a comparison between FRN investments and more conventional bond market investments. The YTM value, like the fixed rate bond yield to maturity, derives an internal rate of return measure of value.

The yield to maturity formula of conventional bond market analysis sets the sum of the bond cash flows (discounted to give present value) equal to the price of the bond. One may use the FRN cash flows in order to derive a similar yield figure. The difference is that unlike a conventional, fixed rate bond the cash flows are not all known. This problem is overcome, as it was for the discounted margin, by assuming a future coupon rate for those cash flows following the first. The yield to maturity formula is thus:

$$P + A = \frac{C_1}{\left(1 + \frac{YTM}{(f \times 100)}\right)^{(f \times T_1)}} + \frac{C_2}{\left(1 + \frac{YTM}{(f \times 100)}\right)^{(f \times T_2)}} + \cdots + \frac{C_n + RV}{\left(1 + \frac{YTM}{(f \times 100)}\right)^{(f \times T_n)}}$$

[7] For additional information see Richard Burden, J. Douglas Faires and Albert C. Reynolds, *Numerical Analysis,* second ed, Boston: PWS Publishers, 1981.

EXHIBIT 11
Sensitivity of Discounted Margin to Changes in Underlying Components

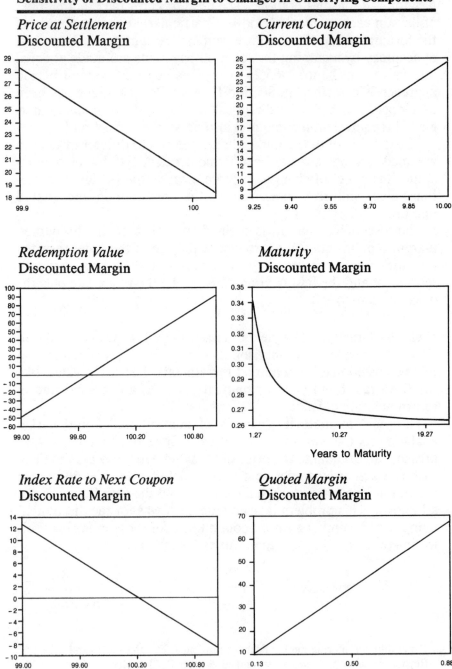

Price at Settlement
Discounted Margin

Current Coupon
Discounted Margin

Redemption Value
Discounted Margin

Maturity
Discounted Margin

Years to Maturity

Index Rate to Next Coupon
Discounted Margin

Quoted Margin
Discounted Margin

where P + A = Price plus accrued, the cost of the note at settlement

        YTM = Yield to maturity

          C_1 = First coupon payment

 C_2 . . . C_n = Assumed coupon payments

         RV = Redemption value

          T_1 = Time to ith coupon payment

            f = Yield basis (e.g., f = 2 given semiannual YTM)

The frequency term, f, in the above formula determines the basis upon which the YTM will be calculated. To calculate an annualized YTM, f = 1 and to calculate a semiannual YTM, f = 2.

Section II shows how YTM can be used to analyze different FRN investments.

YTM Spread. The YTM formulation suggests an alternative method of calculating margin of return of an FRN over its index rate. The YTM spread is determined by calculating the YTM of the FRN's index rate and subtracting this value from the YTM of the FRN. The formula for YTM spread is thus:

$$YTM_{Spread} = YTM_{FRN} - YTM_{Index}$$

where YTM_{Index} is calculated using:

$$100 = \sum_{i-1}^{n} \frac{I_i}{\left(1 + \frac{YTM_{Index}}{(f \times 100)}\right)^{(f \times T_i)}} + \frac{100}{\left(1 + \frac{YTM_{Index}}{(f \times 100)}\right)^{(f \times T_n)}}$$

where I_i = Index rate return over period i

YTM_{Index} = Yield to maturity of index rate.

The value provided by this method is very close to the discounted margin value, in most cases differing by less than a basis point.

FRN Forward Prices

An investor may wish to calculate the price of an FRN at some future date that will secure a given return. For example, what is the price of the FRN at the next coupon date that will secure a return of the index rate for the period from settlement to the next coupon date?

Rollover Price.   An FRN can be bought at a cost consisting of its clean price, P, plus any interest accrued to date, A. An investor could borrow the amount (P + A), and buy the FRN. At what price should the FRN be sold on the coupon (rollover) date in order to cover the cost of borrowing exactly? Borrowing at the index rate of the FRN for the period to the next coupon will cost:

$$(P + A) \times (I/100) \times (d/360)$$

where I is the index rate for the period to the next coupon and d is the number of days to the next coupon.

To pay off the loan on the rollover date, the price of the note should equal the principal amount (P + A) plus the interest charge less the value of any coupon paid by the FRN.

Thus, the price will need to be:

$$(P + A) + \frac{(P + A) \times I \times (d/360)}{100} - \text{Coupon}$$

where P + A = Price plus accrued (the principal amount borrowed).
        I = Index rate of the note for the period to the next coupon.
        d = Number of days to the next coupon.

This is called the *rollover price* of the FRN. The rollover price is the price of the FRN at the next coupon date that will give a return of the index rate over the period to the next coupon. FRNs are frequently traded for settlement at the next coupon date. The rollover price is often quoted for this purpose.

Neutral Price.   The simple and discounted margins are both defined as returns above or below the index rate of an FRN for the life of the note. These definitions imply a return of the index rate plus the margin value between any two coupon dates and between settlement and the first coupon date. Selling the note at the rollover price on the coupon date means that the additional margin of return is not achieved over the period from settlement. This is demonstrated in Exhibit 12.

Define the *neutral price* as the price of the note at the next coupon date that achieves a return of the index rate plus the margin, over the period from settlement to the next coupon date. The formulae for neutral price are as follows:

EXHIBIT 12
Neutral Price vs. Rollover Price
Level of Return Locked in for the Period to the First Coupon

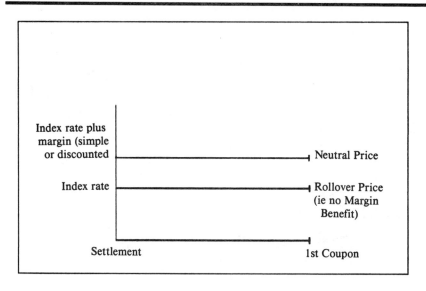

$$\text{Simple Margin Neutral Price} = (P + A) + (I + SM) \times \frac{d}{360} - \text{Coupon}$$

$$\text{Discounted Margin Neutral Price} = (P + A) \times \left(1 + \frac{(I + DM)}{100} \times \frac{d}{360}\right) - \text{Coupon}$$

where P + A = Price plus accrued, the cost of the FRN at settlement
    SM = Simple margin
    DM = Discounted margin

Price Behavior. Values of rollover and neutral price are plotted in Exhibit 13 for the following example:

- Constant clean price = 100, (i)   Index rate constant
                              (ii) Index rate decreasing
                              (iii) Index rate increasing.

Each of these examples assume an FRN paying 25 basis points over the index rate.

EXHIBIT 13
Sensitivity to Changes in Index Rate Curve

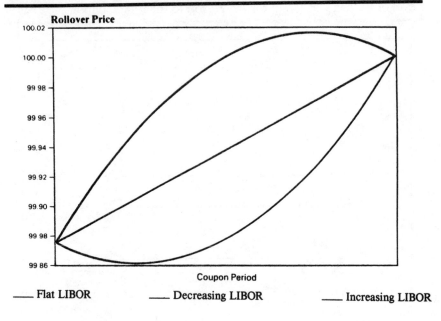

Rollover Price

—— Flat LIBOR   —— Decreasing LIBOR   —— Increasing LIBOR

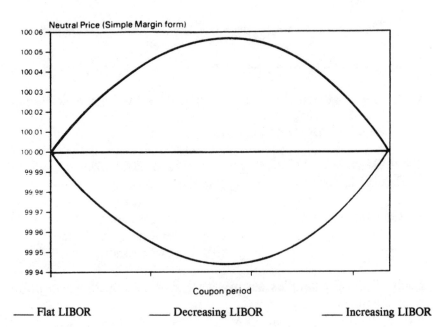

Neutral Price (Simple Margin form)

—— Flat LIBOR   —— Decreasing LIBOR   —— Increasing LIBOR

EXHIBIT 13 *(Continued)*

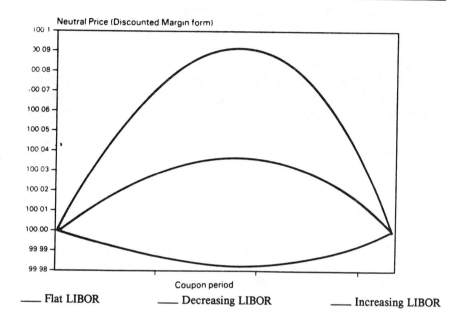

Neutral Price (Discounted Margin form)

_____ Flat LIBOR   _____ Decreasing LIBOR   _____ Increasing LIBOR

Rollover Price Anomaly. It has been noted that to sell an FRN forward for settlement at the next coupon date at the rollover price rather than at the neutral price results in the holder losing any discounted margin benefit over the period to the next coupon date. Buyers of the FRN, however, may benefit from purchasing forward at the rollover price. For FRNs where the discounted margin is positive, the neutral price is greater than the rollover price. The purchase of such an FRN at the rollover price will give the buyer a greater resulting discounted margin (and therefore return) than purchase at the neutral price.

Summary

Early FRN analysis used relatively crude measures of value. These simple margin techniques lacked consistency. Only one simple margin formula provides consistent stable values. Where a more complex, realistic margin value cannot be readily calculated, this simple margin formulation should be used.

Two measures of FRN value, resulting from a more realistic view than is used by simple margin, are discounted margin and yield to maturity. Where an FRN is to be compared directly with its index rate, the discounted margin provides the most consistent measure. Where a longer-term investment view is held, yield to maturity provides a consistent measure for comparison with alternative investments.

The recommended formulae, to be used for calculating each of the above measures, are presented in Appendix A.

II. FURTHER ANALYSIS OF VALUE

Section I discussed the range of FRN evaluation techniques available. This section of the article will present the techniques in greater detail and examine potential applications.

Simple Margin Formulations

In Section I it is noted that the calculation of simple margin at any time, including dates between coupon refixes, is possible using the basic formula:

$$\text{Simple Margin (SM)} = \frac{\text{Redemption Value (RV)} - \text{Adjusted Price (AP)}}{\text{Life}}$$
$$+ \text{Quoted Margin (QM)}$$

where the adjusted price is a price for the FRN at the next coupon date. The adjusted price can be determined in several ways, each one following the same general pattern: the cost of buying the note is carried forward by adding the interest accrued in the period to the next coupon.

The rate used for interest accrual will reflect the return expected over the period to the next coupon. Using the index rate of the FRN alone would result in the rollover price as described earlier. However, as noted in the description of the rollover price, this will not provide any more return from the FRN than if one invests at the index rate. One may, therefore, wish to add some interest rate margin. Possible choices for this margin are:

(a) the quoted margin or
(b) the simple margin itself.

Interest can be considered to accrue on the actual cost of the note or on its par value. Accruing interest on the actual cost of the note gives an interest gain of:

$$(P + A) \times \frac{I^*}{100} \times \frac{d}{360}$$

where P + A = Clean price at settlement + interest gained prior to settlement
    d = Number of days from settlement to next coupon.
    I* = Percent Interest rate used = Index rate alone,
                                Index rate plus quoted margin or
                                Index rate plus simple margin.

Accrual based on par value gives an interest gain of:

$$I^* \times \frac{d}{360}$$

The price of the FRN at the next coupon is the price paid at settlement plus the interest gained less the value of the coupon payment. Thus:

$$AP_1 = (P + A) + (I^*/100) \times (P + A) \times (d/360) - C$$

$$AP_2 = (P + A) + I^* \times (d/360) - C$$

are the two possible versions of adjusted price. AP_1 carries the price forward based on the actual cost of the note at settlement. AP_2 carries the price forward based on par.

AP_2 does not allow interest to accrue on any value gained prior to settlement. This is consistent with the definition of simple margin which employs a straight line approach by forming an average return over the life of the note. AP_1 does not maintain this consistency and may prove to be a source of error in later analysis. Furthermore, AP_2 gains value on a base of par, which is also consistent with the simple margin definition.

Once the price has been adjusted to give the price at the next coupon date it is uncertain what value of life should be used to amortize the return. Should the whole life from settlement be used or has the period to the next coupon date been accounted for?

The two types of adjusted price, the two possibilities for measurement of life and the three possible interest rates to next coupon combine to give twelve possible formulations for simple margin:

(a) $SM = \dfrac{100 - (P + A) \times (1 + I \times (d/36000)) + C}{L} + QM$

(b) $SM = \dfrac{100 - (P + A) - I \times (d/360) + C}{L} + QM$

(c) $SM = \dfrac{100 - (P + A) \times (1 + (I + QM) \times (d/36000)) + C}{L} + QM$

(d) $SM = \dfrac{100 - (P + A) - (I + QM) \times (d/360) + C}{L} + QM$

(e) $SM = \dfrac{100 - (P + A) \times (1 + (I + SM) \times (d/36000)) + C}{L} + QM$

(f) $SM = \dfrac{100 - (P + A) - (I + SM) \times (d/360) + C}{L} + QM$

(g) $SM = \dfrac{100 - (P + A) \times (1 + I \times (d/36000)) + C}{L - (d/360)} + QM$

(h) $SM = \dfrac{100 - (P + A) - I \times (d/360) + C}{L - (d/360)} + QM$

(i) $SM = \dfrac{100 - (P + A) \times (1 + (I + QM) \times (d/36000)) + C}{L - (d/360)} + QM$

(j) $SM = \dfrac{100 - (P + A) - (I + QM) \times (d/360) + C}{L - (d/360)} + QM$

(k) $SM = \dfrac{100 - (P + A) - (P + A) \times (I + SM) \times (d/36000) + C}{L - (d/360)} + QM$

(l) $SM = \dfrac{100 - (P + A) - (I + SM) \times (d/360) + C}{L - (d/360)} + QM$

where SM = Simple margin
      P = Clean price at settlement date
      A = Accrued interest to settlement date
      I = Index rate for period to next coupon from settlement
  QM = Quoted margin
      C = Next coupon payment
      L = Life from settlement to maturity of the FRN
      d = Number of days from settlement to next coupon date.

Note that simple margin formulations (d) and (l) are equivalent. This is shown by collecting all simple margin terms from (l) on to the left hand side, thus:

(l) $SM \times (L - d/360) = 100 - (P + A) - (I + SM) \times (d/360) + C + QM \times (L - d/360)$

$SM \times L = 100 - (P + A) - I \times (d/360) + C + QM \times (L - d/360)$

$SM \times L = 100 - (P + A) - (I + QM) \times (d/360) + C + QM \times L$

(d) $SM = \dfrac{100 - (P + A) - (I + QM) \times (d/360) + C}{L} + QM$

There are therefore eleven possible formulations of simple margin. Formulae (e), (f) and (k) can be rearranged so that all simple margin terms are collected onto the left hand side.

Consistency of Simple Margin Formulation. A simple margin measure must first of all remain unchanged when there is no change in the value of the FRN. In Section I the following example was used to test this requirement for each formulation.

Example: Consider an FRN with a constant price of 100, and a quoted margin of 25 basis points. Let the index rate be a constant LIBOR of 8 percent and the redemption value of the note be 100.

Plotting the path of simple margin against time for each formulation (shown in Exhibit 2) shows that formulae (a), (b), (g) and (h) exhibit jump discontinuities at or around the FRN coupon date. Consider a more general form of the simple margin formula:

$$SM = \frac{100 - (P + A) - I^* \times (d/360) + C}{Life} + QM$$

where Life = L   formulae (a) – (f)

         = L – d/360   formulae (g) – (l)

     I* = I   formulae (b) and (h)

        I + QM   formulae (d) and (j)

        I + SM   formulae (f) and (l)

        (I/100) × (P + A)   formulae (a) and (g)

        ((I + QM)/100) × (P + A)   formulae (c) and (i)

        ((I + SM)/100) × (P + A)   formulae (e) and (k)

On the coupon date of the note we know that:

$$A = C, d = 0 \text{ and } P = 100$$

so,

$$SM_c = QM$$

where SM_c is the simple margin on the coupon date.

On the following day one can assume the following approximate values:

$A = 0$

$d = h$, the inter coupon period

$C = (I + QM) \times (h/360)$, the next coupon payment, and

$P = 100$

so:

$$SM_1 = \frac{-I^* \times (h/360) + (I + QM) \times (h/360)}{Life - (1/360)} + QM$$

where SM_1 is the simple margin on the coupon date plus 1 day.

The difference between these two values is:

$$SM_c - SM_1 = \frac{I^* \times (h/360) - (I + QM) \times (h/360)}{Life - (1/360)}$$

For examples where an FRN has the same price and is subject to the same interest rates on both days, one would expect this value to be zero. However, this is only true for those formulae where:

$$I^* = I + QM$$

Formulae (b) and (h) use $I^* = I$, so they will clearly be subject to the discontinuity identified above.

Formulations (a) and (g) use $I^* = (I/100) \times (P + A)$.

On the day following the coupon $P = 100$, $A = 0$ leaving $I^* = I$ and again the discontinuity appears. (a), (b), (g), and (h) may therefore be rejected as simple margin measures.

Formulations (e), (f), (k) and (l) use values for I^* which incorporate $I + SM$. Their graphs of simple margin against time however, do not exhibit jump discontinuities. This is because the formulae used can be rearranged, as shown earlier for formula (l), to result in I^* dependent upon $(I + QM)$.

To continue, there are now only seven possible variants of the simple margin formula, namely, (c), (d), (e), (f), (i), (j), (k).

A second requirement of a simple margin value is that it should track small changes in FRN value in a stable manner. The following example tests this requirement.

Example: Consider an FRN with constant price 99, quoted margin 25 basis points over LIBOR, redemption value 100. Let the index rate be a constant LIBOR of 8 percent.

Since the price is less than the redemption value in this example, there is an element of capital gain in the simple margin. As the life of the FRN shortens the value of the capital gain becomes more significant, thus increasing the value of the FRN. However, the day-to-day change in this value is small. The paths of the remaining simple margin formulae against time are plotted in Exhibit 3. All the remaining formulae except (d) and (l) exhibit jump discontinuities at or around the coupon date. Consider again the more general simple margin formula:

$$SM = \frac{100 - (P + A) - I^* \times (d/360) + C}{\text{Life}} + QM$$

On the coupon date:

$$A = C, d = 0$$

so

$$SM_c = \frac{100 - P}{\text{Life}} + QM$$

On the following day:

$$A = 0, d = h, C = (I + QM) \times (h/360)$$

so

$$SM_1 = \frac{100 - P - I^* \times (h/360) + (I + QM) \times (h/360)}{Life - (1/360)} + QM$$

The difference between simple margin on the two days is thus approximately:

$$SM_1 - SM_c = \frac{100 - P}{360 \times (Life - (1/360)) \times Life} + \frac{(I + QM) \times (h/360) - I^* \times (h/360)}{Life - (1/360)}$$

$$= \begin{array}{c} \text{change due to increase} \\ \text{in value of capital gain} \end{array} + \begin{array}{c} \text{change due to movement in interest} \\ \text{rates away from coupon rate.} \end{array}$$

Since interest rates have been assumed to be constant, there should be no contribution from the second term of this difference equation. This is only true if $I^* = I + QM$. Formulations (d) and (j) are the ones for which $I^* = I + QM$ exactly. However, (d) is the only one that does not have a jump discontinuity following the coupon date. The difference between formula (d) and formula (j) is the value taken for the life of the FRN. Formula (j) uses the life of the FRN from the next coupon date. By ignoring the period from settlement to the next coupon, formula (j) suffers from discontinuity problems as the life remaining moves from one coupon period to the next. The formulae other than formula (d) may therefore be rejected as simple margin measures.

The stability of formulation (d) is demonstrated in Section I for several different price and index rate scenarios. To conclude, the simple margin definition is restated along with the recommended simple margin formula in Exhibit 14.

Discounted Margin Formulations

The technique used to derive a basic formula defining the discounted margin is described in Section I. The derivation is based upon two alternative views of the return on an FRN. Both views assume that any benefit gained during the life of the FRN is reinvested (or rolled) at an appropriate rate until the maturity of the note.

First, suppose the actual cost of the note could be invested at the index rate of the note plus the discounted margin. Since the value of the index rate following the first coupon date is not known, an

EXHIBIT 14
Simple Margin Definition and Recommended Simple Margin Formula

The Simple Margin is the average cash return on the FRN through its entire life compared with its index rate, with both returns calculated on a base of par.

$$SM = \frac{100 - (P + A) - (I + QM) \times (d/360) + C}{L} + QM$$

where   P   = Price
           A   = Accrued interest
           I   = Index rate for period up to next coupon date
           QM = Quoted margin
           d   = Days to next coupon payment
           C   = Value of next coupon payment
           L   = Life of the FRN (measured in days/360) from settlement to maturity

assumed average rate is a good substitute value. For the period to the first coupon, the value of the index rate is known. Thus the total return gained by the maturity date of the note would be the compound interest product:

$$V1 = (P + A) \times \left(1 + \frac{(I + DM)}{100} \times \frac{d_1}{360}\right) \times \left(1 + \frac{(I_a + DM)}{100} \times \frac{d_2}{360}\right) \times \cdots$$

$$\cdots \times \left(1 + \frac{(I_a + DM)}{100} \times \frac{d_n}{360}\right)$$

where P + A = Price plus accrued, the cost of the FRN
         I = Index rate for the period to the next coupon
        I_a = Assumed index rate for the life of the FRN
     DM = Discounted margin
       d_1 = Number of days to next coupon
$d_2 \ldots d_n$ = Number of days in the 2nd, ..., nth coupon period.

Second, suppose that each of the coupon payments of the FRN could be reinvested at the index rate plus the discounted margin and rolled forward to the maturity date of the note in the same manner. The total return from this procedure would be

$$V2 = RV + C_n + C_{n-1} \times \left(1 + \frac{(I_a + DM)}{100} \times \frac{d_n}{360}\right) +$$

$$+ C_{n-2} \times \left(1 + \frac{(I_a + DM)}{100} \times \frac{d_n}{360}\right) \times \left(1 + \frac{(I_a + DM)}{100} \times \frac{d_{n-1}}{360}\right) + \cdots$$

$$\cdots + C_1 \times \left(1 + \frac{(I_a + DM)}{100} \times \frac{d_n}{360}\right) \times \left(1 + \frac{(I_a + DM)}{100} \times \frac{d_{n-1}}{360}\right) \times \cdots$$

$$\cdots \times \left(1 + \frac{(I_a + DM)}{100} \times \frac{d_2}{360}\right)$$

where RV = Redemption value

C_i = ith coupon payment

Equating these two values to define the discounted margin provides the basic discounted margin formula:

$$(P + A) \times \left(1 + \frac{(I + DM)}{100} \times \frac{d_1}{360}\right) - C_1 = \frac{C_2}{\left(1 + \frac{(I_a + DM)}{100} \times \frac{d_2}{360}\right)} + \cdots$$

$$\cdots + \frac{RV + C_n}{\left(1 + \frac{(I_a + DM)}{100} \times \frac{d_2}{360}\right) \times \cdots \times \left(1 + \frac{(I_a + DM)}{100} \times \frac{d_n}{360}\right)}$$

Points to note about the basic formula are:

1. All coupon payments following the first are not known and have to be estimated as,
   $C_i = (I_a + QM) \times (d_i / 360)$.
2. The cash flows are discounted back to present value using the assumed index rate for each time period except the first. The period to the first coupon is discounted using the actual index rate for the period.
3. It is necessary to know the exact number of days in each coupon period.
4. The current value of the index rate corresponding to the average inter-coupon time period is often taken for the assumed rate. This is not necessarily the best estimate for future values of the index rate since it is only for a six month forward

period. Better estimates may be obtained using forward rates which may be derived from the bond yield curve.

5. The price is carried forward to the next coupon date using a simple interest calculation at the rate (I + DM), the actual index rate for the period plus the discounted margin.

6. The discounted margin is a measure of FRN value that compares the notes against their index rate. This is a short-term money market view that is predominant in European FRN markets. As a result it is clear that comparison of two FRNs using discounted margin is meaningful only if they are both based on the same index rate and pay interest with the same frequency.

7. The basic formula is non-linear in the discounted margin. Iterative rather than direct techniques are used to determine discounted margin values. Some of the possible variations of the formula are examined below.

Equivalence of First Period Discounting and First Period Simple Interest. While describing the development of the discounted margin in Section I, it was stated that carrying the price forward to the next coupon date is equivalent to discounting all cash flows back over that period. This can clearly be demonstrated using the basic formula stated above.

Dividing through by the value:

$$\left(1 + \frac{(I + DM)}{100} \times \frac{d_1}{360}\right)$$

on both sides of the formula, and transferring the first coupon element to the right hand side, results in the price on the settlement date set equal to the FRN cash flows discounted back to the settlement date.

Index Rate for the First Period. It has been suggested, to maintain the analogy with the internal rate of return of conventional bond markets, that the discount rate for the first period should be the assumed index rate. However, it is counter-intuitive to replace a known value with an estimated value. The following example demonstrates that using the assumed rate as the discount rate to the first coupon can provide inconsistent results.

Example: Consider an FRN with a quoted margin 25 basis points over 6 month LIBOR. Let the price remain constant at 99 and LIBOR to the next coupon date remain constant. The discounted margin can be plotted for a range of assumed future index rates using both the basic formula and the formula using the assumed rate over the first period. This is shown in Exhibits 15, 16 and 17.

It can be seen from Exhibits 15, 16 and 17 that the modified formula, by increasing the dependence of discounted margin on the assumed rate has introduced an inconsistency to the measurement of value. The discrepancy is worst immediately following coupon refix. The use of the assumed rate for the first period must therefore be rejected.

This example also reveals that the basic discounted margin formula provides values that are relatively independent of small changes in the assumed rate. The dependence is more apparent

---

EXHIBIT 15
Actual Rate Used for First Period

Discounted Margin

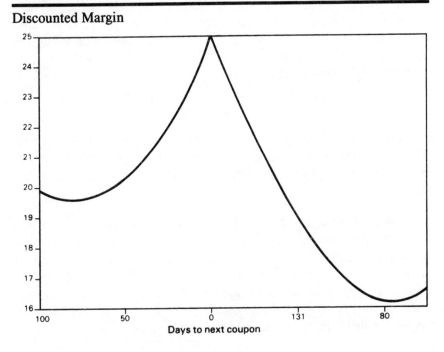

Days to next coupon

EXHIBIT 16
Assumed Rate of 10% Used for First Period

Discounted Margin

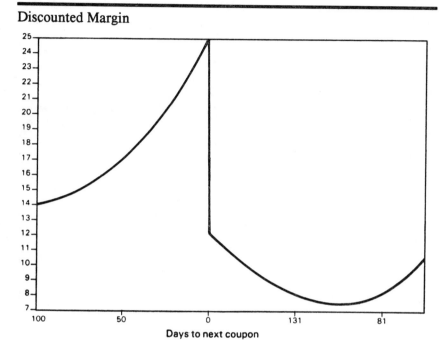

Days to next coupon

for notes trading away from par. A note trading away from par displays a greater dependence upon the assumed rate.

A second reformulation of the discounted margin, which attempts to provide an internal rate of return style, defines discounted margin as follows:

$$P = \frac{C \times \frac{d_0}{360}}{\left(1 + \frac{I_1}{100} \times \frac{d_0}{360}\right)} + \frac{(I_a + QM) \times \left(\frac{d_2}{360}\right)}{\left(1 + \left(\frac{I_1}{100}\right) \times \left(\frac{d_0}{360}\right)\right) \times \left(1 + \left(\frac{I_1}{100}\right) \times \left(\frac{d_2}{360}\right)\right)} + \dots$$

$$\dots + \frac{100 + (I_a + QM) \times \left(\frac{d_n}{360}\right)}{\left(1 + \left(\frac{I_1}{100}\right) \times \left(\frac{d_0}{360}\right)\right) \times \left(1 + \left(\frac{I_1}{100}\right) \times \left(\frac{d_2}{360}\right)\right) \times \dots \times \left(1 + \left(\frac{I_1}{100}\right) \times \left(\frac{d_n}{360}\right)\right)}$$

EXHIBIT 17
Assumed Rate of 9.75% Used for First Period

Discounted Margin

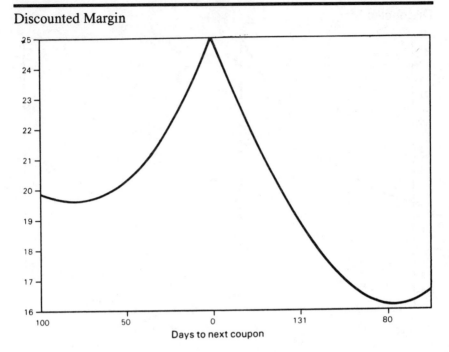

Days to next coupon

where DM = $I_1 - I_a$ where I_1 is determined above
      d_o = number of days from the last coupon to the next
      C = next coupon value.

This method determines what the discounted margin would have been at the last coupon date, assuming that the note had the same flat price as it has at the settlement date. It also assumes that the long run assumed index rate is the market rate at the last coupon date. The method has no intuitive or theoretical justification. The dependence on the assumed rate is increased and the price is assumed unchanged for the period from the last coupon date to settlement. Both of these assumptions can only introduce error. The method is therefore rejected.

Constant Coupon Frequency. The complexity of the basic discounted margin formula has already been noted. The need to know the exact number of days in each coupon period is particularly onerous. A simple modification is to assume that the coupon payments following the first coupon are made at constant intervals throughout 365.25 day years. This at least reduces the amount of data required to use the discounted margin formula. The formula reduces to the discounted margin formula–frequency version:

$$(P + A) \times \left(1 + \frac{(I + DM)}{100} \times \frac{d_1}{360}\right) - C_1$$

$$= \sum_{i=1}^{n} \frac{(I_a + QM) \times h}{\left(1 + \frac{(I_a + DM) \times h}{100}\right)^i} + \frac{RV}{\left(1 + \frac{(I_1 + DM) \times h}{100}\right)^n}$$

where f = number of coupon dates per year (frequency)

n = number of complete coupon periods

$$h = \frac{365.25}{360} \times \frac{1}{f}$$

This formula is more easily programmed on a computer than the basic formula and, as can be seen from Exhibit 18, provides almost identical results for the discounted margin.

A Direct Evaluation Method. A modification to the discounted margin formula to provide a further simplication can be derived as follows.[8]

Consider the basic discounted margin formula modified to use constant frequency coupon payments:

$$(P + A) \times \left(1 + \frac{(I + DM)}{100} \times \frac{d_1}{360}\right) - C_1 =$$

$$\sum_{i=1}^{n} \frac{(I_a + QM) \times h}{\left(1 + \frac{(I_a + DM) \times h}{100}\right)^i} + \frac{RV}{\left(1 + \frac{(I_a + DM) \times h}{100}\right)^n} \qquad (1)$$

The right hand side (RHS) of this equation can be examined as follows:

$$(RHS) = \sum_{i=1}^{n} \frac{(I_a + QM) \times h}{\left(1 + \frac{(I_a + DM) \times h}{100}\right)^i} + \frac{RV}{\left(1 + \frac{(I_a + DM) \times h}{100}\right)^n} \qquad (2)$$

[8] Suggested by Mr. W. Edwardes of Midland Bank.

EXHIBIT 18
Frequency Formula vs. Basic Formula

Percentage Difference

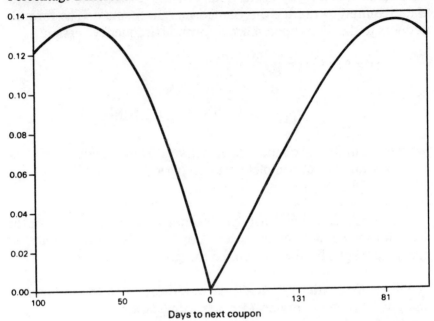

Days to next coupon

Now a conventional fixed rate investment with redemption value of par and coupon equal to yield has a price of par, i.e.,

$$100 = \sum_{i=1}^{n} \frac{C}{\left(1 + \frac{C}{100}\right)^i} + \frac{100}{\left(1 + \frac{C}{100}\right)^n}$$

So if the coupon were $(I_a + DM) \times h$, then:

$$100 = \sum_{i=1}^{n} \frac{(I_a + DM) \times h}{\left(1 + \frac{(I_a + DM) \times h}{100}\right)^i} + \frac{100}{\left(1 + \frac{(I_a + DM) \times h}{100}\right)^n} \qquad (3)$$

Substituting $(I_a + QM + DM - DM)$ for $(I_a + QM)$ in (1) and then applying (3) gives:

$$(RHS) = 100 + \sum_{i=1}^{n} \frac{(QM - DM) \times h}{\left(1 + \frac{(I_a + DM) \times h}{100}\right)^i} + \frac{(RV - 100)}{\left(1 + \frac{(I_a + DM) \times h}{100}\right)^n} \qquad (4)$$

Now the second element of (4) is a geometric sum which can be performed in the normal way to give:

$$(RHS) = 100 + (QM - DM) \times \frac{\left(\left(1 + \frac{(I_a + DM) \times h}{100}\right)^n - 1\right)}{\left(1 + \frac{(I_a + DM) \times h}{100}\right)^n \times \left(\frac{I_a + DM}{100}\right)}$$

$$+ \frac{(RV - 100)}{\left(1 + \frac{(I_a + DM) \times h}{100}\right)^n} \qquad (5)$$

It has been noted that the basic discounted margin formula is relatively insensitive to small changes in the assumed index rate. $(QM - DM)$ is a relatively small value so that $(I_a + QM - DM)$ is an equally valid assumed rate. Substitution of $(I_a + QM - DM)$ for I_a into (5) yields:

$$(RHS) = 100 + (QM - DM) \times K + \frac{(RV - 100)}{\left(1 + \frac{(I_a + QM) \times h}{100}\right)^n}$$

where

$$K = \frac{\left(\left(1 + \frac{(I_a + QM) \times h}{100}\right)^n - 1\right)}{\left(1 + \frac{(I_a + QM) \times h}{100}\right)^n \left(\frac{I_a + QM}{100}\right)} \qquad (6)$$

Returning to equation (1), substitution from (6) gives:

$$(P + A) \times \left(1 + \frac{(I + DM)}{100} \times \frac{d_1}{360}\right) - C_1 = 100 + (QM - DM) \times K$$

$$+ \frac{(RV - 100)}{\left(1 + \frac{(I_a + QM) \times h}{100}\right)^n}$$

The equation is now linear in DM and thus allows direct solution, thus: the discounted margin formula–direct solution version is as follows:

$$DM = \frac{C_1 + 100 + QM \times K - I \times K_1 - (P + A) + \dfrac{(RV - 100)}{\left(1 + \frac{(I_a + QM) \times h}{100}\right)^n}}{K + K_1}$$

where

$$K = \frac{\left(\left(1 + \frac{(I_a + QM) \times h}{100}\right)^n - 1\right)}{\left(1 + \frac{(I_a + QM) \times h}{100}\right)^n \times \left(\frac{I_a + QM}{100}\right)}$$

$$K_1 = \frac{(P + A)}{100} \times \frac{d_1}{360}$$

One can compare the discounted margin results achieved using this formula with those from the frequency based iterative method.

Exhibit 19 shows that the relative error in value from the direct method is small when compared to the value from the frequency based formula. For example, a discounted margin of 10 basis points derived by using the frequency formula, the greatest error of − 1.1 percent would represent a difference between the two formulae of only 0.11 basis points.

EXHIBIT 19
Direct Formula vs. Frequency Formula

Percentage Difference

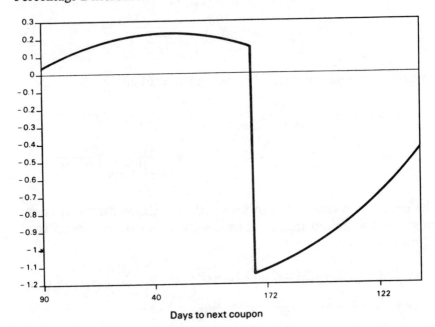

Days to next coupon

Measurement of Time. The discounted margin formulae presented so far have been written in money market accounting form (actual/360). This is valid where the index rate follows money market conventions (e.g., LIBOR rates). However, other FRNs have been issued which follow non-money market indices.

The basic discounted margin can be used to value a FRN which has a non-money market accounting index rate. The measurements of time are simply adjusted as described in Section I.

A modified version of the discounted margin formula has been devised which allows the discounted margin to be calculated to an accounting convention which is different from that of the index rate.[9] The revised formula is:

$$(P + A) \times \left(1 + \frac{I}{100} \times TI_1 + \frac{DM}{100} \times TD_1\right) - C_1$$

$$= \frac{C_2}{\left(1 + \frac{I_a}{100} \times TI_2 + \frac{DM}{100} \times TD_2\right)} + \ldots$$

$$\ldots + \frac{RV + C_n}{\left(1 + \frac{I_a}{100} \times TI_2 + \frac{DM}{100} \times TD_2\right) \times \ldots \times \left(1 + \frac{I_a}{100} \times TI_n + \frac{DM}{100} \times TD_n\right)}$$

where $P + A$ = Price plus accrued

I = Index rate for the period from settlement to next coupon

C_i = ith coupon payment

RV = Redemption value

DM = Discounted margin

I_a = Assumed index rate

TI_i = Time in ith coupon period using index rate accounting

TD_i = Time in ith coupon period using discounted margin accounting.

This formula clearly enables the calculation of discounted margin values, to the same accounting convention, for floating rate securities following different index rates. However, comparison of the floating rate securities using these values takes no account of

[9] See David Muntner, *Analysis of Floating Rate Securities.*

the spread between the two different index rates. Furthermore, one can recall that the motive behind the discounted margin is to compare the FRN with its index rate and not with other floating rate securities.

Time Measured to Infinity–Perpetual FRNs.   There are several FRN issues with no final maturity date. These 'perpetual' FRNs clearly pose a problem when trying to determine a margin measure of value. The simple margin formula presented earlier provides a value equal to the quoted margin as the amortization of the FRN discount/premium is performed over an infinite period. This does not give much guidance as a measure of value.

The discounted margin formula for a perpetual note implies an infinite sum of coupon flows. However, the constant frequency version of the formula can be solved easily using geometric summation techniques. The discounted margin for a perpetual FRN is thus given by:

$$(P+A) = \frac{1}{\left(1 + \frac{(I+DM)}{100} \times \frac{d_1}{360}\right)} \times \left(C_1 + \frac{100 \times (I_a + QM)}{(I_a + DM)}\right)$$

where $P + A$ = Price plus accrued at settlement
I = Index rate to the next coupon date
I_a = Assumed average long term index rate
C_1 = Next coupon payment
QM = Quoted margin
DM = Discounted margin

Note that the frequency of payment element, h, of the constant frequency formula is not present in the perpetual version above, as it is eliminated by the geometric summation process.

Yield to Maturity

The basic formula for the yield to maturity of a floating rate note is:

$$(P+A) + \sum_{i=1}^{n} \frac{C_i}{\left(1 + \frac{YTM}{(f \times 100)}\right)^{(f \times T_i)}} + \frac{RV}{\left(1 + \frac{YTM}{(f \times 100)}\right)^{(f \times T_n)}}$$

where P + A = Price plus accrued, the cost of the note,

C_i = ith coupon payment

n = Number of coupon payments from settlement to maturity

T_i = Time from settlement to the ith coupon payment

YTM = Yield to maturity.

f = Yield basis (e.g., f = 2, semiannual)

This formula enables the calculation of yield values to the same frequency basis for FRNs paying interest at different frequencies. The formula can thus be used for comparing both floating rate investments to floating rate investments and also floating rate investments to fixed rate investments.

Once a YTM value has been calculated to a particular frequency basis it is a relatively simple matter to adjust to other bases. For example, to obtain an annual value from a semiannual value the following is used.

$$YTM_{Annual} = \left(\left(1 + \frac{YTM_{Semiannual}}{200} \right)^2 - 1 \right) \times 100$$

Formulae for conversion to other yield bases are readily available.[10] A detailed discussion of YTM for floating rate securities can be found elsewhere.[11] Here we will review some of the ideas presented by that discussion.

Assumed Coupon Rate Selection.   As with the discounted margin, an assumed coupon rate must be selected to give the coupon payments following the first. Exhibit 20 shows how changes in assumed rate can affect the calculated value of the YTM.

Clearly the assumed index rate can influence significantly the expected yield of the FRN.

Breakeven Analysis.   An alternative approach that avoids the problems of selecting an inappropriate coupon rate is to determine the breakeven index rate needed to produce a specified yield. This type of analysis can be used in two ways.

[10] See *CSFB Investment Manual,* London: Credit Suisse First Boston Limited, 1982.

[11] For additional information see David Muntner, *Analysis of Floating Rate Securities.*

EXHIBIT 20
Sensitivity of YTM to Assumed Index

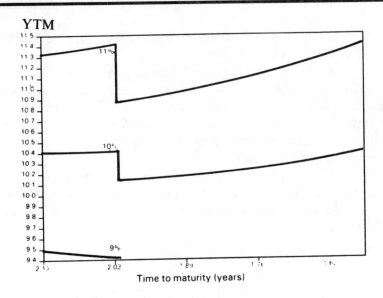

Time to maturity (years)

First, suppose an FRN is to be compared against a fixed rate alternative. For example, consider an FRN paying 25 basis points over its index rate semiannually, its price is 100 and there are 90 days until the next coupon payment of 4.00. The life of the FRN from the next coupon date is two years. Suppose an alternative, fixed rate investment is currently yielding 8 percent. What is the breakeven index rate which will assure a yield of 8 percent from the FRN?

To determine the breakeven rate (BR) one can substitute the details of the FRN into the YTM formula along with a targeted semiannual yield of 8 percent. Thus,

$$100 + 2.00 - \frac{4.00}{\left(1 + \frac{8}{200}\right)^{2 \times 0.25}} - \frac{100}{\left(1 + \frac{8}{200}\right)^{2 \times 2.25}}$$

$$= \frac{(BR + .25) \times 0.5}{\left(1 + \frac{8}{200}\right)^{2 \times 0.75}} + \frac{(BR + .25) \times 0.5}{\left(1 + \frac{8}{200}\right)^{2 \times 1.25}} + \frac{(BR + .25) \times 0.5}{\left(1 + \frac{8}{200}\right)^{2 \times 1.75}} + \frac{(BR + .25) \times 0.5}{\left(1 + \frac{8}{200}\right)^{2 \times 2.25}}$$

The BR calculated directly from this formulation is 7.76 percent. If the index rate is expected to be higher than the breakeven rate, then clearly the FRN will be a better investment, giving a greater return than the fixed rate alternative.

A second use of breakeven rates enables comparison of floating rate securities using different index rates. Here the breakeven spread between the two index rates is determined. Two securities of similar quality and maturity fixing off different index rates can be compared.

On selecting a range of hypothetical values for the first index rate, one can determine the expected YTM values for the security fixing off that rate. For example, hypothetical index rate values of 6 percent, 9 percent and 12 percent may result in expected YTM values of 6.69 percent, 9.34 percent and 11.96 percent for the first security. The breakeven index rates to provide these YTM values for the second security may then be calculated (e.g., 6.99 percent, 10.01 percent and 13.03 percent). The breakeven spread is then the difference between the hypothetical and calculated index rates (e.g., 6.99–6.00 giving 99 basis points, 10.01–9.00 giving 101 basis points and 13.03–12 giving 103 basis points). If the expected spread between the two index rates is less than the calculated breakeven spread, about 101 basis points in the example above, the security reset to the lower index rate will generate a higher return. The breakeven spread calculation is relatively independent of the selected hypothetical rates. In the above example the breakeven spread changed by only 4 basis points for a 6 point change in the first base rate.

YTM Spread. The yield to maturity formulation enables an alternative method of calculating margin of return over the index rate of an FRN. This margin is called the YTM spread. The YTM spread is the difference between the YTM of the FRN and that of the index rate.

The YTM of the index rate is calculated by deriving the expected return from rolling over investments at the index rate.

$$100 = \sum_{i=1}^{n} \frac{I_i}{\left(1 + \frac{YTM_{index}}{200}\right)^{2T_i}} + \frac{100}{\left(1 + \frac{YTM_{index}}{200}\right)^{2T_n}}$$

where YTM_{index} = Yield of the index (assuming semi annual compounding)

I_i = Index rate in the ith coupon period of the FRN

I_1 = Index rate to the next coupon date

$I_2..I_n$ = Assumed index rate for period 2, 3, ...,n

T_i = Time to the ith coupon payment;

The YTM spread is then

$$\text{YTM}_{spread} = (\text{YTM}_{note} - \text{YTM}_{index}) \times 100$$

The value obtained by this method is very similar to the discounted margin value for the FRN.

Perpetual FRNs.   A formula for calculating the yield of a perpetual FRN can be derived in a similar manner to that used for the perpetual FRN discounted margin formula. The yield may be calculated using the formula:

$$(P + A) \times \left(1 + \frac{Y_p}{(f \times 100)}\right)^{(f \times T_1)} - C_1 = C_a \times \left(\left(1 + \frac{Y_p}{(f \times 100)}\right)^{(f \times h)} - 1\right)$$

where P + A = Price plus accrued at settlement

C_1 = First coupon payment

C_a = Assumed long term coupon payments = $(I_a + QM) \times h$

Y_p = Yield for perpetual FRN

T_1 = Time (in years) to first coupon payment

f = Yield basis (1 = annual, 2 = semiannual, etc)

h = Payment interval (1 = annual, 0.5 = semiannual, etc)

Note that this formula differs from the often used 'running yield' formula which simply divides current coupon by clean price. The formula above takes account of both accrued interest and future cash flows.

APPENDIX A—RECOMMENDED FORMULAE

Bond Days Elapsed.   To calculate the number of bond days elapsed in U.S. corporate accounting, the number of days between date 1 (d_1, m_1, y_1) and date 2 (d_2, m_2, y_2) is given by:

$$\text{Bond days elapsed} = (y_2 - y_1) \times 360 + (m_2 - m_1) \times 30 + (d_2 - d_1)$$

Simple Margin.   The recommended simple margin formula is:

$$\text{Simple Margin} = \frac{RV - (P + A) - (I + QM) \times \left(\frac{d}{360}\right) + \text{Coupon}}{\text{Life}} + QM$$

where P + A = Price plus accrued
   I = Index rate from settlement to next coupon date
   d = Number of days to next coupon
   QM = Quoted margin
   RV = Redemption value
   Life = Life from settlement to maturity

Discounted Margin.   The recommended iterative solution formula is:

$$(P + A) \times \left(1 + \frac{(I + DM) \times h}{100}\right) - C_1$$

$$= \sum_{i=1}^{n} \frac{(I_a + QM) \times h}{\left(1 + \frac{(I_a + DM) \times h}{100}\right)^i} + \frac{RV}{\left(1 + \frac{(I_a + DM) \times h}{100}\right)^n}$$

where n = Number of whole coupon periods
   f = Number of coupon payments per year
   $h = \frac{365.25}{360} \times \frac{1}{f}$

Alternatively, the following direct solution formula may be used with only slight loss in accuracy for issues trading close to par:

$$DM = \frac{C_1 + 100 + QM \times K - I \times K_1 - (P + A) + \frac{(RV - 100)}{\left(1 + \frac{(I_a + QM) \times h}{100}\right)^n}}{K + K_1}$$

where

$$K = \frac{\left(\left(1 + \frac{(I_a + QM) \times h}{100}\right)^n - 1\right)}{\left(1 + \frac{(I_a + QM) \times h}{100}\right)^n \times \left(\frac{I_a + QM}{100}\right)}$$

$$K_1 = \frac{(P + A)}{100} \times \frac{d_1}{360}$$

Yield to Maturity.   The recommended iterative solution formula is:

$$(P + A) = \sum_{i=1}^{n} \frac{C_i}{\left(1 + \frac{YTM}{(f \times 100)}\right)^{(f \times T_i)}} + \frac{RV}{\left(1 + \frac{YTM}{(f \times 100)}\right)^{(f \times T_n)}}$$

where YTM = Yield to maturity
C_i = Coupon payment i
T_i = Time (in years) to the ith coupon payment

Neutral Price.   The neutral price assuming constant simple margin between settlement and next coupon date is:

$$\text{Simple margin neutral price} = (P + A) + (I + SM) \times \frac{d}{360} - \text{Coupon}$$

The neutral price, assuming constant discounted margin between settlement and next coupon date:

Discounted margin neutral price =

$$(P + A) \times \left(1 + \frac{(I + DM)}{100} \times \frac{d}{360}\right) - \text{Coupon}$$

APPENDIX B—THE ADJUSTED TOTAL MARGIN

This method of valuation attempts to adjust for one drawback of the simple margin—the current yield effect—but retains straight-line amortization. The current yield effect is overcome using the following approach:

- Adjust the price to allow for the return between settlement and next coupon dates by discounting the calculated price at next coupon date back to the settlement date. Price adjustment based on the amount paid.
- Assume a par base for investment comparison.
- Determine the simple margin using the adjusted price.
- Where the price is below par, adjust the simple margin by adding the additional return possible on a par based investment

(i.e., the return from investing the cash left over after buying the FRN).

- Where the price is above par, adjust the simple margin by subtracting the lost return from the additional cost over par (i.e., the return from extra cash that can not now be invested).

- Rebase the value thus calculated to a par investment.

The general form for the adjusted total margin is a modified version of the simple margin formula, thus:

$$ATM = (\text{Simple Margin} + \text{Yield Adjustment}) \times \frac{100}{\text{Adjusted Price}}$$

The simple margin used here differs from the simple margin described in the body of this article because of the way in which the price is adjusted. The adjusted price is determined by calculating the return to the next coupon date and then discounting back to the settlement date. The simple margin is then:

$$\text{Simple Margin} = \frac{100 - \text{Adjusted Price}}{\text{Whole life of FRN}} + QM$$

The yield adjustment is the return gain/loss derived from investing the difference between the adjusted price and par at money market rates. Thus,

$$\text{Yield Adjustment} = \frac{\text{Index rate}}{100} \times (100 - \text{Adjusted Price})$$

These formulae now prompt the following questions:

- At what rate should the price be carried to the next coupon date?

- At what rate should it then be discounted back again?

- At what rate should the yield adjustment be calculated?

The most common formulation of ATM is:

$$ATM = \frac{\left(\dfrac{100 - P_a}{\text{Life}} + QM + \dfrac{I_a}{100} \times (100 - P_a) \right)}{Pa} \times 100$$

where

$$P_a = P - \frac{\left(c - \frac{I}{100} \times (P + A)\right) \times \frac{d}{360}}{\left(1 + \frac{I_a}{100} \times \frac{d}{360}\right)}$$

and P = Clean price of FRN

    c = Coupon rate

    I = Current value of index rate to next coupon date

    I_a = Assumed average index rate over the life of the note

  QM = Quoted margin

    A = Interest accrued prior to settlement

    d = Number of days to the next coupon date.

This variant of the formula carries the price forward at the current value of the index rate which is a reasonable assumption. However, it is shown with the simple margin in Section I that a

---

EXHIBIT 21
Adjusted Total Margin

ATM

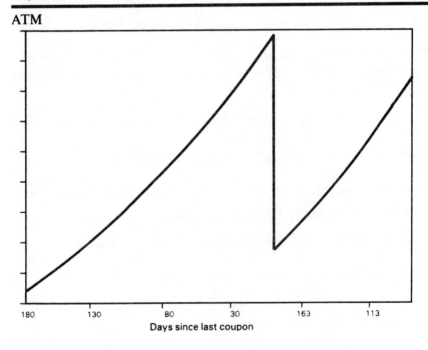

Days since last coupon

more consistent approach carried the price forward at the index rate plus the quoted margin or the simple margin.

The discount factor for the period to the next coupon is an assumed rate. It could equally be the actual rate or a rate plus a margin value.

The interest rate used in the yield adjustment is an assumed rate. This is again a reasonable assumption since it accounts for a return over the whole life of the note. However, as can be seen in Section II, this can lead to problems with the discounting of the period to the first coupon payment.

Exhibit 21 reveals that this version of the ATM suffers from discontinuity problems discussed in connection with some of the possible simple margin formulae.

It is possible to reformulate the ATM formula, as is done for the simple margin in Section I, to obtain a more consistent value. However, as a result of the already complex ATM basic formula and the additional reformulation, this is highly complex and not very worthwhile since the method also retains the unrealistic straight-line amortization assumption. In moving to a more complex method of evaluation it seems desirable, therefore, to adopt a method that overcomes all problems of the simple margin, ideally the discounted margin.

ARTICLE 13

JAMES F. MEISNER holds the position of Vice President and Manager of Financial Futures and Options Research at Merrill Lynch Capital Markets in New York City. He consults with institutional investors and asset/liability managers on the use of financial futures and options to manage risk and enhance return in portfolios.

Prior to joining Merrill Lynch, Mr. Meisner held research and marketing positions at the Chicago Corporation, Prudential-Bache Securities, and the Chicago Board of Trade.

Mr. Meisner's education includes an MBA in finance and a BA in mathematics from the University of Chicago. His articles have appeared in several publications, including *Financial Analysts Journal, The Journal of Futures Markets, Economics Letters, Futures Magazine, Intermarket Magazine,* and *Mortgage Banking.*

JOHN A. RICHARDS is Vice President and Group Manager of Financial Futures and Options at Merrill Lynch Capital Markets. Prior to joining Merrill Lynch, Mr. Richards managed financial futures trading on the floor of the Chicago Board of Trade for Drexel Burnham Lambert. Mr. Richards has also held positions at the University of Hawaii, Continental Illinois National Bank, and ContiFinancial. He received his M.A. in economics from the University of Wisconsin in 1970.

OPTION PREMIUM DYNAMICS: WITH APPLICATIONS TO FIXED INCOME PORTFOLIO ANALYSIS

James F. Meisner
Vice President
Merrill Lynch Capital Markets

John A. Richards
Vice President
Merrill Lynch Capital Markets

A variety of models are available for determining option theoretical values. The Black-Scholes model[1] is widely used despite the restrictive assumptions upon which it is based. These assumptions include (1) the option is European, i.e., it cannot be exercised before the expiration date; (2) the underlying price returns are normally distributed with constant mean and variance; (3) the underlying market is perfectly efficient, with continuous trading and zero transaction costs; (4) no discrete dividends or nonaccruing

---

[1] F. Black and M. Scholes. "The Pricing of Options and Corporate Liabilities." *Journal of Political Economy,* May/June 1973, pp. 637–54.

interest payments; and (5) the short-term interest rate is fixed over the life of the option.

Several option pricing models have been derived which relax some of these restrictions.[2] Despite its many competitors and the restrictive nature of the assumptions which underlie it, the Black-Scholes model has proven itself to be a useful tool for analyzing option price behavior. One of the appeals of the model is its simple closed form, which lends itself to fast computation. The Black-Scholes formula can readily be differentiated, thus facilitating premium sensitivity analysis.

This article presents a generalized form of the Black-Scholes pricing model, along with its derivatives. These formulas are then illustrated graphically in order to shed light on option premium dynamics. Derivative ratios are also examined and illustrated. The final section considers duration and convexity measures for options on fixed income securities. It is assumed that the reader is familiar with basic option terminology.

[2] See, for example: M. Asay. "A Note on the Design of Commodity Option Contracts." *The Journal of Futures Markets,* 3, 1982, pp. 1–7; C.A. Ball and W. N. Torous. "Bond Price Dynamics and Options." Working paper, Graduate School of Business Administration, University of Michigan, 1984; J.N. Bodurtha and G.R. Courtadon. "Relative Pricing of Foreign Currency Options and Foreign Currency Futures Options." Working paper, Ohio State University and New York University, 1985; J.C. Cox and S.A. Ross. "A Survey of Some New Results in Financial Option Pricing Theory." *Journal of Finance,* 31, 1976, pp. 383–402; J.C. Cox and S.A. Ross. "The Valuation of Options for Alternative Stochastic Processes." *Journal of Financial Economics,* 3, 1986, pp. 145–166; J.C. Cox, S.A. Ross, and M. Rubinstein. "Option Pricing: A Simplified Approach." *Journal of Financial Economics,* 7, 1979, pp. 229–6; R.A. Jarrow and A. Rudd. *Option Pricing.* Homewood, Il.: Dow-Jones Irwin, 1983; J.F. Meisner and J.W. Labuszewski. "The Cox-Ross-Rubinstein Option Pricing Model for Alternative Underlying Instruments." Working paper, Merrill Lynch Capital Markets, 1984; R.C. Merton. "Option Pricing when Underlying Stock Returns are Discontinuous." *Journal of Financial Economics,* 3, 1976, pp. 125–44; C.W. Smith. "Option Pricing: A Review." *Journal of Financial Economics,* 3, 1976, pp. 3–52; R.E. Whaley. "Valuation of American Call Options on Dividend-Paying Stocks: Empirical Tests." *Journal of Financial Economics,* 10, 1982, pp. 31–58; R.E. Whaley. "Valuation of American Futures Options: Theory and Empirical Tests." Working paper, Institute for Financial Research, University of Alberta, 1986.

I. A GENERALIZED BLACK-SCHOLES FORMULA

The formulas given below are generalized for options on securities, commodities, currencies, and futures or forward contracts. A cost-of-carry factor is used to distinguish between these various underlying instruments. We use the following notation:

C	= Call premium (price)
P	= Put premium (price)
U	= Underlying security, commodity, or futures price
E	= Strike price
t	= Time to expiration, in years
v	= Price volatility, annualized
r	= Short-term interest rate
h	= Holding cost factor (explained below)
$n(x)$	= Normal probability distribution function at x
$N(x)$	= Cumulative normal distribution function at x

The holding cost factor, h, takes the following forms:

Futures: $h = 0$ (no holding cost or income).

Security: $h = r - y$, where y = security yield.

Commodity: $h = r + x$, where x = storage cost rate, including insurance and spoilage.

Currency: $h = r - r_f$, where r_f = foreign short-term interest rate.

The pricing formulas for puts and calls are given below:

$$C = e^{-rt}[Ue^{ht}N(d_1) - E\,N(d_2)]$$

$$P = e^{-rt}[Ue^{ht}(N(d_1) - 1) - E(N(d_2) - 1)]$$

where $d_1 = \ln(Ue^{ht}/E)/(v\sqrt{t}) + .5\,v\sqrt{t}$
$d_2 = d_1 - v\sqrt{t}$

The derivatives of C and P with respect to U, v, and t are commonly known as *delta*, *vega*, and *theta*, respectively. The formulas are given below:

$$\frac{dC}{dU} = e^{(h-r)t}N(d_1)$$

$$\frac{dP}{dU} = e^{(h-r)t}(N(d_1) - 1)$$

$$\frac{dC}{dv} = \frac{dP}{dv} = U\sqrt{t}\, e^{(h-r)t} n(d_1)$$

$$\frac{dC}{dt} = e^{-rt}[Uv/(2\sqrt{t})\, n(d_1) + Ue^{ht}(h-r)\, N(d_1) + Er\, N(d_2)]$$

$$\frac{dP}{dt} = e^{-rt}[Uv/(2\sqrt{t})\, n(d_1) + Ue^{ht}(h-r)(N(d_1) - 1) + Er(N(d_2) - 1)]$$

The second derivative of the premium with respect to U is known as *gamma*. It is given by:

$$\frac{d^2C}{dU^2} = \frac{d^2P}{dU^2} = [e^{(h-r)t}/(Uv\sqrt{t})]\, n(d_1)$$

II. OPTION PREMIUM COMPONENTS

The option premium has two components: *intrinsic value* and *time value*. Intrinsic value is the amount by which the option is in-the-money; for calls, intrinsic value is the amount by which the underlying price exceeds the strike price and for puts it is the amount by which the underlying price is less than the strike price.

An American option, which can be exercised any business day prior to expiration, should always be worth at least its intrinsic value. A European option, which can only be exercised on the expiration date, may price below intrinsic value if it is sufficiently in-the-money. In general, however, an option is worth more than its intrinsic value. This other component of the option premium is known as time value.

Exhibit 1 illustrates the components of the premium of a call option on a futures contract. When the futures price is less than the strike price of 100, the option has no intrinsic value and the entire premium consists of time value. Note that time value is maximized when the option is at-the-money; i.e., when the underlying futures price equals the strike price of the option.

Time value reflects the potential of the option to gain intrinsic value versus the potential to lose intrinsic value. A deep out-of-the-money option has little potential to gain intrinsic value and therefore has little time value. A deep in-the-money option has about as

EXHIBIT 1
Call Option Premium Components
90 Days, Strike = 100, v = 15%, r = 6%

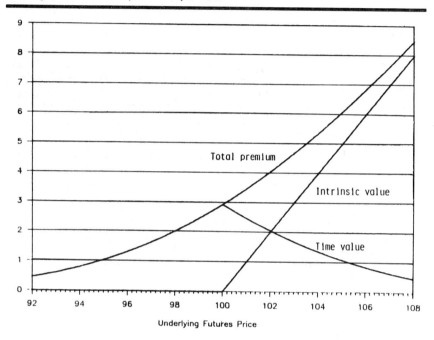

much potential to lose intrinsic value as to gain it, and so also has little time value. An at-the-money option, on the other hand, has no intrinsic value to lose but a roughly 50-50 chance of acquiring it, and therefore has a good deal of time value.

In the next three sections, we will discuss the effect on the option premium of changes in the underlying price, volatility, and time remaining to expiration. It is the interplay of these three factors, along with the short-term interest rate, that determines the option time value and governs the dynamics of the option premium.

Effect of Changes in the Underlying Price

Exhibit 2 illustrates the Black-Scholes premiums of call options with 30, 90, and 180 days remaining to expiration. As the underlying

EXHIBIT 2
Call Option Premiums
Strike = 100, v = 15%, r = 6%

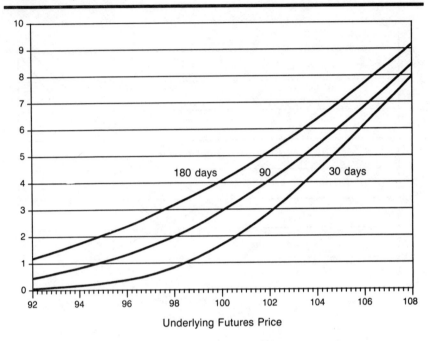

Underlying Futures Price

futures price rises, the call premium rises as well, but not in a linear
fashion. As the option moves in-the-money, it picks up value more
quickly. Conversely, as the option moves out-of-the-money, it loses
value more slowly.

Delta measures the change in the option premium as a proportion of the change in the underlying price. For example, a delta of
.5 suggests that a 1 point change in the underlying price (e.g., from
100 to 101) will cause a .5 point change in the option premium
(e.g., from 3 to 3.5). Exhibit 3 illustrates delta for the same three
options illustrated in Exhibit 2. The deltas in Exhibit 3 are simply
the slopes of the premium curves in Exhibit 2, and are calculated
using the formula for dC/dU given above.

Delta varies between 0 and 1. Deep out-of-the-money options
are little affected by changes in the underlying price and hence
have deltas close to 0. The premium of deep in-the-money options

---

EXHIBIT 3
Call Option Deltas
Strike = 100, v = 15%, r = 6%

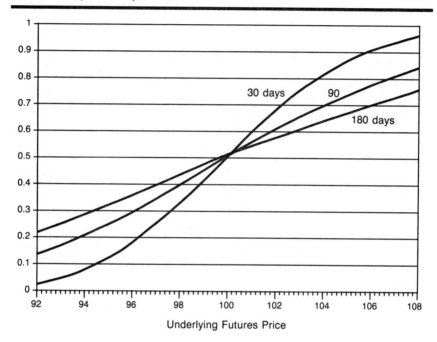

Underlying Futures Price

consists almost entirely of intrinsic value; such options move in lock-step with the underlying price and hence have deltas close to 1. At-the-money options (where the underlying price equals the strike price) have deltas close to .5.

The price elasticities in Exhibit 4 are another measure of an option's sensitivity to changes in the underlying price. These elasticities were obtained by dividing delta by the option premium. A standard price elasticity would also be multiplied by the underlying price; we chose not to do so in order to retain more comparability with delta.

The price elasticity measures the percentage change in the premium given a unit move in the underlying price. For example, an elasticity of 50 suggests that a 1 point change in the underlying price (e.g., from 94 to 95) will result in a 50 percent change in the option premium (e.g., from .1 to .15). The elasticity paints a much

EXHIBIT 4
Call Price Elasticities
Strike = 100, v = 15%, r = 6%

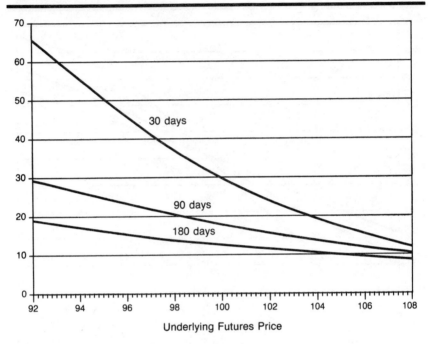

different picture of premium sensitivity than does delta. Delta suggests that out-of-the-money options are least sensitive to changes in the underlying price, while the elasticity suggests the opposite. The reason for this apparent contradiction is that changes in the premiums of out-of-the-money options may be small in absolute terms but large when considered as a percentage of the premium itself.

Gamma, shown in Exhibit 5, is the rate of change in delta; a gamma of .05 suggests that a 1 point move in the underlying price (e.g., from 100 to 101) will result in delta changing by .05 (e.g., from .5 to .55). A high gamma indicates that the slope of the premium curve (Exhibit 2) will change quickly as the underlying price changes, suggesting a high degree of nonlinearity or convexity. The gammas in Exhibit 5 were calculated using the formula for d^2C/dU^2 given above.

EXHIBIT 5
Call Option Gammas
Strike = 100, v = 15%, r = 6%

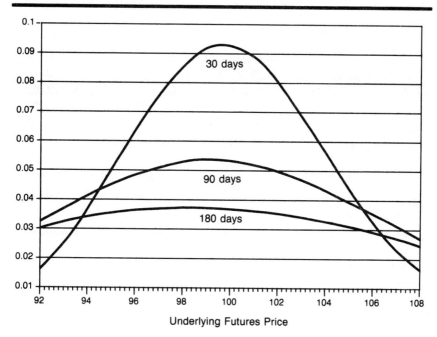

Examination of Exhibit 5 reveals that options which are at-the-money and close to expiration have the highest gammas. Indeed, at expiration gamma is infinite when the option is at-the-money, but 0 when the option is in- or out-of-the-money. This is because the premium at expiration equals the intrinsic value of the option, and delta is either 0 when the option is out-of-the-money or 1 when it is in-the-money.

Gamma is a good indication of the riskiness of a short option position. To understand this, consider the fact that the premium convexity always works to the disadvantage of the option seller: as the option moves in-the-money, delta increases, thus accelerating losses; and as the option moves out-of-the-money, delta decreases, thus attenuating gains. Thus, changes in delta always work against the option seller. If delta is highly sensitive to changes in the underlying price (i.e., gamma is large), then the option is risky from the seller's point of view.

Effect of Changes in the Time Remaining to Expiration

Exhibit 6 illustrates the premiums of three different call options as a function of the time remaining until expiration. The options are at-the-money and either 4 percent or 8 percent out-of-the-money. Since none of the options illustrated in Exhibit 6 have any intrinsic value, the premiums in Exhibit 6 consist entirely of time value. The time value graphs of in-the-money options are similar to the premium graphs of options which are out-of-the-money by the same amount.

Note that as the option approaches expiration, time value diminishes. At expiration, the option is worth only its intrinsic value and

EXHIBIT 6
Call Option Premiums
Futures Price = 100, v = 15%, r = 6%

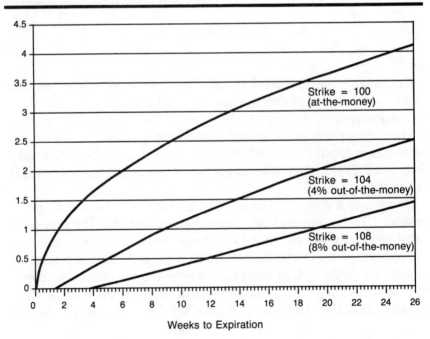

Weeks to Expiration

time value equals 0. The tendency of time value to diminish over time is known as *time value decay;* this feature of option premium dynamics works to the advantage of sellers and to the disadvantage of buyers. Exhibit 6 reveals that time value decay accelerates as an at-the-money option approaches expiration, but may decelerate for in- or out-of-the-money options.

The rate of time value decay is measured by *theta* (see Exhibit 7), also known as the *time delta*. Theta measures the change in the option premium given a 1-day passage of time. For example, a theta of .02 suggests that an option premium will decline by .02 between today and tomorrow, assuming that all other conditions remain the same. The thetas in Exhibit 7 equal dC/dt divided by 365.

High theta options are attractive to option sellers, because such options have a high rate of time value decay. Note from Exhibit 7

EXHIBIT 7
Call Option Thetas
Strike = 100, v = 15%, r = 6%

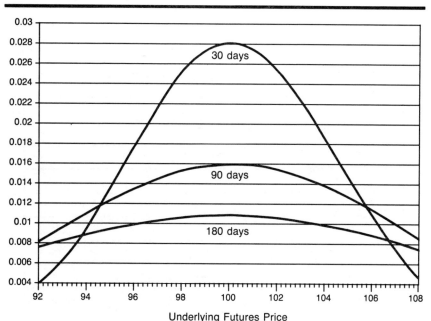

Underlying Futures Price

that options which are at-the-money and close to expiration have the highest thetas. As discussed above, these options also have the highest gammas. Thus, the tradeoff for selling an option with a high theta is that such options also have high gammas, representing a high degree of risk. We will return to the subject of the theta/gamma tradeoff later in this section.

Exhibit 8 is a graph of the time elasticities associated with the three options illustrated in Exhibit 7. The time elasticity is defined here as theta divided by the option premium. The time elasticity measures the percentage change in the option premium given a 1-day passage of time. For example, a time elasticity of 10 suggests that the option premium will diminish by 10 percent between today and tomorrow, holding all other conditions constant.

As in the case of price elasticities, time elasticities are greatest for low-premium options; i.e., out-of-the-money options which are

EXHIBIT 8
Call Time Elasticities
Strike = 100, v = 15%, r = 6%

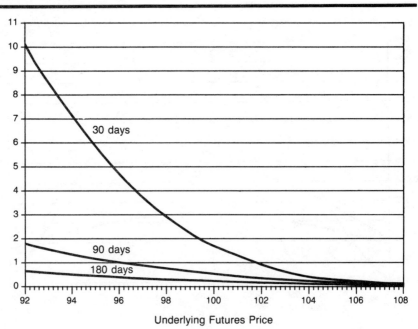

Underlying Futures Price

close to expiration. Although a low-premium option has a large time elasticity, its theta is small. The premium of such an option decays rapidly on a percentage basis, but only slowly in absolute terms.

Effect of Changing Volatility

The volatility of the underlying price is a critical factor affecting an option's premium. As the underlying price becomes more volatile, the premiums of both puts and calls become larger. Volatility measures the fluctuation of the underlying price around its trend; volatility does not measure the trend itself.

To gain an intuitive understanding of volatility, it is helpful to think in terms of 1-day confidence intervals. The following procedure for computing confidence intervals is based on the assumption that the underlying price returns are "normally" distributed, an assumption which is often challenged but is sufficiently accurate for our purposes.

First, since volatility is generally quoted in annual terms, it is necessary to convert it to daily terms. To do so, divide by the square root of the number of trading days in a year, or approximately 16. Thus, an annual volatility of 16 percent translates to daily volatility of 1 percent. Starting with the current day's closing price, plus or minus 1 daily volatility defines a 68 percent confidence interval for the next trading day's closing price. For example, if the underlying price is 100, a plus or minus 1 percent interval would be 99 to 101. We have ignored the price trend in this example, because it is generally negligible over a 1 day period.

Probability theory suggests that there is a 68 percent chance that tomorrow's closing price will fall within this 68 percent confidence interval, and there is a 32 percent chance that it will fall outside of it. Of course, this assumes that the volatility used to calculate the confidence interval is correct.

Unfortunately, volatility is not directly observable and therefore its value is never precisely known. Instead, it must be estimated. There are two common approaches to volatility estimation. The first approach, known as historical volatility, is based on the past behavior of the underlying price. Historical volatility is usually calculated as the standard deviation of price returns over a time period which may be as short as 10 trading days or as long as 1 year. A price return is defined to be the logarithm of the ratio of two prices observed on succeeding days.

Other techniques are available for calculating historical volatilities. These methods employ additional information such as opening, high, and low prices.[3]

The second approach, known as implied volatility, is based on the observable market premium of the option. Implied volatility is the volatility which, when employed in an option pricing formula such as Black-Scholes, results in a model premium which equals the actual market premium.

Exhibit 9 illustrates the premiums of at-the-money call options on futures contracts as a function of implied volatility. Note that the premium rises as volatility increases. The sensitivity of the premium to changing volatility is measured by *vega* (see Exhibit 10). Vega is also known as the *volatility delta*. Vega measures the change in the option premium given a 1 percent change in the implied volatility. For example, a vega of .2 suggests that a 1 percent increase in volatility (e.g., from 15 percent to 16 percent) will result in a .2 change in the option premium (e.g., from 3 to 3.2). The vegas in Exhibit 10 equal dC/dv divided by 100.

Note from Exhibit 10 that vega is maximized for at-the-money options with long terms to expiration. While such high-premium options are most affected in absolute terms by changing volatility, low-premium options (i.e., out-of-the-money and close to expiration) are the most affected in percentage terms. This is illustrated in Exhibit 11, which is a graph of volatility elasticities.

The elasticities in Exhibit 11 were computed as vega divided by the option premium. The volatility elasticity measures the percentage change in the option premium given a 1 percent change in the

---

[3] C.A. Ball and W.N. Torous, "The Maximum Likelihood Estimation of Security Price Volatility: Theory, Evidence, and Application to Option Pricing," *Journal of Business,* 57, 1984, pp. 97–112; M.B. Garman and M.J. Klass, "On the Estimation of Security Price Volatilities from Historical Data," *Journal of Business,* 53, 1980, pp. 67–78; R. Geske and R. Roll, "Isolating the Observed Biases in American Call Option Pricing: An Alternative Variance Estimator," Working paper, Graduate School of Management, University of California at Los Angeles, 1984; M. Parkinson, "The Extreme Value Method for Estimating the Variance of the Rate of Return," *Journal of Business,* 53, 1980, pp. 61–66.

EXHIBIT 9
Call Option Premiums
At-the-Money @100, v = 15%, r = 6%

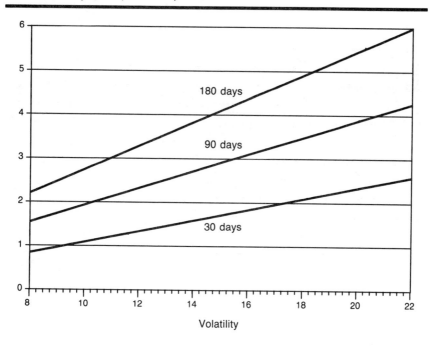

implied volatility. For example, a volatility elasticity of 30 suggests that a 1 percent change in implied volatility (e.g., from 15 percent to 16 percent) causes a 30 percent change in the option premium (e.g., from .1 to .13). It is interesting to note that the volatility elasticity of at-the-money options is relatively constant regardless of the term to expiration.

Sensitivity Ratios

Calculating ratios of the premium sensitivities discussed above can lead to a better understanding of option price behavior. For example, consider the ratio of gamma over theta, illustrated in Exhibit 12. This ratio provides insights into the tradeoff between gamma and theta. As we discussed above, options with high

EXHIBIT 10
Call Option Vegas
Strike = 100, v = 15%, r = 6%

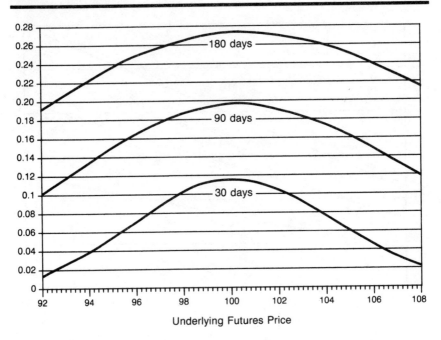

Underlying Futures Price

thetas are attractive to option sellers, but such options also have high gammas, which signal a high degree of riskiness.

The gamma/theta ratio can be interpreted to be the number of units of gamma which must be acquired in order to obtain a unit of theta. Option sellers generally would desire to minimize this ratio. Exhibit 12 shows that the gamma/theta ratio is minimized when the option is somewhat in-the-money. However, the ratio can rise rapidly if the option moves further in-the-money, particularly if the option is close to expiring. Exhibit 12 also shows that the ratio is generally lowest for options which are close to expiration, as long as they are not too far in-the-money.

Exhibit 13 illustrates the vega/theta ratio. This ratio might be of interest to a trader seeking to purchase options in anticipation

EXHIBIT 11
Call Volatility Elasticities
Strike = 100, v = 15%, r = 6%

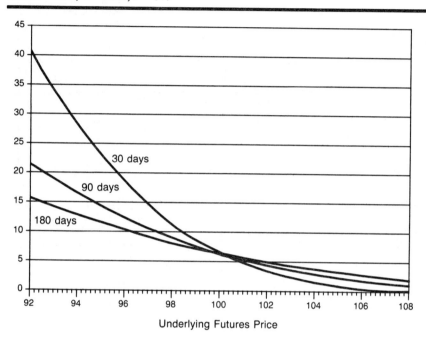

of an increase in volatility. Such a trader would desire a high vega (to profit from increasing volatility) and a low theta (to avoid time value decay), and thus would prefer a high vega/theta ratio. Exhibit 13 shows that this ratio is maximized for options which have long terms to expiration, and is relatively unaffected by whether the option is in- or out-of-the-money.

Exhibit 14 is a graph of the vega/gamma ratio. This ratio is of interest to an option writer who anticipates declining volatility. The option writer is looking for an option with a high vega and a low gamma, and thus a high vega/gamma ratio. As with the vega/theta ratio discussed above, we find that options with long terms to expiration have the highest values of this ratio although, in this case, there is a more substantial bias toward in-the-money options.

EXHIBIT 12
Call Gamma/Theta Ratio
Strike = 100, v = 15%, r = 6%

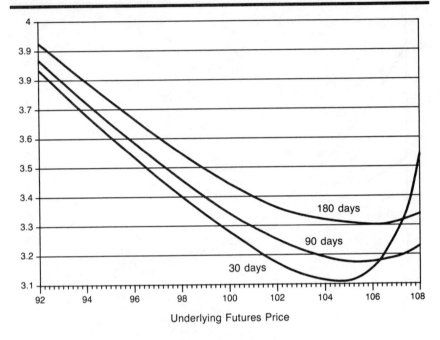

Underlying Futures Price

III. FIXED INCOME PORTFOLIO APPLICATIONS

Fixed income managers are frequently interested in the effect of changing yields on the market value of their portfolios. Since options on fixed income securities and futures contracts are now widely used, they must be included in the analysis of portfolio yield sensitivity.

Two common measures of yield sensitivity are the basis point value (BPV) and modified duration (referred hereafter as duration). The BPV equals the change in the market value of a $1 million position (face value) given a 1 basis point change in the yield to maturity. Duration equals the BPV divided by the security price expressed as a percentage of par (par = 100). Duration can be understood as a measure of the average maturity of the interest and

EXHIBIT 13
Call Vega/Theta Ratio
Strike = 100, v = 15%, r = 6%

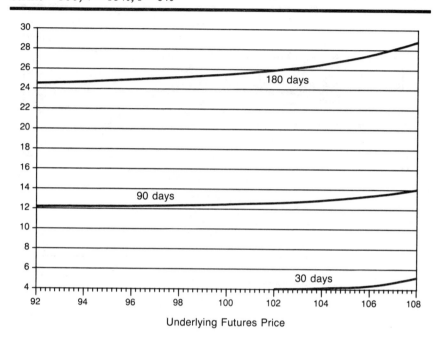

Underlying Futures Price

final principal payments of the security; the duration of a zero coupon bond equals its maturity divided by 1 plus its per-period yield. High values of either BPV or duration indicate that the security price is sensitive to changing yield levels.

The BPV of an option on a fixed income instrument equals the BPV of the underlying instrument multiplied by the option delta:

$$\text{Option BPV} = \text{Delta} \times \text{BPV}$$

It is generally not sensible to calculate option durations; values in excess of 300 years are not uncommon. However, it is sensible to calculate the duration of portfolios which include options. This is easily accomplished using the following formula:

$$\text{Portfolio duration} = .01 \times \text{Portfolio BPV}/\text{Portfolio market value}$$

The portfolio market value must be expressed in millions; e.g., a portfolio market value of $100 million would be 100 in the for-

EXHIBIT 14
Call Vega/Gamma Ratio
Strike = 100, v = 15%, r = 6%

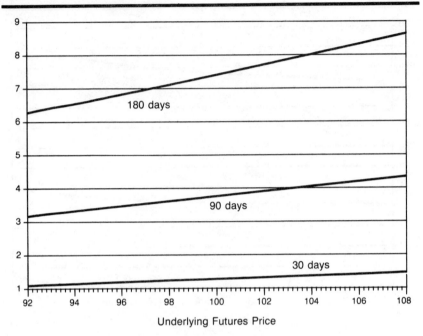

mula above. The portfolio BPV equals the change in the portfolio market value given a 1 basis point change in each yield to maturity, and can be readily computed from the BPVs of each security and option held in the portfolio. For example, if the portfolio BPV equals $1,000 and the portfolio market value equals $1 million, then the portfolio duration equals 10 years (= .01 × $1,000/ 1, since a portfolio market value of $1 million is equal to 1 in the formula).

The portfolio BPV and duration do not remain constant as yield levels change. This nonconstancy is referred to as portfolio convexity and is measured by delta-BPV (d-BPV) and delta-duration (d-duration). These two statistics are usually quoted as 100 times the change in either the BPV or duration given a 1 basis point change in the yield to maturity. The option d-BPV is given by the following formula:

$$\text{Option d-BPV} = \text{Delta} \times \text{d-BPV} + .01 \times \text{Gamma} \times \text{BPV}^2$$

The d-duration of a portfolio may be obtained as follows:

$$\text{Portfolio d-duration} = .0001 \times (A \times C - .01 \times B^2)/A^2$$

where A = Portfolio market value expressed in $ millions
      B = Portfolio BPV
      C = Portfolio d-BPV

The precise BPVs, d-BPVs, durations, and d-durations of fixed income securities can usually be quickly computed from formulas. For example, for a standard bond or note with semi-annual interest payments, we have:

c = Semi-annual coupon (c = .05 for 10% annual coupon rate)

y = Semi-annual yield to maturity

n = Coupons remaining to maturity

a = Accrual fraction of current coupon ($0 \le a < 1$)

P = Price of bond or note (par = 1.0)

$$P = (1 + y)^a [(1 - c/y)(1 + y)^{-n} + c/y] - ac$$

$$\frac{dP}{dy} = (1 + y)^{a-n-1}[(a - n)(1 - c/y) + c(1 + y)/y^2] - c/y(1 + y)^{a-1}(1 - a + 1/y)$$

$$\frac{d^2P}{dy^2} = (a - n)(1 + y)^{a-n-2}[(a - n - 1)(1 - c/y) + c(1 + y)/y^2]$$

$$+ c/y^2(1 + y)^{a-n-1}[a - n - 2(1 + y)/y]$$

$$+ c(1 - a)/y^2(1 + y)^{a-2}[y(1 - a) + 1 + y]$$

$$+ c/y^3(1 + y)^{a-2}[y(1 - a) + 2(1 + y)]$$

BPV per $ million face = $- 50 \times dP/dy$

Duration = $BPV/(P \times 100)$

d-BPV = $d^2P/dy^2/4$

d-Duration = $.01 \times (P \times dBPV - .0001 \times BPV^2) / P^2$

To summarize, all that is needed to calculate the BPV and d-BPV of an option on a fixed income instrument is to know the BPV and d-BPV of the instrument as well as the delta and gamma of the option. Given the portfolio BPV and d-BPV, the portfolio duration and d-duration can easily be calculated.

ARTICLE 14

MICHAEL R. GRANITO is head of J. P. Morgan
Investment Management, Inc.'s Capital Markets Research
Group that specializes in asset allocation research and new
investment product development. He developed Morgan's
bond immunization product and is the author of a book on
immunization published by Lexington Books in 1984.
Mr. Granito is a member of the fixed income strategy group
and Morgan's investment policy committee. Prior to
joining Morgan in 1979, Mr. Granito taught at the
Wharton School while earning a Ph.D. in finance. He is
also an adjunct professor of finance at New York
University.

A SIMPLE APPROACH TO VALUING BOND OPTIONS

Michael R. Granito, Ph.D.
Managing Director
J.P. Morgan Investment Management, Inc.

Option valuation has received widespread interest in recent years both in academia and in application to financial problems. Progress has been limited, however, by the difficulty in analyzing cases that lie much outside the Black-Scholes model. While certain specialized results have been obtained, analysts must often resort to numerical procedures for valuing and replicating options. These methods are often time-consuming and allow less confidence than analytical solutions of models whose properties are better understood.

One of the areas where these problems are particularly acute is in bond option valuation. In a formal development of theory, one often starts with an assumed model for interest rate changes and first derives the associated equilibrium (arbitrage-free) specification of the yield curve. Then option values for various types of securities are derived. The analysis is often more difficult than for stock option values because the assumed interest rate model leads to bond price models that have greater inherent complexity than stock prices. This complexity carries over to the corresponding options.

In this article we provide a simplified framework for deriving European bond option values. We are not able to completely avoid the difficulties mentioned above, but we can often simplify the problem. Specifically, we propose a remarkably accurate method of numerical bond option valuation that uses only information about the equilibrium shape of the yield curve. That is, we go directly from a theory of yield curve behavior to option values, without the intermediate step of a specialized option valuation model. This does not mean that the whole process is easy. We still have to come up with a specification of yield curve behavior—and this can be as difficult as valuing an option directly from an assumed model for interest rate changes. But yield curve theory has been more fully developed than bond option theory so that we are more likely to start with a combined model for interest rate changes and the yield curve whose properties are understood. Moreover, our method allows an empirical development of yield curve movements to stand in place of a theoretical model. This has certain disadvantages, but on balance adds considerable flexibility since the need to solve complex equations can sometimes be avoided.

I. HOW AND WHY THE METHOD WORKS

In valuing an option we normally start with the desired future payoff pattern as of the expiration date of the option. This will be some function of the risky asset price. For instance, in the case of a put on a stock with exercise price $X, the future payoff would be the larger of zero, or $X less the stock price. For a European option, we are only concerned with the payoff at the expiration of the option. For an American option, we would also be concerned about possible payoffs at earlier dates since American options may be exercised at any time before expiration. We consider only European option at present.

In the case of bonds, asset values are functions of interest rates and contract provisions such as maturity, coupon, etc. Consequently, if we have a yield curve theory to price the underlying securities, as we have assumed, we can write the desired future payoff pattern as a function of future interest rates. In other words, corresponding to each possible future interest rate scenario, we can value the security(ies) on which the option is written and thus determine the option payoff.

Graphing the option payoff as a function of interest rates gives us an opportunity to make further use of bond market characteristics and our yield curve theory to value the option. The reason is that we can use the same bond pricing theory to determine and graph the future values of other securities as a function of rates (as of the expiration of the option). In particular, we can graph the values of a group of zero coupon bonds with initial maturities ranging from the expiration of the option to, say, 30 years.

Having obtained the *desired* payoff pattern as a function of rates and the *available* patterns given by the future values of different maturity zeros, we can "fit" the available pattern to the desired pattern. That is, we can determine that combination of zeros which, if purchased today, would provide the desired payoff as of the expiration of the option. Today's cost of the portfolio of zeros that provides the same future payoff pattern as the option will then be the cost of the option. In general, we cannot find a perfect fit except in certain extreme cases. However, it is often possible to obtain a very good approximation using standard fitting techniques such as regression.

The reason that this method can work is that, unlike other assets whose prices are themselves viewed as the underlying risky variable, bond prices are viewed as functions of the risky variable, interest rates. This makes them similar to any option whose payoff is a function of a risky asset price. Bond prices determined through a modern term structure theory thus have certain formal option characteristics in which the bond analogs of theta, delta and gamma (namely, forward rate, duration and convexity) are exactly priced in their appropriate relation to one another. Consequently, it is quite natural to view a particular option payoff pattern as being closely replicated by the "option" payoff patterns implicit in a set of zero coupon bonds (that are themselves priced using methods closely related to formal option valuation methods).

The useful feature of the replicating portfolio of zero coupon bonds is that it remains fixed over the term of the option. In other words, the portfolio of zeros that provides the desired payoff pattern does so at every date between now and expiration of the option. Arbitrage arguments then assure us that the value of this replicating portfolio will be the value of the option at every point of time between now and expiration. This is a consequence of using an equilibrium (arbritrage-free) pricing model for originally determining the prices and future payoffs of the set of zero coupon bonds.

As a practical matter, these findings are useful for valuing and creating options using dynamic hedging techniques. In most cases, the replicating portfolio of zeros will contain short positions which cannot be taken in practice. However, we may still calculate the replicating portfolio at the outset and analyze it through time to determine its duration (or interest sensitivity) and other characteristics. This information can then be used to replicate the option using dynamic hedging.

II. A NUMERICAL EXAMPLE

We illustrate the technique by calculating a particular option's value using the approximation method, and comparing the result to the option's known value.

The yield curve theory used for bond pricing will be a simple version of the Vasicek term structure.[1] Specifically, we assume that the spot rate curve, or the yield curve for zero coupon bonds, has the form

$$r + \frac{k\mu}{2} t - \frac{\sigma^2}{6} t^2 \qquad (1)$$

where r is the instantaneous (over-night) interest rate; t denotes maturity; and the terms k, μ and σ are (all positive) parameters of the formula that specifies changes in r.[2] This version of the Vasicek term structure is the only known arbitrage-free specification for which spot rate curve movements are parallel, and consequently

---

[1] See Oldrich A. Vasicek, "An Equilibrium Characterization of the Term Structure," *Journal of Financial Economics*, v. 5, 1977, pp. 177–88.

[2] The corresponding formula for instantaneous changes in the short rate (dr) is

$$dr = k(\mu - r)dt + \sigma dw$$

where μ is the long-run mean of r; k is the speed of adjustment of r back to the mean; dt represents the change in time; dw is a normal random variable with mean zero and variance dt and σ is the standard deviation of changes in r. We assumed that $\mu = .08$, k = .1 and $\sigma = 0.015$ in our example.

the appropriate risk measure—or duration—of a zero coupon bond is its maturity. [3]

Another unique feature of the Vasicek term structure is that option values for zeros are extremely simple to compute. The reason is twofold. First, holding-period returns on zeros are lognormally distributed (so that continuously compounded returns are normal). Second, the variance of the rate of return is not stochastic. Consequently, we may employ Merton's adjustment to the Black-Scholes model to account for stochastic short rates. [4] The resulting option prices assume the same general form as for stock options. [5] The particular form for the term structure that we have assumed allows the simplest option formula. For instance, the value of an "e" year European call on a "t" year zero with strike price \$X is

$$P_t N(d_1) - X P_e N(d_2) \tag{2}$$

where P_t and P_e are today's prices of t and e year zeros respectively; $N(\cdot)$ denotes the normal distribution function; and

$$d_1 = \frac{\ln(P_t/XP_e) + .5\sigma^2(t-e)^2 e}{\sigma(t-e)e^{.5}}$$

$$d_2 = \frac{\ln(P_t/XP_e) - .5\sigma^2(t-e)^2 e}{\sigma(t-e)e^{.5}}$$

We consider the problem of valuing a European put option on an 8 year zero coupon bond with a \$10 million face amount. The exercise price is assumed to be \$5.5 million and the term of the option is 2 years. This would be the problem faced by someone seeking to provide 2 year portfolio insurance on an 8 year immunized portfolio. The true value of this option for selected initial interest rates (i.e. values of the over-night rate, r, in formula (1)) is given in the second column of Exhibit 1.

---

[3] This form results from setting the market price of risk in the bond pricing equation to −kr. Ingersoll independently discovered this result years ago (see Jonathan E. Ingersoll, *The Theory of Financial Decision Making*, 1985).

[4] See Robert C. Merton, "The Theory of Rational Option Pricing," *Bell Journal of Economics and Management Science*, v. 4, 1973, pp. 141–83.

[5] Although this result has been observed by some option theorists, it does not appear to have been published before.

EXHIBIT 1		
Interest Rate	Estimated Option Value	Theoretical Option Value
5.0%	$ 123,115	$ 109,208
5.5	159,354	152,907
6.0	210,354	207,382
6.5	273,598	272,283
7.0	347,335	346,807
7.5	429,579	429,438
8.0	518,211	518,294
8.5	610,985	611,261
9.0	705,725	706,241
9.5	800,504	801,356
10.0	893,750	895,065
10.5	984,277	986,213
11.0	1,071,227	1,074,018

In this case, our approximate valuation procedure is to calculate the future payoff pattern of the combined portfolio—the zero plus the put. This calculation is made for a range of values of r. We then select a group of zero coupon bonds ranging in maturity from 2 to 30 years and compute the values of each, in 2 years, at the same values of r.

We next "fit" the values of the zeros to the desired payoff pattern in the following way. We treat the vector of market values of the put-plus-zero portfolio (at different future interest rates) as the dependent variable in a regression. The independent variables are the zero coupon bonds (with initial maturities 2 to 30 years). There is one independent variable for each such zero. The data for each that is used in the regression is simply the vector of market values that this particular zero will have 2 years in the future for the range of future values of r that is under consideration. The estimated coefficients that come out of the regression are the number of zeros (of each maturity) that go into forming the replicating portfolio.

In the present example, the maturities of the zeros included in the replicating portfolio, as well as the optimal holding of each, are given in Exhibit 2. The estimated value of the put option is the

EXHIBIT 2	
Zero Coupon Bond Maturities	Optimal Holding
2 yrs	− 21,607
4	148,452
6	− 411,579
8	554,891
10	− 317,466
15	52,524
20	14,340
25	− 38,545
30	20,660

value of the portfolio of zeros less the value of the 8 year zero. These values are provided in column 2 of Exhibit 1 for selected values of today's over-night rate, r. It is evident that the estimated and theoretical option prices in columns 2 and 3 of Exhibit 1 are quite close, suggesting that the approximate solution technique may provide a useful guide in applied circumstances.

We obtained the range of estimated values in Exhibit 1 by repricing the same portfolio of zero coupon bonds at different values of today's rate. The replicating portfolio itself was influenced by the range of future values for r that was considered. This range was selected so as to reflect the distribution of possible values, given an 8 percent starting interest rate level, that is consistent with the interest rate process assumed in the term structure theory. As might be expected from using an approximation method, the accuracy of the estimate is greater for current interest rate levels closer to the assumed starting rate (that is also reflected in the distribution of future values of r). Stated differently, for values of today's rate that differ substantially from the center of the range of future values for r, the approximation is poorer. This is because the fitting technique we used does not reflect the probability in the tails as well as that in the center of the distribution.

A simple way to improve the estimate for extreme values of today's rate is to recalculate the replicating portfolio by estimating a new regression, but this time using a distribution of future values of r that diffuses from the desired (extreme) value of today's rate. Exhibit 3 is identical to Exhibit 1 except it uses a different replicating portfolio valued over different values of today's interest rate. The assumed initial rate for developing the distribution of future values of r was: 2 percent for values of today's rate between 0 and 4 percent; 6 percent for values of today's rate between 4.5 percent and 8 percent; and 10 percent for values of today's rate between

EXHIBIT 3

Interest Rate	Estimated Option Value	Theoretical Option Value
0.0%	$ 0	$ 366
0.5	489	793
1.0	1,552	1,641
1.5	3,219	3,238
2.0	6,073	6,095
2.5	10,873	10,966
3.0	18,596	18,866
3.5	30,447	31,084
4.0	47,774	49,100
4.5	72,425	74,484
5.0	107,887	108,672
5.5	152,533	152,757
6.0	207,374	207,325
6.5	272,509	272,279
7.0	347,201	346,796
7.5	430,027	429,434
8.0	519,047	518,293
8.5	611,078	611,262
9.0	706,174	706,241
9.5	801,376	801,354
10.0	895,159	895,064
10.5	986,397	986,212
11.0	1,074,339	1,074,018
11.5	1,158,542	1,158,007
12.0	1,238,808	1,237,950

8.5 percent and 12 percent. Comparing Exhibits 1 and 3 we see that the fit is significantly improved.

III. DIRECTIONS FOR FUTURE RESEARCH

The valuation method we have outlined may be of help in computing option values when conventional solutions are impractical. This is particularly true for single or multi-factor term structure theories in closed form, but where option prices are difficult to specify. The solution process itself is worthy of academic study as an exercise in approximation theory. For instance, it is extremely important that the range of future values considered for r corresponds to the actual distribution of possible values that results from the interest rate process incorporated in the term structure theory. Similarly, the choice of which zero coupon bonds to use as members of the replicating portfolio may also be optimized. In general, there is a direct link between the finance and the econometrics of this problem that is worth exploring in more detail.

One of the more exciting applications of this method may result from the opportunity to develop option values from empirically derived yield curve models. Specifically, it is possible to have an empirical form for the term structure and empirical distributions for future values of the model's random parameters, even though the theoretical parameters that generate them cannot be isolated. As long as the distributions of random parameters are consistent with the empirical term structure (i.e., there is no implied arbitrage in the model) then option values can be derived using the approximation technique. This requires that the model be estimated in a fashion constrained to be arbitrage-free—and this is not simple. Yet there is the prospect for option valuation without the solution of the complex equations.

PORTFOLIO STRATEGIES

ARTICLE 15

SHARMIN MOSSAVAR-RAHMANI is a vice president of Fidelity Management Trust Company, Boston. A fixed income portfolio manager and strategist, she has published extensively on the bond market as well as on international energy issues. A graduate of Princeton University (A.B. Economics) and Stanford University (M.S. Engineering-Economic Systems), she was formerly vice president and portfolio manager at Lehman Management Co., Inc.

UNDERSTANDING AND EVALUATING INDEX FUND MANAGEMENT

Sharmin Mossavar-Rahmani
Vice President
Fidelity Management Trust Company, Boston

Indexing the performance of fixed income assets to match that of a market benchmark has become widespread in portfolio management. Between 1980 and late 1986, assets under index fund management grew from only $40 million to over $40 billion, with both small and large pension funds accounting for the tremendous growth. Indeed, some of the nation's largest pension funds have begun to index a significant portion, if not all, of their fixed income assets. Among the public funds, all $17 billion of the fixed income assets of the New York City Retirement System have been indexed. In the corporate sector, American Telephone & Telegraph Co. has indexed some $3.5 billion. Smaller funds have also indexed assets through either separate index funds or co-mingled index funds.

Growth in the size of indexed assets has brought with it a proliferation of indices, index fund managers, and index fund management models and software services. In the last two years, three broad market indices were introduced in rapid succession—the Merrill Lynch Domestic Master Index, the Salomon Brothers Broad Investment-Grade Bond Index, and the Shearson Lehman

434 **Article 15**

Aggregate Index. The number of major investment advisors offering index fund management during this period grew from six to over 20, and several index fund optimization models were developed by investment houses and software vendors.

This article provides a detailed review of indexing, starting with a discussion of the motivations for setting up index funds in Section I. An evaluation of the disadvantages of indexing is discussed in Section II. Current indexing methodologies are examined in Section III. Section IV reviews "enhanced indexing" and the requisite use of value-added strategies. The article then examines the more recent interest in customized index funds and the role of the Financial Accounting Standards Board Statements 87 and 88 to the development of such funds in Section V. Section VI concludes with a discussion of the implications of indexing for fixed income management and for the fixed income securities market overall.

I. MOTIVATIONS FOR SETTING UP INDEX FUNDS

Four key factors account for the increased interest in indexing of pension funds. The first motivation for indexing has been the poor past performance of investment advisors as a group. In the past several years, 75 percent of active fixed income managers have underperformed market benchmarks, as illustrated in Exhibit 1. Indexing of assets improves relative performance inasmuch as the returns of an index fund closely track those of a market index; the risk of underperforming an index to the extent illustrated in Exhibit 1 is therefore eliminated by definition.

A second motivation for indexing has been the reduction of advisory fees. Advisory fees for active management normally range from 15 basis points to as much as 50 basis points. Advisory fees for index fund management range from a low of one basis point up to 20 basis points for enhanced and customized index funds, with 10 basis points representing the mode. The consequent savings in management fees, particularly in the case of very large pension funds, can be substantial. It is interesting to note that the advisory fees for indexing are now generally lower for many pension funds than the associated custodian and master trustee fees.

EXHIBIT 1
Annualized Total Return for Fixed Income Funds
(for periods ending September 30, 1986)

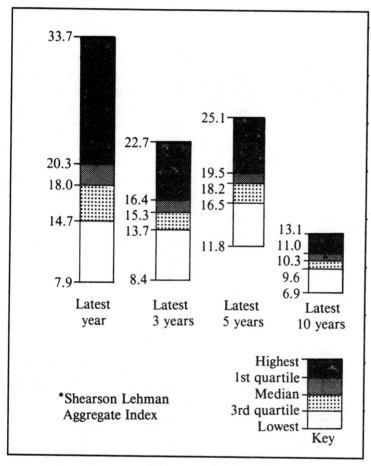

Source: PIPER report © Crain Communications, Inc.

A third and less obvious motivating factor for indexing has been the growth of the nation's pension assets. Between September 1981 (which marked the peak in interest rates) and September 1986, the fixed income market produced a total return of 147.6 percent as measured by the Salomon Brothers Broad Investment-Grade Bond Index, and 149.4 percent as measured by the Shearson Lehman Aggregate Index (the equities market returned a total of 150.8 percent over the same period as measured by the Standard & Poor's 500 Index). The consequent increases in the size of many pension funds have led to increases in the costs associated with the maintenance of these funds. The number of investment advisors hired to manage each fund, for example, has increased, resulting not only in greater advisory fees, but also in greater hidden costs associated with multiple managers. Custodian costs and master trustee costs increase with the number of managers as do the time and effort required for supervision and coordination of multiple managers. Indexing reduces many such hidden costs by reducing the number of advisors responsible for managing any one fund. The size of assets given to any single advisor of an index fund is generally much larger than the size of assets given to any single advisor for active management. In the summer of 1986, for example, the State Universities Retirement System of Illinois transferred fixed income assets from four active and passive managers to a single index fund manager.

A fourth factor behind indexing of fixed income assets has been the increased interest in "structured management." Structured management de-emphasizes interest rate forecasts on the part of investment advisors, and emphasizes instead risk control relative to a market benchmark. Both the benchmark and acceptable risk parameters are specified by the plan sponsor. Examples of structured management are indexing and enhanced indexing, duration-controlled management, management with respect to a normal portfolio, and portfolio insurance. It is important to note that all forms of structured management reflect a gradual shift in control away from the active manager to the plan sponsor.

II. DISADVANTAGES OF INDEXING

The rapid growth in its popularity notwithstanding, indexing does have its doubters and detractors. One key criticism voiced is that while indexing matches the performance of a market benchmark, that benchmark might not reflect optimal performance. Indeed, for the five-year period ending in September 1981, the Shearson Lehman Government/Corporate Index measured a return lower than that of 50 percent of active managers, as shown in Exhibit 2.

EXHIBIT 2
Annualized Total Return for Fixed Income Funds
(for periods ending September 30, 1981)

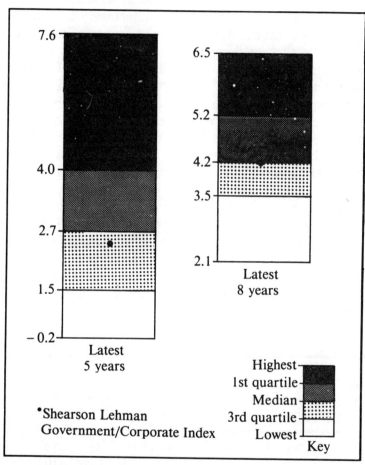

Source: SEI Corporation

Another criticism is that indexing against a broad market benchmark may not meet the specific requirements and objectives of a particular fund, e.g., matching pension assets with pension liabilities.

Index funds are also criticized for lacking flexibility. True (also called "straight" or "vanilla") index funds do not invest in instruments outside the benchmark universe. For example, non-federal agency conventional mortgage pass-throughs such as those issued by Citibank and Sears Mortgage Securities are not included in any of the broad market benchmarks. Excluding this small but growing sector of the market—thereby giving up as much as 25 to 50 basis points of additional yield—is an unnecessary constraint. Among other instruments excluded from the benchmark universes are synthetic assets such as futures, derivative securities such as collateralized mortgage obligations, and Strips and other Treasury zero coupon bonds.

Indexing poses several logistical problems. Pricing of securities in the index universe is one such problem. The fixed income market is an over-the-counter market without a centralized exchange from which reliable closing prices could be obtained. Thus, at a given time, the same securities might be priced very differently from one dealer to the next, as illustrated in Exhibit 3. Even in the more efficient and more liquid Treasury market, prices can vary significantly; at a given time, the 10.75 percent coupon Treasury maturing on August 15, 2005, could be purchased from Dealer B at $128-05 (five thirty-seconds) while the same security could be purchased from Dealer D at $128-09 (nine thirty-seconds). Such pricing differences create two potential problems: first, the benchmarks that represent the same market may produce very different

EXHIBIT 3
Price Spreads

	TSY 10.75% 8/15/05	HCA* 8% 4/15/96	GNSF** 12%
Dealer A	128^{2-6***}	$97^{1/4-3/8}$	108^{2-4}
B	128^{3-5}	$97^{\ -1/4}$	$108^{\ -8}$
C	128^{4-8}	$97^{1/8-3/8}$	108^{1-5}
D	128^{5-9}	$97^{3/8-1/2}$	108^{4-8}
E	128^{6-8}	$97^{1/4-1/2}$	Passed

*Hospital Corporation of America

**GNMA Single Family

***This quote represents a bid price of 128^2 and an ask price of 128^6.

data (see Exhibit 4), and second, the returns of an index fund may not match those of the benchmark. An index fund that purchased a Treasury bond from Dealer B will not match the performance of a benchmark priced by Dealer D.

Another difficulty is caused by the illiquidity of the corporate bond market. The Salomon Brothers Broad Investment-Grade Bond Index contains over 3,700 corporate issues, and the Shearson Lehman Aggregate Index contains over 5,400 such issues. Not only is the pricing of each of these issues unreliable but many cannot be readily found.

A third logistical problem is specific to indexing of the mortgage-

EXHIBIT 4
Variation in Monthly Returns of Market Indices (percent)

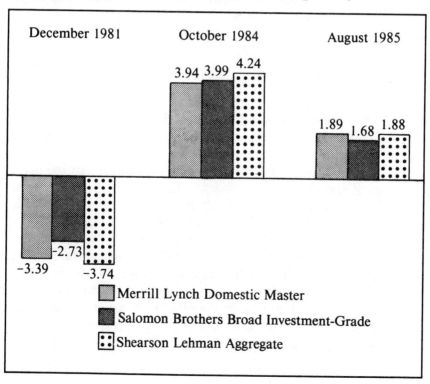

backed securities component of these indices. The three major market indices include the pass-through securities of the Government National Mortgage Association (GNMA or Ginnie Mae), of the Federal National Mortgage Association (FNMA or Fannie Mae), and of the Federal Home Loan Mortgage Corporation (FHLMC or Freddie Mac). Together, these three agencies have issued well over 150,000 specific pools. The indices, however, have consolidated these pools into several hundred issues. There are 8,000 GNMA pools with a 12 percent coupon; yet in the indices, these pools are "collapsed" into only one hypothetical issue whose profile characteristics are intended to reflect the market value weighted average characteristics of all 8,000 pools. Locating pools that precisely match the performance of the hypothetical issue could be extremely difficult.

This problem is compounded by the differences in the risk and reward measurements in mortgage-backed securities indices. The duration and yield-to-maturity of the three major mortgage indices (the Merrill Lynch Mortgage Master, Salomon Brothers Mortgage Pass-Through Index, and the Shearson Lehman Mortgage-Backed Securities Index) vary by a wide margin. The effective duration of the Salomon Brothers Mortgage Pass-Through Index, for example, was 3.20 years as of September 30, 1986, whereas the duration of the Merrill Lynch Mortgage Master was 5.04 years. The difference in the durations of the two indices can be attributed to different prepayment assumptions and options evaluations; nevertheless, these differences do complicate the task of correctly matching the duration of an index fund to that of a benchmark.

Still another logistical problem of indexing stems from the pricing biases of the market benchmarks. The securities in all broad market indices are priced at the "bid side"—the price at which securities can be sold to a broker. Bond index funds, however, purchase securities at the "offer side" or "ask side." The spread between purchase price and sale price, referred to as transaction cost, is not incorporated in the pricing mechanism of the broad market indices. Therefore, the market indices have a total return advantage relative to index funds that can be measured by the bid-ask spread of individual securities. Exhibit 3 provides an example of such spreads in the Treasury, corporate, and mortgage-backed securities market.

III. KEY METHODOLOGIES

There are currently three approaches to managing an index fund: the stratified sampling or the cellular approach; the optimization approach using linear programming; and the variance minimization approach using quadratic programming.

The *stratified sampling method* is the most straightforward and the most flexible of the three approaches. In the stratified sampling method, an index is divided into subsectors, i.e., the index is stratified into "cells." The divisions are made on the basis of such features as sector, coupon, maturity and quality. For example, one cell might contain all Treasury securities with maturities between five and 10 years and coupon rates between nine and 12 percent. Another cell might contain all AA Industrial bonds with maturities greater than 15 years and coupon rates between 10 and 15 percent.

The cells can be defined in much broader terms as well. A market index can be divided into four cells: a Treasury cell that accounts for all the Treasury securities; an agency cell that accounts for all the agency securities; a corporate cell for all the corporate issues; and a mortgage cell for all mortgage-backed securities. Alternatively, the index can be divided into as many cells as there are issues in the index, so that each cell contains only one issue.

Of the factors that determine the number of cells in an index fund, the size of the fund is the most critical. Larger asset size enables the index fund manager to divide the benchmark into a greater number of cells. Indeed, one of the problems with small index funds (under $50 million) is that the fund can be divided into only a few cells, thereby limiting the diversification in the fund.

The next step in the stratified sampling method is the selection of securities to represent each cell. Securities are chosen such that the total return and the profile characteristics (such as yield and duration) of each "sample" of securities representing a particular cell match the average characteristics of all the securities in that cell. The selection of securities enables the index fund manager to impose certain biases on the fund; securities with higher yields but lower convexity may be selected over securities with lower yields and greater convexity.

The product of this approach is a portfolio whose characteristics match those of the index. These characteristics include duration, yield-to-maturity, convexity, maturity and coupon distribution, quality, callability and sinking fund exposure, and, ideally, prepayment risk.

The second methodology, the *optimization approach,* builds on the stratified sampling approach. There are two components to the optimization: the first component is an objective function in which one comprehensive bias is specified, and the second component is a series of constraints in which the cellular breakdown described above is implemented and the portfolio characteristics are forced to match those of the index. Some widely used objective functions are the maximization of yield, convexity, or expected total returns. Typical constraints include cell specifications and duration targets. This optimization methodology based on linear programming is discussed in detail in the next article.

The third approach, or the *variance minimization methodology,* is a form of optimization where the objective is to minimize the variance of the tracking error. Tracking error is defined as the total return deviation of the portfolio from the index. This methodology relies on historical data to generate multi-variate price functions for every bond in the index universe. These price functions are, in turn, used to estimate the variance of returns based on the variance of the term structure of interest rates and of some 80 factors that determine the value of a bond. This optimization model selects a series of bonds whose risk exposure to interest rate changes and to changes in the 80 or so valuation factors will closely match that of the index. As a result of the optimization, the returns of the portfolio will closely match those of the index and minimize the tracking error.

The Relative Merits and Pitfalls of the Methodologies

Of the three approaches, stratified sampling is the most flexible. Attractive yield spread swaps can be implemented within specific cells without affecting the rest of the index fund. Value-added strategies can be implemented without re-optimizing and rebalancing the entire portfolio. Swaps that take advantage of long or short positions of the broker/dealer community can be readily implemented. Yield and convexity biases can be implemented with greater focus; for example, convexity can be maximized in some of the Treasury cells, while yield can be maximized in some of the corporate cells. In addition, strategies that involve sectors outside the index universe (such as CMOs, Strips, and futures) can also be implemented. And, the index fund can be partially rebalanced, resulting in less turnover and hence lower transaction costs. In contrast, in a true optimization, rebalancing can impact the entire portfolio.

The optimization approach is less flexible in other ways as well. A strict implementation of optimization implies use of the model to select issues from a universe of securities, and the purchase and sale of securities according to the solution of the optimization. The problem with such an approach is that it relies completely on a database of bond prices from which the model can choose securities. As mentioned earlier, bond prices in these databases can be very unreliable, due to the over-the-counter nature of the fixed income market. Thus, the model's selection of securities may not be readily traded in the market or, at least, may not be available at prices indicated in the databases. One recourse would be to substitute the securities chosen by the optimization. Such substitution, in effect, results in greater use of the stratified sampling approach and lesser use of an optimization model. Another recourse would be to work with dealers who offer smaller databases (that only contain their own inventories or securities they believe are available in the market) in order to circumvent this pricing problem. The key disadvantage of these databases is the requisite reliance on only one dealer whose major objective is the sale of house inventory or of securities that the dealer can locate and re-sell at a profit. Securities available through another dealer at a lower price are therefore excluded.

Still, the optimization approach does have its advantages. An investment advisor with little or no index fund management experience can readily acquire some index fund management capabilities through access to such a model. Optimization also requires less time and effort on the part of the index fund manager since the model selects all attractive swaps and combinations of securities.

The variance minimization model is the least flexible of the three approaches. Bond swaps, value-added strategies, yield or convexity biases, and partial rebalancings cannot be implemented in this approach. The model can be forced to select various securities by imposing constraints and by limiting the securities in the universe. Again, such tactics imply a move away from the variance minimization model, towards a sampling technique. Complete dependence on historical issue-specific pricing data is another drawback; as mentioned earlier, the pricing of some of the securities may be unreliable and their availability uncertain. Finally, the variance minimization model is based on the assumption that past performance of individual securities is a good indication of future performance; such an assumption is not valid in all market environments. It is also important to note that since the model relies on historical data, new instruments with innovative features cannot be incorporated into the universe, irrespective of their potential value.

Tracking Error

Tracking error is the difference between the total return of an index fund and that of the benchmark. What is acceptable tracking error? And does large positive tracking error imply large negative error (i.e., is tracking error normally distributed)? Salomon Brothers Inc maintains an index optimization system which can be used to generate historical data on the tracking error between an optimal portfolio and the Salomon Brothers Broad Investment-Grade Bond Index or any of its components. A two-year historical analysis found that tracking error varies according to the type of fund (e.g., corporates, mortgage-backed securities, or Treasuries) and the size of assets under management. The corporate component of the Salomon Brothers Broad Investment-Grade Bond Index was the most difficult to track; as shown in Exhibit 5, the standard deviation of the monthly tracking error was 17 basis points, with the largest monthly positive error at 40 basis points and the largest monthly negative error at 26 basis points. However, over the 23-month horizon, the corporate component of the index fund outperformed its respective benchmark by 3.01 percent. Such tracking error in the corporate sector, can be attributed to event risk, call risk, illiquidity, and higher transaction costs.

In the mortgage-backed securities market, tracking error was

EXHIBIT 5
Tracking Error of Monthly Returns in Basis Points (1984-1985)

Sector	Standard Deviation	Mean	High	Low	Total Return	
					Cumulative	Annualized
Broad market	5	2	13	6	69	34
Governments	2	2	5	-1	63	31
Corporates*	17	9	40	-26	301	156
Mortgages	3	0	6	-7	6	3
Broad market (Including trans-action costs)	5	0	11	8	-12	-6

*Analysis between January 1985 and November 1986.
Source: Salomon Brothers Inc, based on Salomon Brothers Broad Investment-Grade Bond Index and its components.

less volatile with a standard deviation of 3 basis points, a high of 6 basis points and a low of negative 7 basis points. The mortgage-backed securities component outperformed its benchmark by 47 basis points over a two-year period. In this sector, prepayment risk and the task of matching the performance of some 150,000 pools account for the tracking error.

Tracking error volatility was lowest in the government sector with a standard deviation of monthly errors of only 2 basis points, a high of 5 basis points, and low of negative 1 basis point. Like the corporate component of the fund, government securities also significantly outperformed their benchmark, albeit by a smaller amount. Yield curve twists and varying spreads between current coupon Treasuries and off-the-run Treasuries underlie most of the tracking error.

In the analysis above, the objective of the optimal portfolio or index fund was to track a specific subsector. For example, the mortgage-backed securities data reflect the tracking error of a portfolio designed to track the mortgage-backed securities component of the Salomon Brothers Broad Investment-Grade Index. Similarly, the data on corporates reflect the tracking error of a portfolio designed to track the corporate component of the Salomon Index. Such a strategy of managing index funds by specialized sectors has, in fact, been implemented by the New York City Retirement System.

The data on the broad market reflect the tracking error of a portfolio designed to track the entire Salomon Brothers Broad Investment-Grade Bond Index. The tracking error statistics of the broader index fund fall between the extreme volatility of the corporate index fund and the relative stability of the government index fund. The cumulative performance of the broader portfolio relative to its benchmark is closer to the cumulative performance of the government portfolio relative to its respective benchmark. Such similarity partly reflects the 60 percent weighting of government securities in the broader benchmark.

When transaction costs are included in the analysis, the broader index fund underperforms the Salomon Brothers Broad Investment-Grade Bond Index by 12 basis points.

Finally, it should be noted that the tracking error of each individual subsector in a portfolio designed to track the entire market will be greater than the tracking error of an individual subsector designed to track its respective benchmark.

IV. ENHANCED INDEXING

The purpose of straight or "vanilla" indexing is to closely track the performance of a benchmark. The purpose of enhanced or "index plus" indexing, on the other hand, is to outperform the benchmark without incurring additional long-term risk. In the short-term, additional risk, defined as greater positive and negative tracking error, is inevitable. Over a longer time horizon, however, the index fund is expected to outperform its benchmark by a small percentage. Three types of strategies can be used to outperform a benchmark while maintaining similar long-term risk exposure as the benchmark: value-added strategies using securities included in the benchmark, value-added strategies using securities and instruments excluded from the benchmark, and trading and execution strategies.

Exhibit 6 illustrates a strategy based on the relative value of specific maturities in the September 1986 current coupon Treasury yield curve. The 5-year current coupon Treasury security is sold and replaced with a 4-year and a 7-year current coupon Treasury security. The swap is implemented such that the duration of the assets sold equals the market value-weighted duration of the assets purchased. In this specific example, the swap results in 15 basis points of additional yield, and a small increase in convexity of 0.01. Furthermore, since the four to seven year spread of 46 basis points

EXHIBIT 6
Treasury Yield Curve Strategy (Barbells versus Bullets)

Issue			Yield	Duration	Convexity
Sell: TSY	6.50	11/15/91	6.706	4.186	.109
Buy: TSY	6.75	9/30/90	6.637	3.364	.070
TSY	7.25	7/15/93	7.098	5.124	.169
Value Added					
Yield Pick-Up	0.15				
Convexity Gain	1.01				
4–7 Year Spread	46				

is at historically wide levels, the expected flattening of the yield curve provides additional value to the index fund. This strategy would be implemented in a cell with a 4- to 7-year maturity range.

Exhibit 7 illustrates the potential value of derivative securities that are not included in the index universe. Similar coupon and weighted average life GNMA-backed collateralized mortgage obligations have outperformed GNMA counterparts in six out of the past 7 quarters.

The returns of an index fund can also be enhanced through efficient trading and execution. Transaction costs can be reduced

EXHIBIT 7
Quarterly Total Returns of Current Coupon GNMAs and
GNMA-Backed Collateralized Mortgage Obligations

Year/Quarter		Current Coupon GNMA (%)	Quarterly Total Returns (%)	CMO Returns Tranche III (%)
1985	I	12	2.90	4.00
	II	12¹/₂	7.95	8.56
	III	11	2.06	2.94
	IV	11	9.41	10.41
1986	I	9¹/₂	5.76	6.04
	II	8¹/₂	−0.45	2.60
	III	9¹/₂	4.33	2.75

Source: The First Boston Corporation.

by taking advantage of long and short positions in the market, by knowing each dealer's particular expertise, or simply by adept placement of buy and sell orders.

V. CUSTOMIZED BENCHMARKS

As mentioned earlier, indexing against one of the three broad market benchmarks may not meet the objectives of a particular fund. A long duration benchmark may be more suited for a pension fund with long duration liabilities, while an intermediate duration benchmark may be more suited for an endowment fund concerned with capital preservation. Customized benchmarks to meet the specific requirements and objectives of a fund offer an alternative to the more standard market benchmarks.

Customized benchmarks are constructed in three steps. First, a duration level is selected. The duration level may be a function of the duration levels of broad benchmarks or of the liabilities of a pension fund. For example, a customized benchmark may have a duration that is 75 percent of the duration of the Shearson Lehman Aggregate Index. Second, the weightings of market sectors are specified. Such weightings are determined by a fund's liquidity and quality preferences and overall risk tolerance. Treasuries may be overweighted relative to the Treasury component of the broad benchmarks while corporates may be underweighted. And third, an information system must be established to measure the performance and the profile characteristics of the customized benchmark and to ensure that the parameters (such as the weighting of Treasuries and the target duration) are internally consistent and practical.

In December 1986, Salomon Brothers Inc. introduced a new benchmark, the Salomon Brothers Large Pension Fund Baseline Bond Index, for large pension funds designed to match the long duration of pension liabilities while taking advantage of the higher yields of corporates and mortgage-backed securities. The motivation in developing such an index was to offer a benchmark that was more suited to the objectives of large long-term oriented pension funds.

Customized benchmarks designed to match or outperform the present value of pension liabilities will become widespread also as companies incorporate FASB Statements 87 and 88 in their income statement and balance sheet reporting. Companies will want to maintain stable and favorable asset-liability ratios by indexing pension assets against a benchmark that fluctuates with their liabilities.

VI. IMPLICATIONS FOR THE FIXED INCOME MARKET

The trend towards indexation has several implications for the investment community. First and foremost, the level of transaction activity will decrease since index funds have less turnover than actively managed funds. In addition, most of the transaction activity will be concentrated at month end when the majority of index funds are rebalanced.

The fixed income market will also witness a decrease in the turnover of each plan sponsor's investment advisors. It is unlikely that plan sponsors will terminate an index fund manager as frequently as they have terminated active portfolio managers in the past; an index fund manager is less likely to underperform a fund benchmark by the magnitudes that result in termination. Furthermore, as the duration of more portfolios, both active and indexed, are clustered around the duration of the broad market indices, the range in the performance of investment advisors will narrow; and the performance of the median manager, the performance of the managers around the mode, and the performance of the broad market indices will all converge.

ARTICLE 16

PHILIP H. GALDI is currently a Vice President in the Merrill Lynch Capital Markets Structured Investments Group. In this position he is responsible for the group's bond indexing products. His previous positions at Merrill Lynch included manager of the Debt Strategy-Product Specialists Group and manager of the Financial Consulting Group. Mr. Galdi is a Certified Public Accountant and holds a degree from Pace University in Accounting and Computer Science.

INDEXING FIXED INCOME PORTFOLIOS

Philip H. Galdi, C.P.A.
Vice President
Structured Investments Group
Merrill Lynch Capital Markets

More and more, managers of fixed income portfolios are turning to indexing techniques for all or a core portion of their portfolios. The result of such a move is investment performance that tracks the market. The reasons many view this as a desirable objective are the same as those that previously made indexing popular with equity portfolio managers: consistent performance relative to the market, and diversification of risk.

The fact that indexing can lead to consistent performance comes as no surprise. The index represents the average return of all investors. By setting up an index fund, the investor is typically looking to protect a core portion of assets from falling below the market average. What may come as a surprise, however, is that moving with the market average does not necessarily result in mediocre performance.

For example, over the 12 months ending 12/31/85, the Merrill Lynch Corporate/Government Master Index measured a total annual return of 21.8 percent, compared to a total return of 21.0 percent for the Trust Universe Comparison System (TUCS) Median Bond Manager (see Exhibit 1). This return ranked the index at the 42nd percentile for the one year period. Over a three year

EXHIBIT 1
**Merrill Lynch Corporate/Government Master Index vs. TUCS Median
Fixed Income Portfolio Performance**
Based on Cumulative Returns as of 12/31/85

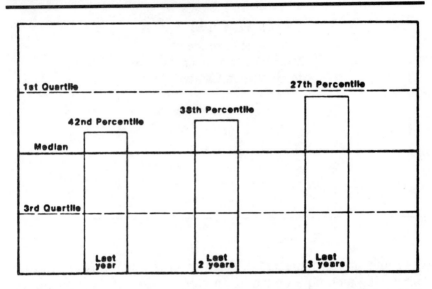

*Source: Trust Universe Comparison System, Wilshire Associates, Santa
Monica, Ca.

term the annualized total return performance of the index exceeded the Median Manager by an even wider margin, 14.8 percent versus 13.8 percent. This three year return earned the index a
ranking in the 27th percentile—a better performance than nearly
three quarters of all portfolio managers included in the study.

A second key benefit of indexing is diversification. By its nature,
an indexed structure for a portfolio implies diversification of risk
within the segments of the market being tracked. If the portfolio is
not overweighted in any one component of the market, it stands to
reason that it does not run the risk of overreacting to significant
negative price movement in any one component.

This article presents an overview of the theories and techniques
involved in establishing and managing an indexed fixed income
portfolio. The article begins with a summary of indexing principles

as they apply to fixed income portfolios and the ways index funds can be used to support investment goals. Several techniques for setting up an indexed portfolio are discussed, including possible modifications of strict indexing principles. Also mentioned are some issues of concern in terms of maintaining the index structure over time and evaluating returns. This article concludes with a case study illustrating the simulated performance of a sample indexed portfolio.

I. GENERAL INDEXING PRINCIPLES

An indexed portfolio is structured to track the market; that is, the total return performance of the portfolio will closely match that of a market index with minimum tracking error. Tracking error is defined as any variance, whether positive or negative, from the desired target. It is by minimizing variances that the index fund achieves reduced performance volatility.

One way to attain strong tracking results would be to purchase a pro rata percentage of every issue in the targeted market. Where bond indexing is concerned, however, this approach is not feasible. First, the overall bond market comprises over 5,000 issues, an impractical size to maintain operationally in an individual portfolio, and one that would require numerous odd lot positions. Second, not all outstanding issues included in the index are available for purchase at a given time. Further, ongoing reinvestment of coupon and principal cash-flows would require fractional purchases if one were to maintain the proper weighting allocated to each of the 5,000 issues.

In practice, an indexed portfolio is constructed by selecting a sample of the bonds that comprise the index. A sampling approach means fewer issues will be required in the portfolio. Therefore those issues that are selected can be purchased in larger, round lot sizes, providing more liquidity for the portfolio. Portfolio selections are limited to issues available for purchase in the open market. These selections must be made so that the portfolio will react, under a variety of market conditions, as if it were in fact a pro rata investment in the entire market. This is a goal that can be achieved by constructing, with the aid of computer analytics, a sample which replicates the characteristic structure of the aggregate market.

Replicating the Market

What is needed to replicate a fixed income market? To begin with, those quantifiable characteristics of a bond that have the greatest influence on its markct value must be singled out and measured for the market at large. A portfolio can then be modeled so as to mirror these characteristics qualitatively, but on a smaller scale.

Generally, duration[1] is considered the most critical characteristic to match in a bond index program. It is the best available measure of relative price volatility of bonds. Therefore, matching the duration of the market protects the portfolio from underperforming the index under a variety of market conditions.

At a minimum, however, a well structured index fund should match not only duration, but also the coupon and maturity structure of the aggregate market. Even though the formula for duration is largely based on coupon and maturity, one must track these two characteristics individually in order to accurately replicate the market. For example, although duration is an effective measure of volatility, two bonds of the same duration but with different coupons may react differently depending on the velocity and direction of the market. This is particularly true when one of the bonds is trading at a discount and the other at a premium. In a similar fashion, maturity must also be considered. Heavy demand in one segment of the market that might result from purchases for a dedicated portfolio or for stripping a Treasury issue, can cause bonds in a given maturity or range of maturities to react in an unusual manner relative to their duration.

An index fund that includes corporate issues must also replicate the distributions among industry and quality sectors of the corpo-

---

[1] Duration is defined as the weighted average term to maturity of the cash flows of a bond, with cash flows expressed in terms of their present value. The duration of any given coupon security is always less than its term to maturity. The duration of a zero-coupon bond equals its term to maturity. It should be noted that the duration of a bond decreases the greater the stated coupon rate. As market yields increase, the duration of a bond decreases. Therefore, a portfolio's duration will change over time with changes in the market.

rate bond market. Furthermore, there is the question of callable issues—often an investment program is designed to provide protection from calls. With an index fund, however, such action might cause poor tracking performance since the index includes callable issues. An effective corporate index program will replicate the call features of the market, not only in percentage of dollars invested in callable issues, but also in the distribution of those dollars among the various ranges of call dates and call prices.

Having singled out the critical characteristics for a particular index program, the next step is to establish what will constitute an acceptable "match" between the market and the portfolio. Either of two approaches, or combinations of the two, can be used.

1. Matching Weighted Average Values. Characteristics that are mathematical in nature, such as duration, maturity and coupon, can be matched using weighted average values. For example, the weighted average maturity of the issues in the portfolio will be equal to that of all issues in the index. The weighting should be based on current market values.

When numeric averages are used in matching, one must be careful to avoid creating a "barbell" structure. For example, to replicate a market with an average maturity of 16 years, one could, theoretically, invest equally in two issues, one with a two year maturity and one with a 30 year maturity. However, this type of structure would be vulnerable to underperforming the index under certain market conditions, such as during a twist in the shape of the yield curve. Therefore, in addition to matching weighted average characteristics, the sample portfolio should also provide for a representative distribution of issues from the selection universe.

2. Matching Pro Rata Distribution Between Classes. Certain characteristics, such as quality and industry segmentation, do not readily lend themselves to numeric averages. The most useful approach is to match the percentage allocation of investment dollars within each category. For example, if 12 percent of the corporate index has a rating of Aa2, then 12 percent of the market value of an indexed corporate portfolio should also be comprised of Aa2 issues. Next, industry classes are matched in a similar fashion. If 14 percent of the index is attributed to finance issues, then 14 percent of the portfolio will be in finance issues.

Issue Selection using Linear Programming Techniques

Matching any one characteristic of a portfolio to the market is not particularly difficult. In order to track well, however, an indexed portfolio must match numerous characteristics simultaneously. Linear programming, a technique for simultaneously solving multiple mathematical equations, can accomplish this task quickly. Linear programming models will identify the best available portfolio given (1) a set of multiple constraints, and (2) an objective function, or optimization goal, for the program.

1. Selection Constraints. The primary constraints on the selection of issues for the portfolio are those that insure that the portfolio replicates the market. Key characteristics are targeted using either the numerical weighted average method or the pro rata distribution method.

In addition to constraints on characteristics, secondary constraints may also be used to tailor the program toward a particular fund's investment parameters. For example, it is possible to place a percentage or dollar cap on the amount invested in any one issue, issuer or group of issuers. Or, combinations of criteria may be used to force the exclusion or inclusion of particular types of issues. There is a limit, however, to the number of secondary constraints that can be accommodated while still constructing a portfolio that meets primary criteria.

2. Objective Function. There may be several combinations of securities that satisfy characteristic and secondary issue constraints. Therefore an "objective function" is used as part of the linear program to establish a quantifiable, objective method for choosing among all possible combinations. The most common approach is to use yield to maturity (YTM) to determine the best portfolio to purchase. The portfolio selected would then be the one with the highest weighted average YTM that meets all constraints.

Maximizing YTM is particularly effective in a program targeted toward the U.S. Treasury index. However, for a program structured to track the corporate market, yield to worst—the lower of yield to maturity or yield to call date—serves as a more effective objective function since call and sinking fund provisions affect the pricing of bonds.

II. INCORPORATING INDEXING IN A BROAD INVESTMENT PROGRAM

Indexing can be used as a strategy for managing all investment assets. However, more often than not, indexed assets constitute a core structure around which other, more active strategies are established. The first step in developing an indexed core is to determine which index the core assets will track. This process can be linked to an asset allocation study, allowing certain classes of assets to be earmarked for indexing. In the absence of a formalized program for allocated investments among classes of assets, an effective starting point is the existing asset composition.

Having made a decision to index some component of fixed income investments, further subdivisions can be specified. For example, assume that an asset allocation study for a hypothetical fund has recommended a structure consisting of 60 percent equities, 30 percent bonds, and 10 percent real estate and venture capital. In addition, a decision was made to use indexing techniques to manage half of the bond component. It would be possible in this circumstance to track the broad fixed income market with the indexed half of the portfolio and at the same time allow for actively managed bonds to be invested in any or all sectors of the same broad market.

A second alternative for this hypothetical fund would be to subdivide the fixed income portfolio between sectors of the market. Each sector is then managed using either indexing or active strategies, but not both. As an example, all government and agency bonds might be indexed while all corporate bonds are actively managed.

These are only two of many possible structures for a core index fund strategy. The availability of numerous sub-indices makes it possible to tailor a particular program in a number of ways. Decisions regarding the core structure should be made only after considering broader objectives for the management of assets.

III. SETTING UP THE INDEXED PORTFOLIO

The mechanics of selecting issues for an indexed portfolio are largely supported by the linear programming model. For this process to work, however, decisions must be made regarding the criteria which guide the computer. For example, which bond characteristics will be targeted? What is the basis for establishing the match: numeric averages, or sample distributions?

The answers to these questions are linked to the selection of the segment of the market that the fund is targeted to track. A government index fund, for example, is structured in a manner that is slightly different from a corporate index fund. The sections that follow illustrate the actual portfolio selection process. The cases presented make use of alternative selection techniques, each adapted to a different type of fund.

Sector-Based Indexing

In addition to tracking broad fixed income markets, such as the Treasury market, the agency market, the corporate market, etc., an indexed portfolio can be made up of numerous sub-indices that segment these broad markets into smaller sectors. These sub-indices, some of which overlap, dissect the major market indices by maturity, quality, issuer type, etc.

Sector-based indexing uses these sub-indices in what might be described as a building block, or "bottom-up" approach to structuring the fund. First, the targeted market, such as the 1–10 year Treasury market, and its associated index (which we will refer to as the "parent" index) are selected. Next, one identifies the sub-indices that comprise the parent index, such as 1–3 year, 3–5 year Treasuries, etc. Each sub-sector of the portfolio is loosely matched by characteristics to the corresponding sub-index. At the same time, the characteristics of the aggregate portfolio are closely matched to those of the parent index, as in the following example.

1. The program was designed to track the intermediate government market. The corresponding 1–10 year government index was used as the parent index. Sectors were constrained around the 1–3 year, 3–5 year, 5–7 year and 7–10 year Treasury sub-indices, as well as the same four maturity sectors of the agency market.

2. Characteristic constraints were as follows:

	Parent Level	*Sector Level*
Duration	Match within +/− .01 years	Match within +/− .1 years
Coupon	Match within +/− .05%	Match within +/− .1%
Maturity	Match within +/− .05 years	Match within +/− .1 years
Dollar Investment	$100 million	Match relative weight of each sub-sector in the 1–10 year government index

3. Other constraints included: no more than 5 percent of the value of the aggregate portfolio in any one issue; no more than 10 percent of the value of the portfolio invested in any one agency; Federal Land Bank and the Federal Farm Credit Bank were not permitted in the portfolio.

Given the constraints outlined in (2) above, linear programming was used to select the optimal indexed portfolio. The resulting portfolio is detailed in Exhibit 2, and an analysis of the characteristics of the portfolio versus those of the index appears in Exhibit 3. The latter analysis illustrates how successful the program was in replicating the structure of the market. Characteristics of the portfolio, at both the aggregate and the sector level, are well within, or near the narrow tolerance levels that were set for matching the index. What makes this even more impressive is that these numerous and diverse characteristic constraints were met with a sample portfolio comprising only 36 issues. In addition, the objective function for the program was to maximize yield to maturity. As a result, the selected portfolio has a seven basis point spread over the average yield to maturity of the aggregate 1–10 year government market.

The matching process in a sector-based program, at both the parent and sector levels, is generally accomplished using the numeric averaging approach. By drawing selections from each sub-sector, a barbell structure is avoided and a more representative distribution attained. Matching requirements are tightly constrained at the parent level since the true goal of the program is to

EXHIBIT 2
Intermediate Government Index Fund

Par Amount (000)	Description	Coupon	Maturity	Flat Price	Yield %	Accrued Int.	Total Full Price
5000	US TREASURY	7.625	11/15/1987	100.970	6.85	1.12	$ 5,104,458.54
2300	US TREASURY	8.500	11/30/1987	102.254	6.77	0.88	2,372,144.55
800	FED NTL MTG AS	10.900	12/10/1987	105.319	6.90	0.85	849,335.17
5000	US TREASURY	8.125	1/31/1988	101.886	6.83	3.55	5,271,633.63
5000	US TREASURY	10.375	2/15/1988	105.265	6.85	4.10	5,468,168.93
5000	US TREASURY	8.000	2/29/1988	101.734	6.86	2.83	5,227,999.45
4500	SALLIE-MAE	9.625	5/25/1988	104.277	7.15	1.15	4,744,181.33
1500	FED NTL MTG AS	13.200	9/12/1988	111.982	7.15	4.25	1,743,529.37
4000	US TREASURY	11.750	11/15/1988	109.895	7.10	1.72	4,464,755.11
1200	FED HOME LN MT	9.375	12/27/1988	104.427	7.38	0.29	1,256,556.88
3000	US TREASURY	10.625	12/31/1988	107.836	7.12	0.23	3,242,008.54
1900	US TREASURY	14.625	1/15/1989	116.969	7.14	7.03	2,355,981.04
4000	US TREASURY	11.250	3/31/1989	109.848	7.20	3.04	4,515,653.51
1900	SALLIE-MAE	7.900	7/06/1989	101.508	7.33	0.04	1,929,495.26
3000	US TREASURY	11.000	2/15/1990	111.041	7.45	4.35	3,461,593.32
4000	US TREASURY	10.500	4/15/1990	109.828	7.45	2.41	4,489,505.76
100	FED HM LN BK B	7.750	6/25/1990	100.669	7.55	0.26	100,927.56

EXHIBIT 2 (Continued)

4000	US TREASURY	10.750	7/15/1990	111.151	7.49	5.17	4,652,730.28
1500	US TREASURY	9.875	8/15/1990	108.370	7.47	3.90	1,684,067.37
3500	US TREASURY	10.750	8/15/1990	111.342	7.49	4.25	4,045,600.33
2200	FED NTL MTG AS	12.500	3/15/1991	116.962	8.07	3.92	2,659,476.49
500	FED HOME LN MT	11.850	8/30/1991	116.166	7.95	4.21	601,896.03
4000	US TREASURY	11.625	1/15/1992	117.871	7.60	5.59	4,938,357.49
2100	US TREASURY	11.750	4/15/1992	119.101	7.59	2.70	2,557,750.91
2400	US TREASURY	10.375	7/15/1992	113.382	7.57	4.99	2,840,864.68
2000	FED HM LN BK B	10.350	8/25/1992	111.380	7.96	3.82	2,304,080.88
700	FED NTL MTG AS	10.900	1/11/1993	114.271	8.04	5.36	837,413.11
1400	US TREASURY	10.125	5/15/1993	113.473	7.57	1.49	1,609,416.13
200	FED HM LN BK B	11.700	7/26/1993	119.171	8.08	5.26	248,872.74
800	US TREASURY	11.750	11/15/1993	122.817	7.63	1.72	996,326.15
2200	US TREASURY	9.000	2/15/1994	108.300	7.54	3.56	2,460,808.12
900	US TREASURY	10.125	11/15/1994	115.460	7.59	1.49	1,052,508.97
2600	US TREASURY	11.250	2/15/1995	122.480	7.64	4.44	3,300,020.30
4000	US TREASURY	11.250	5/15/1995	122.925	7.64	1.65	4,983,051.01
1000	FED NTL MTG AS	11.150	6/12/1995	118.474	8.19	0.81	1,192,793.06
500	SALLIE-MAE	8.085	9/12/1995	100.321	8.03	2.61	514,629.03
							$100,078,591.02

Note: Full price includes accrued interest assuming settlement on 7/8/86.

EXHIBIT 3
Intermediate Government Index Fund
Portfolio Characteristics Versus Index

Aggregate Portfolio:	Index	Portfolio
Duration	3.120	3.120
Coupon	10.325	10.376
Maturity	3.920	3.971
Market Value	$860 bil	$100 mil
Yield to Maturity	7.301	7.375

Subsector Analysis:

	1–3 Year		3–5 Year		5–7 Year		7–10 Year	
	Index	Portfolio	Index	Portfolio	Index	Portfolio	Index	Portfolio
Treasuries								
Duration	1.682	1.734	3.216	3.216	4.525	4.423	5.939	5.838
Coupon	9.785	9.800	10.556	10.656	11.049	11.152	10.652	10.764
Maturity	1.812	1.913	3.883	3.907	5.902	5.873	8.492	8.392
% of Aggregate	37.996%	37.993%	18.501%	18.319%	12.092%	11.937%	12.776%	12.783%
Agencies								
Duration	1.727	1.818	3.264	3.267	4.585	4.537	6.095	6.060
Coupon	10.561	10.440	10.449	10.505	10.580	10.714	10.287	10.414
Maturity	1.884	1.983	3.885	3.974	5.983	6.059	8.833	8.755
% of Aggregate	8.693%	8.587%	4.902%	4.686%	2.980%	3.740%	2.061%	1.955%

track that broad market. Matching criteria at the sub-sector level are not intended to track those individual components, but rather to ensure an effective distribution of selected issues. Therefore, the constraints at that level can be relaxed.

A government index fund readily lends itself to a sector-based approach. Quality and industry segmentation are clearly not of concern in this type of program. The important characteristics for tracking—duration, coupon and maturity—are the type that can be arithmetically quantified for an aggregate group of bonds. Therefore numeric averaging can be used as the basis for replication.

Distribution-Based Indexing

It is not always possible to assemble the combination of sub-indices needed to build a sector based structure for an index fund. This is often true when the parent index is itself a subset of a larger bond universe, such as in a program designed to track only the long term (15–30 year) sector of the Treasury market. One might also face this situation in trying to track certain master indices, such as a Yankee bond index, where a detailed sub-index structure has not evolved.

Distribution analysis works from the top down and therefore does not depend on supporting sub-indices. It is thus possible to create a tailored indexed portfolio for narrowly specified markets such as long-term Treasuries.

The process begins by analyzing the universe of issues comprising the target index to determine the percentage distribution of key characteristics, such as maturity and quality, on a market value basis, within predetermined ranges. A portfolio is then selected that has a similar distribution pattern with regard to each of the key characteristics.

The setting of distribution ranges should be detailed enough to ensure a well dispersed selection, but not so fragmented as to defeat the purpose of sampling. A workable structure for a long-term Treasury fund might match coupon and maturity allocations as follows:

Coupon Ranges (%)	Maturity Ranges (years)
<6	15–17.9
6–7.9	18–20.9
8–9.9	21–23.9
10–11.9	24–26.9
12–13.9	27–30
>16	

Notice that the third critical characteristic necessary to replicate the Treasury market—duration—is not included. For this particular program it is sufficient to match duration only to the weighted average duration of the parent index. The maturity distribution constraint on the portfolio is enough to prevent a barbell type structure, while a requirement to match both duration and maturity on a distribution basis might prove too cumbersome and over restrain the flexibility of the sampling process.

Integrating Sector and Distribution-Based Strategies

The "top down" distribution based technique can also be incorporated within a sector-based strategy, particularly where a sub-index structure can be established but replication of the market depends on matching both qualitative and quantitative characteristics. Such a situation may exist in a corporate index fund. Where appropriate sub-indices can be assembled, the key quantitative characteristics such as duration, maturity and coupon can be matched on a sector by sector basis to corresponding sub-index numeric averages. The more qualitative attributes of that same fund, such as credit ratings, industry segmentation and call features, are then matched on a distribution basis.

Exhibit 4 illustrates an indexed portfolio that was structured to track the Corporate/Government Master Index.

In constructing this portfolio, the Master Index was first segmented by market (i.e., Treasury, Agency, and Corporate). Each market was then segmented into three maturity ranges (i.e., 1–10 years, 10–15 years, and 15–30 years) to develop a nine sector

EXHIBIT 4
Corporate/Government Master Index Fund

Par Amount (000)	Description	Coupon	Maturity	Flat Price	Yield %	Accrued Int.	Total Full Price
1200	FED LAND BK BD	7.250	7/20/1987	100.424	6.81	3.38	$ 1,245,690.92
9800	US TREASURY	7.625	11/15/1987	100.970	6.85	1.12	10,004,738.75
800	FED LAND BK BD	7.850	1/20/1988	101.135	7.05	3.66	838,383.15
1900	US TREASURY	8.000	2/29/1988	101.734	6.86	2.83	1,986,639.79
4400	US TREASURY	6.625	4/30/1988	99.615	6.85	1.24	4,437,716.25
700	FED HM LN BK B	7.250	6/27/1988	100.466	6.99	0.24	704,952.43
1600	FED FARM CR BK	13.050	1/23/1989	112.435	7.58	5.98	1,894,660.99
2300	GMAC	10.500	4/15/1989	106.890	7.68	2.42	2,514,146.87
5300	US TREASURY	14.500	7/15/1989	119.118	7.33	6.97	6,682,624.32
4400	US TREASURY	10.750	7/15/1990	111.151	7.49	5.17	5,118,003.31
400	FED FARM CR BK	10.400	7/23/1990	108.429	7.92	4.77	452,781.91
7000	US TREASURY	10.750	8/15/1990	111.342	7.49	4.25	8,091,200.67
700	MERRILL LYNCH	9.750	12/15/1990	104.176	8.59	0.62	733,590.32
2500	OCCIDENTAL PET	10.000	3/15/1991	97.788	10.60	3.14	2,523,179.72
3300	FED HOME LN MT	11.850	8/30/1991	116.166	7.95	4.21	3,972,513.81
2100	US TREASURY	11.625	1/15/1992	117.871	7.60	5.59	2,592,637.68
1900	FED HM LN BK B	10.350	8/25/1992	111.380	7.96	3.82	2,188,876.84
2200	US TREASURY	11.750	11/15/1993	122.817	7.63	1.72	2,739,896.91
1200	UNION OIL OF C	9.750	3/01/1994	97.205	10.28	3.44	1,207,741.00
3100	US TREASURY	12.625	8/15/1994	129.666	7.64	4.99	4,174,237.72
900	US TREASURY	10.125	11/15/1994	115.460	7.59	1.49	1,052,508.97

EXHIBIT 4 (Continued)

2100	US TREASURY	10.500	8/15/1995	118.863	7.59	4.15	2,583,223.61
2800	INTEGRATED RES	10.750	4/15/1996	99.539	10.82	2.48	2,856,486.42
800	AMER TEL & TEL	4.375	10/01/1996	70.767	8.76	1.18	575,564.96
1000	SALOMON BRO MT	9.900	12/01/1997	105.362	9.13	1.02	1,063,795.00
1200	SOHIO-BP TRNAL	9.750	12/01/1999	102.623	9.40	1.00	1,243,501.00
1600	MINN PWR & LIG	8.125	4/01/2001	91.018	9.25	2.19	1,491,310.98
1500	TENNECO INC.	9.500	6/15/2004	98.057	9.73	0.61	1,479,960.67
2100	GMAC	9.400	7/15/2004	99.425	9.47	4.52	2,182,792.97
1600	US TREASURY	13.750	8/15/2004	154.915	7.97	5.43	2,565,541.37
200	US TREASURY	12.000	5/15/2005	139.437	7.93	1.76	282,394.93
200	ATLANTIC RICHF	10.875	7/15/2005	111.991	9.50	5.23	234,433.88
1800	US TREASURY	10.750	8/15/2005	128.027	7.88	4.25	2,380,919.04
1000	US TREASURY	7.875	11/15/2007	101.334	7.74	1.16	1,024,893.85
1300	COMMONWLTH EDI	9.125	10/15/2008	96.975	9.45	2.10	1,288,020.75
1300	US TREASURY	10.375	11/15/2009	124.308	8.05	1.52	1,635,794.57
200	CITICORP	10.875	6/15/2010	106.466	10.15	0.69	214,321.18
1400	PACIFIC TEL&TE	9.500	6/15/2011	100.372	9.46	0.61	1,413,709.42
1600	US TREASURY	10.375	11/15/2012	125.403	8.04	1.52	2,030,804.22
300	PHILADELPHIA E	11.750	11/15/2014	105.103	11.15	1.73	320,500.08
1100	US TREASURY	11.250	2/15/2015	137.862	7.89	4.44	1,565,366.34
1900	US TREASURY	10.625	8/15/2015	131.274	7.87	4.20	2,573,959.08
1400	COMMONWLTH EDI	11.750	9/01/2015	109.309	10.70	4.15	1,588,357.94
600	SOUTHERN CAL E	9.250	3/01/2016	98.867	9.36	3.26	612,781.17
500	NORTHWSTN BEL	9.500	8/15/2016	100.977	9.40	3.77	523,752.56
1100	SOUWSTN BELL T	9.625	3/15/2019	100.221	9.60	3.02	1,135,662.89
							$100,024,571.20

Note: Full price includes accrued interest assuming settlement on 7/8/86.

program. Duration, coupon and maturity characteristics were matched on the aggregate and sector levels to the Corporate/Government Master Index and the corresponding sub-indices in a manner similar to that used in the preceding example for the intermediate government portfolio.

Since this program included corporate issues, it was also necessary to replicate the industry and quality characteristics of the market. This was accomplished on a percentage distribution basis. As shown in Exhibit 5, the structure of this portfolio very closely matches the distribution of the market between the various industry and quality sectors. This type of structure provides a certain degree of assurance that the portfolio will continue to track the returns of the Corporate/Government Master Index, even in the event that sector spreads shift significantly.

Cash-Flow Sculpturing

To replicate the volatility characteristics of the bond market, the most commonly used measure is duration, since it represents a single, easily matched numeric target. Less often used, but in many ways preferable, is matching the cash-flow structure of the bond universe being indexed.

Cash-flow sculpturing, in which the cash-flow of the index fund matches the cash-flow structure of the corresponding index, is accomplished by aggregating all cash-flows projected for the entire targeted market over a distribution time line. These cash-flows are then scaled down to equate with the current value of the portfolio. Issues are selected so that the resulting portfolio matches these scaled down targets. Exhibit 6 shows an indexed Treasury portfolio (Portfolio A) constructed to replicate the cash-flow structure of the entire Treasury market.

To start with, this program was formulated using a three-sector structure: 1–10 year Treasuries, 10–15 year Treasuries, and 15–30 year Treasuries. Tolerance levels for matching the duration, coupon and maturity characteristics of the aggregate portfolio to the Treasury Master Index were set at +/−0.05, while these constraints were relaxed to +/−0.1 at the sector level. A limit of 5 percent of the total value of the portfolio was placed on the amount that

EXHIBIT 5
Corporate/Government Master Index Fund
Cross Tabulation—Quality versus Industry Distribution

		Quality											
	Cross Tabulation	AGCY	AAA	AA1	AA2	AA3	A1	A2	A3	BBB1	BBB2	BBB3	Total
GOVT	64.4 (63.5)												64.4 (63.5)
AGENCY		11.8 (11.3)											11.8 (11.3)
INDUST			0.5	0.3	0.6	0.6	1.0 (0.2)	1.7 (2.9)	0.8	0.5 (1.5)	1.0 (2.5)	0.5 (1.2)	7.6 (8.3)
S E C T O R UTILITY			0.1	0.1	0.8 (0.6)	0.7	0.9 (1.5)	0.8	1.1 (2.9)	0.7	0.8	0.6 (0.3)	6.5 (5.3)
FINANCE			0.6 (1.1)	0.8 (4.7)	0.2	0.5 (0.7)	0.5	0.5	0.3	0.1	0.3	0.1	4.1 (6.5)
UTIL/COMM			0.3	0.8	0.5 (0.5)	0.6 (0.6)	0.8 (2.5)	0.1	0.1	0.0	0.0	0.0	3.3 (3.6)
BANK			0.1		0.5 (0.2)	0.3	0.2	0.1	0.1	0.0	0.0	0.0	1.3 (0.2)
TRANS			0.0	0.0	0.0	0.1 (1.2)	0.0	0.2	0.0	0.0	0.0	0.0	0.4 (1.2)
OTHER			0.0		0.1	0.0		0.1	0.0	0.1	0.2	0.0	0.5
MARKET:	64.4	11.8	1.6	2.0	2.7	2.9	3.5	3.5	2.4	1.5	2.3	1.4	100.0
PORTFOLIO:	(63.5)	(11.3)	(1.1)	(4.7)	(1.3)	(2.6)	(4.3)	(2.9)	(2.9)	(1.5)	(2.5)	(1.5)	(100.0)

Note: Unbracketed amounts represent the percentage distribution of the market at the time of the structuring. Bracketed amounts represent the corresponding percentage distributions of the indexed portfolio.

EXHIBIT 6
Treasury Index Fund (Portfolio A)
(Structured Using Cashflow Sculpturing)

Par Amount (000)	Description	Coupon	Maturity	Flat Price	Yield %	Accrued Int.	Total Full Price
800	US TREASURY	8.875	7/31/1987	102.301	6.59	3.87	$ 849,400.85
4000	US TREASURY	7.625	11/15/1987	100.970	6.85	1.12	4,083,566.84
3900	US TREASURY	8.125	1/31/1988	101.886	6.83	3.55	4,111,874.24
4000	US TREASURY	8.000	2/29/1988	101.734	6.86	2.83	4,182,399.56
4000	US TREASURY	6.625	4/30/1988	99.615	6.85	1.24	4,034,287.50
2000	US TREASURY	11.250	3/31/1989	109.848	7.20	3.04	2,257,826.76
3000	US TREASURY	11.750	5/15/1989	111.448	7.23	1.72	3,395,180.51
3000	US TREASURY	14.500	7/15/1989	119.118	7.33	6.97	3,782,617.54
3000	US TREASURY	10.500	1/15/1990	109.442	7.40	5.05	3,434,683.15
400	US TREASURY	11.000	2/15/1990	111.041	7.45	4.35	461,545.78
3000	US TREASURY	10.750	7/15/1990	111.151	7.49	5.17	3,489,547.71
1700	US TREASURY	9.875	8/15/1990	108.370	7.47	3.90	1,908,609.68
3000	US TREASURY	10.750	8/15/1990	111.342	7.49	4.25	3,467,657.43
400	US TREASURY	11.750	1/15/1991	115.925	7.53	5.65	486,292.44
1000	US TREASURY	12.250	10/15/1991	120.053	7.56	2.81	1,228,640.14
3000	US TREASURY	11.625	1/15/1992	117.871	7.60	5.59	3,703,768.12
3000	US TREASURY	9.750	10/15/1992	110.887	7.53	2.24	3,393,751.74
2300	US TREASURY	11.750	11/15/1993	122.817	7.63	1.72	2,864,437.68
2600	US TREASURY	12.625	8/15/1994	129.666	7.64	4.99	3,500,973.57

EXHIBIT 6 (Continued)

2700	US TREASURY	10.500	8/15/1995	118.863	7.59	4.15	3,321,287.50
100	US TREASURY	8.500	5/15/1999	105.477	7.81	1.25	106,724.36
200	US TREASURY	7.875	2/15/2000	101.734	7.67	3.11	209,690.28
500	US TREASURY	13.125	5/15/2001	144.941	7.92	1.93	734,336.05
200	US TREASURY	8.000	8/15/2001	102.888	7.67	3.16	212,096.36
200	US TREASURY	13.375	8/15/2001	147.328	7.94	5.28	305,223.56
800	US TREASURY	10.750	5/15/2003	126.234	7.90	1.58	1,022,493.97
200	US TREASURY	11.125	8/15/2003	129.686	7.92	4.39	268,161.80
800	US TREASURY	12.375	5/15/2004	141.739	7.95	1.82	1,148,442.97
900	US TREASURY	8.250	5/15/2005	104.441	7.79	1.21	950,865.79
1200	US TREASURY	10.750	8/15/2005	128.027	7.88	4.25	1,587,279.36
200	US TREASURY	7.625	2/15/2007	99.258	7.70	3.01	204,540.29
100	US TREASURY	7.875	11/15/2007	101.334	7.74	1.16	102,489.38
700	US TREASURY	8.750	11/15/2008	109.308	7.86	1.28	774,146.40
700	US TREASURY	11.750	2/15/2010	137.107	8.18	4.64	992,238.10
700	US TREASURY	13.875	5/15/2011	158.706	8.27	2.04	1,125,193.14
200	US TREASURY	14.000	11/15/2011	160.596	8.26	2.05	325,301.15
800	US TREASURY	10.375	11/15/2012	125.403	8.04	1.52	1,015,402.11
1600	US TREASURY	12.000	8/15/2013	141.978	8.14	4.74	2,347,493.06
1200	US TREASURY	12.500	8/15/2014	147.889	8.14	4.94	1,833,918.69
1400	US TREASURY	10.625	8/15/2015	131.274	7.87	4.20	1,896,601.43
							$75,120,987.02

Note: Full price includes accrued interest assuming settlement on 7/8/86.

could be invested in any one issue. In addition to these criteria, a constraint requiring replication of the cash-flow structure of the Treasury market was also invoked.

It is interesting to see the impact that cash-flow sculpturing has on the structure of the portfolio. Portfolio B in Exhibit 7 below was structured using the exact same constraints as outlined above for Portfolio A with the one exception being the exclusion of cash-flow sculpturing requirements. One difference that becomes immediately apparent is that it is possible to meet all constraints with significantly fewer issues than are generally needed when cash-flow sculpturing parameters are invoked. Examination of the cash-flows and relative yields of the two portfolios, as detailed in Exhibit 8, reveals more important differences between the two structures.

As one might expect, Portfolio B, with its less restrictive constraint parameters achieves an initial yield to maturity that is approximately 11 basis points higher than that of Portfolio A. However, it should also be pointed out that even with the introduction of cash-flow constraints, Portfolio A is slightly higher yielding than the broad Treasury Market—by approximately 8 basis points. Furthermore, the cash-flow structure of Portfolio B is quite substantially different from that of the Treasury market. Therefore in the event of a volatile market environment, particularly one where there is a significant change in the shape of the yield curve, the more conservatively structured Portfolio A would tend to experience better tracking performance than Portfolio B. Whereas in a stable market environment, Portfolio B, with its initial yield advantage will tend to outperform Portfolio A.

The cash-flow structure of the market represents a series of points, whereas duration represents a single numeric target. As such, it is possible to even more accurately measure the volatility of a particular universe of bonds by using cash-flow structure as a basis for replication. An additional advantage of matching cash-flow characteristics is that it opens up a whole new set of options for indexing strategies. For example, rather than using cash-flow to replicate the market's volatility, one could use duration as the measure of volatility and use cash-flow constraints to match some other desired target, such as the actual cash needs of the fund. In this manner, one can integrate certain aspects of a dedication or horizon matching program within an index fund strategy.

EXHIBIT 7
Treasury Index Fund (Structured Without Any Cashflow Sculpturing Constraints)

Par Amount (000)	Description	Coupon	Maturity	Flat Price	Yield %	Accrued Int.	Total Full Price
3000	US TREASURY	7.625	11/15/1987	100.970	6.85	1.12	$ 3,062,675.13
3000	US TREASURY	9.375	9/30/1989	105.959	7.26	2.54	3,254,857.67
1000	US TREASURY	11.875	10/15/1989	112.873	7.36	2.73	1,155,985.19
3000	US TREASURY	10.750	11/15/1989	109.874	7.37	1.58	3,343,540.31
4000	US TREASURY	8.375	12/31/1989	103.404	7.25	0.18	4,143,458.69
3000	US TREASURY	10.500	1/15/1990	109.442	7.40	5.05	3,434,683.15
3000	US TREASURY	11.000	2/15/1990	111.041	7.45	4.35	3,461,593.32
3000	US TREASURY	10.500	4/15/1990	109.828	7.45	2.41	3,367,129.32
3000	US TREASURY	11.375	5/15/1990	112.865	7.46	1.67	3,436,029.08
3000	US TREASURY	10.750	7/15/1990	111.151	7.49	5.17	3,489,547.71
3000	US TREASURY	9.875	8/15/1990	108.370	7.47	3.90	3,368,134.73
3000	US TREASURY	10.750	8/15/1990	111.342	7.49	4.25	3,467,657.43
3000	US TREASURY	11.500	10/15/1990	114.352	7.50	2.64	3,509,732.50
3000	US TREASURY	9.625	11/15/1990	107.973	7.44	1.41	3,281,569.56
3000	US TREASURY	11.750	1/15/1991	115.925	7.53	5.65	3,647,193.33
3000	US TREASURY	9.125	2/15/1991	106.700	7.38	5.44	3,364,187.63
3000	US TREASURY	11.625	1/15/1992	117.871	7.60	5.59	3,703,768.12
1600	US TREASURY	10.375	7/15/1992	113.382	7.57	4.99	1,893,909.78
400	US TREASURY	8.500	5/15/1999	105.477	7.81	1.25	426,897.43
400	US TREASURY	10.750	2/15/2003	126.231	7.89	4.25	521,909.31
3000	US TREASURY	10.375	11/15/2009	124.308	8.05	1.52	3,774,910.54
2500	US TREASURY	11.750	2/15/2010	137.107	8.18	4.64	3,543,707.49
3000	US TREASURY	10.000	5/15/2010	120.611	8.04	1.47	3,662,340.97
2500	US TREASURY	12.750	11/15/2010	147.154	8.23	1.87	3,725,630.80
700	US TREASURY	12.000	8/15/2013	141.978	8.14	4.74	1,027,028.22
							$75,068,077.40

Note: Full price includes accrued interest assuming settlement on 7/8/86.

EXHIBIT 8

Comparison of Indexed Treasury Portfolios With and Without Cashflow Sculpturing Requirements

| Cashflow Periods | | Total Cashflow (000s) | | |
Beginning Date	Ending Date	Treasury Market (Scaled Down)	*Portfolio A* (With Cashflow Sculpturing)	*Portfolio B* (Without Cashflow Sculpturing)
8/86	7/87	8675	7363	6743
8/87	7/88	21835	22081	9573
8/88	7/89	13165	13285	6459
8/89	7/90	10355	10515	31773
8/90	7/91	8258	8423	20975
8/91	7/92	6713	6818	6325
8/92	7/93	5349	5436	1384
8/93	7/94	4403	4455	1384
8/94	7/95	4419	4456	1384
8/95	7/96	4319	4250	1384
8/96	7/97	1407	1408	1384
8/97	7/98	1437	1408	1384
8/98	7/99	1467	1508	1784
8/99	7/00	1581	1600	1350
8/00	7/01	1848	1884	1350
8/01	7/02	1795	1697	1350
8/02	7/03	1996	2076	1750
8/03	7/04	2043	2178	1307
8/04	7/05	1948	1968	1307
8/05	7/06	2041	2130	1307
8/06	7/07	1086	1065	1307
8/07	7/08	941	946	1307
8/08	7/09	1489	1511	1307
8/09	7/10	1424	1481	9652
8/10	7/11	1364	1398	2743
8/11	7/12	771	787	84
8/12	7/13	1316	1332	84
8/13	7/14	1942	1994	742
8/14	7/15	1327	1423	0
8/15	7/16	2490	1474	0
Market Weighted Yield to Maturity		7.413	7.497	7.613

IV. MODIFIED INDEXING FOR
ENHANCED VALUE

In its purest form, an index fund seeks to generate returns that exactly equal those of the targeted index. A point graph of monthly returns in an "ideal" index program might look something like that shown in Exhibit 9, a straight line perfectly dissecting the chart at a 45 degree angle.

One might ask, however, whether it is possible to modify the selection process so as to come close to, but slightly outperform, the index. If so performance results might more closely resemble those in Exhibit 10.

Modified indexing is any strategy in which the manager imparts a particular bias in the selection process. Certain of these "value enhancement" strategies are geared toward generating modest improvements over index returns and can largely be incorporated within the basic constraints of an index structure. Managers seeking larger improvements may require a departure from the matched characteristic structure of a true index fund.

While enhancement programs offer an opportunity for improved performance, they should be approached cautiously. These strategies represent an increase in volatility of performance, hopefully on the positive side. However, there is a risk that the bias could

---

EXHIBIT 9
Performance Goal—Classic Indexed Structure

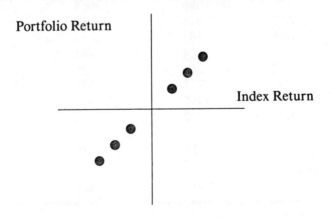

EXHIBIT 10
Performance Goal—Value Enhanced Objective

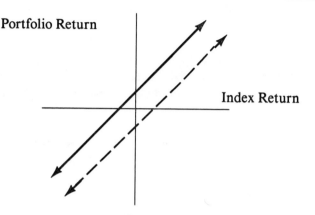

prove incorrect and thereby lead to under-performing the index. A brief discussion of several modified index strategies follows.

Selection of Objective Parameters

Most index programs involve some degree of selection bias. As discussed, the linear programming model is designed to objectively choose among numerous combinations of securities each of which match the characteristic structure of the index. Returns can be enhanced by tilting the selection of securities toward undervalued issues and choosing the portfolio that provides the highest yield to maturity, the highest yield to call, or maximizes some other standard measure of return.

Coupon Strategies. If one's forecast is for interest rates to rise, a possible strategy would be to relax the tolerance levels on coupon constraints and select an objective function that maximizes current yield. Or, as an alternative, the portfolio could be forced to match a coupon target that exceeds the average coupon of the index by some set amount. All other factors being constant, if the market moves as anticipated, a portfolio constructed in either fashion should outperform the market.

Cross Sector Substitutions. A more aggressive enhancement strategy is to replace a bond required in the portfolio with an issue having similar characteristics but coming from another, higher yielding, sector of the market. For example, one might replace a Treasury issue with a corporate bond having the same duration, coupon and maturity. Or a finance issue might replace an industrial in a corporate index fund. Clearly these strategies subject the portfolio to certain additional risks, such as the potential for adverse changes in the spread between the two sectors that have been swapped.

Forecast Tilted Sector Weightings. In the sector-based approach to constructing an index fund, a portfolio is built by matching components to a series of sub-indices that, in the aggregate, comprise the parent index. This approach assumes that investment dollars are allocated to each component consistent with the relative weighting of the corresponding sub-index in the parent index. However, it is possible to alter these weightings to bias issue selection toward those sectors of the market considered attractive. This strategy can be considered "active," in that the manager makes macro level active management decisions, i.e., long sectors versus short, corporates versus governments, etc. Once the decisions are made, however, indexing is used to track performance within desired sectors.

V.   ONGOING MAINTENANCE

Index and sub-index characteristics are constantly changing. One reason is that individual bonds move from sector to sector as their terms to maturity gradually decrease over time. Or an issue may be called, removing it entirely from the master index. A change in credit ratings can change the composite quality of the corporate index. Perhaps most significantly, duration fluctuates constantly with changes in prices and terms to maturity.

Careful use of constraints and parameters in the structuring of an index fund will help to minimize the degree to which the portfolio and the index move out of step. Regardless, there will always be some shifting experienced, such as when new issues are added to the market. To account for this, the portfolio must be analyzed and rebalanced periodically.

The frequency of periodic rebalancing is a judgmental decision. In most cases, either a monthly, quarterly, or even semi-annual rebalancing is adequate. Because of the greater potential for call and sinking fund activity, and the added dimension of possible credit rating changes, the corporate market is more susceptible to the type of structural changes that can affect the performance of an index fund. Therefore a corporate program will generally require more frequent rebalancing than will a Treasury fund.

Aside from maintaining a portfolio that replicates the index, the rebalancing process makes it possible for the fund to remain fully invested in the index. Cash continually flows in and out of a portfolio. Coupon payments are received, new funds may be contributed to the program, or funds may be withdrawn from the program to meet a payment obligation or to be invested in another strategy. As part of the rebalancing process, the linear programming model is given an "invested funds" target to meet. That target is set equal to the current value of the portfolio, plus any coupon payments received since the last rebalancing, plus or minus new contributions/withdrawals from the fund. In this way, cash can be added or withdrawn in the appropriate proportions so as to remain fully invested while the portfolio maintains the overall characteristic structure of the index.

VI. EVALUATING RETURNS

The true measure of performance for an index fund is the accuracy with which it tracks the index. Variance around that standard, whether positive or negative, is referred to as tracking error. In evaluating performance, both the index and the portfolio should be measured on a total return basis. Total return is computed as follows:

$$\text{Total return} = \frac{\substack{\text{Change in} \\ \text{portfolio value}} + \substack{\text{Coupons} \\ \text{received}} + \substack{\text{Income on} \\ \text{reinvested coupons}}}{\text{Portfolio value at beginning of period}} \times 100$$

The above formula provides returns for discreet periods, such as monthly, quarterly, etc. Another formula is used to link a series of discreet period returns:

$$CR = ([(R_1/100 + 1) \times (R_2/100 + 1) \ .\ .\ (R_i/100 + 1)] - 1) \times 100$$

where CR = Cumulative total return

R_i = Individual period return for period i

Once computed, the total return for the portfolio is compared to that of the index to determine the degree to which tracking error, if any, has occurred.

VII.   CONCLUSION

This article has provided a comprehensive review of the techniques and strategies that can be employed in structuring and managing an indexed fixed income portfolio. The review extends beyond the general concepts and principles behind indexing and explores the actual process of implementation.

An indexing approach can be used for managing an entire investment portfolio, but often is used to establish a structured core around which other more active strategies are managed. Since there are numerous sub-indices available, an indexed portfolio is not limited to tracking the entire market but may alternatively isolate one or more segments of the market. Therefore it is possible to tailor the core structure so as to best suit the goals of a particular investment program.

Indexing has long been a popular strategy for managing equity investments. Now, with the advancements made in quantitative analysis, this approach is available for managing fixed income investments as well. Technological advancements alone have not triggered the increasing popularity of fixed income indexing. A more significant factor has been the growing awareness among the investment community that indexing performance is not synonymous with mediocrity. In fact, over an extended investment horizon, an indexing strategy will often outperform the majority of other investment strategies.

ARTICLE 17

MICHAEL R. GRANITO is head of J. P. Morgan
Investment Management, Inc.'s Capital Markets Research
Group that specializes in asset allocation research and new
investment product development. He developed Morgan's
bond immunization product and is the author of a book on
immunization published by Lexington Books in 1984.
Mr. Granito is a member of the fixed income strategy group
and Morgan's investment policy committee. Prior to
joining Morgan in 1979, Mr. Granito taught at the
Wharton School while earning a Ph.D. in finance. He is
also an adjunct professor of finance at New York
University.

THE SECRET OF DURATION AVERAGING

Michael R. Granito
Managing Director
J.P. Morgan Investment Management, Inc.

The notion of averaging is familiar to most investors. Either in stock or bond markets, dollar averaging is thought to be a device that imposes a discipline that forces larger unit purchases at times when prices are depressed—a process that on the surface seems rational if the implied cyclical nature of market levels is true. The purpose of this article is to discuss the investment characteristics of a certain form of averaging in the bond market—duration averaging. Unlike dollar averaging, we do not consider changing the amount of the investment depending on market levels. Instead, we change the duration of our portfolio. Specifically, as yields rise duration is systematically increased, and as rates fall, it is systematically decreased—relative to the neutral level. This notion of averaging is also familiar and intuitively sensible to many investors. We extend these traditional insights by demonstrating that under some simplifying assumptions regarding the behavior of the yield curve, it is possible to derive an exact formula for the performance of this strategy that is simple, highly intuitive and likely to represent an attractive tradeoff for many investors, especially those who would invest in a bond index fund. In particular, the strategy forces the volatility of yield changes to make a significant positive contribution to return, in contrast to the way volatility frequently impacts less disciplined approaches.

Duration averaging may also be studied as a member of class of strategies called Linear Investment Rules (LIRs). These are developed in a previous article.[1] The central feature of these strategies is that asset allocation (in this case duration) is determined by a linear function of an indicator of value (in this case yield). In the general case, if one can make certain assumptions regarding the behavior of the value indicator then it is possible to predict the results of using a Linear Investment Rule. In the present case, these assumptions are automatically made by specifying the behavior of the yield curve. Once these assumptions are established, it is frequently possible to calculate a formula for the performance of the strategy, as we do here for duration averaging.

The advantage of thinking about duration averaging in this way is that its role as a more general investment strategy comes into view. Specifically, we are able to consider circumstances in which some form of duration averaging is an optimal strategy for certain investors. At the same time, examination of the return formula shows that the strategy may be interpreted as a form of portfolio insurance sale. If the sense of the averaging is reversed, so that instead of lengthening we shorten relative to neutral as rates rise, then duration averaging becomes a form of insurance purchase.

We believe these findings to be of theoretical as well as practical interest. The theoretical findings provide new insights into dynamic strategies generally with applications that are not limited to the bond market.[2] As a practical matter, this form of investment

[1] Michael R. Granito, "Investment Rules, Portfolio Insurance and the Implications of Financial Cycles (The Ergodic Hypothesis)," *Journal of Portfolio Management,* Fall 1986.

[2] Averaging has been rigorously examined in other contexts. The theoretical work of Cox and Leland has examined the characteristics of a class of dynamic strategies when certain assumptions regarding the markets are met. (See John C. Cox and Hayne E. Leland, "Dynamic Investment Strategies," paper presented at the American Finance Association Meetings, December 1982.) They find some forms of averaging to be suboptimal in these cases, but do not study this same question when these assumptions are not met. Also see Fischer Black, "Individual Investment and Consumption Strategies Under Uncertainty," Chicago: University of Chicago, Graduate School of Business, Working Paper No. 6C, 1972, for a related analysis.

may be of interest to many investors who wish a disciplined invest-ment strategy with attractive long-run properties as an alternative to a purely passive index. In particular, a passive index has the mathematical characteristic that its duration moves inversely with the level of yields. Following this logic its duration is systematically lowest at yield peaks and highest at yield troughs. Consequently, the index (if thought of as a managed portfolio) is a flawlessly poor market timer. The averaging strategy avoids this index bias.

A full analysis of duration averaging as a Linear Investment Rule is discussed elsewhere.[3] In this article, we confine our atten-tion to the strategy in its more familiar form as an averaging strat-egy in which duration is increased (decreased) relative to a neutral strategy as yields rise (fall). Specifically, we do not consider the portfolio insurance aspects of the strategy. The concept of the strategy and its interpretations are developed in Sections I and II. Section III discusses the results of four empirical studies of the strategy while Section IV provides some practical implications of our analysis.

I. DEVELOPING THE CONCEPT AND RETURN FORMULA

In order to study the duration averaging process, we make the fol-lowing simplifying assumptions. Imagine a world in which the yield curve is flat but has a randomly varying level. This implies that the spot rate curve, or the yield curve for zero coupon bonds, is also flat and is at the same level.[4] The investor is assumed to measure his portfolio relative to an index. We shall take this index to be a zero

---

[3] Michael R. Granito, "Investment Rules, Portfolio Insurance and the Implica-tions of Financial Cycles (The Ergodic Hypothesis)."

[4] It is well known that this yield structure admits arbitrage in a continuous time model with unrestricted trading. Trading is restricted in our model so as to avoid this possibility. We use this framework to develop the duration averag-ing results and not to develop an equilibrium theory of yields. Note that it is not necessary to assume this yield structure to obtain the basic averaging result. For instance, assuming the Vasicek term structure, one can develop a formula analogous to formula (2) in the text (see Oldrich Vasicek, "An Equi-librium Characterization of the Term Structure," *Journal of Financial Eco-nomics,* Fall 1977).

coupon bond, but one whose maturity is constantly reset to some new level so that the index need never mature. The duration of the index is allowed to move in a random but continuous manner. Next, we shall assume that the investor professes no knowledge of short-run movements in the yield curve, but instead is only willing to offer an estimate of what the yield level will tend to average over the very long run.

Based on these assumptions, the simplest and presumably the most inviolable of investment rules is that if any active bets are to be made at all, then it must be the case that portfolio duration should exceed the index duration when the yield level exceeds its long-run expectation. Conversely, portfolio duration should lie below the index duration when yields are below their long-run expectation. Moreover, this broad conclusion should not depend upon the risk preferences or the time horizon of the investor. Our duration averaging rule is the simplest possible mathematical statement of this conclusion. In particular, we assume that portfolio duration equals the index duration plus an amount proportional to the difference between the level of yields and the long-run expectation. That is, at time t,

$$\text{Portfolio Duration} = \text{Index Duration} + A \times [Y(t) - Y^*] \text{ or}$$

$$D_P(t) = D_I(t) + A \times [Y(t) - Y^*] \tag{1}$$

where $D_P(t)$ and $D_I(t)$ are the portfolio and index durations at time t, A is a constant proportionality factor selected by the investor, $Y(t)$ is the level of the yield curve at time t and Y^* is the forecast of the long-run average yield.

Examining formula (1), we see that the implied portfolio management rule is simple and disciplined: increase (decrease) portfolio duration relative to that of the index whenever yields are above (below) long-run expectation; and make the bet size directly proportional to the difference between yield and its long-run expectation. Moreover, this strategy does not depend upon the length of the investor's horizon.

The important insight associated with this investment rule is that under the assumptions of the investment model we have proposed, there is an exact formula that specifies the return of the managed portfolio relative to that of the index. In particular, if this rule is employed for T years (where T is arbitrary), then the continuously compounded total return on the portfolio (R_P) will equal

$$R_p = R_I + \frac{A}{T} \left\{ \left[Y^* - \frac{[Y(T) + Y(0)]}{2} \right] \times [Y(T) - Y(0)] \right\} + \frac{A}{2} VAR(dY) \quad (2)$$

where R_I is the continuously compounded return on the index, $Y(0)$ and $Y(T)$ are the yield on the index at the start and at the end of the period respectively, and $VAR(dY)$ is the average variance of yield changes over the period. In the balance of this section, we explain the terms in the formula, and in the following section interpret its meaning with examples.

Formula (2) decomposes relative return into two components. The first component is the product of several terms. The most important is

$$Y^* - \frac{[Y(T) + Y(0)]}{2}$$

which can be interpreted as the "ERROR" in forecasting the average (where average is defined by the simple average of the beginning and ending yields). ERROR is multiplied by the difference $Y(T) - Y(0)$ or the change in yields from beginning to end of period. Thus, even if the ERROR is nonzero, its contribution is zero if yields end where they begin. Finally, the product of these two are multiplied by A/T. This is a critical insight. Clearly the presence of A is intuitive since if $A = 0$ then the portfolio duration is identical to that of the index so that the relative return should be zero. Division by T is more subtle. This means that, holding the magnitude of ERROR $\times [Y(T) - Y(0)]$ constant, the impact of this entire term is amortized to zero as T becomes large. Intuitively this is saying that a 100 basis point ERROR over one year is just 10 basis points per year over 10 years. *Hence, if it is reasonable to believe that ERROR $\times [Y(T) - Y(0)]$ is bounded by the tendency of yields to fluctuate in normal range, then maintaining the strategy for a long enough period must cause the entire first component to approach zero. That is, total relative performance over the long-run is then independent of the yield forecast or its accuracy.*

Turning to the second component of relative return, we simply have $A \times VAR(dY)/2$, or A times one half the average variance of yield changes over the period. The presence of A is again intuitive since if A = O then this component of relative return must equal zero also. The term VAR(dY)/2, which can only be positive, captures the beneficial logic of the averaging strategy. Namely, even if the forecast is "incorrect," the process of systematically lengthening the portfolio as rates rise and shortening as rates fall imparts a favorable bias to returns. Notice that this term is *not* divided by T so that the benefit is not amortized away, but instead, converges to the long-run average of the variance of yield changes. This term is quite significant. For realistic values of A and the variance of yield changes, it can amount to 1 to 2 percent per year.

II. INTERPRETING THE FORMULA AND EXAMPLES OF USE

Interpreting the Formula

The duration rule given by formula (1) dictates that the difference between portfolio duration and index duration be

$$A \times [Y(t) - Y^*] \tag{3a}$$

or

$$AY(t) - AY^* \tag{3b}$$

where A is a constant selected by the investor to reflect how aggressively the strategy is to be pursued. Examining (3b) it is apparent that the forecast, Y^*, affects relative duration by the constant amount $-AY^*$, independent of changes in rates. Conversely, the effect on duration due to the averaging process is measured by the term $AY(t)$, which is independent of the forecast. This suggests that the relative return can be decomposed into the sum of independent terms—one due to the forecast and one due to the averaging process. Formula (2) is precisely this decomposition. The ERROR term discussed in Section I picks up the impact of the forecast, while the VAR term picks up the averaging process. Insofar as the forecast affects duration by a constant amount, the ERROR term can either help or hurt performance. Other things being equal, a lower forecast (and hence a higher duration) will help if rates fall and hurt if rates rise over the period. Conversely, a higher forecast (and hence a lower duration) will help if rates rise and hurt if rates fall. Given a flat yield curve (by assumption) if rates end up where they began, then the forecast will have no effect at all. That is, having adjusted duration by the amount − AY* will not have an impact on relative return at all in this case. The first term in the return formula merely summarizes all of these effects. To understand the VAR term intuitively the strategy can only contribute to performance if yields change. That is, lengthening into rate increases and shortening into declines is what generates performance due to the averaging process. Hence, the more volatile rates are, the more opportunity to add value.

Illustration

To help illustrate the performance of the strategy, we have compiled two numerical examples. In both examples, the initial yield level is assumed to be 10 percent and the investment period is one year with quarterly rebalancing intervals. At the start of each quarter, the index is assumed to be a 5-year zero coupon bond. Since at the end of a quarter the duration of this index is 4.75 years, the index is then redefined to be the current 5-year zero at the start of the next quarter. Thus, the index amounts to a constant maturity 5-year zero with quarterly reset.

In Example 1 we assume that the forecast, Y*, is 11 percent or 100 basis points above the current level, while in Example 2 we assume that the forecast is 9 percent or 100 basis points below the current level. In Example 1 we assume that over the year rates drop to 9 percent and in Example 2 rates rise to 11 percent. That is, in each example we incorrectly forecast the direction of change by 200 basis points. Within *each* example, we assume that rates arrive at these ending points by two possible routes—rates first rise, then fall to the ending level (Scenario 1), or rates first fall then rise to the ending level (Scenario 2). For instance, in Example 1 rates start at 10 percent and either rise before dropping to 9 percent or fall below 9 percent before rising to 9 percent. In both examples we use formula (1) as the method of setting portfolio duration. Thus, at the start of each quarter,

$$\text{Portfolio Duration} = 5 + A \times [Y(t) - Y^*]$$

We arbitrarily pick A = 100 to reflect the degree of aggressiveness in pursuing the strategy.[5] In Example 1, Y* = 11 percent and in Example 2, Y* = 9 percent. We assume that the portfolio we actually select is a zero coupon bond with the maturity given by the formula, just as the index is a zero coupon bond with duration of five years.

In Exhibit 1, we depict the quarterly yields, durations and returns of the managed portfolio versus the index, along with total returns. Within each example we have both yield scenarios: rising then falling, and falling then rising. In Example 1, rates were forecast to rise but they fell. This reduced performance by an amount conceptually equal to the change in rates times the amount of duration that the forecast error caused us to be short. But rates were also volatile. Consequently, we underperformed the index in Scenario 2 as rates fell below 9 percent, but the formula then caused us to be short enough so that when rates rebounded to 9 percent we substantially outperformed. Overall, we outperformed, even though we were wrong on our forecast by 200 basis points over one year! In Scenario 1, we outperformed as rates rose (as well as when they began to decline), but underperformed as rates fell below 11 percent. Overall, however, we still outperformed.

Example 2 shows a similar pattern. When rates fall in Scenario 2, we substantially outperform so that even though we lose ground when rates rebound, we still outperform. Conversely in Scenario 1, when rates rise we underperform but because this causes our duration to lengthen, we make it back when rates drop, so that we still outperform for the year.

It is clear that the forecast error hurt performance because it biased duration in the wrong direction given the actual change in rates. If we had erred in the opposite duration, it would have helped. Hence, an error is not always a negative. It is also clear that volatility contributed to positive relative performance regardless of the scenario or example. When the forecasts are wrong, outperformance

[5] Realistic values for A range from 50 to 300. A value of A is based on the investor's judgment regarding the desired degree of aggressiveness. A value of 100 simply corresponds to a duration one year longer than the index for every percentage point the yield level exceeds the expected average. Selection of A is analogous to the selection of beta in the capital asset pricing model. In particular, an analogous risk/return tradeoff can be developed.

EXHIBIT 1
Managed Portfolio vs. Index

Example 1: Duration Averaging When Yields Are Expected to Rise But Decline Instead

$$D_p = 5 + 100 \times [Y(t) - .11]$$

	Scenario 1						Scenario 2					
	Yield		Duration		Return		Yield		Duration		Return	
Quarter	Beginning of Period	End of Period	Index	Portfolio	Index	Portfolio	Beginning of Period	End of Period	Index	Portfolio	Index	Portfolio
1	10%	11%	5 yrs.	4 yrs.	-1.90%	-1.01%	10%	8.5%	5 yrs.	4 yrs.	9.31%	7.82%
2	11	12	5	5	-1.64	-1.64	8.5	7	5	2.5	9.04	5.31
3	12	10.5	5	6	9.68	11.17	7	8	5	1	-2.70	1.00
4	10.5	9	5	4.5	9.40	8.66	8	9	5	2	-2.42	0.31
Total					15.79	17.62					13.17	15.04

Example 2: Duration Averaging When Yields Are Expected to Fall But Rise Instead

$$D_p = 5 + 100 \times [Y(t) - .09]$$

	Scenario 1						Scenario 2					
	Yield		Duration		Return		Yield		Duration		Return	
Quarter	Beginning of Period	End of Period	Index	Portfolio	Index	Portfolio	Beginning of Period	End of Period	Index	Portfolio	Index	Portfolio
1	10%	11.5%	5 yrs.	6 yrs.	-3.97%	-5.26%	10%	9%	5 yrs.	6 yrs.	6.95%	7.93%
2	11.5	13	5	7.5	-3.56	-6.73	9	8	5	5	6.75	6.75
3	13	12	5	9	7.55	11.44	8	9.5	5	4	-4.52	-3.20
4	12	11	5	8	7.35	10.28	9.5	11	5	5.5	-4.11	-4.76
Total					6.92	8.59					4.53	6.23

often emerged from rates overshooting their ultimate level leading to an extreme relative gain on the rebound. It is evident, therefore, that too small a volatility relative to the ERROR would not lead to overall outperformance. For instance, if rates simply declined smoothly in Example 1 or rose smoothly in Example 2 we would have underperformed. This result is predicted by the relative return formula (2). If VAR is not large enough relative to ERROR $\times$ [Y(t) − Y(0)], we will underperform the index.

The return formula and examples help illustrate that duration averaging is a disciplined process that is quantifiable and produces results that agree with intuition regarding why the strategy should work. It makes use of a long-term view of the market and does not attempt short-run forecasts, which many view as impossible. The ability to decompose returns into independent components contributes to our understanding of the philosophy for using the strategy. In particular, its ability to make market variance work in a favorable way contrasts with the more frequent negative impact of volatility on return. These factors may make the strategy interesting to many investors. The major question, however, is to what extent would a practical implementation of the strategy beat simpler indices? Stated differently, how sensitive are results to forecast errors versus realized market variance; and if errors are amortized over time, how long must we run the strategy to be confident of outperformance? These are empirical questions that we explore in detail in the next section.

III. PERFORMANCE TESTS OF THE TRADING STRATEGY

As outlined above, duration averaging may be attractive to many investors. In large part this results from the accurate intuition that the contributions to performance made by the forecast and yield variance, respectively, are separate and distinct. However, the theory does not answer the important practical questions: (1) how "accurate" must the forecast be in order to be assured that the variance term will imply outperformance of the index; (2) knowing that forecast error is amortized to zero, how long must we run the strategy to be assured that the variance term (which is not amortized) will dominate; and (3) how would the strategy perform in actual markets that differ from the theoretical model from which we developed the theory. In this section, we discuss four empirical studies that have been undertaken to answer these questions—three historical and one using simulated data. Because of space considerations, we will present results of only two of these studies. The other two, one historical and one simulation, will be summarized. All four strategies cast support for duration averaging as a practical tool.

The First Historical Study

The purpose of this study is to document the basic performance of the duration averaging rule compared with a major market index over a relevant historical period. We wish to avoid the problems associated with using individual security data in making the duration adjustments required by the strategy so that the relative performance due to the strategy is not confused with the effects of individual security pricing, selection, and transaction costs. Consequently, we assume that all duration adjustments required by the strategy are made in the bond futures market.[6] For this purpose we use actual prices for the Treasury bond futures contract (and theoretically constructed futures prices for comparison). This instrument began trading in the fall of 1977 and, hence, our study is limited to the period from 11/77 through 12/84. While a longer history is generally desirable, this entails (as we have indicated) the use of individual security data or sole use of theoretical futures data, both of which are used in the third historical study that is summarized later. Nonetheless the period 1977 through 1984 is of interest to many investors and is representative in several respects.

To compare the strategy to a major market index, we chose the U.S. Treasury bond index consisting of securities with maturities in excess of 15 years. We employ this index because of its interest to many investors as an important benchmark of market performance, but also because, in contrast to corporate indices, detailed histori-

---

[6] Implementing the strategy using the futures market does not imply that relative performance will be exactly as if we used the theoretical zero coupon bonds assumed by the model. This point is further developed later on.

cal yield, duration and return data could be reliably complied.[7] Specifically, we used monthly total return data based on a market-capitalization-weighted index of the bonds in the universe. Index duration data were also capitalization-weighted averages of month-end security durations. The index yield was defined as the capitalization and duration-weighted average of the yields of the securities in the universe.[8] We also used month-end futures prices and durations. While more elaborate methods could be used, the futures duration was defined as simply that Macaulay duration associated with a 20-year, 8 percent bond with price equal to the actual futures price.

The basis of the study is a comparison of holding-period returns of the index versus the duration-averaging strategy over a range of interest rate forecasting accuracies. We construct overlapping one, two, three, four and five year holding periods covering the period 11/30/77 through 12/31/84. The number of holding period returns corresponding to these horizons are 74, 62, 50, 38, and 26, respectively. In the interest of simplicity, we use an aggressiveness factor (A) of 100 throughout. This corresponds to a duration one year in excess of (lower than) the index duration if yields exceed (lie below) their long-run expectation by one percent. We also tested a range of interest rate forecasting accuracies ranging from very good to very bad. Specifically, we defined the yield forecast, Y^*, to be the realized average yield during the period plus a value ranging from -2 percent to $+2$ percent in increments of 0.5 percent. For instance, in the four-year horizon case, we have 38 holding periods within the 11/77–12/84 period, with nine interest rate forecast accuracies each, for a total of 342 (9×38) trials. An error of up to 2 percent in forecasting the average yield is significant, allowing for a much larger implied error in forecasting the end-of-period yield.[9]

---

[7] We did not employ the total government index since the substantial Federal deficits over this period caused patterns of debt issuance that produced significant changes in the yield and duration of that index. This factor, not as significant for the long bond index, would bias performance measurement of the duration averaging strategy since we would have yield changes that were not associated with returns.

[8] This yield measure is theoretically superior to a capitalization weighted yield for our present purposes.

[9] We could also define the error relative to the end-of-period yield but in this case chose the average to be consistent with the return formula as well as with the

EXHIBIT 2
Group One Results—Assuming a "Complete" Zero Coupon Market

Horizon	Forecast Error of Average Yield (in basis points)								
(yrs.)	−200	−150	−100	−50	0	5	100	150	200
Panel 1: Frequency of Outperformance (%)									
1	46	54	62	70	95	96	88	86	85
2	63	66	79	92	95	97	98	97	92
3	66	74	76	88	98	100	100	100	100
4	76	84	100	100	100	100	100	100	100
5	100	100	100	100	100	100	100	100	100
Panel 2: Mean Return Differences (%)									
1	0.44	0.76	1.10	1.44	1.79	2.15	2.52	2.90	3.29
2	0.71	1.02	1.34	1.66	1.99	2.32	2.66	3.00	3.35
3	0.86	1.20	1.53	1.87	2.21	2.55	2.90	3.25	3.60
4	1.22	1.57	1.91	2.26	2.61	2.96	3.32	3.67	4.03
5	1.52	1.85	2.18	2.50	2.83	3.16	3.49	3.82	4.15
Panel 3: Mean/Standard Deviation Ratio									
1	0.11	0.23	0.44	0.79	1.17	1.22	1.06	0.92	0.82
2	0.25	0.45	0.76	1.26	1.78	1.84	1.59	1.36	1.20
3	0.36	0.60	0.94	1.42	1.95	2.26	2.21	2.00	1.80
4	0.97	1.47	2.15	3.03	3.94	4.47	4.45	4.12	3.75
5	4.71	7.44	11.72	16.54	17.10	14.37	11.91	10.19	9.01

We report results in three exhibits with three panels each. The results reported in Exhibits 2 and 3 concern tests that use varying degrees of theoretical (or hypothetical) data. We compare these findings to the results shown in Exhibit 4 which employs only actual price and return data.

Exhibit 2 reports on the performance of the averaging strategy where we ask the simple question: if the yield curve actually was flat, with a randomly varying level given by the yield on the index,

---

seemingly more appealing concept of forecasting the long-run mean rather than its ending value. In the other studies, we define the forecast relative to the ending value.

EXHIBIT 3
Group Two Results—Employing Actual Index Return Data and Assuming an "Ideal" Futures Market

Horizon	Forecast Error of Average Yield (in basis points)								
(yrs.)	−200	−150	−100	−50	0	5	100	150	200
	Panel 1: Frequency of Outperformance (%)								
1	41	51	61	70	92	96	88	86	85
2	56	63	73	90	95	97	98	97	90
3	64	70	76	84	98	100	100	100	100
4	76	79	92	100	100	100	100	100	100
5	100	100	100	100	100	100	100	100	100
	Panel 2: Mean Return Differences (%)								
1	0.09	0.47	0.83	1.18	1.53	1.86	2.18	2.50	2.80
2	0.31	0.67	1.02	1.35	1.68	2.00	2.31	2.60	2.89
3	0.44	0.81	1.17	1.52	1.85	2.18	2.50	2.81	3.11
4	0.76	1.14	1.50	1.86	2.20	2.54	2.86	3.17	3.48
5	1.05	1.40	1.74	2.07	2.40	2.71	3.02	3.31	3.60
	Panel 3: Mean/Standard Deviation Ratio								
1	0.03	0.17	0.39	0.75	1.17	1.23	1.07	0.92	0.81
2	0.12	0.33	0.66	1.18	1.75	1.85	1.60	1.37	1.20
3	0.21	0.46	0.81	1.31	1.89	2.25	2.22	2.01	1.80
4	0.67	1.18	1.88	2.80	3.78	4.41	4.43	4.10	3.71
5	3.72	6.45	10.68	15.41	16.33	14.14	11.94	10.34	9.19

and if we could actually trade zero coupon bonds at these yields, then how would the strategy have performed over the 1977–1984 period? That is, we essentially assume the existence of a complete market in zero coupon bonds with yields given by the level of the yield on the index over this period, and we calculate the performance of this strategy as if we could trade at these yields, and as if the index return was a zero coupon bond return whose maturity equaled the duration of the true index. The purpose of this test is simply to illustrate how the strategy would have performed over this period under ideal conditions.

EXHIBIT 4
Group Three Results—Employing Actual Price and Return Data

Horizon	Forecast Error of Average Yield (in basis points)								
(yrs.)	−200	−150	−100	−50	0	5	100	150	200
Panel 1: Frequency of Outperformance (%)									
1	38	58	62	72	92	95	89	85	84
2	47	60	71	90	95	95	97	87	79
3	58	66	76	80	94	100	100	100	94
4	68	76	82	96	100	100	100	100	100
5	92	100	100	100	100	100	100	100	100
Panel 2: Mean Return Differences (%)									
1	−0.08	0.33	0.72	1.11	1.49	1.86	2.21	2.56	2.89
2	−0.09	0.33	0.73	1.13	1.52	1.89	2.26	2.61	2.96
3	−0.18	0.28	0.72	1.15	1.57	1.98	2.38	2.77	3.14
4	0.11	0.57	1.02	1.46	1.89	2.31	2.71	3.11	3.50
5	0.54	0.96	1.37	1.77	2.16	2.54	2.90	3.26	3.61
Panel 3: Mean/Standard Deviation Ratio									
1	−0.02	0.12	0.35	0.73	1.12	1.12	0.97	0.85	0.76
2	−0.04	0.17	0.51	1.10	1.62	1.54	1.32	1.15	1.03
3	−0.08	0.16	0.51	1.04	1.60	1.85	1.78	1.63	1.49
4	0.09	0.55	1.19	2.05	2.94	3.47	3.52	3.32	3.09
5	1.44	3.11	5.47	8.39	10.66	11.09	10.36	9.41	8.58

Exhibit 3 reports the performance of the averaging strategy where we assume that the index return is that of the true index of coupon bonds, but all duration adjustments required by the strategy are made in an "ideal" futures market. This "ideal" market would reflect a flat yield curve with no bias due to the characteristics of individual deliverable securities or pricing anomalies. For this purpose the futures price is simply taken to be the price of an 8 percent, 20-year bond with yield equal to the yield on the index. The purpose of this test is to see how the strategy performs under the assumption that we do not trade in zero coupon bonds (as the theory assumes) but instead we trade in the actual index with duration adjustments made using an "ideal" futures market that assumes a flat yield curve. This adjustment method differs from the pure theory but is an interesting one in practice.[10] We wish to distinguish however between an "ideal" futures market and the actual market that reflects other assumptions.

Exhibit 4 reports performance of the averaging strategy using actual index and futures data. These results represent a level of performance that almost any investor could have achieved relative to the index. We compare these results to the findings using theoretical data (used in Exhibits 2 and 3) in order to understand how much of any discrepancy is due to the theory itself versus our use of the actual futures market that often contained pricing anomalies and yield curve shape effects over this period. Thus the results in Exhibit 2 (which assume a hypothetical zero coupon market) illustrate what a perfect implementation of this strategy would have done in the 1977–1984 interest rate environment. Exhibit 3 results use actual index return data but assume an "ideal" futures market. This is still an important distinction from the results in Exhibit 2 since using any futures (ideal or not) will not perfectly replicate the mathematical characteristics of the zero coupon bonds that were assumed by the theory. The results in Exhibit 4 can be compared with those in Exhibit 3 to see the effect of using actual futures prices. Thus any differences relate not to the theory but to differences between the actual and our "ideal" futures market.

In each exhibit, panel 1 shows for each horizon and each interest rate forecasting accuracy the percentage frequency with which the strategy outperformed the index. Panel 2 shows the corresponding compound mean return differences of the strategy minus the index. Panel 3 shows the corresponding ratio of mean return difference to the standard deviation of the difference. A higher ratio implies greater certainty in achieving a positive relative return.

Exhibit 2 casts strong support for the basic theory. The frequency of outperformance systematically rises as the horizon is lengthened. Mean return differences in panel 1 are significantly positive and both the mean difference and the ratio of mean to

---

[10] In particular, the second derivative of portfolio value with respect to yield will be different than if true zeros are used.

standard deviation (shown in panels 2 and 3) rise as the horizon lengthens. Exhibit 3 illustrates a similar qualitative and quantitative pattern. Mean returns are slightly less due in part to the theoretical difference between the duration adjustment using zero coupon bonds and using futures. Overall, the strategy appears to reliably outperform the index as the horizon lengthens. The findings in Exhibit 4 are broadly similar although generally not as strong. This is particularly true in the case of the minus 200 basis-point forecast. As we have indicated, differences with the results in Exhibit 3 are due to the difference between the actual and "ideal" futures prices. While the average of the "ideal" prices was close to the actual average (the average monthly price difference was only $4.82 for a $100,000.00 face value contract) the difference over this period was correlated with the shape, level and variance of the yield curve in a way that reduced performance. In particular, as rates decline short rates tend to decline more and the variance of yield changes tends to decline. The increased spread between long and short rates causes actual futures prices to rise relatively less than otherwise. This effect is most severe when we underforecast rates. In this case, duration tends to be larger on average and we are long more futures. In fact, the effect can be a benefit when we overforecast. Alternative procedures could be used to mitigate these effects, such as using Treasury bill futures contracts or combinations of bond futures (spreads) to hedge the impact of yield curve shape changes on the spread between the bond futures yield and the index yield.

Notwithstanding the fact that the strategy produced a relatively weaker result in the minus 200 basis point case using actual futures data, a significant outperformance still emerged (92 percent frequency of outperformance) with a long enough holding period. Moreover, this was true using the simple investment media prescribed here rather than some more complex hedging method. Over the long run, total relative performance still appears to tend toward a positive level under real-world conditions. In theory this level is not closely related to the forecast error, but is instead related to the realized average variance of yield changes.

In order to gain further insight into the performance of the strategy, it is useful to examine the accuracy of the relative return formula (2) for predicting return. To study this question, we regressed (without a constant) returns from data employed in Exhibits 3 and 4 on their theoretical determinants as expressed in formula (2).[11] It should be stressed that the usual tests of significance are not accurate in the regressions because the sample consists of returns from overlapping periods. Nonetheless, we report the normal statistics— coefficients, t-statistics and R-squareds. Because of space considerations, Exhibit 5 reports these regression results for returns using data employed in Exhibit 3 for only the one, three and five year horizons and the −200 basis point, 0 basis point and +200 basis point forecast errors. Exhibit 6 reports the corresponding data from employing actual data.

In forming these regressions we defined variables 1 and 2 as the corresponding two calculations in formula (2). Hence the theoretically expected coefficient is one in every case. Predictably, results in Exhibit 5 appear better than the results in Exhibit 6. A more surprising observation, however, is that the estimated coefficients are normally fairly close to their predicted values (especially in Exhibit 5) and explain a large percentage of the variance in return even though the actual shape of the yield curve differed markedly over this period from the theoretical model of a flat curve. That is, the model's explanatory power is fairly robust regardless of the horizon or rate forecast error.[12]

The Second Historical Study

Here we report the results of historical performance tests of duration averaging versus the index most frequently employed by market practitioners—the Shearson Lehman Government/Corporate Index. The basic analysis compares holding-period returns on the

---

[11] For this purpose, we defined the ERROR term exactly as in formula (2) and the variance term as the annualized variance of monthly yield changes times A/2.

[12] The lowest R-squared, 49 percent, took place for the 5 year horizon in the −200 basis points case, even though the frequency of outperformance was much higher here than for shorter horizons. This is due to the phenomenon mentioned earlier relating to the performance of the actual futures market when short rates decline substantially relative to long rates—a problem exacerbated by the longer duration (or larger contract holdings) implied by an interest rate underforecast.

EXHIBIT 5
Regression Results Employing Actual Index Return Data and Assuming an "Ideal" Futures Market*

Forecast Error	Variable 1	Variable 2	R-Squared
	One-year Horizon		
− 200 bp	0.930	0.791	.998
	(203.38)	(88.24)	
0 bp	0.854	0.900	.989
	(45.47)	(111.07)	
+ 200 bp	0.937	0.914	.998
	(168.84)	(88.79)	
	Three-year Horizon		
− 200 bp	0.935	0.791	.999
	(339.43)	(240.13)	
0 bp	0.914	0.900	.998
	(103.14)	(270.26)	
+ 200 bp	0.975	0.899	.999
	(229.25)	(202.30)	
	Five-year Horizon		
− 200 bp	0.853	0.756	.969
	(27.30)	(79.29)	
0 bp	0.842	0.925	.973
	(30.92)	(91.77)	
+ 200 bp	0.967	0.898	.999
	(481.45)	(447.71)	

* Numbers in parentheses are t-statistics

index to holding-period returns using duration averaging. To employ the averaging strategy, it is again assumed that we own the index and execute duration adjustments using the Treasury bond futures market. This approach is illustrative because it does not confuse the impact of the strategy with the impact of individual security selection that has attendant problems of transaction costs, pricing sources, etc.

EXHIBIT 6
Regression Results Employing Actual Price and Return Data*

Forecast Error	Variable 1	Variable 2	R-Squared
	One-year Horizon		
– 200 bp	0.930	0.619	.963
	(42.42)	(14.40)	
0 bp	0.865	0.883	.957
	(22.73)	(53.82)	
+ 200 bp	0.978	1.021	.974
	(46.62)	(26.26)	
	Three-year Horizon		
– 200 bp	0.977	0.494	.988
	(64.55)	(27.29)	
0 bp	0.932	0.759	.947
	(21.75)	(47.16)	
+ 200 bp	1.164	0.810	.979
	(46.64)	(29.06)	
	Five-year Horizon		
– 200 bp	0.732	0.474	.493
	(4.31)	(9.14)	
0 bp	0.453	0.945	.750
	(3.93)	(22.16)	
+ 200 bp	1.044	0.827	.989
	(48.46)	(38.43)	

* Numbers in parentheses are t-statistics

The data we report illustrate relative performance over the 11/77 through 6/85 period assuming seven different horizon lengths, assuming nine degrees of long-term-average rate forecasting accuracy, and assuming two degrees of aggressiveness in executing the strategy. Specifically, we examined holding-period lengths of one through seven years. In each case, we computed returns over all possible (overlapping) horizons within the 11/77–6/85 period. There were 80 one-year periods; 68 two-year periods; 56 three-year periods; 44 four-year periods; 32 five-year periods; 20 six-year periods; and eight seven-year periods. For each horizon (and for each starting period) we tested performance assuming a forecast error (in forecasting the average interest rate to occur over the period) ranging from minus 200 basis points to plus 200 basis points in increments of 50 basis points. It should be noted that a 200 basis-point error in forecasting the average yield corresponds to a much larger error in forecasting the end-of-period yield. Finally, we tested two values of the aggressiveness parameter A—A equal to 100 or 200. This corresponds to setting duration equal to one or two years longer than the index duration if rates are one percent above their long-run expectation.

Exhibits 7 and 8 report the basic performance tests. Panels 1–5 in Exhibit 7 show various statistics of the difference between the strategy return and the index return for A = 100. Panels 1–5 in Exhibit 8 show corresponding data for A = 200. Each panel shows results for the full range of assumptions on horizon and forecast accuracy. Panel 1 shows the frequency that the strategy outperformed the index as a percentage of the total number of cases in each cell. For example, in Exhibit 7 for A = 100, a horizon of five years and a forecast error of −200 basis points, there are 32 overlapping periods in the sample. The data in the corresponding cell in panel 1 of Exhibit 7 would be the number of times that the strategy outperformed the index as a percent of 32. Panel 2 shows the mean return difference. Using the same example, this would be the average of the 32 differences of the five year strategy performance minus the five year index performance. Panel 3 shows the ratio of the return difference to the standard deviation of the return difference. In the example, this would be the corresponding number in panel 2 divided by the standard deviation of the 32 five year return differences. Panel 4 shows the worst relative performance. In the example, this would be the worst difference in the 32, or the lowest value of the strategy return minus the index return. Panel 5 shows the difference in the standard deviation of return (as opposed to the standard deviation of the difference). In the example, this would be the standard deviation of the 32 strategy returns minus the standard deviation of the 32 index returns.

These data broadly support duration averaging as an alternative to indexation. Even for poor forecasting accuracy, the frequency of outperformance is fairly high for short horizons and converges to

EXHIBIT 7
Strategy Return vs. Index for A = 100

Horizon	Forecast Error of Average Yield (in basis points)								
(yrs.)	−200	−150	−100	−50	0	5	100	150	200
	Panel 1: Frequency of Outperformance (%)								
1	54	61	68	79	91	95	88	84	80
2	60	76	88	93	93	90	91	90	79
3	70	75	80	93	98	100	100	100	93
4	75	82	93	100	100	100	95	95	95
5	100	100	100	100	100	100	100	100	100
6	95	100	100	100	100	100	100	100	100
7	100	100	100	100	100	100	100	100	100
	Panel 2: Mean Return Difference (%)								
1	0.95	1.21	1.46	1.70	1.93	2.15	2.36	2.57	2.76
2	0.69	1.01	1.32	1.63	1.92	2.20	2.48	2.74	2.99
3	0.78	1.08	1.38	1.66	1.93	2.19	2.44	2.69	2.92
4	0.72	1.04	1.36	1.66	1.95	2.23	2.50	2.76	3.01
5	1.03	1.33	1.62	1.91	2.18	2.44	2.69	2.93	3.17
6	0.90	1.21	1.52	1.82	2.11	2.39	2.67	2.93	3.18
7	1.11	1.35	1.57	1.79	2.00	2.20	2.39	2.57	2.75
	Panel 3: Mean/Standard Deviation Ratio								
1	0.24	0.38	0.59	0.87	1.09	1.05	0.90	0.77	0.67
2	0.28	0.53	0.90	1.33	1.51	1.39	1.21	1.07	0.96
3	0.33	0.57	0.93	1.41	1.81	1.82	1.60	1.38	1.21
4	0.61	1.12	1.82	2.51	2.68	2.44	2.16	1.92	1.74
5	2.46	4.31	6.26	6.33	5.35	4.51	3.92	3.50	3.19
6	1.71	2.82	4.46	7.04	10.96	14.48	13.72	11.16	9.14
7	10.89	26.14	52.28	24.60	15.82	12.11	10.07	8.76	7.84
	Panel 4: Worst Relative Return (%)								
1	−7.83	−6.18	−4.53	−2.90	−1.28	−1.97	−3.25	−4.55	−5.85
2	−5.53	−4.53	−3.54	−2.55	−1.57	−1.12	−1.79	−2.48	−3.18
3	−4.67	−3.50	−2.33	−1.18	−0.03	0.75	0.68	0.03	−0.62
4	−2.01	−1.21	−0.41	0.38	0.71	0.34	−0.05	−0.43	−0.88
5	0.40	0.92	1.12	1.11	1.09	1.06	1.02	0.97	0.91
6	−0.06	0.42	0.89	1.35	1.80	2.13	2.22	2.29	2.36
7	0.98	1.26	1.54	1.67	1.79	1.90	2.00	2.09	2.17

EXHIBIT 7 *(Continued)*

Horizon (yrs.)	Forecast Error of Average Yield (in basis points)								
	−200	−150	−100	−50	0	5	100	150	200
Panel 5: Standard Deviation Difference (%)									
1	3.61	2.76	1.91	1.07	0.25	−0.56	−1.35	−2.12	−2.84
2	2.15	1.57	1.00	0.43	−0.13	−0.68	−1.21	−1.72	−2.21
3	2.16	1.65	1.14	0.64	0.15	−0.34	−0.83	−1.30	−1.75
4	1.08	0.77	0.46	−0.15	−0.15	−0.46	−0.75	−1.05	−1.33
5	0.37	0.21	0.06	−0.09	−0.24	−0.38	−0.53	−0.67	−0.80
6	0.50	0.41	0.31	0.21	0.12	0.02	−0.08	−0.17	−0.27
7	0.10	0.04	−0.01	−0.07	−0.12	−0.18	−0.23	−0.29	−0.35

one as the horizon lengthens (panel 1 of Exhibits 7 and 8). The mean return difference is significantly positive in every case (even for short horizons) with evidence of the expected tendency to become more stable across forecast accuracies as the horizon lengthens (panel 2). The ratio of mean return difference to the standard deviation of return difference rises dramatically confirming a sharp increase in the likelihood of outperformance as the horizon lengthens (panel 3). The worst case relative performance also confirms the rising probability of outperformance as it systematically rises from a negative to a positive number as the horizon lengthens (panel 4). The difference in the standard deviation of total performance is positive when rates are underestimated and negative when they are overestimated. This is because underestimates lead to higher duration portfolios (based on the duration control formula (1)) and overestimates lead to lower duration portfolios. But as the horizon lengthens this difference converges to zero regardless of forecasting accuracy. This is because, from formula (2), the variable term relating to the forecast is amortized to zero leaving only the more stable variance term. Thus over the long run, the strategy and the index have equal volatility (panel 5).

Finally, in comparing Exhibit 7 with Exhibit 8, the differences are exactly those predicted by formula (2). Specifically, the probabili-

EXHIBIT 8
Strategy Return vs. Index for A = 200

Horizon (yrs.)	Forecast Error of Average Yield (in basis points)								
	−200	−150	−100	−50	0	5	100	150	200
Panel 1: Frequency of Outperformance (%)									
1	53	61	68	79	91	95	88	84	80
2	59	75	88	93	91	90	90	90	78
3	66	73	80	89	98	100	100	98	93
4	75	82	89	100	100	100	95	95	93
5	100	100	100	100	100	100	100	100	100
6	90	100	100	100	100	100	100	100	100
7	100	100	100	100	100	100	100	100	100
Panel 2: Mean Return Difference (%)									
1	1.68	2.27	2.82	3.34	3.82	4.26	4.67	5.04	5.38
2	1.09	1.81	2.49	3.14	3.75	4.33	4.86	5.36	5.82
3	1.23	1.91	2.56	3.17	3.74	4.28	4.78	5.24	5.66
4	1.06	1.79	2.49	3.14	3.76	4.34	4.88	5.38	5.84
5	1.69	2.38	3.03	3.64	4.22	4.76	5.27	5.73	6.16
6	1.42	2.15	2.83	3.48	4.10	4.68	5.22	5.73	6.21
7	1.86	2.41	2.93	3.42	3.88	4.30	4.69	5.05	5.37
Panel 3: Mean/Standard Deviation Ratio									
1	0.21	0.36	0.58	0.87	1.09	1.05	0.90	0.76	0.65
2	0.22	0.47	0.85	1.29	1.49	1.38	1.20	1.05	0.93
3	0.26	0.50	0.85	1.34	1.77	1.79	1.58	1.35	1.18
4	0.44	0.93	1.64	2.36	2.60	2.40	2.12	1.88	1.69
5	1.93	3.68	5.68	6.06	5.24	4.44	3.86	3.44	3.11
6	1.33	2.43	4.03	6.54	10.39	14.01	13.35	10.77	8.74
7	8.71	22.01	53.16	24.53	15.56	11.85	9.82	8.49	7.54
Panel 4: Worst Relative Return (%)									
1	− 15.95	−12.54	− 9.18	− 5.87	− 2.60	− 3.97	− 6.56	− 9.19	−11.91
2	− 11.30	− 9.24	− 7.20	− 5.18	− 3.19	− 2.34	− 3.69	− 5.10	− 6.55
3	− 9.75	− 7.31	− 4.91	− 2.54	− 0.21	1.39	1.30	− 0.02	− 1.37
4	− 4.59	− 2.87	− 1.18	0.48	1.30	0.57	− 0.20	− 1.00	− 1.92
5	0.46	1.58	2.07	2.09	2.07	2.02	1.93	1.81	1.65
6	− 0.49	0.55	1.56	2.53	3.47	4.15	4.32	4.44	4.53
7	1.60	2.24	2.86	3.19	3.46	3.69	3.90	4.06	4.20

EXHIBIT 8 *(Continued)*

Horizon (yrs.)	Forecast Error of Average Yield (in basis points)								
	−200	−150	−100	−50	0	5	100	150	200
	Panel 5: Standard Deviation Difference (%)								
1	7.36	5.65	3.98	2.35	0.78	−0.70	−2.03	−3.14	−3.88
2	4.44	3.27	2.13	1.03	−0.03	−1.02	−1.90	−2.61	−3.07
3	4.47	3.45	2.44	1.45	0.49	−0.43	−1.28	−2.03	−2.59
4	2.27	1.66	1.05	0.45	−0.13	−0.67	−1.17	−1.58	−1.83
5	0.79	0.49	0.19	−0.10	−0.38	−0.63	−0.83	−0.96	−0.97
6	1.04	0.85	0.65	0.46	0.26	0.07	−0.13	−0.31	−0.48
7	0.21	0.10	−0.02	−0.13	−0.24	−0.35	−0.46	−0.54	−0.48

ties of outperformance are virtually identical and the ratios of mean to standard deviation are very similar. However, absolute performance measures (panels 2, 4, and 5) are roughly doubled, as would be expected if A is doubled. In considering these results, it is apparent that the strategy not only works well relative to the index—it performs much as formula (2) predicts. However, several discrepancies appear. Specifically, the results are not quite as symmetrical for over and under rate forecasts as might be predicted. Moreover, the results for rate underforecasts are somewhat, although not significantly, weaker than might be expected. For instance, mean return differences in the −200 basis point forecast case are significant but are not as large as for other accuracies (although they are rising with increasing horizon length); and in comparing panel 2 of Exhibits 7 and 8, mean differences do not increase by as close to a factor of two as for the other forecasting accuracies.

In trying to explain these observations, it is important to keep several factors in mind. First, because of our limited sample period, 1977–1985, we do not have equal numbers of observations for each horizon nor are our observations independent of one another. This can bias comparisons across horizons. Second, the period under study was one of generally rising interest rates. This implies that, on average, lower duration portfolios would outperform higher duration portfolios. Hence, cases of rate overestimate should perform better than cases of rate underestimate over this period. Third, basis risk in the futures market is a problem. Specifically, when rates fall generally, we often find short rates falling by more which causes futures prices to fall by less. This tends to penalize higher duration portfolios and benefit lower duration portfolios. In the case of rate underestimates, duration would be biased upwards, leading to more futures contacts and hence more exposure to this problem. Fourth, the theory was developed assuming a flat yield curve where futures yields move in perfect alignment with the index yield. In fact, the theoretical difference between the futures yield and the index yield is primarily due to yield curve slope, which we have assumed away. Thus, the presence of a volatile slope would have added further distortions to the basic relationships over this period.[13] This can be thought of as another form of basis risk.

Finally, the Shearson Lehman Government/Corporate Index yield is generally more volatile than the futures yield due to corporate spreads changing. Overall this suggests that the strategy works better for mixed government/corporate indexes because the strategy capitalizes on greater volatility; but the imperfect link between the futures and cash markets introduces an element of imprecision that would be more significant for portfolios using greater numbers of futures.

To cast further light on the ability of the theory to explain the actual results, as in the first study, we performed a regression analysis of realized return differences on their theoretical determinants given by formula (2). Specifically, we calculated the theoretical values of both the ERROR and VAR terms based upon realized sample information and used these as independent variables in a regression of the realized return differences.[14] This analysis will help summarize the goodness of fit of the basic theory in light of the

[13] More complex developments of the theory directly account for slope problems and imply corresponding adjustments to the regression analysis.

[14] Unlike calculations in the first study, we slightly modified the definition of the ERROR term so that in place of $[Y(T) + Y(0)]/2$ (i.e., the average of beginning and ending yield) we used the average monthly yield over the period, believing that this would conform more sensibly when the index yield and futures yield were not in as perfect alignment. To reflect to the theory of formula (2) we omitted a constant from the regression.

observations made above. Exhibits 9 and 10 contain the regression findings. To save space, we report results on the one, three and five-year horizons only, and for the −200, −100, 0, +100 and +200 basis point forecasting accuracies. Longer horizons have insufficient observations to produce meaningful conclusions. Because we perform the regressions without a constant term, but more importantly because of the overlapping periods used to compute return differences, the standard regression statistics do not have their normal interpretation. Nevertheless, we report the usual statistics. Variables 1 and 2 in the tables correspond to the ERROR and VAR terms respectively. Based on formula (2), the theoretical value of each coefficient is 1.

Exhibits 9 and 10 report findings for A = 100 and 200 respectively. In examining these exhibits, five observations stand out. First, while the regression coefficients are not as close to their theoretical values as in the first study (using Treasury data) they are nonetheless quite significant and appear to have a stable pattern across horizons and forecast accuracies. Second, the R-squareds are high indicating that the basic theory developed in formula (2) explains most of the relative return. Third, the R-squared tends to be larger for more extreme forecasting accuracies, again indicating that the theory is correctly identifying the determinants of relative return. Fourth, the regression statistics—coefficients, t-statistics, and R-squareds—have roughly the same magnitude regardless of the horizon. This indicates that the formula (2) is accurate over the short run as well as the long run. Fifth, the coefficients in Exhibit 10 (A = 200) are almost identical to those in Exhibit 9 (A = 100), a result that is also predicted by the theory.

These results substantiate the accuracy of the basic theory. The goodness of fit is not as impressive as in our first study where the index was the long Treasury Bond index. In particular, the R-squareds are lower and the coefficients are not as near their theoretical values. This would seem to be due to the reduced alignment of the index and the futures market. Nonetheless, we believe that the results provide strong general support for duration averaging. They illustrate the ability of the proposed theory to substantially explain relative returns with roughly equal effectiveness regardless of horizon, forecasting accuracy or aggressiveness. This places in context the questions raised earlier regarding symmetry and alignment.

EXHIBIT 9
Regression Results for A = 100*

Forecast Error	Variable 1	Variable 2	R-Squared
	One-year Horizon		
– 200 bp	0.772	0.386	0.824
	(18.381)	(8.080)	
– 100 bp	0.808	0.485	0.688
	(11.679)	(12.339)	
0 bp	0.004	0.491	0.574
	(2.115)	(10.245)	
+ 100 bp	0.666	0.654	0.832
	(12.626)	(21.828)	
+ 200 bp	0.702	0.724	0.924
	(25.052)	(22.740)	
	Two-year Horizon		
– 200 bp	0.695	0.303	0.676
	(11.996)	(6.184)	
– 100 bp	0.687	0.414	0.276
	(6.559)	(9.323)	
0 bp	0.007	0.352	0.225
	(2.273)	(4.372)	
+ 100 bp	0.728	0.601	0.715
	(8.083)	(15.759)	
+ 200 bp	0.720	0.678	0.883
	(16.266)	(18.065)	
	Three-year Horizon		
– 200 bp	0.925	0.379	0.805
	(15.624)	(9.334)	
– 100 bp	1.092	0.480	0.601
	(10.256)	(13.137)	
0 bp	0.004	0.417	0.237
	(1.092)	(4.093)	
+ 100 bp	0.439	0.648	0.729
	(4.855)	(20.859)	
+ 200 bp	0.607	0.715	0.897
	(13.714)	(23.521)	

EXHIBIT 9 *(Continued)*

Forecast Error	Variable 1	Variable 2	R-Squared
	Four-year Horizon		
− 200 bp	0.781	0.352	0.903
	(20.225)	(20.390)	
− 100 bp	0.801	0.453	0.744
	(10.187)	(25.798)	
0 bp	− 0.010	0.787	0.770
	(− 3.823)	(11.863)	
+ 100 bp	0.741	0.621	0.852
	(7.905)	(29.713)	
+ 200 bp	0.760	0.689	0.915
	(14.309)	(29.023)	
	Five-year Horizon		
− 200 bp	0.628	0.407	0.778
	(11.278)	(27.311)	
− 100 bp	0.411	0.490	0.566
	(4.256)	(37.985)	
0 bp	0.015	1.031	0.851
	(− 5.425)	(13.111)	
+ 100 bp	1.304	0.622	0.922
	(12.035)	(42.966)	
+ 200 bp	1.087	0.670	0.943
	(16.295)	(37.609)	

*Numbers in parentheses are t-statistics.

The one asymmetry that the results do illustrate is that, while the R-squareds are not lower, the coefficients on the VAR term (variable 2) are lower for rate underestimates than for overestimates, although they are still very significant. It should be recalled, however, that this result was also found in the first study, and is evidently due to the basis risk in the futures market that adversely affects rate under-forecasts and benefits rate over-forecasts.

We have discussed the goodness of fit of our empirical results in terms of formula (2), which was developed under simplified yield

EXHIBIT 10
Regression Results for A = 200*

Forecast Error	Variable 1	Variable 2	R-Squared
One-year Horizon			
– 200 bp	0.771 (18.567)	0.355 (7.524)	0.827
– 100 bp	0.807 (11.752)	0.470 (12.047)	0.688
0 bp	0.004 (2.137)	0.483 (10.140)	0.569
+ 100 bp	0.666 (12.695)	0.645 (21.649)	0.831
+ 200 bp	0.702 (25.134)	0.706 (22.249)	0.924
Two-year Horizon			
– 200 bp	0.691 (11.988)	0.263 (5.387)	0.683
– 100 bp	0.683 (6.532)	0.392 (8.842)	0.278
0 bp	0.007 (2.267)	0.340 (4.229)	0.213
+ 100 bp	0.731 (8.155)	0.588 (15.476)	0.714
+ 200 bp	0.724 (16.475)	0.655 (17.578)	0.883
Three-year Horizon			
– 200 bp	0.925 (15.537)	0.335 (8.186)	0.807
– 100 bp	1.096 (10.236)	0.455 (12.380)	0.605
0 bp	0.004 (1.061)	0.404 (3.947)	0.224
+ 100 bp	0.442 (4.902)	0.633 (20.423)	0.726
+ 200 bp	0.613 (13.991)	0.689 (22.889)	0.897

EXHIBIT 10 *(Continued)*

Forecast Error	Variable 1	Variable 2	R-Squared
	Four-year Horizon		
– 200 bp	0.792	0.303	0.895
	(19.191)	(16.461)	
– 100 bp	0.821	0.425	0.731
	(9.950)	(23.094)	
0 bp	– 0.010	0.773	0.753
	(– 3.792)	(11.330)	
+ 100 bp	0.739	0.605	0.847
	(7.827)	(28.697)	
+ 200 bp	0.768	0.663	0.914
	(14.434)	(27.918)	
	Five-year Horizon		
– 200 bp	0.635	0.357	0.759
	(10.500)	(22.070)	
– 100 bp	0.427	0.462	0.525
	(4.107)	(33.266)	
0 bp	– 0.016	1.017	0.845
	(– 5.417)	(12.782)	
+ 100 bp	1.300	0.606	0.919
	(11.873)	(41.434)	
+ 200 bp	1.092	0.646	0.942
	(16.208)	(35.847)	

*Numbers in parentheses are t-statistics.

curve assumptions. Other theoretical work extends these findings to other yield curve models. These other models predict varying degrees of modification to formula (2), although not its basic message. It is likely, however, that the use of a modified equation to reflect such factors as yield curve slope will improve our regression findings by altering and/or introducing variables that are currently omitted from the analysis.

Summary of the Third Historical Study

This study is analogous to the first study in that we employ historical data from the U.S. Treasury market. However, most of the
strategies tested involve the construction of portfolios composed of
individual securities. We also test strategies where varying degrees
of duration adjustments are assumed to be made in the futures
market. But since the actual Treasury bond future did not begin
trading until 1977, we must use a hypothetical pricing mechanism
for futures prices for prior periods. This mechanism is based on
principles of arbitrage that connect long rates, short rates and futures prices.

We began with the U.S. Treasury universe of notes and bonds
covering the period May 1972 through June 1983. Earlier data were
not used due to the sparsity of this universe for prior periods.
Monthly total rates of return were computed for each security.

Next we evaluated what index or indices should be employed as
the benchmark. Although equal-weighted indices have some merit
when considering the Treasury market, capitalization-weighted indices are more normally used for performance comparisons, so this
is what we used, as in the first study. In deciding how to construct
the index, consideration had to be given to the fact that the theory
assumes that the characteristics of the index do not change significantly over the horizon for performance measurement. While this is
generally true of indices used in practice, it is not true of the total
index of Treasury notes and bonds over this period. Specifically,
the enormous increases in the Federal deficit over the 10 years in
our sample caused significant changes in the duration and yield of
the index, especially over the second half of the period. Any such
changes which are due to issuance rather than to market moves can
undermine our results because such issuance should induce a modified interest rate forecast to be included in the duration formula. As
a consequence of these problems (and as in the first study), we
decided to employ the Treasury long bond index as our benchmark
since the characteristics of this fund (duration and yield) were much
less affected by issuance than the total index of notes and bonds. It
should be added that we generated results on several of the other
definitions as well and found qualitatively similar results, which
were often even more supportive of the theory, although we report

only those results for the capitalization-weighted Treasury bond index.

As with the other studies, the broad design of this study was to test various strategies under several assumptions. For every strategy tested we computed holding period returns versus the index over one, two, three, four and five year horizons. Over the entire sample, there are 109 one-year (overlapping) holding periods, 97 two-year (overlapping), 85 three-year (overlapping), 73 four-year (overlapping) and 61 five-year (overlapping) holding periods. Within each holding period, portfolios were rebalanced monthly with an assumed *one-way* transaction cost of .25%, which is fairly high for Treasury securities. In every case, the securities held were constrained to be those contained within the bond universe. We did not allow purchase of notes or bills since the duration required by the formula is sometimes beyond that of the largest or shortest securities in the universe, this biases the results against the strategies we are testing versus the index. In order to simulate the duration-averaging rule, it was necessary to develop a mechanism for altering the duration of the portfolio beyond that allowed by the shortest or longest bonds in the universe. Allowing holdings of notes and/or bills would have helped on the short end but not on the long end. Consequently, we continued to restrict holdings to bonds only, but used the Treasury bond futures to handle both short and long exposure. Specifically, we created a financial future rate based upon arbitrage pricing that reflected long and short rates as well as the time to expiration of the contract. That is, the contract was assumed (and priced) to expire on the same months it actually does. Whenever a futures position was held in the simulation, we always assumed that we rolled over the nearby contract. Transaction costs on futures trades were assumed to be $30 round trip per $100,000 principal value contract. Overall, we built a basis risk into the future pricing and a transaction cost that we expect would cause this method to closely reflect what actual experience would have been had such a market existed as early as 1973 (actual prices were used after 1977). As in the first study, our reasoning for adopting this approach using futures is its simplicity. First, it allows a clean and symmetrical treatment of extending versus shortening portfolio duration relative to the index duration. Second, it established a record for this low transaction cost alternative, which is a strong candidate for practical application.

To test the duration-averaging rule we developed seven strategies. In every case an aggressiveness factor (A) of 100 was used. Strategies 1 and 2 set duration as close to the target duration specified by the formula as could be achieved using bonds in the universe. Strategy 1 did this while optimizing a simple average yield concept, while strategy 2 optimized a theoretically superior concept (the market and duration weighted yield). In each case, rebalancing was not done if the yield pickup did not overcome the transaction costs. Instead, slight adjustments to existing holdings would be made to satisfy the duration target.

Neither of these two strategies strictly conformed to the duration-averaging rule because that rule often called for durations outside the range of what could be achieved using bonds in the Treasury bond universe—shorter or longer. To remedy this, strategies 3 and 4 are identical to 1 and 2 except that futures are used to make up any shortfall in duration. In contrast to strategies 3 and 4, strategies 5 and 6 select bonds to maximize respective yield concepts in setting portfolio duration to index duration, but achieve the entire adjustment to duration prescribed by the formula through use of the futures only. Thus all of the impact of the duration averaging is achieved using futures. The final strategy (7) does not select individual securities at all but instead assumes that the index itself is purchased and that futures alone are used to achieve the duration specified by the rule. This strategy reflects the value added of the technique alone without reference to any yield pickup due to trading actual bonds and is analogous in this sense to the first historical study.

The object of this study is to evaluate the historical contribution of the duration averaging rule compared with a representative index, assuming realistic transactions parameters and covering both stable and volatile interest rate periods. We must also consider various degrees of forecasting accuracy. Accordingly, for each strategy tested and for each holding period we consider five variations on the accuracy of forecasting the end-of-period yield on the index. This is in contrast to the first study where we forecast the average yield. Specifically, we assumed that the end-of-period yield equaled the actual end-of-period yield plus 200 basis points, plus 100 basis points, plus 0 basis points, minus 100 basis points, and minus 200 basis points. For instance, in testing the first strategy for a one-year holding period, we would test 109 overlapping one-year periods in which for each of the 109 trials, the end-of-period rate forecast equaled the actual end-of-period rate plus or minus the given range of values, for a total of 545 (109 × 5) trials. We believe this range of values to be representative for practical purposes with the results allowing extrapolation to further extremes of error.

The results of the study are a striking confirmation of the duration averaging rule. First, mean relative returns (of the strategy versus the index) are almost always positive, and the probability of outperformance is almost always comfortably in excess of 50 percent. Second, the second half sample results are almost always superior to the first half as predicted by theory, regardless of the specific strategy. This is because of the greater volatility of yields in the second half of the sample. Third, allowing the use of futures to obtain the correct duration meaningfully improves returns. Strategies 3 and 4 illustrate this as they use futures to extend duration beyond the levels obtained using the portfolios in strategies 1 and 2. Fourth, it is better to make all duration adjustments required by the duration averaging using the futures market. Strategies 5 and 6 illustrate this since they are duration matched to the index except that the entire duration change necessary for applying the rule is accomplished in the futures market. This is in contrast to strategies 3 and 4, which use futures to obtain only the duration that could not be achieved using bonds. The reason for this finding appears to be due to the impact of lower transaction costs allowed for by the use of futures, and to the reduced exposure to certain types of yield curve shifts which are more detrimental when the actual cash market portfolio duration differs significantly from the index duration. As suggested before, strategy 6, based upon the improved yield concept, outperforms the simple yield concept in strategy 5. Finally, strategy 7 employs the index and futures only. As with the results for other strategies it shows a clear and reliable outperformance, although not as great as a strategy which also allows us to beat the index based on both the duration averaging rule and security selection.

To broadly summarize these results, this analysis agrees with the other studies that show duration averaging has a compelling value added which is persistent even under systematic errors in forecasting end-of-period yields. Moreover, the results agree entirely with the intuition that: (1) the superior yield definition should perform better, (2) the results are better as yields become more volatile; (3) the use of futures is important as a vehicle to reduce transaction costs and avoid certain types of adverse yield curve shape moves, although they are still vulnerable to spread changes between long and short rates that produce basis risk.[15]

Aside from demonstrating the general performance of the averaging strategy, one of our objectives is to measure the literal accuracy of formula (2) for predicting relative returns. On the one hand, that formula is exact only if the yield curve and portfolio selection conforms to the theoretical yield model that we employed in developing the formula. On the other hand, the empirical results in actual markets broadly substantiate the theory so that we would expect formula (2) to do a reasonably good job of explaining relative return. To test this hypothesis, we performed regressions of realized relative returns on a constant and their two theoretical determinants, i.e., the two terms in formula (2). If the yield model held exactly, we would expect the estimated constant to be close to zero and the estimated coefficients to be highly significant and close to 1 (their theoretical values), with the overall regression having a high R-squared.

These regressions were performed for each strategy and for each horizon (one through five years). As with the first study, the tests of significance are biased by the fact that the returns are calculated from overlapping periods. Nonetheless, we consider the usual statistics.

Despite several instances where the predicted results do not emerge, the analysis strongly supports the theory. This is most clearly indicated in the case of strategy 7 where the index is assumed to be purchased and futures are employed to make all duration adjustments. In this case, there is no ambiguity in explaining relative return because of the performance of individual securities held;

[15] Our calculation of the futures price in this study differs from the "ideal" market concept used in the first study. Using our present concept in the first study would have, we believe, produced results between those shown in Exhibits 3 and 4.

all of the return difference is caused by the futures. In addition, there is a smaller potential impact from omitted variables associated with yield curve slope factors outside of our simple model. This allows a clear identification of the impact of duration averaging.

In examining the strategy 7 regression results, we find remarkably high R-squareds and significant coefficients. The coefficient on yield variance is close to its theoretically predicted value of 1, while the coefficient on the error term is strongly significant. The constant is close to zero and is often insignificant. Notwithstanding the statistical caveats to the significance tests, these results demonstrate that the theoretical equation works remarkably well in explaining the returns generated through use of duration averaging when the assumptions of the theory are more closely met, even though the yield curve does not obey all of the assumptions used in developing the formula.

Summary of the Simulation Study

This study is an extensive simulation using hypothetical data that is intended to measure the performance of the strategy over a range of conditions that could not be easily tested using history. We used an econometric model to simulate three yield scenarios, each consisting of 56 quarterly yield curves—a high yield, an intermediate and a low yield environment. Along with each simulated yield curve was a dynamically evolving (simulated) universe of bonds with semi-annual coupons. We tested the strategy assuming two holding periods, four years (for which we had 40 observations per scenario) and eight years (for which we had 24 observations per scenario). We compared results of the strategy to two categories of indices. The first were constant duration indices with durations of four, five and six years. The second were constant maturity range indices, 1–5 years, 6–15 years, 16–30 years, and 1–30 years.

In the case of the constant duration indices, we compared the index performance versus the duration-averaging strategy assuming three different selections for the aggressiveness factor, $A = 100$, $A = 200$, $A = 400$, and nine different forecasting accuracies in calculating ERROR (see the discussion following formula (2) for a definition of ERROR), ranging from very bad to very good. We also tested two methods for selecting the specific holdings within the index and the managed portfolio: maximize yield subject to the duration constraint, and minimize cash flow dispersion (convexity) subject to the duration constraint. For the constant maturity range indices, we performed a somewhat different test. Specifically, since the duration of such an index is a function of the yield level, we computed the realized high, low and average duration of each index during each holding period. We then constrained the durations of the managed portfolio to one of these values for the entire holding period. This is based on the principle derived from the duration averaging concept that a constant duration index will outperform a constant maturity index whose duration fluctuates around the constant value. In these cases, there was no selection of "A" or ERROR since these were not part of the experimental design.

The results of the study, contained in 106 tables of simulated evidence, strongly support the theory as well as the practical significance of duration averaging. With just three exceptions (to be discussed), all major predictions of the theory are substantiated: (1) relative returns were positive even for poor forecasting accuracy, (2) relative returns improve as forecasting accuracy improves, (3) relative returns improve as aggressiveness increases, and (4) relative returns improve as the horizon lengthens. Two of the exceptions apply only to some of those cases where portfolio construction maximizes exposure to yield curve shape by selecting barbell portfolios. In these cases relative returns were not always positive for a zero insight or better return forecasting accuracies, and did not always improve as aggressiveness increased. These exceptions were shown to be due to a combination of two factors: portfolio construction that minimized the ability of the duration model to explain returns, and the literal inability to construct portfolios with the proper duration as aggressiveness increased due to the lack of bonds in the universe with required duration. The third exception relates to the fact that mean relative returns did not necessarily increase as the horizon lengthened although the standard deviation of relative return dropped so that the probability of achieving this relative return becomes extremely high.

To help understand this result we computed for both horizons the mean contribution from the ERROR term that would be expected if the theoretical yield curve model held perfectly and compared these means to the associated standard deviations of the contributions from the ERROR term. Although the means change in the expected direction as the horizon lengthens, and the standard deviation drops, the change in mean is small relative to the standard deviation. Consequently, we need more observations or a longer horizon to strongly observe the effect.

The key finding, pervasive throughout the study, is that assuming portfolio construction methods and degrees of aggressiveness that are realistic, the strategy performs well relative to an index even with poor forecasting ability. For this purpose, and for comparison to the other (historical) studies, we defined the forecast yield as equal to yield at the start of the horizon plus a fraction of the difference between the end-of-period yield and the starting yield. The fractions (nine of them to make the nine degrees of accuracy tested) ranged from 1.33, 1, 0.67, 0.33, 0, −0.33, −0.67, −1, −1.33. For example, if the initial yield was 10 percent and the ending yield was 12 percent, the forecasts would range from 12.67 percent to 8.33 percent in increments of 0.67 percent. In the other studies we assumed an arithmetic error. In this study errors are proportional and hence reflect the prospect that in practice, the magnitude of forecast error is more likely to be related to the volatility of yields (and hence to their level) than to any particular numerical amount.

IV. CONCLUDING REMARKS

In this article, we have considered the empirical characteristics of a particular bond strategy that is a member of a general family of strategies we call Linear Investment Rules. The particular rule tested is called duration averaging because it appeals to the averaging concept associated with lengthening and shortening the portfolio duration as yields rise and fall. Based on the properties that we believe characterize yield curve behavior, this strategy increases long-run compound return, and can even be thought of as selling a type of bond portfolio insurance.

We believe that these results have considerable practical interest. First, these basic ideas extend to other markets and rebalancing rules, and cast more light on why certain intuitive strategies perform well. More importantly, the compelling empirical evidence supports a theory that may provide an important alternative to indexation for many bond investors. It avoids the negative index bias (outlined at the beginning of this article) caused by duration moving inversely to yields. It is a disciplined technique that does not attempt short-run rate forecasting but does employ a long-run belief about interest rates. It imposes a sensible trading rule that systematically capitalizes on rate changes. The strategy is quantifiable and can provide a clear and simple concept of what relative return will be and why. Based on the decomposition of return into the ERROR term and the variance term, the impact of the rate forecast is amortized to zero over the long run, leaving only the contribution of the variance of yields to reliably and meaningfully improve returns. Based on data from the last seven years, this amounts to an improvement of 100 to 200 basis points per year using a moderate degree of aggressiveness. That is, volatility is forced to work *for* rather than *against* the portfolio. Finally, the strategy is simple to implement. The investor merely chooses the aggressiveness parameter, A, and the means of execution. Our work illustrates that the futures market is a simple and effective vehicle. Moreover, use of the futures market implies that the strategy can be run independently of the underlying portfolio. Thus, for instance, an index fund could be owned, with a separate futures account maintained elsewhere to implement the averaging strategy.

ARTICLE 18

ROBERT W. KOPPRASCH is a Director in the Bond Portfolio Analysis Department of Salomon Brothers Inc. He directs the activities of the Hedge Group, which is responsible for research and development related to customer and trading desk hedging in fixed income, commodity, currency and related markets. The group is actively involved in arbitrage analysis, derivative and new security pricing, and special projects.

Before joining Salomon Brothers Inc, Dr. Kopprasch was an assistant professsor at The American University in Washington, D.C., on the business faculties of the graduate and undergraduate schools.

Dr. Kopprasch received his B.S. and M.S. in Management and Ph.D. in Finance from Rensselaer Polytechnic Institute. He completed the Chartered Financial Analysts Program in 1980.

CAL JOHNSON is a Vice President in the Bond Portfolio Analysis Hedge Group at Salomon Brothers Inc. Before joining Salomon Brothers in 1980, he was an associate professor of mathematics at Bowling Green University.

Dr. Johnson received his B.S. in Mathematics from the California Institute of Technology and his Ph.D. also in Mathematics from the University of Massachusetts.

ARMAND H. TATEVOSSIAN is a senior research analyst in the Bond Portfolio Analysis Hedge Group at Salomon Brothers Inc. He received his B.S. in Economics from the Massachusetts Institute of Technology.

STRATEGIES FOR THE ASSET MANAGER: HEDGING AND THE CREATION OF SYNTHETIC ASSETS

Robert W. Kopprasch, Ph.D., C.F.A.
Director
Salomon Brothers Inc

Cal Johnson, Ph.D.
Vice President
Salomon Brothers Inc

Armand H. Tatevossian
Senior Analyst
Salomon Brothers Inc

As the markets in financial futures and options have matured in recent years, the formerly academic notion of a synthetic financial instrument has entered the world of the practitioner. Arbitrageurs and a broad spectrum of asset managers create and use synthetic assets daily. Some synthetic assets are structurally similar to hedges. For example, a manager who hedges the value of a long-term bond by selling it three months forward is creating a short-term asset that will earn a short-term rate, although the position contains a bond

525

that is earning a long-term rate. Other synthetic assets, particularly those involving options, are best viewed as a form of insurance that protects a portfolio against unfavorable interest rate movements. Still others are attempts to capture mispricings that occur in an option or futures contract.

Although a synthetic asset may be structured like a hedge, the two are used to achieve different objectives. Hedging is usually a defensive act, while the intentional creation of a synthetic asset is typically an aggressive attempt to add value by exploiting mispricings that a manager perceives. Reflecting this fundamental difference, this article is divided into two sections—Section I dealing with hedging techniques and Section II with the creation and use of synthetic assets.

I. HEDGING TECHNIQUES

The following discussion assumes that the reader understands the basic considerations that should underlie a decision to hedge (identification of the risk, consideration of alternatives and selection of the hedge vehicle).[1] It also assumes familiarity with futures contracts on Treasury securities, conversion factors, the break-even repo rate, and the basics of determining the hedge ratio when hedging a single bond.[2]

Hedging the Value of a Portfolio

Many potential constraints lead portfolio managers to hedge—rather than liquidate—their portfolios. In some cases, the securities—like private placements—may not be liquid enough for quick sale. For other managers who have spent time accumulating a particular portfolio, hedging may be more attractive than selling

---

[1] See Robert W. Kopprasch, *Introduction to Interest Rate Hedging,* New York: Salomon Brothers Inc, 1982.

[2] See Robert W. Kopprasch, *An Introduction to Financial Futures on Treasury Securities,* New York: Salomon Brothers Inc, December 1981, and Robert W. Kopprasch, "Understanding Duration and Volatility," Chapter 5 in Frank J. Fabozzi and Irving M. Pollack, eds., *The Handbook of Fixed Income Securities,* (Homewood, IL: Dow Jones-Irwin, 1987).

because the securities may be difficult to replace at a later date. Institutions—like life insurance companies—that carry securities on their books at cost or accreted cost rather than at market value may find hedging attractive if these securities are below cost to the point where their sale would cause the recognition of greater losses than the institution desires. Finally, the synthetic sale of assets through hedging may produce a higher price than would be obtained through their actual sale. Relative value considerations will be discussed in Section II, but they may also be appropriate when hedging in a defensive posture. For example, a mortgage portfolio that would ordinarily be hedged by selling GNMAs forward might be hedged with Treasury notes if the spread is expected to narrow.

The manager who has decided to hedge an asset portfolio has two basic alternatives—to sell short or to purchase put options.

The Short Hedge. The short hedge consists of a short sale, a forward sale or a sale of futures, usually in the Treasury market. Because the short hedge is used instead of selling the assets, the economic consequence of selling the assets suggests what can be achieved. When a long bond portfolio is sold, the proceeds are normally invested in the money market until the bond market becomes attractive again. Thus, in three months, the portfolio would be worth its value today moved forward at some short-term rate. In an upward sloping yield curve environment, the manager would forfeit some income to eliminate price risk.

The same principle applies to the familiar cash-and-carry trade, in which one buys a cash bond and simultaneously sells it forward with the intention of making delivery. This creates a short-term investment with a known return, and if forward or futures prices are fair (set by arbitrage), the investor will earn a short-term rate. Thus, the hedge of a Treasury bond with futures or forwards is nothing more than a cash-and-carry transaction, and it should earn a short-term rate, not the rate on the long-term bond.[3] *It is not*

---

[3] Arbitrage is not as straightforward in the equity market. Dealers (the most active arbitrageurs) find that the capital haircut required for equity arbitrage is far more onerous than for debt arbitrage. As a result, stock index futures are often mispriced, and cash-and-carry hedges may return far more than the short-term rate. See H. Nicholas Hanson and Louis I. Margolis, *Using Stock Index Futures to Create Synthetic Money Market Instruments,* New York: Salomon Brothers Inc, February 1985.

possible to earn the long-term rate, without price risk, for short periods of time. Hedging cannot perform yield curve magic.

Hedgers sometimes expect to eliminate risk without giving up yield (as must be done in a positive yield curve environment) and blame the failure of a hedge on basis risk. There is indeed some basis risk in futures hedging, but because cash and futures converge in a predictable manner, this risk is minimal. Basis risk should not be used as a catchall for the hedger's failure to properly determine the target market value of the portfolio.

These points can be illustrated with numerical examples: Assume that a decision has been made to hedge the U.S. 12½s of 8/15/14 by selling forward the U.S. 11¼s of 2/15/15. The hedge ratio computation is shown in Exhibit 1, and a scenario analysis is given in Exhibit 2. The hedge ratio computation using futures as the hedge vehicle is shown in Exhibit 3.[4] In Exhibit 2 two items stand out. First, the returns in the first three scenarios are nearly identical and are at the level of short-term rates, not the long-term yield (10.60%) on the bond. The fact that they are nearly the same means that, in the absence of a change in the yield spread between the two securities, the hedge would be quite effective.

The last two scenarios in Exhibit 2 show that hedging results are much more sensitive to unanticipated changes in the yield spread between the hedged and hedging vehicles than they are to changes in the overall level of interest rates. This is particularly relevant to the manager who is attempting to hedge corporate bonds. (See the discussion on the corporate cash and carry in Section II.)

The only way to hedge the part of the Treasury-corporate spread that is not level-dependent is to use hedge vehicles that are directly

---

[4] In this article, we treat futures contracts as if they were forward contracts. The major difference between futures contracts and forward contracts is that with forwards, gains or losses are recognized on the delivery date. With futures, gains or losses are recognized immediately through the variation margin mechanism. A futures position can be made to approximate a forward position by "discounting" the number of forward contracts from the delivery date to the present using the overnight rate expected to prevail over this period. This results in a futures position that is somewhat smaller than the equivalent forward position. For a more detailed discussion of this adjustment, see H. Nicholas Hanson and Robert W. Kopprasch, "Pricing of Stock Index Futures," Chapter 6, in *Stock Index Futures,* Frank J. Fabozzi and Gregory M. Kipnis, eds., (Homewood, IL: Dow Jones-Irwin, 1984).

EXHIBIT 1
Forward Market Short Asset Hedge

The following example illustrates a short asset hedge for the U.S. 12.50 of 8/15/14. The hedge is implemented with a forward sale of the U.S. 11.25 of 2/15/15. The hedge is set on June 19, 1985, and is lifted on September 19, 1985.

Step 1. Determine Forward Rates and Hedge Ratio

Settlement Date:			6/19/85
Three-Month Finance Rate (Bond Equivalent):			7.20%

		— Spot — (6/19/85)	— Forward — (9/19/85)
Target Asset: U.S. 12.50 of 8/15/14:	Price: Yield:	116.969 10.604%	115.955 10.702%
Hedge Vehicle: U.S. 11.25 of 2/15/15:	Price: Yield:	108.000 10.373%	107.137 10.462%

Dollar Value of 0.01% on Forward Date (9/19/85):

U.S. 12.50 of 8/15/14:	$0.10154 per $100 Face
U.S. 11.25 of 2/15/15:	$0.09663 per $100 Face

Calculate the Hedge Ratio

$$\text{Hedge Ratio} = \frac{\$VAL01 \text{ Asset}}{\$VAL01 \text{ Hedge Vehicle}} * \text{Beta}^a$$

$$= \frac{0.10154}{0.09663} * 1.0 = 1.05081$$

Step 2. Establish Hedge Position on June 19, 1985.

Face Amount of U.S. 12.50 of 8/15/14 Owned:	$100,000,000
Face Amount of U.S. 11.25 of 2/15/15 to Sell Forward:	$105,081,000

[a] The beta term in the hedge ratio is the relative yield volatility as determined by regression analysis. A beta of 1.2 would mean that the yield of the security being hedged has tended to move 1.2 basis points for each basis point move in the yield of the security being used as the hedge vehicle. A yield spread that changes in proportion to changes in interest rate levels is incorporated into a hedge ratio via the beta term. All examples assume a beta of 1.

EXHIBIT 2
Forward Market Short Asset Hedge Scenario Analysis

Unwind Hedge Position in Exhibit 1 on September 19, 1985.

Examine the outcome of the hedge under a variety of interest rate scenarios. For illustrative purposes, the calculation of the rising rate scenario return is detailed in a footnote.

Scenario	Annualized CD Return Over Hedge Period	
Interest rates rise to 100 basis points above forward rates.[a]	7.00%	
Spot rates converge to forward rates.	7.06%	Yield Spread Remains Unchanged
Interest rates decline to 100 basis points below forward rates.	6.95%	
U.S. 12.50 yields ten basis points over forward rate; U.S. 11.25 converges to forward rate.	3.80%	Spread Widens
U.S. 12.50 yields ten basis points under forward rate; U.S. 11.25 converges to forward rate.	10.36%	Spread Narrows

[a] Interest rates rise to 100 basis points above forward rates:

Settlement Date:		6/19/85
Purchase:		
U.S. 12.50 of 8/15/14 @ 10.604%	Flat Price:	116.969
	Accrued Interest:	4.282
	Full Price:	121.251
Sell Forward (to 9/19/85):		
U.S. 11.25 of 2/15/15 @ 10.462%	Flat Price:	107.137
	Accrued Interest:	1.070
	Full Price:	108.207

Horizon Date:		9/19/85
Sell:		
U.S. 12.50 of 8/15/14 @ 11.702%	Flat Price:	106.541
	Accrued Interest:	1.189
	Full Price:	107.730
Purchase to Close Out Forward:		
U.S. 11.25 of 2/15/15 @ 11.462%	Flat Price:	98.198
	Accrued Interest:	1.070
	Full Price:	99.268

EXHIBIT 2 *(Continued)*

Loss on U.S. 12.50 of 8/15/14:

Full Purchase Price (6/19/85):	<121.251>
Coupon Flow (8/15/85):	6.250
Interest on Coupon (8/15/85 - 9/19/85):	0.048
Full Sale Price (9/19/85):	107.730
Loss:	<7.223>

Profit on U.S. 11.25 of 2/15/15:

Proceeds of Forward Sale:	108.207
Purchase to Close Out Forward:	< 99.268>
Profit per $100 Face:	8.939
Hedge Ratio:	1.05081
Profit:	9.393

Net Profit:	2.170

Annualized CD Return: $\dfrac{2.170}{121.251} * \dfrac{360}{92} = 7.00\%$

---

related to the corporate market. Since corporate futures do not exist, the hedger of a corporate bond portfolio is exposed to quality-spread risk.

Exhibit 4 illustrates the creation of a short asset hedge for a portfolio of bonds—corporate bonds in this case—being hedged in the Treasury market.

Purchase of Put Options. A short hedge, which is intended to protect the value of an asset, locks in today the price of a sale to be made in the future. If prices go down, the asset value is protected; if they go up, the holder of the asset does not benefit. The purchase of puts, with their asymmetric payoff pattern, makes it possible to protect an asset against a price decline and also to participate in a market rally, should one occur. Puts, however, unlike futures contracts, have an up-front premium that must be paid regardless of the outcome. In this respect, they are exactly like insurance: A premium is paid in exchange for protection against disaster, and different deductibles can be selected by varying the strike price. Options provide a manager great flexibility, and because their cost is known in advance, interest rate views can be assessed in terms of the amount that it will cost to express them.

EXHIBIT 3
Calculation of the Hedge Ratio—Futures Market Hedge

The short asset hedge detailed in Exhibit 1 can also be implemented in the Chicago Board of Trade Treasury bond futures market. In this example, the U.S. 12.50 of 8/15/14 will be hedged with the September 1985 futures contract.

Step 1. Calculate Forward Rates

Settlement Date:		6/19/85

Target Asset: U.S. 12.50 of 8/15/14	Price: Yield:	116.969 10.604%

Hedge Vehicle:
SEP 85 Treasury Bond Futures Contract

Cheapest to Deliver: U.S. 11.25 of 2/15/15	Price: Yield:	108.000 10.373%

Determination of Forward Rates on 9/19/85 as Implied by Futures:

SEP 85 Contract Price:	77.6880
U.S. 11.25 Conversion Factor:	1.3650
Final Contract Basis:[a]	0.1875 Points
Forward U.S. 11.25 Price:[b]	106.2316
Forward U.S. 11.25 Yield:	10.5561%
Expected Yield Spread (Assumed to Remain Unchanged):	23 Basis Points
Forward U.S. 12.50 Yield:[c]	10.7861%
Forward U.S. 12.50 Price:	115.1020

Step 2. Calculate Hedge Ratio

Dollar Value of 0.01% on Forward Date (9/19/85):

U.S. 12.50 of 8/15/14:	$0.10022 per $100 Face
U.S. 11.25 of 2/15/15:	$0.09518 per $100 Face

Futures Hedge Ratio per $100,000 Face US 12.50 of 8/15/14:

$$\text{Hedge Ratio} = \frac{\$VAL01\ Asset}{\$VAL01\ Futures} = \frac{\$VAL01\ Asset}{\$VAL01\ Cheapest\ to\ Deliver} * \text{Conversion Factor}$$

$$= \frac{0.10022}{0.09518} * 1.3650 = \textbf{1.4373}\ \text{SEP 85 Contracts}[d]$$

[a] Because of various delivery options available to the short, the bond contract closes slightly cheaper than cash. The number used here is a Salomon Brothers's estimate of the SEP 85 final basis of the U.S. 11.25.

[b] The forward price calculation is 106.2316 = (77.6880 • 1.3650) + 0.1875. The forward price implied by the futures market is lower than the cash market forward price (used in Exhibit 1) because of cheapness in the futures contract.

[c] Forward U.S. 12.50 Yield = Forward U.S. 11.25 Yield + 23 Basis Points.

[d] For purposes of computational accuracy, fractional contracts will be assumed throughout this article.

EXHIBIT 4
Forward Market Short Asset Hedge for a Portfolio

This example illustrates a short asset hedge for a portfolio of corporate bonds. The hedge is implemented with a forward sale of the U.S. 11.25 of 2/15/15. The hedge is set on June 19, 1985, and is lifted on September 19, 1985.

Hedge Vehicle:
U.S. 11.25 of 2/15/15

Forward Price:		107.137
Forward Yield:		10.462%
Forward Dollar Value of 0.01%:		0.09663[a]

Portfolio Position:

Ticker	Coupon	Maturity	Forward Yield	Forward $VAL01	Position Size[b]	Hedge Ratio	Hedge Position[b]
GMAC	8.250	11/15/06	10.99	0.06643	700	0.687	481
ALP	12.625	6/ 1/10	11.89	0.08337	400	0.863	345
ABT	11.800	2/ 1/13	10.74	0.09504	1,000	0.984	984
CPT	12.375	9/ 1/17	11.79	0.08638	800	0.894	715
Total					**$2,900**		**$2,525**

An asset manager wishing to hedge this portfolio to September 19, 1985, would execute a forward sale of $2,525,000 face amount U.S. 11.25 of 2/15/15.

[a] Same as Exhibit 1, Step 1.
[b] Dollars in thousands

The primary difference between hedging with futures and hedging with puts is shown in Exhibit 5. The effect of the cost of the premium is shown, because the put hedger's return (value of portfolio) is never the maximum amount possible. If the market rallies, the hedger participates but loses the premium. If the market declines, the hedger is protected but still pays the premium.

Portfolios with puts can also be used in the more speculative positions taken by active managers who trade the yield curve based on their expectations of future interest rate levels. Options and futures allow these managers to express their views without having to dismantle their portfolios and pay large transaction costs. Long puts are generally considered to be bearish instruments, but when they are added to an existing portfolio they can be viewed as bullish, giving a combined payoff pattern resembling that of a call. For example, if a manager expects rates to fall and locks in today's high rates with a long-term investment, the purchase of a put (or perhaps a putable bond) adds some insurance, providing extra income if

EXHIBIT 5
Put Option Asset Hedge (Fixed Value versus Floor Value)

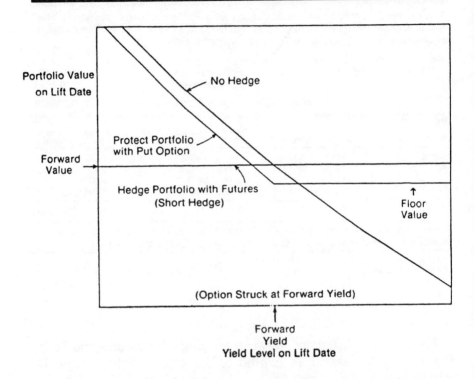

rates increase. A similar strategy available to a bullish short-term money manager is to buy a two-year note at par and a one-year put struck at par on a one-year note, with the intention of holding them for one year. If, after one year, rates have gone down as expected, the note will be sold at a profit and the put will expire unexercised. If rates rise, the then one-year note will be sold at par by exercising the option. The put provides a floor return that protects the manager. As with hedging, it is not possible to perform yield curve magic using options. If the put option in the present example were free, a high two-year rate could be transformed into a floor return on a one-year investment. In fact, the price of the put will be high enough to make the one-year floor return less than the available one-year rate.

Hedging Timing Differences Between Commitment and Receipt of Funds

Several types of timing differences create risk that can be hedged away. Consider the case of an insurance company portfolio manager who knows that funds from a Guaranteed Investment Contract (GIC) or thrift plan will be received over the next year and that a rate to be paid on the funds has already been set. The portfolio manager is mismatched and is at risk, due to the timing difference between the commitment to pay a rate and the receipt of the funds. If market rates decline before the funds are received, the manager will be unable to meet the investment requirements of the committed rate. This situation is often aggravated by the fact that the amount of funds invested will increase above projections when rates have declined below the promised rate. If rates rise prior to receipt of the funds, the portfolio will produce a surplus above the original expectation. Yet, if the amount invested is sensitive to rate levels, a lower amount will probably be received when alternative rates have moved higher.

A timing difference also occurs when a portfolio manager expects a cash inflow—such as a pension fund contribution or maturity proceeds—and wishes to lock in a rate today for the investment of the funds when they become available. If the portfolio has obligations on which the rate has been set, this manager also is at risk in the mismatched sense. If the portfolio has no such obligations, the manager's performance may be at risk but the problem is one of market timing and not the hedging of a timing difference.

Long Futures or Forwards.   The forward purchase of securities locks in the *forward yield* as of the settlement date of the forward purchase. Taking a long position in futures serves the same purpose. Today's rate cannot be locked in by hedging, except by coincidence. The method for determining the hedge ratio is the same for a long hedge as for a short hedge. The forward yield on a corporate is usually assumed to be the sum of today's corporate yield spread and the forward yield of the Treasury bond to be used as a hedge vehicle. If the corporate is deemed to be especially cheap and a narrowing of the spread is expected, the forward yield of the corporate can be the expected spread for the bond plus the Treasury forward yield. This would increase the hedge ratio slightly. An example of a long hedge and its outcome is given in Exhibit 6.

Purchase of Call Options.   A portfolio manager who is bearish on the market sector in which future funds are to be invested has the option of doing nothing today and simply investing future cash

---

EXHIBIT 6
Forward Market Long Asset Hedge

The following details a long asset hedge for the Niagara Mohawk Power Company (NMK) 12.875 of 11/1/12. The hedge is implemented with a forward purchase of the U.S. 11.25 of 2/15/15. This transaction serves to lock in a target purchase price for the corporate bond. The hedge is set on June 19, 1985, and is lifted on September 19, 1985.

Step 1. Determine Forward Rates and Hedge Ratio

Settlement Date: 6/19/85

Target Asset:
  NMK 12.875 of 11/1/12   Price: 105.279
                                     Yield: 12.20%

Hedge Vehicle:		— Spot —	— Forward -
U.S. 11.25 of 2/15/15		(6/19/85)	(9/19/85)
	Price:	108.000	107.137
	Yield:	10.373%	10.462%

Calculate Forward (Target) Yield on Corporate on 9/19/85:

  Quality Spread to Treasury on 9/19/85
  (Assumed to be Unchanged):   182.7 Basis Points

  Forward Yield of NMK 12.875 of 11/1/12[a]   12.289%
  Forward Price of NMK 12.875 of 11/1/12   104.546

Compute Hedge Ratio:
  Dollar Value of 0.01% on Forward Date (9/19/85):
  NMK 12.875 of 11/1/12:   0.08144 per $100 Face
  U.S. 11.25 of 2/15/15:   0.09663 per $100 Face

$$\text{Hedge Ratio} = \frac{\$VAL01 \text{ Asset}}{\$VAL01 \text{ Hedge Vehicle}} = \frac{0.08144}{0.09663} = 0.84280$$

---

[a] Forward NMK 12.875 Yield = Forward U.S. 11.25 Yield + 182.7 Basis Points.

EXHIBIT 6 *(Continued)*

Step 2. Establish Hedge Position on June 19, 1985

Face Amount of NMK 12.875 to Purchase on 9/19/85: $100,000,000

Face Amount of U.S. 11.25 to Buy Forward: 84,280,000

Step 3. Unwind Hedge Position on September 19, 1985

Examine the outcome of the hedge under a variety of interest rate scenarios. For illustrative purposes, the calculation of the rising rate scenario effective yield is detailed in a footnote.

Scenario	Effective Purchase Yield of NMK 12.875 (Target = 12.29%)	
Interest rates rise to 100 basis points above forward rates[a]	12.30%	Treasury - Corporate Spread Remains Unchanged
Spot rates converge to forward rates	12.29%	
Interest rates decline to 100 basis points below forward rates	12.30%	

In the absence of a change in the Treasury-corporate yield spread, the forward purchase of the U.S. 11.25 of 2/15/15 results in a highly effective hedge.

[a] Interest rates rise to 100 basis points above forward rates:

Settlement Date:		6/19/85
Buy Forward (to 9/19/85): U.S. 11.25 of 2/15/15 @ 10.462%	Flat Price:	107.137
	Accrued Interest:	1.070
	Full Price:	108.207

Horizon Date:		9/19/85
Purchase: NMK 12.875 of 11/1/12 @ 13.289%	Flat Price:	96.943
	Accrued Interest:	4.935
	Full Price:	101.878
Sell to Close Out Forward: U.S. 11.25 of 2/15/15 @ 11.462%	Flat Price:	98.198
	Accrued Interest:	1.070
	Full Price:	99.268

EXHIBIT 6 *(Continued)*

Full Price of Asset (NMK 12.875 of 11/1/12):	<101.878>
Loss on Hedge Vehicle (U.S. 11.25 of 2/15/15):	
Full Price of Forward Purchase:	<108.207>
Sell to Close Out Forward:	99.268
Loss per $100 Face:	< 8.939>
Hedge Ratio:	0.8428
Loss:	< 7.534>
Effective Full Price of Asset (Inc. Accrued):	<109.412>
Effective Flat Price of Asset:	104.477
Effective Yield of Asset:	12.30%

EXHIBIT 7
Long Asset Hedge (Fixed Rate versus Floor Rate)

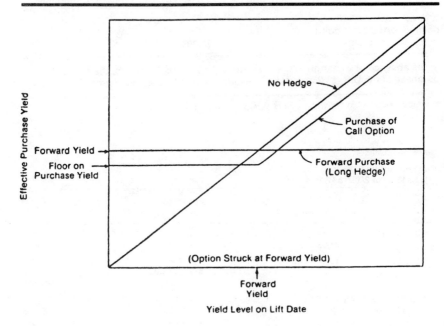

flows when they arrive at the hoped-for higher rates. Purchasing call options, if they are available, on what might otherwise have been the hedge vehicle can insure against the risk of being wrong. This serves to put a floor on the portfolio yield while allowing potential benefit from higher yields. The expense involved, which affects the floor rate, will depend on the amount of insurance desired (the number of options purchased and their strike prices) and its cost (the option premiums). The difference between locking in a target yield with a forward purchase and establishing a floor yield with call options is shown in Exhibit 7.

II. THE USE OF SYNTHETIC ASSETS TO ENHANCE PORTFOLIO RETURNS

The strategies that we have discussed so far have all involved protecting a portfolio against adverse market movements. We will now examine several more positive strategies through which these new financial instruments can be used to enhance asset portfolios. These strategies allow a manager to view the entire spectrum of fixed-income securities, find value in the market and then tailor a position to fit particular needs.

Creating Synthetic Short-Term Assets

We have seen how the forward sale of an asset creates a short-term investment earning a short-term rate. It follows that the sale of an overvalued futures contract could produce a short-term rate in excess of those available directly in the money market. We have looked at the cash and carry from the point of view of a manager with a legitimate need to hedge; however, the manager could have observed rich futures in the marketplace and done the same transaction for the express purpose of capturing the excess short-term return.

One might assume that any excess return would be quickly arbitraged away, but this is not necessarily so, principally because the investor usually views the short-term cash-and-carry return in comparison with the Treasury bill rate. When viewed by the dealer/ arbitrageur, however, it is compared with the rate at which the cash security can be financed. Since dealers cannot borrow at Treasury rates, the break-even rates of the investor and arbitrageur differ. This difference makes excess returns to the investor possible. A futures contract will not always appear rich to the investor, since many other factors are involved, but profitable opportunities are not uncommon.

Treasury Cash and Carry. Exhibit 8 details how a long-term bond, the U.S. 12½ of 8/15/14, can be converted to a short-term investment by selling an appropriate number of Treasury bond futures against it. Notice that the hedge ratio is the same as if this bond were being hedged by selling futures. This is the same transaction: The only difference is that, when hedging, the fact that the hedged portfolio will earn a short-term rate is simply accepted, whereas now the short-term rate is being computed and compared with other money market rates. The hedger would be aware of the short-term rate—the implied repurchase rate—only to the extent that the decision to hedge or the choice of hedge vehicle depended on how rich bond futures were.

Notice in Exhibit 8 that the short-term cash-and-carry return is 2.62 percent—an unattractive rate—because bond futures have been relatively cheap since the end of 1982. This persistent cheap-

---

EXHIBIT 8
Treasury Cash and Carry

For the investor, the Treasury cash and carry creates an alternative short-term investment. In this example, the holding period return of the U.S. 12.50 of 8/15/14 will be converted to a short-term rate through the sale of Treasury bond futures.

Step 1. Determine Hedge Ratio

		6/19/85
Settlement Date:		
Long Position: U.S. 12.50 of 8/15/14	Price: Yield:	116.969 10.604%
Short Position: SEP 85 Treasury Bond Futures Contract		
Cheapest to Deliver: U.S. 11.25 of 2/15/15	Price: Yield:	108.000 10.373%

EXHIBIT 8 *(Continued)*

Since the hedge ratios of a Treasury cash and carry and a futures market asset hedge are identical, the hedge ratio of 1.4373 derived in Exhibit 3 may be applied here.

Step 2. Establish Cash-and-Carry Position on June 19, 1985

Purchase:

U.S. 12.50 of 8/15/14 @ 10.604%	Flat Price:	116.969
	Accrued Interest:	4.282
	Full Price:	121.251

Sell:
SEP 85 Treasury Bond Futures Contracts @ 77.688

1.4373 Contracts per $100,000 Face U.S. 12.50 of 8/15/14.

Step 3. Deliver U.S. 12.50 into the Expiring SEP 85 Futures Contract (9/19/85)

The U.S. 12.50 of 8/15/14 can be delivered into the SEP 85 contract with a conversion factor of 1.4749. If the SEP 85 futures contract closes unchanged at 77.688, the sale proceeds per $100 face U.S. 12.50 via the delivery[a] are 114.5820 = 77.688 * 1.4749, plus accrued interest of 1.189 from 8/15/85 through 9/19/85.

Horizon Date:	9/19/85
SEP 85 Contract Price:	77.688

Profit on Cash and Carry:

Full Purchase Price (6/19/85):	<121.251>
Coupon Flow (8/15/85):	6.250
Interest on Coupon (8/15/85 - 9/19/85):	0.043
Full Sale Proceeds (9/19/85):	
(114.5820 + 1.189) =	115.771
Profit:	0.813

Annualized CD Return: $\dfrac{0.813}{121.251}$ * $\dfrac{360}{92}$ = **2.62%**[b]

[a] Delivery would be made against one contract per $100,000 face U.S. 12.50. The remaining 0.4373 contracts would be closed out (at a purchase price equal to the sale price).

[b] The return on the Treasury cash and carry will be somewhat higher than 2.62% if the U.S. 12.50 is not actually delivered into the expiring contract. Since the bond contract closes slightly cheaper than cash, an investor could simultaneouly close out the futures position (at a purchase price equal to the sale price), and sell the U.S. 12.50 of 8/15/14 in the cash market. Based on recently settled contracts, a reasonable estimate of the SEP 85 final basis of this bond is 0.4063 points. If this spread prevails, the full sale proceeds become 116.177 = 115.771 + 0.4063. This produces an annualized CD return of 3.93%.

ness is explained by the fact that this contract is widely used by hedgers (who sell) and that dealers find it difficult to short Treasury bonds in enough size to hedge the futures that they would have to buy in order to arbitrage cheap futures back to fair value. Some cheapness has also been incorporated into the bond contract as users have become aware of various delivery options available to the short and have learned to value them properly.

There is no reason for bond futures to stay cheap indefinitely, and the cash-and-carry return need not always be unattractive. Even when futures are cheap, however, attractive returns are sometimes available with the corporate cash and carry (see below), although extra risk is involved. The best way to use cheap futures is to capture their value by buying them together with Treasury bills, creating a synthetic bond that will outperform real bonds. The synthetic bond strategy is discussed at greater length later in this section.

The trade described in Exhibit 8 could be done using note futures instead of the bond futures by increasing the hedge ratio by an appropriate amount. The resulting short-term investment would be exposed to yield curve risk, but it would be attractive if note futures were rich *and* an upward sloping Treasury yield curve was expected to flatten in the ten- to 20-year range.

Corporate Cash and Carry.   The synthetic short-term instrument created by selling Treasury bond futures against a deliverable Treasury bond has a return that is virtually riskless. When the futures are sold against a corporate bond (corporate cash and carry), the return is no longer riskless, since the position contains unhedgeable quality spread risk. With this risk, however, comes the possibility of higher returns. Exhibit 9 shows the computations involved in setting up a corporate cash-and-carry trade, together with a scenario analysis. An examination of the first three scenarios in Exhibit 9 shows that, with no changes in quality spread, the short-term return is relatively insensitive to overall yield changes and higher than the return from the Treasury cash and carry, reflecting the higher yield and lower price volatility of the corporate. (The returns in these scenarios differ more than those in the first three scenarios of Exhibit 2 because of convexity differences. The more the hedged asset and the hedging vehicle differ in convexity, the greater the potential

EXHIBIT 9
Corporate Cash and Carry—Futures Market

As an alternative to holding short-term securities, an investor may prefer a long position in a cash security and a short position in the appropriate number of futures contracts. In this example, the return from the following strategy will be examined under varying interest rate scenarios: (1) Hold the NMK 12.875 of 11/1/12 on June 19, 1985; (2) sell the September 1985 Treasury bond futures contract; and (3) close out both positions on September 19, 1985.

Step 1. Calculate Forward Rates

Settlement Date: 6/19/85

Long Position:
NMK 12.875 of 11/1/12

Price:		105.279
Yield:		12.20%

Short Position:
SEP 85 Treasury Bond Futures Contract

Cheapest to Deliver:
U.S. 11.25 of 2/15/15

Price:		108.000
Yield:		10.373%

Determination of Forward Rates on 9/19/85 as Implied by Futures:

SEP 85 Contract Price:	77.6880
U.S. 11.25 Conversion Factor:	1.3650
Final Contract Basis:[a]	0.1875 Points
Forward U.S. 11.25 Price:[b]	106.2316
Forward U.S. 11.25 Yield:	10.5561%
Expected Quality Spread: (Assumed to Remain Unchanged):	182.7 Basis Points
Forward NMK 12.875 Yield:[c]	12.3831%
Forward NMK 12.875 Price:	103.785

Step 2. Calculate Hedge Ratio

Dollar Value of 0.01% on Forward Date (9/19/85):

NMK 12.875 of 11/1/12:	$0.08037 per $100 Face
U.S. 11.25 of 2/15/15:	$0.09518 per $100 Face

Futures Hedge Ratio per $100,000 face NMK 12.875 of 11/1/12:

$$\text{Hedge Ratio} = \frac{0.08037}{0.09518} \cdot 1.3650 = \textbf{1.15261} \text{ SEP 85 contracts.}$$

[a] Because of various delivery options avaliable to the short, the bond contract closes slightly cheaper than cash. The number used here is a Salomon Brothers's estimate of the SEP 85 final basis of the U.S. 11.25
[b] The forward price calculation is 106.2316 = (77.6880 • 1.3650) + 0.1875.
[c] Forward NMK 12.875 Yield = Forward U.S. 11.25 Yield + 182.7 Basis Points.

EXHIBIT 9 *(Continued)*

Step 3. Establish Cash-and-Carry Position on June 19, 1985

Purchase:

NMK 12.875 of 11/1/12 @ 12.20%	Flat Price:	105.279
	Accrued Interest:	1.717
	Full Price:	106.996

Sell:

SEP 85 Treasury Bond Futures Contracts

1.15261 Contracts per $100,000 Face NMK 12.875 of 11/1/12.

Step 4. Unwind Cash and Carry on September 19, 1985

Examine the outcome of the hedge under several interest rate scenarios. For illustrative purposes, the calculation of the rising rate scenario return is detailed in a footnote.

Scenario	Annualized CD Return Over Hedge Period	
Interest rates rise to 100 basis points above forward rates[a]	6.05%	Treasury - Corporate Spread Remains Unchanged
Spot rates converge to forward rates	6.31%	
Interest rates decline to 100 basis points below forward rates	5.98%	
NMK 12.875 yields 20 basis points over forward rate; U.S. 11.25 converges to forward rate.	0.51%	Spread Widens
NMK 12.875 yields 20 basis points under forward rate; U.S. 11.25 converges to forward rate.	12.27%	Spread Narrows

---

[a] Interest rates rise to 100 basis points above forward rates:

	9/19/85
Horizon Date:	
NMK 12.875 of 11/1/12	96.2790 @ 13.3831%
U.S. 11.25 of 2/15/15	97.4243 @ 11.5561%

A price of 97.4243 on the U.S. 11.25 implies a futures price of 71.2358 = (97.4243 − 0.1875)/1.3650.

Sell:

NMK 12.875 of 11/1/12 @ 13.3831%	Flat Price:	96.279
	Accrued Interest:	4.935
	Full Price:	101.214

Purchase:

SEP 85 Treasury Bond Futures Contracts @ 71.2358

1.15261 Contracts per $100,000 Face NMK 12.875 of 11/1/12

EXHIBIT 9 *(Continued)*

Loss on NMK 12.875 of 11/1/12:		
Full Purchase Price (6/19/85):		<106.996>
Full Sale Price (9/19/85):		101.214
Loss:		< 5.782>
Profit on Futures Position:		
Purchase Price (9/19/85):		71.2358
Sale Price (6/19/85):		77.6880
Profit Per Contract:		6.4522
Hedge Ratio:		1.15261
Profit:		7.4369
Net Profit:		1.6549

Annualized CD Return: $\dfrac{1.6549}{106.996} * \dfrac{360}{92} = 6.05\%$

---

hedge error.[5]) Exhibit 9 shows how much the short-term return can be affected when the quality spread changes. It follows that the corporate cash and carry may be very attractive, even with cheap futures, if the quality spread is expected to narrow, but it carries the risk that the spread will widen. The investor doing a corporate cash-and-carry trade should understand this cross-hedge risk and, if spreads widen, not blame the result on basis risk.

Extending the Maturity of Short-Term Assets

The synthetic strategies discussed so far have involved selling futures to shorten the maturity of a long-term asset—giving up the long-term rate in exchange for a short-term rate. This strategy is

[5] The convexity of a portfolio is the sensitivity of its volatility to changing yields. Put another way, it is a measure of how nonlinear (or curved) its price/yield curve is. Loosely speaking, if all price/yield curves (bonds, futures and options) were linear, then all hedges would be perfect and all the synthetic strategies that we will be discussing would work perfectly, assuming parallel yield curve shifts. The greater the convexity differences among the instruments being used or synthetically created, the less perfect the results will be and the more closely a position will have to be monitored and adjusted. Convexity is discussed more thoroughly in Richard G. Klotz, *Convexity of Fixed-Income Securities,* New York: Salomon Brothers Inc, October 1985. This article makes a distinction between convexity per dollar invested and convexity per unit of (dollar) volatility. Technically, it is the second quantity that is relevant to the assessment of convexity-related hedge error.

particularly attractive when futures are trading rich. It is also possible to extend the maturity of a short-term asset by purchasing futures. In this case, one gives up a short-term rate in exchange for a long-term rate, a strategy that is more attractive when futures are cheap. As an example, we consider the creation of a synthetic one-year Eurodollar time deposit.

Using Futures to Set a Target Rate.　On June 17, 1985, an asset manager could have invested in a one-year Eurodollar time deposit with a yield of 8.19 percent. Alternatively, this manager could have created a synthetic one-year investment with the purchase of a three-month Eurodollar time deposit and three successive IMM Eurodollar futures contracts (known as a strip). This strategy is diagrammed in Exhibit 10, and the computations, using then-available prices, are given in Exhibit 11. These show the synthetic asset giving a target return of 8.35 percent, or 16 basis points over the one-year time deposit. A similar strategy could have been employed using a cash position in 90-day Treasury bills and a strip of Treasury bill futures to create a synthetic one-year Treasury bill.

As in hedging, the use of futures locks in a target rate. If in Exhibit 11, the cash Eurodollar rate in September had turned out to be 5.80 percent, the futures contract would have provided a profit of 200 basis points, making the effective reinvestment rate 7.80 percent (5.80 percent plus 200 basis points). Similarly, if the cash September rate had been 9.80 percent, the effective reinvestment rate

---

EXHIBIT 10
The Buy Money Market/Buy Futures Approach

● Roll Short-Term Asset

● Lock in Today Rate at Which the Asset Reprices Each Time

● Compound Each Roll Rate to Determine Longer-Term Yield

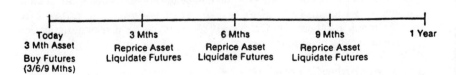

| Today
3 Mth Asset
Buy Futures
(3/6/9 Mths) | 3 Mths
Reprice Asset
Liquidate Futures | 6 Mths
Reprice Asset
Liquidate Futures | 9 Mths
Reprice Asset
Liquidate Futures | 1 Year |

EXHIBIT 11
A Synthetic One-Year Asset With a Fixed Return

On June 17, 1985, an asset manager could have invested in a one-year Eurodollar time deposit at a yield of **8.19%**. As an alternative to an investment in this time deposit, the manager could have created a synthetic one-year investment with the purchase of a three-month Eurodollar time deposit and a strip of IMM Eurodollar futures contracts. On the same day, a three-month Eurodollar time deposit was available at a yield of 7.563%, and a strip of IMM Eurodollar futures contracts was trading at the following levels:

	Price	Yield
SEP 85:	92.20	7.80%
DEC 85:	91.72	8.28
MAR 86:	91.29	8.71

The futures positions required to create the synthetic asset are computed as follows:

Settlement Date:	6/17/85
Initial Investment in Three-Month Time Deposit:	$1,000,000
Three-Month LIBOR:	7.563%

Contract Month	Number of Contracts[a]	Face Amount of Contracts
SEP 85	1.0000 * (1 + 0.07563 * 91/360) = 1.0191	1,019,100
DEC 85	1.0191 * (1 + 0.07800 * 91/360) = 1.0392	1,039,200
MAR 86	1.0392 * (1 + 0.08280 * 91/360) = 1.0610	1,061,000

On June 17, 1986, the time deposit made in March 1986 would be worth $1,084,620 = $1,061,000 * (1 + 0.0871 * 92/360). This 365-day investment has a target return of **8.35%** = 8.462 * 360/365 (on a 360-day CD equivalent basis.)

A yield of 8.35% represents a pickup of 16 basis points over the one-year time deposit rate.

[a] In practice, these amounts are adjusted slightly to allow for the effects of cash settlement of the futures and to hedge variation margin.

would again have been 7.80 percent (9.80 percent less the futures loss of 200 basis points).

Consider one ramification of this ability to move the maturity structure of an asset from one part of the yield curve to another. Suppose that one is offered, by different dealers, two floating-rate assets that are identical in all respects except that one floats at 200 basis points over the three-month Treasury bill and the other floats at 170 basis points over the one-year Treasury bill. If the spread between the three-month bill and the one-year bill is 60 basis points, which asset has more value? Initially, it might seem that 200 basis points over the three-month Treasury bill is like 140 basis points over the one-year bill and that, therefore, the second asset, at 170 basis points, is really 30 basis points better than the first. Just as a three-month bill can be made into a one-year bill with a strip of futures, the asset floating at 200 basis points over the three-month bill can be converted to an asset floating at 200 basis points over the synthetic one-year bill, thus extending the repricing from a three-month to a one-year horizon. If the synthetic one-year Treasury rate compares favorably with the cash one-year rate, the asset floating at 200 basis points over the three-month rate is preferable to the one floating at 170 basis points over the one-year rate. This example shows how a manager unfamiliar with the use of synthetic assets can overlook real value.

Using Calls to Set a Floor Rate. The purchase of a strip of Eurodollar futures converted the three-month Eurodollar time deposit in Exhibit 11 into a synthetic one-year investment with a locked-in target return. If, instead of the futures, calls on a corresponding number of Eurodollar futures (or over-the-counter calls on 90-day LIBOR) had been purchased, a floor rate would have been locked in without giving up the potential benefits of an increase in rates. The level of such a floor rate depends on the amount of insurance purchased and its price—on the rates at which the calls are struck and the amount of the premiums paid up-front. The example in Exhibit 11 is modified in Exhibit 12 to show how a strip of calls on three-month LIBOR could have been used to establish a floor rate. It is important to note that the one-year floor rate in Exhibit 12 is less than the one-year Eurodollar time deposit rate. The creation of synthetic assets cannot perform yield curve magic. If a synthetic two-year Treasury note is created with a one-year note and a one-year call on another one-year note, the floor rate on the synthetic two-year note will be less than the cash two-year rate.

Converting Floating-Rate Assets to Fixed-Rate Assets. Portfolio managers purchase floating-rate notes for many reasons. Some managers view them as defensive investments to be held until the market

EXHIBIT 12
A Synthetic One-Year Asset With a Floor Return

On June 17, 1985, the asset manager in Exhibit 11, instead of locking in a target rate, could have locked in a floor rate — or minimum return — with the purchase of a three-month Eurodollar time deposit and a strip of call options on three-month LIBOR. In this example, the asset manager purchases options struck at the target rate of 8.35% computed in Exhibit 11.

Option Expiration	Premium per $1-Million Face Amount
Sep 16, 1985	$1,800
Dec 16, 1985	1,100
Mar 17, 1986	650

The principal amounts on which the calls should be purchased are computed as follows. (It is assumed that rates remain below 8.35% and all the calls are exercised.)

Settlement Date:	6/17/85
Initial Investment in Three-Month Time Deposit:	$1,000,000
Three-Month LIBOR:	7.563%

Option Exp. Month	Number of $1-Million Units[a]	Face Amount of Contracts
Sep 1985	$1.0000 \cdot (1 + 0.07563 \cdot 91/360) = 1.0191$	$1,019,100
Dec 1985	$1.0191 \cdot (1 + 0.08350 \cdot 91/360) = 1.0406$	1,040,600
Mar 1986	$1.0406 \cdot (1 + 0.08350 \cdot 91/360) = 1.0626$	1,062,600

The dollar cost (paid on June 17, 1985) of these options is:

Option Exp. Month	Number of $1-Million Units	Premium Per Unit	Cost
Sep 1985	1.0191	$1,800	$1,834
Dec 1985	1.0406	1,100	1,145
Mar 1986	1.0626	650	691
Total			$3,670

On June 17, 1986, the time deposit made in March 1986 would be worth $1,085,300 = $1,062,600 \cdot (1 + 0.08350 \cdot 92/360)$. Since the initial cash outlay was $1,003,670, the 365-day holding period return is 8.133% = $100 \cdot (1.0853/1.00367 - 1)$.

The 360-day CD equivalent is **8.02%**, which is the floor return for this investment.

[a] In practice these amounts are adjusted slightly to allow for the effects of cash settlement of the option contracts.

outlook improves. Others will be aggressive buyers when they think that the floating-rate sector (or specific notes) is undervalued. Floating-rate notes tend to have price fluctuations that are not too large; thus, they do not usually fall into a category that warrants hedging. It is possible, however, to purchase floating-rate notes and hedge the future level of floating payments. A successful hedge essentially transforms a floating-rate note into a synthetic fixed-rate instrument with a known rate of return. A floating rate note can also be converted to a synthetic fixed-rate note by entering into an interest rate swap as the floating-rate payer and the fixed-rate receiver.[6]

A floating-rate note is similar enough to the rolling over of certificates of deposit or Eurodollar time deposits that the examples of the past two sections will illustrate how a strip of futures or call options can be used to set a target rate or a floor rate. When reset dates differ significantly from dates in the futures cycle, a composite contract approach, using a combination of contracts, can be used to minimize the error of the hedge.[7] In this case, the target return must be high enough to allow for the additional possibilities for error that are introduced.

Hedging with futures is usually not perfect in exactly matching the target rate, and some error is to be expected. This error can be positive or negative to the hedger, and should average out over time. When the rate that is being hedged is closely related to the rate on the hedge instrument—as with a LIBOR-based floating-rate note and the Eurodollar contract—these errors should be small. When the rates are not directly related, as in a cross hedge, the error may be larger, but this too should average out over time if the model of

---

[6] Interest rate swaps are beyond the scope of this article. See Robert Kopprasch, John Macfarlane, Daniel R. Ross, and Janet Showers, "The Interest Rate Swap Market: Yield Mathematics, Terminology and Conventions," Chapter 56, in *The Handbook of Fixed Income Securities,* (Homewood, IL: Dow Jones-Irwin, 1987).

[7] See Robert W. Kopprasch and Mark Pitts, *Hedging Short-Term Liabilities with Interest Rate Futures,* New York: Salomon Brothers Inc, April 1983, and Mark Pitts and Robert W. Kopprasch, "Reducing Inter-Temporal Risk in Financial Futures Hedging," in *The Journal of Futures Markets,* Vol. 4 (1984), pp. 1–13. Although these papers specifically address liabilities, the methods described apply equally to hedging asset rates.

rate relationships is correct for the periods hedged. The hedger must determine, given the possible risk, whether a hedged position has less risk than an unhedged position.

Creating Synthetic Long Bonds

Given that long Treasury bonds exist, why should anyone bother to create them synthetically, with the added inconvenience of variation margin? *A synthetic asset can often be created with a higher yield than its real counterpart in the market.* In a perfect capital market, this would not be possible. But all investors do not have the same borrowing rates, tax rates, volatility assumptions, and time horizons, and these variations lead to price imperfections. Futures sometimes trade rich and sometimes cheap. When they are rich, they can be sold short in a portfolio of longer securities to create short-term instruments with higher yields than real short-term instruments. When they are cheap, they can be purchased together with short-term instruments to create synthetic long-term instruments with better yields than real long-term instruments.

The creation of a synthetic long bond using three-month Treasury bills and Treasury bond futures is demonstrated in Exhibit 15 (where it is compared with a synthetic asset created by replacing the bond futures with calls on bond futures). The approach is to equate the volatility of the cash bond with that of a portfolio consisting of Treasury bills and Treasury bond futures, which is accomplished by finding the volatility of one bond futures contract and then determining the number of contracts that will make the volatility of the bill/futures portfolio equal that of the cash bond.

How well does such a methodology work? Exhibit 13 demonstrates how a simple strategy (synthetically creating the newest long bond from the Treasury bill on the first day of each delivery month and holding it for one quarter) would have worked from 1981 through the second quarter of 1985. The graph shows that the real long bond outperformed the synthetic in the earlier periods, when futures were overpriced. When futures became systematically underpriced toward the end of 1982, the synthetic investment began to outperform the cash bond. Exhibit 14 shows the difference in return between the cash and synthetic bond positions. It is evident that both overpricing and underpricing can prevail for extended

EXHIBIT 13
Synthetic Long Bond versus Cash Long Bond—Annualized Returns

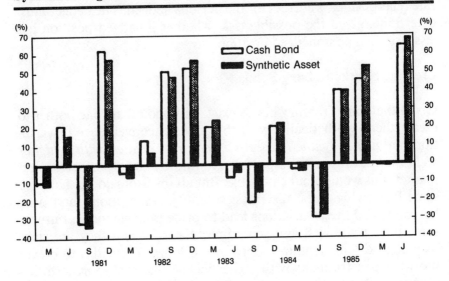

EXHIBIT 14
Synthetic Long Bond versus Cash Long Bond—Difference in Annualized Returns

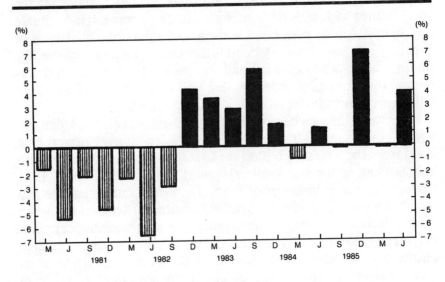

periods of time. During 1981 and 1982, investors in money market instruments could have increased their yields by buying long bonds and selling overvalued bond futures to create synthetic short-term instruments. In 1983 and 1984, investors in long bonds could have improved their returns by switching their portfolios to a combination of Treasury bills and futures.

The graphs in Exhibits 13 and 14 represent a mechanistic approach to replicating the long bond positions. No attempt was made to time the market or to replicate cheap Treasury bonds, and it is likely that a manager could apply judgment to the trading and achieve superior results. Another improvement that could be made would be to replace the Treasury bills used in this simulation with a higher yielding money market instrument or a floating-rate note, although this would entail extra credit risk and would, therefore, not be directly comparable to a position in Treasuries.

What about the manager who wants to hold a long-term bond for longer than a few months? During a prolonged period of underpricing, one contract can be rolled into another to extend the holding period of the synthetic instrument. If one contends that the systematic cheapness of the past two years will not be arbitraged away, a synthetic bond could be held indefinitely. Moreover, bond futures have a certain amount of cheapness built into them because of uncertainty about the most deliverable bond and the presence of various delivery options available to the short. Thus, an investor rolling from one contract into the next has a technical advantage that arbitrage cannot completely remove.

Using Options to Create Synthetic Assets. The synthetic long bond discussed above had the disadvantage of tracking the long bond not only in market rallies but in down markets as well. If this risk is one that the portfolio manager does not want to bear, call options can be substituted for the long futures position. This option strategy is compared with the synthetic long bond strategy in Exhibit 15, which shows how the two instruments are created and compares their performances with that of a cash bond under three different interest rate scenarios (see Exhibit 16 for a graphical comparison).

The performance of the bill/option portfolio reflects the levels of premiums paid and the ultimate direction of the market, but some

---

EXHIBIT 15
Creation of Synthetic Long Bond

An asset manager may capture cheapness in the futures market to create synthetic long-term instruments with higher returns than real long-term instruments. Alternatively, a manager with a bearish view on the market may substitute call options for the long futures position. In this example, (1) $100-million face amount of the U.S. 12.50 of 8/15/14 will be synthetically created by purchasing Treasury bills and Treasury bond futures; and (2) this synthetic bond will be converted to an instrument with a floor return by substituting call options on Treasury bond futures for the Treasury bond futures. The initial transaction is set on June 19, 1985, with a horizon date of September 19, 1985.[a]

Step 1. Compute Synthetic Positions

Settlement Date: 6/19/85

Bond to be Synthetically Created:
U.S. 12.50 of 8/15/14 @ 10.604%

Flat Price:	116.969
Accrued Interest:	4.282
Full Price:	121.251
Face Amount:	$100,000,000
Market Value:	$121,251,000
Forward Dollar Value of 0.01%:	$100,220[b]

---

(1) Creation of Synthetic Bond:

Long Treasury Bond Futures Position:
1,437 SEP 85 Contracts @ 77.688

Face Amount per Contract:	$100,000
Dollar Value of 0.01% per Contract:	$ 69.73[c]

Money Market Investment:
Treasury Bills Maturing 9/19/85   Discount: 6.76%

Market Value:	$121,251,000
Face Amount:	$123,383,000

To derive the correct number of long futures contracts, the price volatility of the target asset on the horizon date is equated with the net price volatility of the futures position. (The Treasury bills have zero volatility since they mature on the horizon date.) The resulting position for $100-Million face U.S. 12.50 of 8/15/14 is 1,437 SEP 85 contracts (1,437 =$100,220/$69.73).

---

[a] In practice, slight adjustments are made to allow for the fact that the SEP 85 Treasury bond futures options actually expire at the end of August. The pattern of returns is essentially unaffected.

[b] See Figure 3 for forward yield and $VAL01 data.

[c] $VAL01 Futures = $\dfrac{\$VAL01 \text{ of Cheapest to Deliver}}{\text{Conversion Factor}}$

$\qquad = \dfrac{0.09518}{1.36500} = \$.06973 \text{ per } \$100 \text{ face.}$

See Exhibit 3 for $VAL01 data on the cheapest to deliver.

EXHIBIT 15 *(Continued)*

(2) Conversion to an Instrument With a Floor Return:

Long Option Position:		
SEP 85 Treasury Bond Futures		
Call Options Struck at 78.	Premium:	$1,563 per Contract
Purchase 1,437 Options.	Market Value:	$2,246,000
Money Market Investment:		
Treasury Bills Maturing 9/19/85	Discount:	6.76%
	Market Value:	$119,005,000
	Face Amount:	$121,097,000
	Total Market Value:	$121,251,000

Step 2. Compare Synthetic Returns with Cash Bond Returns

Examine the outcome of the synthetic positions and cash bond under three interest rate scenarios at the horizon date. For illustrative purposes, the determination of the rising rate scenario loss is detailed in a footnote.

	Annualized CD Return		
Strategy	Spot Rates Rise by 100 Basis Points[a]	Spot Rates Unchanged	Spot Rates Decline by 100 Basis Points
(1) Futures and Bills	-17.91%	12.89%	49.07%
(2) Options and Bills	- 0.50	4.07	40.26
(3) Cash Bond	-20.55	10.28	46.35

The futures/bills strategy provides a higher return (or smaller loss) than the cash asset, while the options/bills strategy provides a floor return by sacrificing some of the upside potential.

---

[a] Spot rates rise by 100 basis points.

(1) Futures and Bills:

Futures:	Contracts	Market Value	Net[a]
Purchase:	1,437	77.688	111.638
Sell:	1,437	72.343	103.957

Futures Loss: <$7.681>

Bills:	Face	Market Value	Net[a]
Purchase:	123.383	98.272	121.251
Sell:	123.383	100.000	123.383

Bills Gain: $2.132

Net Loss: <$5.549>

Annualized Return (CD Basis): -17.91%

EXHIBIT 15 *(Continued)*

(2) Options and Bills:

Options:	Amount	Market Value	Net[a]
Purchase:	1,437	1.563	2.246
Sell:	1,437	0.000	0.000

Options Loss: <$2.246>

Bills:	Face	Market Value	Net[a]
Purchase:	121.097	98.272	119.005
Sell:	121.097	100.000	121.097

Bills Gain: $2.092

Net Loss: <$0.154>

Annualized Return (CD Basis): –0.50%

(3) Cash Bond:

	Face	Market Value	Net[a]
Purchase:	100.00	121.251	121.251
Sell:	100.00	108.590	108.590

Loss: <$12.661>
Coupon Flow: 6.250
Coupon Reinvestment: 0.043

Net Loss: <6.368>

Annualized Return (CD Basis): –20.55%

[a] Dollars in millions.

EXHIBIT 16
Cash Bond versus Two Synthetic Bonds—Annualized Returns

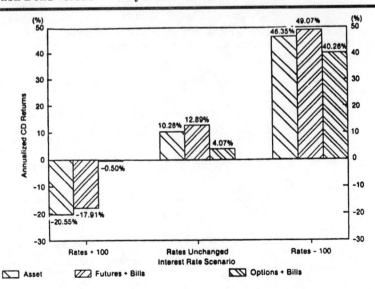

generalizations can be made. In strong rallies, the portfolio will reap most of the increase in value of a long bond portfolio, lagging only because of the premiums paid. In strong down markets, the portfolio will outperform a long bond portfolio, and will lose only the value of the premiums and the difference in income between short and long instruments. Such a portfolio is really a call on higher rates: If rates go up, the money market instrument provides funds to invest at a higher rate, and the call expires worthless; if rates go down, the call generates profits to provide a floor return.

Altering Duration[8]

Thus far we have discussed how a synthetic money market instrument can be created by selling bond futures against a long bond portfolio and a synthetic long bond can be created by buying bond futures with a portfolio of short-term instruments. These are only two of the ways that futures can be used to alter the maturity, or duration, of a portfolio. If we think of duration as a measure of price volatility, then the general principle is that selling futures shortens the duration of a portfolio, and buying futures lengthens the duration of a portfolio.

Several types of portfolio managers may wish to alter the duration of their portfolios. Managers of immunized portfolios may wish to rebalance using futures instead of cash market transactions. These managers may deliberately select securities with the wrong durations but with other desirable characteristics (yield, liquidity or protective covenants) and achieve the desired duration with futures. Macro hedgers may wish to lower the volatility of their portfolios with futures for general risk reduction or until securities are sold. Taken to its extreme, a macro hedge can be used to entirely remove the bond market risk from a portfolio (see the discussion on asset allocation below).

Exhibit 17 details how futures can be used to reduce the Macaulay duration of the U.S. 12½s of 8/15/14 from 8.97 to 6.00. To alter the duration of an entire portfolio, the price sensitivity of the portfolio would be calculated, using either weighted dollar values of a 0.01 percent change in yield ($VAL01s) of the individual securities or an overall portfolio duration measure.

---

[8] See Robert W. Kopprasch, "Understanding Duration and Volatility."

EXHIBIT 17
Altering the Duration of a Bond with Futures

An asset manager who wishes to increase (decrease) the duration of a bond held in a portfolio may purchase (sell) an appropriate number of futures contracts. The net price volatility of the combined position can be matched to a desired target price volatility. In this example, the Macaulay duration of a Treasury bond will be reduced from 8.97 years to 6.00 years through the sale of Treasury bond futures.

Settlement Date: 6/19/85

Asset:
U.S. 12.50 of 8/15/14   Price: 116.969
                                                                              Yield: 10.604%

Face Amount:	$1,000,000
Market Value:	$1,212,510
Macaulay Duration:	8.97 Years
Modified Duration:	8.52 Years
Dollar Value of 0.01%:	$1,033.04
Target Macaulay Duration:	6.00 Years
Equivalent Dollar Value of 0.01%:	$690.88[a]

SEP 85 Treasury Bond Futures:
Face Amount per Contract:	$100,000
Dollar Value of 0.01% per Contract:	$69.73[b]

To derive the appropriate number of futures to sell, the following equality is solved:

Target Volatility	=	Asset Volatility	−	Futures Volatility	•	Number of Contracts
($690.88)	=	($1,033.04)	−	($69.73)	•	(Number of Contracts)

In the above example, the target Macaulay duration of 6.00 years may be achieved by selling 4.9 SEP 85 Treasury bond futures contracts.

---

[a] $\$VAL01 = \dfrac{\text{Macaulay Duration}}{(1 + \text{Yield}/2)} \bullet \text{Yield Change} \bullet \dfrac{\text{Full Price}}{100.000}$

$= \dfrac{6.00}{1.05302} \bullet 0.01 \bullet \dfrac{121.251}{100.000}$

$= \$0.069088$ per $100 face.

See *Understanding Duration and Volatility*, Robert W. Kopprasch, Salomon Brothers Inc, September 1985, for discussion of the $VAL01 computation.

[b] $\$VAL01\ \text{Futures} = \dfrac{\$VAL01 \text{ of Cheapest to Deliver}}{\text{Conversion Factor}}$

$= \dfrac{0.09518}{1.36500} = \$.06973$ per $100 Face.

See Exhibit 3 for $VAL01 data on the cheapest to deliver.

When altering duration as in Exhibit 17 and especially for an immunized portfolio, a pool of liquid assets must be available for variation margin purposes. This may mean that some of the portfolio must be sold for cash, and the portfolio volatility must be recalculated after any liquidating transactions.

Will the newly structured portfolio actually behave like a natural portfolio with the same duration? This depends on how we define the natural portfolio and on the assumptions made about how portfolios should behave. Because futures can be used to reduce duration significantly, as well as to increase it to levels achievable only with zero-coupon bonds, it may be difficult to specify an objective measure of performance. If the duration is lengthened significantly using futures because there are no securities available with the desired duration, which portfolio becomes the comparison portfolio? In Exhibit 17, with the duration set at 6, is one bond with a duration of 6 the benchmark, or is it a laddered or a barbell portfolio that is to be the standard? These questions must be answered, because nonparallel shifts of the yield curve will alter the values of these portfolios differently, and none of them is necessarily a better measure. Even the parallel shifts assumed by most immunization models will affect these portfolios differently because of their differing convexity values.[9]

A portfolio with its duration altered by futures will react to at least two points on the yield curve and perhaps many if the portfolio contains many bonds with varying maturities. The futures used to alter the duration will react to the bond(s) underlying the futures contract used; thus, the overall performance is tied to that part of the yield curve. If long bonds have a downward yield move that exceeds the rest of the market, a portfolio whose duration has been shortened by selling bond futures will perform poorly relative to many other portfolios with the same duration. This reflects the short position in a sector of the market that is outperforming the rest of the market. Similarly, such a portfolio will perform favorably if the long bond sector performs poorly.

Allocating Assets Between Fixed Income and Equity

Portfolio managers and pension plan sponsors can utilize futures to allocate assets between fixed income and equity. Assets do not have

---

[9] See footnote 5 for a brief discussion of convexity.

to be sold to change the allocation within a portfolio. Sponsors need not transfer funds from a fixed-income manager to an equity manager, because that transfer can be accomplished synthetically with futures.

Using futures to allocate assets has several advantages. The individual managers are not forced into selling decisions that unintentionally restructure their portfolios. The costs of reallocating are substantially lower than with cash market transactions. The speed with which the transfer takes place is greatly improved, and the impact on the market is minimized due to the high liquidity in the futures market.

The logic of allocating assets with futures relies on the relationships that we have been discussing: A position in the underlying combined with a short position in stock or bond futures is equivalent to a money market investment; a money market investment together with a long position in stock or bond futures is equivalent to a position in the underlying.

Let us proceed by using an example of a $100-million portfolio currently structured at 50 percent stocks and 50 percent bonds. Assume that the sponsor wishes to change the allocation to 60 percent stock and 40 percent bonds. Exhibit 18 demonstrates the necessary transactions and their effects.

Determining the numbers of contracts involved is relatively straightforward. In Exhibit 18, $10-million (10 percent of $100 million) in bonds must be shortened in effective maturity or duration to three months. This involves fully hedging the $10 million and would be accomplished using the hedging techniques that we discussed in Section I.

Assume that the bond portfolio has a $VAL01 of 0.080 per $100 face amount and that the bonds have a market value of 90. $10-million market value would then be approximately $11,111,000 face amount. The $VAL01 of these bonds together would be $8,888. Assuming that the $VAL01 of the bond futures is $70, the number of contracts to sell would be 127.

To add $10-million market value of equity exposure with futures, we need to buy 125 contracts. This is determined by noting that the S&P futures contract at a price of 160 covers a market value of $160 \times \$500 = \$80,000$. To buy $10 million of equity we need $\$10,000,000/\$80,000 = 125$ contracts.

EXHIBIT 18
Using Futures to Alter the Structure of a Portfolio

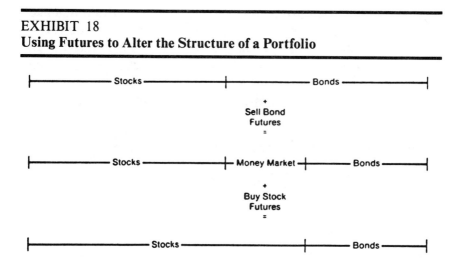

The decision to allocate assets with futures involves many considerations, and the relative pricing of the futures is important. In determining whether or not futures are an attractive method of allocating, the sponsor must recognize that the necessary contracts may be unattractively priced for the desired transactions. In the example above, if stock futures were rich and bond futures were cheap, the strategy would be less attractive.

III. CONCLUSION

The availability of these new synthetic instruments makes the portfolio manager's task more challenging and more complicated because of the increased number of markets and combinations of securities that must be tracked. Managers prohibited from using the new instruments (by charter or board decision) will find it more difficult to perform in the top tier of managed funds. Financial institutions that must compete for funds will find that they cannot afford *not* to know how to value these instruments and use them, since knowledgeable competitors who can reinvest more profitably will be offering more attractive rates.

In other ways, the portfolio manager's job has been made easier.

When synthetics can produce extra return, the portfolio manager can add incremental return to a portfolio with very little risk— probably much less than would be required to generate the incremental return through speculative trading or some other technique. The flexibility provided by the new instruments makes it possible to search the entire debt market for value relative to Treasuries.

ARTICLE 19

MICHAEL R. ROSENBERG is Director of International
Fixed Income Research for Merrill Lynch. The
international fixed income research group publishes a
weekly review of global bond market and currency trends
(including recommended global portfolio strategy), a
bi-weekly review of yield curve and yield spread
developments in all major bond markets, and a monthly
international economic and financial calendar. Two new
publications include a monthly review on new issue activity
and financial innovations in the international bond
markets and a quarterly perspective of currency and
interest rate developments around the world.

Mr. Rosenberg joined Merrill Lynch in August 1984.
Prior to joining Merrill Lynch, he was Director of
International Bond Management for Prudential Insurance
Company of America (1982–84). At Prudential he
managed a $400 million multi-currency bond portfolio.
Prior to joining Prudential, he was an international
economist for Chase Manhattan Bank (1976–77) and a
senior currency and international money market analyst
for Citibank (1978–81).

Mr. Rosenberg holds a Bachelor of Science degree in
Accounting from the State University of New York at
Albany, a Master of Arts degree in Economics from
Queens College and a Ph.D. in Economics from Penn
State University.

GLOBAL BOND PORTFOLIO MANAGEMENT: STRUCTURING THE INVESTMENT PROCESS

Michael R. Rosenberg, Ph.D.
Vice President and Manager
International Fixed Income Research Department
Merrill Lynch

Investment managers are increasingly taking an international perspective in their asset allocation decisions. Our purpose here is to provide globally minded investors, particularly new entrants in the international arena, with general guidelines for setting up and constructing an international bond portfolio, and a framework for designing active global bond portfolio strategy.

Managing a global bond portfolio is more complex than managing a domestic bond fund. Variations in government regulations, market practices, settlement procedures, yield conventions, and secondary market liquidity means that the international investment manager must be thoroughly knowledgeable of numerous institutional details. Moreover, transaction costs in the form of commissions, taxes, bid/offer spreads, custody fees, and settlement charges differ widely among markets, thereby requiring that the international investment manager have a thorough understanding of trading, regulatory and accounting practices as well. Finally, and perhaps most important, the international fixed income strategy process requires that the investment manager evaluate the complex interaction of currency movements, interest rate changes, inter- and intra-market yield spread developments, and yield curve shifts in all of the major markets.

I. GETTING STARTED: SETTING UP AN INTERNATIONAL BOND PORTFOLIO

The first step in setting up an international bond portfolio is to determine the investor's financial objectives. Is the portfolio to be designed to maximize return or to minimize risk, or is some risk level tolerable, whereupon the portfolio can be actively managed to maximize return subject to a predetermined risk constraint. Once this is decided the international investor should select an optimal time horizon to make his investment decisions, both to achieve his stated total return goals and for performance measurement purposes. For instance, investors may select either a short-term investment time horizon so as to catch short-run swings in exchange rates and interest rates, or a long-term time horizon to capture the general trend in currency and bond market movements. To a large extent, the investment time horizon decision will be dictated by:

1. the general objective of the fund;
2. one's views as to the relative merits of aggressive, active and passive management; and
3. the time and resources investors can and will devote to the active management of the international bond portfolio.

In the initial stages of setting up an international bond portfolio, the investment manager should draw up a delegation of authority list. Such a list should indicate which foreign markets and credits will be approved for purchase. Based on an assessment of country and credit risk, as well as an assessment of tax and liquidity considerations, an approved list of issuers should be drawn. More names could be added and some dropped over time as conditions warrant.

For example, a risk-averse fund may choose to invest only in government and government-guaranteed issues. Another fund may approve the purchase of AAA and AA corporate issues. And so forth. The delegation of authority list should also detail what percentage of the fund's assets can be assigned to any single credit.

Once it is clear which markets and credits will be approved, the international investor should select a global custody service (usually a large international bank with an extensive overseas branch and correspondent banking network) to arrange for the delivery and settlement of bought and sold securities and foreign exchange, the collection of coupon income, the reclaiming of any coupon tax due the investor because of double taxation treaties, maintaining cash balances in various markets on deposit, and the receipt of comprehensive and timely reports on portfolio activities and the valuation of total assets under management. It would be wise for the investment manager to set up an internal bond operations unit to review all trade details (i.e., price, settlement date, and accrued interest), specify delivery instructions, and contact the global custody service to arrange for settlement and safe custody.

II.   ESTABLISHING PORTFOLIO MANAGEMENT GUIDELINES

Once these housekeeping duties are taken care of, the international investment manager should turn his attention to the establishment of portfolio management guidelines for the distribution of the global bond fund's assets. These self-imposed asset allocation guidelines should assign minimum, normal, and maximum positions that can be held in any single currency bloc or market. The purpose of the guidelines is to underscore the desire for diversification and at the same time provide ample latitude for active management. For example, Exhibit 1 highlights the asset distribution guidelines for a hypothetical global bond fund. The guidelines define the proportion of the portfolio's funds which can be assigned to the major currency blocs: U.S. Dollar, German Mark, Japanese Yen, and British Pound.

The normal weights chosen should reflect the approximate relative current market value of each of the major markets in the total world bond market, or perhaps even better, reflect the relative

EXHIBIT 1
Asset Allocation Guidelines for Structuring a Hypothetical Global Bond Portfolio

Currency Bloc	Minimum Position	Normal Position	Maximum Position
U.S. Dollar*	25%	50%	75%
German Mark**	10%	20%	60%
Japanese Yen	10%	20%	60%
British Pound	5%	10%	55%

* Includes U.S. and Canadian Markets.

** Includes German, Dutch, Swiss, French, and ECU Markets.

liquidity and tradeability of each market. If investors use a widely followed external benchmark (or bogey) for performance evaluation purposes, they might want to use the benchmark's fixed weights as the normal weights.

The minimum and maximum guideposts should reflect the operational constraints facing the active portfolio manager. Within the limits defined by the minimum and maximum position guideposts, the portfolio manager should be free to allocate funds among currencies and maturities. Within the assigned portfolio constraints, the investment manager can then decide which currency blocs (and which markets and sectors within each currency bloc) will be overweighted, which currency blocs will be underweighted, in which markets funds will be invested long, and in which markets funds will be invested short. These decisions can only be made by assessing what direction exchange rates and interest rates will take.

III. TOTAL RETURN ANALYSIS

Although management styles differ, one will generally find that the active management of multicurrency bond portfolios lends itself much more to a top/down rather than a bottom/up approach. That is, investors will find that the rewards from choosing the right currencies and maturities to invest in far outweigh the rewards from individual bond selection. This is not to say that individual bond selection should be dismissed as unimportant, since, if done correctly, it can add valuable incremental return to a portfolio. What it does suggest is that the allocation of an investor's time and resources should be handled carefully so that those areas representing the greatest sources of return, as well as risk, receive the greatest attention.

A top/down assessment of total return outcomes in the various markets requires that the projected return on multicurrency bond investments be made comparable in terms of a single base currency. That is, from a dollar based investor's perspective, the projected returns on dollar and non-dollar bond investments must be translated in dollar terms first before a ranking based on dollar-adjusted performance can be made. In dollar terms, the principal sources of return on multicurrency bond investments are: (1) currency changes versus the dollar; (2) coupon income; (3) interest on interest; and (4) changes in local currency bond prices. Mathematically, the total return in dollar terms on a non-dollar bond investment for a single period is shown below:

$$(1 + R_\$) = (1 + LC) * (1 + \$)$$

or

$$R_\$ = LC + \$ + (\$ * LC)$$

The equation states that the total return in dollar terms ($R_\$$) on a foreign bond investment equals the local currency return (LC), plus the currency gain or loss ($), plus a small product term which measures the impact of the currency change on the local currency return ($ * LC). For example, if the local currency return on a foreign bond is 10 percent and the respective foreign currency appreciates by 5 percent, the total return in dollar terms on the foreign investment would be 15.5 percent. The reason that the total return is not 15 percent (LC + $ = 10 percent + 5 percent = 15 percent) is that the currency gain applies to both the principal and to the local currency return. Thus, in the example above, a $1,000 investment in a foreign bond would yield a 5 percent currency gain on the initial $1,000 investment ($50) and a 5 percent currency gain on the $100 local currency return ($5). Totalling the different sources of return would yield $100 (10 percent local currency return on the initial $1,000 investment) plus $50 plus $5 to equal $155, which amounts to a 15.5 percent total return.

The ranking of markets according to projected total return outcomes requires a careful assessment of what direction exchange rates and interest rates will take over the relevant investment time horizon. The interest rate forecasts should include projections of government note and bond yields for all relevant maturities in all markets. The initial focus should be on government note and bond yields, after which an analysis of key sectors could be made to search for incremental yield opportunities.

A straight-forward procedure to derive total return projections is to first estimate what local currency returns will be along all points on each of the major government bond yield curves and then to translate these local currency return forecasts in terms of a single base currency such as the dollar. For example, in Exhibit 2, a projected local currency return curve (solid line) is constructed for a hypothetical foreign bond market. The local currency return curve plots projected local currency returns against each of the relevant points on the foreign bond yield curve. In the exhibit, the local currency return curve is drawn with an upward slope, indicating that the longer maturities in the foreign bond market are expected to outperform the shorter maturities. If the longer maturities were expected to underperform the shorter maturities, the local currency return curve would be drawn with a downward slope.

Translating local currency projections for each market into a single base currency such as the dollar is a fairly straightforward exercise, using the total return equation described above. Given one's assessment of the change in the relevant foreign currency versus the base currency, total returns in terms of the base currency can be calculated. In Exhibit 2, a projected total return curve in dollar terms for our hypothetical foreign bond market (dashed line) is drawn on the assumption that the relevant foreign currency is expected to appreciate against the dollar. The total return curve lies above the local currency return curve because the expected appreciation of the foreign currency versus the dollar raises the total return on the foreign bond in dollar terms to a U.S. investor. Had the foreign currency been expected to depreciate, the total return curve would instead have laid below the local currency return curve.

EXHIBIT 2
Investing in a Hypothetical Foreign Bond Market
Projected Total Returns (In Local Currency and Dollar Terms) Along
Different Points on the Foreign Bond Yield Curve

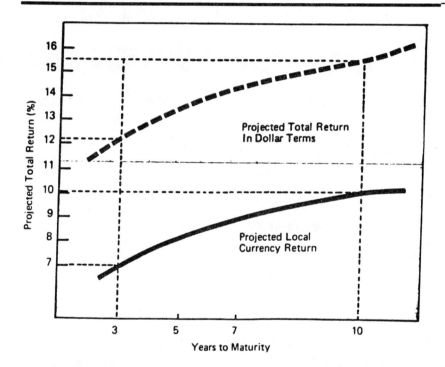

It should be noted that although the gap between the projected
total and local currency return curves reflects the contribution of
the expected currency change, the two curves are not parallel. As we
showed in the total return equation above, the contribution of the
currency change to total return affects not only the value of
the principal but the local currency return as well. Thus, if the
longer maturities are expected to outperform the shorter maturities
in local currency terms, the contribution of the currency change
will be more heavily felt at the long end of the yield curve. For
example, assume that the projected local currency return on a
hypothetical short-term foreign note is 7 percent and on a similar
but longer-term foreign bond it is 10 percent (see Exhibit 2). Then,
if the relevant foreign currency is projected to rise by 5 percent

against the U.S. dollar, the projected total return in dollar terms for short- and long-term foreign securities would 12.35 percent and 15.5 percent, respectively. The gap between the projected total and local currency return curves at the short end would be 5.35 percent and at the long end would be 5.5 percent. Since the gap is wider at the longer end than at the shorter end, the curves are not parallel.

Once total return projections in terms of a single base currency are calculated for all markets, the international manager must begin the process of ranking the markets according to best expected performance. At times, the ranking process will be fairly straightforward, i.e., the best performing markets will be associated with the best performing currencies. For example, in Exhibit 3, hypothetical projected total return curves for the United States and two foreign

---

EXHIBIT 3
Hypothetical Projected Total Returns in Dollar Terms on U.S. and Foreign Bonds

---

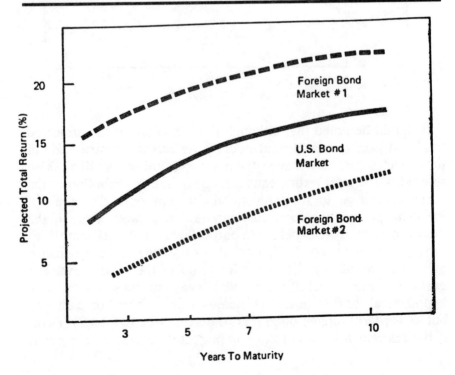

bond markets are drawn. Foreign bond market #1 is expected to post the strongest performance in U.S. dollar terms because its currency is expected to gain ground on the dollar. Foreign bond market #2 is expected to post the weakest performance in U.S. dollar terms because its currency is expected to lose ground to the dollar. Based on a simple ranking according to expected performance, an international manager would overweight foreign bond market #1, normally weight the U.S. bond market, and underweight foreign bond market #2 in his global bond portfolio.

However, there will be many occasions when the ranking process will be more complex. It is not always true that the best performing markets are associated with the best performing currencies. For example, in Exhibit 4, the projected total return curve for foreign bond market #3 is drawn on the assumption that the currency is

EXHIBIT 4
Hypothetical Projected Total Returns in Dollar Terms on U.S. and Foreign Bonds

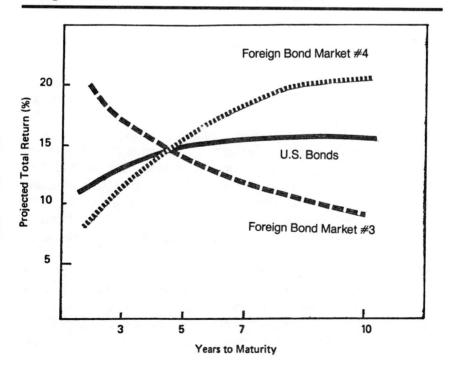

expected to appreciate against the dollar, but the bond market in local currency terms is projected to experience a sharp setback. As a result, the total return curve slopes downward, with the highest projected returns being at the short end of the maturity spectrum. The projected total return curve for foreign bond market #4 is drawn on the assumption that the underlying currency is expected to depreciate against the dollar, but a strong performing bond market in local currency terms lifts the projected returns on longer-term securities. As shown, despite the weakness of the currency, long-term bonds in foreign bond market #4 are expected to perform favorably in U.S. dollar terms because of the strong local currency performance. In terms of establishing a ranking according to projected performance, the international manager would recommend overweighting the short end of foreign bond market #3 and the long end of foreign bond market #4 and underweighting the U.S. market.

IV.   MANAGING CURRENCY AND INTEREST RATE RISK

The precise assignment of portfolio weights in a global bond fund will be largely dictated by the investment manager's assessment of currency and interest rate trends. However, since there are significant risks inherent in any currency or interest rate forecast, prudent managers should ensure that minimum diversification standards are met, i.e., that all or most of the fund's assets are not allocated to a single currency or market. Instead, by requiring that the precise assignment of portfolio weights conform to prescribed asset allocation guidelines, the fund manager can be certain that minimum international diversification requirements are met and at the same time be confident that ample scope exists to overweight and underweight the various currency blocs and markets to enhance total return.

The establishment of internal portfolio management guidelines should be accomplished before the actual currency and security selection process begins. Exhibit 5 is similar to Exhibit 1 in that it highlights how internal guidelines can be structured for a hypothetical global bond fund. These guidelines define minimum, normal,

EXHIBIT 5
Global Bond Portfolio Strategy Determining the Optimal Asset Mix for an
Actively Managed Global Bond Fund

Currency Bloc	Minimum Position	Fundamentally Bearish	Normal Position	Fundamentally Bullish	Maximum Position
U.S. Dollar*	25%		50%		75%
German Mark**	10%		20%		60%
Japanese Yen	10%		20%		60%
British Pound	5%		10%		55%

* Includes U.S. and Canadian markets.
** Includes German, Dutch, Swiss, French and ECU markets.

and maximum positions that a global bond fund can assign to each
of the major currency blocs. The selection of appropriate portfolio
weights for each currency bloc (and the markets and sectors within
each currency bloc) along the min-norm-max spectrum in Exhibit 5
should involve a two stage process. First, based on an analysis of
underlying economic fundamentals, the investment manager should
rank each of the markets according to their projected total return
performance. This ranking will dictate which range along the min-
norm-max spectrum each market's weight should fall. Those markets projected to post the strongest total return performance will be
assigned portfolio weights in their prescribed norm-max ranges,
whereas those markets projected to record the weakest total return
performance will be assigned portfolio weights in their prescribed
min-norm ranges.

The second stage of the active management decision process
should require the investment manager to integrate his longer-run
fundamental view with his shorter-run technical view of currency
and interest rate trends. Based on the investment manager's technical reading of market trends, he can determine how much to overweight or underweight a particular market. For example, if the fund
manager's technical reading of the market confirms a generally
bullish fundamental assessment, then the assigned portfolio weight

to that market should lie closer to the maximum position along its prescribed norm-max range. Likewise, if the fund manager's technical reading of the market confirms a generally bearish fundamental assessment, then the assigned portfolio weight to that market should lie closer to the minimum position along its prescribed min-norm range. If the technical reading does not confirm the fundamental assessment, then the assigned portfolio weight should gravitate closer to the normal position along the relevant min-norm or norm-max range.

The only time a fund manager would recommend the maximum allocation to a particular market or currency bloc would be when he is both fundamentally and technically bullish on that market's prospects, and, at the same time, is both fundamentally and technically bearish on the prospects for all other markets. Otherwise, the actual portfolio mix should fall somewhere between the prescribed minimum and maximum guideposts for each market.

Active international bond managers must constantly assess and reassess the fundamental and technical outlook for the major currencies and respective bond markets. Total return projections should be reviewed on a frequent basis, perhaps monthly. This is because unforeseen developments may alter the fundamental outlook for currencies and interest rates, and also because the workout time required for a total return projection to be realized may have to be shortened or lengthened.

There will be many instances when new developments may contribute to a cloudy picture for the currency and interest rate outlook, and it is at such times when the portfolio manager's mettle is truly tested. Fortunately, there are many avenues open to the global portfolio manager to hedge short-term currency and interest rate risk. Futures and options markets are available in many currencies and the investor can use such markets to temporarily protect a heavily overweighted or underweighted position in one or more currencies. For example, if a portfolio manager wishes to hold onto an overweighted Deutschemark bond position, but is nervous about the near-term outlook for the currency (not the underlying bond), he can hedge the currency risk in the short-run by selling the nearby Deutschemark futures contract (or by selling Deutschemarks forward in the interbank forward market), or he can hedge himself by buying a put on the nearby Deutschemark options contract. There are fewer futures and options contracts available to protect against interest rate risk in all of the major bond markets, but the more volatile bond markets such as the United States, United Kingdom, Canadian, Australian and Japanese markets do have such hedging vehicles available.

For those markets where no adequate interest rate hedging vehicle is available, the portfolio manager is always free to alter the maturity/coupon profile of his portfolio. However, investors will probably find that those markets which do not offer adequate interest rate hedging vehicles also exhibit considerably less volatility than those markets that do. When markets exhibit little overall volatility it often proves expensive to adjust the maturity/coupon mix too finely. In most cases, it may be preferable to ride out any storms that do develop in such markets, rather than to try to fine tune the portfolio exactly.

V.   MONITORING PORTFOLIO PERFORMANCE

The only way a fund manager can accurately evaluate portfolio performance and design portfolio strategy is by monitoring his asset mix through carefully constructed security valuation and asset allocation reports. Exhibit 6 shows a security valuation report for a hypothetical global bond fund. The report provides the fund manager with a snapshot of his security holdings, broken down by market. The report reveals both the local currency and dollar value of each security held, the purchase price and current price, the par value (i.e., the total amount) of each issue held, and the share that each security comprises in the total portfolio. Such a snapshot is valuable for fund managers who seek diversification across currencies, markets and credits and for investors who attempt to periodically upgrade their holdings to enhance coupon income or yield.

Exhibit 6 is a useful tool for monitoring the fund's security holdings, but in order to get a clear and concise snapshot of the fund's exposure to currency and interest rate risk, a more compact, less comprehensive report is needed. A fund manager may wish to construct a report similar to Exhibit 7, which shows the broad currency/bond market mix profile for a hypothetical global bond fund. Such a table indicates the net currency exposure that the global bond

EXHIBIT 6
Hypothetical Global Bond Fund
Security Valuation Report for the Week Ending:

Market	Issue	Par Value	Purchase Price	Current Price	Local Currency Value	U.S. Dollar Value	Percent of Portfolio
U.S.	XXXXX						
	XXXXX						
	XXXXX						
	XXXXX						
	XXXXX						
Japan	XXXXX						
	XXXXX						
	XXXXX						
	XXXXX						
	XXXXX						
Germany	XXXXX						
	XXXXX						
	XXXXX						
	XXXXX						
	XXXXX						
United Kingdom	XXXXX						
	XXXXX						
	XXXXX						
	XXXXX						
	XXXXX						

EXHIBIT 7
Hypothetical Global Bond Fund—Asset Mix Report

Currency Bloc	Currency Decision		Market Decision			Composition of Bond Portfolio								
	Net Currency Position	Currency Hedge	Gross Currency Position	Cash Equiv.	Bonds	Maturity Structure						Sector Breakdown		
						1-3 Years	3-5 Years	5-7 Years	7-10 Years	10-15 Years	Long	Gov't.	Euro	Foreign
US$*	-()	–	–	–	–	-()	-()	-()	-()	-()	-()	-()	-()	-()
DM**	-()	–	–	–	–	-()	-()	-()	-()	NA	NA	-()	-()	-()
YEN	-()	–	–	–	–	-()	-()	-()	-()	NA	NA	-()	-()	-()
STG	-()	–	–	–	–	-()	-()	-()	-()	-()	-()	-()	-()	-()
Total	100	0	100	–	–	-()	-()	-()	-()	-()	-()	-()	-()	-()

- Portfolio Weight

( ) Performance Benchmark Weight

* Includes U.S. and Canadian Markets

** Includes West German, Dutch, Swiss, French and ECU Markets fund has in each of the major currency blocs, any currency positions that are hedged, the cash/bond mix that the portfolio holds in each market, and the maturity structure and sector breakdown of the bond holdings in each market. The table can be drawn to show how the portfolio weights stand in regard to the weights of a benchmark performance index (or bogey). This would then indicate which currencies, maturities, and sectors are being over and underweighted.

VI. CONCLUSION

Only through active global bond portfolio management can fund managers be successful in enhancing return above the level that can be earned on a pure domestic bond portfolio. In fact, without the benefit of active management, there is no reason to believe that over the long-run the returns on passively managed foreign bond funds should outperform the returns on passively managed domestic bond funds, and this is borne out by the facts. What active management tries to do is to exploit the existence of sizable differences in the year-to-year total return performance among the various bond markets around the globe, which should provide the international manager with significant opportunities to enhance return if he correctly adjusts currency and market weightings. This also means that there are great risks if asset allocation is done incorrectly. The steps outlined here should help investors to manage such risk.

ARTICLE 20

FRANK J. JONES is a Managing Director of Kidder, Peabody & Co., Incorporated. As the Director of the Financial Futures Department-Customer Business, he is responsible for the marketing, sales and research in interest rate, stock index, foreign currency and petroleum futures and options contracts. Dr. Jones is also currently on the Board of Directors of the New York Futures Exchange and on the Board of Directors of the Intermarket Clearing Corporation, a subsidiary of the Options Clearing Corporation.

Dr. Jones was formerly Senior Vice President of the New York Stock Exchange and Executive Vice President and C.E.O. of the New York Futures Exchange. Dr. Jones is author of several books, including *The Futures Game: Who Wins, Who Loses and Why?*, McGraw Hill Book Company (1987) and *Macro Finance—The Financial System and the Economy*, Winthrop Publishers (1978), and several articles and chapters in books on the financial futures and options markets, the financial system, and other related topics. He is a frequent speaker on topics related to financial futures, the financial markets, and futures exchanges.

BETH A. KRUMHOLZ, Assistant Vice President, is a member of the Product Development Group and works closely with Dr. Frank Jones in research strategies and applications on the interest rate futures and options contracts. Ms. Krumholz joined Kidder, Peabody in 1978 in the Retail Sales Department, and became a member of the Financial Futures Department in 1980. She is licensed as a registered securities agent by the National Association of Securities Dealers and as a registered commodities representative by the Commodity Futures Trading Commission. Ms. Krumholz received her B.A. in Economics from Rutgers College.

DURATION ADJUSTMENT AND ASSET ALLOCATION WITH TREASURY BOND AND NOTE FUTURES CONTRACTS

Frank J. Jones, Ph.D.
Managing Director
Kidder, Peabody & Co., Inc.

Beth A. Krumholz
Assistant Vice President
Kidder, Peabody & Co., Inc.

Duration management and asset allocation are strategies commonly used by fixed-income and balanced portfolio managers. These strategies have typically been implemented by using the cash bond, note and bill markets. This article discusses how the liquidity, low transactions costs, flexibility and, at times, the pricing of the Treasury bond and note futures contracts can be used to accomplish these portfolio strategies more effectively.

The objective of duration management is to either passively maintain the duration of a portfolio equal to that of a specific target portfolio or index or to change the duration of a portfolio consistent with an active strategy. Asset allocation involves changing the market value of the bond portion of the portfolio relative to

the cash and/or equity portions. In general, buying Treasury bond
or note futures contracts can extend the duration of a fixed-income
portfolio, while selling Treasury bond or note futures contracts
can achieve the opposite purposes. To accomplish either of these
results, however, the appropriate number of futures contracts
to buy or sell must be determined. This article discusses the
method for calculating the appropriate number of futures and provides examples.

I.   SYNTHETIC RELATIONSHIPS UNDERLYING STRATEGIES

In a duration adjustment strategy, the market value of the portfolio
is typically kept constant while the duration is changed. In this
application, it is necessary to calculate the number of futures contracts to buy or sell in order to change the duration by the desired
amount while maintaining the initial market value of the portfolio.
On the other hand, in an asset allocation strategy, the duration of
the fixed-income component of the portfolio is typically kept constant while the effective market value of the portfolio is changed.
In this application, therefore, the number of futures contracts to
buy or sell to change the market value of the bond portfolio by the
desired amount, while maintaining the initial duration of the portfolio, must be calculated. Both calculations are based on the same
concept.

The use of Treasury bond and note futures contracts for either
portfolio strategy is based on two synthetic relationships:

Bond (Note) + Short Bond (Note) Futures Contract = Bill

and

Bill + Long Bond (Note) Futures Contract = Bond (Note).

Therefore, selling Treasury bond futures contracts against a Treasury bond holding converts the Treasury bond into a Treasury bill
(more accurately into a term repo agreement, the mechanism for
financing Treasury securities). The combination of a bond and a
short bond futures position is called a hedge. On the other hand,
buying Treasury bond futures contracts in conjunction with a

Treasury bill position (or a term repo investment) converts the Treasury bill (or term repo investment) into a Treasury bond. The combination of a bill and a long bond futures position is typically called a synthetic bond. These relationships apply exactly if the futures contract is priced fairly—if the futures price equals the cash price adjusted for the net carry cost of the underlying asset. If futures contracts are priced cheaply relative to fair value, however, as recent Treasury bond and note contracts have been, there may be an advantage to buying these cheap contracts and a disadvantage to selling them. In this situation, a hedged bond position (bond plus short bond futures) would underperform a bill; a "synthetic bond," (bill plus long bond futures) would outperform a bond. On the other hand, if the futures contracts are rich relative to fair value, a hedged bond would outperform a bill and a synthetic bond would underperform an actual bond, as summarized below:

	Pricing of Futures	
Futures Position	Cheap	Rich
Long	Outperform Bond	Underperform Bond
Short	Underperform Bill	Outperform Bill

Treasury bond and note futures contracts may be used for both duration adjustment and asset allocation on either a temporary or a permanent basis. The futures contracts may be used on a temporary basis to accomplish the duration adjustment or the asset allocation quickly, with low transaction costs and via very liquid markets. For example, once a decision is made to increase the allocation of bonds, long Treasury bond futures contracts can be used to implement this decision immediately. The portfolio manager could subsequently determine which particular bonds to buy without either time pressure on the analysis or the possibility of missing a major interest rate move. When the analysis of the specific bonds to buy is completed, these bonds can be bought and the long futures positions liquidated. Futures contracts may also be used as substitutes for either bonds or bills on a longer-term basis to take advantage of the richness/cheapness of the futures contracts.

Although Treasury bond and note futures contracts can be used for adjusting duration or asset allocation in either direction, the frequent cheapness of these contracts provides a bias toward buying them and away from selling them in most circumstances. Managers who use futures contracts to achieve a target duration for their portfolios should, when Treasury bond and note futures contracts are priced cheaply, keep the duration of their actual bond portfolio at the lower end of the range of likely targets and use long futures contracts to extend the duration, rather than the opposite. In this case, the portion of the portfolio consisting of synthetic bonds may outperform the actual bonds for which they were substitutes. On the other hand, if short "cheap" futures are used to reduce duration, the portion of synthetic bills in the portfolio may underperform the actual bills for which they were substitutes. Similarly, when using futures contracts for asset allocation, managers should keep the bond allocation at the lower end of its likely range and use long futures to increase the bond allocation rather than taking the opposite approach when futures contracts are cheap.

However, the disadvantage of using short futures positions when they are cheap for either portfolio strategy can be reduced by rolling these short positions from the nearby contract to the next contract month at least a month and a half before the beginning of the delivery month of the nearby contract. The reason for this timing is that during the last six weeks before the delivery month the cheapnesses of both the Treasury bond and note futures contracts typically decrease more rapidly to the disadvantage of short positions. For example, a short position in the December contract should be rolled to the March contract by mid-October. Long futures positions, on the other hand, should be maintained until as late as possible if they are cheap relative to fair value because the decrease in cheapness serves to the advantage of the long position. The portfolio manager may, however, wish to roll long positions to the next contract month on the first notice day of the contract—two business days before the first business day of the delivery month—to avoid wild card deliveries, particularly if a high coupon bond or note is the cheapest or close to the cheapest deliverable instrument. However, some cheapness will probably remain in the futures contract at the beginning of the delivery month, and for this reason some managers may choose to maintain their long positions well into the delivery month.

II. CALCULATION OF HEDGE RATIOS

The number of futures contracts to buy or sell to accomplish either duration adjustment or asset allocation changes results directly from the definition of modified duration:[1]

$$D = \frac{dP/P}{dY} \qquad (1)$$

where D is the modified duration, P is the market value (including accrued interest), Y is the yield and dP and dY are the changes in the market value and yield, respectively. The typical objective of a portfolio manager relates to the change in market value, dP, in response to a change in yield, dY. This change in the market value of a portfolio, dP, can be expressed in terms of the definition of duration as follows:

$$dP = D \times P \times dY. \qquad (2)$$

Assume portfolio managers want to modify the change in the market value of their initial portfolios, dP_I, to a target level, dP_T, by using futures contracts F:

$$dP_T = dP_I + (N \times dP_F), \qquad (3)$$

where dP_F refers to the change in the market value of one futures contract, and N is the number of futures contracts necessary to accomplish this change (a positive N refers to a long futures position and a negative N to a short futures position).

Expressing equation (3) in terms of equation (2) gives:

$$D_T \times P_T \times dY_T = (D_I \times P_I \times dY_I) + (N \times D_F \times P_F \times dY_F). \qquad (4)$$

[1] Strictly speaking, modified duration is equal to:

$$D = -\frac{dP/P}{dY}$$

The omission of the negative sign in this article does not affect the analytical results derived.

Solving equation (4) for N gives:

$$N = \frac{(D_T \times P_T \times (dY_T/dY_F)) - (D_I \times P_I \times (dY_I/dY_F))}{D_F \times P_F}. \tag{5}$$

The two terms involving yields in the numerator, dY_T/dY_F and dY_I/dY_F, are the changes in the yields of the target and initial portfolios with respect to a unit change in the yield of the futures contract (usually measured by the yield of the cheapest deliverable instrument as discussed below), typically called "yield betas." These yield betas are often considered to be 1.0 although, for example, to adjust the duration of a corporate bond portfolio with Treasury futures contracts, different yield betas can be used. With yield betas of 1.0, the above equation becomes:

$$N = \frac{(D_T \times P_T) - (D_I \times P_I)}{D_F \times P_F}. \tag{6}$$

Equation (6) is the basis for using futures contracts for both duration adjustment and asset allocation.

Duration Adjustment

Using equation (6) to determine the number of futures contracts to adjust the duration of the portfolio from its initial D_I to its desired D_T, assuming the market value of the cash portfolio remains the same, that is, $P_T = P_I$, gives:

$$N = \frac{(D_T - D_I) \times P_I}{D_F \times P_F}. \tag{7}$$

If portfolio managers wish to reduce the duration of their portfolios to 0, that is $D_T = 0$ (or make the portfolio equivalent to overnight funds), then:

$$N = -\frac{D_I \times P_I}{D_F \times P_F}. \tag{8}$$

From equation (1), $D \times P = dP/dY$, where the term dP/dY, the change in the portfolio value for a given change in yield, is often called the "basis point value," denoted by "BPV(.01)" in the futures literature. Equation (8) can be rewritten:

$$N = -\frac{BPV(.01)(\text{Initial Portfolio})}{BPV(.01)(\text{Futures Contract})}. \tag{9}$$

Equation (9) is the standard futures "hedge ratio," which is, thus, equivalent to the number of futures contracts necessary to sell in order to reduce the duration of the bond or portfolio to 0, as shown by equation (8). The standard futures hedge ratio, equation (9), is also equivalent to a duration-based approach shown in equation (8). Equation (6) can be considered as a general "hedge ratio equation" which indicates the number of futures contracts to sell (or buy) for any desired change in duration to D_T.

Asset Allocation

Equation (6) can also be used for asset allocation. The number of futures contracts necessary to change the effective market value, or asset allocation, of the fixed-income component of a portfolio from the initial P_I to the desired P_T, while retaining the duration of this fixed-income component of the portfolio at D_I, can be determined from equation (6) by assuming $D_T = D_I$ as follows:

$$N = \frac{D_I \times (P_T - P_I)}{D_F \times P_F}. \qquad (10)$$

Comparing equation (7) for duration adjustment with equation (10) for asset allocation, the numerator in the former is the change in duration multiplied by the initial market value, while the numerator in the latter is the change in the market value times the initial duration. Both numerators result directly from the definition of modified duration.

The denominator in both equations (7) and (10) is $D_F \times P_F$. The market value of a futures contract, P_F, is an arbitrary concept; in fact, various definitions of the market value of a futures contract can be proposed, including zero. The method chosen is irrelevant, however, since the product of $D_F \times P_F$ is dP_F/dY_F, the BPV(.01) of a futures contract discussed above. Thus, the denominator in equations (7) and (10) is the BPV(.01) of the futures contract.[2]

---

[2] In these examples, the BPV(.01) of the futures contract is assumed to be equal to the BPV(.01) of the cheapest deliverable bond (note) on the contract divided by the conversion factor of this bond (note), which is the standard approach. Alternative hedge ratio approaches are considered later in this article.

III. EXAMPLES

Consider examples which illustrate the use of Treasury bond futures for duration adjustment and asset allocation. On February 14, 1986, the BPV(.01) of the Treasury bond futures contract, the change in its price (on the basis of 100) in response to a 1 basis point change in yield, was .08424. Converting this price to the $100,000 futures contract and adjusting for a one basis point yield change provides the denominator of $842,400 for equations (7) and (10).

Consider a portfolio with an initial market value (including accrued interest) of $60 million and an initial duration of 4.5. The number of Treasury bond futures contracts which must be sold to reduce the duration of the portfolio to 4.3 but maintain its market value at $60 million is given by equation (7) as:

$$N = \frac{(4.3 - 4.5)(60,000,000)}{\$842,400}$$

$$= -14.2.$$

Thus, 14 Treasury bond futures contracts must be sold to reduce the portfolio duration to 4.3.

The number of futures contracts necessary to increase the effective market value to $75 million while maintaining the duration of 4.5, can be calculated from equation (10):

$$N = \frac{4.5(\$75,000,000 - \$60,000,000)}{\$842,400}$$

$$= 80.1.$$

Thus, to accomplish this asset allocation toward bonds, 80 Treasury bond futures contracts must be bought.

As indicated, Treasury bond or note futures contracts may be used for duration adjustment or asset allocation on either a temporary or a permanent basis. If used on a permanent basis, small adjustments in the number of futures contracts may occasionally have to be made. In equation (7), the duration of the portfolio is in the numerator while the duration of the futures contract is in the denominator. The durations of both the portfolio and the futures contract change as market levels change, specifically both are convex. These changes, thus, tend to offset each other, although not perfectly. The duration of the futures contract may also change because of a change in its cheapest deliverable instrument. Therefore, certain small adjustments may have to be made in the number of futures contracts outstanding as the market level or the cheapest deliverable instrument changes. For this purpose, the duration (or the BPV(.01)) of the futures contract should be monitored as a basis for adjusting the number of open futures positions. While such adjustments should be made, these adjustments are of such small magnitudes that the effectiveness of using futures contracts for duration adjustment or asset allocation remains intact.

For example, between January 30 and February 14, 1986, the BPV(.01) of the Treasury bond futures contract changed from .07935 to .08424. Over the same period, the BPV(.01) of the 10 3/8 percent Treasury bond, considered as a benchmark for the portfolio, changed from .10060 to .10725. These increases occurred as the market level rose due to the convexity of the futures contract (the cheapest deliverable bond on the futures contract was the same on both dates) and the 10 3/8 percent bond, and tended to be offsetting in their effect on the appropriate number of futures contracts. Nevertheless, the ratio of the BPV(.01)'s of the 10 3/8 percent Treasury to the futures contract increased from 1.268 (.10060/.07935) to 1.273 (.10725/.08424), during this period; that is, the offset was not perfect. Ignoring the offset completely in the above examples, and using the two BPV(.01)'s for January 30th and February 14th in the above asset allocation example provides:

$$\text{January 30} \quad N = \frac{4.5(\$75,000,000 - \$60,000,000)}{\$793,500} = 85.1$$

$$\text{February 14} \quad N = \frac{4.5(\$75,000,000 - \$60,000,000)}{\$842,400} = 80.1.$$

In this example, over this month-and-a-half period, it would have been necessary to gradually liquidate five long Treasury bond futures to achieve the desired bond allocation.

IV. BALANCED PORTFOLIOS

The discussion of asset allocation in this article relates to the balance between bonds of a given duration and cash. For balanced

managers (managers with both fixed-income instruments and securities), however, the other side of the fixed-income asset allocation may require a reallocation of equities. The equity component
of the portfolio can also be decreased by selling stock index futures contracts or increased by buying these contracts. When stock
index futures contracts are rich relative to fair value, a shift from
stocks to bonds by selling rich stock index futures and buying
cheap Treasury bond futures is optimal for a balanced manager in
terms of richness/cheapness, rather than the opposite shift. Thus,
when stock index futures are rich, the actual bond component of
the portfolio should be kept at the lower end of its intended range
and the equity component at the upper end of its intended range,
with adjustments made toward bonds and away from equities with
long Treasury bond and short stock index futures contracts. This
strategy, however, is most appropriate only when Treasury bond
futures are cheap and stock index futures rich.

The duration of a fixed-income portfolio is analogous to the
"beta" of an equity portfolio. Typically, during asset allocations,
while the duration of the bond portfolio is maintained, the beta of
the equity component is also maintained. Similarly in the same
way that Treasury bond and note futures contracts can be used to
change the duration of fixed-income portfolios, stock index futures
contracts can also be used to change the effective beta of equity
portfolios. If stock index futures contracts are rich, the bias is toward decreasing the beta by selling stock index futures contracts
rather than by increasing beta by buying stock index futures contracts. Therefore, in an environment where equity futures are rich
relative to fair value, the beta of the stock portfolio should be kept
at the upper end of its desired range and adjusted downward with
short stock index futures.

The equation that relates the number of stock index futures contracts to the value of a stock portfolio and its beta is:[3]

$$N = \frac{\text{Value of Portfolio} \times \text{Beta}}{\$500 \times \text{S\&P 500 Index}}.$$

[3] The beta of a stock or portfolio is a measure of the change in the return of the
stock or portfolio relative to the change in the return on the reference index
over a specific holding period. Most equity betas are calculated on the basis of
monthly returns over a five-year period. Betas calculated on this basis, how-

This equation is equivalent to equation (6) for bonds and notes and can be used for both beta adjustment and asset allocation.

V. THE BPV, DURATION AND MARKET VALUE OF TREASURY BOND AND NOTE FUTURES CONTRACTS

As indicated, calculating the number of Treasury bond or note futures contracts to transact for a duration adjustment, asset allocation, or hedge ratio strategy requires the calculation of the BPV (basis point value, that is the change in price or value due to a change in yield) of the futures contract or, alternatively, the duration and the market value of a futures contract. This section discusses the method of calculating the BPV, the duration and the market value of Treasury bond and note futures contracts.

There is a simple mathematical relationship among the BPV, the duration and the market value of a Treasury bond or note futures contract. The BPV of a Treasury futures contract (or a fixed-income instrument) can be defined as dP/dY, that is the change in price for a unit change in yield. Since the duration is defined as

$$D = \frac{1}{P} \times \frac{dP}{dY},$$

then

$$BPV = dP/dY = P \times D,$$

where P is the market value.

Determining the duration of a futures contract differs from determining the duration of a bond in two significant ways. The first is that the market value of a futures contract, due to its leverage, is not easily defined. The definition of the market value of a futures contract is, however, of no consequence in using futures contracts for duration adjustment or asset allocation because the duration of a futures contract does not appear alone in the duration adjust-

---

ever, may not be reliable for short-term hedging, such as daily or intra-day hedging. In fact, in many cases, the estimated "daily beta," when the error of estimation is considered, is not significantly different from one.

ment or asset allocation equations, but as a product of the market value of the futures contract as shown in equation (6):

$$N = \frac{(D_T \times P_T) - (D_I \times P_I)}{D_F \times P_F}$$

where D and P refer to the duration and market value of the relevant portfolio, respectively; the subscripts I and T refer to the "initial" and "target" variables of the portfolio, respectively; the subscript F refers to the futures contract; and N refers to the number of futures contracts to buy (+) or sell (−) to change from the initial variables to the target variables, for example from D_I to D_T (duration adjustment) or P_I to P_T (asset allocation).

The product of the duration of a futures contract, D_F, and the market value of a futures contract, P_F, in the denominator of the equation is:

$$D_F \times P_F = \frac{dP/P}{dY} \times P = \frac{dP}{dY}. \qquad (11)$$

The market value of the futures contract, thus, cancels out in the product of D_F and P_F, the denominator of equation (6). Specifically, the product $D_F \times P_F$ equals dP/dY, denoted by BPV(.01). While the market value of the futures contract is not needed explicitly to calculate $D_F \times P_F = dP/dY$ it is, however, needed to calculate the duration of the futures contract.

One potential definition for the market value of a futures contract is zero since it has no intrinsic value. The measure of the market value of the futures contract used herein, however, is the price of a futures contract, P_F. The rationale for this definition is that it is consistent with the definition of P used in calculating the dP/dY or BPV(.01) of a futures contract. Thus, the definition of the P in dP/dY and the definition of P used as the market value of the futures contract are both, consistently, defined as the futures price.

The second difference between the duration of a bond and the duration of a bond futures contract refers to the yield related to the price of these instruments. The price of a Treasury bond or

---

[4] While a bond price depends on only one yield, its yield to maturity, this price/ yield relationship assumes that the yields at which the coupons subsequently

note depends on only one yield, its yield to maturity.[4] On the other hand, the price of a Treasury bond or note futures contract depends on two yields, the yield of the cheapest deliverable instrument and the financing cost (or repo rate) of the instrument over the period until delivery. That is, the futures price depends on both a long-term yield and a short-term yield. The fair value futures price, also called the theoretical futures price, in terms of the price of its cheapest deliverable instrument (CTD), PC (which corresponds to the yield YC on this instrument), and the short-term yield, R, is provided explicitly by:[5]

$$F \times PF = PC + \left[\frac{N}{360} \times R \times (PC + AI1)\right] - AIE \qquad (12)$$

where: PF is the theoretical (fair value) of the futures price;

PC is the cash market price of the cheapest deliverable Treasury bond or note (excluding accrued interest);

F is the conversion factor of the CTD;

R is the financing rate (term repo rate) of the CTD to the futures delivery day;

N is the number of days to the futures delivery day; and

AIE is the accrued interest earned, which is equal to AI2 – AI1 + C where AI1 is the accrued interest paid when the CTD is purchased, AI2 is the accrued interest received when the CTD is sold and C is the coupon received during the holding period, if any (equal to 1/2 the annual coupon).[6]

___

received are reinvested, the reinvestment rates, equal the yield to maturity. Different assumed reinvestment yields will, however, affect the total bond returns over time.

[5] This equation is based on a "cash and carry" value of a futures contract and, thus, ignores the value of the delivery options implicit in the Treasury bond and note futures contracts. These delivery options reduce the fair value of the futures price to below its cash and carry value. For a discussion of this issue, see Frank J. Jones and Beth A. Krumholz, "The Cheapness of the Treasury Bond and Note Futures Contracts," Financial Futures Department, New York: Kidder, Peabody & Co., Inc., March 1985.

[6] This equation ignores the reinvestment of any "coupon drop" during the holding period.

The BPV of a Futures Contract

To determine the dP/dY or the BPV(.01) of a futures contract, an assumption is required about the relationship between the changes in the two yields which affect the theoretical futures price, the short-term yield, R, and the long-term yield, YC, the yield associated with the price of the CTD, PC. Different assumptions can be made about the relationship betw een these two yields. The general equation for the change in the theoretical futures price with respect to the changes in the yield of the CTD, YC, and the short-term yield, R, based on equation (12) is:

$$F \times dPF = (dPC) + \left(\frac{N}{360} \times R \times dPC\right) + \left(\frac{N}{360} \times (PC + AI1) \times dR\right)$$

$$= \left(1 + \frac{N}{360} \times R\right) dPC + \left(\frac{N}{360} \times (PC + AI1) \times dR\right) \qquad (13)$$

Note that when YC increases (that is, PC decreases), dPF is negative; that is, PF decreases. However, when R increases, dPF is positive; that is, PF increases. Specifically, $dPF/dYC < 0$ and $dPF/dR > 0$. Thus, changes in the same direction in the two yields that determine PF, R and YC, affect PF in opposite directions.

The general approach to determining the change in the futures price with respect to a change in "the yield" of the futures contract requires the specification of the relationship between the changes in PC (or the related yield, YC) and R; that is, dR/dPC (or dR/dYC) in the context of equation (13). Equation (13) can be rewritten in terms of the change in the yield of the cheapest deliverable bond, YC, by taking the derivative of PF with respect to YC in equation (13), that is:

$$F \times \frac{dPF}{dYC} = \left(1 + \frac{N}{360} \times R\right) \frac{dPC}{dYC} + \left(\frac{N}{360} \times (PC + AI1) \times \frac{dR}{dYC}\right) \qquad (14)$$

where the term dPC/dYC is the standard price/yield relationship for the CTD and the term dR/dYC can be considered as the yield beta of the term repo rate relative to the yield on the CTD. Consider various alternative relationships between the changes in R and YC, that is, alternative specifications of dR/dYC.[7]

---

[7] In this article, the term BPV(.01) and dP/dY are used interchangably. An alternative convention is to define BPV(.01) as dP rather than dP/dY. Either

First Assumption. The standard assumption in duration analysis concerning changes in the yields of instruments of different durations is that of a parallel shift in the yield curve, that is equal basis point changes in the short-term and long-term yields. This assumption provides the relationship: $dR/dYC = 1$. Denote the measure of dP/dY (or, in general, BPV) based on the assumption of equal one basis point changes in the short- and long-term rates of a futures contract by "BPV(.01/.01)(FC)." Calculating dPF/dYC from equation (14) on the basis of the assumption that $dR/dYC = 1$ provides:

BPV(.01/.01)(FC) =

$$\frac{dPF}{dYC} = \frac{1}{F}\left[\left(\left(1 + \frac{N}{360} \times R\right)\frac{dPC}{dYC}\right) + \left(\frac{N}{360} \times \left(PC + AI1\right)\right)\right]. \tag{15}$$

Second Assumption. A second assumption with respect to the relationship between the short-term yield and the long-term yield

---

definition, in concept, refers to the change in price for a one basis point change in yield. According to this definition, the specification of the duration, D, becomes $D = BPV(.01)/(P \times dY)$ rather than $D = BPV(.01)/P$ as in the article. The difference in the definitions affects only establishing the decimal point in the duration.

In addition, to be precise, the BPV(.01/.01) should refer to a basis point change in the bond equivalent yield of the CTD and the bond equivalent implied repo rate. This involves expressing the yield term specifying the cost of carry or financing cost in the theoretical futures price equation as $(1 + BIR/2)^{2N/365}$ where BIR is the bond equivalent implied repo rate, rather than $(1 + N \times IR/360)$ where IR is the implied repo rate on an add-on basis. Expressing equation (12) in terms of the bond equivalent implied repo rate, denoted by BIR, provides:

$$F \times PF = \left[\left(1 + \frac{BIR}{2}\right)^{2N/365} \times (PC + AI1)\right] - AI2 \tag{F1}$$

Taking the derivative of this equation with respect to yield, and specifying that BIR is a linear function of yield (that is, $BIR = A + (B \times Y)$) provides:

$$F \times dPF/dY = [(1 + BIR/2)^{2N/365} \times (dPC/dY)] + [(PC + AI1) \times 2N/365 \times B/2 \times (1 + BIR/2)^{2N/365 - 1}] \tag{F2}$$

which is an equivalent but more precise form of equation (14). The specification $B = A + (B \times Y)$, implies that $dBIR/dY = B$. Thus, the constant, B, is the change in the bond equivalent short-term rate relative to the change in the bond equilavent long-term rate ($B = dBIR/dY$).

is that the short-term yield does not change when the long-term yield changes, that is, $dR/dYC = 0$. In this case, equation (14) becomes:

$$\frac{dPF}{dYC} = \frac{1}{F}\left(1 + \frac{N}{360} \times R\right)\frac{dPC}{dYC}. \tag{16}$$

Denoting dPF/dYC on the basis of this assumption by "BPV(.01)(FC)" and dPC/dYC by "BPV(.01)(CTD)," equation (16) becomes:

$$BPV(.01)(FC) = \frac{1}{F}\left(1 + \frac{N}{360} \times R\right) \times BPV(.01)(CTD). \tag{17}$$

Third Assumption. A further simplifying assumption which supplements the second assumption is that the term $(1 + ((N/360) \times R))$ equals 1, that is the term $(N/360) \times R$ is ignored. According to this assumption, and denoting the corresponding dPF/dYC by $BPV(.01)(FC)'$, equation (17) becomes:

$$BPV(.01)(FC)' = \frac{1}{F} BPV(.01)(CTD). \tag{18}$$

Equation (18) is the basis for the standard hedge ratio, asset allocation and duration adjustment calculations.

Comparison

Thus, overall, there are three formulations of the dPF/dYC or BPV of a futures contract which differ in their assumptions about the change in the short-term yield relative to the long-term yield, that is dR/dYC. While the general formulation of dPF/dYC is provided in equation (14), the three formulations based on explicit assumptions about the relationship between R and YC are summarized as:

1. *Assumption: $dR/dYC = 1$*

   $BPV(.01/.01)(FC) =$

   $$\frac{1}{F}\left[\left(\left(1 + \frac{N}{360} \times R\right) \times BPV(.01)(CTD)\right) + \left(\frac{N}{360} \times (PC + AI1)\right)\right]. \tag{15}$$

2. *Assumption: $dR/dYC = 0$*

   $$BPV(.01)(FC) = \frac{1}{F}\left(1 + \frac{N}{360} \times R\right) \times BPV(.01)(CTD). \tag{17}$$

3. *Assumption: dR/dYC = 0 and 1 + ((N/360) × R) = 1*

$$\text{BPV}(.01)(\text{FC})' = \frac{1}{F}\,\text{BPV}(.01)(\text{CTD})\,. \tag{18}$$

Consider the relative magnitudes of these three formulations of dPF/dYC or BPV. Obviously, comparing equations (17) and (18):

$$\text{BPV}(.01)(\text{FC})' < \text{BPV}(.01)(\text{FC})$$

since the multiplicative term

$$\left(1 + \frac{N}{360} \times R\right),$$

which is greater than one, is assumed to be 1 in the BPV(.01)(FC)′ formulation.[8]

A second relationship is:

$$\text{BPV}(.01/.01)(\text{FC}) < \text{BPV}(.01)(\text{FC}),$$

which can be demonstrated as follows. The term involving BPV(.01)(CTD) or dPC/dYC in both the BPV(.01/.01)(FC) and BPV(.01)(FC) formulations is negative due to the inverse relationship between bond prices and yields. The second term in the BPV(.01/.01)(FC) formulation, however, which is (N/360) × PC and results from assuming dR/dYC = 1, has a positive sign, and, thus, countervails the first term. Hence, the assumption that dR/dYC = 0 in the BPV(.01)(FC) approach increases the magnitude of dPF/dYC and causes:

$$\text{BPV}(.01/.01)(\text{FC}) < \text{BPV}(.01)(\text{FC}).$$

Thus, overall:

$$\text{BPV}(.01)(\text{FC})' < \text{BPV}(.01)(\text{FC}),$$

and

$$\text{BPV}(.01/.01)(\text{FC}) < \text{BPV}(.01)(\text{FC})\,.$$

An unequivocal relationship between BPV(.01)(FC)′ and BPV (.01/.01)(FC), however, cannot be derived from either these two inequalities or by comparing equations (15) and (18).

---

[8] Because of the inverse relation between price and yield, the BPV's are negative in sign. In comparing the BPV's in this article, however, only their magnitudes are considered.

Which is greater depends on the relative magnitudes of $((N/360) \times R) \times BPV(.01)(CTD))$ (which is negative) and $(N/360)$ $(PC + AI1)$, both in equation (15), (which is positive) and both of which are ignored in equation (18).

Exhibit 1 provides an example of the calculation of these three BPVs for the Treasury bond futures contract. In the example, note that:

$$BPV(.01/.01)(FC) < BPV(.01)(FC)'.$$

Thus, in this example, the effect of assuming $dR/dYC =$ zero in the transition from $BPV(.01/.01)(FC)$ to $BPV(.01)(FC)$ is less than the effect of ignoring the $((N/360) \times R)$ term in the transition from $BPV(.01)(FC)$ to $BPV(.01)(FC)'$.

Overall, the relationship among the BPVs are:

$$BPV(.01)(FC)' = (1/F)BPV(.01)(CTD) \tag{19}$$

$$BPV(.01)(FC)' < BPV(.01)(FC) \tag{20}$$

$$BPV(.01/.01)(FC) < BPV(.01)(FC) \tag{21}$$

$$BPV(.01/.01)(FC) \, ? \, BPV(.01)(FC)' \tag{22}$$

where the "?" in equation (22) refers to the relationship between these two terms on a theoretical basis. But based on the data in Exhibit 1, the "?" could be replaced by a "<". The $BPV(.01)(FC)'$ approach is the standard approach used to calculate hedge ratios. The data in Exhibit 1 indicate that the differences in these BPV calculation methods are material.

These relationships can be explained as follows. Equation (19) indicates that the factored $BPV(.01)(FC)'$ of the futures contract equals the $BPV(.01)(CTD)$, which is true because in the $BPV(.01)(FC)'$ approach the effect of the short-term yield, R, is ignored and, hence, the resulting BPV depends only on the change in the yield of the CTD. Equation (20) is true because in the $BPV(.01)(FC)'$ formulation, the term $(1 + (N/360) \times R)$ is assumed to be 1, which reduces $BPV(.01)(FC)'$ from $BPV(.01)(FC)$. Equation (21) is true because while the $BPV(.01/.01)(FC)$ formulation assumes that $dR/dYC = 1$, the $BPV(.01)(FC)$ formulation assumes that $dR/dYC = 0$. Since R and YC have opposite effects on the futures price, as shown by equation (13), by ignoring the effect of R as a result of assuming $dR/dYC = 0$ in $BPV(.01)(FC)$, the result-

---

EXHIBIT 1
Example of BPV and Duration Calculation

A. **Assumptions**
   Calculation Date: November 21, 1986
   Settlement Date: November 24, 1986 (127 days to delivery)
   Cheapest Deliverable Bond (CTD)
      Coupon: 14%
      Maturity: 11/15/11-06
      Price: 159–16
      Yield (to call):   7.9889%
   Futures Contract:
      Delivery Month: March 1987
      Futures Price: 98–24
      Factor: 1.5875
      Implied Repo Rate (to March 1987):   3.86%

B. **BPV and Duration***
   *BPV***:
      CTD
      BPV(.01)(CTD):   14.31633
      Futures Contract
      BPV(.01/.01)(FC):   8.7857
      BPV(.01)(FC):   9.1410
      BPV(.01)(FC)':   9.0182
   Duration:
      CTD
      Duration (CTD):   8.9758
      Futures Contract
      D(.01/.01)(FC):   8.8969
      D(.01)(FC):   9.2567
      D(.01)(FC)':   9.1324

Calculations
   BPVs

$$\text{BPV}(.01/.01)\text{FC} = \frac{1}{1.5875}\left[\left(\left(1 + \frac{127}{360} \times 0.0386\right) \times -14.31633\right)\right.$$
$$\left. + \left(\frac{127}{360} \times \left(1.595 + 0.00348066\right)\right)\right]$$

$$= \frac{1}{1.5875}\left((-14.51128) + (0.56391)\right) = -8.7857$$

EXHIBIT 1 *(Continued)*

$$\text{BPV(.01)FC} = \frac{1}{1.5875}\left(1 + \frac{127}{360} \times 0.0386\right) \times -14.31633 = -9.1410$$

$$\text{BPV(.01)FC'} = \frac{1}{1.5875} \times -14.31633 = -9.0182$$

$$\text{BPV(.01)(CTD)} = 14.31633$$

Durations

$$\text{D(CTD)} = 14.31633 \times \frac{1}{1.595} = 8.9758$$

$$\text{D(.01/01)(FC)} = 8.7857 \times \frac{1}{.9875} = 8.8969$$

$$\text{D(.01)FC} = 9.1410 \times \frac{1}{.9875} = 9.2567$$

$$\text{D(.01)FC'} = 9.0182 \times \frac{1}{.9875} = 9.1324$$

***These BPV refer to the change in price of $100,000 par value of the instrument for a 1 basis point change in yield.*

Note: This example can be analyzed using the equations in footnote 7 of this article. Using the futures price (98-24), the factor of the CTD (1.5875), the cash price of the CTD (159-16) and the AI1(0.348066) and AI2(5.2596685) specified in the example in equation (F1) provides:

BIR = 3.92621 (the implied repo rate of the above bond relative to the futures price on a bond equivalent basis)

Then, by changing the yield of the CTD by 1 basis point up and down and taking the average of the change:

$$\text{dPC (per dollar of par value)} = -.14327$$

Given PC + AI1 = 1.598481, equation (F2) provides:

$$\text{dPF} = 1/F \times \{[(1 + \text{BIR}/2)^{2N/365} \times \text{dPC}] + [\text{dY} \times (\text{PC} + \text{AI1}) \times 2N \times B/730$$
$$\times (1 + \text{BIR}/2)^{2N/365 - 1}]\} = -.09147959 + (.01 \times .3482868)$$
$$= -.08800507$$

Thus:

$$\text{BPV} = \frac{\text{dPF}}{\text{dY}} = -8.800507$$

The duration corresponding to this dPF/dY is:

$$\text{D} = \frac{\text{dPF}}{\text{dY}} \times \frac{1}{\text{PF}} = -8.800507 \times \frac{1}{98.75} = -8.911905$$

EXHIBIT 1 *(Continued)*

These BPV and D measures, since they are based on 1 basis point changes in the short- and long-term yields, should be compared to BPV(.01/.01)(FC) and D(.01/.01)(FC) shown in the "Calculations" rather than the other measures. In fact, the BPV and D in this footnote are slightly greater than their BPV(.01/.01)(FC) and D(.01/.01)(FC) counterparts in Exhibit 1, as summarized in the table below, because 1 basis point in the bond equivalent implied repo is slightly smaller than 1 basis point in the add on repo rate.

	"Calculations" (Add-On Yield)	"Footnote" (Bond Equivalent Yield)
BPV(.01/.01)(FC)	−8.7857	−8.800507
D(.01/.01)(FC)	−8.8969	−8.911905

ing BPV(.01)(FC) is larger, as indicated by equation (21). However, even though both BPV(.01)(FC)′ and BPV(.01/.01)(FC) are less than BPV(.01)(FC), the relationship between BPV(.01)(FC)′ and BPV(.01/.01)(FC) cannot be determined in concept—the example in Exhibit 1, however, shows that BPV(.01/.01)(FC) is less than BPV(.01)(FC)′.

The Duration of a Futures Contract

The previous discussion relates the dP/dYC or BPV of a futures contract to that of the CTD. Here we consider the duration of a futures contract relative to the duration of the CTD. As indicated, the duration of a futures contract is the product of two terms, the dP/dYC or BPV of the futures contract and the market value of the futures contract, P:

$$D = \frac{dP/P}{dY} = \frac{dP}{dY} \times \frac{1}{P} = BPV \times \frac{1}{P}.$$

Relating the duration of the futures contract D(FC) to the duration of the CTD, D(CTD), requires comparing the BPVs' and Ps' of the futures contract and the CTD. As indicated, the definition of the market value of the futures contract, P(FC), used in this article is:

$$P(FC) = PF,$$

the futures price. When the yield curve is positively sloped, the factored basis of the cheapest deliverable bond is positive, that is:

$$P(CTD) - F \times PF > 0,$$

or

$$P(CTD)/F > P(FC).\tag{23}$$

Consider the relationship between D(FC), the duration of the futures contract, and D(CTD), the duration of the CTD, on the basis of the three measures of the BPV(.01) of the futures contract.

First, according to the standard BPV(.01)(FC)′ formulation:

$$BPV(.01)(FC)' = \frac{1}{F} BPV(.01)(CTD).\tag{24}$$

The corresponding measure of duration, denoted by D(.01)(FC)′, can be derived by using equations (23) and (24):

$$D(.01)(FC)' = BPV(.01)(FC)' \times \frac{1}{P(FC)}$$

$$= \frac{1}{F} BPV(.01)(CTD) \times \frac{1}{P(FC)} \qquad \text{via equation (24)}$$

$$> \frac{1}{F} BPV(.01)(CTD) \times \frac{1}{(1/F) \times P(CTD)} \qquad \text{via equation (23)}$$

$$= BPV(.01)(CTD) \times \frac{1}{P(CTD)}$$

$$= D(CTD)$$

Thus, $D(.01)(FC)' > D(CTD)$, that is the duration of the futures contract based on the BPV(.01)(FC)′ formulation is greater than that of the CTD bond. This conclusion applies, however, only when the yield curve is positively sloped because $BPV(.01)(FC)' = (1/F) \times BPV(.01)(CTD)$ and, with a positive yield curve, $P(CTD) > F \times P(FC)$. With an inverted yield curve the relationship would be reversed. And with a flat yield curve, the duration of the futures contract according to this measure would equal the duration of the CTD.

These results occur because in the BPV(.01)(FC)′ formulation, the short-term interest rate is ignored completely both because dR/dYC is assumed to be zero and the term $(N/360) \times R$ is assumed to be zero. Thus, the BPV(.01)(FC)$'$ of the futures contract is simply related to the BPV(.01)(CTD), that is, it equals $(1/F) \times$ BPV(.01)(CTD). Therefore, other than the conversion factor adjustment, the relationship between the duration of the futures contract and the duration of the CTD will be determined based only on the relationship between P(CTD) and P(FC) or more precisely between P(CTD)/F and P(FC). This relationship refers to the factored basis of the CTD and is either positive or negative when the yield curve is positively or negatively sloped, respectively. That is, D(.01)(FC)$'$ is greater than D(CTD) when the yield curve is positively sloped, less than D(CTD) when the yield curve is negatively sloped and equal to D(CTD) when the yield curve is flat.

Consider next the relationship between D(FC) based on the BPV(.01)(FC) formulation, denoted by D(.01)(FC), and D(CTD). Since BPV(.01)(FC) > BPV(.01)(FC)$'$; and D(.01)(FC)$'$ > D(CTD) when the yield curve is positively sloped; then D(.01)(FC) is also greater than D(CTD) when the yield curve is positively sloped. The opposite inequality, however, may not apply when the yield curve is negatively sloped. In addition D(.01)(FC) > D(.01)(FC)$'$.

Finally, consider the relationship between the D(FC) based on BPV(.01/.01)(FC), denoted by D(.01/.01)(FC), and D(CTD). Since BPV(.01/.01)(FC) < BPV(.01)(FC) and, in concept, the relationship between BPV(.01)(FC)$'$ and BPV(.01/.01)(FC) is indeterminate, it cannot be determined whether D(.01/.01)(FC) is greater than or less than D(CTD). In addition, since the example in Exhibit 1 indicates that BPV(.01/.01)(FC) < BPV(.01)(FC)$'$, on this basis D(.01/.01)(FC) may be either greater than or less than D(CTD).

Thus, overall, when the yield curve is positively sloped:

$$D(.01)(FC) > D(.01)(FC)' > D(CTD),$$

and

$$D(.01/.01)(FC) \ ? \ D(CTD) \ .$$

Based on the example in Exhibit 1, however:

$$D(.01)(FC) > D(.01)(FC)' > D(CTD) > D(.01/.01)(FC).$$

VI. SUMMARY

This article demonstrates that the Treasury bond and note future contracts can be used for both duration adjustment and asset allocation. Similarly, stock index futures contracts can be used for both beta adjustment and asset allocation. Because of their liquidity, low transaction costs and ease of execution, these futures contracts can be effectively used by portfolio managers to implement these common strategies. The pricing of the futures contracts may also provide higher returns in the implementation of these strategies.

The calculation of the number of Treasury bond or note futures contracts to transact requires the BPV or duration of the futures contract. This article also discusses conceptual and numerical issues in determining the BPV and duration of Treasury bond and note futures contracts for calculating hedge ratios and for asset allocation and duration adjustment calculations. The conceptual issues and the assumptions involved in these calculations are important and provide insights in the nature of hedging. In addition, at least for large transactions, in practice the number of futures contracts transacted will be also affected by methods used. Calculations, such as in Exhibit 1, should be done on a regular basis by those using the Treasury bond and note futures contracts for hedging, duration adjustment and asset allocation.

ARTICLE 21

RICHARD BOOKSTABER is Principal in the Fixed Income Research Group at Morgan Stanley & Co. He is responsible for options and futures research and is Product Manager for dynamic hedging and portfolio insurance at Morgan Stanley.

Mr. Bookstaber received a B.A. from Brigham Young University, and a Ph.D. from the Massachusetts Institute of Technology. Prior to joining Morgan Stanley, he was a professor at Brigham Young University, Boston University, and was a Visiting Professor and Senior Fulbright Fellow at the Hebrew University at Jerusalem. In his academic career, he was instrumental in the development of the applications of option technology to portfolio management and hedging.

He is the author of three highly regarded books and many papers in the field of options and portfolio strategies.

HAL B. HEATON is currently an assistant professor of finance in the School of Management at Brigham Young University, where he teaches advanced corporate finance and policy. Prior to receiving his Ph.D. in finance from Stanford University, Mr. Heaton was a consultant with the Boston Consulting Group (BCG). While at BCG, he performed strategic planning services for clients in the electronics, lumber, banking, farm equipment and other industries. Mr. Heaton has published research articles in *The Journal of Finance, The Journal of Financial and Quantitative Analysis, The Journal of Money, Credit and Banking,* as well as other journals.

ON THE HEDGING PERFORMANCE OF THE NEW MUNICIPAL BOND FUTURES CONTRACT

Richard Bookstaber, Ph.D.
Principal
Morgan Stanley and Co., Inc.

and

Hal Heaton, Ph.D.
Assistant Professor of Finance
Brigham Young University

Despite the explosive growth of financial futures and hedging instruments, up to recently the risk management demands of the municipal bond market have remained unanswered. The most common hedging instrument, Treasury futures, is largely ineffective with municipal bonds because it does not address the major sources of risk in the municipal bond market. This is particularly evident in light of recent trends in the tax-exempt security market: the increased changing default patterns and the prospects for new tax legislation. These are risks that are unique to municipal bonds. They can only be addressed through a municipal bond market instrument. The new municipal bond futures contract gives municipal bond issuers, investors, and dealers a new hedging and risk management tool to meet that demand.

The municipal bond futures contract is based on the Bond Buyers Municipal Bond Index. This index is made up of 40 high-quality municipal bonds. The index price is computed by averaging the bond prices together after making adjustments for differences in coupons and time to maturity. Since the actual bonds comprising the index will change over time—some bonds will be eliminated because they no longer meet the criteria for inclusion in the index, and other bonds will be added to the index in their place—the resulting price average is adjusted by a coefficient to assure continuity in the Index price.[1]

Hedging demand is found in many areas of the municipal bond market. As a tool for reducing the risk of an investment position, a hedge may be applied against an anticipated position.[2]

For example, the most common hedging objective is to secure investment holdings against loss. This objective may be sought by a bond dealer wishing to preserve the value of his inventory, or a portfolio manager wishing to lock in the value of his portfolio. The value of these positions can be safeguarded by taking a short position in an instrument that closely tracks changes in the holdings. If the holdings drop in value, the short position should experience an offsetting rise.

Issuers may be more interested in hedging the value of an anticipated position. For example, a municipality may find the current market interest rate environment attractive for offering an issue, but face a delay before the issue comes to the market. The issuer can hedge the anticipated position, in effect fixing the rate of return for the forthcoming issue, by taking a short hedge position. The short hedge position will increase in value with a rise in interest rates, and provide compensation for the increased issuing cost.

If interest rates rise, making the issue less attractive, the short

[1] The computation of the Bond Buyer Municipal Bond Index, as well as the criteria for the selection of the Index bonds, is explained in detail in *The Chicago Board of Trade's Municipal Bond Futures Contract,* a publication of the Chicago Board of Trade.

[2] A detailed exposition of the various types of hedges and the mechanics of implementing them is presented in Alden Toevs and David Jacob, "Interest Rate Futures: A Comparison of Alternative Hedge Ratio Methodologies," in Frank J. Fabozzi and Irving M. Pollack, (eds), *The Handbook of Fixed Income Securities,* Homewood, IL: Dow Jones-Irwin, 1987.

position will increase in value. Of course, while a hedge eliminates the potential for loss, it eliminates the opportunities for gains as well. If interest rates drop, leading to a more attractive issuing environment, the hedge position also drops in value. The decline in the hedge position will offset the gains realizable from the interest rate shift.

An alternative to the conventional hedge, a hedge which eliminates the opportunities for gains along with the risks of loss, is to create a one-sided hedge—a hedge which protects against loss while leaving any gains in the position open for capture. Such a strategy, which amounts to an insurance policy against loss, is useful for creating interest rate caps on floating rate municipal bond obligations. The payoff from the policy compensates for any loss from an interest rate rise above some specified ceiling, assuring an effective cap on interest costs. This one-sided protection is also useful for the issuer who wishes to insure against unfavorable interest rate shifts before an issue comes to market, but **does** not wish to do so at the cost of eliminating the opportunities to profit from favorable interest rate movements. The insurance protection makes no claims on the returns if the unfavorable risk does not occur. Instead, it extracts an upfront cost.[3]

For many participants in the financial market, the ability to control interest rate exposure, either with a conventional hedge or with one-sided, insurance-type protection, will make financing choices possible which would otherwise have been over-shadowed by the specter of unfavorable turns in the market. In this article, we will consider only the conventional hedging effectiveness of the municipal bond

---

[3] This type of protection is provided by following a dynamic hedging strategy. The size of the hedge is adjusted over time, according to the price of the underlying bond and other factors. The protection is similar to that provided by buying a put option. (A put option increases in value as the underlying asset drops in value, and expires worthless if the underlying asset increases in value.) As a result, such insurance strategies are often called protective put strategies. Given the relationship between this insurance protection and option payoffs, it is not surprising that the mathematical formulation for the hedge is based on option theory. The dynamic hedging strategy, and the procedure for creating such hedges through the use of futures contracts is covered in Richard Bookstaber, *The Use of Options in Performance Structuring: Molding Returns to meet Investment Objectives,* New York: Morgan Stanley Fixed Income Research, 1984.

futures. However, the potential for using the futures contract in creating insurance-type payoffs is directly related to the performance of the contract in its conventional hedging role.

The value of the new municipal bond futures depends on two considerations: the efficient pricing and trading of the contract, and the comparative hedging ability of the new futures in managing municipal bond risk.

The contract is only useful if positions can be quickly transacted without large price spreads. For the municipal bond futures, the depth of the market is particularly important, since most of the market participants will be institutions with large positions. In Section I we discuss the underpinning of pricing efficiency: the determinants of futures pricing, and the implications these have for the Municipal Bond Index futures contract.

Sections II through IV then cover the most critical aspect of the municipal bond futures contract: its relative hedging efficiency. Sections II and III introduce some important tools for creating a hedge and for measuring hedging effectiveness. Section IV then evaluates the hedging potential of the municipal bond futures contract, comparing it to the hedging performance of Treasury instruments. The results of these tests indicate that the municipal bond futures contract has the potential of fulfilling an important risk management role in the municipal bond market, but still leaves some bond-specific risk difficult to hedge.

I. THE PRICING OF THE MUNICIPAL BOND FUTURES CONTRACT

For many of the municipal market participants, the pricing of the municipal futures contract is of foremost concern. Particularly important for those wanting to use the futures to hedge cash bond positions is how the futures price will relate to the cash bond price. Since the municipal futures contract is traded for cash settlement against the Bond Buyer Municipal Bond Index, a potential hedger must also examine how his municipal portfolio relates to the actual Index value. The spread between the Index value and the futures price, known as the *basis* of the contract, is of central concern. Since the cash settlement of the futures on the delivery date is equal to the actual value of the Index, it is obvious that the basis between them will converge to zero on any futures contract delivery day.[4] However, in the months preceding the delivery day, the pricing relationship in the basis and the resulting basis risk require a closer examination. This examination of the basis will help to illustrate the market forces that will determine the cash-futures relationship in the municipal bond market. The major market force at play is the ability to trade between the markets and extract profits if the correct pricing relationships and basis are not maintained.

Understanding the Basis: A Simple Example

To illustrate the basis, consider the pricing of a less complex futures contract: gold. Suppose an investor wants to take a position in gold. There are two markets for doing this, the cash gold market (spot market), which gives immediately physical delivery of the gold, and the futures market, which gives a contract to take delivery of the gold at a specified future date. The question facing the investor is which alternative is less expensive, to take delivery now and hold the gold, or to buy a futures contract that allows delivery at a future date.

To answer this question, consider the following example: Suppose gold is trading at $400 an ounce in the spot market, and is trading in the futures market for delivery in one year for $440 an ounce. In either case, the investor will have physical possession of the gold in one year. If the investor's time horizon is one year, both of these markets give exactly the same opportunity to gain from an appreciation in the price of gold. Buying the gold in the cash market will lead to an interest cost, since $400 will be tied up for the year gold is carried. By contrast, no funds are tied up when entering into a futures transaction.[5] So the decision to purchase the gold in either

---

[4] A delivery date schedule of March, June, September and December has been established for the new contract. This is the same as Treasury bond futures schedule.

[5] Since interest bearing securities may be used as margin for a futures contract, there is no cost of carry. See Alden Toevs and David Jacob, "Interest Rate Futures: A Comparison of Alternative Hedging Ratio Methodologies."

the cash or futures market depends on whether the interest carrying cost is less than $40. If so, then the cash market will be cheaper, while if the interest cost is greater than $40, then the futures market will be cheaper. The $40 basis difference between the cash and futures market tells us that the implied interest rate, or cost of carry for one year for the $400 gold in the cash market is 10 percent. If the actual interest rate in the cash market for the cost of carrying the gold does not equal this implied rate then the cash and futures markets are out of alignment with each other. The cost of an ounce of gold is cheaper in one market than the other. Since one market is cheaper than the other it is possible to extract a profit by trading between these two markets. Buying in the cheaper market and selling in the overpriced market will yield an arbitrage profit. This action will cause the two rates to return to equality with each other. For example, let the current carrying cost be 5 percent for the $400 gold. It will cost $420 to buy gold and carry it for one year, the $400 cost of the gold plus the $20 interest cost of carry. In the futures market, let the cost for one year be $440. Buying the gold in the cash market and simultaneously selling gold in the futures market would lock in a $20 profit with zero risk.[6]

In this example, the actual interest cost of carry was less than the implied interest cost of carry. To capitalize on this disparity, we bought the basis. Buying the basis is defined as buying the cash market and selling the futures. If the actual interest cost of carry was greater than the implied interest cost of carry, one would reverse the positions described above, or sell the basis. Selling the basis is defined as selling the cash market and buying the futures. Shorting the cash market requires special conditions, which we will assume for now, but which will be examined more thoroughly later in this section. Exhibit 1 summarizes the above strategies.

The Pricing Mechanism of the Municipal Bond Futures Contract

Applying the concepts of basis trading to understand the pricing mechanism in the bond market requires more sophistication than was used in our gold example. Since a bond is made up of both

[6] This profit will be locked in only if both positions are closed on the delivery date of the futures.

EXHIBIT 1

Given:
  Cash market price = $400
  Futures market price for delivery one year out = $440

Strategy 1: Buying the Basis
  Actual interest rate carrying cost ≈ 5%

Opening transaction:
(1) Borrow funds	+ 400
(2) Buy gold in cash market	− 400
(3) Sell gold futures contract	–0–
Net investment	–0–

Closing transaction (one year later):
(1) Deliver gold at contract price	+ 440
(2) Pay off loan	− 420
Net profit	+ 20

Strategy 2: Selling the Basis
  Actual interest rate carrying cost = 15%

Opening transaction:
(1) Short gold in cash market	+ 400
(2) Invest funds	− 400
(3) Buy gold futures contract	–0–
Net investment	–0–

Closing transaction (one year later):
(1) Buy gold at contracted price	− 440
(2) Receive payment on loan	+ 460
Net profit	+ 20

---

principal and coupon payments, calculating the implied interest carrying cost is more difficult. Added to this difficulty is the fact that there are many different types of bonds with varying maturities, call provisions, coupons and, particularly important for the municipal bond market, tax consequences.

To begin to understand how the cash-futures arbitrage concept would be applied to the bond market, assume an investor needs to purchase an 8 percent, 20-year bond at the end of one year. As in the gold example, this may be done in either of two ways: purchase the bond in the cash market and hold it for one year, or buy the futures contract and take delivery in one year. We will assume for now that a constant life 8 percent, 20-year bond may be purchased in the cash market.[7] Suppose this hypothetical 8 percent coupon bond is currently trading at $92 in the cash market and the corresponding futures contract for delivery one year from today is currently trading at $91. The decision to purchase the bond in either the cash or futures market depends on whether the interest carrying cost or repurchase rate (also called the repo rate) in the cash market is smaller or larger than the $10 premium in the cash market.

At first glance it would seem foolish to purchase the cash bond at 92 and then carry it for a year when we can purchase the futures contract on that same bond for less than the cash price of 92. The important difference between the bond market and the gold market is that the owner of a cash bond will receive coupon payments while holding the bond. The purchaser of the constant-life 8 percent bond will receiver $80 each year he holds the bond. In a normal, upward sloping yield curve environment, the futures contract should always trade at a discount to the cash market, to reflect the fact that short term rates are less than long term rates.[8] The calculation of the implied cost of carry must take into account not only the difference in the cash and futures price, but also the amount of coupon to be received or paid out. As in our gold example, whether we buy or sell the basis is going to be determined by whether our implied cost of carry is greater than or less than the actual cost of carry in the cash market.

If we were to buy the basis when interest rates were 5 percent, we would have to pay $46 in interest on the $920 we borrow to purchase the cash municipal bond. But, we would also be receiving $80 worth of coupon payments for the year, leaving us with a net profit from the carry of $34. After taking the $10 loss in price associated with closing out the short futures position, an arbitrage profit of $24 would have been earned. Thus, at an interest rate of 5 percent, it is

---

[7] This assumption is not unreasonable. It will be shown later in this section how it is possible to equate any cash bond to a constant 8 percent, 20-year bond on a yield-equivalent basis.

[8] The inverse relationship between bond prices and yields explains this phenomenon.

profitable to buy the basis. A similar argument can be made for selling the basis when interest rates are at 15 percent and the cash and futures positions are at the same prices, 92 and 91, respectively. In this case the investor receives $138 interest, a $10 price premium, and a debit of $80 leaving him with a $68 net profit. Exhibit 2 summarizes the cash-futures arbitrage results.

EXHIBIT 2

Given:
$1,000 per bond with an 8% coupon currently trading at 92 and the 8% futures contract currently trading at 91.

Strategy 1: Buying the Basis
Actual interest rate cost of carry = 5%

Opening transaction:

(1) Borrow funds	$ + 920
(2) Buy bond in cash market	– 920
(3) Sell bond futures	–0–
Net investment	–0–

Closing transaction (one year later):

(1) Deliver bond at contract price	$ + 910
(2) Pay off loan principal	– 920
(3) Pay off loan interest	– 46
(4) Coupon payment received	+ 80
Net profit	$ + 24

Strategy 2: Selling the Basis
Actual interest rate cost of carry = 15%

Opening transaction:

(1) Short bond in cash market	$ + 920
(2) Invest funds	– 920
(3) Buy bond futures	–0–
Net investment	–0–

Closing transaction (one year later):

(1) Buy bond at contracted price	$ – 910
(2) Receive loan principal	$ + 920
(3) Receive loan interest	$ + 138
(4) Payout coupon payment	– 80
Net profit	$ + 68

The Conversion Factor: A Method for Equilibrating the Prices of Different Bonds

Coupon payments and time to maturity differ from one bond issue to the next. For any given market yield, bonds with different terms will all be priced differently. In order to provide pricing consistency to the Municipal Bond Buyers Index, the prices of the many bonds comprising the index are all converted into the prices these bonds would have if they all had an identical coupon and time to maturity. The factor that relates the price of a given bond to the 8 percent, 20-year base is called the bond's *conversion factor.* For example, the 10 1/2 percent Clark County Airport Revenue Bond maturing on 7/01/97 with settlement on 7/01/97 was priced at 98 1/2. The conversion factor is found by calculating the price at which this bond will yield 8 percent. The Clark County Bond callable at par on 7/01/97 with settlement on 7/01/84 will yield 8 percent at a dollar price of $1,199.78. For the Clark County Bond example the conversion factor is 1.1998, the dollar price of the bond is divided by 1000 and rounded to the nearest 4 decimal places. The cash bond price of 98 1/2 is divided by this factor to obtain the converted futures bond price that is entered in the construction of the municipal index. The converted futures bond price for the 10 1/2 percent Clark County Bond is 82.097.

The conversion factor is a useful means of smoothing over the different terms and equilibrating the prices of the many bonds to make the bond prices comparable for the Index.[9]

The Implication of the Index Market Basket on Cash-Futures Pricing

The opportunities for basis trading between the Bond Index and the cash municipal bond market will determine how the proposed municipal futures contract will be priced. In our previous bond example the interest rate cost of carry is the key to basis trading, and to the fair pricing of each market with respect to one another. Determining the implied repo rate in the municipal market in relation to

[9] The conversion factors are tabulated in a booklet available from the Chicago Board of Trade.

the municipal futures contract is more involved. Since the Municipal Index upon which the futures is based is comprised of 40 bonds, one would in effect need to buy or short all the bonds in the Index for an exact cash position versus the futures.[10] Since each bond has its own coupon schedule, maturity date and call provisions, the calculation of the implied cost of carry will be considerably more complex.

Suppose that when interest rates were 10 percent an investor purchased $12 million of all the municipal bonds that make up the Bond Index. Feeling that there was an arbitrage profit to be made by buying the basis, he then shorted $12 million worth of the municipal futures, which equates to 125 contracts at a price of 96. Three months later he decided to close out the positions by selling all the cash municipal bonds to meet his futures cash settlement obligation. A net profit of $75,000 is locked in after netting out the $300,000 interest payment from the $375,000 worth of coupon payments received. Selling the basis may also be performed in the right interest rate environment. If the interest rate cost of carry was 15 percent, selling the basis, that is selling short $12 million of all the bonds in the Municipal Index and simultaneously buying $12 million of Municipal Index futures would also leave a net profit of $75,000. Exhibit 3 summarizes these results.

Practical Considerations: The Impact of Short Sale Barriers and Other Factors

The cash-futures arbitrage examples were developed to give the investor an idea of how a basis trading position would be set up. However, it is important to note the practical considerations that could effect the performance of the trade. The first consideration is that the basket of cash municipal bonds bought or sold will have a different dollar value than the Municipal Index. This is because the Index is made up of converted bond prices whereas the actual market basket contains non-converted or actual prices. A second factor to be considered is that the amount of futures contracts bought or sold against a cash position will almost never equal the

---

[10] Such market baskets are already used in trading other index-based futures, most notably the S&P 500 index futures.

EXHIBIT 3

Buying the Basis

Interest Rate = 10%

Opening Transaction:

(1) Borrow $12 million	$ + 12,000,000
(2) Buy $12 million of all bonds in Bond Index	– 12,000,000
(3) Sell 125 futures at 96.	–0–
Net Investment	–0–

Closing Transaction: (3 months later)

(1) Pay off loan principal	$ – 12,000,000
(2) Pay off loan interest	– 300,000
(3) Sell cash bonds (to close out futures position)	+ 12,000,000
(4) Coupon payments	+ 375,000
Net Profit	+ 75,000

Selling the Basis

Interest Rate = 15%

Opening Transaction:

(1) Buy 125 futures at 96	$ –0–
(2) Loan out $12 million	– 12,000,000
(3) Short $12 million of all bonds in Bond Index	+ 12,000,000
Net Investment	–0–

Closing Transaction: (3 months later)

(1) Receive loan principal	$ + 12,000,000
(2) Receive loan interest	+ 450,000
(3) Coupon payments	– 375,000
(4) Cover short position in cash market	– 12,000,000
Net Profit	$ + 75,000

dollar value of the cash portfolio. In contrast to the example presented in Exhibit 3, an investor will have to exercise his own judgment to determine the exact number of futures contracts he will trade to best match his cash position. A third consideration is that the Municipal Index is updated twice monthly. Bonds are added and dropped from the Index depending on certain criteria. To keep a position current, it will therefore be necessary to update the cash portfolio. A fourth consideration is encountered if the basis trade is closed out before the delivery date of the futures. The convergence of the futures price to the Index value is only guaranteed on the delivery date of the futures. Thus, any action before this date is subject to basis risk, a widening or narrowing of the basis from the time the position was initially placed.

The final practical concern is the difficulty involved in the short sale of municipal bonds in the spot market. Short sale difficulties may make it impossible to execute a basis trade. This may lead the basis relationship to be inexact, especially if the imbalance requires taking a short position in the cash market. Lack of liquidity, reflected by the wide bid/ask spreads, makes it very expensive to cover a short.[11, 12] The lack of an efficient long-term forward market also hampers short selling. The majority of short sales that do occur are usually done with term issue bonds and are held for a time frame of less than two weeks. Traders take these short-horizon positions to capitalize on what they perceive as market disparities between issues. Tax consequences, though usually not fully considered, are also reasons for only short term holdings of short positions.[13] A final reason for the difficulty in short sales in municipals can be illustrated by the fact that no market repurchase rate or cost of carry rate exists for this market.[14] As a rough guide, traders usually add a fixed number of basis points to the current Federal Funds rate to determine their interest expense. The advent of a liquid futures market should have a noticeable effect on the current short selling procedure and practices of the municipal marketplace.

The Cost of Carry Implied by Municipal Bond Futures Contract Prices

The relationship that we have just discussed between interest rates, the Municipal Bond Buyers Index value, and the price of the futures contract can be expressed as:

$$F = I[1 + (r_s - r_L)T/360] \tag{1}$$

---

[11] The payment in the event of a short sale is usually more than the coupon payment amount since the short seller must also pay for the use of the bonds.

[12] Covering a short in the municipal market can be expensive due to the illiquidity in many issues.

[13] Shorting a municipal bond creates tax free income to the purchaser.

[14] In contrast, there is an active repurchase market for Treasury bonds.

where F = theoretical price of the futures contract.
I = the Municipal Bond Buyer Index value.
r_L = coupon rate on constant maturity 20 year bond.
r_s = cost of carry.
T = number of days to futures contract settlement.

If the cost of carry (r_s) implied by the prevailing futures price, index value and long-term coupon rate is not equal to the short-term borrowing rate then the futures contract price might either allow direct arbitrage, subject to the barriers previously discussed, or reduce the effectiveness of the futures contract as a hedging instrument. Exhibit 4 shows the cost of carry implied by the actual municipal bond futures contract prices over the period of June 1985 to February 1986. Actual futures prices together with the Municipal Bond Buyers Index value and the yield of the Index portfolio were substituted into equation (1) for F, I, and r_L, respectively. Equation (1) was then solved for r_s, the cost of carry to produce Exhibit 4.

EXHIBIT 4
Implied Cost of Carry; Municipal Bonds

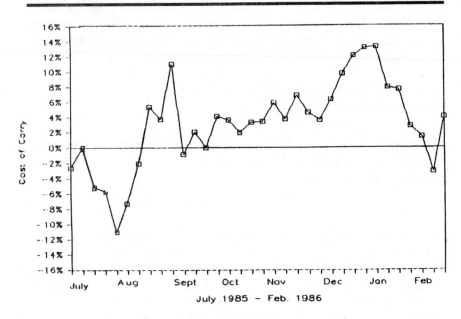

July 1985 – Feb. 1986

Note that in the early weeks of the contract the implied cost of carry was negative, then rose to a peak in December 1985, and then dropped off again in 1986. During late 1985 an unusually large volume of tax-exempt bonds were issued, presumably to avoid any restrictions that pending tax legislation might impose on bonds issued after 1986. However, at no point did short-term tax-exempt rates or other short-term rates exceed 9–10 percent. These data indicate that the futures price was less than the theoretical price in the early weeks of the contract and greater in the latter part of 1985.

Whatever the reason for this mispricing, it indicates that the barriers to the arbitrage relationships must be relatively effective. Otherwise, investors engaging in the arbitrage portfolios described earlier would have brought the prices into the relationship specified by equation (1). The fact that the cost of carry diverges from short-term borrowing costs indicates that the futures price does not exhibit a stable relationship to the Index value. The fluctuation of the futures price relative to the Index adds basis risk that may reduce the effectiveness of the municipal bond futures contract as a hedging instrument. This issue will be addressed in more detail in Section IV.

The 'MOB Spread'

Since the introduction of the Municipal Index Futures contract, there has been substantial interest in a portfolio position that has become known as the 'MOB Spread' (for 'municipal over bond'). This portfolio is formed by taking an opposite position in the Municipal Index futures contract and the Treasury bond futures contract.

Perhaps the apparent underpricing of the Municipal Bond futures contract reflected in the negative cost of carry in the early weeks of the contract generated the interest. A long position in the Municipal Index contract together with a short position in the Treasury bond contract to reduce or eliminate the risk of changes in overall interest rates might allow one to benefit from the mispricing. However, this position does not eliminate the risks associated with possible changes in the relative yields of Municipal versus Treasury debt.

It is more likely that investors in the 'MOB Spread' are interested in hedging or speculating on the relative prices of Municipal and

Treasury debt. The legislation for major tax reform in 1986 may have created hedging or speculative demand for a portfolio position, such as the 'MOB Spread,' which can be dramatically affected by tax legislation. For example, a reduction of marginal federal tax rates may reduce the investment attractiveness of municipal bonds vis-a-vis taxable debt. This might narrow the difference between the yields on taxable and tax-exempt securities. A long or short position in the 'MOB Spread' would have allowed parties affected by the legislation to hedge the risk that the legislation would or would not be accepted.

Whatever the reason for the interest, the key question for this research is whether the interest in the 'MOB Spread' would distort the prices of the two futures contracts in such a way as to reduce the effectiveness of the Municipal Index contract as a hedging instrument for municipal bonds. Perhaps the interest in the 'MOB Spread' explains the divergence of the implied cost of carry from short-term borrowing rates.

II. THE INGREDIENTS OF AN EFFECTIVE HEDGE

Hedging is a means of risk reduction. Hedging offsets an undesirable risk through a position in an instrument which moves inversely with the risky position.

The most obvious means of hedging a risk is simply to sell off the risky asset. Of course, this approach skirts the usual objective of a hedge: eliminating the risk of a position without physically selling the position out. To fulfill this objective, a surrogate for the asset being held must be sold off in place of the risky asset. The best hedge will be formed by finding an asset which comes as close as possible to the ideal of selling off the asset directly. The more the hedging instrument shares the price behavior of the asset being hedged, the more perfectly this goal will be met.

For example, if an investor holds a position in a Treasury bond, and wishes to reduce his risk exposure to the effect interest rate changes may have on the price of that bond, he can short a Treasury bond futures contract against it. Since Treasury futures prices are based on the price of the underlying Treasury issues, the futures price and the Treasury bond price will move very closely with one another. The short position in the Treasury futures will therefore move opposite the price of the bond; when interest rates rise, leading to a drop in the bond price, the price of the futures will also drop, and the short position will go up in value. By taking the proper proportion of futures positions relative to the bond being held, the two effects can be made to balance out almost exactly, and any change in the bond price can be offset by the change in the futures position.

As was discussed in the previous section, the futures and cash prices do not move exactly in line with one another. There is always some basis risk which limits the effectiveness of the hedge. Since no two instruments move completely in step with one another, the basis risk will be a factor in hedging effectiveness any time a surrogate security is used to counteract the movements in the asset to be hedged. The greater the basis risk, the greater the number of cases where the hedging instrument will fail to trace changes in the price of the risky bond, and the less effective the hedge will be.

Exhibit 5 provides a simple illustration of the effect of basis risk on hedging. Exhibit 5-A shows the price path taken by the target bond—the bond to be hedged—and the two prospective hedging instruments. The volatility of these instruments, as well as the correlation of their prices with the target bond, is evident from the variation in their prices over the time period. The first hedging instrument displays less variability than the other hedging instrument and the target bond. However, it does not track the fluctuations in the price of the target bond as well as the second hedging instrument does. Exhibit 5-B and 5-C combine the target bond with a short position in each of the hedging instruments. The short position moves exactly opposite to the price changes in the instrument—when the instrument rises a dollar in value, the short position will lose a dollar.

As Exhibit 5-B shows, the first hedging instrument is clearly ineffective. This would be expected, given the basis risk reflected by the poor tracking between its price and the price of the bond. On some occasions, this hedging instrument tends to move in the opposite direction of the target bond, and on other occasions it does not move strongly enough in the same direction. The result is that the short position does not offset the bond's price movements.

EXHIBIT 5
An Illustration of the Determinants of Hedging Effectiveness

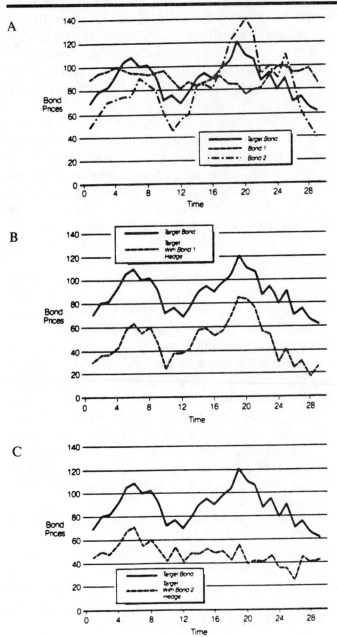

Indeed, despite the low volatility of its price, this first hedge actually leads to greater price variability than for the unhedged target bond.

The second hedge performs its objective far better. Exhibit 5-C overlays a short position in the second hedging instrument with the target bond, and shows the effect of this combined position. Since the second instrument tracks the bond more closely, its short position also offsets the bond's price movements more fully. The residual basis risk from this position is far lower than the risk of the unhedged bond. The result is a position that is subject to only a fraction of the risk of bond price shifts.

Taking the target bond as a municipal bond position, what types of vehicles would the first and second hedging instruments represent? Clearly, the second instrument is one that has more in common with the bond. The first instrument reflects some of the factors that lead to shifts in the price on the target bond, but misses out on other important factors. As we will see in the following sections, the first hedging instrument is representative of Treasury bond futures, while the second is more representative of the performance of municipal bond futures. Treasury bond futures can capture some of the interest rate risk inherent in the municipal bond market. When the bond price movement is attributable to the overall interest rate environment, the Treasury futures will serve as a hedge. However, the Treasury bond hedge fails to capture several other important aspects of the municipal bond market which are reflected in the municipal bond futures.

The message of Exhibit 5, that hedging effectiveness is higher the more similar the hedging vehicle is to the bond being hedged, is also brought forth in Exhibit 6. Conventionally, hedging effectiveness is measured by the amount the hedge reduces the variance of the bond position. Since price variance is the most common measure of risk, the percent reduction in variance is a natural statistic for measuring hedging effectiveness. The percent variance reduced is calculated by dividing the variance of price changes for the hedged position in the target bond by the variance of price changes for the unhedged position, and subtracting the resulting value from one. That is:

$$\text{Percent Variance Reduced} = 100 \times \left(1 - \frac{\text{Variance of Hedge Position}}{\text{Variance of Unhedged Position}} \right)$$

EXHIBIT 6

Bond	Percent Variance Reduced
U.S. Treasury 8.75% 11/15/08	94%
U.S. Treasury 7.875% 2/15/93	88
U.S. Treasury 14% 11/15/11	84
Bethlehem Steel 8.45% 3/1/05	40
Valdez (Sohio) 6% 7/1/07	35

If the hedge is perfect, the hedge position will have zero variance, and the percent variance reduced will be 100 percent. If the hedged position contributes no value to risk reduction, then the variance of the unhedged position will equal the variance of the hedged position, and the percent variance reduced will be 0 percent. Note that the percent variance reduced will be negative if the variance of the hedged position is greater than the value of the initial, unhedged position. As we will see in Section IV, negative values for the percent variance reduced are not an uncommon occurrence when hedging municipal bond prices.

Exhibit 6 shows the effects differences in maturity, coupon, and bond quality and type have on the percent variance reduced. In this exhibit, the underlying bond is the 7 5/8 percent Treasury bond of 2007. The first bond in Exhibit 6 is a 8 3/4 percent Treasury that matures in 2008. The percent variance reduced for this bond is quite high, at 94 percent. The next two issues are also Treasuries, but differ from the first Treasury in terms of time to maturity (2/15/93 versus 2/15/07) and coupon (14 percent versus 7 5/8 percent), respectively. As is clear from the exhibit, these differences in terms lead to a less effective hedge.

The greatest drop in hedging effectiveness, however, comes from the last two factors, quality difference and differences in the type of bond. For the corporate issue, a bond with an A rating, the percent variance reduced is 40 percent, and for the Valdez (Sohio) municipal bond, it is only 35 percent.

As we will show in the next section, differences in coupon or maturity can be adjusted for by the proper selection of the hedge ratio. However, differences in bond quality and the bond type can only be controlled by selecting a hedging instrument that shares these attributes with the bond being hedged.[15] The entire motivation for the municipal bond futures contract is to facilitate this selection. The implications of these two factors on the relative hedging effectiveness of the municipal bond contract will be treated in Section IV.

III. THE USE OF DURATION TO CONSTRUCT THE MOST EFFECTIVE HEDGE RATIO

Bonds with different maturities and coupons will react differently to changes in interest rates. A long time to maturity and a lower coupon both increase the price sensitivity of a bond to interest rate changes. It is possible to develop an expression to relate the relative price sensitivity of bonds, and use it to make adjustments for the differences in price behavior. The key to doing this is the duration of the bond.[16]

Bond Duration and Interest Rate Sensitivity

Consider two semiannual zero coupon bonds, one with twenty years to maturity, and another with five years to maturity.[17] Suppose the interest rate for both bonds is initially at 10 percent. The price of the 20-year bond will be $14.20, and the price of the 5-year bond will be $61.39. Now suppose interest rates jump to 12 percent.

---

[15] Until recently, the quality component of a bond was considered unhedgable. A new methodology for hedging quality and credit risk has recently been introduced by Bookstaber and Jacob (see Richard Bookstaber and David Jacob, *The Composite Hedge: Controlling the Credit Risk of High Yield Bonds,* New York: Morgan Stanley Fixed Income Research, 1984). This methodology is particularly effective in hedging low-quality issues, where credit risk is the greatest contributor to price risk.

[16] A detailed discussion of duration is presented in Alden Toevs, *Uses of Duration Analysis for the Control of Interest Rate Risk,* New York: Morgan Stanley Fixed Income Research, 1984.

[17] A semiannual zero is a zero coupon bond priced with interest compounded semiannually.

The price of the two bonds will drop to $9.72 and $55.84, respectively. For the 20-year bond, this is a 32 percent drop in price, while for the 5-year bond, it is only a 9 percent price drop. The longer maturity issue has greater price sensitivity to interest rate changes. For zero coupon bonds, this relative interest rate sensitivity is easy to determine.[18]

The method of measuring the interest rate sensitivity of a zero coupon bond can be applied directly to coupon bonds. A coupon bond can be thought of as a portfolio of zero coupon bonds.[19] For example, a 4-year bond with $100 par value, paying an 8 percent coupon in semiannual payments, gives a payout stream that is identical to the payout stream from holding a portfolio consisting of zero coupon bonds with $4 face value and with maturities of half a year, one year, and one and a half years, up to three and a half years, and a zero coupon bond with $104 face value (to cover the final coupon payment and principal) and a maturity of four years.

Since we can compute the interest rate sensitivity of each of the zero coupon bonds that comprise this portfolio, we can compute the interest rate sensitivity of the overall portfolio. And since the coupon bond is identical to this portfolio, we can compute the interest rate sensitivity of the coupon bond.

Exhibit 7 shows the steps in doing this computation. Column (1) gives the years to the semiannual cashflow. The next column gives the payouts on those dates. These payouts represent the principal amounts of the replicating zero coupon bonds. Column (4) gives the weight of each of these zero coupon bonds and the next column gives the weight of each of these zero coupon bonds in the replicating portfolio. For example, since the overall dollar value of the portfolio is $100, and the cost of the first zero coupon bond is $3.85, it represents 3.85 percent of the overall portfolio value.

The portfolio has interest sensitivity equal to the weighted aver-

---

[18] Since the price of a zero coupon bond is simply the discount factor times the face value, the interest rate is calculated by differentiating the discount factor with respect to the interest rate, r.

[19] The concept of a coupon-paying bond as a portfolio of zero coupon bonds is utilized in creating zeros. Zero coupon bonds are constructed by stripping the coupon components from coupon-paying Treasuries.

EXHIBIT 7

(1) Years to Cash Inflow	(2) Cash Inflow Amount	(3) Cash Inflows Discounted at 8%	(4) Price Weights	(5) Price Weighted Maturities
.5	$ 4.00	$ 3.85(a)	.0385(c)	.0193(d)
1	4.00	3.70	.0370	.0370
1.5	4.00	3.56	.0356	.0534
2	4.00	3.42	.0342	.0684
2.5	4.00	3.29	.0342	.0823
3	4.00	3.16	.0316	.0948
3.5	4.00	3.04	.0304	.1064
4	104.00	75.99	.7599	3.0396
		$100.00(b) (Current Price)	1.00	3.5011(e)

Duration = 3.5011(e)

(a) Column 2 divided by $(1.04)^T$

(b) Current price sums all cash inflows discounted by the 4% yield to maturity per period (half-year)

(c) Column (3) divided by 100

(d) Column (4) × Column (1)

(e) Duration is the sum of all price weighted maturities.

age of the interest sensitivity of all the zero coupon bonds that make up the portfolio. We can therefore compute the interest rate sensitivity of the coupon bond by averaging together the interest rate sensitivity of each of the zero coupon bonds that make up the coupon bond.[20] Or, we can simply look at the weighted average maturity of

[20] For example, since the first payment represents 3.85 percent of the overall portfolio value, the portfolio has interest sensitivity that is 3.85 percent the interest rate sensitivity of the half year zero. Since the second payment represents 3.7 percent of the overall portfolio value, the portfolio also has interest sensitivity that is 3.7 percent the interest rate sensitivity of a one-year zero. By going through the same process for each of the zero coupon bonds, we can obtain a measure of the interest rate sensitivity of the coupon bonds.

the zeros, and compute the interest rate sensitivity of a zero with that as its maturity.[21]

By taking the maturity of each of the zeros and weighting it by the proportion of the portfolio it represents, we can compute the maturity of the coupon bond that mimics the interest rate sensitivity of the portfolio. This is done in the final column of Exhibit 7. The weighted average maturity of the bond is 3.5 years.

This weighted average maturity is called the bond's *duration*. The bond will have the same interest rate sensitivity as a zero coupon bond with a maturity equal to the bond's duration.

Since the duration of this bond is 3.5 years, the bond price will react to interest rate changes the same as will a zero coupon bond with 3.5 years to maturity.

Given the simplicity in computing the interest rate sensitivity of zero coupon bonds, this information makes it straightforward to compute the interest rate sensitivity of this coupon paying bond as well. Using the duration of a bond, its price sensitivity to interest rate changes can be expressed in the following simple form:

$$\text{Change in P per unit change in } r = -D^* \times P, \qquad (2)$$

where P is the bond price, r is the interest rate, and D^* is the modified duration of the bond.[22]

Duration Hedging: The Hedge Ratio for Maximizing Hedging Performance

The hedge ratio for minimizing the variance of a hedged position is the price sensitivity of the hedged bond divided by the price sensitivity of the hedging instrument. For example, if the hedging instrument is twice as sensitive to interest rate changes as is the bond being hedged, then the bond being hedged should be held in a two-to-one ratio to the hedging instrument in order for the interest rate-induced price changes of the two positions to offset one

---

[21] This can be done because the interest sensitivity of a portfolio of zero coupon bonds is equal to the interest rate sensitivity of a bond with a maturity equal to the weighted average maturity of the portfolio.

[22] Modified duration is the duration of the bond divided by $1 + (r/2)$, where r is the yield to maturity of the bond.

another. We can use equation (2) to express this in terms of duration. This leads to the equation for the duration-based hedge ratio:

$$N^* = \frac{P_b \times D_b^*}{P_h \times D_h^*} \qquad (3)$$

The ratio of the hedging instrument to the bond being hedged, N^*, equals the modified duration of the bond being hedged times its price divided by the modified duration of the hedging vehicle times its price.[23]

Notice that the dollar-value matched hedge (the naive one-for-one hedge which matches the number of dollars of principal value of the bond being hedged with an equal principal value in the hedging instrument), will only be correct when both the price and duration of the hedging instrument and the bond being hedged are the same. The variance-minimizing hedge will almost always require a hedge ratio other than one.[24]

To illustrate the calculation of the duration based hedge, consider hedging the MAC 10 1/4 percent bond due in 1993 with the Municipal Bond Buyers Index. The modified duration of this bond was 5.52 years, and its price was $108. The Municipal Bond Buyers Index had a value of $85 17/32 and a modified duration of 10.01 years.[25]

---

[23] An alternative approach to using the duration measure to determine interest rate sensitivity is to use a regression model on past price data to measure the interest rate sensitivity empirically. The regression-based approach is shown in Toevs and Jacob (see Alden Toevs and David Jacob, "Interest Rate Futures: A Comparison of Alternative Hedge Ratio Methodologies") to lead to hedging effectiveness similar to the duration-based hedge. However, it is a more involved approach to use, since past data are required to perform the regression. Furthermore, if the price history is not representative of current interest rate levels, the interest sensitivity arising from the regression model may give an inaccurate picture of the current sensitivity.

[24] The hedge ratio presented in equation (3) is the proper hedge ratio for eliminating interest rate risk. Often, the objective of a hedge is to match a bond position with the interest rate sensitivity of a particular liability. Such asset/liability matching can be facilitated by a slight adjustment in the hedging position. For example, suppose the bond position needs to meet an interest-sensitive liability with a particular duration, D_1. The hedge ratio will then be:

$$N^* = \frac{(D_1^* - D_b^*)}{P_h^* \times P_h} P_b.$$

[25] The prices and duration for this example are determined as of the start of the simulation period for our study, June 1985. The duration of the bond, from

Using these values given a hedge ratio of:

$$N^* = \frac{108 \times 5.52}{85.531 \times 10.01} = .696.$$

From this hedge ratio, we see that since the Index has a longer duration than the MAC bond, its price will be more sensitive to interest rate changes: the MAC bond will move only $.696 in value for every $1 in price that the municipal bond Index moves. This means that for every long MAC bond being hedged, a short position in .696 Municipal bond futures should be held.

We have had to use an estimate of the duration of the Municipal Bond Buyers Index in this example, because the duration of the Index is not published. Given the importance of the duration in determining the optimal hedge position, it would be useful for the duration to be calculated and published with the Index price and composition.

IV. THE VALUE ADDED FROM THE MUNICIPAL BOND FUTURES

The principle of duration hedging is applicable to any hedging instrument. The duration hedge will overcome the errors that arise due to a mismatch of maturity or coupon between the hedging instrument and the underlying bond. However, as was evident from Exhibit 6, this alone is not sufficient to assure an effective hedge. Bond sector and quality must also be matched as closely as possible. Obviously, this means that the logical hedging vehicle for municipal bonds is another municipal bond.

The Treasury bond hedge provides a natural benchmark for judging the value added by the municipal bond futures. The Treasury bond hedge, generally implemented through the Treasury bond futures contract, is often used as a hedging vehicle for municipal bonds. It is a viable alternative to the municipal bond futures, if only because of its great liquidity and popularity. The major questions regarding the value of the municipal bond futures contract are

---

which the modified duration is computed, was 5.75 years, and for the Municipal Bond Buyers Index was 10.46 years.

how well it hedges, i.e., what can be expected in terms of percent variance reduced, and how well its performance compares to that of the Treasury bond futures.

To answer these questions, we have performed tests of hedging effectiveness on a set of 25 widely-followed municipal bonds. We used weekly price data on these bonds and the Treasury bond and Municipal Bond Buyers Index futures contract for the period since the introduction of the Municipal Bond Index contract, June 1985 through February 1986.

A complete list of the bonds is presented in Exhibit 8, along with summary statistics for the tests in this section.

The Dangers of Using Treasury Bonds for Hedging Municipal Bonds

Since Treasury bonds are pure interest rate instruments, they will be ineffective in hedging municipal bonds unless the spread between municipals and Treasuries stays relatively constant, i.e., unless no factors other than the default-free interest rate affect municipal bond prices. However, as we have already shown, there is more involved in making municipal bond prices move. For example, quality effects, both for individual municipal bond issues and for the tax-exempt sector in general, changes in tax laws, and shifts in the average tax liability among investors will have a significant impact on this spread. As a result, the Treasury bond hedge may be ineffective, and in fact may actually increase the risk of the municipal bond position.

Exhibit 8 compares the hedging effectiveness of the Treasury bond futures contract hedge with the use of the Municipal Bond Buyers Index futures contract. The hedging effectiveness is measured by the percent variance reduced. As this exhibit shows, the percent variance reduced using the duration-based Treasury bond hedge ranges from a high of 85 percent to a low of −2041 percent. In 13 of the 25 cases, the Treasury bond hedge, rather than serving as a risk-reduction vehicle, actually added more variance to the position. For ten cases it more than doubled the variance of the position.

For a portfolio which included one of each of the twenty-five bonds, the Treasury bond futures contract reduced variance by only 19 percent.

EXHIBIT 8
Summary Statistics for Hedge Positions

Bond	Coupon	Maturity	Percent Variance Reduced For Treasury Bond Hedge	Percent Variance Reduced For Municipal Index Hedge
Alabama G.O.	8.375	3/1/01	26%	71%
Chelan Cnty Auth NY	5	7/01/13	− 170	− 2
Clark Cnty Arpt Rev	10.5	7/01/07	− 73	45
Dela River Port Auth	6.5	1/15/11	63	83
Ga Mun El Auth Pwr Rev	8	1/01/15	79	85
Intermountain Pwr	10.5	7/01/18	85	79
Intermountain Pwr	14	7/01/21	− 114	23
Loop	6.5	9/01/08	− 225	− 132
MAC	8	7/01/86	− 76	− 42
MAC	10.25	2/01/93	− 2041	− 1007
Massachusetts G.O.	6.5	8/01/00	72	85
Mass Wholesale	13.375	7/01/17	69	62
Michigan Public Pwr	10.675	1/01/18	− 142	20
NJ Turnpike Auth	5.7	5/01/13	47	72
NY Mtgr Agency Rev	9.5	10/01/13	− 110	24
NY State Pwr	9.875	1/01/20	− 308	− 71
NY State Pwr Escr	9.5	1/01/01	− 379	− 109
NY State Urban Dev Crp	6	11/01/13	48	82
NC East Mun Pwr Agcy	11.25	1/01/18	39	82
Port of NY & NJ	6	2/01/06	− 127	− 14
Port of NY-Delta	10.5	2/01/08	− 980	− 399
SC Pub Svc Auth	10.25	7/01/20	− 7	74
Valdez (Exxon)	5.5	5/01/07	69	62
Valdez (Sohio)	6	7/01/07	72	64
Washngtn PPSS#3	13.875	7/01/18	66	70
Portfolio			19	77

The Municipal Bond Hedge: A More Effective Hedging Vehicle

Exhibit 8 also shows the reduction in variance that came from using the Municipal Bond Buyers Index futures contract as a hedge. This hedge was generally superior to the Treasury bond hedge in reducing the variance of the bond. In 21 out of 25 cases, it performed better than the hedge with the Treasury bond futures contract. In five cases, the municipal hedge gave over 80 percent reduction in variance—an extremely high level of hedging effectiveness.[26] For a portfolio which included one of each of the twenty-five bonds, the Municipal Index hedge reduced variance by 77 percent.

However, the successes for the municipal bond hedge are shared with number of cases when the hedge was ineffective. In eight of twenty-five cases, the municipal bond hedge actually increased the variance of the position. In one case it increased the variance by more than 1000 percent. There is a great deal of variation in the municipal bonds in bond quality and sector. Given the heterogeneity of this group, it is not surprising that a single bond index, although in some sense representative of average long-term municipal bonds, cannot capture the price changes of all the issues. The bond index will not be effective in all cases.

Over the 34 week period of this test, interest rates fell by more than 150 basis points. This dramatic shift in interest rates provides an excellent test for the hedging effectiveness of the municipal bond contract. The performance of the Municipal Index hedge, although generally better than the Treasury bond hedge, still leaves much to be desired. In a stable interest rate environment, price movements for individual bonds will be mostly driven by changes in the underlying creditworthiness of the issuer. Since the Municipal Bond Buyers Index represents only the average creditworthiness of the bonds included in the index, the municipal bond futures contract is not an effective instrument to hedge changes in bond-specific credit risk.[27] However, the period of this test does not provide one of the best scenarios for which one would expect the municipal bond futures contract to provide the most effective hedge. Over the period of this test, the relative yield of municipal bonds versus Treasury bonds remained relatively stable. Despite the large volume

---

[26] Even the most homogeneous bond group, the long-term Treasury bonds, frequently does not have a percent variance reduced of greater than 90 percent.

[27] Hedging bond-specific credit risk requires a different approach. See Richard Bookstaber and David Jacob, *The Composite Hedge: Controlling the Credit Risk of High Yield Bonds*.

increase in new issues of tax-exempt securities during late 1985, the yield on 20-year prime grade municipal bonds only varied between 78 percent and 85 percent of the yield on 20-year Treasury bonds.[28] The greatest improvement in hedging efficiency of the Municipal Index futures contract over the Treasury bond futures contract would be in a period of major shifts in the relative yields of municipal versus government bonds. Despite the stable relative yield over the period of the test, it is clear that the municipal bond futures contract did improve on the Treasury bond futures contract. However, its inability to hedge individual-security risk appears to be a major weakness in its effective use for single bond portfolios. These data suggest that the primary hedging use of the Municipal Index futures contract will likely be for investors holding diversified municipal bond portfolios.

V. CONCLUSION: WHAT CAN WE EXPECT FROM THE MUNICIPAL BOND FUTURES CONTRACT

The first task of any bond hedge is to find a hedging instrument which matches the price movements of the target bond as closely as possible. If all bond prices moved identically, then any bond could be used to hedge any other bond with perfect results. Less than perfect hedges arise because of differences in price behavior in the hedging instrument and the bond being hedged. These occur from two sources: differences in bond terms and differences in bond type. Different bond term—different coupon rate or time to maturity—can be easily adjusted by using the duration hedge discussed in Section III. However, the mismatch that arises from differences in bond type—differences in quality and tax status—are not so easily corrected. Because the municipal bond futures provides a better match than the Treasury bond futures for these last two factors, the contract has great potential for facilitating the hedging of municipal bonds.

This potential is investigated in the hedging comparisons of Section IV. The Bond Buyers Municipal Bond Index correlated more

---

[28] See *An Analytical Record of Yields and Yield Spreads,* Salomon Brothers, Inc.

closely with the municipal bonds in our sample than did the Treasury bond. It led to greater hedging effectiveness as measured by the reduction in the variance of price change in the bond position for most of the bonds. The municipal bond hedge led to variance reductions in 17 out of 25 cases, whereas in 13 of the 25 bonds we considered, the Treasury bond position actually led to an increase in risk. Rather than offsetting price changes in the target bond, the Treasury bond simply added a new, largely uncorrelated price uncertainty to the position. And in only four of the 25 cases did the Treasury bond exhibit superior hedging effectiveness than the Municipal Index futures.

However, the fact that in eight of 25 cases the municipal bond hedge actually increased the variance of the position indicates that the heterogenous nature of individual municipal bonds reduces the hedging effectiveness of the new contract. It is likely that the most effective use of the municipal bond contract will be in hedging diversified municipal bond portfolios rather than single bonds.

The potential for the hedging effectiveness of the Municipal Index futures contract may be greater than these tests suggest. Although there was a dramatic shift in the level of interest rates over the period of our test, the time a municipal bond hedge would be expected to perform best relative to the alternative Treasury bond hedge is during times of a municipal bond market crisis. For example, as a result of the moratorium on the payment of New York City notes in 1975, or after the WPPSS default in 1983, the municipal bond market suffered dislocations relative to the other bond markets, and the spread between municipal issues and Treasuries widened precipitously. It is in such times of crisis—at the very time when the risk in the municipal bond market is greatest—that the municipal bond futures contract will tend to be a superior hedging instrument. In addition to crises of default, an increase in price risk can occur with changes in the political environment. The restructuring of the tax code in the United States that was imminent in early 1986 is the most obvious case in point. Only a hedge with tax-exempt securities can capture the implications of such a restructuring on municipal bond price risk.

This article supports the hedging role of the Municipal Index futures contract. But many important questions regarding the use of the municipal bond futures must remain unanswered until more data are available. The early weeks of any new contract are unsettled, thus longer run results may differ from these.

Liquidity and the size of the cash municipal bond pool underlying the market basket are the most obvious hurdles for the success of the municipal bond futures contract. The very structure of the municipal futures contract magnifies their importance. The futures contract is based on a market basket of securities. This market basket concept has been used successfully as the basis for the many stock index futures contracts. However, there are two critical differences between the market basket used for stock indexes and the market basket proposed for the municipal bond futures: the municipal bond futures contract market basket is based on securities that are not as liquidly traded, and the capitalization of the municipal bond futures contract market basket is an order of magnitude smaller than that of the market baskets underlying the stock index futures.

These two differences lead, in turn, to two dangers in the market behavior of the contract.

First, it is natural for many of those using the contract to hold the bonds underlying the futures contract in their cash portfolios. Investors interested in cash-futures arbitrage obviously will need to hold a representative set of the underlying bonds. And, investors who want to take advantage of the hedging potential of the futures in managing their bond portfolio will be inclined to weight their portfolio toward holdings of the bonds that comprise the index. This extraordinary demand for the bonds underlying the futures contract will have an impact on the price behavior of the bonds. The bonds in the market basket will no longer be representative of the general municipal bond market price behavior. The very use of the bonds as a proxy for the municipal bond market will lead to distortions in their pricing, and will compromise the function of their selection. Such problems are not as great for the stock index contracts because of the sheer number and size of the issues. We suggest further research to investigate this issue once data become available.

The second problem is also a direct result of the relatively small size of the issues. The total dollar value of the market-basket bonds outstanding is on the order of $10 billion. A large share of the bonds are essentially locked away, out of the market circulation. This brings the size of the market down to the level where a number of individual market participants could materially affect the price of the market basket, and thereby control the course of the futures contract price as well.

These potential problems are not unique to the municipal bond market. Many successful futures contracts are based on an underlying asset with small market capitalization. For example, the outstanding size of the current Treasury note, which makes up the primary delivery instrument for the Treasury note futures, is roughly that of the forty municipal bonds in the futures market basket, yet this has caused no dislocations for that contract. The same argument can be made, to a lesser extent, about the most deliverable bonds in the Treasury bond market. In any case, the hedger can overcome the risks from distortions in the pricing of the market basket-futures relationship by rolling over the next delivery month when cash settlement approaches, when the mix of participants in the market shifts more towards the larger speculators and locals.

There are three types of participants needed for a futures contract to be successful. First, there must be hedgers who use the market to help them meet portfolio risk objectives. Second, there must be trading depth on the floor of the exchange. The market makers and spreaders are the primary source for market liquidity. They also keep the bid-asked spread tight, and are particularly important for maintaining a market in the less active, distant contract months. Third, there must be speculators who are sensitive to pricing inefficiencies. The speculators assure that the futures price maintains the proper relationship to the value of the underlying asset, thereby reducing the large fluctuations in the basis. And, as with the floor traders, the speculators are a major source of liquidity for the hedgers. The larger the speculative component of the market, the less the price has to change from its equilibrium value to elicit the desired contract supply.

The opening of the municipal bond futures contract seems to indicate that there is an adequate number of the first two types of participants, the hedgers and floor traders. The municipal bond contract has a clear hedging constituency for whom there is no attractive alternative. We would expect, as has occurred in other futures markets, that a continually increasing number of municipal bond market participants will enter into hedging activity once the opportunities for risk control become apparent. It is the third leg of the triad, the speculative demand, which remains an open question. The fact that the implied cost of carry estimated in this research fluctuates both well above and well below short-term borrowing rates indicates that speculators and arbitragers may not be able to force a stable relationship between the futures price and Index value.

ARTICLE 22

MARCELLE ARAK is Vice President and Head of the Capital Markets Analysis and the Options and Arbitrage Units of Citicorp's North American Investment Bank. The CMA group analyzes developments in the fixed income markets and provides strategies for traders and investors.

Prior to joining Citicorp, she was Vice President in the Research area of the Federal Reserve Bank of New York. She has taught at Baruch College (CUNY). Ms. Arak has written on a wide variety of financial topics including financial futures, tax exempt bonds, and original issue discount bonds and is especially known for her analysis of tax structure effects on financial markets.

Ms. Arak earned her doctorate in economics from M.I.T. and her B.A. from the University of Rochester.

LAURIE S. GOODMAN is a Vice President in the Capital Markets Analysis Unit of Citicorp's North American Investment Bank. She specializes in research and analysis of fixed income financial instruments, with an emphasis on futures and options.

Prior to joining Citicorp, Ms. Goodman was a senior economist at the Federal Reserve Bank of New York. She has also served on the finance faculty of the Graduate School of Business at New York University. Ms. Goodman holds a Ph.D. in Economics from Stanford University, and a B.A. from the University of Pennsylvania.

RAJ DARYANANI has been an analyst in the Capital Markets Analysis Unit of Citicorp Investment Bank since 1985. His specialties include research in the areas of governments, interest rate swaps and municipals.

Mr. Daryanani has a B.A. in Politics, Economics, Rhetoric and Law from the University of Chicago.

THE MOB: PRICING
AND ARBITRAGE

Marcelle Arak, Ph.D.
Vice President
Capital Markets Analysis
Citicorp Investment Bank

Philip Fischer, Ph.D.
Vice President
Public Finance
Citicorp Investment Bank

Laurie Goodman, Ph.D.
Vice President
Capital Markets Analysis
Citicorp Investment Bank

Raj Daryanani
Research Analyst
Capital Markets Analysis
Citicorp Investment Bank

Soon after the June 1985 debut of the municipal futures contract, market participants began to track the "MOB"—the spread between municipal and Treasury bond futures prices.[1] As shown in Exhibit 1, the MOB has been very volatile, ranging from a Septem-

[1] Municipal bond futures are discussed in the previous article.

Exhibit 1, the MOB has been very volatile, ranging from a September 1985 high of $348/32$ to a low of $-190/32$ on April 14, 1986. This volatility has made the MOB a point of interest for futures market participants; MOB trading far dominates transactions involving municipal futures alone.

The MOB is traded for several different reasons:

- Portfolio managers want to hedge municipal bond portfolios. They could short municipal futures, but the MOB is more liquid. Thus they short the MOB and then short Treasury bond futures.

- Traders think that municipal futures are priced too high (or too low) relative to municipals in the cash market. For example, in January 1986, the price of municipal futures exceeded that of the municipal bonds themselves. Theoretically, munic-

EXHIBIT 1
MOB (Front Contracts, 11 June 1985 to 15 September 1986)

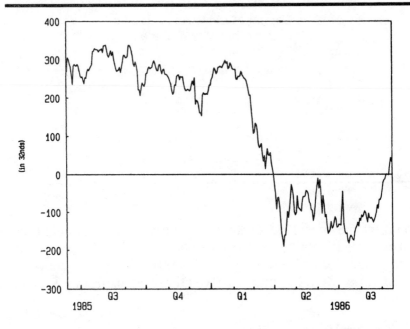

ipal futures should trade at a discount from the cash market, as holders of the cash instrument earn carry. Municipal futures should (and did) fall relative to a portfolio of municipal securities. In 1986, if a market participant was short municipal futures and long a portfolio of municipal securities, a gain of close to 2 points could have been achieved between January 7 and January 9.

- Market participants feel that the futures market spread, the MOB, is misaligned with the cash market relationship between municipals and Treasuries.

- Market participants believe municipal rates will change relative to Treasury rates and find it more convenient to place this bet in the futures markets rather than in the cash markets. For example, on March 19, 1986 when Senator Packwood proposed subjecting all municipal securities to the alternative minimum tax, municipal prices dropped sharply. If a market participant felt that chances of passage of this legislation were slight and that municipal prices would recover, he or she could have bought the MOB March 19, 1986, sold the spread March 21, 1986, and gained $54/32$ by the widening.

Anyone using the MOB in connection with any of these trades should be aware of the slippage between the MOB—a futures market spread—and cash market events. For example, municipal prices might improve relative to Treasury prices in the cash market while the MOB declines. To help evaluate such risks, we have developed arbitrage bands for the MOB, derived mathematically in Section I. Futures contracts generally trade within these theoretical trading bands. Because these bands are fairly wide, however, there is significant MOB basis risk. Section II discusses trades involving the MOB and the importance of the theoretical bands in MOB trades.

I. ARBITRAGE BANDS FOR THE MOB

To develop arbitrage bands for the MOB, we must first develop upper and lower bounds for each market individually.

Municipal Upper Bound

Municipal futures are overpriced if a riskless profit is possible by shorting the future. Suppose an investor:

- borrows money
- buys the bonds in the municipal index in the exact proportions as the index
- receives the municipal coupons
- sells municipal futures

Suppose one unwinds this position at the expiration of the futures by:

- selling the bonds
- buying municipal futures
- repaying the amount borrowed with interest

The sale price of the municipal market basket will equal the purchase price on the municipal futures. Therefore, any profit locked in by the initial transaction is guaranteed, unaffected by subsequent events. Municipal futures should be priced such that one cannot profit by this risk-free transaction.

Introducing some notation, let

$\overline{M}(n)$ = upper bound for the municipal futures contract at time n
$\underline{M}(n)$ = lower bound for the municipal futures contract at time n
$I(n)$ = municipal index at time n
$r_{t/e}$ = tax-exempt rate
r_s = short-term Treasury rate
δ = tax-deductible portion of borrowings used to carry municipals
t_g = marginal income tax rate
C_F = transaction costs of buying or selling futures
C_I = transaction costs of buying or selling municipals
N = time held (portion of a year)

The upper bound is given by (1).

$$\overline{M}(n) = I(n) - I(n)[r_{t/e} - r_s(1 - \delta t_g)]N/(1 - t_g) + C_F + C_I \qquad (1)$$

The first term is simply the cost of purchasing the cash index. The second term adjusts for the interest costs and benefits of holding the cash instrument; the holder of the cash instrument earns tax-free interest on the municipal securities, although money must be borrowed to buy the securities.

Prior to 1986, the cost of carrying municipals was 80 percent tax deductible for banks. The 1986 tax bill prohibits banks from deducting interest paid to carry municipals acquired after August 7, 1986. Because this tax legislation was expected to reduce deductibility to 0 percent effective 1/1/86, the market behaved as if $\delta = 0$ during 1986. Assume a bank broker/dealer is the marginal price setter in this market. If the carry costs are 7 percent, the bank's marginal tax rate is 46 percent, and 80 percent is tax deductible, the after-tax cost of carry is .07 $(1 - .8 \times .46)$ or 4.42 percent. If δ is reduced to zero, the after-tax cost of carry is raised to 7 percent.

The coupon gain less the costs of shorting must be multiplied by the fraction of a year during which the position is held. The carry term is then divided by $1 - t_g$ or .54 to place it on a before-tax basis so that it can be compared to Treasuries.

The final two terms are the transactions costs of creating the position. The cost of buying or selling a $100,000 municipal futures contract is $20, which amounts to $.02 per $100. The final term is the cost of buying municipal bonds. We estimate that, for a dealer, bid-ask spreads are about 1/8 of a point.

To see how equation (1) might be implemented consider the following: On March 31, 1986, the municipal cash index was at 100.156 and the tax-exempt rate was roughly 8 percent. The short-term Treasury rate was 7.0 percent, and there was assumed to be no deduction for carrying municipal bonds. The time until expiration on the June contract was 80 days and the investor's marginal tax rate was 46 percent. Thus, the upper bound is given by:

$$\overline{M}(n) = 100.156 - 100.156(.08 - .07(1 - 0 \times .46))(80/360)/.54$$
$$+ .02 + .125 = 99.89$$

Municipal Lower Bound

Now, consider the lower bound for the municipal futures contract. Suppose one:

- sells short municipal securities
- invests the proceeds from the short sale (if possible)
- pays the municipal coupon
- buys municipal futures

The profit on this transaction is locked in since the transaction can be unwound at expiration by buying the municipal index to cover the short position and selling municipal futures, both at an identical price.

Shorting municipal securities is very expensive because institutional restrictions on shorting municipal bonds require the short seller to actually "fail." Settlement is postponed when he fails to deliver the bonds. The short is responsible, however, for accrued interest from the initially specified delivery date until actual settlement. Thus while the short does not receive the cash from the sold bonds until delivery, he owes the tax-exempt coupon on the bonds for the entire period that the short position was on. Essentially, the short foregoes interest on the proceeds from the short sale.

The lower bound for the municipal futures contract may be determined by (2)

$$\underline{M}(n) = I(n) - I(n)r_{t/e}N - C_I - C_F \qquad (2)$$

The first term in (2) is the value of the cash index. The second term is the cost of paying the tax-exempt interest rate, while receiving no proceeds from the short sale. The final two terms are the transactions costs of selling municipal bonds and buying futures contracts.

A sample calculation for the lower bound as of March 31, 1986 appears below. The tax-exempt municipal rate is assumed to be 8 percent and the transactions costs are identical to those used in the previous example.

$$\underline{M}(n) = 100.156 - (100.156).08(80/360) - .125 - .02 = 98.23$$

Thus for the municipal futures market, the lower arbitrage bound, 98.23, and the upper arbitrage bound, 99.89, are 1.66 points apart.

Where the municipal future does not lie within its upper and lower bounds, arbitrage opportunities exist. If it lies above its upper bound, one would arbitrage by buying the municipal index and shorting the futures. If it lies below its lower bound, one can arbitrage by selling the municipal index and buying the futures. Thus we have:

$$\overline{M}(n) > M(n) > \underline{M}(n) \tag{3}$$

where $M(n)$ is the actual value of the municipal futures contract at time period n.

Municipal Futures versus Arbitrage Bands

Exhibits 2 and 3 show the upper and lower bounds and the actual prices for the March 1986 and June 1986 municipal bond futures

EXHIBIT 2
Municipal Futures, March 1986
—————— Lower and Upper Bounds
. . . . Municipal Bond Futures

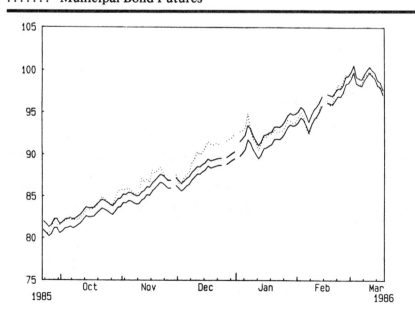

EXHIBIT 3
Municipal Futures, June 1986
_____ Lower and Upper Bounds
. . . . Municipal Bond Futures

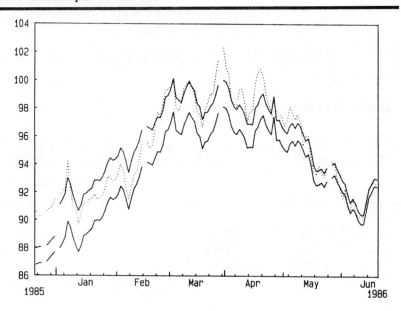

contracts. In general the contract has behaved fairly well. However, it was slightly above its upper bound in December, indicating that arbitragers could have made money by shorting the municipal futures and buying municipal bonds approximating the index.

A substantial widening of the bands in January 1986 reflected expectations that banks could no longer deduct interest for carrying municipal securities after 12/31/85. δ declined from .8 to 0, more than doubling the width of the arbitrage bands.

The June municipal futures was again above its upper bound in March and April 1986, reflecting uncertainty about the provisions of the tax legislation. This situation presented another opportunity for arbitragers.

Treasury Bond Futures

The upper and lower bounds for the Treasury bond futures contract can be computed in much the same way as for municipal futures. If the Treasury futures is "too expensive" to cash, it is advantageous to short the futures contract and buy Treasury bonds in the cash market. The steps are:

- Borrow money at the short-term interest rate
- Buy the deliverable bond (the amount purchased should be the deliverable bond divided by the factor)
- Receive the current yield on the bond
- Short bond futures

On the last day of futures trading, the transaction can be unwound by:

- Selling the deliverable bond
- Buying the futures
- Repaying amount borrowed plus interest

This transaction presents a problem insofar as there is no necessary convergence between cash and futures prices at the end of the delivery month: the Treasury bond futures contract lacks a cash settlement feature and traders have one week after trading ends to make delivery of an eligible bond.

The holder of the short futures position can elect which bond to deliver and when to deliver it. There are two main options inherent in this contract. First, the futures trading day ends before the cash market trading day. The short has until 9:00 PM each day during the delivery month to decide whether or not to deliver. If he or she decides to deliver, $100,000 par amount is presented and is invoiced based on the closing (3:00 PM) futures price. Thus if there is a large price decline in the late afternoon, the short can take advantage of it. Second, trading stops one week prior to the end of the month, while delivery may occur until the last day at the pre-established price.[2]

Because of the advantage to the short, the futures price must be lower than one would anticipate from carry considerations alone. The value of the delivery options can be calculated as the difference between the repurchase agreement (repo) rate and the repo rate implied in a cash and carry transaction. For the June 1986 contract, it was roughly $13/32$ three months before expiration. The value of the option will depreciate as the contract nears expiration at the rate of $.75/32$ per day during the delivery month and $.375/32$ per day prior to the delivery month until its value is gone.[3]

The upper bound for the Treasury bond futures contract is given by (4).

$$\overline{B}(n) = G(n) - P(n) - G(n)(cy - r_s)N + C_F + C_G \qquad (4)$$

where $G(n)$ = the value of the Treasury bond at time n (cheapest to deliver bond divided by the factor)

$P(n)$ = the value of the delivery options at time n

cy = the current yield on the cheapest to deliver Treasury bond

r_s = the short-term taxable interest rate

C_F = the transactions cost of buying or selling a futures contract

C_G = the transactions cost of buying or selling a government bond

[2] The value of these options is discussed in more detail in Marcelle Arak and Laurie S. Goodman, "Treasury Bond Futures: Valuing the Delivery Options," a paper presented at the Financial Management Association Meetings, Denver, Colorado, October 9-12, 1985.

[3] The value of the options is calculated as follows. The difference between the repo rate and the interest rate implicit in a long cash-short futures position (the so-called "implied rp" rates) for the June contract was 160 basis points three months before maturity. We divide this number by 4 because it is annualized. We then multiply by the average value of $1.00 par of the futures contact, which at the time of this writing was approximately 1.0. This gives us roughly $13/32$. This number can vary considerably from contract to contract. For example, for the September 1985 contract the delivery options were worth roughly $25/32$, calculated as follows: there was a 400 basis point difference between the repo and implied repo rates and the value of the futures contract at that point was roughly $.80 per $1.00 par.

The first two terms are the value of the cash bond less the value of the delivery options. The third term is the net carry, and the final two terms are the transaction costs.

We can establish a lower bound for the Treasury bond futures contract in a similar manner. If Treasury bond futures are too cheap to cash, we short the cash instrument and buy the futures contract:

- Sell short the deliverable bond

- Invest the proceeds from the short sale in a short-term asset earning the short-term rate

- Pay the current yield on the bond

- Buy bond futures

On the last day of futures trading, the transaction can be unwound by buying the deliverable bond and selling the futures. The lower bound must therefore be set such that (5) holds.

$$\underline{B}(n) = G(n) - P(n) - G(n)(cy - r_s + h)N - C_F - C_G \qquad (5)$$

where h is the "haircut" or cost of shorting the Treasury security and $r_s - h$ is the interest rate on the money lent.

Note that two differences exist between the upper and lower bounds for Treasury futures. First, the transactions costs are added for the upper bound and subtracted for the lower bound. Second, the short seller must pay the "haircut" on the Treasury securities.

To illustrate the calculation of the upper and lower bounds, we will consider values as of March 31, 1986 on the June contract. The cheapest to deliver bond was the 12 1/2 of 2014. The price was 151.1875. The factor was 1.4699. The price divided by the factor is thus 102.8556. The value of the delivery options was 13/32, and the short-term rate was 7.0 percent.

$$\overline{B}(n) = 102.8556 - 13/32 - 102.8556(.08268 - .07)91/360$$
$$+ .125 + .02 = 102.26$$
$$\underline{B}(n) = 102.8556 - 13/32 - 102.8556(.08268 - .07 + .005)91/360$$
$$- .125 - .02 = 101.84$$

In theory, the Treasury bond future must lie within its upper and lower bounds.

$$\overline{B}(n) \geq B(n) \geq \underline{B}(n) \tag{6}$$

That is, if (6) doesn't hold, arbitrage opportunities exist.

Exhibits 4 and 5 show that the bounds for Treasury bond futures are very narrow, less than $1/2$ point or $16/32$, for the March 1986 and June 1986 contracts. The futures contracts usually trade within their bounds.

MOB Bounds

Suppose the Treasury bond futures contract was trading at the lower end of its band, and the municipal futures contract was at

---

EXHIBIT 4
Treasury Futures, March 1986
_____ Lower and Upper Bounds
. . . . Treasury Bond Futures

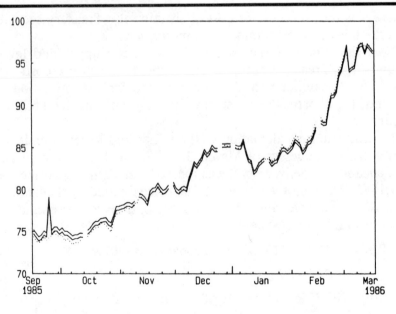

EXHIBIT 5
Treasury Futures, June 1986
   ——— Lower and Upper Bounds
   ...... Treasury Bond Futures

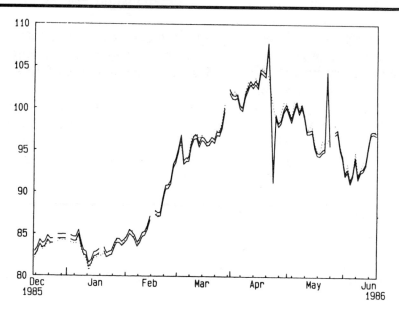

the upper end of its band. The MOB was still within appropriate bounds. Similarly, if the Treasury bond futures contract was trading at the upper end of its band, and municipal futures contract was at the lower end of its band the MOB would still be within appropriate bounds. The arbitrage bounds for the municipal-Treasury futures spread are given by (7).

$$\overline{M}(n) - \underline{B}(n) \geq MOB(n) \geq \underline{M}(n) - \overline{B}(n) \tag{7}$$

where $\overline{M}(n)$ and $\underline{M}(n)$ are the upper and lower bounds for the municipal futures contract and $\overline{B}(n)$ and $\underline{B}(n)$ are the upper and lower bounds for the Treasury bond futures contract. Let us assume:

$$\overline{M}(n) = 100; \underline{M}(n) = 97; \overline{B}(n) = 101; \underline{B}(n) = 100$$

MOB upper bound $100 - 100 = 0$

MOB lower bound $97 - 101 = -4.0 = -128/32$

In order for the MOB to be misaligned, it is a necessary, although not a sufficient condition that one of the two futures contracts be trading outside its arbitrage bands.

The upper and lower bounds for the September 1985 MOB are shown in Exhibit 6. The MOB was outside its arbitrage range in late June–early August of 1985 because the municipal future was outside its arbitrage range.

Exhibits 7, 8, 9, and 10 show the upper and lower bounds for the MOB on the December 1985 and March, June, and September 1986 contracts. While the MOB has generally been within its bounds, there were periods in November and December 1985

EXHIBIT 6
MOB, September 1985
_____ Lower and Upper Bounds, in 32nds
. . . . Actual September MOB, in 32nds

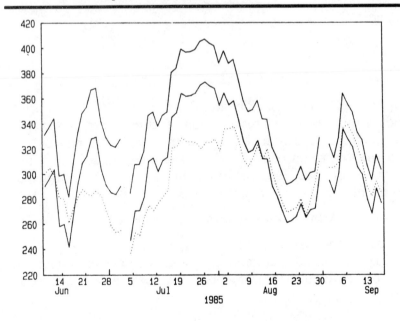

EXHIBIT 7
MOB, December 1985
———— Lower and Upper Bounds, in 32nds
. . . . . . Actual December MOB, in 32nds

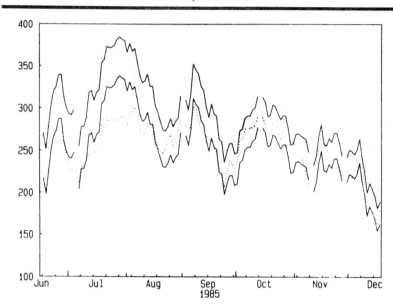

when the March contract was above its upper bound. There were also periods in March and April 1986 when the September 1986 contract traded above its upper bound. In both these instances, however, the nearby contracts (December 1985 and June 1986, respectively), were within their bounds.

II. TRADING THE MOB

Individuals who want to trade the MOB will need to consider these arbitrage bounds. Let's consider several different types of trades.

EXHIBIT 8
MOB, March 1986
_____ Lower and Upper Bounds, in 32nds
. . . . Actual March MOB, in 32nds

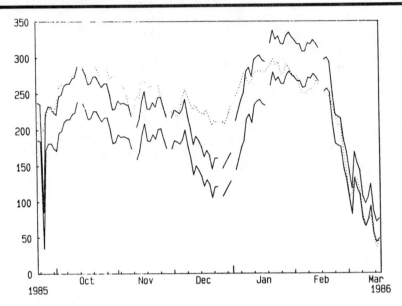

Hedging Transactions

Consider a municipal portfolio manager who holds $20,000,000 par of long-term municipal securities. He thinks municipal yields will rise for several weeks, but is reluctant to sell the securities. Instead, he wants to hedge these securities by going short 200 municipal futures since each contract is for $100,000 par value.

If the municipal futures market were deep enough, this transaction would not involve the MOB spread. However, the municipal market is often not sufficiently liquid to execute 100 or 200 contracts without moving the price. The MOB spread, which is traded by another group of traders, is always liquid enough to handle that volume. Someone wanting to sell 200 municipal

EXHIBIT 9
MOB, June 1986
——— Lower and Upper Bounds, in 32nds
……. Actual June MOB, in 32nds

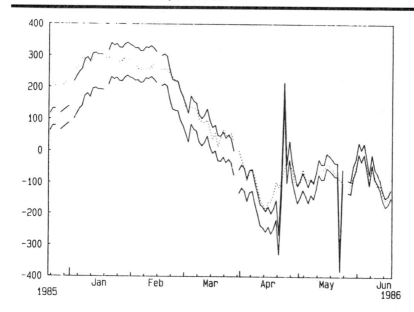

futures contracts could do so by selling 200 MOBs (selling 200 municipal futures and buying 200 Treasury futures). The Treasury bond futures could simultaneously be resold. These steps are illustrated below:

Desired Position: Short 200 municipal futures
Problem: The municipal contract is insufficiently liquid

Solution: – Sell the MOB *and*
     Sell Treasury Bond futures
     – 200 Municipal futures
     + 200 Treasury futures | –200
     – 200 Treasury futures | MOBs
     ————————————————
     – 200 Municipal futures

EXHIBIT 10
MOB, September 1986
_____ Lower and Upper Bounds, in 32nds
. . . . Actual September MOB, in 32nds

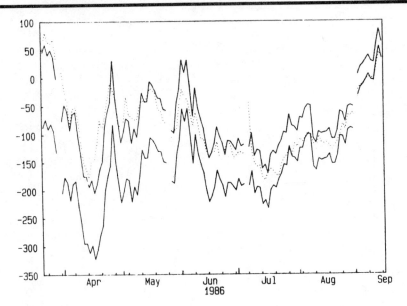

One would be more apt to put on a short position in municipal futures to hedge if the municipal futures were trading toward the upper end of their arbitrage bounds, because then any movement within the band would tend to be downward, and therefore in favor of the short. Suppose, however, the municipal futures were trading near the bottom of their arbitrage bands. In this case, if the municipal cash market stays relatively constant, and the futures move to the top of the bands, the portfolio manager would experience a loss in the futures not offset by a gain on the cash; this is the basis risk between municipal bonds and municipal futures.

A graph of this basis risk is shown in Exhibit 11. The basis risk can be substantial, up to $2 per $100 of par (that is, ± 64/32). If a hedger expected it to move in his favor, a hedge would be much more desirable than if he expected it to move against him. None-

EXHIBIT 11
**Basis Between the Bond Buyer 40 and the September 1986
Municipal Futures Contract**

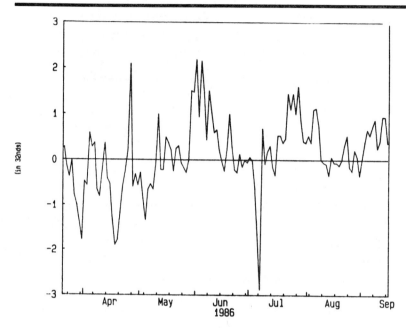

theless, if a sizeable upward move in yields is expected, say 25 basis points or more, the cost of not hedging might exceed the basis risk between cash and futures. The portfolio manager may therefore want to hedge even though the futures contract is close to the lower end of its bands.

An arbitrage transaction between the municipal cash market and the municipal futures market would not involve the MOB, were it not for liquidity considerations. Since the municipal market is often not liquid enough to execute 100 or 200 contracts without moving the price, the trade is effected by shorting (going long) the MOB, and simultaneously selling (buying) the Treasury bond futures.

Another type of "arbitrage" transaction can be used when the MOB is outside its bounds. This situation occurs somewhat less frequently than the situation in which the municipal futures contract is outside its band. (Since the Treasury futures contract is almost always within its bounds,[4] a necessary, but not sufficient condition for the MOB to be outside its band is that the municipal futures contract be outside its band.)

It is clear that if the MOB is outside its bounds, and the bounds do not change, an arbitrage trade would be profitable. On January 6, 1986 the June contract had the following parameters:

$$\overline{M}(n) = 91.78; \ \underline{M}(n) = 86.11; \ \overline{B}(n) = 84.65; \ \underline{B}(n) = 84.17$$

$$\text{MOB upper bound} = 91.78 - 84.17 = 7.61 = 244/32$$

$$\text{MOB lower bound} = 86.11 - 84.65 = 1.46 = 47/32$$

Arbitrage

MOB trades can also be attractive when the municipal futures or the MOB is trading outside its arbitrage bands. A trade could be put on to take advantage of this temporary aberration.

Suppose municipal futures are trading above their upper bound. In this situation, municipal futures are expensive relative to cash. An arbitrager could short the municipal futures contract and buy bonds approximating the index. If this position is held to the expiration of the futures contract, a risk-free profit can be locked in. Or, if the market retreated inside the arbitrage bounds before the contract's expiration, the position could be liquidated at that point at a profit.

Consider the following example: On March 31, 1986 the June municipal futures contract was $77/32$ points above its upper bound. If the municipal cash index was purchased and municipal futures were sold at this point, and then reversed on April 3, 1986 when the municipal futures contract returned to the top of its band, the gain would have been $2.40 per $100 par.

Similarly, if municipal futures are trading below their lower bound, municipal futures are cheap relative to cash. This situation

---

[4] The Treasury bond futures market is so efficient that it is rare to see situations where the Treasury contract is trading outside its bands. Moreover, what appears to be a small aberration is often due to small differences between the timing of the cash and futures contract.

is extremely rare—not since August 1985 have municipals traded below their lower bound. In this case, however, the futures contract should be purchased and the municipals should be shorted. If the position is held until the expiration of the futures contract, a profit would be locked in, even allowing for the cost of failing. The position could be closed out at a profit if the municipal futures go within their band before the contract expired. On that day the MOB traded at $27^2/32$, $2^8/32$ above its upper bound. If one sold the MOB (sold municipal futures and purchased Treasury futures), and next day the MOB fell to $24^3/32$—just below its upper bound— the profit would be $2^9/32$.

But in this case the MOB stayed above its band until January 10. By this point the bounds had moved up to:

$$\overline{M}(n) = 91.08; \ \underline{M}(n) = 85.59; \ \overline{B}(n) = 82.90; \ \underline{B}(n) = 82.42$$

$$\text{MOB upper bound} = 91.08 - 82.42 = 8.66 = 2^{77}/32$$

$$\text{MOB lower bound} = 85.59 - 82.90 = 2.69 = 8^6/32$$

So with the MOB now trading at its new upper bound of $2^{77}/32$, the position would be bought back at a $5/32$ loss.

Thus, arbitrage if the MOB is outside its bounds represents a potential profit opportunity only if the bounds do not change. It is not a riskless arbitrage as in the case where municipal futures are outside their bounds.

Basis Trading

The MOB can also be used to position for a change in municipal interest rates relative to Treasury interest rates.

Exhibit 12 illustrates that the ratio of tax-exempt to taxable rates has varied greatly—from a low of .81 to a high of 1.12. If one can predict changes in this ratio, there is obviously a lot of money to be made.

Consider this concrete example of how expectations about rates can be used in trading the MOB. Assume that in February 1986 one thought that municipal securities would be cheaper relative to Treasuries, i.e., tax-exempt rates would rise relative to taxable rates. To take advantage of this, one could have sold the MOB (sold municipal futures and purchased Treasury futures). If one

EXHIBIT 12
Ratio of Tax Exempt to Taxable Yields
(Bond Buyer Revenue Index/30 Year Treasury Yield)

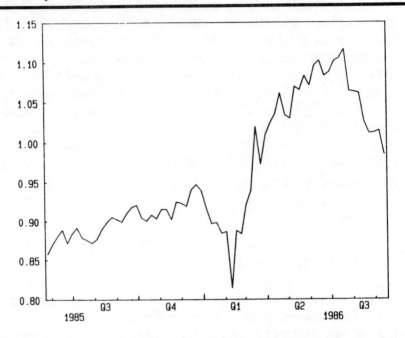

had done this at the close on February 10 and offset the trade on April 11, the profits would have been phenomenal. The municipal futures would have been sold for $92.50 and repurchased for $97.09—a loss of $4.59. However, the Treasury futures would have been purchased for $85.68 and sold for $103.41—a gain of $17.73. The total profit on the trade would have been $13.14.

The tax-exempt to taxable spread has always varied, but from October 1985 to August 1986 it varied considerably because of changing expectations about tax legislation.

This situation has generated several worthwhile trading opportunities.

• In December 1985, new issues of municipal bonds were at an all-time high, due to the provisions in the House of Representatives' tax reform bill on restricting certain types of revenue bonds, effective 1/1/86. This increase in supply narrowed the MOB spread on the March contract to a low of 6 13/32 from its September high of 9 7/32. One could have taken advantage of this situation by selling the MOB—selling municipal futures and buying an equivalent number of Treasury futures—in September, when the spread was wide.

- In January 1986, the demand for municipal bonds remained strong but supply fell drastically due to uncertainty about the effective date of the tax legislation, slated to be January 31, 1986 according to the House's bill. Thus municipal bonds outperformed Treasury securities in early January. On January 10, the MOB spread had risen to 8 18/32. An investor who bought the spread (bought municipal futures and sold Treasury futures) in December would have gained quite a bit by the widening of the spread.

- In March of 1986, the Senate Finance Committee began consideration of tax reform proposals. A careful analysis of this legislation suggested some good trades. On March 19, for example, when Senator Robert Packwood of the Finance Committee announced plans to subject all municipal bond interest to the alternative minimum tax, the market seemingly overreacted. If one considered a prompt negative vote by the Senate Finance Committee likely, which did occur, one could have bought the MOB (buying municipal futures and sold Treasury futures) and unwound the position two days later 54/32 richer.

- In August of 1986, when the House-Senate Conference Committee reached an agreement and the bill was passed, it was clear that the municipal market was pricing municipals to reflect a worst case scenario that did not materialize. Hence, the MOB began to rise. If one had purchased the December MOB on August 15, 1986, at −103/32 and sold it on October 1 at −12/32, a profit of 91/32 would have resulted.

Even after the passage of the tax legislation, it is likely that profit opportunities will remain. Some of these opportunities will result from uncertainties about provisions of the new law. For example, the legislation's effect on the supply of municipal bonds is unclear, as is its effect on individual demand for long-term municipals. Instruments such as taxable municipals and stripped municipals, made possible by the 1986 tax legislation, alter the relationship between the *Bond Buyer 40* and Treasury securities.

Not all profit opportunities in MOB trading stem from tax reform. Even before discussion of tax reform, the ratio of tax-exempt to taxable yields was not constant. Credit premiums and liquidity premiums for municipal securities can fluctuate considerably over time. Thus while the market may not be quite as volatile as it was historically, MOB trades warrant continued attention.

A Few Caveats

While most market participants tend to think in terms of yields, it is actually the cash index that is traded. Potential calls on outstanding municipals (and some Treasuries) can affect the price-yield relationship. For example, from February 10, 1986 to April 11, 1986 yields on long-term revenue bonds declined by 61 basis points. On a 15-year instrument, this translates into a price rise of $5.39. Because of call provisions, which makes the effective life much shorter, the actual increase in the cash index was $2.50.

The attractiveness of a basis trade will also be influenced by where the MOB is within its bounds. If the MOB is at the upper end of the bands, to sell it would appear even more attractive than otherwise. Even if the bands do not move, the MOB seller would have a profit as the MOB moves toward the center of the bands. Similarly if the MOB is at the lower end of its bands, buying the MOB would seem more attractive than otherwise.

Those who expect municipal rates to change relative to Treasury rates must consider call provisions on municipal bonds, as well as where the MOB is trading within its bounds.

III. CONCLUDING COMMENTS

The municipal futures market, and the MOB, allow attractive new trading strategies. During the first year of the municipal futures contract when uncertainty about tax legislation existed, there were enormous opportunities for arbitrage. We anticipate these markets will continue to present significant profit potential. It is important for those who wish to trade the MOB to examine the trading bands and determine whether movement within the bands is likely to work for or against the trade.

INDEX